EXCEEDING EXPECTATIONS:

A USER'S GUIDE TO IMPLEMENTING
BRAIN RESEARCH IN THE CLASSROOM

by Susan J. Kovalik
and
Karen D. Olsen

FIFTH EDITION

D1307417

Exceeding Expectations:
A User's Guide to Implementing Brain Research in the Classroom
Fifth Edition

by Susan J. Kovalik and Karen D. Olsen

Edited by Kathleen Wolgemuth
Graphics, Layout, & Illustrations by Lanitta Jaye Delk

Published by The Center for Effective Learning
www.thecenter4learning.com

Distributed by Books for Educators
P.O. Box 468
Black Diamond, WA 98010
360-825-6633
E-mail: books4@q.com
www.books4educ.com

ISBN # 978-1-878631-98-5

Printed in the United States of America

Table of Contents

Preface

This fifth edition of *Exceeding Expectations: A User's Guide to Implementing Brain Research in the Classroom* brings a fresh face to a 25-year track record of training thousands of teachers throughout the world how to use brain research in the classroom to vastly improve both the learning environment and student outcomes.

The fresh face is a change in name of the model—from ITI (Integrated Thematic Instruction) to *HET* (Highly Effective Teaching). The shift reflects the strengthened messages from brain research. The name ITI no longer best describes the goals and purposes of the model it spawned. Here's why:

- The context of learning is critical. Learning is greatly speeded up, and is more accurate, when what is to be learned is experienced where it is found and used in the real world.

  The real world is the most effective, efficient, and natural integrator of content and skills to be learned. If curriculum is based in real-world, being there locations, there is no need to integrate content as a separate goal. **I** T I

  Also, real-world contexts significantly increase sensory input and engage the power of the brain's mirror neurons.

- The brain learns through pattern seeking and building programs to use what is learned, until it wires that learning into long-term memory.

  Concepts—because they are intrinsic in the real-world and are also found tucked into state standards—are a better target for curriculum development and make stronger neural glue than themes. I **T** I

- The job of teaching demands orchestration of all of the tools of bodybrain-compatible curriculum development and instructional strategies.

  Instruction is only a part of the overall job of teaching. Curriculum—developed for the classroom with brain research in mind and tweaked to best fit the students in that classroom—is an extremely powerful tool. I T **I**

Therefore, a new name but the same commitment to using brain research to redefine teaching and learning for the 21st century.

Another feature of this edition is setting the goal of teaching effectively the first time. Effective First Teaching (EFT) is an economic imperative, an assessment must, and a layperson's reason for implementing brain research. In short, EFT provides:

- A singular criteria for making budget decisions—cutting and/or adding money

- A clear purpose for formative and summative assessment instruments and processes that provide in-the-moment feedback to teachers for improving instruction, and

- A framework for organizing curriculum development and instructional strategies

And, most important, EFT adds political urgency to getting on with the task of implementing brain research in the classroom.

This fifth edition also opens the door on two important areas of brain research—mirror neurons and gender differences. Although in their infancy, they foreshadow the need for profound changes in both curriculum and instruction tools and practices.

Acknowledgements

"The very least you can do in your life is to figure out what you hope for.

And the most you can do is live inside that hope."

— Barbara Kingsolver

The "hope" of Susan Kovalik and Associates is to facilitate learning communities that are dynamic environments for teaching and learning, providing multiple opportunities for meaningful content, which will enable students to become responsible and informed citizens.

The associates of Susan Kovalik and Associates, all classroom teachers or administrators, are responsible for the training and coaching of thousands of educators in the United States and around the world. They perform the dual roles of sage on the stage and guide on side, leading and supporting educators who are committed to creating true learning communities. Their contributions to the development of the ITI/HET model are many and varied:

Karen D. Olsen, who has held the intellectual conscience and integrity of the ITI/HET model since 1987. She is author, co-author, or contributing editor of all our publications.

Patty Harrington, who patiently helped us understand the need to build a strong sense of community in classrooms and schools as a means of improving academic learning. A master communicator, she provides individuals and schools with clear direction and inspiration. Her schoolwide assessments provide insight and practical steps for change.

Judy Eacker, whose talent and spirit gave the LIFESKILLS a voice through song and a sensitive ear to the needs of students and teachers. Judy also orchestrated the *Sign On* video at the Colorado School of the Deaf so that everyone can learn to teach and use the Lifelong Guidelines & LIFESKILLS in American Sign Language.

Dean Tannewitz, who leads with wisdom and intention, building community wherever she goes and inspiring schools to go the distance toward success. A gifted group process facilitator, she offers guidance to administrators as they seek to move their schools. Her authentic presentations inspire belief and a "can do" attitude.

Sue Pearson, whose efforts and commitment produced the LIFESKILL book, *Tools for Citizenship and Life: Using the ITI/HET Lifelong Guidelines and LIFESKILLS in Your Classroom*. Sue's deep knowledge of the HET model is instrumental in moving educators to create model HET classrooms and schools. She is the organization's ListServ facilitator for teachers and administrators and co-creator of the HET Certification process.

Linda Jordan, Professor at Hope College, Michigan, who co-developed an exceptional teacher training program to prepare college students with the HET tools necessary to become highly effective teachers. She is also co-creator of the HET Certification process. A gifted keynote presenter, Linda moves audiences of all ages to make significant changes on behalf of students.

T. J. Mears, whose vibrant personality brings his understanding of the HET model to secondary schools. His talents and skills as a model teacher, coach, and master of group process for district leadership staff makes him a very effective change agent.

Denise White, a gifted secondary language arts teacher whose great communication skills with students and adults allow her to demonstrate her deep understanding of *HET* curriculum development and instructional strategies. Her positive energy is contagious to all who work with her.

Alisa Braddy, a dynamic classroom teacher who guides teachers to orchestrate curriculum and instruction while integrating movement into all that she does. A literacy specialist, she provides practical insights to teachers as they integrate language arts standards into meaningful content.

To the associates who are no longer on the road but have influenced the model: Jo Gusman, Barbara Pedersen, Robert Ellingsen, Martha Kaufeldt, Ventura Lopez, Jacque Melin, Sally Johnson, Pattie Mills, Joy Raboli, Kathy Theuer, Jane McGeehan, Sister Patt Walsh, Ann Ross, Kari Kling, and Nicole Miller.

None of this is possible without the support of the people back home. A big thank you to all the families out there who realize the power of knowledge and commitment and who share those they love with other people's children.

Also, a heartfelt thank you to the people who make it all happen at the office. Every organization is dependent on its foundation. In particular, Debora Schweikl and Nita Delk have been heroic in supporting our mission of Highly Effective Teaching.

To all the teachers who have worked with us during model teaching weeks and summer institutes, thank you for enriching the model through your enthusiasm, talents, and insights. Multiple schools and entire school districts all over the country have caught the vision of the HET model and have joined the quest for excellence in their state: Alaska, Arizona, California, Colorado, Florida, Georgia, Indiana, Iowa, Kansas, Kentucky, Michigan, Minnesota, Missouri, Nebraska, Nevada, New Mexico, New Jersey, New York, North Carolina, North Dakota, Ohio, Oklahoma, Oregon, Pennsylvania, South Carolina, Tennessee, Texas, Utah, Virginia, Washington, and Wisconsin.

Thanks also to those teachers in Slovakia, the Czech Republic, Italy, Switzerland, Denmark, Saudi Arabia, Australia, Jakarta, and Japan for embracing the idea of applying brain research to the classroom and proving that the *HET* model works with all children in all circumstances anywhere in the world.

Thousands of students and teachers go to school each day excited by the possibilities. Each of you, in countless ways during untold hours, has contributed to that possibility.

This book is a labor of love. Representing a lifetime of thinking and teaching, it holds forth the hope that we will find the political will to use brain research to transform our schools and, in so doing, transform our world. It's heartening to hear from those implementing *HET* that this hope is taking wing and that, in ways big and small, *HET* is contributing to making the world a better place.

To all who have had a hand in growing the *HET* model, thank you isn't a big enough phrase, but we do thank each of you for allowing us to "live inside that hope." For in the end, as Baba Dioum as pointed out:

We will conserve only what we love.

We will love only what we understand.

We will understand only what we are taught.

We invite all of you to move forward with us into the coming years under a new banner—Highly Effective Teaching (*HET*)—and to do so with renewed commitment.

The Authors

Introduction

ORIGINS OF THE HET MODEL

As a new sixth grade teacher, I worked my intuition overtime to come up with the best ways to teach my students. As an Italian, that meant providing plenty of enthusiasm, exuberant gestures, laughs, hugs, and food. My formula worked; my students loved school and loved learning. Then I became a K-6 science teacher for 1,200 students. To my basic Italian instructional strategies, I added lots of hands-on-of-real-things—your basic nightmare for a custodian and for the music teacher with whom I shared space. Snakes, rats, chickens, you name it. More good results with kids. Then one day the custodian told me he had seen a notice for a new job opening—teacher for the gifted and talented (GT). He told me I should apply! Whether it was because he had noticed the enthusiasm of my students or hoped longingly for a more traditional science teacher with fewer critters and exploratory items, I'll never know. But I took his suggestion. My work with GT students led me to giving workshops, in the course of which I was noticed by a talent scout for an organization that sponsored conferences across the country. Fully convinced that we needed to save students from the boredom and tedium of textbooks and worksheets—so why not start with the gifted!—I hit the road.

As I'd promised my three teenage children that I would take each of them on the road with me for a week, I soon found myself in Indiana with my youngest son, Marshall. The GT coordinator, our dinner hostess, was very enthusiastic about her mission, effusive about the needs and achievements of GT students. As the testimonials rolled on, my son spun his corner-fold napkin to make a loop and pretended to hang himself, gagging for added effect. As I stared in disbelief at my son's rudeness, I was further shocked as he burst out: "Do you really believe that the only students who want a good teacher and something interesting to learn are the ones that score high on a one-hour test?" In response our dinner hostess said he seemed a little hostile. "Yes," he said, "my brother and sister [who were in a GT program] get all the good teachers and I get the leftovers. And no one ever asked me what I wanted."

Marshall was right. Every kid deserves a good teacher. I left the field of gifted education and turned my attention to learning for all students.

The most important lessons in life often come from our own family experiences.

Three years later, Marshall came home from high school in January of his senior year and said to me, "I know what you believe and I know what you stand for, but I'm quitting school. Before you say anything, you go sit in my classes for a day. If, at the end of the day, you can look me in the eye and tell me that six more months of this will really enhance who I am as a person, then we'll talk about it." After sitting through his classes, I could not look him in the eye and say, "Yes, it would." Marshall left school.

Marshall was right again.

My quest for answers intensified. I scoured bookstores for books about learning and happened upon Leslie Hart's *Human Brain and Human Learning* in 1983. At last . . . an explanation about how the brain learns from a scientific perspective. New doors began to open. To my wonderment, many of my earlier intuitions about instructional strategies and curriculum development were confirmed by brain research. I was ecstatic! I began to analyze my teaching strategies. They worked not because I was an extroverted Italian but because they allowed students' brains to work the way they naturally work; the strategies were, as Hart coined the term, "brain-compatible." In fact, anyone could learn the techniques and they worked for all students—not just GT, not just reluctant learners, but all students. The *HET* model was born.

The *HET* model reflects another side of my family experience, that of the political activism of my parents, Malcolm and Josephine Jafferies. They imprinted on me early in life that the purpose of an educated life is citizenship—active participation in our democratic processes.

Over the next 18 years, the *HET* model (Integrated Thematic Instruction) continued to evolve to stay current with emerging brain research and the ongoing efforts by my associates and me and *HET* teachers across the country. In this quest to develop the best possible curricular and instructional practices to translate brain research into practical applications, it has become clear that the name Integrated Thematic Instruction no longer fits. Curricular focus should not be on creating themes but on being conceptual and organized around concepts—which enhances the brain's ability to detect and understand patterns and thus makes content generalizable and transferrable.

Similarly, integration should no longer be the goal, the result of carefully (and often artificially) weaving together pieces of multiple subjects, but rather the automatic outcome of basing curriculum in sensory-rich, *being there* experiences in the real world. The new goal should be developing new ways to massively increase sensory input by studying the world as it occurs outside of the classroom.

And, of course, our childhood and adolescent pictures of instruction from our own educational process need to be replaced with strategies aimed at teaching the brain the way it learns, not how our bureaucracy has found it convenient to teach in the past.

The name that now seems to best fit—that sets a goal for how we develop curriculum and the instructional strategies we choose—is *Highly Effective Teaching (HET)*.

For those who have held to your commitment to implement the ITI model over the years, welcome home to the future. The *HET* model is truly a 21st century version of your old friend, ITI.

So, on behalf of all the Marshalls out there who want, and deserve, good teachers and something interesting to learn and in deep gratitude for my parents who modeled citizenship, knowing how precious and fragile a democratic society is, I welcome you to the *HET* model.

Susan J. Kovalik
April, 2010
Federal Way, Washington

THE CHALLENGES AHEAD

The first decade of the 21st century held many surprises—in our personal lives, in our schools, and worldwide. While we still fumble for answers, it's clear that we can ill afford to continue business as usual. As failure to meet rising standards and economic crises collide, we need to rethink what we have been doing—policy at all levels and educational practice within schools and districts.

Starting in the 1960s, Congress started public education along the path of remediation as part of the war against poverty. In hindsight, perhaps that wasn't the best public policy decision—useful in the short run but problem-ridden in the long run. Another case of yesterday's solution becoming today's problem.

Every version of the Elementary and Secondary Education Act over the past 50 years has continued heavy investment in remediation and testing to determine the need remediation—all furthering the notion that remediation as the solution to improving education.

However, half a century later, the unspoken assumption that remediation is inevitable and necessary is killing any chance at real improvement efforts because staffing and resources for remediation—as currently required by the three-tier model of RTI—compete directly with dollars needed to improve teaching outcomes in the classroom by each classroom teacher. Such approaches, while sounding well intentioned and funded by weary taxpayers to the tune of billions of additional dollars, undermines improvement efforts.

Continued focus on remediation is is poor policy because it:

- Diverts critical funding away from needed professional development for classroom teachers. Case in point, the United States now lags behind its western counterparts in investing in professional development for its teachers.[2]

- Blunts any true quest for accountability. If the need for remediation programs is accepted as a given, then accountability for classroom teachers is a meaningless soundbite.

The economic realities of our time are clear. We can no longer afford to pursue a two competing directions. We must choose, either to:

1) Invest in classroom teachers to raise student achievement and eliminate the need for remediation

OR

2) Continue investing in resources outside of the classroom—remediation and subject specialists—to make up for what should, but doesn't, happen in the classroom.

New Policy Is Needed

Clearly, a radical change in goals, policies, and practice is needed here. I offer a modest proposal: Invest in classroom teachers and teach them to teach effectively the first time!.

Effective First Teaching (EFT) means teaching for understanding and the ability to apply what is understood until it is wired into long-term memory the first time. For example, teach long division in a single day and be done with it (see pages XXX), or multiplication in a week, or addition facts in two days. Imagine the "extra" time this would create for a robust, daily science program, a rich arts program, study trips that matter, and more.

Brain Research and the HET Model Makes EFT Possible

Fifty years ago, EFT was simply not possible. However, with today's brain research into how the human brain learns, EFT is not only possible, it is a moral imperative. And the HET model is an approach to curriculum development and instructional strategies that makes EFT possible. It translates brain research into into practical, doable steps in the classroom, which is the subject of this book. The goal of public education reform in the 21st century must become Effective First Teaching.

OVERVIEW OF THE HET MODEL

The *HET* model has two main goals:

- To create participating citizens, willing and able to engage in our democratic processes to improve life now and for future generations

- To help educators translate current brain research into practical strategies for the classroom and schoolwide, and to so in ways that make teaching Effective First Teaching a reality, not just a dream

Pursuing one goal without the other is an empty activity. The world has urgent problems to solve and we have children waiting to learn and grow and hoping to have meaningful work to do.

The *HET* model is based in current brain research. Our knowledge of how the human brain learns—the biology of learning—informs us about what's worth teaching as we develop curriculum and instructional strategies that will work best.

Few will be surprised by the core concepts of brain research presented in this book; they ring true with our intuitions. We believe that schools of the 21st century must develop curriculum and instructional strategies illuminated by brain research, not by educational tradition and habit.

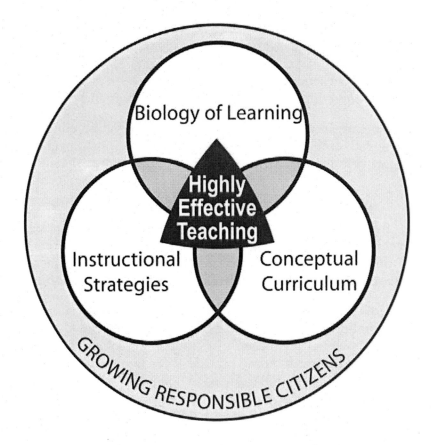

BRAIN BIOLOGY— THE FOUR HET LEARNING PRINCIPLES

The *HET* model is based on four basic principles from brain research, each of which is discussed in Chapters 1-5:

1 *Intelligence* as a function of experience (see Chapter 1)

2 Learning is an inseparable partnership between **brain** and **body** (see Chapter 2):

— Emotion is the gatekeeper to learning and performance

— Movement enhances learning.

3 There are **multiple intelligences** or ways of solving problems and/or producing products (see Chapter 3).

4 Learning is a **two-step process**:

— Step one: Making meaning through pattern seeking (see Chapter 4)

— Step two: Developing a mental program for using what we understand and wiring it into long-term memory (see Chapter 5).

THE NINE BODYBRAIN-COMPATIBLE ELEMENTS OF CURRICULUM DEVELOPMENT AND INSTRUCTION

The bodybrain-compatible elements of the *HET* model are the primary ways of translating brain research into action in the classroom. These nine elements are:

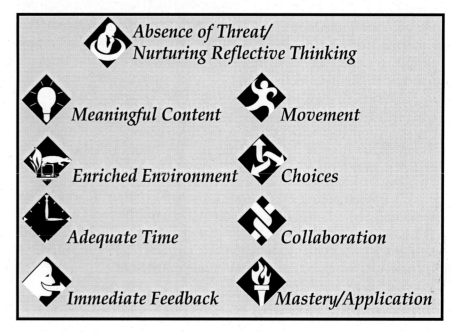

These nine bodybrain-compatible elements appear at the back of each of the five chapters dealing with an *HET* Learning Principle (see Chapters 1-5). This intermix of theory and practical applications are the heart of *HET* model.

TOWARD BODYBRAIN-COMPATIBLE TEACHING/LEARNING

Although little about the four *HET* Learning Principles from brain research and their relationship to the nine bodybrain-compatible elements may surprise you, implementing them in the face of a system that is brain-antagonistic in so many ways is indeed a challenge.

Coherence, Not Piecemeal. Achieving bodybrain-compatibility for your students is not the result of following a check list. The concepts from brain research cannot be implemented by a few simple strategies. Effective implementation will only come through full understanding of the brain research and the richness of its implications. As you study each of the *HET* Learning Principles in Chapters 1-5, do ask yourself, "So what?" What does this mean to my students? What does this suggest that I change about my classroom? What does it mean to base my teaching in brain research rather than traditional practices?

Implementing *HET* is not a piecemeal affair in which one picks and chooses what to implement. Perhaps the most important thing to say about brain research and its implementation is this: *If even one of the bodybrain-compatible elements is not in place, the learning environment is not bodybrain-compatible.*

Old Yet New. It is important to recognize that the curricular and instructional strategies described in the *HET* model are not new. Good teachers have implemented them over the years but did so intuitively. However, intuition alone is insufficient when putting together a coherent, comprehensive approach to curriculum and instruction for a schoolwide program improvement effort.

Basing our improvement efforts on brain research requires us to use old tools differently and for new purposes. It would, in fact, be easier to implement brain research if it required all new curricular and instruction strategies: Just throw out and start fresh. Hardest of all is to use old strategies in new ways for new purposes.

What makes this so hard is that it's extremely difficult to maintain a clear vision of old tools used anew when one lives in an old structure with its old pictures, old habits, and old vocabulary with its old ideas. Before we know it, we're back where we started. And old tools used in old ways will not produce the results for students that we desire. But when old tools are used in new ways, with the purpose of translating brain research into action, you will be amazed at the changes in student behavior, attitudes, and test scores. You'll also find yourself enjoying teaching more than you ever thought possible.

HOW TO USE THIS BOOK

This book is not designed to be read straight through. Rather, read as you implement, stage by stage over three-to-five years. These stages, which follow the *HET Classroom Stages of Implementation,* describe how to implement the *HET* model from before school begins through full implementation of a brain research-based, fully bodybrain-compatible learning environment. The stages of implementation are:

- Stage 1: Getting Started.

— Before the first day of school (Stage 1.1)

— The first day of school and beyond (Stage 1.2)

— What to accomplish before moving on to Stage 2 (1.3)

- Stage 2: First Steps to Integrating Curriculum

- Stages 3-5: Working Toward Total Integration in a Fully Bodybrain-Compatible Learning Environment

This book is designed to carry the reader through each of these stages.

 Part A is your touchstone. Read it and re-read it until you feel you have a grasp of the vision it forecasts. Revisit it each time you begin a new part of the book.

Read **Part B** when you're ready to begin implementing Stage 1*—what to do before school starts, what to do the first day of school (includes an outline and lesson plan for the first day of school) and beyond, and what to accomplish before moving on to Stage 2.

Once you have your bodybrain-compatible learning environment firmly in place (which typically takes a year of concerted effort), review Part A and read **Part C**. Part C explains how to begin integrating curriculum, your first step in Stage 2.

Part D describes how to make curriculum more powerful while working toward total integration as described in Implementation Stage 3. Stage 3 assumes that you have mastered the environmental and instructional strategies of previous stages. Before you begin, review Part A, the summary of brain research. It is essential for all stages but especially so for curriculum development.

Part E explains how to achieve full integration of curriculum through Stages 4-5 of the ITI Classroom Stages of Implementation by creating more quality and more time within your brain-based curriculum. This part also describes how to grow responsible citizens through social/political action projects and how to create a micro-community, a true-to-life simulation of the real world, especially its civic and economic facets.

 Part F discusses tools for living with change. Read it when you begin implementing Stage 1.2. Revisit it as you begin planning for each subsequent stage.

As you use this book, notice that we have provided quick graphic references for you. Every page carries one of the distinguishing symbols above, quickly identifying where you are. Also, the first page of each part can be quickly located by looking for the gray stripe along the right edge of the book.

As you read through Parts A and B, keep in mind the curriculum development structures for the ITI model that appear on the next page. Key points are what you want students to understand cepts, significant knowledge, and skills) and inquiries are wh want students to be able to do with what they understand should be familiar with them from the very beginning of you ney into the ITI model.

Examples of *key points are accompanied by a strip of puzzle pieces* along the left margin, symbolic of the brain's pattern-seeking processes as it attempts to make meaning of its surroundings.

Examples of *inquiries are accompanied by a strip of action elements* along the left margin, symbolic of the brain's drive to use what it understands through doing—taking action, applying what is being learned in order to wire it into long-term memory.

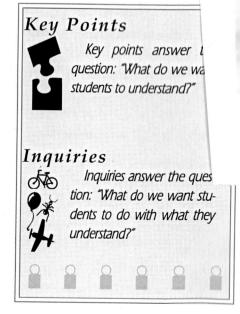

Key Points

Key points answer t question: "What do we wa students to understand?"

Inquiries

Inquiries answer the ques tion: "What do we want stu dents to do with what they understand?"

A NOTE TO LONG-TIME FRIENDS OF THE ITI/HET MODEL

For those who have been using the ITI/*HET* model during the past quarter century, we welcome you to an even greater sense of urgency about the need for change and the need for a rallying cry that all stakeholders can intuitively grasp and work together to achieve, regardless of their knowledge of brain research and educational practice. We believe that rallying cry should be *EFFECTIVE FIRST TEACHING*.

The idea of *EFFECTIVE FIRST TEACHING* captures key elements for all stakeholders:

- Urgency. *Do it now!*

- Laser sharp focus:
  Do the job right the first time!
  The focus for improvement efforts shouldn't be to just to improve some, but rather learning to do the job right the first time.

- Clear criteria for allocating resources:
  Invest only in what ensures getting the job done right the first time.
  Eliminate all expenses that do not directly improve the possibility of doing so.

- Clear focus for evaluation:
  The most critical information is not end-of-the year standardized tests but instruments that provide *feedback to teachers in the moment* so that they can alter their lessons to provide more practice or to recycle through reteaching using a different approach and resources.

- For students, *expect to learn it NOW!* Not tomorrow, next week, or next year.

- For parents, *failing to learn is not an option*. Expect your child to succeed. Expect the school staff to implement *EFFECTIVE FIRST TEACHING* and support them in doing so by doing your part at home with your child and providing informed support.

Part A:

Brain Research

And Its Practical Applications

BRAIN RESEARCH AND THE HET MODEL

The *HET* model starts with brain research to determine best practice—everything from curriculum development to instructional strategies, assessment of student progress to budgeting. For every step we propose to take and for every dollar we allocate, we should ask ourselves this question: "Will this help implement what we know from brain research and is it the best available option for doing so?"

The challenges facing students, teachers, and administrators are greater now than ever before and are not likely to be solved until we change our ways of thinking about learning and teaching. As Einstein commented: "Problems can't be solved by the same thinking that created them." This is the 21st century. Traditional ways of teaching and the habits of mind that go with them must give way to using best knowledge.

BODYBRAIN BIOLOGY

Teachers need and deserve a comprehensive view of brain research coupled with practical applications to the classroom. Piecemeal views, however fascinating the pieces, remain vague and unconvincing. The good news is that the four learning principles which form the basis of the *HET* model ring with our own experience as learners. We can recall times when our brain operated just like the brain principle described. Certainly we can name students we have taught who were the perfect poster child for each of the brain principles.

Part A of this book describes the four learning principles from brain research that provide a biological base for a comprehensive view of the instructional strategies and curriculum development. Embedded in the four concepts is a discussion of the nine bodybrain-compatible elements of the *HET* model. These elements translate brain research insights into practical, everyday applications

in the classroom and school. They appear in the order of their power to implement that particular learning principle.

Four Learning Principles from Brain Research

Although the enormous complexity of the brain and the dizzying, science fiction-like capabilities of today's research technologies can make for heavy treading, descriptions of how the human brain learns can be expressed in relatively simple conceptual terms. And although we may not know as much as we will, we certainly know enough to get started.

The learning principles outlined on the next page are, we believe, fundamental to establishing a working theory of human learning for the 21st century. Corroborated by researchers studying the human brain from many different fields, they provide a powerful template for making decisions about curriculum and instruction and other issues for systemic rethinking of American education.

> "Most school practice arises from tradition, ritual, and the context within which schools are conducted. Only during the 20th century has scientific learning theory had an influence and then only in a minor way. The school is a kind of subculture in which are preserved the relics of former times, with a few practices added or subtracted because of contemporary thought."
>
> *Foshay*

The Four HET Learning Principles About How the Human Brain Learns Are:

- *Intelligence as a function of experience[1]* (Chapter 1)

  Learning is the result of real, observable physiological growth in the brain[1] that occurs as a result of sensory input and the processing, organizing, and pruning it promotes. Genetics is not the immutable determiner of intelligence it is generally believed to be; although it sets parameters, experiences with high levels of sensory input can significantly increase development of one's potential.

- *Learning is an inseparable partnership between the brain and body[2]* **(Chapter 2)**
  - Emotion is the gatekeeper to learning and performance
    Much of the information processed in the brain comes from "information substances" produced throughout the body, many of which are the "molecules of emotion" that drive attention which in turn drives learning and memory.
  - Movement enhances learning
    The movement centers of the brain also help sequence our thoughts.

- *There are multiple intelligences* — ability to solve problems and/or produce products[3] (Chapter 3)

  We have not one, generic intelligence but at least seven,[4] each of which operates from a different part of our brain. As defined by Howard Gardner, intelligence is "a problem-solving and/or product-producing capability."[5]

- *Learning is a two-step process:[6]*

  Step One — The brain makes meaning through pattern seeking. As it does so, it is not logical or sequential. **Step one of learning** *is the extraction, from confusion, of meaningful patterns.[7]* (Chapter 4)

  Step Two — Most information we use is embedded in **programs**, a planned sequence to accomplish a purpose or goal; information not embedded in programs is generally unretrievable and thus unusable. **Step two of learning** *is the acquisition of a mental program.[8]* (Chapter 5)

Each of these five chapters describes how to translate the brain principle into practical, and powerful, classroom applications using the nine bodybrain-compatible elements:

- Absence of threat/ Nurturing reflective thinking
- Meaningful content
- Movement
- Enriched environment
- Choices
- Adequate time
- Collaboration
- Immediate feedback
- Mastery/Application

The bodybrain-compatible elements are described in each chapter in the order of their importance to that particular learning principle.

ENDNOTES

1 Recommended first book to read is *Magic Trees of the Mind: How to Nurture Your Child's Intelligence, Creativity, and Healthy Emotions from Birth Through Adolescence* by Marion Diamond (New York: Penguin, 1998).

2 Recommended first books to read are *Molecules of Emotion: Why We Feel the Way We Feel* by Candace Pert (New York: Touchstone, 1997) and *Smart Moves: Why Learning Is Not All in Your Head* by Carla Hannaford (Alexander, NC: Great Ocean Publishers, 1995).

3 For a user-friendly introduction to the multiple intelligences, we recommend *Multiple Intelligences in the Classroom* by Thomas Armstrong (Alexandria, VA: ASCD, 2000).

4 Howard Gardner originally proposed seven intelligences. To qualify, each intelligence had to meet many criteria. The key criteria for us was that the intelligence operated from a different part of the brain. Recently, Gardner has proposed an eighth candidate, the naturalist, that he explores quite thoroughly (see *Intelligence Reframed: Multiple Intelligences for the 21st Century*, Chapter 4). However, the naturalist intelligence does not appear to operate from a distinct part of the brain and, even more troublesome for us, its description parallels general functions of the brain as a whole as described by Leslie Hart, pattern seeking, and by Elkhonon Goldberg (*The Executive Brain: Frontal Lobes and the Civilized Mind. Oxford: University Press, 2001*) and others (notably Nobel Prize-winning psychologist Herbert Simon). Another reason we do not address the naturalist intelligence here is that it would add yet another issue for teachers to tussle with, one we feel is best addressed under *HET* Learning Principle #4, the first step in learning: pattern seeking.

5 This definition of intelligence was developed by Howard Gardner in the early 1980s. See *Frames of Mind: The Theory of Multiple Intelligences*. He has updated and expanded that definition: "A biopsychological potential to process information that can be activated in a cultural setting to solve problems or create products that are of value in a culture." (See *Intelligence Reframed: Multiple Intelligences for the 21st Century*. New York: Basic Books, 1999, 33-34.) Says Gardner, "Although we all receive these intelligences as part of our birthright, no two people have exactly the same intelligences in the same combinations. After all, intelligences arise from the combination of a person's genetic heritage and life conditions in a given culture and era." (*Intelligence Reframed*, 45.)

6 Recommended first book to read is *Human Brain and Human Learning* by Leslie A. Hart (Black Diamond, WA: Books For Educators, Inc., 2002).

7 This definition of step one of learning comes from the work of Leslie Hart, *Human Brain and Human Learning*, 127.

8 This definition of step two of learning comes from the work of Leslie Hart, *Human Brain and Human Learning*, 161.

Chapter 1: Intelligence* As a Function of Experience

Learning is the result of real, observable physiological growth in the brain[1] that occurs as a result of sensory input and the processing, organizing, and pruning it promotes. The richer the sensory input, the greater the physiological growth in the brain and thus the greater the learning that will be wired into long-term memory. This factor is the important issue in the great nature versus nurture debate about intelligence. It now appears that there is plenty of scientific evidence to establish the power of both. Genetics was once thought to be an immutable determiner of intelligence—what you were born with was what you would end up with. Not so, but it does set a range of potential. However, within those parameters, experiences matter greatly. An undeveloped potential or capacity is just that, an undeveloped brain capable of less intelligent behaviors. It is our responsibility as educators to provide the kinds and amounts of sensory input that will ensure that each child's brain is developed to the full range of its potential.

The work of Marian Diamond, UC Berkeley, Reuven Feurstein, Israel, and many others refutes the long-held beliefs that intelligence is a genetically fixed, singular quality. Feurstein and his associates have even gone so far as to stipulate that "Genetics is no barrier to learning."[2] Marian Diamond's work[3] shows that an enriched environment results in measurable physiological growth in the brain. In short, if we know how the brain learns—what happens physiologically when learning occurs—we can provide the sensory input that will assist a learner to create new "hardwiring" in the brain to carry new learnings. Intelligence, the capability to solve problems and create products, is significantly influenced by environment and experience. For example, most "gifted" students in our programs for the gifted and talented are not "gifted" as in the realm of such people as Einstein, Mozart, David Packard, Eleanor Roosevelt, Steve Wozniak, Sacajawea, or Maria Montessori. Rather, they are advantaged; they are students whose parents provided an enriched environment which nurtured physiological development of neural networks which became long-term memory of knowledge, skills, and greatly expanded vocabulary.

> ## HET Learning Principles
>
> - Intelligence as a function of experience
> - Inseparable bodybrain partnership
>   — emotion as gatekeeper
>   — movement to enhance learning
> - Multiple intelligences
> - Learning is a two-step process

---

* The HET model builds on Howard Gardner's definition of intelligence— "a problem-solving and/or product-producing capability."[4]

An enriched environment spurs brain growth; a sterile and/or hostile environment retards mental growth and can even lead to a decline in capacity. Here is the story.

JUST WHAT DOES GO ON IN THERE?

Due to fantastic advances in technology such as PET scans, MRI, and fMRI, our understanding of how learning takes place has radically expanded in the past two decades. While the story is fantastically more complex than we need to delve into here, a simplified accounting of the biology of learning provides, we believe, valuable images that can help teachers enhance student learning. "Just what does go on in there?" is a question of undeniable human curiosity. The answers are critical to improving teaching and learn-

Intelligence

"Intelligence is a problem-solving and/or product-producing capability."
- Howard Gardner

ing. As Leslie Hart says, "Although we don't know as much as we may and will, we know sufficient to change our ways."[5] And we can do so without taking "a bridge too far."[6]

A Cautionary Tale

In the midst of our deep discouragement over our failures to deliver on the promise that all students can learn, it is easy to fall victim to the old belief that genetics sets intelligence and capability in an immutable way. Today what we know about the genetics versus environment debate is summed up beautifully by Dr. John Ratey: "We are not prisoners of our genes or our environment. Poverty, alienation, drugs, hormonal imbalances, and depression don't dictate failure. Wealth, acceptance, vegetables, and exercise don't guarantee success. Our own free will may be the strongest force directing the development of our brains, and therefore our lives. . . . the brain [child and adult] is both plastic and resilient, and always eager to learn. ***Experiences, thoughts, actions, and emotions actually change the structure of our brains.***"[7] As Ratey says, everything affects brain development and development is a lifelong process. The challenge of educators and parents is to provide the best possible environment for learning—one in which experiences are powerful enough to engage full sensory input (the subject of this chapter)—so that thinking becomes reflective and analytical not just reactive, actions/movement are used to enhance learning, and emotions open the door to learning and performance (the subject of Chapter 2).

When standing before a group of 30-35 students, we must believe in our hearts, and know without a shadow of a doubt, that all students can learn, that all students can succeed and that, with help from brain research and this book, that it is in everyone of us to make such learning happen.

THE BASIC BUILDING BLOCKS OF LEARNING

The basic building blocks of learning are: neurons, brain organization, and information substances.

Neurons, Dendrites, and Axons

There are, by conservative estimate, 100 billion brain cells (neurons). Each neuron has one axon and as many as 100,000 dendrites. The resulting intertwining forms 100 trillion *constantly changing* connections. There are more possible ways to connect the brain's neurons than there are atoms in the universe.[8]

How neurons organize themselves and how they connect with each other results in the outward manifestations of learning and the quality we call intelligence. For example, the graphic below illustrates the increase in complexity of dendrites and axons from birth to age two. As a result, the brain becomes measurably denser and heavier (during infancy, the overall size of the skull increases as well, reaching full size by age five).

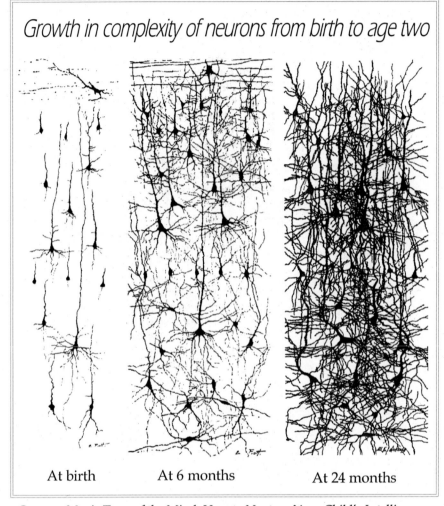

Growth in complexity of neurons from birth to age two

At birth   At 6 months   At 24 months

Source: *Magic Trees of the Mind: How to Nurture Your Child's Intelligence,*
Creativity, and Healthy Emotions from Birth Through Adolescence
by Marian Diamond, Ph.D., and Janet Hopson, 106-107.

Such growth—multiple branching of the dendrites, myelination of axons, enlargement of synapses and overall size of the neurons—is the brain's response to rich sensory input from an enriched environment. In contrast, sterile, boring environments not only result in significantly less growth but in actual shrinking of existing dendrites. A period of drastically reduced enrichment, even as short as four days, can result in measurable shrinkage of dendrites.[9] "Use it or lose it"[10] is a universally acknowledged premise among neuroscientists and is powerful advice when it comes to growing and maintaining a healthy brain. Parents and educators alike, take heed. Your job is to help children (and fellow adults) grow dendrites[11] and to nurture continued use of what is grown.

Exactly how learning occurs is still a mystery, hidden at the molecular level. But the story is rapidly unfolding. In simple terms, there are two ways that neurons in the brain communicate with each other. The means of communication that has been understood for decades is an electrical-chemical process. The sending neuron transmits an electrical signal down its axon to its tip which is very close to the bulbous ending on the dendritic spines of the receiving cell. Chemical messengers, neurotransmitters, travel from the axon to the dendrite across the synaptic gap. If the information is compelling enough[12] to the receiving neuron, it in turn will spark an electrical transmission down its axon to the dendrites of another cell and on and on until the communication is complete, all at the rate of up to a billion times a second.[13] This means of communication carries the bulk of academic learning, particularly symbolic and abstract content, but is heavily influenced by emotion. (See the discussion of information substances in Chapter Two.)

Enrichment Theory. The story of neurons, axons, and dendrites and how to make them develop and grow leads us to the new field of brain enrichment pioneered by Dr. Marian Diamond. The kinds of questions such researchers ask are closely akin to those that educators raise with the timeless question, "How can I best help Johnny learn X (math or geography or spelling)?" Dr. Diamond suggests that the question "How can I help Johnny?" should be re-phrased: "How do I best stimulate Johnny's brain to make it grow, to increase the number and strength of connections being made, and to "hardwire" learning into long-term memory?"

In short, learning is the result of actual physical growth in the brain. To talk about learning is to talk about the physiology of the brain and how to enhance its physical growth and thus learning. According to Dr. Diamond, a number of physiological changes occur when the brain is immersed in an enriched environment:[14]

1. Dendritic spines grow, change shape, or shrink as we experience the world. Neurons grow larger. The brain becomes denser and heavier. Therefore, choose the types of input that will produce the greatest physiological change in the brain.

2. The stimulation of an enriched environment results in significant physiological change in the brain—as much as 20% compared to brains in sterile, boring environments.

3. There is a correlation between brain structure and what we do in life—what we spend time doing and not doing.[15] In other words, how we spend our time—what we ask our brain to do on a daily basis—actually alters its physical structure. Vast amounts of time spent on television and/or video games (4-6 hours daily) wires the brain to do television and video games and does not wire the brain for other things such as physical exploration or high facility for initiating and processing language. If students cannot do what you expect of them, such as learn phonics, take time to build the neural wiring and structures that will enable them to do what is expected of them.

4. Much of the increase in the physical size of the brain (at birth, the brain is one quarter of its eventual adult size) is due to myelination, a process by which fatty tissue forms around the axons of frequently-firing neurons which act like rubber insulation on electrical cords. This allows for speedier and more reliable transmission of electrical impulses thus improving communication among neurons. While much of this process occurs with the unfolding maturation of the brain,[16] much can be deliberately enhanced through ample practice in using the knowledge or skill being learned, particularly in real-world settings which allow for rich sensory input and feedback. See Chapters 4 and 5 for a discussion of developing mental programs.

5. Use it or lose it is a maxim for all ages—birth through old age. "Brains don't just steadily make more and more connec-tions. Instead, they grow many more connections than they need and then get rid of those that are not used. It turns out that deleting old connections is just as important as adding new ones."[17]

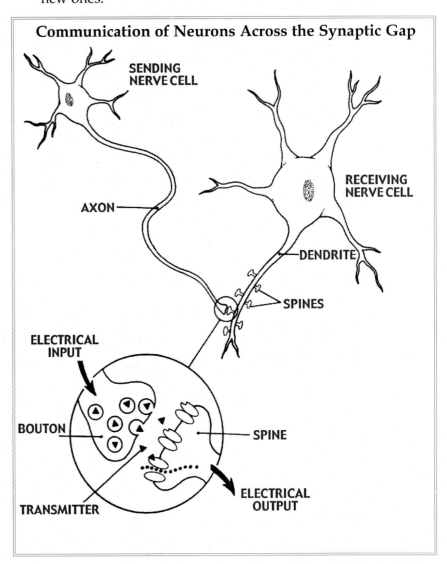

Source: *Magic Trees of the Mind: How to Nurture Your Child's Intelligence, Creativity, and Healthy Emotions from Birth Through Adolescence* by Marian Diamond, Ph.D., and Janet Hopson, p. 26.

Implications: If learning is the result of such physiological changes, then the question for teachers becomes: What should the classroom teacher do to maximize growth in the brain? The answers aren't mysterious or complicated yet they fly in the face of our traditional curricular tools and instructional processes.

1. Eliminate or drastically reduce low-sensory input materials and processes such as textbooks, worksheets, and working in isolation. Provide large amounts of sensory input from *being there* experiences in the real world. Remember, dittos don't make dendrites!

2. Demanding performance when the requisite wiring is not in place is akin to keeping the high jump bar over someone's head when he/she doesn't have the physical skills for jumping it at waist height. In track sports, this would be instantly recognized as both cruel and a foolish waste of time.

3. Design curriculum and instructional strategies that encourage practice and mastery in real-world situations, rather than aiming at quick quiz responses that usually stop at the ability to *recognize* content but don't demand students *understand and and are able to use it.* Using knowledge and skills in real-world applications greatly increases development and maintenance of neural connections.

Brain Organization

Our understanding of how the brain organizes itself is currently undergoing a major paradigm shift. In the 1980s and early 1990s, our view was that the brain was very modular, that different parts of the brain control different abilities and these parts (or modules) operate independently. In this view, words and their meaning were stored in certain places and functions such as vision and hearing were also operated by other parts of the brain.[18]

In contrast, the gradiental/distributive view of the brain holds that different aspects of word meaning are stored close to the sensory and motor areas that participated in acquiring information about these objects.[19] For instance, naming animals activates the left occipital areas (name plus picture) whereas naming tools activates the left premotor regions in charge of right-hand movements (name plus movement when using the tool). For further discussion of the gradiental/distributive view of the brain, see pages 4.2-4.3.

This is exciting stuff! It provides hard brain science to back up what teachers know from working with students. Learning the meanings of 20 vocabulary words a week, when presented for straight memorization, is harder for students to learn and remember than those same 20 words used in real-world conversation at a *being there* location. Inviting the brain to associate words meanings in multiple locations in the brain makes the learning and recall easier and faster plus increases the number of memory "hooks" that can be used to recall. It also builds a stronger structure upon which to build new, related information.

Information Substances

The description of neurons, dendrites, and axons described in this chapter has been bedrock knowledge for some decades. Recently, however, the story has expanded quite dramatically. In short, it seems that the Greeks were onto something 2,000 years ago when they emphasized the importance of educating and training both mind and body.

Another means of communication among neurons, and one that interconnects the entire body, is wholly chemical. These chemicals, often called "information substances"[20] include transmitters, peptides, hormones, factors, and protein ligands. They carry information throughout the body. Some of these substances are created in other organs in the body but, wherever they are produced and wherever else they are received (the heart and respiratory center are major "hot spots"), all are received by neurons in the brain. See the discussion of information substances in Chapter.

TRANSLATING BRAIN RESEARCH INTO ACTION USING THE NINE BODYBRAIN-COMPATIBLE ELEMENTS

Intelligence as a function of experience—active, full-bodied participation in the world—presents a very different picture of learning than the traditional one based on seat time with students quietly working in rows and credits earned for specified hours of lecture and reading of assigned textbooks. Curriculum content cannot be inserted into students' heads but must be assembled by each student through his/her sensory system. Admittedly this is not a tidy or orderly process as it differs dramatically with the uniqueness of each and every brain. Nor are there any guarantees. The major lesson for teachers is that the only way to achieve uniform results is to radically vary the sensory input, giving each student what he/she needs to develop accurate and comprehensive understandings and then learn to apply what they understand.

Bodybrain-Compatible Elements

- Enriched Environment
- Meaningful Content
- Collaboration
- Movement
- Choices
- Adequate Time
- Immediate Feedback
- Mastery
- Absence of Threat & Nurturing Reflective Thinking

The *HET* model presents nine ways to translate brain research into action in the classroom and school. Each of the nine bodybrain-compatible elements is discussed in the order of their power to translate this body of brain research—intelligence as a function of experience—into practical strategies in the classroom.

ENRICHED ENVIRONMENT

Our window on the world is far more powerful than conventional thinking indicates. Human beings have at least 19 senses, not five.[21] And, not surprisingly, there is a direct correlation between the number of senses activated and the amount and locations of brain activity. Quite simply, the greater the range of sensory input, the greater the physiological activity and growth in the brain. The result is more learning and a greater likelihood that such learning will be retained in long-term memory.

While the names of some of these senses may seem foreign, your use of them is not. Consider this story for example, a childhood memory of co-author Karen Olsen that is as vivid today as it was almost half a century ago.

An Example of Vivid Memory Based on High Sensory Input

Age eight, with her older brother, engaged in the thoroughly hopeless but intriguing task of attempting to dam up the creek south of the family home; sunshine on their backs, reflections dancing on the water; bare feet scrunching in the pebbly gravel and gooey mud; the tepid, slow-moving water with darting minnows disturbed by rearranging of rocks and the shovels full of smelly mud; the sweat from their efforts dripping down their faces; their laughter rippling across the creek; her brother's nearness; his patience with a little sister who "never stayed home like the other girls did" …the lessons of that day, the wonder of the creek, the beauty of family relationships.

Such moments of acute sensory awareness stay with us always.[22] To see examples of what information each of the 19 senses processed, see the chart on the following page.

An enriched environment is a learning environment that focuses sensory input—through all 19 senses—on the concept or skill to be learned. Maximizing sensory input is a fundamental

HET goal when developing curriculum and planning instructional strategies for a number of reasons. First, input through the senses is the brain's only way to bring in information from the outside world; there are no short cuts. Second, large amounts of sensory input enable students to grasp the concepts/information accurately and completely, thereby eliminating misunderstandings. Third, large amounts of sensory input is what causes physiological changes in the brain, resulting in the phenomena of learning.

Lesson Planning for the 19 Senses

A fundamental *HET* goal when developing curriculum and planning instructional strategies is to maximize sensory input focusing on the concepts and skills to be taught. When lesson planning, the senses can be grouped into six categories or kinds of input to consider.

The 19 senses activated by each of these kinds of input are illustrated on pages 1.8 and 1.10.

The two kinds of input **least used** in classrooms, *being there* and *immersion,* provide the **most sensory input.** Conversely, the two **most commonly used,** *secondhand* and *symbolic,* provide the **least sensory input.** The definitions of these six kinds of input and the senses they feed are described on pages 1.10 and 1.11.

In the typical classroom, 90 percent of the input consists of secondhand and symbolic input and most hands-on experience comes from manipulating representational items. In the *HET* classroom, the goal is to flip those percentages so that 90 percent of the sensory input during initial learning (meaning-making and practicing how to use what is learned in real-world ways) is from *being there* and immersion experiences and 10 percent from hands-on experience with the real thing.

Secondhand input—principally reading materials, Internet, and video—is then a useful way to extend what has been learned through *being there* experiences supplemented with immersion, and hands-on experiences with the real thing.[23]

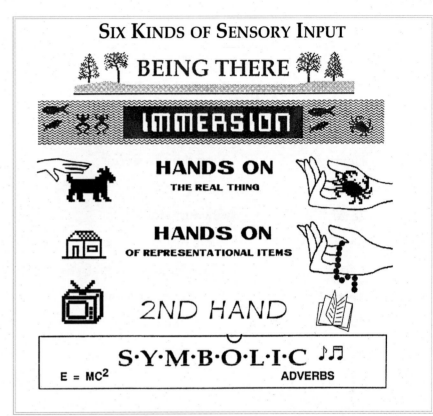

If this information seems disturbing and too impossible to be true, think back to an attempt to learn something "from scratch" that was fraught with difficulties and failures. For co-author Karen Olsen, it was her first experience trying to "learn" computers. This is her story: A colleague and his wife offered computer literacy classes in their home (at the time, they had more computers in their spare bedroom for such a class than the local university did). I was thrilled at the opportunity, paid my $30, and sat in the front row. My instructor-friend dove right into "what goes on inside the box." "Wow," I thought, "If I understood how things work, writing programs, never mind word processing, would be a piece of cake. This is the class for me!"

The story that unfolded boggled my mind. Whoever thought up this stuff in the first place? If I didn't understand something, I raised my hand and kept it there until I got an explanation

THE 19 SENSES

SENSES	KIND OF INPUT	EXAMPLES OF SENSORY INPUT FROM STORY
Sight	Visible light	Reflections dancing on the water; darting minnows, dams breaking, etc.
Hearing	Vibrations in the air	Laughter, gravel scrunching; mud sucking; rocks clashing, splashing
Touch	Tactile contact	Bare feet scrunching in the pebbly gravel; tepid, slow-moving water
Taste	Chemical molecular	Sweat dripping down their faces; an occasional splash of creek water
Smell	Olfactory molecular	Smelly mud
Balance	Kinesthetic geotropic	Keeping balance wading in the deep gravel; moving rocks/mud
Vestibular	Repetitious movement	Re-arranging rocks and shoveling smelly mud
Temperature	Molecular motion	Warm summer day
Pain	Nociception	Thankfully, none!
Eidetic imagery	Neuroelectrical image retention	The vivid picture of the scene and its details
Magnetic	Ferromagnetic orientation	The location of the creek—south of the family home
Infrared	Long electromagnetic waves	The warmth and power of the sun's rays
Ultraviolet	Short electromagnetic waves	The warmth and power of the sun's rays
Ionic	Airborne ionic charge	The refreshing feeling from being around water
Vomeronasal	Pheromonic sensing	Primal sense of smell—body odors, sweat, rotting vegetation
Proximal	Physical closeness	The nearness of the brother
Electrical	Surface charge	The humidity of the creek eliminated any perceivable static electricity
Barometric	Atmospheric pressure	The steady, unchanging atmospheric pressure of a calm summer day
Geogravimetric	Sensing mass differences	Density (weight to mass) of material—pebbly gravel versus gooey mud

I could understand. The night was fascinating. I left the class thrilled to my toes. It was, after all, quite understandable conceptually despite its sci-fi veneer.

The next morning, my mother, who was visiting me at the time and whom I tried to talk into coming with me to the class, asked reasonably enough, "Well, what did you learn last night?"

> # A Maxim:
>
> *There is a direct correlation between the number of senses activated and the amount and locations of brain activity. Human beings have at least 19 senses, not five. Use them!*

"Holy moley, Mom! You should have come. You would've loved it. It was our kind of workshop. He explained what goes on inside the box. It was fabulous!"

"Oh," she said, "So, just what does go on in there?"

"Well, when you plug it in and turn it on, it . . . ah, er."

Egad, how is this possible? I couldn't remember a thing except for my clear recollection that I understood it at the time. But nothing else stuck in my brain! What a waste! What happened?

Two things conspired against my getting the information into long-term memory. First, I had no prior experience with what goes on inside the black box, no mental post office box address for the information. Second, the only sensory input for this new learning was auditory and thus provided no context to help learn about the goings on in the box. Consequently, the information evaporated from my short-term memory during the night.

Remember, there is no such thing as bypassing the sensory system; it is the bodybrain partnership's[24] way of taking in information. We cannot expect to set aside millions of years of evolution in favor of our traditional textbooks, lectures, worksheets, and, yes, computers. Again, the moral of the story here is that dittos and worksheets don't make dendrites!

Even in the area of language arts, sensory input is essential. For example, success in creative writing and poetry, even much of descriptive narrative, depends heavily upon sensory input and reflecting those experiences in words in order to evoke similar feelings and thoughts in the reader. Revisit co-author Karen Olsen's half-century-old memory of playing with her brother in a creek (see page 1.9). A quick, off the cuff reminiscence, it is a vivid descriptive narrative, the stuff from which poetry is written. Now, looking back and comparing it to each of the 19 senses, it is startling to see that the fullness of the memory relied on input from each and every sense.

There are many lessons here for teachers. If we want vivid creative writing, edge-to-edge painting with real detail, deep understanding of concepts, or accurate use of skills, to name but a few areas of learning, we must provide students with full sensory input. *Being there* experiences—visits to real-life locations—are the most powerful way to do so.

For example, choose a favorite work of fiction, such as Pat Conroy's *Prince of Tides,* a short story by Hemingway, a poem you memorized long ago and still recall. Analyze it against the 19 senses. If it's powerful enough to make you feel like you're there, looking at or participating in the scene, you're reading language encoded by all 19 senses or piggybacking on input that was. Once the high levels of sensory input have worked their magic, secondhand and symbolic input "makes sense" and can support learning.

Using Enriched Environment to Enhance Development of Intelligence

The bodybrain-compatible element of enriched environment enhances development of the multiple intelligences in many ways.

Curriculum

- Base curriculum planning at the classroom level on *being there* interactions with the real world. Provide them as early in the study of a concept or skill as possible. Then, revisit the location often and go again at the end of study as a means to assess students' ability to

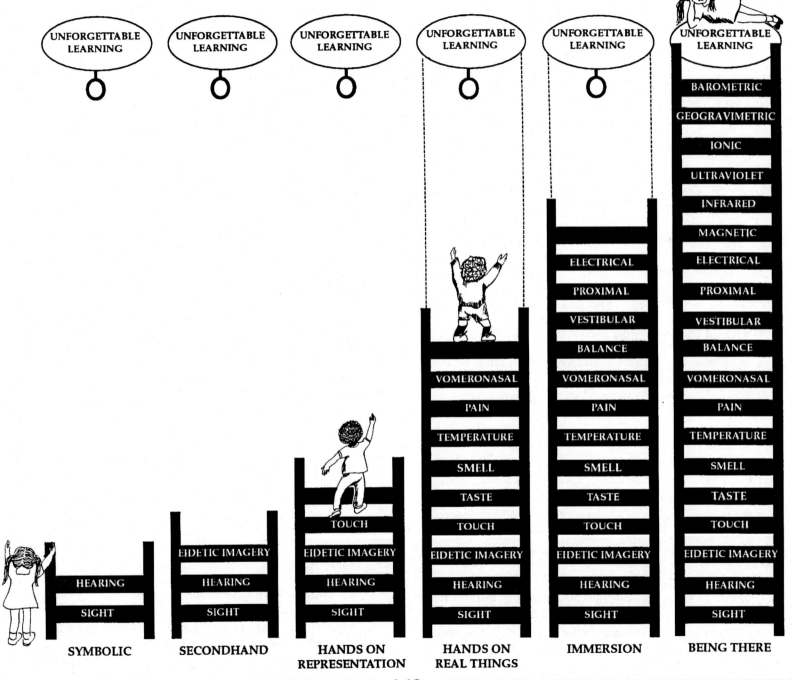

Being there input occurs when real things are studied in their real-world context, such as a pond, lake or wetlands area, a mall, a factory, or a neighbor's backyard—literally *"being there."* All 19 senses are activated, producing maximum electrical and chemical activity in the brain. Input is rich, varied, and plentiful.

Immersion input replicates the real world context of the *being there* experience in the classroom as fully as possible. For example, if a pond is the *being there* site, a classroom pond (a child's swimming pool with a black plastic drape) is created with as many real pond critters and plants as possible. The classroom itself is then made to look like a pond with the water line slightly above the teacher's head when standing. Blue film covers the windows to simulate the water line of the pond. Replicas of animals and plants at the water's edge and underwater cover the walls. The CD plays the sounds of water and pond animals. At least 100 books and other printed materials about ponds, and other multi-media resources fill the room. Models and pictures of pond animals and plants are available for close analysis and exploration. The immersion environment provides input for 13 of the 19 senses.

Hands-on of the real thing provides input through examination of real world things but without the context of *being there* or *immersion*. In the case of the pond, there would be frogs and polliwogs, cattails, and so forth for students to handle and examine closely, engaging 9 of the 19 senses.

Hands-on of representational items provides input from models of real things such as plastic frogs and polliwogs. Without the context of *being there* or *immersion* or the experience of the real items, hands-on of representational items elicits response from only 4 of the 19 senses. Such limited sensory input provides limited brain activation and thus limits pattern-seeking capabilities for many learners. Program-building opportunities are all very limited because real world applications are so difficult to create with only representational items. Hands-on of representational items activates only four senses.

Secondhand input can be found in books, computers, DVDs, and other multi-media presentations which can activate only sight, hearing, and eidetic imagery. Such limited input makes pattern-seeking difficult and provides no opportunities for program-building. Secondhand input evokes only three senses.

Symbolic is the most difficult input to process. High linguistic and spatial intelligence is needed to make use of symbolic input, plus prior *being there* experiences related to the new learnings. Activates only two senses. Fewer than 20 percent of students can learn well through this type of input which includes such things as mathematical sentences, parts of speech, and most of physics, and so forth.

apply what they understand and whether the concepts and skills have been wired into long-term memory.

- Based on the *being there* experience, develop lots of group and individual inquiries* that provide opportunities for solving problems and producing real products, including social/political action projects.

- Take time to access prior experiences of students. Tapping existing memory gives a "post office" address in the brain making new learning more efficient and giving the teacher an opportunity to detect and correct misconceptions.

- Develop inquiries for "homework" which ask the student to apply the information/skill in settings relevant to the student's life (home, neighborhood, friends' interests, hobbies and workplaces of parents, extended family, family friends).

Instructional Strategies

- Make the classroom a complete immersion experience reflecting the *being there* location upon which your curriculum is based.

- Have at least 100 resources (print and nonprint) related to the current topic of student available in the room — real things, models, diagrams, blueprints, sketches, and art objects, as well as the traditional sources such as books, magazines, multimedia, including the Internet.

- Invite guest speakers who are experts on the topics of interest to the classroom.

- Take away all materials — posters, bulletin boards, books, displays, models, etc. — not directly related to the key points and inquiries of the current monthly component or weekly topic.

---

* Inquiries, or activities, are a key structure for developing curriculum in the *HET* model. Inquiries provide opportunities to practice using the concepts and/or skills of the key points. For a discussion of inquiries and key points, see Chapters 15 and 14.

MEANINGFUL CONTENT

No one — student or teacher — gets up in the morning and says, "Oh, boy, I hope this day is boring!" Quite the opposite; children and adults dread boredom. For the brain, it's the equivalent of a heart monitor showing a straight-line . . . death by multiple paper cuts. So what makes content meaningful? Meaningfulness, like beauty, is in the eye of the beholder. But there are some universal truths to follow. Intrinsically meaningful are:

- Real-life situations with high and varied sensory input

- Content that relates to an existing interest, hobby, or favorite activities

- Content with which the learner has prior experience, especially with some facet of a real-world location (If the association is positive, the learner will actively search for meaning.)

- Content relates to the learner's future aspirations

- Novel (to the learner) situations that pique our curiosity

- Activities/knowledge that respected Learning Club members do/find fascinating

- Concepts and/or skills that help the learner meet Glasser's four fundamental needs —

  — Belonging (want to learn what others in the club do)

  — To love and be loved (learning the personal/social skills necessary to be successful in collaborative environments; the deep sense of personal satisfaction and connection to others that comes from service projects)

  — Power (knowledge and skills to become a competent person)

  — Fun (the teacher's classroom leadership style makes learning enjoyable and joyous)

- Problem-solving/product-producing situations in which no one knows the answer or how to go about making the product (challenging but doable) and thus all are needed to accomplish the task

Words and Making Meaning. Traditionally, the study of a new topic begins with memorization of "vocabulary words." The country author remembers, with cold dread, the seemingly endless lists of vocabulary words at the end of every chapter in every textbook for every subject throughout elementary school. Following that were weekly lists of 20 words each and every week throughout her sophomore English class. Such processes are needlessly painful and inefficient.

Why? Because as Leslie Hart explains, "Words fail to convey much meaning except as the hearer already has experience and extracted patterns that give meaning to the words. For example, consider these two statements. A stock broker: "If you sell a security to establish a loss, you just wait 30 days to buy it back or it will be viewed as a wash sale but the waiting period doesn't apply to gains." Or, a musician, "Since the B-flat clarinet is a transposing instrument, the note you play from the written music will actually sound a full tone lower." These are perfectly understandable statements if we bring prior experience to bear. Without prior experience, the words are meaningless. The need for sensory input as the starting point for learning is well illustrated by the following. As the saying goes, 80 percent of reading comprehension is based on prior knowledge.

If you doubt so much hangs on prior knowledge and experience, try your hand at this one:

"*Cayard* forced *America* to the left, filling its sails with 'dirty air,' then tacked into a right-hand shift. . . .That proved to be the wrong side. *America,* flying its carbon fiber/liquid crystal main and headsails, found more pressure on the left. *Cayard* did not initiate a tacking duel until *Il Moro* got headed nearly a mile down the leg. . . . *Cayard* did not initiate a jibbing duel to improve his position heading downwind and instead opted for a more straight-line approach to the finish."[25]

We can assume this paragraph has something to do with sailing and we could answer questions such as these:

1. What kind of air filled America's sail?
2 What kind of sail did America have?
3. How far down the leg did Il Moro get before Cayard initiated a tacking duel?
4. What strategy to the finish did Cayard use?

Does answering these questions about Cayard and America really mean you understand what is happening in this race or, even more importantly, could you participate in the race yourself? For over 99 percent of us, the answer is no. Why? Because we have never been sailing. We lack *being there* experiences from which concepts and skills are developed. This passage could be understood with teacher explanation and the use of a dictionary but arrival at a level of comprehension needed to read and understand other short descriptions of sailing would likely not occur.

This statement bears repeating: Understanding of concepts, as opposed to memorizing factoids, requires large amounts of sensory-based input; the best source of sensory input (richness and variety) comes from *being there* experiences in real-world settings (see the sensory input ladders on page 1.10). Sensory experience is not a luxury; it is a prerequisite for understanding.

The lesson from this story is that it is possible to be an A student because you are a good reader yet not really understand what you've read. Most standardized tests of content, such as science and social studies, are tests of reading ability, not of mastery of content.

We must accept that words convey only limited meaning when our students lack relevant prior experience. Whether from speech or print, understanding words demands bringing information to the situation.[26] Even in social conversation, a comment or question off the subject usually produces a "Huh?" response until the new topic is settled on and relevant prior experience is brought into focus.

In a bodybrain-compatible learning environment, learning occurs like this:

SENSORY INPUT FROM
  BEING THERE   APPLICATION
  EXPERIENCE ➡ CONCEPT ➡ LANGUAGE ➡ TO THE REAL
                                                 WORLD

In contrast, conventional schooling starts with language and definitions *about* things and attempts to move to concept development. The fading ink illustrates the drop off in learning.

LANGUAGE ➡ ➡ ➡ CONCEPT ➡ ➡ ➡ APPLICATION

Frank Smith, in *Insult to Intelligence: The Bureaucratic Invasion of Our Classrooms*, makes the point that when meaning is reached, "learning" occurs automatically and simultaneously.[27] The learner is always asking, What does this situation/information mean to me? How can I use it? How does it affect me now and in my future? "Making sense of the everyday world in relation to ourselves, our needs (physical, emotional, mental), and motivations (interests and need for fun in our lives) is our greatest concern and motivator."[28]

Overcoming Inequities. Brain research and our common sense tell us that the more you know about something, the more meaning you can extract. Given the disparity of experiences that students bring to the classroom, the playing field is anything but level. Only massive sensory input through *being there* experiences simultaneously provides the needed "catch up" experiences for those with no prior relevant experience as well as challenge for those who have "been there, done that."

Luckily for readers of this book, the subject area in which the gaps among students can most readily be overcome is science, a subject that begs for *being there* experiences, immersion, and hands-on of the real thing. Within minutes, enough sensory input can be provided to level the playing field for all students.

The subject area in which the gaps among students is the greatest and takes the most time and work to bridge is language

arts. Why? Because it trades primarily in second-hand input and symbolic input.

Powering Up Second Language Acquisition. Everything that's just been said about words and making meaning and overcoming inequities is doubly true for second language acquisition students.

Making Meaning

According to Leslie Hart, *input* is a key and necessary ingredient for making meaning. "Input is critically important in any kind of learning situation, whoever the learner and whatever is to be learned. The process of learning is the extraction, from confusion, of meaningful patterns. Input is *the raw material* of that confusion, what is perceived through the senses by the individual"[29] that relates to the pattern. (See Chapter 4 for further exploration of this concept.)

In other words, powerful, bodybrain-compatible learning for students occurs when high levels of sensory input from *being there* experiences are processed by the pattern-seeking brain to construct meaning which can be expressed by language (the attachment of a word to this new understanding). Having language then makes possible further exploration and application (program building for long-term retention and use). The brain readily learns (makes meaning) and applies (builds a program for using) information learned in this sequence.

Please note: This paradigm of learning is especially important for second language acquisition.

In contrast, conventional schooling relies heavily on lecture and reading (textbooks/worksheets, Internet, and other second-hand explanations). Beginning with and staying focused on language or vocabulary—definitions of things and processes, whether via lecture or reading—works only when students have had prior experience with what is being discussed or have unusually high linguistic skills. Although such an approach may, and often does, result in high test scores for highly verbal students, it fails to enable students to apply knowledge and skills. The remarkable lack of transfer to long-term memory is represented by the fading ink in the graphic on the previous page.

School As Counter Balance

Every child's brain is unique; a portion of this uniqueness comes from genetic wiring, much is shaped by environment. According to Jane Healy, in her book *Endangered Minds: Why Our Children Don't Think*, "Experience—what children do every day, the ways in which they think and respond to the world, what they learn, and the stimuli to which they decide to pay attention—shapes their brains. Not only does it change the ways in which the brain is used (functional change), but it also causes physical alterations (structural change) in neural wiring systems."[30] What is taken in by the senses makes for profound differences in the structure of the brain. In short, the brain of Video Kid is quite different in structure than that of the Child of Print (the child whose parents have immersed him/her in books, stories, conversation, etc.).

The differences between Video Kid and Child of Print are profound from the teacher's point of view. Whereas Child of Print comes to school with a "well-muscled" left hemisphere and language center, Video Kid, on the other hand, arrives with a Joe Puny left hemisphere and undeveloped language capacity (albeit an active right hemisphere and visually-oriented brain). In the "use it or lose it" environment of the brain, connections form and rapidly die. If Video Kid watches television an average of 130 minutes seven days a week but spends less than four minutes a day on reading,[31] it is clear that Video Kid's preparation is not only highly language-deficient but, in fact, such a daily diet is also very language-antagonistic in terms of developing needed neural networking for language processing. Numerous studies suggest that the brains of spectators, however rich the visual images, are no different from those brains which live in impoverished environments.[32] In other words, if there is no active involvement, there is minimal activity in the brain.

It is not our purpose here to catalog the impact on the modern brain of TV, computers, and other visual, non-interactive technologies. We intend only to make the point that many of today's students come with very little direct experience of the real world and thus with minimal conceptual understanding of what makes the world work. Accompanying this deficit is minimal language development; without receptive and expressive language capability, the seven scientific thinking processes[33] are simply not possible. Thinking demands language; according to Healy, "language is the scaffolding for thought."[34]

In the past we could assume that students came to school with a wide range of experience of the real world and the concepts and language that come with such experience. After all, a working farm was a virtual gold mine of real life experience—animal husbandry, crops of all kinds, the economics of supply and demand, problem-solving spurred by equipment that breaks down in a remote field, and the geometry and mathematics involved in building fences and new buildings. City kids who were a part of the street markets and who had family members living in different neighborhoods had a range of firsthand experiences as well—economics, supply and demand, varied forms of transportation. Consequently, schools of the past could use a wide range of "secondhand" sources during instruction—books, textbooks, workbooks, worksheets, dittos, pictures, models, and, more recently, videos, the internet, blackberries, and so on—because children came to school possessing a rich tapestry of real experiences to build upon and learning continued apace.

Today's students, on the other hand, come with scant experience with the real world and the concepts and language that accompany them because in many areas of the U.S. it is not considered safe to

Scientific Thinking Processes

- Observing
- Communicating
- Comparing
- Organizing
  –ordering
  –categorizing
- Relating
- Inferring
- Applying[35]

be out exploring the neighborhood. These students arrive at school ill-equipped to learn from our "secondhand" sources. As 80% of reading comprehension is based on prior knowledge, one can only take from a book what one brings to the book. Books can expand our knowledge but cannot create it from scratch. According to Frank Smith, "Much of today's school failure results from academic expectations for which students' brains were not prepared—but which were bulldozed into them anyway. Deficits in everything from grammar to geography may be caused by teaching that bypasses the kind of instruction that could help children conceptually come to grips with the subject at hand."[36]

Using Meaningful Content to Enhance Development of Intelligence

The bodybrain-compatible element of meaningful content enhances development of the multiple intelligences in many ways.

Curriculum Development

- State curriculum as concepts and base them in real-world locations, situations, and events.

- Ensure that curriculum is age-appropriate—comprehensible to the student given his/her stage of brain development.

- When planning your curriculum and daily lessons, find out what prior experiences students have had. What concepts and skills do they already understand and can apply? Don't assume that students have the necessary conceptual building blocks from prior experience to understand what your curriculum is about. Investing the time to get to know each student pays big dividends.

- Be alert to misconceptions. To correct them, provide massive amounts of sensory input.

Instructional Strategies

- Provide being there interactions with the real world—people, processes, things. Allow students to explore

beyond what you envision in order to construct their own meaning-understandings that are accurate, complete, and comprehensive.

- Base second language acquisition on being there and immersion experiences which convey the fullness of what the words of the new language mean.

- Use cooperative learning strategies that encourage students to connect prior knowledge with the new.

Collaboration

Research over the past 50 years provides a very compelling endorsement of the power of collaboration to increase learning, improve the quality of products, and make the work/learning environment more pleasant and productive.[37]

Also, from a brain perspective, Leslie Hart, *Human Brain and Human Learning, Updated,* talks about the need for great quantities of input to the brain which collaboration helps provide. Frank Smith, in *Insult to Intelligence: The Bureaucratic Invasion of Our Classrooms,* lists opportunity for manipulation of information as one of the key ingredients for learning. Active learning processes result in active brains. Collaboration is not just a bow to the social needs of students, it is a vital way of enhancing academic learning.

Full understanding of what is being learned and the ability to apply it in real-life settings—creative problem solving and flexible use of what is learned—depends upon ample opportunity to manipulate information in our heads, to test it, expand it, connect it with prior learnings. Collaborating with others allows us to examine our own thinking while expanding our knowledge base. According to both authors, one teacher facing a classroom of thirty brains, each with very different ways of learning, is insufficient to the task. Collaboration—students teaching each other and providing a sounding board for each other—is an essential classroom structure in a bodybrain-compatible learning environment.

Powerful rationales for collaboration come also from business. In 1989, the U.S. Department of Labor released its commission report entitled, *Investing In People*. An entire chapter was devoted to what education needs to do in order to improve the quality of the American work force. This is one of their observations:

"Business can make additional contributions by providing schools with the information that they need to develop course content and instructional methods that meet the current and emerging needs of the work place. Increasingly, employees will have to work in cooperative groups, be able to make decisions about production problems and processes, and develop the ability to acquire new skills and behavior on the job. We urge schools to adjust their instructional methods to match more closely the situation students will later face in the work place."

The requisite skills for running one's own business are and have always been problem-solving, decision-making, and the ability to communicate with peers and adults—be it farmer, homemaker, inventor, engineer, or a businessman (even as a shoeshine boy or delivery girl). However, with the growth of huge, multi-national corporations and large bureaucracies, a significant portion of our population are now employees, not entrepreneurs. Thus, significant numbers of students are growing up in homes where the work of the parents or other adults is not known to them and the standards of successful business (such as the drive to master skills and provide quality customer service) are rarely modeled with a sense of consequence to the survival of the business or to one's personal reputation in the community. Collaboration in the classroom over real problems to be solved and real products to be created goes a long way to filling in that experiential gap for students.

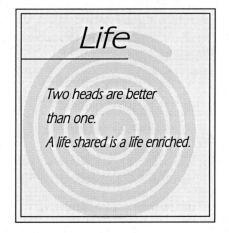

Life

Two heads are better than one.

A life shared is a life enriched.

As previously cited, collaboration increases understanding and improves quality of output. And this brings us back to the classroom. Collaboration dramatically increases opportunities for the bodybrain partnership to play an active rather than passive role in learning thus spurring physiological change in the brain. It is an essential instructional strategy for the classroom and should be used daily. Do note, however, that collaboration needs to be balanced with times for reflective thinking (see Chapter 2).

Using Collaboration to Enhance Development of Intelligence

The bodybrain-compatible element of collaboration enhances development of intelligence in many ways.

Curriculum Development

- The content for good collaboration should be:

  1) A challenge that no one group member working alone can do. Thus, genuine inclusion of all is a must rather than a sociological nicety.[38]

  2) Reflective of real life and engage the 19 senses.

- The content of inquiries assigned for collaborative work should include social/personal skills as well as curriculum content.

- In the HET model, collaborative groups are called Learning Clubs.[39] The goal of collaborative tasks should always be increased achievement and higher quality products. Collaboration is a means to an end (learning), not an end in itself. Never use collaboration as a social event. If you want to have a party or allow chatting to fill in an odd moment or two, have the party or allow chatting in pairs. Collaboration should be viewed by students as genuine work, serious study. The value of the work should be obvious to all during collaborative work.

Instructional Strategies

- Change the composition of the Learning Clubs monthly or at least every six weeks. Getting to know others well accelerates learning, prevents cliques, and increases opportunities to practice applying the Lifelong Guidelines and LIFESKILLS.* Changing group members gives an opportunity for a fresh start for students who get off on the wrong foot with their first Learning Club group. Learning how to get to know others, and be comfortable doing so, is a critical personal/social skill.

- In addition to the ongoing class family group, create groups for skills and interests.

  Skill groups—short-term, ad hoc groups for studying specific skills or concepts among which students shift from group to group as mastery is attained

  Interest groups—opportunities to share/work on a topic of special interest

- The two primary purposes of collaboration are to:

  1) Enhance achievement by increasing input to the bodybrain learning partnership and increasing emotional engagement and opportunities to apply what is learned and

  2) Equalize social status in the classroom. .

MOVEMENT

It's humbling to think that our amazing, science fiction-like technology of the 21st century has finally reached a level that it can tell us what the Greeks knew 2,500 years ago. The body and mind are a partnership affair—you can't develop one without the other. They are in fact a single operating system.

---

* The Lifelong Guidelines and LIFESKILLS are the behaviors guiding both students and adults. They form the basis for creating a sense of community and for ongoing classroom leadership and management. See Chapters 9 and 10.

What took us so long?

What the Greeks understood through observation of the human condition and applied to the education of their young, we now know from scientific fact. However, our society seems resistant to applying the implications to our schools and youth. But, I'm getting ahead of myself. For an explanation of the brain research behind movement as a tool for enhancing learning, see Chapter 2. For our purposes here, three things are key:

- Movement is fundamental to the very existence of a brain. In fact, only an organism that moves from place to place even requires a brain.[40]

- The entire front half of the brain is devoted to organizing action, both physical and mental. "Higher" brain functions have evolved from movement and still depend on it.[4]

- Movement is crucial to every brain function, including memory, emotion, language, and learning.[42]

This being the case, it is obvious that having students sit quietly in rows is a worst case scenario for the brain. What it needs is active participation from its partner, the body. However, *being there* experiences are tailored made for the bodybrain partnership. There is action, emotion, and plenty of raw material for cognitive processes.

Using Movement to Enhance Development of Intelligence

The bodybrain-compatible element of movement enhances development of intelligence in many ways.

Curriculum Development

- Add to your key points an example of how the concept is used so the movement inherent in using the concept is part of the brain's encoding. Do the same with skill key points unless the use of the skill is obvious. Whenever possible, point out applications of the key point that affect students now at home, school, their favorite mall, etc., not just down the road later in life.

- Base your inquiries in *being there* locations. Make them action oriented, requiring that a problem typical of that location be solved or a product needed or sold at that location be produced.

- Code your inquiries according to the multiple intelligences as a way of reminding yourself how well you are including movement. Make sure you develop plenty of inquiries for bodily-kinesthetic, musical, spatial, and interpersonal intelligences, all of which emphasize movement.

Instructional Strategies

- During direct instruction, illustrate using hands-on of the real thing

- When selecting inquiries for whole class, group, or individual work, assign those that include movement first. Assign linguistic inquiries (e.g., write a paragraph or essay, make a list, look up in the dictionary, write a poem or lyrics for a rap song) only after students have developed a full and accurate understanding of the concept or skill and are able to apply what they understand. In fact, as a rule of thumb, assign last those inquiries that are wholly linguistic.

- Use movement throughout the day to:
    - Reset emotions (to energize or to slow the pace as needed)
    - Pique interest by illustrating how things are used
    - Use the body to do memorable simulations (such as make the shapes of the letter of the alphabet, mimic animal movements, perform plays, skits, and hand signs, and so forth)

 ## Choices

The most mind-numbing quality of bureaucracy is its assembly line sameness. Common sense and brain research to the contrary, "the system" is based on the misguided assumption that the same input (textbook and lecture) will produce the same learning, that the same equals equity, that the same equals fairness, and that because of the misbehavior of a few, all must be restricted from an activity or punished with a blanket treatment.

In reality, nothing could be more unfair than giving two very different brains—and no two brains are alike—the same input and expecting the outcome to be the same. It's not only unfair, it's cruel. If we want the same learning outcomes from different brains, we must provide different input to each—whatever each brain needs to arrive at the standard end point. And given the huge differences in prior experiences, intelligence strengths, personality preferences, and brain processes, reliance on the textbook and lecture are patently ridiculous.

To some, however, the idea of offering choices to students (and teachers) may seem like warmed-over "Do your own thing" from the 60s. Somehow offering alternatives is viewed as antithetical to high standards or the notion of core curriculum for all. Some might believe that having choices is fluff or, more to the point, that it runs against the grain of having clear standards and high expectations: one can't just go around doing what one wants all the time; learning after all is serious business and therefore should be expected to hurt a little.

But in reality, offering students choices—ones well crafted/ selected by the teacher to ensure mastery of key points—has enormous power to enhance learning. In addition to its many positive emotional effects, having choices allows students to select the kind of input that they most need in order to understand and apply concepts and skills. Although this demands that teachers develop a rich variety of inquiries in the short run, in the long run it's much more time and energy efficient because it significantly reduces the amount of re-teaching and remedial teaching needed when initial instruction fails.

The choices to be offered should vary greatly due to age, ability to stay focused on the task, and experience with making and sticking with decisions.

For example, for the young learner, choice can be as simple as chalk versus crayon or paint and the number of options need to be limited to two or three. Although learning to speak and write standard English is not an item of choice for an educated person, the content of essays could and should take into account student interests. Also, students who have never been to the ocean, need more time exploring tidepools and more time discussing what they find than students who frequently visit the ocean. First timers would also benefit from construction projects creating an immersion experience of the tidepools while the frequent visitor might be ready to move to secondhand resources at the library.

The truth is that offering choices is essential if one's goal is mastery and application of concepts and skills, not to mention creating lifelong learners who possess a passion for learning.

Using Choices to Enhance Development of Intelligence

> ## Choices
>
> *In reality, nothing could be more unfair than giving two very different brains—and no two brains are alike—the same input and expecting the outcome to be the same. It's not only unfair, it's cruel.*

The bodybrain-compatible element of choices enhances development of intelligence in many ways.

Curriculum Development

- Develop at least 5-10 inquiries for every key point.
  - Design some for whole class work, some for collaborative choice, and some for individual choice.
  - Make sure that you build in choice based on the multiple intelligences and Bloom's taxonomy (see Chapter 3) plus personality preferences (see Chapter 6).

- Make them action-oriented requiring students to apply concepts and skills to real-life problems and products.

- Encourage students, after teaching them the format, to write their own inquiries. Select those you think will provide the best application and practice of concepts and skills.

Instructional Strategies

- During meaning-making/gaining an understanding of concepts and skills, invite students to select inquiries that rely on intelligences in which the student is strong; during practice applying what is understood, encourage students to select inquiries requiring intelligences that they wish to strengthen.

- Provide opportunities for students to tutor each other. Looking for ways to explain and demonstrate what we understand to another person increases our mental processing and creates new " Aha's."

Adequate Time

It was Albert Einstein who said that man invented the concept of time and has spent the rest of his life being controlled by it! It seems all the more true today when technology has literally added 20 percent to our work week, mainly because we take on larger and larger undertakings due to the fabled promise of assistance from our technological helpers—computers, fax machines, cellular telephones, and instantaneous worldwide communication.

In addition, knowledge continues to accumulate daily at an ever-expanding rate. As it does so, it is more essential than ever that we constantly reevaluate what we believe students should know in order to become contributing members of society. As higher expectations—state standards, benchmarks, tests, etc.—wind their political course, too often the result is more of the same—more dates, more facts, more definitions, more homework.

We need to reduce the number of standards by writing them conceptually so they can take us deeper into meaningful content which in turn allows students to immerse themselves in understanding and learning to use what they understand in real-world ways. Skills likewise should be grouped into meaningful wholes. Until then, we need to pull the standards, however fragmented they might be, into real-world settings that can help give them a sense of coherence, relevance, and importance. *Being there* experiences provide a powerful glue. Both understanding and learning to use what we understand require time for the brain to engage and make those mysterious physiological changes that result in long-term memory.

Simply put, physical growth—of the body or of the brain—requires time. Time to explore, time to reflect, time to act, time to evaluate, time to try again and again until we get it right, until we master the concept or skill to be learned. And, clearly, the amount of time needed varies wildly from brain to brain depending on the amount of prior knowledge relevant to the current task, the brain's processing preferences, personal likes and passions, and so forth.

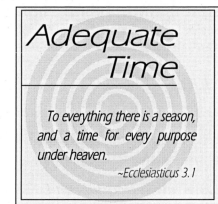

Adequate Time

To everything there is a season, and a time for every purpose under heaven.

~Ecclesiasticus 3.1

To understand the power of this brain-compatible element, it might be helpful to apply it to our own lives first. For example, how many of us would sit down to complete our income taxes on a short weekend, knowing that the task will take at least three to four days of uninterrupted work to figure it out and then get it computed? Or, how many of us are eager to take a two-hour task out of our in-basket when we don't have a two-hour time block and we know that, with interruptions, it will end up taking us six hours? How many of us jump into learning a new software program at work because we don't have the needed chunk of time? Answer: a very rare few.

Similarly, how many of our students refuse to engage in a learning task when they feel certain that they won't have enough time to complete it successfully? In too many classrooms the clock is the commander. Ten minutes for recess, 40 minutes for language arts, 20 minutes for P.E., 35 minutes for music. What percentage of misbehavior and acting out has its roots in the frustration that comes from knowing time is inadequate and failure a certainty? Just a guess, more than half.

Adequate time is a critical element for successful learning and performance. We must begin to value learning more highly than bureaucracy's demand for lock step schedules.

Using Adequate Time to Enhance Development of Intelligence

The bodybrain-compatible element of adequate time enhances development of intelligence in many ways.

Curriculum Development

- Reduce the number of things to be learned by teasing out the underlying concepts and presenting them in meaningful chunks. Once students understand the concept, additional related knowledge can be learned much more easily. As Frank Smith says, "Understanding takes care of learning." Learning then becomes nearly effortless and automatic.

- Clarify in your own mind exactly what you want students to understand and then what you want them to do with it. Factoids can then easily be left behind.

Instructional Strategies

- Before you begin planning the sensory input students will need, carefully assess the extent of their prior experience and knowledge relevant to the concept or skill. Then allocate the time needed for *being there, immersion,* and *hands-on of the real thing* in the initial time block so students move beyond recognition to understanding. For subsequent instruction and inquiries, make sure students can complete their work without interruption. Long-term projects are the exception but even then adequate blocks of time should be allocated to allow students to "get into it" and make satisfying progress.

- Teach students to manage their time and to recognize plateau points in their work—natural breaking points at which a pause would be productive rather than disruptive.

- Make time for reflecting on what was accomplished—individually and as a group.

IMMEDIATE FEEDBACK

Immediate feedback is a necessary element in the learning environment—both for pattern seeking and for program building (see Chapters 4 and 5). In all learning environments except the school, it is present in abundance. Consider, for example, when children first begin to talk. Each time they say something incorrectly, we immediately give them the correct word, usage, and pronunciation. Imagine letting all their mistakes pile up during the week and correcting them on Friday!

Or, think back to the time you learned to drive a car. Feedback was instantaneous and continuous. If you returned home with no dents and no tickets, your parents knew you had a fairly successful time! Similarly, when learning to play a game or sport or beginning a hobby, feedback is built in, immediate, and continuous. In such cases, the learning materials or the conditions themselves provided the immediate feedback, or your fellow adventurer interpreted your progress toward mastery. This is a far cry from the classroom setting where students must press for information with the often asked questions: "Is this right, teacher?" "Teacher, is this the way it's supposed to be?"

Frank Smith, in *Insult to Intelligence: The Bureaucratic Invasion of Our Classrooms*,[43] states that learning does not require coercion or irrelevant reward. Learning is its own reward. Feedback that tells

us we have succeeded at a learning task produces a burst of neurotransmitters, producing a "chemical high" that is readily observable in the spark in a child's eye as the " aha" registers.

The more immediate, intrinsic, and unambiguous the feedback, the faster and more accurate the learning. For example, learning to ride a bike. If you don't get the balance right, you hit the ground. Ambiguous? Not! In contrast, taking an essay test that will be graded and returned next week (and that is fast as essay exams go!) or doing all the odd number problems for math homework and getting a response from the teacher hours or days after the task is done violates all the important rules for learning. By then, the brain either learned it wrong or didn't learn it at all.

Few worksheets or dittos provide feedback that is self-correcting or intrinsic. As a consequence, children feel rudderless, confused, powerless, dependent on someone else, and either anxious or bored. Hardly the characteristics of a bodybrain-compatible learning environment. Without immediate feedback, learning is seriously impeded and students are left to tug at their teacher's shirt sleeve to ask, "Teacher, teacher, is this right?"

Using Immediate Feedback to Enhance Development of Intelligence

The bodybrain-compatible element of immediate feedback enhances development of intelligence in many ways.

Curriculum Development

- Re-evaluate the starting point of your curriculum content. Shift the point of view of your curriculum content from disciplines to a need to understand the real world: locations, events, settings. "Disciplines" are an artifact of Western culture's way of talking about the world, a classic example of the parts not adding up to the whole. Start with the whole—the real world and *being there* experiences that offer intrinsic feedback rather than external (teacher or expert) feedback. Focus on doing, on applying concepts and skills in productive ways.

- Design action-oriented inquiries whose tasks provide natural, real-world feedback as the students carry out the inquiry.

- Teach students how to use/adapt the 3Cs of assessment and other self-assessment tools. The 3Cs are: correct, complete, and comprehensive (see Chapter 19).

Instructional Strategies

- Teach students to identify what they will need before they begin a learning task—what LIFESKILLS, prerequisite skills and knowledge, and how to tell if they are being successful at coming to an accurate understanding of and ways to apply concepts and skills. Model/Teach them to use self-talk to help them when they feel confused, bogged down, or discouraged.

- Help sensitize students to the feedback built into the real world; help them learn to direct self-talk to guide reflection on their own work and thus develop confidence in their own ability to provide feedback for themselves.

- Increase the number of "teachers" by organizing students into Learning Clubs; empower them to provide feedback. Also, eliminate tracking (students are equally unable to help each other), create multi-age classrooms (at least three grade levels is ideal), and arrange for cross-age tutoring.

- Limit your direct instruction to 16 minutes or less; during inquiry work, circulate among the students to give them immediate feedback individually and as a group.

- Allow sufficient time for students to be thoughtful about what they're doing and the progress they're making.

- Teach them to use simple, self-constructed or teacher-made rubrics by which they can assess their progress. Often just asking a self-assessment question helps guide learning.

MASTERY/APPLICATION

One of the greatest frustrations for teachers is "I taught them but they didn't learn." What happened?

In the *HET* model, mastery means completion of both steps in the new definition of learning (see Chapters 4 and 5); it means being able to apply what is understood in real-world ways and practicing how to use that skill or knowledge until it becomes wired into long-term memory.

Mastery in the *HET* model does not mean achieving adult-level expertise; it means acquiring competence at understanding and using concepts and skills at a level appropriate for a child at his/her age.

The goal of mastery is achieving competence at navigating through life. This is in stark contrast to accepting a score of 80 percent or higher on a quiz or standardized test as proof of "learning," an unacceptable outcome for the billions we spend on education and testing.

A Dash of Common Sense

To assess mastery/competence in the *HET* classroom, we recommend asking two common sense questions:

"What do you want students to understand?"

and

"What do you want them to do with it?"

These two questions parallel the two-step definition of learning used in the *HET* model.

The Caines, in their book *Making Connections: Teaching and the Human Brain*, suggest four indicators to guide your evaluation:[44]

- The ability to use the language of the discipline or subject in complex situations and in social interaction

- The ability to perform appropriately in unanticipated situations

- The ability to solve real problems using the skills and concepts

- The ability to show, explain, or teach the idea or skill to another person who has a real need to know

These guidelines are imminently genuine and authentic; they also require both *being there* experiences and real-world practice using concepts and skills before the assessment process begins. For a discussion of learning to the level of mastery as a two-step process, see Chapters 4 and 5; also see Chapter 19 on assessment.

Using Mastery/Application to Enhance Development of Intelligence

The bodybrain-compatible element of mastery/application enhances development of intelligence in many ways.

Curriculum Development

- Make sure what you're asking students to understand and be able to do is genuinely useful in the real world. Eliminate factoids* and always provide examples of uses for concepts and skills beyond the school walls.

- Base your curriculum in real-life locations. Use the real-world standards of mastery inherent in the roles of those who work/use the location. What concepts and skills from your curriculum must these people understand and be able to use? To what levels?

Instructional Strategies

- Help students tune in to real-world standards that apply to what you are teaching. Eliminate any double standards—this is good enough for school but would get you fired on the job.

- Encourage students to question. "What is this good for?" "So what?" "Why is this important for me to know and be able to do?" Be prepared to answer such questions.

---

* When developing curriculum, there is no bigger enemy than factoids. They kill student interest, elicit little emotion to assist the learning process, and aren't memorable. They therefore are difficult to record in long-term memory. For example, Columbus sailed in 1492.

ABSENCE OF THREAT / NURTURING REFLECTIVE THINKING

In simple terms, fear limits exploration. Threat—real or perceived—significantly restricts, if not eliminates, students' ability to fully engage in the learning process. To explore the new and different and to be open to new ideas requires confidence that one is in a safe environment, one in which mistakes and difficulty in understanding/doing something are considered just part of learning, not an opportunity for sarcasm and put-downs.

Building intelligence—the capability to solve problems and produce products—requires exuberant and curiosity-driven exploration, full focus on the learning at hand, maximum activation of the senses and bodybrain partnership. For this, absence of threat is an absolute must, a prerequisite for reaching the mental state of reflective thinking.

For a fuller discussion of the role of emotion as a gatekeeper to learning and performance, see Chapter 2.

Using Absence of Threat/Nurturing Reflective Thinking to Enhance Development of Intelligence

The bodybrain-compatible element of absence of threat/nurturing reflective thinking enhances development of intelligence in many ways.

Curriculum Development

- Know your students. Make sure that your curriculum is age-appropriate and thus understandable to them. Nothing rips apart a student's sense of confidence faster than knowing that he/she doesn't understand what is going on when others do.

- Develop, and begin with, inquiries that help students bring forward any prior experiences related to the key point.

Instructional Strategies

- Help students make connections between what they are now studying and their lives now—at school, at home, wherever they go. If you can't find a connection, don't waste your students' and your time teaching it. The world is full of urgent things for students to learn—for their safety, their health, their well-being, not to mention their future capacity to succeed at work and family life and be a contributing member of society.

- Provide a good mix of collaborative time and intrapersonal time, stimulation and time to be reflective.

- Provide immediate feedback in order to keep self-doubt and frustration at a minimum.

ENDNOTES

1   For an extraordinary look at this physiological growth in the brain first became available in 1995, see Diane Sawyer, "Your Child's Brain," *ABC News Prime Time* (January 25, 1995).

2   Reuven Feurstein is an eminent cognitive psychologist, known for his groundbreaking research in cognitive mediation and practice. He has established the principle that "all children can learn" while working with culturally deprived, retarded, and autistic children. Professor Feurstein developed a classroom curriculum designed to build the cognitive functions of students diagnosed by others as incapable of learning. His program, Instrumental Enrichment, provides students with the concepts, skills, strategies, operations, and techniques necessary to become independent thinkers.

3   Marian Diamond, author of several books on the brain, was a Professor of Anatomy at Berkeley for over thirty years and director of the university's Lawrence Hall of Science from 1990 to 1996. A pioneer brain researcher, she conducted numerous lines of research into the effect of the environment and hormones on the forebrain. She also has investigated structural changes in the cerebral cortex induced by an enriched environment and structural changes in the cerebral cortex as influenced by sex steroid hormones. Her groundbreaking work in the 1970s and '80s studying the effect of enriched and impoverished environments on the brains of rats, which she later extended to humans, resulted in her "enrichment theory." Enrichment theory should be read by all teachers, administrators, and parents. A layman's description can be found in *Magic Trees of the Mind: How to Nurture Your Child's Intelligence, Creativity, and Healthy Emotions from Birth Through Adolescence.* (New York: A Dutton Book, 1998 and by Plume/Penquin Group, 1999).

4   This definition of intelligence, developed by Howard Gardner, is the most useful definition for the classroom that we have found. See *Frames of Mind: Theory of Multiple Intelligences* (New York: Basic Books, Inc., 1985 and 1993), x and *Intelligence Reframed* (New York: Basic Books, Inc., 1999 and 2000), 44. For other models of intelligence, see David Perkins and Strauss.

5   Leslie A. Hart, *Human Brain and Human Learning,* 3rd ed. (Black Diamond, WA: Books for Educators, Inc., 2002), 87.

6 John Bruner, in his article, "A Bridge Too Far" (*Educational Researcher*, August, 1997) has challenged that a jump from brain research to classroom application is too far a leap, that we don't have grounds for doing so, that we should, instead, base educational practice on the work of cognitive psychologists (he being one). While his cautionary tale is important—education is infamous for its leaps to unfounded fads—there are brain research findings that have been confirmed and reconfirmed over the past twenty years. These concepts also resonate with our intuitions and experiences, personal and professional. Furthermore, the curriculum development and instructional strategies recommended to translate them into action are not "new." They are proven strategies from the fields of psychology, sociology, and education. See page 18. In truth, it would be easier to implement the implications brain research if the strategies were completely new. It's much harder to implement an old strategy differently and for a different purpose (a why from brain research). Old habits take us quickly back to old practices done the old way. It takes considerable ongoing vigilance to stay true to the new why and the new twist to the old.

7 John J. Ratey, *A User's Guide to the Brain: Perception, Attention, and the Four Theaters of the Brain* (New York: Pantheon Books, 2001 and 2002), 18.

8 Ratey, 20.

9 Marian Diamond observed the impact of boredom on young and adolescent rats: "A boring environment had a more powerful thinning effect on the cortex than an exciting environment had on cortex thickening. Young rats are obviously very susceptible to losing mental ground when not challenged, and that shrinkage shows up after just four days. In rodent teenagers, at least, the shrinkage can begin to be reversed again after four days of enrichment." Given the number of parallels between the effects of enrichment and boredom on the brains of rats and humans that have proven true, this is quite disturbing. Among many things, it should cause us to reexamine the school calendar. It would appear that the traditional agrarian calendar with three months of summer vacation works strongly against those who most depend upon the public schools for learning. See *Magic Trees of the Mind: How to Nurture Your Child's Intelligence, Creativity, and Healthy Emotions from Birth Through Adolescence*.

10 "Use it or lose it" is more than a catchy phrase or metaphor. It applies to the brain "directly and literally." See Elkhonon Goldberg, *The Executive Brain: Frontal Lobes and the Civilized Mind* (Oxford: University Press, 2001 and 2009), 209.

11 The visual image of how dendrites grow and connect in the brain—captured on video as early as 1995 ·see Diane Sawyer, "Your Child's Brain," *ABC News Prime Time*, January 25, 1995) is one teachers should hold in their mind—and teach toward—every day.

12 William Calvin, author of *How Brains Think: Evolving Intelligence, Then and Now,* talks about competing choruses, each singing its own message or answer and trying to get others neurons to agree. The chorus best able to recruit neighboring neurons into singing its song determines which competing message wins out. An example of this is when we "can't make up our mind." Choice A or B, is it a cheetah or a leopard? (Conversations with William H. Calvin, January, 1997, Covington, Washington.)

13 Diamond and Hopson, 26.

14 Diamond and Hopson, 26.

15 Jane Healy, *Endangered Minds: Why Children Don't Think — And What We Can Do About It* (New York: Simon & Schuster, 1990 and 1999).

16 Diamond and Hopson, 26.

17 Another method of brain organization is pruning, the result of a chemical wash of neurons that are not connected. The synapses that carry the most messages get stronger and survive, while weaker synaptic connections are cut out. Experience determines which connections will be strengthened and which will be pruned: connections that have been activated most frequently get preserved. Between about age ten and puberty, the brain will ruthlessly destroy its weakest connections, preserving only those that experience has shown to be useful. See A. Gopnik, A. Meltzoff, and Patricia Kuhl, *The Scientist in the Crib: Minds, Brains, and How Children Learn* (New York: William Morrow and Company, 1999), 186-187. Also see Ratey, *User's Guide to the Brain*, 24-26. See also pages 19-26 for an electrifying description of how the fetal brain forms, connects, organizes, prunes, and operates.
Pruning plays a particularly significant role in adolescence.

18 Goldberg, 209.

19 Goldberg, 65.

20 Candace Pert, *Molecules of Emotion: Why You Feel the Way You Feel* (New York: Scribner, 1997), 179.

21 Our first introduction to the existence of at least 19 senses came from Bob Samples, *Open Mind, Whole Mind* (CA: Jalmar Press, 1987). See also Robert Rivlin and Karen Gravelle, *Deciphering Your Senses* (New York: Simon and Schuster, 1984). There is an interesting history here. Robert Rivlin and Karen Gravelle present the scientific evidence underpinning the 19 senses and give a historical perspective explaining why the mistaken notion of the five senses has persisted for so many centuries despite scientific evidence to the contrary. ". . . according to the Medieval philosopher Cornelius Agrippa, arguing Plato's philosophy, 'Divinity is annexed to the mind, the mind to the intellect, the intellect to the intention, the intention to the imagination, the imagination to the senses, and the senses at last to things. For this is the bond and continuity of nature.'"

"It used to be so simple. There were five senses and they created a picture of the world inside your head. But new ways of probing the brain are transforming this view of sensory perception. For starters, we have far more than five senses; the consensus is that there are at least 21." *New Scientist,* (New York: Schnell Publishing Co. Inc., January 29, 2005).
"There was, in fact, a divine relationship between the senses and the world they sensed. And, like many things in God's divine plan for the universe, the senses were seen to occur in fives—a prime number with considerable symbolic significance. How convenient, then, to think of the body as having five senses, corresponding roughly to the sensory organs (eyes, ears, nose, tongue, and skin). That the skin could feel both temperature and touch, to say nothing of pain, was somehow conveniently overlooked in order to align the essential unity of the human body with a metaphysical plan of the universe; to say we had eight or eighteen senses simply wouldn't do." (Rivlin and Gravelle, *Deciphering Your Senses*, 15).
Since the work of these early pioneers, the link between sensory input and physiological growth in the brain has been well established. John Medina provides the best contemporary summary in his book *Brain Rules: 12 Principles for Surviving and Thriving at Work, Home, and School* ((Seattle, WA: Pear Press, 2008), 111-113: "All sensory encoding processes have these common characteristics:

• The more elaborately we encode information at the moment of learning, the stronger the memory,

• A memory trace appears to be stored in the same parts of the brain that perceived and processed the initial input, and

• Retrieval may best be improved by replicating the conditions surrounding the initial encoding."

22 The power of the 19 senses is easily verified by our own experiences. Simply ask yourself to recall one of your most vivid memory from childhood. Analyze the scene in your mind's eye. You will discover input from most, if not all, of the 19 senses.

23 One can't overstress the importance of full sensory input through *being there* experiences in building the necessary neural wiring for understanding the concepts involved. Once understanding through sensory input and prior experience is brought together, secondhand input allows the learner to extend and expand learning.

24 Candace Pert's pioneering research (discovery of the opiate receptor, 1972) on how the chemicals inside our bodies form a dynamic information network, linking mind and body, was revolutionary. By establishing the biomolecular basis for our emotions, Pert has come to the brilliant conclusion that it is our emotions and their biological components that establish the crucial link between mind and body. This does not repudiate modern medicine's gains; rather her findings complement existing techniques by offering a new, scientific understanding of the power of our minds and our feelings to affect our health, well being, and learning.
See also John Medina's summary of the power of emotion, Rule #4: Attention . . . Emotion matters, *Brain Rules: 12 Principles for Surviving and Thriving at Work, Home, and School*, 71-94. The DVD that accompanies the book.provides a useful introduction to and overview of the concepts presented in the book.

25 *USA Today*, May 13, 1992, 9.

26 Leslie A. Hart, *Human Brain and Human Learning* (Black Diamond, WA: Books for Educators, 2002), 18.
A good example of the anemic power of words without sensory input from current or prior experience is illustrated by the video, *A Private Universe*. Interviewers ask Harvard University graduates in their caps and gowns the answer to this question: "Explain the reasons for the seasons." Over 80 percent of the randomly selected students and faculty—despite their middle school and university science classes—give the "stove is hot" theory, i.e., in the summer the earth is much closer to the sun and is therefore hotter. In fact, the earth's orbit is nearly round; distance from the sun is not a factor. This despite the amount of formal teaching received—varying from none to classes in advanced

planetary motion—yet another example of the power of the *being there* experience over secondhand information! The toddler's experience with hot stoves prevails.

Therefore, meaningfulness for elementary students must begin with firsthand, *being there*, here and now experiences. They provide the mental scaffolding for the words which represent the concepts and definitions of things they have experienced. The number of "experiences" must continuously increase so that students will have a basis for relating and applying new information.

27 Frank Smith, *Insult to Intelligence: The Bureaucratic Invasion of Our Classrooms* (New York: Arbor House, 1986).

28 Smith.

29 See the discussion of the brain as pattern seeker, Chapter 4, especially the excerpts from *Human Brain and Human Learning* by Leslie Hart.

30 Healy, *Endangered Minds*, 50-51 and 70.

32 Jane Healy, *Failure to Connect: How Computers Affect Our Children's Minds—And What We Can Do About It* (New York: Simon & Schuster, 1998), 110.

33 Larry Lowery, "Scientific Thinking Processes," *California State Science Curriculum Framework*, 1986.

34 Healy, *Endangered Minds*, 69.

35 Susan J. Kovalik and Karen D. Olsen, *Kid's Eye View of Science: A Teacher's Handbook for Implementing a Conceptual, Integrated Approach to Teaching Science, K-6* (Federal Way, WA: The Center for the Future of Public Education, 2008), Chapter 7, pages 183-200.

36 Frank Smith, *Insult to Intelligence: The Bureaucratic Invasion of Our Classrooms* (New York: Arbor House, 1986 and 1999).

37 There are many collections of data about the power of collaboration to improve learning and performance. The *Handbook of Research on Improving Student Achievement*, 2nd ed, edited by Gordon Cawelti cites over two dozen studies beginning in 1985 (Arlington, Virginia: Educational Research Service, 1999, 159). Robert J. Marzano, in *Classroom Instruction That Works: Research-Based Strategies for Increasing Student Achievement*, summarizes nine synthesis studies on collabora-

tion, from 1987-1996 (Alexandria, VA: ASCD, 2001) 86-87. An author who makes important connections to curriculum development for collaborative work is Elizabeth Cohen; see *Designing Groupwork: Strategies for the Heterogeneous Classroom* (New York: Teachers College Press, 1994).

38 This sage advice comes from Elizabeth Cohen. She provides the best guidance for developing curriculum for collaborative tasks that we have found to date. See *Designing Groupwork*, Chapter 5.

39 Learning Clubs is a term used by Frank Smith who describes the glue of "clubs" in real life. For example, when we join a golf club, our sense of belonging propels us to learn what others in our club know—golf, the style of dress of the members, stock market, etc. See Smith, *Insult to Intelligence*.

40 Ratey, 37.

41 Ratey, 150, 148.

42 Ratey, 148.

43 Frank Smith, *Insult to Intelligence*, 29-30, identified emotion for the powerful force on learning that it is. Since then, the issue is no longer debatable; it is fact. See the groundbreaking work of neuroscientist Candace Pert who uncovered the molecules of emotion (*Molecules of Emotion: Why You Fee the Way You Feel*, 1997) and John Medina's savvy summary of brain principles (*Brain Rules: 12 Principles for Surviving and Thriving at Work, Home, and School*, (2008).

44 Renata and Geoffrey Caine, *Making Connections: Teaching and Human Brain* (California: Addison-Wesley, 1994), 103.

Chapter 2: The Inseparable Bodybrain Partnership— Emotion and Movement

There are two aspects of the bodybrain partnership that are critical to the classroom:

- Emotion—the gatekeeper to learning and performance. In the words of Dr. Robert Sylwester, "Emotion drives attention which drives learning, memory, problem solving, and just about everything else."[1] The role of the limbic system, highly interconnected with all parts of the brain and thought to be the core of emotion, has been studied for more than 50 years. Researchers now believe that most of the brain systems, including the limbic system, participate in emotion and its connection to cognition. A second biological system of emotion was discovered in the 1990s. This chemical system operates through the body, making an inseparable bodybrain partnership.[2]

- Movement to enhance learning—in many respects the mobility of the body grows the brain[3] and the motion centers in the brain are responsible for sequencing thought.[4] This area of brain research is changing our perception of brain development and processing. At one level it is absolutely astonishing; at another, it resonates with our intuition. The implications here for classroom life are enormous.

EMOTION AS GATEKEEPER TO LEARNING AND PERFORMANCE

Given the Western world's love affair with science and technology, with their underpinnings of rational, logical thought, investigating the biological basis of emotion has been slow in coming. But once begun, brain research in this area has exploded, especially in the last 15 years of the 20th century and early 21st century. Today we must talk in terms of a bodybrain partnership, an inseparable partnership running parallel complementary information systems. One system is a combination of electrical and chemical, one wholly chemical.

HET Learning Principles

- Intelligence as a function of experience
- Inseparable bodybrain partnership—
  —Emotion as gatekeeper to learning and performance and
  —Movement to enhance learning
- Multiple intelligences
- Learning as a two-step process

Years of Research: Learning from Fear

One of the earliest attempts to analyze the role of emotion in brain function emerged from Dr. Paul MacLean's work at the National Institute for Health in the 1950s. In describing the basic functions of the various structures of the brain, MacLean was the first to make clear that emotions significantly affect brain functions and thus learning, memory, and behavior. However, MacLean mistakenly perpetuated the assumption that we mostly operate from our cerebral cortex, known for its logic and rational thinking and home of academic learning, and only occasionally "downshifted" into our limbic system. Now we know that emotions are a function of the entire bodybrain partnership and are with us all of the time. Emotions, in fact, filter incoming sensory input, modulating what the cerebral cortex attends to, processes, and stores in long term memory. Emotions truly are the gatekeeper to learning and performance.

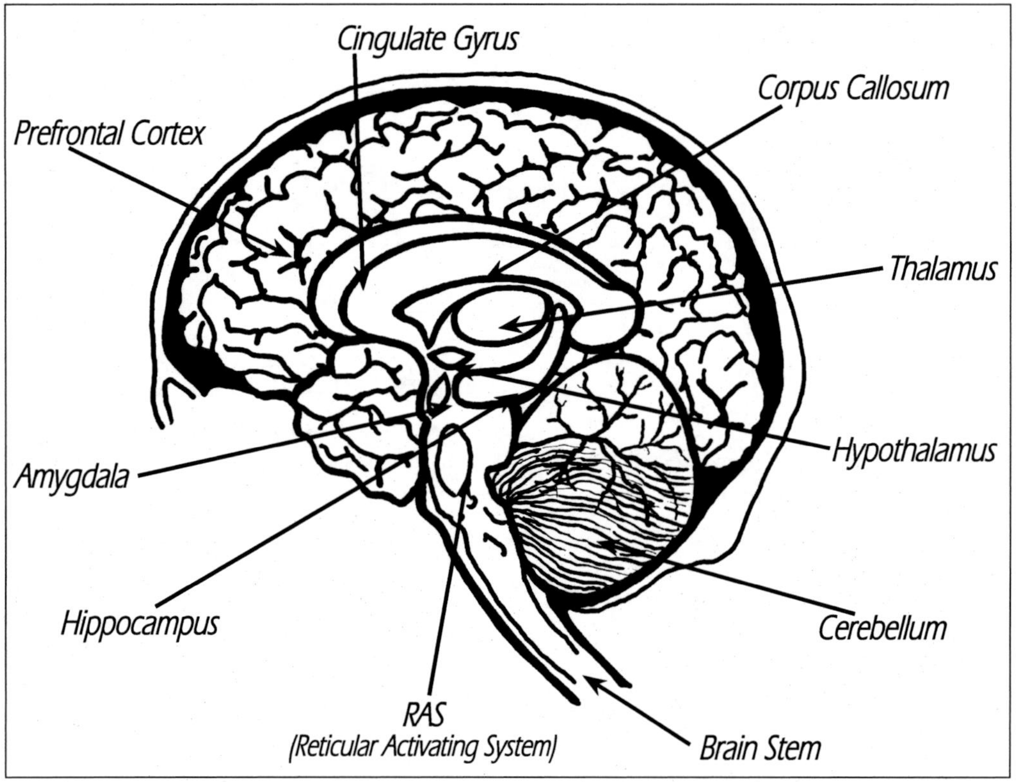

As researchers explore the brain and its responses to emotion, they are discovering how enormously complex the brain is. Because fear is essential to survival and was easier to study, it has been studied more than any other emotion.

So what did researchers find? Somewhat to our surprise, we have discovered that emotions are processed throughout the entire brain and all of its structures—particularly the interconnected structures of the amygdala, hippocampus, thalamus, hypothala-

mus, and cingulate gyrus, an area once referred to as the "limbic system."

How Emotion Affects Learning

What happens in our brains when emotionally charged sensory data comes in? A great deal. Here's how:[5]

• The walnut-sized thalamus, located in the center of the brain, receives, sorts, and forwards almost all input from the sensory organs. It is the relay station for all of the 19+ senses, except the olfactory or sense of smell, which goes directly to the cortex. Some sensory information from the thalamus travels to the amygdala, which is essential to decoding certain emotions, particularly those related to potential dangers in the environment.

• The almond-shaped amygdala is located close to the hippocampus, in the frontal portion of the temporal lobe. Sensory information arrives at the amygdala via either the short, fast, but imprecise route directly from the thalamus or the long, slow, precise route from the various sensory cortexes. Information coming to the amygdala directly from the thalamus arrives very quickly and helps us prepare for potential danger before we even know exactly what it is. After receiving the information from the thalamus, the amygdala sends signals to the hypothalamus, informing it of potential danger.

Figure labels:
- Cingulate Gyrus
- Corpus Callosum
- Prefrontal Cortex
- Thalamus
- Amygdala
- Hypothalamus
- Hippocampus
- Cerebellum
- RAS (Reticular Activating System)
- Brain Stem

- The hypothalamus, a pecan-sized structure below the thalamus, unleashes a host of chemicals that raise blood pressure, increase heart rate, release fat into the blood stream and in many other ways prepare the body to fight, flight, or freeze. This rapid automatic response often means the difference between life and death. (In women, the response is befriend and nurture.)

- The hippocampus, Greek for "seahorse" because of its shape, seems to be primarily responsible for helping form and find long-term memories which are actually stored elsewhere in the cerebral cortex.

- The cingulate gyrus, located on top of the corpus callosum that connects the two hemispheres of the brain, helps resolve ambiguous situations. The cingulate gyrus reviews incoming sensory data from the 19+ senses and determines whether the data has emotional significance. It then coordinates the retrieval and analysis of memories about previous similar situations and relays information to the prefrontal cortex for a decision about what to do.

The prefrontal cortex acts like the CEO of the brain, coordinating and integrating almost all basic brain functions. Unlike most other animals that can primarily react to sensory input, humans have a large prefrontal cortex that permits proactive behavior that anticipates and prepares for challenges. When there is sufficient time, it is the prefrontal cortex that analyzes possible choices and makes the decision as to the best action for the bodybrain to take.[6]

Sensory information sent directly from the thalamus to the amygdala and then on to the hypothalamus for the appropriate fight, flight, or freeze response helps get us out of danger fast. Information sent via the long, slow, precise route from the sensory cortex to the amygdala arrives after the brain has had a chance to process the input and decide if it really is threatening. The prefrontal cortex also seems to be involved in the final phase of confronting a danger, where, after the initial automatic, emotional reaction, with input from the cingulated gyrus, the brain must react and choose the course of action to move us out of the dangerous situa-

tion. The connections between the prefrontal cortex and the amygdala help the amygdala store additional information such as perceptions of sight and sound to create an automatic response the next time a similar dangerous situation is perceived. Meantime, our memory immediately stores details of where we are, what we are doing, who we are with, what we are feeling, and when this is happening in the hippocampus.

The connections between prefrontal cortex and amygdala are also involved with anxiety. At times the prefrontal cortex can gain some control over anxiety, but at other times our creative prefrontal cortex generates anxiety through imagination of failure or presence of dangers that do not actually exist. When students are anxious or fearful for either real or imagined reasons, the amygdala may begin its automatic response and hijack the thinking, reasoning prefrontal cortex. The only learning that takes place during this time is the amygdala's recognition of another potential danger to add to its list of automatic responses to remove the body from danger. Reflective thinking and long-term learning do not take place during times of real or perceived threat.

Emotions in the Classroom

It is clear that emotion does drive attention. Goldberg suggests that the prefrontal cortex becomes particularly active during emotional experiences. "The function of the prefrontal cortex is to calculate 'what is good for the organism,' more than to calculate 'what is true' in an abstract, dispassionate sense."[7] Engaging the prefrontal cortex in determining what is good for the organism seems to be critical for the formation of new cognitive routines and patterns so that learning can take place.

Providing opportunities for full sensory input through study trips or *being there* experiences allows students to look for novel solutions to problems or situations and take in sensory data from a variety of sources. The brain is constantly scanning the environment for patterns in the form of sensory data. This sensory data is stored throughout the brain and is then available to help form neural connections as further learning takes place. However, we can not take in all of the sensory information available to us. If you focus your attention on listening, you will become aware of sounds that you hadn't heard before. If you focus your attention on feeling, you will become aware of your clothes as they touch your body. If every bit of the sensory data available to us came into the brain all at once, we would suffer sensory overload. The brainstem, the thalamus, and the sensory cortex together form the RAS or reticular activating system. The RAS acts somewhat like a dimmer switch or volume control to filter the amount of sensory input that makes it to our cortex. Important data that we are paying attention to makes it past the filter to the cortex where the patterns are manipulated, processed, combined with other future learnings, and turned into programs and long-term memories.[8]

In *HET* classrooms, teachers greet students at the door to welcome them back to class and take their emotional temperature, providing a time for students who are anxious or fearful to have a short conversation with the teacher to help center and focus themselves. When classrooms are safe and free from threats, the thalamus allows life to go on in a "normal" pattern and learning is possible. Providing relevant and meaningful curriculum that students can experience both emotionally and cognitively encourages involvement of the prefrontal cortex and helps it to determine what is good for the organism and can be moved to long-term storage. Lack of engagement often happens when information and skills are broken down into small discrete parts that do not allow students to see patterns and search for novel solutions. Using instructional strategies that tap the power of emotion such as collaborative learning, simulations, music, and drama enable students to engage more systems in their brains and make learning powerful and memorable.

Testing can be a scary time for students—and teachers. Practicing deep breathing, movement activities such as those found in *Brain Gym*[9], and using the steps of *Freeze Frame*[10] can help students cope with anxiety. When students can't remember the answer to a question, they need to allow their hippocampus time to retrieve the information. Knowing that by breathing deeply and calming themselves, they can refocus their brains and "find" the answer will give them the confidence they need to do their best.

So it would seem that the structures of the brain make learning and performance an emotionally driven function. As summarized by Dr. Robert Sylwester, "Emotions drive attention which drives learning, memory, problem-solving and just about everything else."[11] But there's more to the story. The groundbreaking work now done on the chemical origins and operations of emotions by Dr. Candace Pert and others in the past 20 years suggests that there is a chemical information system used by the brain that parallels the electrical-chemical synaptic gap system. These chemicals, according to Pert are the "molecules of emotion."[12] Collectively referred to as "information substances," they are, as Paul Harvey would say, the rest of the story begun in Chapter 1. In effect, we learn through the cooperative interaction of multiple systems of the brain and body working together as an inseparable unit.

Information Substances: The Rest of the Story

Just as Paul Harvey's "The Rest of the Story" adds a stunning twist that makes us view the earlier part of the story differently, so it is with brain research. For 100 years, scientists have understood the basic electrical-chemical building blocks of learning in the brain: nerve cells (neurons) grow dendrites (structures that receive information from other neurons) and axons (structures that send information to other neurons). Electrical impulses travel down the axon, turn into chemical messengers that jump (actually float across) the tiny gap (synapse) to the dendrites of the next neuron. Although there were many mysteries yet to be understood, such as how this all results in learning and memories, the basic explanation still holds true. During the 1950s, structures in the brain that process emotion were discovered; over the next 30 years, it became clear that emotion has a powerful impact on learning. Dr. Robert Sylwester's summary is no exaggeration: Emotion drives our attention, what we attend to determines what we perceive and thus drives learning, memory, problem-solving, behavior, and on and on.[13]

The neurotransmitters in the brain responsible for the synaptic leap, discussed at some length in Chapter 1, are but one category of "information substances" found throughout the body and brain that carry out the process we call learning. Likewise, the limbic system is only one source of "emotional messages" in the bodybrain partnership. The term "information substances" was coined initially by Francis Schmitt, elder statesman of neuroscience from the Massachusetts Institute of Technology, to describe a variety of transmitters, peptides, hormones, factors, and protein ligands that make up a second system. In this system, chemical information substances travel the extracellular fluids circulating throughout the body to reach their specific receptors, receptors on cells located not just in the brain but throughout the body.[14]

This second system parallels the conventional model of neuronal circuitry with its dendrites, axons, and synaptic leaps. Some neuroscientists now speculate that less than two percent of neuronal communication actually occurs at the synapse.[15] Less than two percent! Most of the information received by a neuron is taken in by the receptors at the cell's surface. And no wonder. The number of receptors on a neuron is staggering; current estimates are tens of thousands to a million plus per neuron.[16] That's a lot of potential for conversation! It would appear that the ability to perceive understandable patterns and learn from them is so important to survival that it cannot be posited only in one place or with one method of communication—not just one part of the neuron (at the synaptic gap) nor just in the brain. The entire body is involved.[17]

So just what are these "information substances" and what is their role in learning? These molecules, or ligands, are the basic units of a language used by cells throughout the organism to communicate across systems such as the endocrine, neurological, gastrointestinal, and even the immune system. As they travel, they inform, regulate, and synchronize.[18] Peptides are the largest category of information substances; one kind or another is produced in every cell in the body, not just by cells in the brain. Furthermore, every peptide now known to be produced within the body has receptors in the brain, thus qualifying each peptide to be considered a "neuropeptide." This means that the body talks to the brain, giving it information that alters its messages back to the body and vice versa.

According to Dr. John Ratey, "We are learning that emotions are the rules of multiple brain and body systems that are distrib-

uted over the whole person. We cannot separate emotion from cognition or cognition from the body."[19]

The Molecules of Emotion: The effect of such "conversations" on the organism is to change physical activity cell by cell and as a total organism, *"including behavior and even mood—the closest word to emotion in the lexicon of hard science."*[20] Examples of outward manifestation of such inner "conversations" include a "gut feeling" about something; a first impression of someone as untrustworthy; a physical restlessness that something is wrong before you can put your finger on it; a spark in the eye that says, "I get it even though I can't yet explain it"; a passion for one's hobby; deep love for the beauty of nature; the contentment of a quiet hour spent with a special friend. As was foreseen by the now virtually abandoned triune brain theory,[21] core limbic brain structures such as the amygdala, hippocampus, and hypothalamus—which were long believed to be involved in emotional behavior—contain a whopping percent of the various neuropeptide receptors studied to date, perhaps as high as 85 to 95 percent.[22] Now add to that the startling finding that several of the key emotion molecules such as endorphins can be found in single-cell animals as well as on up the evolutionary trail. Peptides, it appears, have been carrying information since before there were brains, leading researchers such as Antonio Damasio to assert that "emotion is the highest part of our mindbody survival kit."[23] One of their key roles is to tell the brain what's worth attending to and the "attitude" with which one attends. Again, as so nicely summarized by Dr. Robert Sylwester, "Emotion drives attention and attention drives learning and memory, problem solving, and just about everything else."

Emotion As Filter. Another important piece of this new view of learning as a bodybrain partnership is the discovery that there are other locations in the body where high concentrations of almost every neuropeptide receptor exist. One example is the dorsal horn (the back side of the spinal cord) which is the first synapse with the nervous system where all somatosensory information is processed. In fact, in virtually all locations where information from the five senses—sight, sound, taste, smell, and touch—enter the nervous system, there are high concentrations of neuropeptide receptors.

Such regions, called nodal points or hot spots, seem to be designed so that they can be accessed and modulated by almost all neuropeptides as they go about their job of processing information, prioritizing it, and biasing it to cause unique neurophysiological changes. Thus, peptides filter the input of our experiences, significantly altering our perception of reality and the input selected and allowed in during any learning situation.[24] According to Dr. Candace Pert, author of *Molecules of Emotion: Why You Feel the Way You Feel,* "Emotions and bodily sensations are thus intricately intertwined, in a bidirectional network in which each can alter the other. Usually this process takes place at an unconscious level but it can also surface into consciousness under certain conditions or be brought into consciousness by intention."[25]

Implications: In summary, this wholly chemical system of learning, that parallels the electrical-chemical system of neurons, dendrites, axons, and synapses as described in Chapter 1, expands our definition of learning in multiple ways. We now know that:

1) The body and brain form an inseparable learning partnership. Each sends messages out to the other which alters the messages that are sent back. Most sensory input (if not all) is filtered through/modulated by our emotions which direct our attention. What we attend to then drives learning, problem solving, and memory. Conversely, if we do not attend, learning and memory cannot occur.

2) Therefore, the environment of the body is critical—the physical surroundings and the quality of interrelationships of those in it (student to student and student-adult). Consequently, implementation of the *HET* model begins with ensuring that the classroom and school-wide environment enhance rather than impede students' abilities to focus on the learning at hand. Two essential aspects are an absence of threat (real and perceived) and the creation of a sense of community. [26] See Part B, Chapters 8-10.

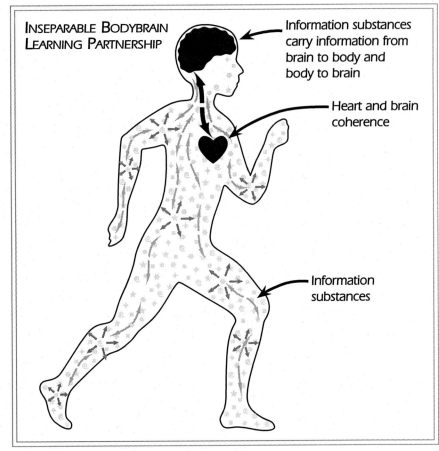

INSEPARABLE BODYBRAIN LEARNING PARTNERSHIP

Information substances carry information from brain to body and body to brain

Heart and brain coherence

Information substances

A Word about Emotions and Gender Differences

Gender differences in the brain, an important emerging area of brain research, are significant and have far reaching implications for all areas of curriculum and instruction. Emotions—positive and negative—are processed differently in the male and female brain. According to Dr. Leonard Sax, the gender differences are so specific that, in many ways, a second grade girl is more like a 25-year old woman than a second grade boy.[27]

The following examples regarding emotions are merely the tip of the iceberg.

Perspective on Learning. According to Sax, girls are more likely to do their homework, even it the assignment doesn't interest them. They are eager to please the teacher and are more likely to listen to adults and see their perspective. Boys don't share that motivation; they are less likely to affiliate with adult goals and aims.[28] Boys are less motivated unless they find the material intrinsically interesting.[29]

Stress. The gender differences regarding stress are dramatic. According to Sax, stress improves learning in males but impairs learning in females. In males it enhances the growth of neural connections in the hippocampus; in females, it inhibits grown of hippocampal connections.[30]

Also, moderate stress improves boys' performance on tests; the same stress levels in young girls degrades their test performance.[31]

Handling Disagreements. Boys can be mean to each other and when they are it is obvious to those around them. Typically, they then punch each other and get sent to the principal's office. One day later they are better friends than before.[32]

In contrast, the surface of a girl fight can be silent and smooth as marble. Tensions can simmer and build for weeks or months, corroding a friendship until there is no friendship left.[33]

In boys, as in men, the part of the brain where emotions happen is not well connected to the part of the brain where verbal processing and speech happen. The opposite is true in girls and women.[34]

MOVEMENT TO ENHANCE LEARNING

The Western world's view of the brain is that it is rational, logical, ruler of all; the body in this scheme has been primarily viewed as merely the vehicle that carried the brain from one cerebral task to another. And, if it was good looking and athletic to boot, so much the better! Now, however, it is clear that there is no hierarchy, no separation between the body and the brain. What the Greeks knew 2,500 years ago is being confirmed by today's high tech brain research—if you want the best performance from your brain, tune the body and brain together.

During the 1980s and 1990s, the popular press has extolled and sold the virtues of physical fitness as a means of increasing mental sharpness and reducing stress, to overall health and well-being. But the story now emerging from brain research is amazing. As Carla Hannaford is fond of saying, "The body grows the brain."[35] Indeed, animals that don't move, don't have a brain. And those like the sea squirt that move early in its life cycle, later reabsorb their brain when they permanently affix themselves to a stationary object.[36]

What Brain Research Is Telling Us

The brain research into the relationship between movement and cognition is nothing less than startling. The major findings that we believe are key for classroom teachers are:

- Movement is fundamental to the very existence of a brain. Only an organism that moves from place to place requires a brain.[37]

- The entire front half of the brain—the newest in evolutionary terms—is devoted to organizing action, both physical and mental.[38] "Higher" brain functions have evolved from movement and still depend on it.

- Movement is crucial to every brain function including planning and executing plans, memory, emotion, language, and learning.[39]

- The ability to mimic, one of young human's most powerful avenues for learning, is movement based.[40]

- Aerobic exercise kick starts brain chemicals essential for forming new memories and wiring learning into long-term memory.[41]

Movement Is Fundamental. Only an organism that moves from place to place even requires a brain.[42] This is not a casual link! The brain and body are an inseparable partnership. As Dr. John Ratey points out, "What the brain communicates to the body depends largely on what messages the body is sending to the brain. Together they collaborate for the good of the whole organism."[43] In classroom life, this means that the body and brain are always talking and working together. When one member of the bodybrain learning partnership is shut down, told to sit still and not move, the functioning of the other partner is deeply affected.

As we think about the traditions of the educational system we inherited, we can't help but marvel at how far off the mark some of its features are. Children sitting quietly in rows, not moving, not talking. What a recipe for failure to learn!

This suggests that the pendulum swings in school reform over the past century may have failed not because they were inherently flawed but because throughout those reforms the bodybrain partnership remained divided and thus ineffective at learning.

Half of the Entire Brain Is Devoted to Organizing Action.
This is another powerful message for teachers. Half the brain! And the newest, most powerful parts of the brain at that. The frontal cortex learns, routinizes, and processes motor and mental functions in parallel. Movement, then, becomes inextricably tied to cognition.[44]

This feature of the physiology of the brain underscores the importance of defining learning as a two-step process: understanding and then *using* what is understood. It turns out that the brain *expects* to use what it understands.

Movement Is Crucial to Every Brain Function.
Although our Olympic-level athletes have discovered the impressive power of the brain to improve the performance of its partner, the body, we in the U.S. are slow to acknowledge reciprocal power of the body on the brain. According to Ratey, "our physical movements can directly influence our ability to learn, think, and remember. Evidence is mounting that each person's capacity to master new and remember old information is improved by biological changes in the brain brought on by new activity."[45]

What does this all mean for the classroom teacher? Nothing short of a revolutionary shift in our view of our students as learn-

ers. What this means is that the bodybrain partnership perceives, processes, and stores in long-term memory concepts and skills in terms of their usability and usefulness. Not useable (who cares?), not useful (relevant now), then, not worth learning. We must reframe what we teach and why we teach it. Learning not for the sake of learning but for the sake of using what we learn—for our own lives and as contributing citizens.

Ideally, the resources spent on textbooks, workbooks, blackline masters, and copy paper and machines should be redirected to *being there* experiences. Knowing how concepts and skills are *used* in the real world greatly enhance building long-term memories.

Mimicry.
Startling research is emerging that suggests the presence of "mirror neurons," a subset of movement-related neurons in the premotor cortex area [46] that buzz away when we watch someone do something that interests us. Whether these neurons merely assist us to understand or to mirror gestures or actions is still uncertain. Some researchers such as Ramachandran believe that mirror neurons play a bigger role than is generally appreciated. Ramachandran believes that not only are they the missing link between gesture and language but they help explain human learning, ingenuity, and culture in general. "Language, imitative learning, and mind reading, seemingly unrelated human developments, may all be shown to be linked through these intriguing nerve cells."[47]

Aerobic Exerise.
Aerobic exercise kick starts brain chemicals essential for forming new memories and wiring learning into long-term memory. Here are a few examples of the changes high aerobic exercise (heart rate at 70% or higher) for 35 minutes daily can kick start in the brain:[48]

In the hippocampus — [49]

- Stimulates regenesis, the growth of new stem cells

- Spurs new stem cells to develop into new nerve cells

- Can cause a shrunken hippocampus (due to inactivity or aging) to return to normal size

These changes are crucial to learning because the hippocampus is where new memories are formed.

Production of chemicals to spark attention, learning, and long-term memory —

- Elevates BDNF (brain-derived neurotrophic factor), a protein that builds, protects, and maintains neuron circuitry, giving neurons the tools they need to learn — to process, associate, put in context, and remember.[50]

  BDNF is especially important in the formation of long-term memories.

- Rate of learning is directly correlated with levels of BDNF. Levels rise as the amount of exercise increases.[51]

  In summary, BDNF gives the synapses the tools they need not only to take in information but also to process it, associate it, put it in context (with prior experiences and other elements in the current situation), and remember it.

Vastly improves most mental health conditions, particularly depression, anxiety, ADD, and addiction by stimulating the production of serotonin, norepinephrine, and dopamine and balancing them for optimum performance of the brain.[52]

- Serotonin helps keep brain activity under control by influencing mood, impulsivity, anger, and aggressiveness. (Note: Prozac is a serotonin substitute.)

- Norepinephrine amplifies brain signals that influence attention, perception, motivation, and arousal.

- Dopamine is thought of as the learning, reward (satisfaction), attention, and movement neurotransmitter. (Note: Ritalin is used to increase dopamine levels.)

According to John Ratey, "Voluntary exercise has a profound impact on cognitive abilities and mental health. It is simply one of the best treatments we have to most psychiatric problems."[53]

The amount of movement matters — The amount of exercise has a profound effect on the number of new stem cells that are formed.

The kind of movement matters — The more complex the movements, the more complex the synaptic connections. Aerobic exercise should also include new learning — acquisition of new physical skills and/or new mental skills and knowledge used for problem solving.

Academic impact. Studies by the California Department of Education have consistently shown that students with higher fitness scores also have higher test scores.[54]

- In 2002, fit kids scored twice as well on academic tests as their unfit peers.[55] Those fifth-, seventh-, and 9th-grade students passing all six portions of the fitness test significantly outranked their unfit peers. In reading, scores doubled (27th percentile to the 54th percentile); in math, scores jumped from the 35th to the 68th percentile.[56] Even when socioeconomic status was factored in, the trend remained. And, among low-income students, fitter students scored better than unfit students.[57] In 2004, the similar story.

- Six areas of fitness were tested — aerobic capacity, percentage of body fat, abdominal strength and endurance, trunk strength and flexibility, upper body strength, and overall flexibility.[58] When researchers at the University of Illinois near Naperville replicated the CDE study, they found that two areas of the test were particularly important in relation to academic performance: increased aerobic fitness had a strong, positive relationship and increased body mass had a strong, negative influence.[59]

Researchers discovered that an EEG (electroencephalogram) showed more activity in fit kids' brains, indicating that more neurons were being recruited for the assigned tasks. Hillman also discovered that even a single, acute bout of exercise had a positive impact on learning. The formula goes something like this: aerobic exercise = faster cognitive processing speed = better attention (greater attentional control resulting in more accurate responses) = better learning.[60]

In summary, physical activity has a positive influence on attention, concentration, memory, and classroom behavior. Clearly, fitness should not be looked upon as extracurricular but rather as a vital component in students' academic success.[61]

Despite such research, the increase in minutes for reading and math in response to No Child Left Behind, has pulled the nation in the opposite direction. Many districts have cut or eliminated their P.E. programs. Some districts have even eliminated morning recess. Illinois, because of PE4Life, is now the only state that requires daily P.E.

While many classroom teachers may dread the thought of becoming an aerobics instructor, we can no longer afford to ignore the extensive impact aerobic exercise has on the learning brain. For more information, see *Spark: The Revolutionary New Science of Exercise and the Brain* by John Ratey.

A Word about Movement and Gender Differences

Gender differences in the brain, an important emerging area of brain research, are significant and have far reaching implications for all areas of curriculum and instruction. The following examples regarding movement are merely the tip of the iceberg.

Male Brain Geared to Action. It comes as no surprise that the kind and amount of movement needed by students differs greatly by gender. Among the hardwired physiological differences between the genders, boys focus on movement. Their brains are geared to the question, "Where is it going?"[62]

On the other hand, girls focus on the question, "What is it?" As expressed in art, boys draw verbs, girls draw nouns.[63]

This fundamental difference comes from biological structure of the eye itself.[64] Rods within the retina, which are color blind,

send their signals to large ganglion cells and are senstive to motion. They has the questions, "Where is it now and where is it going?"

Cones, which are sensitive to color, connect to smaller ganglion cells. They answer the questions, "What is it and what are the colors and textures?"

The male retina has mostly the larger, thicker M (magnocellular) cells, which are essentially a motion detector and can track objects anywhere in the field of vision. Conversely, the female retina has predominantly the smaller, thinner P (parvocellular) cells that are concentrated in and around the fovea, the center of the field of vision.[65]

The eye structure of boys is geared to motion—looking out the window, out the classroom door, watching the classroom action, anything moving—will catch their attention. They can't help themselves . . . they are wired for that. Looking at a worksheet, in the center field of vision, is better designed for the girls and their retinas. Seatwork assigned to male students working at individiual desks is the antithesis of an effective learning environment for boys. [66]

Movement Activities for Boys (And Not So Bad for Girls Either). As one might guess, daily aerobic exercise (35 minutes at 70+% heart rate) is made to order for boys. Equally important is Dewey's "learn by doing" approach to curriculum, such as project-based assignments and study trips to the field.

In many ways, action replaces language for boys. The developmental language area of a five-year old boy looks like the language area of a three and a half year-old girl.[67]

To ignore the vast biological gender differences in the need for movement has dreadful consequences for young boys. The good news is that the needed curriculum and instructional fixes for boys also improve the learning environment for girls.

Movement is fundamental to learning.

TRANSLATING BRAIN RESEARCH INTO ACTION USING THE NINE BODYBRAIN-COMPATIBLE ELEMENTS

The *HET* model presents nine ways to translate brain research into action in the classroom and school. Each of the nine is described here. They are discussed in the order of their power to translate this area of brain research—the bodybrain partnership—into practical strategies in the classroom.

Bodybrain-Compatible Elements

- Absence of Threat/Nurturing Reflective Thinking
- Movement
- Collaboration
- Meaningful Content
- Choices
- Enriched Environment
- Adequate Time
- Immediate Feedback
- Mastery

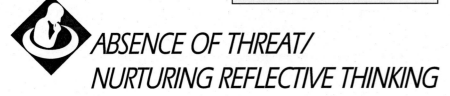

ABSENCE OF THREAT/ NURTURING REFLECTIVE THINKING

Given the primacy of emotions to drive attention and thus memory, problem-solving, and virtually every other aspect of learning and performance, the number one job of a teacher is creating and maintaining an environment free from threat. Once this is in place, that environment must also actively nurture reflective thinking. These two qualities form the heart and soul of bodybrain-compatibility and are at the very heart of the *HET* model. They are also the beginning point of implementation and the ongoing touchstone of *HET*. Once created, they cannot be ignored but must receive consistent, on-going, **daily** attention from teacher and students.

Creating Absence of Threat

When creating absence of threat, it is important to consider two truisms:

- Like beauty, what constitutes threat—even perceived threat—is in the eye of the beholder. What is threatening to one person may not be considered threatening to another. However, that does not minimize the sense of perceived threat held by that person. Its affect on the functions of the bodybrain partnership are profound.

- Absence of threat does not mean absence of consequences. Misbehavior and failure to complete work have consequences in the real world and so should they in the classroom. What matters is fairness, consequences appropriate to the nature of the infraction, and emotional consistency of those who apply the consequences.

For some traditionalists, a little bit of threat is often considered a good thing,—"keeps 'um on their toes" and "shows them who's in charge." But, as Dr. John Ratey points out, the excess mental noise that goes on in the brain as a result of dealing with threat and stresses "can make it difficult to perceive what's going on, overloading other circuits of attention, memory, learning, cognition, emotional stability, or any other brain function." In effect, the system goes into information overload, which is precisely what can happen when highly anxious people take tests. "They will look at a test question and literally not see certain words, which causes them to misinterpret it and give the wrong answer. They may even miss seeing entire questions on the page.

Absence of Threat

Absence of threat does not mean absence of challenge or lack of consequences for misbehavior or bad choices. It does mean lack of real and perceived threat to physical and emotional safety.

Their brains are so busy dealing with the noise that the visual channels in the brain aren't open to perceive accurately. *Our brains are not infinite.* They run out of space, run out of gas, as it were. If the brain is busy trying to filter uncomfortable and frustrating noise, worries, or other concerns, there is less 'brain stuff' available for perceiving.[68] There are many aspects of our traditional curriculum and instructional strategies that are threatening to students and cause excess mental noise.

Curriculum and Threat. Curricular aspects that have a strong bodybrain–antagonistic effect include:

- Boring when too hard or too easy

- Difficult to understand if there is no perceivable relevance to their life; humiliating when they can't get it; source of acting out

- Frustrating because content is not understandable — the material is not age appropriate and/or is composed of factoids

Instructional Strategies and Threat. Instructional strategies that have a strong bodybrain-antagonistic effect include:

- Low standards for cleanliness, maintenance, and decor (lower than for most other public and private settings)

- Lack of community building

- Lack of personal relationship between teacher and students

- Poor leadership — students uncertain about what's happening and why or what will happen next

- Restricting body movement in the classroom, limited to recess, lunch, and P.E.

- Adherence to rigid time lines, inadequate time to complete tasks

- Threat of bad grades (potential negative consequences from teacher, parent, and fellow students)

An environment with absence of threat is fundamental to learning and a prerequisite for reflective thinking.

Using Absence of Threat to Enhance the Bodybrain Learning Partnerhship

The bodybrain-compatible element of absence of threat enhances the effectiveness of the bodybrain learning partnership in many ways.

Curriculum Development

- Teach students about the power of emotion to enhance or impede learning and performance; present this through both formal introductory lesson and through ongoing pre- and post-lesson processing

- Teach students the personal and social skills they need to succeed with their peers and teachers.

- Eliminate fear of failure by ensuring that content is age appropriate, and thus understandable, that inquiries are doable given current skill levels, and that students have the option to choose inquiries based on intelligence(s) of strength when needed.

- Base curriculum in being there locations that are kid-grabbers, ones that require that they do something and actively participate in. Study trips that are "look and listen" experiences don't readily engage the emotions.

- State curriculum as concepts; include how the concept is/can be used in the students' world.

- Allow students to make choices — among inquiries (how they learn required curriculum), about social/political action projects, yearlong projects, and other study tasks as appropriate.

Instructional Strategies

- Use the Lifelong Guidelines and LIFESKILLS 100 percent of every day (see Chapters 7, 9, 10). Ask guest experts to share which Guidelines/ LIFESKILLS are used in the workplace.

- Ensure full membership in a community — the class family — plus being in relationship with the teacher.

- Use daily agendas and written procedures (see Chapters 7 and 8).

- Provide active, purposeful body movement in the classroom every hour to re-focus (release energy or re-energize as needed) the brain and body using activities that are an extension of what is being studied.

- Eliminate all pull-out programs except for short-term, urgent interventions.

Nurturing Reflective Thinking

The ability—and the inclination—to think reflectively is an invaluable habit of mind. It lowers stress, improves learning and decision making, and enhances performance. In learning situations, reflective thinking allows students to move from "So what?" to "How can I use this now and in the future?" Without such automatic questioning, learning will be on the surface in the short run and will probably fail to trigger the brain's decision to store learning in long-term memory.

While reflective thinking may seem a vague or elusive term[69], each of us can recall times when we were so immersed in something that we lost track of time and external distractions stayed at bay. Mihaly Csikszentmihalyi (pronounced CHICK-sent-me-high-ee) provides a wonderful description of the state of mind that is home to reflective thinking, a state he calls "flow experience."[70] This state of mind is attained in exceptional moments when we find ourself totally and completely immersed in a place where our heart, mind, and will are simultaneously interacting and to the point that outside distractions are not able to penetrate. This metaphor of "flow" is one that we have

Reflective Thinking

The ability—and the inclination—to think reflectively is an invaluable habit of mind. It lowers stress and improves learning and decision making.

experienced and can reflect upon as some of the best times of our lives. It is also a state of mind ideal for learning because engagement is extremely high and learning seems effortless.

Reflective Thinking As an Act of Discipline. Reflective thinking doesn't just happen automatically. It is an act of either conscious discipline or habit of mind. We must first slow down,[71] clear away distractions, focus our thoughts on what we're learning and doing and why, and use self-talk to guide our thinking when puzzled or stuck.

Second, to be reflective is a choice, a decision that can be made only by the learner. No teacher can hammer thoughtfulness into a student; it must come from within. The Greek/Latin base for the word educate means "to draw forth." As part of drawing forth, we need to set up conditions that nurture reflective thinking. Most importantly, we must model it and then provide ample opportunities for students to develop and practice it.

Impact of the Physical Environment. Humans beings are, as alertness to ensure survival demands, extremely sensitive to their environment. Children are even more so than adults. The ongoing impact of the physical environment of the classroom is extremely powerful. If you doubt this, think of your favorite environment, the one that relaxes you yet you remain alert and aware, fully enjoying your time there. Be that Yosemite Falls or your favorite five-star hotel, you know what an impact it has on your emotions and mental processing. In contrast, think of the environment that has the opposite effect on you—perhaps the teachers' lounge at your school with its machines and their fumes, messy coffee station, and old, uncomfortable furniture.. Or, maybe it's parts of your own aging school . . . the cafeteria/gym with stained ceiling tiles, unremitting, high-decibel noises (no sound dampener). Or, maybe it's the drab, dirty, crowded vehicle licensing office with its long lines and no place to sit while you wait; and, when your turn comes up you feel pressed to complete your tasks and so you hurry through, only half engaged in the tasks at hand. Wherever this is, it's a place you dread going to and a cloud of gloom settles over you every time you even think about having to go there.

If any of this rings a bell with you, you already know that one's physical environment strongly affects one's ability to slip into a reflective state of mind and stay there. So it should come as no surprise that your first step—even before school begins—is to address the physical environment of your classroom. At a minimum, it should be:

- Healthful—clean, well lighted, pleasant smelling, and free from harmful chemicals and allergens

- Aesthetically pleasing—calming colors and music, living plants, comfortable furniture, and well organized

- Uncluttered yet reflects what is being learned

An environment that meets these benchmarks eliminates competing sensory input to the learning at hand from within and from outside of the body thus making it easier for students to focus on what they're learning and to reflect on how and when and why they can use the concepts and skills they are studying. Without this reflective time, school is a blur and seems largely unrelated to their life. This is especially true in departmentalized settings.

Nurturing Reflective Thinking to Enhance the Bodybrain Learning Partnerhship

The bodybrain-compatible element of nurturing reflective thinking enhances the effectiveness of the bodybrain learning partnership in many ways.

Curriculum Development

- Teach students how to redirect themselves when things get in the way of their learning, for example, when any of the four psychological needs identified by William Glasser are not in place (belonging, fun, power, and freedom).[72]

- Teach students simple techniques, such as Freeze Frame, [73] for bringing themselves to a reflective state of mind.

- Teach students how to direct their own learning—a foundational building block for becoming lifelong learners—by

allowing them to exercise self-direction when appropriate. For example, choice of inquiries and helping develop inquiries, selecting their role to play in social/political action projects, and conducting a yearlong research project on a topic of their own choosing.

Instructional Strategies

- Ensure that the physical environment is healthful, aesthetically pleasing, and uncluttered (see Chapter 7).

- Offer rich input from being there, immersion, and hands-on-of-real-things so students can construct meaning rather than have to rely on attempts to memorize as a coping strategy.

- Provide adequate time for group and independent exploration.

- Be readily available to refocus, reenergize, and redirect students; during student work time, keep circulating through the classroom taking advantage of the teachable moment and building a personal relationship with each student.

- Balance time for collaborative learning with personal time for applying skills and knowledge to individual interests, exploring related ideas, and reflect on what one is learning and how it could be used now and in the future (vocations and hobbies).

- Institute a mastery-based instruction with a pass/not-yet passed accountability system coupled with in-class and cross-age tutoring as needed until each student achieves mastery of the concepts of the curriculum.

MOVEMENT

With a nod to classical education, primarily the Greek tradition of training body and mind in a mutually supportive partnership, American education has long required physical education. Unfortunately, in practice P.E. is primarily training in sports, particularly competitive team sports such as football, baseball, basketball, with purported mental and character carry over bonuses.

Given what we know today, competitive sports should be extracurricular and P.E. should be renamed "movement to enhance learning" and become the province of the classroom teacher. In other words, we should teach students how to enhance their ability to learn through movement of their body.

Why? Memory of knowledge and skills also records the emotional state of the learner at the time the learning took place. If the emotion was negative and unpleasant, we prefer to suppress the content as well as the emotion. Statements such as, "I hate reading" or "I hate math" are really someone's way of saying, "Every time I think of reading or math, I feel bad. I remember the frustration and humiliation, feeling stupid and feeling like an outcast."

How many of us know people who know how to read but choose not to? They choose not to because there are so many negative memories. This suggests that teachers battle not only for the minds of their students (getting knowledge and skills into long-term memory) but also for their hearts (wanting to use what they have learned and doing so of their own volition).

Why do we bring this up under a discussion about the importance of movement and emotion? Because movement is the quickest and most reliable way to add fun to the moment. Movement resets our emotional state. It provides opportunities for wiggly students to let off steam, tired students to get reenergized. When movement is planned as an extension or application of the concepts or skills being learned, additional parts of the brain wake up and content gets encoded in additional areas of the brain.

For the teacher searching for the key to his/her students' minds and hearts, eureka! You have found it.

Remember, movement in this context means using the bodybrain partnership fully and joyously to learn the concepts and skills of the curriculum—science, social studies, arts, language arts, science, and technology. Movement for sports, the traditional view of P.E., is not included in this discussion.

Remember that movement, as discussed in this chapter, is not about "jumping around." The intent is movement that enhances brain chemistry and the neural networking needed to hard wire academic learning into long-term memory.

Bodymapping is a popular strategy whereby the teacher (and then finally the learner) use the body and its potential movements to map out information—and, by moving, show relationships among the parts. It is, in effect, a mindmap of the body's shapes and actions in space.[74]

Using Movement to Enhance the Bodybrain Learning Partnerhship

The bodybrain-compatible element of movement enhances the effectiveness of the bodybrain learning partnership in many ways.

Curriculum Development

- Use movement as an extension or application of content rather than as a separate activity.

- Invite students to help you plan movement sequences that will help the class master concepts and skills.

- Teach students the skills for reading and using body language effectively. For example, miming, role playing, acting, public speaking, and dancing.

- The curriculum addresses movement both as a content itself (e.g., teaching students of the importance of movement in learning and positive emotional states) and as a means of enhancing academic learning (e.g., using the body to explore through the 19 senses and using the body to role play, react, and so forth).

Instructional Strategies

- Use movement every hour. Whenever possible, make it an extension of the concepts or skills being studied. However,

movement to reset emotions and prepare the bodybrain for a change of pace is also worthwhile.

- Add music and singing to your movement sequences. Melody, rhythm, rhyme, and words add fun and increase retention.

- Include these movement sequences during Celebrations of Learning,75 parent nights, and cross-age tutoring.

- List the movement activities you currently use. Identify which contribute to learning curriculum content and which are "sponge activities," worthwhile ways to use up small amounts of time while waiting for the next event or scheduled activities to begin. Add to your list as needed.

COLLABORATION

Almost all learning occurs in a social context. From birth we are genetically wired to connect with others[76] and to learn through imitating others—be it learning to speak, the rules and strategies of a playground game of Red Rover or organized sports, or etiquette at a community BBQ. We are social animals; collaborating isn't something we do, it is who we are and the context in which we live. Over the millennium, collaboration has often meant the difference between life and death. The John Wayne mythology of the Old West—of individualism writ large— runs counter to what really goes on in rural living, then and now. Collaboration, with few exceptions, has always increased the likelihood of success. However, like most social skills, collaborating— with family, friends, and in the workplace—must be learned, through modeling and practice. Done poorly, it is a lifelong source of emotional upset. Done well, it is the key to satisfaction and success throughout one's life.

The jury has weighed in on this instructional strategy. Its power to improve the learning environment and increase academic learning is indisputable.[77] In short, learning how and when to collaborate is essential to our emotional health, our capacity to learn, and our performance levels throughout life. In the classroom, skills and knowledge that help students keep their emotional state geared to learning are precursors to the rest of the curriculum.

The instructional strategies to implement collaboration, usually referred to as cooperative learning, are well known and proven. Three excellent resources are *Designing Groupwork: Strategies for the Heterogeneous Classroom* by Elizabeth Cohen for research and practical curriculum and instructional strategies, *Cooperative Learning, All Grades* by Spencer Kagan, and *Reaching All by Creating TRIBES Learning Communities* by Jeanne Gibbs. In addition to these, the *HET* model recommends numerous curriculum development and instructional strategies to ensure that students' collaborative work is consistent with what we now know about emotions as gatekeeper to learning and performance.

Building Collaboration

The three stages[78] of building a Learning Club in the HET model are:
- Developing a sense of inclusion/ belonging
- Creating common ground
- Taking action

Using Collaboration to Enhance the Bodybrain Learning Partnerhship

The bodybrain-compatible element of collaboration enhances the effectiveness of the bodybrain learning partnership in many ways.

Curriculum Development

- Have students analyze historical events and literature for instances when collaboration, or lack of, was key in changing the course of national/world events and human lives.

- Make sure that the curriculum content of collaborative work is specifically designed for collaboration, not just putting students together to answer questions at the back of the chapter. An appropriate task for collaborative work is one that the brightest student can't do alone; every member of the group is needed to be successful. Otherwise, collaborative work negatively reinforces low social status for middle and lower achieving students and the brightest students end up doing all the work.79

• Have students review the content of the Lifelong Guidelines/ LIFESKILLS they will most need to be successful at their task and make decisions about how they will apply it to their work.

• At every being there location, have students focus on the most important Lifelong Guidelines/LIFESKILLS needed to be an informed participant at that location and those needed to be an employee there.

• Whenever feasible, require content-related movement during collaborative work.

Instructional Stategies

• Keep in mind that collaboration has but two critical goals: increasing achievement and equalizing social status in the classroom (raising status of all to that of equal peer among peers).80

• Insist that students consistently use the Lifelong Guidelines/ LIFESKILLS; no exceptions. As the adult in charge, you must ensure that the classroom environment is free from threat at all times.

• To equalize social status in groups, rotate the role of group leader frequently and equally. If you think that a lower achieving student will have difficulty with the content of a task which will then impede his/her leadership role, work with the student in advance so that he/she can carry out the leadership role successfully and thus grow in social status.81

• Invest in reflective thinking: After students finish with each collaborative task, have them analyze how well they utilized

the Lifelong Guidelines/LIFESKILLS, how they felt about the process of working together, how they could have improved both process and product, and, very importantly, what they learned about their personal and social skills for working together. How will they put that knowledge into action during the next collaborative work session.

• Convene Town Hall meetings at least once a day.

• Read student-written acknowledgments from the Acknowledgments Box at least once a day.

MEANINGFUL CONTENT

"You can lead a horse to water but you can't make him drink" is an old rural proverb that is equally true in the city and especially true in the classroom. Horses drink water only when they're thirsty. Students drink in what they find meaningful to them. Meaningfulness starts with an emotional reaction and continues with the "aha" experience that makes the eyes dance.

Renata and Geoffrey Caine describe the role of emotion and passion in learning in their description of what they call "natural thinking knowledge, " a combination of "felt meaning" and "deep meaning." "Felt meaning," is that "aha" response that occurs when something we've been trying to learn suddenly clicks into place and we "get it." It begins as "an unarticulated general sense of relationship and culminates in the 'aha' experience that accompanies insight."[82] According to the Caines, "such insight is much more important in education than is memorization."[83]

The second concept is "deep meaning," defined by the Caines as ". . . whatever drives us and governs our sense of purpose."[84] It includes all the instincts embedded in our reptilian brains, our needs for social relationships and an emotionally rich life, and our intellectual and spiritual needs.[85] These drives are sources of individual meaning, what people live for, and they are meaningful and drive our inner engines whether they are articulated or not and even whether or not we are conscious of them.[66] The important thing for us here is that ". . . people access passion when deep meanings are engaged." Deep meanings, therefore, ". . . provide a sense of direction because they govern what people look for and what they are willing to do, whether in sports, computing, music, finance, or writing poetry, or teaching. And, in part, deep meanings are a source of the energy that people are capable of bringing to bear on a task or activity."[87]

According to the Caines, when information, felt meaning and deep meaning come together, the result is "natural knowledge," knowledge so much a part of us that we refer to it as "second nature."[88] For example, "I love cars. I can't walk through a parking lot without diagnosing motors from the sounds they make. Fixing problems is second nature to me." With natural knowledge, "the learner has acquired a felt meaning for the subject or concept or procedure so that new information and procedures fit together. In addition, there is a sufficient connection with the learner's interests or deep meanings so that the information and procedures are personally relevant."[89]

Clearly, "natural knowledge" is arrived at by young children—outside of school and without the benefit of worksheets. What draws them on is the emotion of belonging to various "clubs"[90] (family, neighborhood play group, scouts club, school Learning Club, etc.) and through the exuberance of their natural search for meaning to their "why" questions begun as two year-olds.[91] Emotion and meaningfulness go hand in hand. You can't have a decision of meaningfulness without an emotional hook—something that grabs attention and elicits a strong desire to know more.

Using Meaningful Content to Enhance the Bodybrain Learning Partnership

The bodybrain-compatible element of meaningful content enhances the effectiveness of the bodybrain learning partnership in many ways.

Curriculum Development

- When selecting being there locations, look for ones that:
  - Are innately appealing to your students and will generate high levels of emotion
  - Students will consider useful to know about (from their perspective, of course)
  - Offer a high level of interaction and participation ("doing" raises emotional responses).

- Restate your curriculum as concepts rather than as lists of factoids (dates, definitions, etc.). Because concepts are generalizable to other situations, you will be more likely to intersect with students' existing areas of felt meaning and deep meaning.

- Develop inquiries allowing children to follow their natural curiosity—their whys and wherefores—when applying the skill and knowledge you want them to master.

- Allow students to participate in curriculum development so they can build in ways of using knowledge and skills that most interest them; invite them to write inquiries and then you select those you think are the best use of students' time.

Instructional Strategies

- Build in "doing"—a natural blend of body and brain working in partnership which always produces more neurotransmitters that excite learning than sitting at one's desk.

- Utilize the power of membership in the Learning Club and classroom to expand and deepen what students find meaningful.

- Bring resource people to the classroom that students can respect and admire—the experts, the everyday heroes.

- Be passionate about what you teach! Show your love of learning, model the excitement and joy of being a lifelong learner.

CHOICES

As every parent quickly learns, offering a two-year old a choice of A or B—do what I've asked or go to time out—significantly defuses a potential power struggle and improves the child's attitude toward the task chosen. The same is true in the classroom. Giving students a choice of inquiry A or inquiry B—often makes the difference between sloppy work performed with indifference or a project given one's personal best. Yet despite our experience and common sense, in schools we too often succumb to the law of bureaucracies: mind-numbing insistence on assembly-line sameness. We must leave behind the foolish insistence that the same input (textbook and lectures) will produce the same learning outcomes, that same equals equity and fairness, that misbehavior of a few should result in all receiving the same punishment regardless of circumstances. In our opinion, public education's worst, and most deadly, enemy is bureaucracy.

Offering choices is a frontal assault against the bureaucratic mentality of sameness and control and a huge emotional boost for the bodybrain partnership. Offering students choice strengthens their commitment to learn because:

- Having choices allows students to design their own path between too hard (leading to failure) and too easy (leading to boredom). It also allows them to alternate between intelligences already well developed and those they are working on.

- The higher the level of interest, the higher the level of motivation and commitment to learn, and thus the higher the level of neurotransmitters generated to assist the learning process.

- The power to choose gives students a measure of power and control over their own learning, prerequisites for emotional stability92 and becoming a lifelong learner.

- Having choices increases the likelihood of students' success in learning skills and knowledge and wiring them into long-term memory.

In many ways, having choice makes learning easier. As Frank Smith points out, thinking is made easy and effective when two fundamental requirements are met: 1) we understand what we are thinking about; and 2) the brain itself is in charge, in control of its own affairs, going about its own business.[93] "Thinking," he points out, "becomes difficult and inefficient when the brain loses control, when what we try to think about is contrived . . . it throws the brain out of gear. Something that in less forced circumstances might be thought about with ease becomes an obstacle, a blurred focus of contrary purposes, aggravated often by frustration and irritation." "The most difficult kind of thinking is that which is imposed on us by someone else. . ."[94]

Using Choices to Enhance the Bodybrain Learning Partnership

The bodybrain-compatible element of choices enhances the effectiveness of the bodybrain learning partnership in many ways.

Curriculum Development

- Develop inquiries which offer real choice rather than more of the same; this is particularly important for the practice and mastery of skills (reading, writing, speaking, and mathematics). Do so by building on the multiple intelligences and using real-life situations. Also make sure there are inquiries for Learning Club work and for individual exploration as well as for whole class assignment.

- Develop a sufficient number of inquiries to allow for real choice. For example, being assigned one's choice of three out of 12 rather than three out of four is real choice. However, it takes time to up students' capacity to handle choice. Start small and build upward as quickly as you can.

- Invite students, from third grade and up, to develop their own inquiries from which you as teacher select the best. Learning to pose our own questions is more important to lifelong learning than being able to answer someone else's questions. Encourage students to apply the concepts and knowledge of your curriculum to areas of their personal interest.

Instructional Strategies

- Begin offering choices on a small scale. Start with a choice of two and set a time limit for the decision, after which you will make the choice for them.

- Shift your role from "sage on the stage" to "guide on the side" as quickly as you can. Nothing interrupts the deep state of reflective thinking called "flow" more completely than someone cutting across your thoughts; nothing kills exploration faster than someone giving the answer or obvious clues. In the HET model, more teacher time and energy is spent developing, organizing, and orchestrating learning than "teaching" through direct instruction, controlling students and events, and adhering to a rigid schedule.

- Provide choice through activities, all of which you deem equally effective to help students learn the agreed upon curriculum for your school. Do so whenever possible. Be open to thoughtful proposals from students; always ask them how their proposal will ensure that they learn concepts X and skill Y (those in the key points) that is part of your curriculum. Help them monitor their progress. Learning to "know when you know" and "know when you don't know" is essential to becoming a successful lifelong learner.

◆ ENRICHED ENVIRONMENT

Given the choice of spending a day in a five-star hotel or in an old, ramshackle, chaotic house on the corner of the busiest street in the city, which would you choose? Or, a day at Disney World/Epcot versus time at the nearby strip mall? In which environments would you smile the most, in which would time seem to pass quickly and without your notice? In which would you most likely form long-lasting pictures of what you experienced? Clearly, we'd choose the environments that were planned using the best available science about the impact of environment to support the visitor becoming engaged and learning (especially Epcot). Not only that, but the creators of such environ-

ments used the very best scientific research available at the time about the impact of color, interior design.

Using Enriched Environment to Enhance the Bodybrain Learning Partnerhship

The bodybrain-compatible element of enriched environment enhances the effectiveness of the bodybrain learning partnership in many ways.

Curriculum Development

- Plan for role models/experts.

- Create an immersion wall(s) that best simulates the real thing.

- Add hands-on-of-the-real-thing items, models, posters, videos, computer software, books, and so forth that directly support your key points and inquiries.

- Provide an area of the room for movement that will enhance learning the key points and wiring those skills and knowledge into long-term memory.

Instructional Strategies

- Revisit the *being there* location, each time digging for greater understanding of how the conceptual and significant knowledge key points of your curriculum are used in real life.

- Request that your guest speakers/experts bring as many hands on and immersion items as possible. Work with them in advance to create scenarios for role playing, problem solving, and groupwork assignments. Emphasize *how to use* the knowledge and skills in as realistic a setting as possible.

◆ ADEQUATE TIME

Lack of time is our society's number one cause of anxiety and stress. It starts early when infants must awake according to the family schedule instead of their own internal time clock. In school, our rigid schedules ensure that most children will fail to finish the initial task or, if speedy, run out of time on the second task. Or, and equally nightmarish for children, is too much time with nothing engaging to do and thus boredom sets in. The "baby bear" experience of time being "just right" is exceedingly rare. Few children learn good time-management skills because time is not under their control nor are most of the elements important to the task.

The more important to us the completion of a task is, the greater the stress, anxiety, and frustration—all elements that add up to perceived threat. Consequently, many students unconsciously withdraw their commitment to completion with high standards as a way of protecting themselves against high levels of emotional stress. In effect, our rigid schedules train students to not care, to be surface thinkers and mediocre performers. In most secondary systems, the departmentalized learning environments of junior and senior high fit such trained behavior perfectly and continue to further shape attitudes and behaviors that run counter to becoming effective lifelong learners.

Using Adequate Time to Enhance the Bodybrain Learning Partnerhship

The bodybrain-compatible element of adequate time enhances the effectiveness of the bodybrain learning partnership in many ways.

Curriculum Development

- When writing inquiries, keep in mind the time frames in which you will have students use them, e.g., all morning or all afternoon, for an hour before the schoolwide assembly, the 30 minutes before the bus arrives for your *being there* experience, and so forth. If the inquiry requires more time than the schedule permits, even after using maximum flexibility, think through natural breaking points in advance.

- Teach students useful ways to organize their work and related materials. Help them find a balance between efficiently organized for tasks and their personality preferences, e.g., judging

versus perceiving.[95] An optimum balance here will do much to reduce threat and enhance reflective thinking now and for the rest of their lives.

- Embrace "less is more." Make it your number one goal for the year. Teach conceptually rather than "covering" all the chapters of a textbook.

Instructional Strategies

- Develop, with student input, written procedures for what to do when they finish their assignment early. Include "looking back" questions—questions that help them evaluate whether the information has reached their long-term memory, introspections about how they might use such information in the future, and other questions that help students realize that their learning is for them, not for the teacher or the grade point or other external audiences or purposes.

- Create an agenda every day and use it throughout the day to organize your time and your students'.

- Teach students time management skills through modeling, mini-lessons during teachable moments, and through reflective thinking questions before, during, and after collaborative work and individual assignments, especially those lasting over multiple days. Give students genuine control over relevant elements of their work so that they can realistically practice effective time management.

- Model good time management practices and "talk out loud" as you think your way out of time crunch dilemmas and your stress reactions to them.

IMMEDIATE FEEDBACK

Immediate feedback that tells us if we're on track or not is one of the greatest sources of motivation. Lingering on with a task that we suspect we're doing "all wrong" and therefore will have to do over again and, worse, makes us feel stupid in the process, is a recipe for giving up, not caring, not wanting to try again.

Another motivation killer is having to rely on external sources for our feedback, especially a control figure such as one's classroom teacher. The older students get, the more they, like we adults, begin to resent being dependent on someone else and feeling powerless.

In just these two examples, it is clear that inadequate feedback produces highly charged negative emotions. It is critical that teachers master this late phase in the learning process; otherwise, all earlier efforts are in vain. In contrast, feedback that tells us we have succeeded at a learning task produces a burst of neurotransmitters, producing a "chemical high" that is readily observable in the spark in a child's eye as the "Aha" registers. As Frank Smith points out in *Insult to Intelligence: The Bureaucratic Invasion of Our Classrooms*, learning does not require coercion or irrelevant reward. Learning—driven by immediate feedback—is its own reward.

Using Immediate Feedback to Enhance the Bodybrain Learning Partnerhship

The bodybrain-compatible element of immediate feedback enhances the effectiveness of the bodybrain learning partnership in many ways.

Curriculum Development

- When developing an inquiry, make it clear and specific enough that students can judge for themselves whether they've completed it correctly, completely, and comprehensively. Use real world standards of performance whenever possible.

- Base the inquiries on real world settings and situations. The less abstract the assignment, the more likely students are to have a sense of what high standards are.

Instructional Strategies

- Select materials from the real world that have feedback built in naturally.

- Utilize peer review and feedback systems.

- Help students develop their own rubrics for judging their work.

MASTERY/APPLICATION

The emotional side of mastery is the foundation of positive self-concept, of seeing ourselves as a competent person, capable of handling whatever life puts in front of us. Such positive, learning-enhancing emotions are the life blood of the lifelong learner and, in the short run, they make the classroom sizzle with excitement and love of learning. The bodybrain partnership lives here—using what we understand, putting to use what we know and can do in ways **we** value.

Just as successful implementation of a mental program is its own reward, accompanied by feelings of accomplishment and increased satisfaction, having to abort a mental program that doesn't work is emotionally unsettling because it leaves us unsure of what to do next and decreases our sense of self confidence.[96] In other words, the brain has its own built-in means of evaluating whether we've achieved mastery. The brain knows the difference between scoring 100% on a quiz versus being capable of performing something needed and valued in the real world.

Using Mastery/Application to Enhance the Bodybrain Learning Partnerhship

The bodybrain-compatible element of mastery/application enhances the effectiveness of the bodybrain learning partnership in many ways.

Curriculum Development

- When developing an inquiry, make it clear and specific enough that students can judge for themselves whether they've completed it correctly, completely, and comprehensively. Use real world standards of performance whenever possible.

- Base the inquiries on real world settings and situations. The less abstract the assignment, the more likely students are to have a sense of what high standards are.

- Encourage students to write their own inquiries applying what they understand to problems and situations important to them. Make sure they state what actions would convince them they have mastered the knowledge or skill in the inquiry.

Instructional Strategies

- Select materials from the real world that have feedback built in naturally.

- Utilize peer review and feedback systems.

- Help students develop their own rubrics for judging their work. Whenever possible, reinforce their efforts to assess themselves in realistic ways.

ENDNOTES

1   Robert Sylwester has synthesized a good deal of research into a very useful and memorable phrase: "Emotion drives attention, attention drives learning/memory/problem-solving/just about everything else." Quoted in an unpublished paper entitled "The Role of the Arts in Brain Development and Maintenance." See also *A Celebration of Neurons: An Educator's Guide to the Human Brain* (Alexandria, VA: ASCD, 1995), especially Chapter 4.

The power of emotions to enhance, inhibit, and prevent learning is a well-established fact in the world of brain research. To ignore this information at the turn of the 21st century is both foolish and unacceptable. The traditional classroom with its isolated seating in strict rows and no talking except to respond to the teacher's questions is completely out of step with current knowledge.

2   Candace Pert, *Molecules of Emotion: Why You Feel the Way You Feel* (New York: Scribner, 1997).

3   Conversations with Carla Hannaford, Summer Institutes sponsored by Susan Kovalik & Associates, summer, 1999. Also see *Smart Moves: Why Learning Is Not All in Your Head*, 2nd ed. (Salt Lake City, UT: Great River Books, 2005) which expands as well as updates the book.

4   John J. Ratey, *A User's Guide to the Brain: Perception, Attention, and the Four Theaters of the Brain* (New York: Pantheon Books, 2001).

5   Robert Sylwester, *How to Explain a Brain* (Thousand Oaks, CA: Corwin Press, 2005), 160-161, 18, 85-86, 82, 46, 69-70.4

6   John J. Ratey.

7   Elkhonon Goldberg, *The Wisdom Paradox: How Your Mind Can Grow Stronger As Your Brain Grows Older.* (New York: Gotham Books, 2006), 229.

8   Patricia Wolfe, *Brain Matters: Translating Research into Classroom Practice.* (Alexandria, VA: ASCD, 2001), 76– 86.

9   Isabel Cohen and Marcelle Goldsmith, *Hands On: How to Use Brain Gym in the Classroom* (Ventura, CA: Edu Kinesthetics, 2002).

10 Doc Childre, *Freeze Frame: One Minute Stress Management – A Scientifically Proven Technique for Clear Decision Making and Improved Health* (Boulder Creek, CA: Heartmath Llc, 1998).

11 Sylwester.

12 Pert, Chapters 1 and 7.

13 Sylwester.

14 Pert, 139.

15 Pert, 139.

16 Conversations with Dr. Candace Pert, Best of the Best Invitational sponsored by Susan Kovalik & Associates, Tukwila, Washington, May, 1998.

17 An amazing but still mysterious discovery is the presence of cells through the digestive track—from mouth to anus—that are identical to neurons in the brain. Dr. Candace Pert and other scientists wonder aloud if these cells may be the source of our "gut feelings."

18 Pert, 26-27.

19 Ratey, 223.

20 Pert, 38.

21 Joseph LeDoux, "The Emotional Brain," presentation at Emotional Intelligence, Education, and the Brain: A Symposium, Chicago, IL, December 5, 1997. See also *The Emotional Brain: The Mysterious Underpinnings of Emotional Life* (New York: Simon and Schuster, 1996 and 1998).

Given the typical time lag between findings within the brain research community and education, it will likely be some years into the 21st century before reference to the triune brain is abandoned and new ways of talking about, and implementing, the power of emotion in the bodybrain partnership are developed and put into widespread use.

22 Pert, 133.

23 Antonio Damasio, "Thinking about Emotion," presentation at "Emotional Intelligence, Education, and the Brain: A Symposium," Chicago, IL, December 5, 1997. See also *Descartes' Error: Emotion, Reason, and the Human Brain,* (New York: G. P. Putnam Sons, 1994).

24 Sylwester, *How to Explain a Brain*, 141-142. Somasensory refers to any bodily sensations or feelings, whether it is the touch of another's hand on our skin or sensations arising from the movement of our own organs as they carry on our bodily processes.

25 Pert, 142.

26 There are many useful definitions of community that can be readily and powerfully applied to the classroom. In *Creating Community Anywhere*, Carolyn Shaffer and Kristin Anundsen define community as "a dynamic whole that emerges when a group of people participate in common practice, depend on one another, make decisions together, identify themselves as part of something larger, and commit over the long term to their own, one another's and the group's well-being." See *Creating Community Anywhere* (New York: Putnam's Son, 1993), 10. Also published San Francisco, CA: CCC Publishing, 2005.

27 Leonard Sax, *Why Gender Matters* (New York: Doubleday, 2005), 35.

28 Sax, 81

29 Sax, 81.

30 Sax, 89.

31 Sax, 90.

32 Sax, 73.

33 Sax, 74.

34 Sax, 29.

35 Carla Hannaford, presentation at Summer Institute sponsored by Susan Kovalik & Associates, 2000.

36 Ratey, 156.

37 Ratey, 156.

38 Ratey, 150, 148.

39 Ratey, 148.

40 Miror neurons were first discovered by XXXXX when studing monkeys. The existence of this handful of very large neurons is considered a major breakthrough in brain research, likened by Bob Sylwester andmany others to the discovery of DNA in biology. The implications for education are enormous. K-12 faculties should update themselves on this information annually.

41 The most eyepopping book summarizing this information is *Spark: The Revolutionary New Science of Exercise and the Brain* by John Ratey with Eric Hagerman (New York: Little, Brown and Company, 2008).

42 Ratey, 156.

43 Ratey, 159.

44 Ratey, 158.

45 See *Spark: The Revolutionary New Science of Exercise and the Brain* by John J. Ratey, MD with Eric Hagerman (New York: Little, Brown and Company, 2008). Also see *What Brain Research Can Teach Us About Cutting School Budgets* by Karen D. Olsen; pages 6.7-6.9 summarize the effects that a daily exercise/aerobics exercise regimen of 35-minutes (with heart rate at 70% or higher) can stimulate in the brain.

46 William Calvin, "The Mind's Big Bang and Mirroring," unpublished manuscript, Seattle: University of Washington, 2000.

47 See *Mirrors in the Brain: How Our Minds Share Actions and Emotions* by Giacomo Rizzolatti and Corrado Sinigaglia, translated by Frances Anderson (New York: Oxford University Press, 2006) and *The New Science of How We Connect with Others: Mirroring People* by Marco Iacoboni (New York: Farrar, Straus and Giroux, 2008).

48 See *Spark* by John Ratey with Eric Hagerrman.

49 This area of research is well-established. For one of many surveys, see "The Effects of Exercise on the Brain" by M. K. McGovern, serendip.brynmawr,edu/bb/neuro/neuro05/web2/mmcgovern.html.

50 Numerous studies have explored the role of BDNF in learning; they overlap and confirm. For more information, see Carl W. Cotman, Activity Dependent Plasticity in the Aging Brain, University of California Irvine, 2004. For a brief, user-friendly overview, also see M. K. McGovern.

51 It is important to note that there is a point beyond which increased aerobic exercise does not continue to increase BDNF. However, few push their exercise regimen beyond this point. And certainly 35 minutes daily comes nowhere close to reaching this plateau.

52 See M. K. McGovern for a reader-friendly summary (serendip.brynmawr,edu/bb/neuro/neuro05/web2/mmcgovernhtml).

53 Ratey, 7.

54 According to Jim Grissom, although "the overall health benefits of organized

physical activity are probably much more important than possible academic benefits ... when policy makers need to make difficult decisions about where to spend public funds and administrators need to make decisions about where to focus resources in a climate of academic accountability, a proven relationship between physical fitness and academic achievement could be used as an argument to support, retain, and perhaps even improve physical education programs." "Physical Fitness and Academic Achievement" (Journal of Exercise PhysiologyOnline (JEPonline), Vol 8, Number 1, February 2005), 12.

55 See the summary, "California Physical Fitness Test: A Study of the Relationship Between Physical Fitness and Academic Achievement in California Using 2004 Test Results" by Jim Grissom (California State Department of Education, 2004). For a more academic discussion, see "Physical Fitness and Academic Achievement," Journal of Exercise PhysiologyOnline (JEPonline), Vol 8, Number 1, February 2005.

56 Grissom, JEPonline. Stanford Achievement Test/9 mean curve equivalent increases were from 42 to 60 in reading (roughly a 33 percentile increase) in reading and a 37 to 52 MCE increase (24 percentile increase) in math. See page 16.

57 Grissom, CDE study, 5-6.

58 The CDE physical fitness test, called the Fitnessgram, was developed by the Cooper Institute for Aerobics Research in Dallas, Texas. Included in the CDE study were 371,198 fifth graders, 366,278 7th graders, and 298,910 ninth graders.

59 Castelli, Darla, C. H. Hillman, S. M. Buck, and H. E. Erwin, "Physical Fitness and Academic Achievement in Third- and Fifth-Grade Students, Journal of Sport & Exercise Psychology, 29, 2007, 239-252.

60 See C. H. Hillman, M. B. Pontiflex, L. B. Raine, D. M. Castelli, E. E. Hall, and A. F. Kramer, "The Effect of Acute Treadmill Walking on Cognitive Control and Academic Achievement in Preadolescent Children," Neuroscience 159, 2009, 1044-1064. In preadolescents, a single acute bout of moderately-intense aerobic exercise improves cognitive performance in reading, increases response accuracy (improved cognitive control). According to the researchers, acute exercise might serve as a cost-effective means for improving specific aspects of academic achievement and enhancing cognitive control during preadolescence (1059-1060).

Hillman also found that in adults, single bouts of exercise may increase attentional resource allocation and improve cognitive processing speed (from a 2003 study reported in the above 2009 article, 1046). In schools, what's good for the goose is also good for the gander. Staff, and parent volunteers, should explore the benefits of becoming fit and consider becoming role models.

61 Conversation July 13, 2009 with Jim Grissom, Ph.D., Research and Evaluation Consultant, Standards & Assessment Division, California Department of Education.

62 Sax, 20.

63 Sax, 20.

64 Sax, 19.

65 Sax, 21.

66 See *Boys Adrift: The Five Factors Driving the Growing Epidemic of UnMotivated Boys and Underachieving Young Men* by Leonard Sax (Philadelphia, PA: Basic Books, 2007). Sax presents a grave indictment of our schools, especially elementary grades. From curriculum content to instructional practices, a major overhaul is needed if our schools are to meet boys' biological learning needs.

67 Sax, 35.

68 Ratey, 61-62.

69 There are many terms for an established, on-going performance review process. "Metacognition" is used by Costa and Garmston in their peer coaching model. "Thinking about thinking" is used by Caine and Caine. Jeanne Gibbs uses the phrase "processing the process." Following through on brain research findings, we've chosen to use the term "reflective thinking."

Warnings against the unexamined life are as old as Socrates: "The unexamined life is not worth living." Because there are so many personal and social skills that need to be honed for successful group work, we recommend that the you make reflective thinking a regular part of your classroom life—before, during, and after groupwork on a daily basis.

70 Mihaly Csikszentmihalyi provides a useful definition for assessing engagement for learning. He identifies several necessary ingredients: See *Flow: The Psychology of Optimal Experience* (New York: Harper Row, 1990), 74-75. Also published New York: Harper Perennial Modern Classics, 2008.

71 Part of "slowing down" is allowing the brain and heart to come into coherence. See Doc Childre and Howard Martin with Donna Beech, *The HeartMath Solution* (San Francisco: HarperSan Francisco, 2000). This fascinating book opens new windows on the relationship between brain and heart, a connection not considered important by neuroscience until very recently. See also *Transforming Stress: The Hearmath Solution for Relieving Worry, Fatigue, and Tension* by Doc Childre and Deborah Rozman (Oakland, CA: New Harbinger Publications, 2005).

72 We are mistaken if we believe that discipline, dropouts, and drugs are what is wrong with today's schools. These are merely symptoms of a much

larger underlying problem: Far too many capable students make little or no effort to learn. In his landmark book *Control Theory in the Classroom*, William Glasser, MD (New York: Harper & Row Publishers, Inc., 1986), explains the roots of this behavior and how we can begin to solve it through learning teams.

73 See Doc Childre and the well-known HeartMath Freeze Frame technique that shows how to manage thoughts and emotions in the moment by applying five simple steps, which enhance performance and creativity.

74 For a description of Celebrations of Learning, an important instructional strategy in the *HET* model, see Chapter 15.

75 Bodymapping is a learning strategy in which parts of the body as assigned attributes of a concept or process; specific movements illustrate the idea or action. See *Minds in Motion: A Kinesthetic Approach to Teaching Elementary Curriculum* by Susan Griss, a dancer, educator, curriculum consultant, and faculty member at Lesley University, Cambridge, MA.

76 See *Hardwired to Connect: A New Scientific Case for Authoritative Communities*, a publication by the YMCA of the USA, Dartmouth Medical School, and Institute for American Values (New York: Institute for American Values, 2003) and the work of Sigurd Zielke.

77 Our own experiences as social beings tell s us that there are levels of knowing others, levels of trust we are willing to ascribe to another, and degrees of intimacy we allow at different stages of getting to know someone. These levels are described in different ways by gurus of group building, sociologists, and psychologists. Tuckman, in 1965, described three stages as forming, storming, and norming, the result of which is performing (see "Reconsidering Group Process in Challenge Education: Paradigmatic Shifts" by Don DeGraaf and Jeff Ashby). Tuckman also added a later stage, to describe the process of disbanding and moving on.

78 There are innumerable collections of data about the power of collaboration. A user-friendly source is *TRIBES: A New Way of Learning Together* by Jeanne Gibbs for classroom-oriented summaries of research from sociology, psychology, anthropology, as well as educational psychology. The book does a beautiful job of blending research and practical applications. Jeanne's newest work is *Reaching All by Creating TRIBES Learning Communities* (2006). See also the ground breaking work of Johnson and Johnson.

79 Cohen, Elizabeth, *Designing Groupwork: Strategies for the Heterogeneous Classroom*, 2nd ed. (New York: Teachers College Press, 1994), Chapter 3. This book offers an extremely straightforward, clear discussion of the social and psychological benefits of groupwork done well. Inclusion this book in your school's professional library.

80 Cohen, Chapter 3.

81 Cohen, Chapter 3.

82 Geoffrey and Renata Caine, *Making Connections: Teaching and the Human Brain* (Virginia: ASCD, 1991), 95.

83 Caines, 95.

84 Caines, 97.

85 Caines, 97.

86 Caines, 97.

87 Caines, 97.

88 Caines, 99

89 Caines, 99.

90 See Frank Smith's discussion about Learning Clubs.in *Insult to Intelligence: The Bureaucratic Invasion of Our Classrooms* (New York: Teachers College Press, 1990).

91 Why questions are very powerful. The "why" progression is:

• "What are you doing?"

• "Why are you doing this? Is your 'why' important to me, too?"

• "May I join you?"

• "What do members of this club do and know and how do they go about it?"

  According to Frank Smith, "We underrate our brains and our intelligence. . . . Learning is the brain's primary function, its constant concern, and we become restless and frustrated if there is no learning to be done. We are capable of huge and unsuspected learning accomplishments without effort." In attempting to debunk learning myths, he states, "Learning is not the occasional and difficult thing it is often thought to be. That learning requires effort is another myth. The stress and strain comes from **trying to learn and failing**. When learning is successful, it's totally inconspicuous." (See Smith, 27-30).

92 See William Glasser's Control Theory.

93 Smith, 27.

94 Smith, 27.

95 Keirsey, David. *Please Understand Me II: Temperament Character Intelligence* (Del Mar, CA: Prometheus Nemesis Book Company, 1998).

96 Hart, 160-161.

Chapter 3: The Multiple Intelligences

As any parent with two or more children knows, children's brains are different—in how they process experiences and information, in their talents and challenges, in their likes and dislikes, and more. So, if even the same gene pool can and does produce enormous variations, imagine the range of differences in a classroom of 30 students. However hard some schools may seek homogeneity by sorting students according to age, I.Q. number, achievement levels, and so forth, teachers will always face a group of students whose brains are more different than alike. For handling such dizzying differences among learners, Howard Gardner's theory of multiple intelligences[1] is, in our opinion, one of the most powerful and practical areas of brain research to apply in the classroom. His first gift to us is an imminently commonsense and intuitive definition of intelligence: ". . . a problem-solving and/or product-producing capability."[2]

Gardner's work not only sheds light on how and why students approach learning differently but also points toward very practical strategies for dealing with such differences in ways that can significantly improve the classroom learning environment and curriculum for all—for each student and also the teacher.

This chapter describes each of the multiple intelligences and discusses specific—and practical—ways to use them when developing curriculum and selecting instructional strategies.

CHANGING THEORIES OF INTELLIGENCE

Since the 1980s, our definition of intelligence has changed dramatically. We used to be told that intelligence was a singular, general characteristic set by genetics—people were either across-the-board smart or not so smart. Of course, all of this was determined by a paper-pencil test that distilled human capability down to a single number, an intelligence quotient or IQ number. And, clearly, to have an IQ of 120 was far more desirable than 100.

> ## HET Learning Principles
>
> - Intelligence as a function of experience
> - Inseparable bodybrain partnership—
>   —Emotion
>   —Movement and aerobic exercise
> - Multiple intelligences
> - Learning as a two-step process

Nature Versus Nurture

The current, broad-based view of intelligence refutes the belief that intelligence, however defined, is immutably set by genetics, that what you were born with is what you will end up with. Although genes do play a significant role, experiences from conception to death also shape intelligence. As science and our own common sense and personal and professional experiences tell us, lots of practice solving real problems and creating products of value in the real world does increase capacity to do so. In the *HET* model, we call this increase in capacity to make connections in order to solve ever more complex problems and create more resourceful and valuable products *an increase in intelligence*.

For example, co-author Karen Olsen, having decided at age five that what she would do with her life was become a teacher, hoped desperately to become a vocal music teacher. Her genetic gifts, however, did not include perfect pitch or even an ear that would allow her to play anything but a fixed-pitch instrument such as a piano. Yet, through her thousands of hours of practice, double and triple what students with innate musical capability spent, she did succeed in significantly increasing her musical intelligence— her problem-solving and product-producing capability in music. However, her product, holding her own in eight-part harmony, was accomplished through compensating measures—using the feel of the vibration in her throat (if it was "off," she knew she had either the wrong note or poor tone; in either case, stop for a bar and then pick up again). But she also knew she would never be able to rise to the level of excellence that those with inborn musical intelligence could achieve quite easily. Nor could she rise to a level of adequacy to train and direct musical groups. She therefore switched her teaching career to language arts, an area of innate gifts.

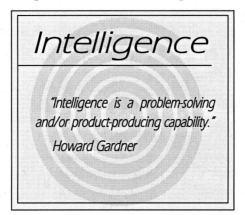

Intelligence

"Intelligence is a problem-solving and/or product-producing capability."

Howard Gardner

The decision to abandon music was deeply disappointing but an important lesson to Karen as a future educator. Even though she couldn't hit the pinnacle of music performance, there wasn't a moment of her musical experiences—singing with community and church groups and as a music minor in college—that she doesn't cherish to this day. Although painful, the lesson she learned is that

the purpose of public education ought to be that of assisting students to develop all of Howard Gardner's intelligences. Our goal should be giving students options in life—options which make life rich and deeply satisfying for both work and personal interests.

Karen's story is not uncommon. Parents everywhere have watched their children struggle and triumph, embracing a vocation or hobby challenging to them or pursuing another area that they find easier to develop. In effect, each of us has our own experiences and observation of the nature-nurture debate and will readily recognize it in discussion in the first five chapters of this book, Volume One. As the "nature-nurture" debate rages on,[3] becoming more hotly contested with each passing decade, most observers believe it's a roughly 50-50 proposition. However, the new field of epigenetics will likely significantly reframe the nature-nurture discussion.

We believe that it is the responsibility of every teacher to develop curriculum and select instructional strategies that will enable every student to develop all his/her intelligences, to become Renaissance citizens, capable of rendering informed decisions in the voting booth, developing rich relationships within family and community, and nurturing a wide range of interests and skills by which to earn an adequate living and pursue a satisfying life richly lived.

GARDNER'S THEORY OF MULTIPLE INTELLIGENCES

Gardner's definition of intelligence is an infinitely practical as well as theoretical way to look at human potential and behavior across cultures. As he developed his theory of multiple intelligence, he used several criteria:[4]

- Each intelligence had to be relatively independent of the others, with its own timetable for development, peak growth, and the like.

- Each had to operate from a different part of the brain.

- Each had to be valued in cultures around the world.

Multiple Intelligences Versus Modalities

To grasp the power of Gardner's theory of multiple intelligences, one must make a distinction between how students take in information (the visual, auditory, tactile, and kinesthetic modalities) versus how students process information inside their brains in order to first make meaning of the input and then use it to act upon the world. Remember that these intelligences are sets of problem-solving and product-producing skills/knowledge, not merely gateways through which information passes to reach the brain. Do not equate modalities with Gardner's intelligences.[5]

The Multiple Intelligences Defined

According to Gardner, intelligence ". . . entails a set of problem-solving skills, enabling the individual to resolve genuine problems or difficulties that he or she encounters and, when appropriate, to create an effective product; it also entails the potential for finding or creating problems, thereby laying the groundwork for the acquisition of new knowledge."[6]

And although each intelligence is a distinct entity meeting his research requirements, Gardner acknowledges that ". . . only the blend of intelligences in an individual makes possible the solving of problems and the creation of products of significance."[7] And, very importantly, an individual's intellectual gifts in one area cannot be inferred from his/her capacities in another.[8] For example, high mathematical ability doesn't necessarily mean the student will also be reading above grade level.

In his first book published in 1983, *Frames of Mind: The Theory of Multiple Intelligences,* Gardner identified seven intelligences. In the 1990s, he added an eighth intelligence, naturalist, and discusses a basis for two others—existential and spiritual.[9]

The following brief descriptions of the original seven intelligences, plus the naturalist intelligence, will provide curriculum designers and classroom teachers alike with beginning outlines for restructuring curriculum for the classroom. The task is a signifi-

cant one because most of today's curriculum addresses only two of the multiple intelligences—logical-mathematical and linguistic—yet all seven are needed to succeed in life.

From core curriculum standards to homework assignments to extra credit work, we must ensure that our curriculum speaks to all learners, not just those high in linguistic and logical-mathematical intelligences, as most teachers are.

Also, the multiple intelligences should be woven into our lesson planning and instructional strategies. During direct instruction we should make sure that we use all the intelligences, not just linguistic and logical-mathematical. And all other choices of strategies should selected with the goal of including all the intelligences.

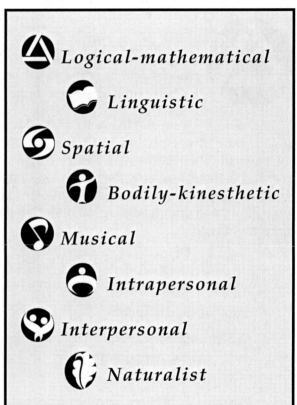

- Logical-mathematical
- Linguistic
- Spatial
- Bodily-kinesthetic
- Musical
- Intrapersonal
- Interpersonal
- Naturalist

Practical Applications

As you read this definition of the multiple intelligences, keep in mind real-life examples, such as the occupations of your extended family and friends, the intense interests and capabilities of students you've known over the years. After reading each one, jot down the name of at least three people you know well who typify that problem-solving and/or product-producing capability. You'll find you already know a great deal about these intelligences. Although considered "theoretical" in science, they seem more like common sense in real life.

Logical-Mathematical Intelligence–
operates primarily in the left hemisphere, front and back of both sides of the brain

This problem-solving and/or product-producing capability is the home of science and math. The core function of this intelligence is the interaction with the world of objects—ordering and reordering them, assessing their quantity, comprehending numerical symbols, appreciating the meaning of signs referring to numerical operations, and understanding the underlying quantities and operations themselves.[10]

Children* high in logical-mathematical intelligence:

- Compute arithmetic problems quickly in their head

- Enjoy using computers

- Ask questions such as, "Where does the universe end?" "What happens after we die?" and "When did time begin?"

- Play chess, checkers, or other strategy games, and win

- Reason things out logically and clearly

- Revise experiments to test out things they don't understand

- Spend time working on logic puzzles such as Rubik's Cube[11]

* These descriptors for each intelligence are equally true of adults.

This intelligence appears early and the most productive work is done by age forty if not by age thirty. The basis for all logical-mathematical forms of intelligence springs from the handling of objects; later these processes become internalized ("done in one's head"). One proceeds from objects to statements, from actions to the relations among actions, from the realm of the sensorimotor to the realm of pure abstraction—ultimately to the heights of logic and science.

The classical description of the development of this intelligence, the home of science and math, is that by Piaget. His work remains an accurate description of the development of logical-mathematical intelligence. However, his work does not describe development of the other intelligences.

Linguistic Intelligence–
operates predominantly in the left hemisphere, temporal and frontal lobes

Linguistic competence is the most widely and most democratically shared across the human species. As Gardner says, "one could not hope to proceed with any efficacy in the world without considerable command of phonology, syntax, semantics, and pragmatics."[12]

The core operations of language, used with special clarity, include sensitivity to the following: the meaning of words; the order among words, such as using the rules of grammar, and on carefully selected occasions, choosing to violate them; the sound, rhythm, inflection, and meter of words; and the different functions of language— its potential to excite, convince, stimulate, convey information, or simply to please.

The major uses of linguistic intelligence:

- Rhetoric—the ability to use language to convince others of a course of action

- Mnemonics—a tool to help one remember information

- Explanation—the ability to use oral and written language to teach and learn

- Metalinguistic analysis— the use of language to reflect upon language, to explain its own activities[13]

Without question, high linguistic intelligence is over 80 percent of the formula for success in traditional schooling. Without it, schooling is painful and frustrating to students and the failure rate is obscenely high despite their competence in the other intelligences. Current brain research makes clear that there are many ways of knowing, of taking in information about the world. The most powerful of these is not through reading or lecture, but rather, through full sensory input from the real world.

Children strong in linguistic intelligence:

- Like to write

- Spin tall tales or tell jokes and stories

- Have a good memory for names, places, dates, or trivia

- Enjoy reading books in their spare time

- Appreciate nonsense rhymes and tongue twisters; typically spell words accurately and easily

- Enjoy crossword puzzles or games such as Scrabble or anagrams[14]

Spatial Intelligence—

operates predominantly in the right hemisphere

The core operations of this intelligence depend on the ability to image. It also involves the capacity to perceive the visual world accurately, perform transformations and modifications upon one's initial perceptions, and recreate aspects of one's visual experience, even in the absence of relevant physical stimuli. This intelligence should be arrayed against and considered equal in importance to linguistic intelligence. Loosely put, *the mind's link to language is through pictures, not sound.* This intelligence is as critical as linguistic intelligence because the two are the principal sources of information storage and solving problems.[15]

Spatial intelligence is a collection of related skills. The images produced in the brain are helpful aids to thinking; some researchers have gone even further, considering visual and spatial imagery a primary source of thought.[16]

For many of the world's famous scientists, their most fundamental insights were derived from spatial models rather than from mathematical lines of reasoning. Einstein once commented: "The words of the language, as they are written and spoken, do not play any role in my mechanisms of thought. The psychical entities which seem to serve as elements in thought are certain signs and more or less clear images which can be voluntarily reproduced or combined. . . . The above mentioned elements are, in my case, of visual and some muscular type."[17] Examples of imaging as a primary source of thought are Darwin and the "tree of life," Freud and the unconscious as submerged like an iceberg, and John Dalton's view of the atom as a tiny solar system.

It is important to note that spatial intelligence should not be equated with the visual sensory modality. Even people who are blind from birth can develop spatial intelligence without direct access to the visual world.

A keenly developed spatial intelligence is not only an invaluable asset in our daily lives but is also essential for understanding the application of what is learned in school.[18] This is particularly true in areas where the elements are abstract and unseen (microscopic in size or invisible physical science areas such as the forces of gravity, electricity/magnets, etc.).

Children strong in spatial intelligence:

- Visualize while reading

- Spend free time engaged in art activities

- Report clear visual images when thinking about something

- Easily read maps, charts, and diagrams

- Draw accurate representations of people or things

- Like it when you show movies, slides, or photographs

- Enjoy doing jigsaw puzzles or mazes

- Daydream a lot[19]

Bodily-Kinesthetic Intelligence–
tendency for left hemisphere dominance in right-handed people and right hemisphere dominance in left-handed people

Characteristic of this intelligence is the ability to use one's body in highly differentiated and skilled ways for expressive as well as goal-directed purposes, such as the mime, actor, athlete, and tradesman. This intelligence also brings the capacity to work deftly with objects, both those that involve the fine motor movements of one's bodily motions and the capacity to handle objects skillfully.[20]

Not only is the body an instrument for acting on knowledge, to a degree greater than previously understood, the body is also an active partner in learning (see Chapter 2).

Children strong in bodily-kinesthetic intelligence:

- Use body language to communicate thoughts and emotions

- Do well in sports and recreational hobbies requiring physical skill and effort

- Move, twitch, tap, or fidget while sitting in a chair

- Engage in physical activities such as swimming, biking, hiking, or skateboarding

- Need to touch people when they talk to them

- Enjoy scary amusement rides

- Demonstrate skill in a craft like woodworking, sewing, or carving

- Cleverly mimic other people's gestures, mannerisms, or behaviors[21]

- Easily remembers information when given movement cuing systems. For example, the algorithm for long division could be expressed as: first you divide (clap-clap), multiply (tap crossed hands twice), subtract (outward slicing movement of both hands twice), and then bring it down (two hands pulling imaginary pipe down as if chinning yourself). (See *I Can Divide And Conquer* video and companion book by Martha Kaufeldt, available through Books For Educators. See back of this book.)

Involving the rest of the body in any learning event increases the neural activity of the brain, activates the motor areas of the brain which assist in sequencing thought, increases the positive flow of epinephrine which aids transfer from short-term memory to long-term memory, and releases positive molecules of emotion.

Recent research, reported convincingly by both Elkhonon Goldberg and John Ratey, reveals that movement plays a critical role in learning and life and may not be as separate a function as first suggested by Howard Gardner. In *The Executive Brain: Frontal Lobes and the Civilized Mind*, Goldberg states that various features of cortical representations of objects and of word meanings denoting objects "are stored close to the sensory and motor areas that participated in acquiring information about these objects."[22] Furthermore, it is the motor part of the brain that sequences our thoughts. Ratey, in *A User's Guide to the Brain: Perception, Attention, and the Four Theaters of the Brain*, states that "movement is crucial to every other brain function, including memory, emotion, language, and learning . . . our 'higher' brain functions have evolved from movement and still depend on it." He goes on to say that "Motor function is as crucial to some forms of cognition as it is to physical movement. It is equally crucial to behavior, because behavior is the acting out of movements prescribed by cognition. If we can better understand movement, we can better understand thoughts, words, and deeds."[23]

Musical Intelligence–
operates primarily in the right hemisphere

This intelligence is the most separate from the other intelligences and is the earliest to appear. For individuals high in this intelligence, composing and performing at age five, as Mozart did, is not unusual. It makes itself known as early as age three. Core functions include pitch, melody, rhythm, timber (tone), and pattern.

Students who are unusually high in musical intelligence and relatively low in linguistic intelligence will use their musical intelligence skills to "translate" language into rhythmic patterns. An example of this type of student is the one whose body begins to jive and tap the instant the teacher begins to speak, stopping the second the teacher stops talking, restarting with the next burst of speech—all in rhythm with the teacher's words. Content in rhyme can be readily absorbed by these students while the same information in an uninspiring lecture or in the stilted prose of a science textbook can be completely indigestible. Monotone speakers have particularly deadening effects on highly musical students.[24]

Children high in musical intelligence:

- Play a musical instrument and/or sing
- Remember melodies of songs
- Tell you when a musical note is off-key
- Say they need to have music on in order to study
- Collect records or tapes
- Sing songs to themselves
- Keep time rhythmically to music; hum and drum[25]

Intrapersonal and Interpersonal Intelligences

Both intrapersonal and interpersonal intelligence are far more diverse and culturally dependent than the other intelligences.

Extreme circumstances such as times of war, subjugation, famine, disaster in general, recession/depression, life or death situations, and death itself greatly affect the expression of these intelligences. All of these circumstances make demands for action that most people don't practice. They are one-time or seldom experienced happenings. Yet the cultural beliefs and premises held by society demand that we respond to these events and express ourself in certain ways, depending upon locale, age, status in the community, etc. In short, these are problem-solving situations requiring problem-solving intelligences. Although not so dramatic, daily living demands the same kinds of problem-solving from us.

 Intrapersonal Intelligence involves the examination and knowledge of one's own feelings, the "sense of self"—the balance struck by every individual and every culture between the prompting of inner feelings and the pressures of others.

The core capacity of intrapersonal intelligences is access to one's own "feeling life"—the range of our emotions; our capacity to instantly discriminate among these feelings and, eventually, to label them, to draw upon them as a means of understanding and guiding our behavior.[26]

At its advanced level, intrapersonal knowledge allows one to detect and to symbolize complex and highly differentiated sets of feelings, e.g., the novelist who can write introspectively about feelings, the patient or therapist who comes to attain a deep knowledge of his own inner world of feelings, the wise elder who draws upon his/her own wealth of inner experiences in order to advise members of the community.

Children strong in intrapersonal intelligence:

- Display a sense of independence or a strong will

- React with strong opinions when controversial topics are being discussed

- Seem to live in their own private, inner world

- Like to be alone to pursue some personal interest, hobby, or project

- Seem to have a deep sense of self-confidence

- March to the beat of a different drummer in their style of dress, their behavior, or their general attitude

- Motivate themselves to do well on independent study projects[27]

Interpersonal Intelligence involves looking outward toward the behavior, feelings, and motivations of others.

The core capacity of interpersonal intelligence is the ability to notice and make distinctions among other individuals and, in particular, among their moods, temperaments, motivations, and intentions.[28]

In an advanced form, interpersonal knowledge permits a skilled adult to read the intentions and desires of many other individuals—even when those have been hidden. This intelligence also permits us to act upon such knowledge, such as when influencing a group of disparate individuals to behave along desired lines; it's what we call leadership. We see highly developed forms of interpersonal intelligence in political and religious leaders (a Mahatma Gandhi or a John Fitzgerald Kennedy), in skilled parents and teachers, and in individuals enrolled in the helping professions, be they therapists, counselors, or concerned friends.

Children with high interpersonal capability:

- Have a lot of friends

- Socialize a great deal at school or around the neighborhood

- Read people's intentions and motives

- Get involved in after-school group activities

- Serve as the "family mediator" when disputes arise

- Enjoy playing group games with other children

- Have a lot of empathy for others[29]

Naturalist Intelligence*—allows people to distinguish among, classify, and use features of the environment.[30]

Howard Gardner suggests that this intelligence develops on its own in most children, " . . . particularly those who have a chance to spend time out of doors—in both rural and urban/suburban settings. The real trick is to maintain it, in the face of different pressures in school."[31] The naturalist pays attention to flora and fauna, noticing critical distinctions. Charles Darwin exemplifies the keen observation, curiosity, and awareness of patterns essential for strength in this intelligence. In a farming or hunting culture, persons strong in the naturalist intelligence are highly valued to ensure the group's continued success.

Placed in a culturally diverse environment, the naturalist picks up on characteristic patterns of speech, movement, dress, and the like with the result that he can both recognize group members and choose to conform and fit into the setting. People who move

---

* Gardner's description of the naturalist intelligence parallels Hart's discussion of how the entire brain operates as a pattern seeker. We therefore do not use the naturalist intelligence in curriculum development as it is unnecessary.

easily from mainstream to minority cultural environments are strong in naturalist intelligence.

Children who are naturalists:

- Ask many questions about their environment
- Delight in large collections of natural objects, e.g., insect collection
- Enjoy scouting or similar activity allowing them to pursue an interest at their own pace
- Stay intensely involved in an activity, not wanting to stop
- Are sensitive to patterns in the environment such as at the lake, in the woods, on the street, and in the classroom
- See structure and order where others see only noise or random elements[32]

A MESSAGE TO TEACHERS

The multiple intelligences, each of which operates from a different part of the brain, identify important ways for students to solve problems and produce products. If students are having difficulty learning a concept or skill, provide inquiries which call on their well-developed intelligence(s).[33] Later, when their understanding is solid and they're practicing how to use concepts or skills in order to wire them into long-term memory, teachers should provide inquiries which call on other intelligences, giving students opportunities to develop them. This wide input and processing not only helps cement long-term memory but strengthens students' problem-solving and product-producing capabilities in all areas of intelligence.

Do the activities within each category strike a familiar chord? They should. Each of us is born with all of these intelligences but we tend to develop those valued by our culture (home, school, church, community). It is the goal of the *HET* classroom to make sure that all intelligences are developed and used on a daily basis.

TRANSLATING BRAIN RESEARCH INTO ACTION USING THE NINE BODYBRAIN-COMPATIBLE ELEMENTS

The multiple intelligences are a major curriculum development tool in the *HET* model. They are key when developing inquiries because they help the teacher build in choices and meaningfulness for students. (See Chapter 17.) They also serve as a check list for the teacher when creating an enriched environment.

Bodybrain-Compatible Elements

- *Choices*
- *Meaningful Content*
- *Enriched Environment*
- *Adequate Time*
- *Absence of Threat/Nurturing Reflective Thinking*
- *Collaboration*
- *Immediate Feedback*
- *Mastery*
- *Movement*

CHOICES

Choice based on variety just for the sake of variety is a one-way ticket to hard work for teachers and an investment with minimal return for students. Choice must be purposeful—specifically planned ways to provide input and/or apply concepts and skills that will enable each student to achieve at high levels.

Using Choices to Enhance Development of the Multiple Intelligences

The bodybrain-compatible element of choices enhances development of the multiple intelligences in many ways.

Curriculum Development

- Teach the theory of multiple intelligences to your students. Help them distinguish between the intelligences as ways of thinking to solve problems/produce products versus a subject content of the same name, such as music or language arts. For example, writing lyrics for a song is not necessarily using one's musical intelligence; it's likely just another linguistic activity. But figuring out how to use music composition skills as a study technique (to go from Ds to As in college) is a way of using musical intelligence to solve problems and produce products.[33] Also, doing arithmetic, carrying out the mechanics of a long division problem, is not the same as thinking mathematically to solve a problem in your environment as in the TV show *Numbers*. *The intelligences are a way of thinking, not a subject, not a modality.*

- For every key point, develop at least 5-12 inquiries; ensure that there are two or more for each of the following intelligences: spatial, musical, bodily-kinesthetic, and mathematical intelligences. Then check that interpersonal and intrapersonal intelligence are addressed among the above five. Also check that inquiries address Bloom's taxonomy (see Chapter 13) and the way we take in information (see temperament, Appendix A).

- Encourage students to write inquiries for themselves and for the class. Select those you think will provide the best application and practice of concepts and skills for students.

Instructional Strategies

- Have students identify their strongest intelligences and those they would like to develop further. Have them set goals and strategies for developing their intelligences on a weekly basis.

- Prepare resource people to talk about how they use the multiple intelligence most critical to their area of expertise. Prep them for such questions from students as: "When did you first know you had this capability?" "How did you build it when you were a student?" "What other occupations could you have chosen using this intelligence?" Explore these same issues with people at your *being there* locations.

- Teach students to observe how fellow Learning Club members use their intelligences. After every collaborative task, have students (individually and as a group) reflect on what they have learned from each other about using the intelligence(s) needed to successfully complete their work.

- Model respecting different ways of learning, solving problems, and producing products.

- When planning direct instruction and its immediate follow up, build in all of the first seven intelligences.

- Make the multiple intelligences a daily focus of your teaching. It is probably your most powerful means to empower students as learners now and throughout their lives.

MEANINGFUL CONTENT

Have you ever sat in a class and thought to yourself, "Why am I struggling so? This stuff can't be this hard. What's going on here?" If so, you were probably responding to a learning environment that didn't allow you to use your intelligence(s) of strength thus crippling your ability to learn. The moral of the story here is that much of meaningfulness is a function of how we go about learning rather than any innate quality of the concept or skill to be learned. For example, high interpersonal-intelligence people will happily absorb all kinds of concepts and skills if allowed to process them interpersonally. The same content approached intrapersonally may hold little interest and meaning to them. Likewise, study of the physics of sound waves may hold little interest to someone high in musical intelligence but low in logical/mathematical intelligence until he/she is allowed to apply the concepts to sound waves of various orchestral instruments from tuba to piccolo, bass viola to violin, piano to guitar.

Frank Smith, in *Insult to Intelligence: The Bureaucratic Invasion of Our Classrooms*, makes the point that when meaning is reached, "learning" occurs automatically and simultaneously.[34] The learner is always asking, What does this situation/information mean to me? How can I use it? How does it affect me now and in my future? "Making sense of the everyday world in relation to ourselves, our needs (physical, emotional, mental), and motivations (interests and need for fun in our lives) is our greatest concern and motivator."[35] According to Hart, "How much is learned by rote is a direct function of time and effort. But when the learning is meaningful we learn much faster and without effort."[36]

Using Meaningful Content to Enhance Development of the Multiple Intelligences

The bodybrain-compatible element of meaningful content enhances development of the multiple intelligences in many ways.

Curriculum

- Help students discover and track their own intelligences.

- Know your students. Create curriculum that builds on their strengths while they are attempting to understand something new and learning how to apply it.
  During practice to cement such learning into long-term memory, encourage students to stretch using intelligences that aren't as well developed.

- The easiest way to respond to the fact that every brain is unique and therefore processes information, solves problems, and produces products differently is to ensure that your inquiries offer a range of mental engagement. For example, create inquiries that invite use of those intelligences that are most developed in students and also some that invite students to use their least developed intelligences. The goal is to create Renaissance minds, competent, flexible, powerful.

Instructional Strategies

- Ask students what it would take to make the concept or skill to be learned meaningful to them. Know that each student's brain is different and that they will therefore process differently. Commit yourself to providing the kinds of input that they need to arrive at your levels of expectation.

- During direct instruction, provide input for all the intelligences; this increases students' understanding of the concept/skill and the perception of relevance.

- Provide opportunities for students to reflect on how well they're developing all of their intelligences.

- When students are reading literature, studying famous people, or attending a career day, have students analyze the intelligences most critical to that person and/or task.

- Until you have developed a mental program for engaging and supervising students in developing their multiple intelligences, create a class graph that allows you to track the intelligences required by the inquiries that students complete. Be ready to encourage students to stretch themselves.

ENRICHED ENVIRONMENT

The brain can't learn new things or make connections among previously learned concepts and skills without new input—a problem to be solved or a product to be made that forces us to "reshuffle the deck" of new sensory input. Thus, the elements we select to make learning come alive for students are crucial. In addition to taking into account the six kinds of input—with special emphasis on *being there* locations, *immersion*, and *hands on of the real thing*—we also need to take into account if and how that input will encourage and challenge the multiple intelligences. (For a discussion of levels of sensory input, see Chapter 1.)

There are many examples of apparent fit that, once examined closely, don't accomplish the desired result. For example, a study trip to a grocery store would, on the surface, seem to address bodily-kinesthetic intelligence. But if the visit is a look-see-listen event, the body is walking and standing but not necessarily involved in solving problems or producing products. Similarly, a presentation by a visiting artist may challenge spatial intelligence or the visit may only be a linguistic experience on the topic of art.

Keep in mind that Gardner's theory of multiple intelligences is about how the brain solves problems and makes products. An enriched environment, therefore, must provide the substance for such thoughts and projects. Thus, the input must invite—even demand—action. An enriched environment is a purposeful environment that walks the tight rope between enough to activate the multiple intelligences and too much that results in clutter.

Using Enriched Environment to Enhance Development of the Multiple Intelligences

The bodybrain-compatible element of enriched environment enhances development of the multiple intelligences in many ways.

Curriculum

- Check the power of every item you bring into your classroom to encourage solving a problem or producing products relating to your curriculum. Eye appeal is nice, interesting is nice, but the important questions are: "Does it invite problem solving? Will it play an integral role in producing a product?" If not, don't bring it into the classroom; your space is too limited. If yes, keep it and use it to build your curriculum, especially to design engaging inquiries.

Instructional Strategies

- Select *being there* locations that call upon and/or illustrate all the intelligences.

- Replicate/Simulate in your classroom the important elements of the immersion wall. If your replication/ simulation is a mirror of the location, all the intelligences will be included automatically because real life is integrated and rich in its problems to be solved.

- Analyze hands-on-of-the-real-thing items; make sure their use (as a group) addresses all of the intelligences.

- Realize that what you find acceptable or endearing may have very opposite effects on some students due to their different strengths. Base your classroom decor and music on carefully researched principles of interior design and musicality, not on personal preferences.

ADEQUATE TIME

Solving problems and producing products are a far cry from rote memorizing; they require thinking and reflecting, searching for and understanding connections among prior and current learnings—all of which takes time.

Each of us can recall a time when we were deeply immersed in something and then were interrupted. Not only do we immediately feel irritated—a sense of loss—but when we can again return to the task, the enjoyment is gone. Worse, it takes some time before we are able to figure out where we were in our thinking process. Inadequate time causes tremendous stress and kills motivation for all of us.

For teachers, inadequate time is lethal. Many a worthwhile and widely-supported school improvement effort has died a premature death because of inadequate time to plan together, study together, prepare together, and implement together. In fact, without adequate time, together does not and cannot happen.

For students strong in logical-mathematical intelligence, inadequate time to complete a project or come to a logical breaking point is intolerable.

When learning—especially when learning the skills and attitudes for becoming a lifelong learner and developing intelligences that are not our strengths—it is important to remember that the race is not to the swift but to the thorough. Working with the multiple intelligences is not just a means to an end but a worthy goal in its own right because of the long-term benefits.

Using Adequate Time to Enhance Development of the Multiple Intelligences

The bodybrain-compatible element of enriched environment enhances development of the multiple intelligences in many ways.

Curriculum

- Always remember, developing an intelligence is not about getting the right answer but about practicing new ways of thinking to solve problems and produce products and becoming more proficient in doing so. This takes time—lots of time and lots of practice. Always have more inquiries on hand than you think you'll need.

- Help students understand the importance of developing all of their intelligences so that they will challenge themselves to do so.

- Assign practice in applying concepts or skills to real-world situations through homework. Use class time the next day to process what students learned about their intelligences. What they learn about themselves as a learner is far more useful over a lifetime than memorizing any one concept.

- Encourage students who need more practice to use spare time during the school day and at home to complete inquiries. Invite them to develop their own inquiries to practice with.

Instructional Strategies

- Be flexible; reduce or eliminate "regular schedules" with their specified time blocks.

- Let students' interests and excitement lead them. Learning to learn, learning how to steer one's own learning takes time.

- Provide adequate wait time; let students mull and stew and benefit from self-talk or dialogue with Learning Club members before you accept an answer to your question. Make answering a question an adventure in reflective thinking rather than a competition to be first.

- If students are to work at developing all their intelligences, create an environment that encourages students to slow down so they can talk their way through their work, shifting from strengths to weaknesses and weaknesses to strengths, comfort level to extreme challenge and back again. Allow students to tell you if they need more time and then alter the schedule accordingly.

- Plan direct instruction that uses all intelligences. Alternate short periods of direct instruction (maximum of 11-16 minutes) with inquiries that invite the use of several different intelligences.

ABSENCE OF THREAT/NURTURING REFLECTIVE THINKING

In Chapter 1 we made the case that absence of threat is a prerequisite for but not the same as reflective thinking. Reflective thinking assumes absence of threat but requires that we are allowed to think and solve problems and produce products thinking the way we think best, that is, using our developed intelligences. It also requires, however, that we have multiple ways to tackle a problem so that we can have many avenues to pursue, not just one approach.

Absence of Threat. Stress in all its forms, including threat (real or perceived), almost always makes us retreat to more familiar territory, coping strategies, and habits of mind. For example, when under stress, we tend to revert to old eating habits and styles of interacting with others. In the classroom, this translates into reverting to our problem-solving/product-producing strengths. If linguistic intelligence is not our strength and we are confronted with a paper-pencil test situation we believe we will fail, we are likely to revert to our strong intelligence. If that is interpersonal, we are likely to begin talking with our neighbor; if bodily-kinesthetic, moving about. Neither strategy assists in successful test taking.

Traveling the multiple intelligences is a balancing act between using our dominant strengths when content and situations are challenging versus learning to stretch ourselves to build our problem-solving/product-producing strategies and approaches. The most effective learners and performers are those who can, and are willing to, dance between the two. Again, our goal in public education ought to be the creation of Renaissance people, the Leonard da Vincis and everyday geniuses of the 21st century.

Reflective Thinking. According to Einstein, "Imagination is more important than knowledge." His greatest insights came when he was in a dreamlike state, another kind of reflective thinking.

This is an important awareness. Nose to the grindstone, never taking time to look up or rethink what one is doing is a recipe for pain and inefficiency. Advances in thinking come from seeing with new eyes, an aha! preceded by a quiet moment of introspection and/or undirected, free-flowing thought.

The key here is to use your classroom leadership to create frequent times for students to work quietly on their own, developing their intrapersonal intelligence and helping them learn to use it to guide their problem solving and product producing efforts.

Using Absence of Threat and Nurturing Reflective Thinking to Enhance Development of the Multiple Intelligences

The bodybrain-compatible element of absence of threat and nurturing reflective thinking enhances development of the multiple intelligences in many ways.

Curriculum

- Teach students the theory of multiple intelligences. Have them assess their strengths and areas yet to be developed. Develop key points and inquiries just as you would for science or social studies.

- Make sure that the inquiries for each key point address all of the first seven intelligences. (For a discussion of each of the kinds of key points and inquiries, key curriculum structures in the HET model, see Chapters 14 and 15.)

- When selecting inquiries for whole class use, select first those that use the greatest sensory input and manipulation of the information or skill, e.g., inquiries designed for bodily-kinesthetic and interpersonal intelligences and that are application-based. Select last those that are linguistic, especially those based on the knowledge and comprehension levels of Bloom's Taxonomy (see Chapter 13).

- Invite students to write inquiries that they consider a stretch for themselves, inquiries that require them to use an intelligence they want/need to develop.

Instructional Strategies

- Create classroom procedures for instituting daily time periods for intrapersonal time. They are an important part of classroom leadership. For more information about procedures, see Chapter 7.

- Provide time for and model using intrapersonal time; orchestrate conditions that encourage reflective thinking.

- Invite students to reflect on their progress in developing one or two intelligences they don't normally use.

- Use reflective thinking questions after collaborative learning to ensure that students see the value of multiple intelligences, e.g., "Which intelligences did we use/could we have used to complete this task?"

- During intrapersonal time, invite and encourage students to choose the inquiry they will work on or write their own.

- Involve students in writing inquiries they believe will best help them stay engaged and learn most effectively.

Collaboration

When it comes to teaching students how to develop and use the first seven intelligences, collaboration is your most powerful tool. Why? Because a Learning Club composed of students with strengths in different intelligence provides ongoing modeling of how each intelligence operates and contributes to a more effective result. And since imitation is a core learning strategy of all children, daily modeling of an intelligence by someone they like and respect is very powerful indeed. Understanding how the different intelligences work is a first step toward appreciating intellectual differences rather than being intimidated by them or feeling superior about them.

Likewise, collaboration among staff produces better products when differences are acknowledged and consciously used to achieve a better result.

Using Collaboration to Enhance Development of the Multiple Intelligences

The bodybrain-compatible element of enriched environment enhances development of the multiple intelligences in many ways.

Curriculum

- Make sure that the content of each inquiry assigned for collaborative work requires several intelligences so that no one student by him/herself can do it.[37] This ensures that each student must contribute and thus each intelligence is demonstrated to be important to successfully completing the task.

- Ensure a balance of inquiries using interpersonal (collaborative work) and intrapersonal (working solo) intelligences.

- Consider the match between the intelligences required by an inquiry and the intelligence strengths of the student assigned to be the leader of the group for that task. Develop additional inquiries if needed so that each student leader can be successful as leader as well as learner.

Instructional Strategies

- When establishing the membership of your collaborative groups, called Learning Clubs in the HET model, use problem-solving/product-producing strengths as a major criteria. In your groups of four to five students,[38] do your best to have strengths in at least four intelligences represented.

- Whenever students work on a group inquiry, have them analyze what intelligences they will most need to complete the assigned task(s). This will alert students not strong in that intelligence to tune into that mode of solving problems or producing products. Similarly, during reflective thinking after a collaborative task, have students analyze how they used/didn't use the multiple intelligences as they worked together. (Reflective thinking is an important strategy for maximizing learning in group settings—both of subject content and ability to work together as a group.)

- Have students analyze what intelligences are required by the most frequently assigned group roles, e.g., recorder, leader, materials gatherer. Encourage them to observe how specific roles and intelligences make the group successful.

IMMEDIATE FEEDBACK

Each intelligence has its own built-in ways of thinking, e.g., shifting immediately to mindmapping information or creating a mathematical formula to show relationships, reading the directions first or "playing with it" first to figure it out. To learn new ways of thinking, immediate feedback is essential. The issue here is not about getting the right answer but about actually thinking differently. After-the-fact feedback is therefore useless. What is needed is "in-flight" assessments and adjustments. External feedback from teachers and fellow Learning Club members is therefore invaluable.

However, since external feedback is not always available, in the long run students must learn to expand their capacity for self-talk, a key factor in intrapersonal intelligence. Self-talk can provide a running dialogue for students. It can ask pertinent questions to guide the next attempt at solving the problem or get around a production problem to complete a project.

For example, co-author Karen D. Olsen has learned to rely on self-talk a great deal when writing a book. When writer's block appears, the self-talk begins. "Now, why am I stuck on this? Is it the content I'm hung up on or how to express it? Are my examples only linguistic or have I provided pictures of how it would look in the classroom (spatial input) and ways students could act on this idea (bodily-kinesthetic)?" And the internal dialogue continues. Are some of my questions hard to answer? You bet! Musical intelligence is my low suit still and interpersonal isn't my first preference but the beat goes on. Problem solving even for a linguistic task such as writing a book is greatly enhanced by use of all of the intelligences.

Lifelong learners and effective performers learn to use intrapersonal intelligence to redirect use of all the other intelligences. In effect, conscious use of the intrapersonal intelligence is a way to provide ourselves instant and ongoing feedback.

Using Immediate Feedback to Enhance Development of the Multiple Intelligences

The bodybrain-compatible element of enriched environment enhances development of the multiple intelligences in many ways.

Curriculum

- Structure inquiries so that the materials used and/or the processes required provide intrinsic feedback, i.e., the student can determine on his/her own whether his/her effort worked (solved the problem) or the product meets expected standards (real-world work standards)

- Include in group inquiries reflective thinking questions that invite students to reflect on:
  - Which of the multiple intelligences, and/or what combinations of them, did they use to complete their inquiry
  - How did they use these intelligences (give examples)
  - How well they used those intelligences
  - What they learned about the strengths of the group and how well the group modeled each intelligence
  - What each member learned about his/her ability to use each of the intelligences.

- Consider student misbehavior an indicator of curricular weaknesses. Analyze the intelligences required by the curriculum and those intelligences you have observed the misbehaving students to use most effectively. Fill in the gap.

Instructional Strategies

- Use rubrics which invite students to ask themselves questions about their work—a "guided practice" of intrapersonal intelligence.

- After reflecting upon the process of completing a collaborative task, invite students to record their thoughts in their journals. Have them create a section of their journals called "Me and My Shadow" or "Are You Listening?" and record how they used self-talk to increase their power as a learner.

- Use student misbehavior as an indicator of limited range of instructional strategies, especially during direct instruction. After analyzing the intelligences most effectively used by the misbehaving students and the intelligences you use during direct instruction, be more deliberate in your lesson planning and fill in this gap.

- Find someone to provide immediate feedback to you about how well you provide immediate feedback to your students (and other issues you may choose).

MASTERY / APPLICATION

In the *HET* model, the focus of mastery is one's ability to apply concepts and skills in real-life settings in accordance with real world standards and expectations. Rote memory therefore is a small piece of success in the *HET* model—a means to an end but not valued as an end in itself. What's important is the ability to use what is understood, not just repeat it back, that is valued.

Clearly, the ability to use what is understood requires facility in handling a wide range of circumstances and tools. The best way to acquire this flexibility and expertise is to develop the capacity to solve problems and produce products in each of the multiple intelligences. Until then, allow students to demonstrate what they understand using their strengths rather than their weaknesses and to practice what they know in various ways until the new information becomes stored in long-term memory.

Using Mastery/Application to Enhance Development of the Multiple Intelligences

The bodybrain-compatible element of mastery/application enhances development of the multiple intelligences in many ways.

Curriculum

- When developing ways to determine student mastery—tests, rubrics for self-assessment and group feedback, and so forth—avoid only paper-pencil tools. Require ability to use concepts and skills in real world ways; instead of multiple choice answers to a single question, offer students their choice of assessment options based on spatial, bodily-kinesthetic, musical, and logical-mathematical intelligences which require students to "do" something, not just talk.

Instructional Strategies

- Have students manipulate information in a variety of ways that can lead to mastery.

- Model how to use the different intelligences to assess a product or a problem-solving process.

- Help students develop a sense of "knowing when they know" and "knowing when they don't know." If a little knowledge is a dangerous thing, a person with a little knowledge who perceives it to be a lot is a detriment to himself and to others. For example, the on-line investors who lose their retirement nest egg because they failed to recognize what they didn't know about investing. Or, meetings with people who hog the agenda yet have no grasp of the extent of their ignorance on the topic (but nonetheless were adamant in their opinions)—a nightmare in a democratic society when citizens gather together to solve a problem!

- Provide time for students to reflect in their journals about how they can tell if they know enough about a topic to make decisions responsibly and when they need to gather more information

- Provide models of quality products so students can see what mastery looks like.

- Involve students in designing portfolios that demonstrate mastery.

MOVEMENT

The multiple intelligences are rarely used in isolation—one at a time. Almost any real-world task requires a rich mixture of intelligences. *Being there* experiences are especially effective in making us move about and use a combination of intelligences. In such active learning situations, movement and bodily-kinesthetic intelligence meld together. Thus, if you plan explorations of *being there* locations, you will automatically engage both movement and bodily-kinesthetic intelligence. Our only word of advice is this: Assign authentic action. Avoid that which is contrived.

Using Movement to Enhance Development of the Multiple Intelligences

The bodybrain-compatible element of movement enhances development of the multiple intelligences in many ways.

Curriculum

- Remember that bodily-kinesthetic intelligence is a problem-solving and product-producing capability. Inquiries should offer important problems to be solved and worthwhile products to be produced. Anything less is a waste of time and insulting to students. Always ask yourself, "If I were the age of my students, would I find this task worthy of my time? Would the task help me understand that concept or skill or learn to apply it? Would the task help me remember the concept or skill 10 years from now?

- Think movement, think action, think doing something worthwhile while practicing how to use key points.

Instructional Strategies

- Because the motor areas of the brain sequence thinking, the more students *do* things with what they know, the more solid the learning. Add movement to every possible aspect of your instructional processes—from direct instruction to independent study and everything in between.[39]

- Design inquiries that ask students, in Learning Clubs or in pairs, to create movements as mnemonics for applying and remembering the concept or skill of a skill point.

- Develop an active cross-age tutoring or buddy program that invites your students to demonstrate what they know to younger students. The tutor/buddy rule: Demonstrate, don't tell.

ENDNOTES

1 Howard Gardner's theory of intelligence is widely received and well ensconced; it is also our choice for the *HET* model because it can be easily applied in the classroom and with great power. However, Dr. Robert Sylwester points out that Gardner's theory isn't the only credible theory of multiple intelligences. He believes that the work of David Perkins and Robert Sternberg (see below) is also intriguing and useful, fitting well with *HET* and the brain functions explored by Elkhonon Goldberg (see Chapter 4).
David Perkins defines intelligence as "knowing one's way around" seven realms of human experience: dispositional, challenge, tool, technical, field, situational, and contextual. See *Outsmarting IQ: The Emerging Science of Learnable Intelligence* (Free Press, 1995).
Robert Sternberg's triarchic brain model identifies three intelligences: creative, analytic, and practical. Sylwester sees close parallels between these intelligences and the capabilities of the principal brain, especially the frontal lobes: 1) the ability to develop a useful solution to a novel challenge, 2) the ability to develop effective cognitive routines to use when confronted by familiar challenges, and 3) the ability to anticipate the motives, intentions, and behaviors of others. See *Successful Intelligence How Practical and*

Creative Intelligence Determine Success in Life (New York: Plume, 1997). The views of Dr. Robert Sylwester about this area are taken from discussions based on his August 4, 2003 letter to the authors.

2   We use Gardner's work because it rings with our experiences with children and adults and because it so readily lends itself to practical applications when developing curriculum and selecting instructional strategies. See *Frames of Mind: The Theory of Multiple Intelligences* (New York: Basic Books, Inc., 1985).

3   For fascinating accounts of the interacting of genes and environment, see Richard Restak, MD, *The New Brain: How the Modern Age Is Rewiring Your Mind* (Emmaus, PA: Rodale Inc., 2003). Also see the discussion of epigenetics in the DVD documentary *Ghost in Your Genes, a* BBC production, 2008).

4   For a description of the criteria used by Gardner to define an area of intelligence, see *Frames of Mind*, x.

5   According to Howard Gardner, "Intelligences are not equivalent to sensory systems" (*Frames of Mind*, 68). The theory of multiple intelligences expands and replaces our previous understandings of sensory input, such as the modalities. Such frames of reference were based upon observing *from the outside,* variations in student learning behavior and then, based on such observations, making assumptions about how students learn.

In contrast, current research into how the human brain learns—the focus of this book—is based on high-tech observations *of the inside* of the brain as it is operating. These observations about what the brain is actually doing as it thinks and learns then allow us to determine what educational practices will assist the brain to do its job most naturally and thus most powerfully.

This difference is critical because although you may find considerable overlap in recommended instructional strategies for modalities and multiple intelligences, implementation of each of those instructional strategies must differ in subtle but powerful ways because the whys and whats behind what you are trying to achieve are different. In simple terms, modalities focus on instructional approaches and materials that provide input through different pathways to the brain—kinesthetic, taste, and smell as well as visual and auditory. In contrast, multiple intelligences focus on how the brain processes information once it gets to the brain—how it uses what it learns to solve problems and/or produce products. The difference is between the route through which input arrives versus ways of processing and thinking about what comes in.

6   Gardner, 60-61.

7   Gardner, x.

8   Gardner, xiii.

9   Since his initial work in the 1980s, Gardner has considered evidence for three additional intelligences: naturalist, spiritual, and existential. See Chapters 4 and 5, *Intelligence Reframed: Multiple Intelligences for the 21st Century* by Howard Gardner (New York: Basic Books, 1999). The naturalist intelligence is considered the strongest candidate so far. However, as you read through this chapter and Chapters 9 and 10 about how to develop curriculum in the *HET* model, you will notice that we do not utilize the naturalist intelligence. There are several reasons: Gardner himself states that the naturalist intelligence develops on its own in most children. We believe that well constructed *being there* experiences, along with teaching the scientific thinking processes, will provide ample practice in observing, classifying, and using features of the environment. Also, it is our contention that Gardner's comment that the "pattern-recognizing talents of artists, poets, social scientists, and natural scientists are all built on the fundamental perceptual skills of naturalist intelligence" is incorrect. In our opinion, "pattern-recognition" as described in Chapter 4 is a **general function of the entire brain**, not just that of the naturalist intelligence. This is consistent with the fact that Gardner does not assign the function of naturalist intelligence to a particular region of the brain as he does the first seven intelligences. In effect, the naturalist intelligence does not meet Gardner's initial criteria for identifying distinct intelligences.

Howard Gardner's definition of intelligence is an extremely useful alternative to the standard I.Q. number. See *Frames of Mind*, x.

10 Gardner, Chapter 7.

11 Thomas Armstrong, *In Their Own Way*, Revised Edition (New York: Tarcher Press, 2000).

12 Gardner, Chapter 5.

13 Gardner, Chapter 5.

14 Armstrong, 20.

15 Gardner, 177.

16 Armstrong, 18.

17 Gardner, 190.

18 For a teacher-friendly tool for strengthening spatial intelligence, the best resource we have found is by Nanci Bell, *Visualizing and Verbalizing for Improved Language Comprehension: A Teacher's Manual* (CA: Academy of Reading, 1991).

19 Armstrong, 21.

20 Gardner, Chapter 9.

21 Armstrong, 23.

22 Elkhonon Goldberg, *The Executive Brain: Frontal Lobes and the Civilized Mind* (Oxford: Oxford University Press, 2002), 65-66. See also *The New Executive Brain: Frontal Lobes and the Civilized Mind* (Oxford: Oxford University Press, 2009).

23 John Ratey, *A User's Guide to the Brain: Perception, Attention, and the Four Theaters of the Brain* (New York: Pantheon Books, 2001), 48 (Chapter 4) and by Abacus, 2003.

24 Gardner, Chapter 6.

25 Armstrong, 22.

26 Gardner, Chapter 10.

27 Armstrong, 24.

28 Gardner, Chapter 10.

29 Armstrong, 23-24.

30 For reasons discussed in footnote 9, we do not use the naturalist intelligence in our curriculum work for the *HET* model.

31 E.F. Shores, "Howard Gardner on the Eighth Intelligence: Seeing the Natural World," *Dimensions of Early Childhood* (Summer, 1995), 5-7.

32 Shores, "Howard Gardner," 5-7.

33 Co-author Karen Olsen interviewed a young man who had given up on college—frustration and low grades. After touring with a band for several years, he returned to college. Determined to succeed, and armed with information about Gardner's multiple intelligences, he began to figure out ways to use his considerable musical talent as study aids. For classes with a lot of details and definitions, he would first choose a letter or word representing each element and then compose a short melody using those letters/words. Before long, he was composing and singing his way to high grades— consistently As and B+s.

34 Frank Smith, *Insult to Intelligence: The Bureaucratic Invasion of Our Classrooms* (New Hampshire: Heinemann, 1986), 62. Also see revised edition, 1988.

35 Smith.

36 Leslie A. Hart, *Human Brain and Human Learning*, (Black Diaimond, WA: Books for Educators, 2002), 67.

37 This sage advice comes from Elizabeth Cohen. She provides the best guidance for developing curriculum for collaborative tasks that we have found to date. See Elizabeth Cohen, *Designing Groupwork: Strategies for the Heterogeneous Classroom*, 2nd ed. (New York: Teachers College Press, 1994).

38 Learning Clubs with three to four members are an ideal size (see Robert J. Marzano et al, *Classroom Instruction That Works: Research-Based Strategies for Increasinsg Student Achievement*), 88. However, if students have never worked collaboratively before, you will likely need to start with groups of two and work up to five. This could take days or months depending on the personal and social skills of your students. The Lifelong Guidelines and LIFESKILLS are a crucial tool for teaching students how to work together. And, don't be dismayed if you must begin with a group of one. Start where your students are.

39 This recent area of brain research is critical to educators. More than any other area we know of, it explains why traditional classrooms, with their "sit quietly and work on your own" assignments, produce such minimal results. For more information, see John Ratey, *A User's Guide to the Brain: Perception, Attention, and the Four Theaters of the Brain*, especially Chapter 4, and *The Executive Brain: Frontal Lobes and the Civilized Mind* by Elkhonon Goldberg, especially 65-66.

Chapter 4: Pattern Seeking— Step One of Learning

A NEW DEFINITION OF LEARNING

Recent brain research is revolutionizing our understanding of teaching and learning by revealing how we learn—how the brain processes raw sensory input into long-term memory. Leslie Hart, a pioneer in synthesizing and applying brain research to education, defines learning as a two-step process.[1]

> ### Learning Is a Two-Step Process
>
> Step One — Input stage: Pattern seeking & meaning making
> First, the brain must detect/identify a pattern.
> Second, the brain must make meaning of the pattern, including its relationship to other patterns.
>
> ### AND
>
> Step Two — Output stage: Building programs to use what we understand
> Begins with conscious effort (often with guidance)
> *and then*
> With practice, becomes almost automatic and wired into long-term memory.

Hart's definition of learning is much more stringent than what is currently used. In his view, students must not only be able to detect and understand patterns but also to use use them, first with guidance in familiar settings and then in varying situations on their own until the ability to use the knowledge or skill is readily at hand, almost automatic.

This definition of learning carries us far beyond that assumed by makers of standardized tests. The typical multiple choice and true/false questions can be answered based on a faint ring of familiarity of one answer over another. "Choice B rings a bell. . . ." "Hmm, that statement doesn't sound familiar, so it must be false. . . ." The test taker doesn't even have to understand the content.

HET Learning Principles

- *Intelligence as a function of experience*
- *Bodybrain partnership—emotion as gatekeeper to learning and performance* and *movement and aerobic exercise to enhance learning*
- *Multiple intelligences*
- *Learning as a two-step process — pattern seeking/meaning making — program building/wiring for long-term memory*

And step two of learning—being able to use what is understood and then to apply it until it becomes stored in long-term memory—isn't even considered by test makers.

Does it shock you that we spend billions of dollars on standardized testing based on ever-increasing state and federal standards but don't care whether learning can be be applied or will last beyond the exam? We hope so. We hope it will motivate you and your school to sit down and seriously apply brain research in all your program improvement efforts.* A beginning point is to adopt a definition of learning that all can work toward. Hart's two-step definition on the next page is the most useful and useable we have found. And, 20 years after he proposed it, there is even more convincing evidence from brain research to substantiate it.

THE GRADIENTAL/DISTRIBUTIVE VIEW OF THE BRAIN

The newly emerging gradiental/distributive view of the brain suggests that the brain—especially in contextually rich, meaningful, real-lifelike settings—is extremely active and more integrated than the modular theory first envisioned. Activity shifts over time as the new learnings are used and committed to long-term memory.

These shifts parallel the definition of learning on the next page. For example, when something new is encountered (vertical column A, naive), pattern seeking begins in the right frontal lobe (identification of the pattern). For making meaning of the pattern (comparing to prior information and testing information in the current experience), the brain shifts to the left frontal lobes.

As the learning is used (a program to apply what is learned) and becomes practiced, brain activity shifts downward and toward

---

* For a fascinating look at applying brain research principles during budget cutting, see *What Brain Research Can Teach Us About Cutting School Budgets* (Corwin Press, 2010). Available through books4educ.com

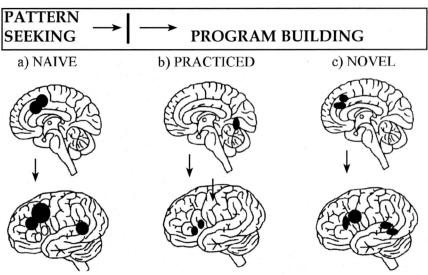

PATTERN SEEKING → | →	PROGRAM BUILDING

a) NAIVE   b) PRACTICED   c) NOVEL

Source: *The Executive Brain* by Elkhonon Goldberg, page 70. [Adapted from M. E. Raichle, J. A. Fiez, T. O. Videen, A. M. MacLeod, J. V. Pardo, P. T. Fox, S. E. Petersen, "Practice-related changes is human brain functional anatomy during nonmotor learning," *Cerebral Cortex* vol. 4, no. 1 (1994)].

the back to older structures in the brain—the program created to use the concepts or skills becomes wired into long-term memory (vertical column B, practiced). Frontal activation drops with task familiarization.

The third vertical column, C, novel, shows brain activity when the brain encounters something somewhat familiar (as in Column B—Practiced) but in a novel setting. The frontal lobes become partially activated again (reexamining the pattern) when a somewhat different or novel task is introduced (similar to a known one but not identical to it). For example, when the learner is asked to apply the concept of habitat that was studied in a rain forest to a grassland habitat.

These right to left, front to back, and top to bottom shifts illustrate the widespread involvement of the brain in learning and the significant physiological activity and growth/change that is the process of learning—a process unique to each brain and with a timeline that cannot be dictated by bureaucratic convenience.

Brain Organization and the HET Definition of Learning

Perhaps the most fascinating aspect of Goldberg's gradiental model—with its shifts from right to left frontal, from front to back, and neocortex to older structures—is that it provides a physiological explanation for Leslie Hart's definition of learning as a two-step process (see the first column in the graphic below). To assist teachers in planning curriculum and instructional strategies, we have broken each of those steps into two phases. The correspondence of the two views is striking.

Admittedly, these are broad brush strokes but knowing that different parts of the brain must be engaged to move learning from an initial "Aha" to long-term memory of how to *use* the knowledge or skill gives us a larger view of learning. It allows us to key in to what sensory and motor input students need, what practice *using* the knowledge or skill will move the learning from new to practiced, and the time it takes to make those physiological shifts in the brain. Suddenly, "covering" content and relying on paper-pencil tests to indicate mastery can be seen as the useless strategies that they are.

New definition of learning	Brain activity when learning something new
▪ Step One: Pattern-Seeking	
Identifying patterns.....................................	Primarily right frontal lobes shifting to
Making meaning/understanding................	Primarily left frontal lobes
▪ Step Two: Program-Building (See Chapter 5)	
Able to use learning with support..............	Shift from front toward back of brain
Ability to use the learning becomes automatic and part of long-term memory.......	Shift to back and lower/older brain structures

This chapter addresses the first step of learning—identifying patterns and making meaning of them, the shift from right to left in the frontal lobes. Chapter 5 addresses step two of learning.

THE MOST NOTABLE CHARACTERISTIC OF THE HUMAN BRAIN

The most notable characteristic of the human brain is its phenomenal penchant for seeking and detecting patterns. In his book, *Human Brain and Human Learning*, Leslie A. Hart stipulates that no part of the human brain is naturally logical while it is learning,"[2] i.e., making meaning. (This is distinguished from its ability to use information already learned in a "logical" or sequential way if the situation so requires.) Instead, the brain learns by sifting through massive amounts of input that is arriving simultaneously from all the senses, processing thousands of bits of information per minute. Obviously, such information is processed in a multi-path, multi-modal way with the brain attending to changes in the pattern of incoming data.

The simultaneity of its processing makes patterns obvious while processing along one avenue at a time, however speedily, would produce no "aha," no sense of an overall picture whatsoever. Imagine if the brain processed only one set of information at a time, e.g., first vision, then hearing, then bodily-kinesthetic, etc. Like the three blind men, recognizing an elephant would, at best, be an extremely time consuming and laborious task.

> *"The brain detects, constructs, and elaborates patterns as a basic, built-in, natural function. It does not have to be taught or motivated to do so, any more than the heart needs to be instructed or coaxed to pump blood. In fact, efforts to teach or motivate the pattern detection, however well meant, may have inhibiting and negative effects."*
>
> Leslie A. Hart

Pattern seeking progresses along a continuum: detection, identification, and understanding.

What Is a Pattern?

Hart defines a pattern as:

"An entity, such as an object, action, procedure, situation, relationship or **system**, which may be recognized by substantial consistency in the **clues** it presents to a brain, which is a pattern-detecting apparatus. The more powerful a brain, the more complex, finer, and subtle patterns it can detect. Except for certain **species wisdom** patterns, each human must learn to recognize the patterns of all matters dealt with, storing the **learning** in the brain. Pattern recognition tells what is being dealt with, permitting selection of the most appropriate program in brain storage to deal with it. The brain tolerates much variation in patterns (we recognize the letter *a* in many shapes, sizes, colors, etc.) because it operates on the basis of **probability**, not on digital or logic principles. Recognition of **patterns** accounts largely for what is called insight, and facilitates transfer of learning to new situations or needs, which may be called creativity."[3]

Examples of patterns include those shown in the graphic in the next column.

As the brain attempts to make sense out of the chaos which surrounds each of us, it constantly searches for patterns that can impose meaning on the input received. Its "aha" arises from detection of a recognizable (from the learner's perspective) pattern or patterns. This pattern detection propensity is seen in the operation of each of the senses. The ear registers every sound wave within its perceivable frequency but it attends only to those that provide a meaningful pattern. Sounds of traffic or workshop chatter are ignored and only the presenter's voice is tuned in or noted as a pattern to attend to. Similarly, the eye recognizes a chair, be it a three-legged milking stool, a church pew, the chair at the kitchen table, or a log in the forest; it does so by looking for the pattern or **collection of attributes** necessary for something to be a chair when one wants to sit down.

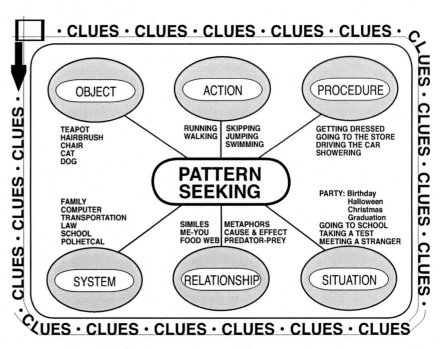

From the time we are born until we die, the brain takes in these patterns as they present themselves, sorting and categorizing in an attempt to make sense out of our complex world. Learning takes place when the brain sorts out patterns using past experiences and current clues to make sense out of new input the brain receives.

According to Hart, the first step in learning is ". . . the extraction, from confusion, of meaningful patterns." In real-life settings, information comes at the learner in a way that can best be described as rich, random, and even chaotic.[4] Over the millenniums, the brain has perfected learning within such an environment.

This pattern-detecting aspect of the brain can be clearly seen in the brain's mastery of one of its biggest accomplishments: learning the mother language. Watch mothers just home from the hospital with their newborns (or even listen to them talk to their child in utero!). Mothers know how to teach language. They do not "dumb down" their language to the infant to single syllable communications. Instead, mothers discuss the everyday happenings of life and share their hopes and dreams for their little one—"When you grow up, you'll go to Stanford and become an astronaut. You'd like that very much, I think. Very, very exciting occupation." "Yikes, there are so many choices at this grocery store. Which brand was it that we tried last week that was so good?" "Come, it's time to toss in a load of laundry; we'll do the whites first with hot water." Why do mothers do this? Because it works. Because every noun and verb in the English dictionary (and in our curriculum) is a pattern. Each has attributes that distinguish one word from another. The more experience with the attributes, the finer the patterns so that choosing among words such as pensive and melancholy is not a random choice but a decisive match with someone's emotions at the moment.

Such a barrage of sounds coming at the child in real-life fashion would at first seem a hopeless environment in which to master language. But an environment similar to the one previously mentioned—rich, random, even chaotic—gives large amounts of input to the child, and thus provides his or her mind with the opportunity to search for patterns. As educators, we have been carefully and logically taught that such an environment would make the task of learning a language impossible. Consequently, we teach English as a second language logically and carefully, "This is a pen. What is this? This is a _____." Unfortunately, the human brain does not learn well from such logical, tidy, greatly restricted input because it is so antagonistic to the learning methods the brain has perfected over the ages.

In short, the mind is genetically designed to learn from the natural complexities of the natural world. To the extent that schools oversimplify, or make logical, or restrict the world's natural complexity is the extent to which schools inhibit the natural workings of the mind and restrict a student's ability to learn. In contrast, input from the real world engages all of the senses. Logical, sequential curricula are highly brain-antagonistic. Comments Hart, "Perhaps there is no idea about human learning harder to accept for people familiar with classrooms and schools than this: that *the ideal of neat, orderly, closely-planned, sequentially logical teaching will, in practice with young students, guarantee severe learning failure for most.*"[5] A common mistake of the public schools is stripping down the input to a small amount of content, all analyzed and dissected into small bits, so that the "right"

answer seems inescapable. This does not work. Patterns are the building blocks of meaning, the heart of curriculum development.

Stripping a learning situation of its real-life richness also robs the child's mind of the possibility of perceiving patterns and thus making sense of what is in front of him/her. Ironically, we do this consistently with students who need special help. If they are slow, conventional wisdom has dictated that the task be broken into smaller and smaller pieces. We've now achieved pieces that are so small and so "easy"— only one item to focus on—that there is no longer any pattern to perceive. Consequently, Chapter 1 students with their finely-chopped, oversimplified diet say "I don't get it" which confirms to us that they are "slow." However, most Chapter 1 students are adept learners from real-world input. They come to us having learned their mother tongue and a wide range of skills for coping with life. Consider the immigrant child who is the translator for the entire family, the urban child with street savvy, the migrant child with flexibility and resourcefulness to figure out each new setting from town to town.

The amazing flexibility of the brain in its pattern seeking is apparent in its ability to recognize the pattern of the letter *a*; we

> ## *Learning:* Step One
>
> *Pattern-matching is inherently pleasing because that is what our minds are designed (or programmed) for. . . . Quite apart from anything the teacher does. . . the student, being human, is a pattern-finder and a pattern-maker. Possibly the greatest obstacle to our making use of this not very startling principle is our ingrained notion that education is the acquisition and mastery of new material. What we "teach" and they do not "learn" is the "material."*
>
> —David B. Bronson[6]

recognize it amid an amazing range of fonts, sizes, shapes, positions. This speed and flexibility can occur because the brain naturally works on a probabilistic basis. The brain does not add up, for example, all the parts of a cat until all parts are perceived and accounted for: four legs, a tail, fur, meows, purrs, etc. Rather, the mind "jumps to the conclusion" that the pattern "cat" applies when only one or a few characteristics have been noted. While this jumping to conclusions sometimes gets us in trouble, it is crucial to rapid completion of myriad actions minute by minute. The rapid reader, for example, does not see every letter before deciding what the word is. Context clues or the mere outline of the word are used, in probabilistic fashion, to jump to conclusions.

In the example of our infant learning its mother tongue, language pours around the child for hours and hours a day. The more input, the more readily the child learns. The first patterns perceived are those that are most meaningful—the child's name and then the name of mom and dad. Patterns are at first quite gross, i.e., "Dadda" means any man in trousers. Over time, with continued rich input and immediate feedback, the patterns become more and more refined until, finally, the educated adult ends up with a vocabulary of 10,000-plus words with subtle shades of meaning and the ability to use them with considerable precision.

The entire structure of language is based on pattern. For example, plurals mostly end in *s* except for mice, moose, fish, etc. Past tense ends with *ed*. Words ending in *ing* are a real thrill for most children. When they first grasp the *ing* pattern, everything is jumping, leaping, hitting, running, and so forth for several days until another pattern of language gets discovered. Every noun and verb in our language reflects a pattern.

Pattern-seeking is the brain's way of striving to extract meaning from the thousands of bits of input pouring into the brain each minute through the 19 senses. And, very importantly, what is one learner's pattern is another learner's hodgepodge. This is to say, we cannot predict what any one particular child will perceive as a pattern because so much depends upon prior knowledge, the

existing neural networking of the brain used to process the input, and the context in which the learning takes place.

However, if the input is rich and varied, all learners can arrive at an understanding of the pattern to be learned.

The First Fundametal of Learning: Making Meaning*

Over 80 years ago, for example, Aldous Huxley remarked that "What emerges most strikingly from recent scientific developments is that perception is not a passive reception of material from the outside world; it is an active process of selection and imposing of patterns."[7]

The findings Huxley referred to were well known in fields more scientifically oriented than education then and that are thoroughly established now. Brain researchers of the 1990s accept this as a given.[8] We do not have to look far for confirmation—our own daily experience tells us most convincingly that the brain has this ability and has it to an astounding degree.

Examples from Personal Experience

Imagine that you are attending a sporting event. People by the thousands stream by as you find your seats. The merest glance tells you they are all strangers. But now you see two figures that immediately seem familiar and in a moment you have identified them as former neighbors, Francine and Peter. Somehow, your brain has picked them out of this vast crowd; somehow it has separated them from all the other people you know so that you can identify them and greet them warmly by name. There is no question that our human brain can do this—usually effortlessly. (If we simply look at what we all can do, we begin to glimpse the enormous powers of the brain.)

---

* The text in this font, from here through page 4.10, indicates excerpts from *Human Brain and Human Learning* by Leslie A. Hart. (Black Diamond, Washington: Books for Educators, 2002). Used by written permission of the publisher.

The feat is even more impressive because you haven't seen these friends for three years, didn't expect to run into them here. Both are wearing clothes you have never seen them in. Francine has a new hair style, Peter wears sunglasses that partly hide his features. Yet, you recognized them as familiar while they were still 50 feet away.

Clearly, the recognition does not stem from any logical process. You did not check Francine's height in inches or Peter's weight in kilos. You put no measure to their middle finger bones, Bertillon fashion,[9] nor did you use a color-comparison guide to determine the shade of skin and hair. While Peter has a distinctive walking movement and Francine an animated manner, trying to measure or describe these exactly would be an impossible task. Let us grasp firmly the clear fact that your brain does not work that way but that it did quickly and accurately accomplish recognition and identification by some other means.

Nor was this an isolated, unusual phenomenon. If I were to display a teakettle, a paint brush, a handsaw, a necklace, a bunch of carrots, a pencil sharpener, a violin, a telephone, a sweater, a microscope, a toothbrush, a slice of Swiss cheese . . . you would recognize and name each in the same effortless way. You were plainly not born knowing these objects, so this recognition has been learned at some time between birth and the present.

We are so used to looking at something and immediately knowing what it is that we come to think of the process as automatic. Comparisons of eye and camera may also mislead us. A camera can't recognize anything; our brain can, using not only vision but also hearing, smell, touch, and other aspects of our senses.

When we are exposed to something quite unfamiliar, we simply do not see it in any meaningful way. To look inside some complex machine, for example, we may see only a confusion of forms. In a museum, observing some fossilized remains of various ancient animals, we may see only vague shapes, in contrast to what the curator sees. I often dramatize this in workshops by showing a newspaper in Arabic or Chinese. The participants see only squiggles that a moment later they are hopelessly unable to reproduce—although a person knowing the language would see headlines and news, information at a glance.

If we place a teakettle before a month-old infant, the baby will regard it with momentary interest but plainly have no notion of what it is. As adults we can see a vessel, a handle, and a spout; the baby can see none of this arrangement, only edges, shapes, and surfaces.

Even if the teakettle were made of unfamiliar materials or shaped like an elephant, we would recognize it as a teakettle. Any familiar item, from a paint brush to a necklace, would be identifiable. Moderate differences do not bother us a bit.

Examples from Classroom Life

Consider, for instance, the 20 different forms of the letter *a* that appear below. Despite the range of shapes they cover, we have no difficulty seeing any one as *a*. We could, of course, carry this recognition much

A ᴬ A **A** A a a *A* a *a* **a**

ꟼ a 𝓐 AAA a A̲ ᴅ A

further, to letters of many larger sizes, in different colors, formed of lights or dots, put into three-dimensional materials, tilted, laid on the floor, or seen on the side of a moving vehicle. Even holding just to typefaces available for printing, there are literally thousands of alphabets; handwritten, drawn, or printed forms add thousands more. There is no letter *a*, only a pattern we conventionally call *a*.

In the same sense, teakettle, paintbrush, carrots, violin, and the rest are patterns. Our knowledge of the pattern is what enables us to say what object is what. But we are by no means limited to hard, visual patterns. We can detect and learn patterns far more subtle or complex. In time, adults normally become quite familiar with such patterns as cat, city park, affection, boss, fraction, racial bigotry, jealousy, or adventurousness.

Just how the brain detects and recognizes patterns cannot be easily or quickly explained. Yet, it is an astoundingly powerful, subtle, living computer with billions of neurons at its command. We do know in a general way that *the brain detects characteristics or features and also relationships among these features.*

The lower-case letter *a*, for example, may consist of a hook facing left which may take a variety of forms,

connected to a more or less round enclosure form.

The relationship between these shapes has a key role. If the hook were 20 centimeters tall and the enclosure only a millimeter high, one might have much difficulty seeing it as an *a*. On the other hand, there

is a different pattern for small *a* that lacks the hook altogether that we can readily learn to accept as an alternate. It is illogical to have two forms but, as we have seen, logic is the least of the human brain's concerns.

Key Factors in Pattern Seeking

When looking at the brain as a seeker of patterns, consider five key factors: Use of clues and cues, use of multiple sensory input and prior experience, sensitivity to negative clues, categorizing down through patterns within patterns, and using probability.

Use of Clues and Cues

Our brain's ability to detect and identify patterns is impressive for its flexibility. We can be certain about our identification of something without needing to perceive most or even many of its features and relationships. With experience, in fact, we normally become extremely expert in using *clues* (sometimes the term *cues* is used in the same sense) to make very rapid judgments. We would not be able to read at all if we had to study all the features of letters. The capable reader goes much further and uses clues for whole words and even phrases.[10]

Use of Multiple Sensory Input and Prior Experience

In practice our pattern-detecting ability depends on clues from vision, hearing, touch, or other senses, on behavior and relationships, and/or on the situation. In short, *the ability to detect and recognize pat-*

terns depends heavily on our experience, on what we bring to the act of pattern detection and recognition. The more that experience tells us what we are likely to be looking at, or dealing with, the less detailed, feature-type information we need to jump to a probably correct conclusion.

Sensitivity to Negative Clues

One reason we can rely on little information is the sensitivity of the brain to *negative* clues. When clues do not fit together rapidly within a pattern, or when one or more are jarringly strange or contradictory, our pattern-detecting apparatus quickly senses something wrong. Suppose that I am going to the house of people I have visited a couple of times before, on a dark suburban street where house numbers are hard to find. As I walk toward what seems to be the house, I come to a flagstone walk. It "doesn't feel right," prompting me to retreat and try the house next door. Or, perhaps another day I identify an all-black bird as a Brewer's blackbird. When I see a flash of color on the wing, I must revise my identification to "red-winged blackbird."

Patterns Within Patterns: Categorizing Down

In the example of recognizing friends Francine and Peter, only a yes/no kind of decision was involved—they were or were not those individuals. But more common is the detection and recognition of patterns *within* patterns, which leads to finer and finer discriminations, a process called *categorizing down*, a most important aspect of learning. For example, we can detect the pattern "animal," then categorize it down to "dog," and then to "Afghan hound." Or, observing a number of people at a gathering, we may categorize further by noting that the people are festively dressed, a "party," and then on seeing a cake with candles, conclude it's a "birthday party."

But we must note that a person from a country where birthday cakes are not a custom would not be prepared to interpret that clue the way we so easily do. Again, what the observer brings to the recognition act—in terms of prior relevant experience and previously acquired knowledge—plays a critical part. (It is startling to observe that in conventional teaching this absolutely fundamental principle is largely ignored.)

In small children, the process of enlarging pattern detection and extending and refining categorizing-down chains is often clearly observable. A girl just starting to talk may say "Daddy!" while pointing to any man who comes into sight—we gather she is using *daddy* in the sense of *man*. A little later, guided by such feedback as "No, that is not Daddy—Daddy is at his office," the child may point to any man who comes into the home, whether young cousin or elderly grandfather, as *daddy*. With further feedback, categories gradually get straightened out and *daddy* is used to mean only one person. It may take much longer for the child to become clear on the fact that her friend also has a daddy (and some years to grasp the relationship). It may take still more time to be able to categorize surely from people to males, to relatives and friends, neighbors, policeman, mailman, Mr. Jackson (who lives next door), as well as boys, girls, and many other subtle relationships.[11]

It seems apparent that the brain must have some kind of organizational process that enables humans to rapidly categorize down patterns as they are detected, so that they can be identified quickly.

Matching. The principle of *matching* is well understood. In simplest terms, one receives an input from outside the brain—for example, visual input that comes from a door. Inside the brain, stored, is a pattern, *door*.[12] If the current input and the stored pattern pretty well match, recognition occurs. Looking in the night sky, one may see any one of several patterns that match up with stored patterns for *moon*. Hearing some sound waves that compose a certain pattern, we recognize it as the word *scarecrow*, since it fairly well fits our stored pattern for scarecrow. The matches do not have to be precise—another principle, *probability*, applies. This permits us to recognize "scarecrow" whether spoken by a child in a thin, high voice or by a man or woman in other pitches, and despite various pronunciations. *The brain searches for a probable match.* (If this were not so, we would all have a terrible time trying to read English, with its frequently weird spellings!)

Parallel Processing. But to operate effectively, the brain cannot afford to search sequentially through tens of thousands of stored patterns to find the match. It seems likely that patterns are grouped in categories within hierarchies, or layers, much as mail is addressed (reading from the bottom up and right to left):

> The country (USA).
>
> The state (Connecticut).
>
> The city or town (Bethel).
>
> The street (Maple Avenue).
>
> The house number (628).
>
> The person in that house (Mr. or Mrs.)

This method, we know, quite efficiently makes a match between the letter and one out of more than 250 million inhabitants. If the address (the input) is a little wrong, the letter may still be delivered but if the error is large, no match can be made, no delivery can occur.

Experimental studies suggest that the brain does not usually need as many as six steps to categorize down. (That investigation is beyond the scope of this book.) Nor is the brain limited to one linear chain of categorizing down (such as that illustrated above in addressing a letter). It can employ many such chains simultaneously, as we have noted. This "parallel processing" enormously speeds recognition. It's like having 1,000 clerks sorting the mail rather than just one.

Using Probability . . . Jumping to Conclusions

A variety of studies indicate that the brain naturally works on a *probabilistic* basis. The brain skillfully jumps to conclusions! It isn't an adding machine that must reach a correct total. For example, seeing a creature that has four legs, a tail, fur, and barks at a friend's home, we jump to the conclusion that the pattern "dog" applies. Why not "cat"? Because we pick up negative clues: Cats don't bark and ordinarily don't come aggressively to the door when a stranger enters. Why isn't it a monkey? Because the relationship of limbs is different. The situation also gives clues; we expect to find a dog in a home. If we visited a zoo, however, and found this same animal exhibited in a cage, we would assume it was not a dog but some similar creature. Our experience tells us that dogs are not displayed this way.

The Brain—A Master at Extracting Meaning from Confusion

This is the process of learning that Frank Smith and others aptly call "making sense of the world."[13] The ability that even infants have to gradually sort out an extremely complex, changing world is nothing short of astounding. And it's natural. But even more surprising still is that we learn *from input presented in a completely random, fortuitous fashion*—unplanned, accidental, unordered, uncontrolled, the polar opposite of didactic classroom teaching.

Consider, for example, the sorting-out problem a child has to grasp for such patterns as *dessert, pie, and cake.* Since a great variety of dishes may constitute dessert, the child must extract the idea that meals have a sequence (program) and dessert is the last course. He or she must also learn that *dessert* does *not* mean a particular dish, or even a tight group or class of dishes. *Pie* presents few problems to an adult with years of experience to draw on but, to a toddler, an open pumpkin pie, a crusted blueberry pie, and a lemon pie heaped with meringue topping present little in common. Or does pie mean *round*, the most obvious feature? Unfortunately many desserts are round, particularly cakes—which vary from pie-like cheesecake, to coffee cake, to layered birthday cake elaborately iced and decorated.

While adults and older siblings may provide gentle, casual, and almost incidental corrective feedback when the child calls a pie a cake or doesn't regard a fruit dish as dessert and cries in frustration, it would be most unusual for anything resembling teaching or instruction to deal with dessert, pie, and cake as subjects. Yet in a few years, from this confused, random exposure and experience, the child has extracted the patterns, gradually coming to see which features and relationships have significance in which settings, and which can be ignored. Frequently, however, the child extracts a pattern that sooner or later has to be revised in the light of new information. For example, everything if let go falls—until someone presents a gas-filled balloon. Children often find the need to revise something disturbing. The world keeps proving more complicated, with more exceptions, than they had previously thought. Adults have a similar problem; in time, they may become less flexible, cling to old ideas, refuse to revise, and even try to avoid the input that forces the contradiction. "Nonsense . . . that's crazy . . . I won't listen . . . don't bother me!"

Even more amazing is the obvious ability of preschool children to extract rules about language from the quite random speech they hear about them and engage in. We hear such expressions as *sheeps* and *deers,* plurals plainly not picked up from adults or older children. The added *s* makes unmistakably clear that the small child has extracted a general rule for plurals—end with the *s* sound—and is applying it even to what will later be learned as special exceptions. In the same way, most youngsters will use such constructions as "Tommy hitted me," or "I falled down," showing that they have extracted the pattern of past tense and the use of the *ed* sound, again even where there are common exceptions. Yet it would be absurd to expect a three- or four-year-old to explain *plural or past tense.*[14]

These familiar experiences and others like them are so prevalent that we cannot reasonably doubt that all of us, at whatever age, *do extract patterns from the quite random, confused mass of input we are exposed to in the course of normal living. Nor can it be easily denied that the great bulk of practical knowledge we have and use to get along in the world is acquired in this way.*

A Word About Rote Memory. The great bulk of general learning occurs through extracting meaningful patterns from confusion. The only other important method is via rote memory. But while "pure" rote learning—straight memorization—appears to suffice, as in the case of learning the alphabet in sequence, even rote learning is greatly helped by detecting the patterns involved where patterns clearly exist, as in the multiplication tables. Or consider the marching band, very much a rote activity. If the patterns in the music and in the maneuvers are understood, learning can be far faster and surer.

In Summary

In embracing a new definition of learning, it is important that we recognize a new view of the brain:

- The brain is by nature a magnificent pattern-detecting apparatus, even in the early years.

- Pattern detection and identification involve both features and relationships, processes that are greatly speeded up by the use of clues and a categorizing down procedure. (i.e., round ears or barks . . . not a house cat).

- Negative clues play an essential role.

- The brain uses clues in a probabilistic fashion, not by digital "adding up" of clues.

- Pattern recognition depends heavily on the experience one *brings* to a situation.

- Children must often revise the patterns they have extracted, to accommodate new experience.

TRANSLATING BRAIN RESEARCH INTO ACTION USING THE NINE BODYBRAIN-COMPATIBLE ELEMENTS

Pattern seeking is the bodybrain partnership's way of making meaning of our world. The early phase of this process is detecting the existence of a pattern and then, through more experience with the concept or skill, coming to understand that pattern by exploring it and its uses to make sure that we understand it correctly and fully. The nine bodybrain-compatible elements will help you help your students to perceive and understand patterns in the curriculum and in their lives.

Although memorization does have a role in learning, it should have a minor one. As Frank Smith and Leslie Hart both affirm, *understanding takes care of learning.* **Things that are understood and used are readily retained in long-term memory.** Memorization is generally used as a teaching/learning tool only when there is no discernible meaning to the learner such as the order of the alphabet or when fast, automatic repetition is needed as with the multiplication tables.

Bodybrain-Compatible Elements

- *Meaningful Content*
- *Movement*
- *Enriched Environment*
- *Adequate Time*
- *Immediate Feedback*
- *Mastery*
- *Absence of Threat/ Nurturing Reflective Thinking*
- *Choices*
- *Collaboration*

The most critical job for a teacher is making learning meaningful for students. That being the case, teachers must go about curriculum development and choosing instructional strategies with a primary goal in mind: enhancing students' capacity to perceive and understand patterns.

MEANINGFUL CONTENT

Meaningfulness, like beauty, is in the eye of the beholder. But there are several things that teachers can do to increase the likelihood that students will perceive something as meaningful.

State Key Points As Concepts, Not Factoids

First, state what is to be learned as concepts (or significant knowledge directly linked to and necessary to support the concepts) rather than as factoids. Factoids have few attributes that give a sense of pattern. For example, "In 1492, Columbus sailed the ocean blue." Although catchy and cute, there is little for the brain to work on in terms of meaningfulness. This is a statement that only rote learning could lock into long-term memory.[15]

On the other hand, a concept is a rich collection of attributes that can provide a sense of pattern. For example: "Interactions among animals and plants to meet the need for food within a habitat are called a 'food chain' or 'food web'."

Rote memory is not needed here. In this conceptual statement, virtually every noun and verb is a pattern, each of which, with the possible exception of "habitat," is a pattern already familiar to students. Prior experience that can be pulled forward to help the students learn new content is a powerful ally. Furthermore, this concept allows students to place the information in a context they care about, e.g, their family and/or classroom pet(s), their favorite zoo animal, a local endangered animal, and so forth. (For a discussion of key points, see Chapter 14.)

Place Inquiries in Real-World Contexts

Second, for concepts or skills with which students have little or no prior experience, place the concept or skill to be learned in a real-world context. Develop inquiries that ask students to use the concept or skill in real-life situations. This heightens the sense of seeks patterns in an attempt to create meaning. Also help them avoid "jumping to conclusions" based on a couple of clues that may be true but not key by becoming sensitive to negative clues. Create activities such as playing a modified version of the old TV game show, "I Can Name That Tune in . . . Notes." Instead of notes, use the attributes of a concept or skill.

Instructional Strategies

- Ensure massive amounts of sensory input through all 19 senses. Schedule frequent *being there* field studies—early in students' study of the concepts/skills described in the key points, at the end, and in between.

- Make the classroom a complete immersion experience for the *being there* location your curriculum is based on.

- Invite guest speakers that will present their experiences using *hands on of the real thing*. Insist that students include examples of their concepts/skills from their experiences.

- Deliberately use collaboration as a way of increasing input and use of concepts and skills.

- Have at least 100 resources related to the current topic of study available in the room—real things, models, diagrams, blueprints, sketches, and art objects, as well as books, magazines, multimedia, and the Internet.

- Use analytical tools that help students key in on important attributes of a concept or skill. For example, T-charts that compare what something is and what it is not, Venn diagrams that compare similarities and differences between two items, and organizers that help students identify prior related experience (KWL charts that identify what we now think we know, want to know, and, afterwards, what we learned). For young children, dot-to-dot puzzles are useful to help them reveal visual attributes of things such as a frog or butterfly. (For more information on these organizers, see Chapter 10, 10.13-10.15.)

MOVEMENT

Seeing firsthand how concepts and skills are used in real-world settings provides the richest possible environment for learning, especially when learning something new. Why? Because things in use have movement and motion to them. Who, what, why, and how are all attention-getting patterns. When the who becomes "I," patterns become richer, more engaging.

Furthermore, as discussed in Chapter 2, movement activates different areas of the brain and body, thus increasing the likelihood of retrieval later on. Many believe that some forms of memory, especially those associated with high emotional states, are stored in the body; others that movements of the body awaken memories that were being used when the memory was wired into long-term memory. In either case, the lesson for classroom teachers is that we *must* make the process of learning about concepts and skills mirror the ways those concepts and skills are used in real-world settings.

Using Movement to Enhance Pattern Seeking

The bodybrain-compatible element of movement enhances pattern seeking in many ways.

Curriculum

- Before you begin to write key points and inquiries, go experience how the concepts and skills are used in the real world. Practice them and the movements inherent in them until you have mastered them. Then, look around for other settings these same skills are used in, particularly settings/locations that students experience, e.g., a mall, home, school, neighborhood. Your curriculum should require the use of concepts and skills.

- Make your curriculum an experience in **doing**, not just reading about or hearing about.
  — Include in the statement of the key point examples of settings or uses that students can recognize from their

usefulness, an important trigger for the brain in transferring information to long-term memory.

For example: "A system is a collection of things and processes (and often people) that interact to perform some function. To study a system, one must define its boundaries." In this conceptual key point, every noun and verb is a pattern with which students are familiar. But, when put together in the above sentence, students may initially have no idea what is meant. However, when the concept is illustrated using first a bicycle and then one's school (transportation system, food system, classroom system and so on), the pattern becomes memorably clear and readily transferrable.

Similarly, few high school sophomores are innately interested in geometry but there are many who would be interested to learn how it applies to taking the best angle to run down and tackle a ball carrier, reading a map, driving a car, plotting the correct angle for a pool shot, and so forth.

Be Realistic

Third, when under the pressure of ever higher expectations, be realistic. Don't assume that because a concept is assigned to your grade level, it can be made understandable to students at your grade level. Some patterns require simultaneous attention to numerous variables before the intended pattern can emerge. Many such ideas must be considered age-inappropriate.[16] For example, the chemical processes of photosynthesis for sixth graders, tectonic plate movement as a cause of earthquakes for third graders. For more information about age-appropriateness, see Appendix D, Volume Three. (Also see *Thinking and Learning: Matching: Matching Developmental Stages with Curriculum and Instruction* by Lawrence F. Lowery.)

Input Is Essential for Pattern Development

In Hart's view of learning, *input* is a key factor. "Input is critically important in any kind of learning situation, whoever the learner and whatever is to be learned. The process of learning is the extraction, from confusion, of meaningful patterns. Input is *the raw*

material of that confusion, what is perceived through the senses by the individual that bears on that particular pattern in any way."[17]

By way of example, Hart recounts how a suburban teenager might go about learning the concept of *city*:[18]

"Think of a 13-year-old suburban male who as yet has no clear concept of what is meant by city, although his teachers, his texts, and other sources have often presented that term. It easily can seem incredible to adults that children or adults less experienced in some specific area do not grasp a pattern that is already so familiar to those who already understand it. Once we have done the pattern extraction—a gradual process—and melded the concept into our collection of patterns, it seems so obvious that we have trouble putting ourselves into the brain of someone who has not acquired that pattern!

But how could this 13-year-old come to understand the main connotations of city? If he is told in school that a city is a place where many people live close together, he may fail to see why his suburb (or at least those denser parts of it) is not a city. If he has contact with commuters, he may assume that city means Boston or St. Louis or Los Angeles, or whatever city his community is near. If he visits that city occasionally, he may be impressed by traffic, noise, many stores, busy sidewalks, bridges, tall buildings, apartments, or development houses—yet a visit to another city may present quite different features, such as zoo, museum, or historic places. Going to the downtown part of a nearby suburb may impress him as being to a city, since he experiences crowded sidewalks, many stores, movie houses, considerable dirt, and apparent crowding—yet if he refers to this place, technically a village, as city he may be corrected or receive some negative feedback, such as being tolerantly laughed at.

It seems simple enough to tell him what city means. But it isn't simple, when we get down to trying it. A dictionary may say something like "a closely settled place of significant size," or "a chartered, incorporated municipality," but such definitions simply introduce new questions. With little effort, the boy can learn by rote a "right answer" to give in school but that hardly amounts to pattern extraction. It may function more as a cover-up answer to conceal uncertainty or lack of insight. The distress of teachers who by accident discover that students able to give "correct" answers actually don't understand the topic at all has long been familiar. Most adults, too, experience chastening moments when by some circumstance they discover that conventional right answers are like thin ice over a deep lake of ignorance or misconception. From personal and professional experience, educators have long been aware that "telling" methods can prove extremely ineffective in instruction.[19] Despite much evidence to the contrary, they are heavily used in conventional teaching."

The bottom line here according to Hart is that "words fail to convey much meaning except as the hearer already has experience and extracted patterns that give meaning to the words. Consider two statements. A stock broker: "If you sell a security to establish a loss, you just wait 30 days to buy it back or it will be viewed as a wash sale but the waiting period doesn't apply to gains." Or, a musician, "Since the B-flat clarinet is a transposing instrument, the note you play from the written music will actually sound a full tone lower." These are perfectly understandable statements if we bring prior experience to bear.

We must accept that words convey only limited meaning and that if our students lack relevant prior experience, we must rely on input from the real setting. Hearing speech intelligibly demands bringing information to the situation.[20] Even in social conversation, a comment or question off the subject usually produces a "Huh?" response until the new topic is settled on.

As Hart says, "While input via telling or lecture may be the most common and usually the easiest to provide in the classroom, it can prove ludicrously ineffective, even in supposedly simple situations."[21] The best environment for detecting and understanding patterns is to see them in their real-world context.

The power of real-world examples can't be overestimated. For example, the idea of 3/4 becomes clear only when it is recognized and used in multiple contexts such as those in this example:

Using Meaningful Content to Enhance Pattern Seeking

The bodybrain-compatible element of meaningful content enhances pattern seeking in many ways.

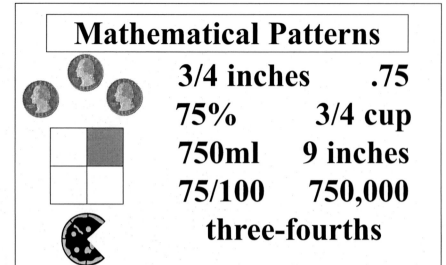

Curriculum Development

- Because meaningfulness is in the eyes of the beholder, expect that your students' perceptions of what is meaningful will likely differ from yours. Thus, don't expect to start where you want students to end up. In other words, if a concept is substantive, don't begin teaching it in the form you want them to remember it, e.g., $E=mc2$. If you do, you will force students into memorization as a coping strategy rather than allowing them to construct their own understandings. Therefore, make sure that your curriculum has starting points that can reasonably bridge students' prior experience/ knowledge to current sensory input to understanding the concept or skill. For example, include in the statement of the key point examples of settings or uses that students can recognize from their daily experiences. Include common objects as examples such as a multi-speed bicycle to evoke students' prior knowledge about chains (only as strong as its weakest link, potential to connect to multiple gears large and small) as a precursor to learning about the food chain/web.

- Teach students to become aware of how they know what they know. Help them become conscious of how their brain

daily experiences.
— State your key points conceptually; eliminate factoids.
— Develop inquiries that require application of concepts and skills to students' prior experiences and to other real-life situations so that students can readily understand what the concept/ skill is, why it's important, and how and when to use it.

• Develop, and involve students in developing, movements to mimic or act out the key attributes of the patterns within the concept or skill you are teaching. Include these in your direct instruction and in inquiries.

• When writing inquiries, first develop those that address bodily-kinesthetic intelligence and Bloom's taxonomy levels of application and analysis.

• When writing inquiries for linguistic intelligence, add movement through music, dance, rhythm (such as rap), and bodily-kinesthetic mnemonics.

• When developing immersion experiences, include role playing of the actions of people working and conducting commerce at your *being there* locations. Go for richness; focus on the most important attributes of the patterns of the concepts/skills in the key point.

Instructional Strategies

• In direct instruction, always address the questions of a journalist—who, what, when, where, how, and why in the real world—for the concept or skill you are teaching. Emphasize the how and why—the movement of how used and why.

• When selecting inquiries to follow up on direct instruction, lead with bodily-kinesthetic inquiries and those spatial and musical inquiries that call for movement. As with young children, the first step in understanding and using what we learn is often through mimicking.

• Because the movement centers of the brain are also responsible for sequencing thought, encourage students to create and use movements that mimic the sequence, steps, or actions of the concept/skill when in use. For example, reenactments of events or processes (a famous historical event such as the Boston Tea Party or the blood/oxygen flow through heart and lungs), miming (the travails of the Westward Movement), bodily movements that mimic shapes or actions (letters of the alphabet or a butterfly emerging from its cocoon), and hand jives (to represent the steps in computing a long division problem).

ENRICHED ENVIRONMENT

The pattern-seeking penchant of the brain is in diametric opposition to the assumptions underlying our traditional curriculum—its structure and content. Several erroneous assumptions are:

• Small, isolated pieces automatically add up to large pictures of real life

• The small, isolated pieces provide focus for the brain, making them easier to learn, especially for slow or limited ability students

• Study of "subjects" explains the world to students

When these small pieces are presented through the sparse sensory input of lecture and textbooks/worksheets, pattern-seeking is paralyzed for lack of input and learning grinds to a halt.

Consequently, conceptual curriculum in an enriched environment is not a luxury, it is a necessity. Pattern seeking is only possible when there is sufficient sensory input for the learner's brain to

> ## Sensory Input
> *In reality, nothing could be more unfair than giving two very different brains—and no two brains are alike—the same input and expecting the outcome to be the same. It's not only unfair, it's cruel.*

sift for patterns. And, very importantly, prior experience, existing mental wiring, and temperament guarantee that what one student sees as a pattern will remain invisible or a tangle of confusion to another. Thus, "Different Strokes for Different Folks" is more than that title of a TV sitcom. In the realm of the brain, it is utter truth. An enriched environment—*being there experiences, immersion, and hands on of the real thing*—provides something for everyone, ensuring that every student can succeed in understanding the concept or skill at hand. ***When input for a concept or skill is rich and varied, all learners can arrive at an understanding of the pattern to be learned.***

Using Enriched Environment to Enhance Pattern Seeking

The bodybrain-compatible element of enriched environment enhances pattern seeking in many ways.

Curriculum

- Knowing there is a fine line between an enriched environment and a cluttered environment, make sure you have finished writing your key points and inquiries before you begin to gather resources to create an enriched environment. Once you know exactly what you want your students to understand and how you will have them use what they understand, be selective. Remove input about other topics from the room. Then, for each key point and inquiry, plan your input in descending order: first being there, then immersion, then hands on of the real thing, and so on. If possible, eliminate hands on of representational items in favor of the above three kinds of input. Include secondhand and symbolic input last; plan to use them during the latter stages of Step One of Learning—Pattern-Seeking.

Instructional Strategies

- Select materials and other resources appropriate to the lesson that provide contrasting points of view so that the attributes of issues become clear through their comparison with each other, such as that of the polluter and of the family whose child developed cancer, land use through the eyes of the cattleman and the farmer.

- Include resource people, preferably from the *being there* locations upon which your curriculum is based. Work with them in advance so they understand what students have done prior to their coming and what new input would be most valuable.

- Use student-generated role playing and skits as formats for students to demonstrate the attributes of a concept/skill they are learning to use. Follow up these presentations with a discussion of what attributes of the concept/skill were demonstrated. Add any new ones to KWL chart and correct any misconceptions.

ADEQUATE TIME

Just as every brain is different, so is each student's approach to detecting patterns and making meaning. So, too, is the amount of time needed.

Factors that directly affect the amount of time students need to detect patterns and construct their own meaning are:

- Prior experience
- Whether the concept/skill is studied in its real-life context
- The kind and amount of input involves an intelligence of strength (see discussion of the multiple intelligences in Chapter 3)
- The wiring of the learner's brain

Regardless of why a student may need more time, the critical point is that we must provide it. To close the grade book on a student because he/she didn't master something in the allotted time is discrimination of the worst kind. The implicit message is that if you aren't like everyone else, you will be cut off and abandoned. In such an environment the focus is not on mastery but on the lock-step demands of bureaucracy.

In the *HET* classroom, the "grade book" is held open until the end of the year. Demonstration of mastery the last day of school is as good as mastery the first day the key point is studied.

But we're getting ahead of ourselves here. Step One of Learning is pattern-seeking, constructing meaning, *understanding* the concept or skill described in the key point.

Using Adequate Time to Enhance Pattern Seeking

The bodybrain-compatible element of adequate time enhances pattern seeking in many ways.

Curriculum

- Review the curriculum you have planned for your monthly components and weekly topics. Do you have more than students can come to understand and learn to apply, not just get 80% on a pop quiz? If so, start cutting back. Be realistic! Resist the political pressures to "cover" what looks good (for more information about components and topics, see Chapter 14).

- To help you cut back, use the principle of "selective abandonment." Put at the end of your curriculum those things you believe are least important for students to understand and be able to apply. Chief among these are factoids that won't affect their lives five or ten years from now. Then, if you run out of time—and who doesn't!—you will have given students the gift of what will most serve them later in life.

- Create time by stating your curriculum as conceptually as possible and using examples of how that concept is used in contexts that students experience in their daily life. For example, science is everywhere around us and is directly experienceable; the fundamental concepts in social studies have their parallel wherever people congregate.

(However, concepts in social studies are not as hands on as science; also, for young children, because they've grown up with something doesn't mean it's any easier to see than water is for a fish.)

Instructional Strategies

- Just as there is a silent period before vocalization when learning another language, so there is a quiet period when students are learning a new concept or skill. Don't rush through such silences or periods of delayed responses. Allow students time intrapersonally to observe and sift through what they already know and how this new concept/skill relates to what they already understand and can do (the patterns and the interrelationships among the patterns). Allow them time to explore the patterns involved and to arrive at their own understandings—about how things work, what makes things tick, why they might be important to them. Allow time for personal exploration through sketching or diagramming/graphing/mindmapping the patterns they see and how they interrelate with other patterns. Allow interpersonal time to try out what they understand, to correct and/or add to what they understand with nonjudgmental, supportive peers. Only then ask for personal performances that will be "graded" or critiqued by an audience. New understandings are not layered into the brain as separate things; they are integrated into prior understandings or patterns.

- Take time to plan for and effectively teach a concept or skill the first time. Effective first teaching is a huge time saver but you must invest time up front.

- Deep understanding comes from identifying attributes of things and their uses and coming to understanding interrelationships among them. Such mental work requires rewiring and new wiring—physiological tasks of the brain that require time and processing of new input. Be patient. Allow adequate time for this wiring to occur.

- Revisit the *being there* location at least once or twice between the initial and culminating visits. Assign inquiries to be completed, including adding to their KWL chart and answering questions such as "How do you know that _____?" and "Where else would you find this occurring and why?"

IMMEDIATE FEEDBACK

Leslie Hart points out that the most difficult thing for a brain to do is unlearn something. We're all familiar with this one. Is it *maintanence* or *maintainence* or *maintenance?* And every time we have to spell the word, all three choices pop up with competing intensity? Why? Because each time they simultaneously come to mind as options, the wiring of the three is equally reinforced. Or, how about the < and > signs. Is the number off the pointed end the smaller? Or does it depend on the order in which you say them? Or, hang it, I don't know! And you have trouble learning it because the confusion is wired in just as strongly as the right answer each time you try to recall which of the options is the correct one.

The number one purpose of immediate feedback is to prevent this kind of mental sputtering. Give feedback to students before they begin to practice something incorrectly or incompletely. Immediate feedback helps ensure that students come to a full and accurate understanding of a skill or concept—that they discover the critical attributes and understand how they fit together. This is especially important when students begin to integrate new experiences with prior learnings. For example, the videotape *A Private Universe*[22] provides an astounding example of how childhood experiences with heat (the closer you get, the hotter it becomes) override lecture and textbook. As the interviews with graduating Harvard students illustrate, even course work in advanced planetary motion can fail

to dispel the assumption put together in childhood—that summers are hot because the earth gets closer to the sun.

The recent emphasis on effective first teaching and ensuring that students learn something correctly and thoroughly the first time is right on track.

Using Immediate Feedback to Enhance Pattern Seeking

The bodybrain-compatible element of immediately feedback enhances pattern seeking in many ways.

Curriculum

- Build checking for accuracy of understanding and performance—by Learning Club, partners, and self—into inquiries.

- Develop inquiries that require students to develop and use their own internal voice as they go through the two steps in learning—asking questions, checking their understanding, insisting upon looking for ways a concept or skill can be used in the real world, and so forth.

- Include in inquiries the criteria to be used in assessing performance or where such criteria exist.

- If students' understanding or performance is inaccurate, incomplete, or not yet wired into long-term memory, provide additional inquiries applying the same concept or skill until mastery occurs. Invite students who have reached an accurate and complete understanding of the concept or skill to write additional inquiries that might help create an "aha" for classmates. Have students review each other's inquiries using the 3Cs of Assessment (see Chapter 19, pages 19.6-19.7) as they are developing them and immediately upon their completion.

- Use the language of pattern-seeking and program-building in inquiries so that students may assess their understanding and performance along the continuum of learning as a two-step process—pattern seeking to make meaning and program building to use what they understand.

Instructional Strategies

- Develop a repertoire of ways you can provide students with immediate feedback and use them often:
  - Brief "talk with your neighbor" breaks during presentations to reflect on a question or check for understanding about something just presented
  - "Walk abouts"—opportunities to observe/listen/ask questions as students work collaborative
  - Journal writing assignments asking students to reflect on what they've just learned and how they might use it in their lives now and in the future
  - Self-check procedures of many kinds, such as rubrics, answer sheets, self-developed criteria
  - Creating tasks to be completed while visiting resource person is still available to give feedback.

- Develop a repertoire of ways classmates can provide each other with immediate feedback and use them often:
  - Use of rubrics by Learning Club members and study partners to check each other's work immediately (thereby eliminating overnight grading by teachers)
  - "Think-pair-share," reflective thinking (before and after an activity), and other similar cooperative learning strategies[23]
  - Peer review and assessment; cross-age buddies.

- Develop opportunities for immediate feedback outside the classroom and use them frequently through:
  - Developing legitimate audiences who hold real-world expectations for work by students
  - Using inquiries during *being there* study trips that require students to compare notes and check for accuracy.

MASTERY / APPLICATION

Given the *HET* definition of learning as a two-step process—pattern-seeking for understanding and program-building for using what we understand—mastery must also be examined in these two steps because the ability to use what is understood begins with and builds upon how correct, complete, and comprehensive that understanding is.

When we become expert in a field, we know when we don't know something. When new to a field, a little bit of knowledge seems like great stuff and we often launch off with false certainty that we can do something. This is the source of the expression, "Taking off half cocked" or "Hell bent for leather" or "He's going fast to nowhere" and so forth. We've all been there. We thought we understood what to do and how to do it but once we got into it, disaster struck! We were humbled into an awareness that we knew only a fraction of what we needed to know.

Mastery, a Habit of Mind

Checking for mastery of understanding, the equivalent of looking before leaping, is an important habit of mind for students to develop. And it comes with two cornerstones: a notable lack of arrogance that we know all that needs to be known and the self-confidence that we are capable of learning what we need to know.

Teachers nurture these two qualities by providing bodybrain-compatible learning experiences. Satisfaction with surface knowledge is counteracted by providing curriculum that explores concepts in depth and demands high levels of skill performance. Confidence in ability to learn blossoms in an atmosphere of success at learning—an environment that has high but appropriate expectations, that grades on mastered/not yet mastered, that provides plenty of learning support from both teacher and peers, and that holds the grade book open for mastery any time during the school year.

High But Appropriate Expectations

The clamor for higher expectations is a double-edged sword. Without question, the contribution of K-12 schooling to students' pool of knowledge and skills is inexcusably low. Yet the raising of the bar often results in state standards written by politicians, not educators. The results would be laughable if not so detrimental to students. For example, state curriculum standards from a southeastern state expects third graders to grasp an introduction to atomic fusion. Another led second graders to ponder the Preamble of the Constitution of the United States.

We cannot expect mastery of understanding of things that students' brains are incapable of processing due to the stage of their development—development that unfolds with age. Understandable curriculum—as compared to memorizable curriculum—is a must if we are to expect mastery. (For a discussion of age-appropriateness, see Appendix B.)

The Powerful Role of Mirror Neurons

Every parent of a teenager intuitively understands the power of mirror neurons. "Falling in with the wrong crowd" is a concept that sends shivers down their spines and keeps them up awake at night. And with the young, the same concept surfaces with the certainty that "Do as I say, not as I do" is unlikely to bring on desired results.

According to Bob Sylwester, professor emititus at Oregon Univerwity, the discovery of mirror neurons is akin to the discovery in biology of DNA. Although in its infancy, this area of brain research has the power of completely redraw our pictures of teaching and learning and completely revolutionize instructional strategies. And, because the new definition of learning calls for applying what is understood, and wiring that ability to apply into long-term memory, it is critical that we purposely take advantage of mirror neurons to mimic the applications that can be experienced through *being there* experiences.

Using Mastery/Application to Enhance Pattern Seeking

The bodybrain-compatible element of mastery/application enhances pattern seeking in many ways.

Curriculum

- Make sure that the curriculum you present to students is in fact "getable" or understandable by children their age. If not, mastery is not possible. (If in doubt, see *Thinking and Learning: Matching Developmental Stages with Curriculum and Instruction* by Larry Lowery.)

- Embed the curriculum in *being there* experiences, preferably at real-life locations where people work and conduct commerce or where mother nature is at her most undisturbed. Make these experiences action-oriented rather than look and hear events. Seeing concepts and skills used by real people in real life settings makes recognition of patterns and their attributes much easier for students. It also increases motivation to learn and master.

- Include observation skills in your curriculum and teach students the verbal skills to report to themselves and others what they are witnessing. For example, see the discussion about using structure words to help students wire their brains for more effective language processing and comprehension in *Visualizing and Verbalizing for Improved Language Comprehension* by Nanci Bell. Better observation leads to more accurate and complete identification of the attributes of a thing, action, concept, or skill and thus a more comprehensive and in-depth degree of understanding.

Instructional Strategies

- Front load initial instruction with a wide variety of sensory input—*being there*, immersion, and hands-on-of-the-real thing. Stop frequently to provide students opportunities to experience and share observations; check frequently for accuracy and completeness of understanding.

- Have students use visual organizers for notetaking, such as KWL (what students think they _k_now before you start, what they _w_ant to know, and later what they have _l_earned), mindmaps to show multiple relationships, Venn diagrams to compare attributes, and so forth, rather than the standard outline format. Have students compare their notes within their Learning Club, checking for accuracy and completeness, and resolving any differences in pattern-seeking before you move on. If more than one group has the same difference in understanding, bring the issue to the whole class. Tease out what previous learnings are interfering with correct understanding of the current concept or skill and then reteach by giving correct information about both prior and current concepts/skills. Then, recheck for understanding. Ask students, grades three and up, to write inquiries that would help them understand the differences between prior and current concepts. Select the best ones and allow students to choose which one or two they will complete.

ABSENCE OF THREAT / NURTURING REFLECTIVE THINKING

The complaint du jour of 21st century living seems to be "I'm too busy to think." We're too busy to do anything but react. For fight-flight circumstances, this is workable. But not for academic learning.

Our classroom environments must not only be safe, they must also show students how to slow themselves down enough to be reflective. Why? Because pattern recognition depends heavily upon bringing together prior experiences with current input. To do so, students must be able to take time to put together several possible lines of inquiry rather than blurting out a guess. This requires uninterrupted time for sustained reflection.

Using Absence of Threat/ Nurturing Reflective Thinking to Enhance Pattern Seeking

The bodybrain-compatible element of absence of threat/nurturing reflective thinking to enhances pattern seeking in many ways.

Curriculum

- Teach students the elements of Mihaly Csikszent-mihalyi's "flow" experience[24] as applied to optimal learning. Help students recognize how to adjust their state of mind and/or learning environment so that they are in the best possible frame of mind for learning and remembering.

- Allow students to propose alternative ways of approaching a concept or skill that "makes more sense to them" and choice of additional situations for applying what they are learning, e.g., Freeze Frame.

Instructional Strategies

- During whole-class instruction
  - Eliminate distractions
  - Provide a peaceful yet businesslike atmosphere with background music, non-vocal with 50-60 beats per minute
  - Provide wait time
  - Allow students to volunteer an answer rather than worry about being called on
  - Provide reflective time before journal writing.

- During collaborative work

— Build in time for students to jot down their own thoughts before joining a brainstorming or discussion session

— Teach group leaders to insist on wait time when questions are posed to the group

— Use collaborative strategies such as think-pair-share and three-before-me.

• Provide a range of individual performance formats such as individual study projects, inquiries for personal choice, and journal writing.

• Invite students to learn to nurture the environmental elements that produce their own "flow" experiences.

CHOICES

Unless our goal is blind uniformity of both process and outcome, there is no justifiable reason for insisting on only one way of doing something. For example, we teach and accept only one algorithm (a mathematical term for pattern) for multiplication when there are more than 16 that do the job just as well. And likewise for long division, addition, and on and on.

As each brain is wired differently due to genetics, environment, and prior experiences, we should allow students to choose the patterns for solving a problem that work best for them while still producing accurate answers and useful products. Demanding that a brain operate in a specific way is the quickest way to frustration and a major disruption to reflective thinking.

Using Choices to Enhance Pattern Seeking

The bodybrain-compatible element of choices enhances pattern seeking in many ways.

• Teach students that there are usually multiple ways to go about solving problems. Provide several examples

and then let them devise others. Once you determine that the child has a pattern that they prefer—and that unfailingly produces correct answers—stop teaching other ways/patterns, even if they are the traditional ones.[25] Accept their method/pattern if it consistently gives them correct answers. As the saying goes, "If it ain't broke, don't fix it." Examples include many areas of mathematics such as multiplication, division, subtraction, addition, and percentages and areas of language arts such as decoding and spelling.

Instructional Strategies

• The world outside of school doesn't offer simplistic options such as true or false, *a* or *b*. Encourage students to begin to develop their own alternatives. When only one option is presented and not well understood, students must resort to memorization. When several patterns are examined and are understood well enough to make a choice among them, students needn't resort to memorization; learning is effortless, absorbed in the act of making meaning.

• When teaching a concept or skill, always illustrate several ways it can be used and give several examples of what it is not. Such attributes assist pattern seeking and meaning making by clarifying the pattern and making it more specific. Also, the fuller their sense of the pattern, the more likely they are to recognize it in their prior experiences.

COLLABORATION

A close-knit collaborative group such as a Learning Club is an ideal medium for pattern seeking. If you have constructed your Learning Clubs to ensure a range of intelligences (see Chapter 3), temperament (see Appendix A), and interests, then you have supplied your students with a veritable gold mine of patterns. Working closely with people representing such diversity in ways of thinking, organizing, carrying out tasks, and so forth opens a whole new vista on life—with new patterns come new possibilities. Collaboration is a powerful way to enrich the mental life of your students. It also encourages students to sharpen their strengths and learn the value of enhancing their undeveloped areas.

Using Collaboration to Enhance Pattern Seeking

The bodybrain-compatible element of collaboration enhances pattern seeking in many ways.

Curriculum Development

- Teach students to look for patterns. Model it in your questioning strategies and when leading approaches to solving problems and producing products.

- Teach them the patterns in thinking and behavior in the multiple intelligences, personality preferences, and their own habits of mind.

Instructional Strategies

- Ask students to use reflective thinking frequently by having them discuss if and how their Learning Club's process helped them learn the content and reach social and personal goals in the process. Companion questions include what they have learned from answering these questions and what they could have done differently to make their group process more effective. Also ask such questions of the class as a whole; have students reflect, verbally and in their journals, on what they've learned.

- Incorporate the terms "patterns" and "attributes of a pattern" into your direct instruction and assessment questions. Help make students aware of the pattern-seeking operation of their brain.

ENDNOTES

1   With each succeeding book he wrote about how the brain learns, Leslie Hart continued synthesizing his conceptualization of the two fundamental brain concepts: pattern detection, addressed in this chapter, and program building, described in Chapter 5. His initial definition was simple and to the point:

> *The process of learning is the extraction, from confusion, of meaningful patterns*
> **and**
> *Learning is the acquisition of useful programs.*

The revised edition of his book takes yet another step forward, further defining these two steps and the learning phases within them. Step one involves input; step two involves output. Each step is in turn divided into two stages.

This conceptualization of learning is an extremely important contribution to the field of learning because it is comprehensive enough to cover the wide range of practicalities that teachers, administrators, and parents face on a daily basis—from establishing curriculum to instruction to assessment.

For example, if we use Hart's two-step definition of learning when we examine current standardized testing instruments, we see that the ubiquitous multiple choice and true-false items call for no more than identification of a pattern (this choice *sounds* more familiar than that choice). *Understanding* the pattern is not necessary. Knowing how to use the information is well beyond the scope of the test and long-term memory of how to use it isn't even an issue.

This fuller, more comprehensive view of learning provides a set of lenses for examining all issues of curriculum, instruction, and assessment. It also provides a useful perspective when considering resource allocation and the success of improvement efforts.

See Leslie A. Hart, *Human Brain and Human Learning,* 3rd ed (Black Diamond, Washington: Books for Educators, 2002).

This shift from understanding (pattern seeking) to program building is reflected in Elkhonon Goldberg's discussion of learning as a "transition from novelty to routinization [right brain to left brain] . . . the universal cycle of our inner world." He describes a "cognitive continuum, a gradient." See Elkhonon Goldberg, *The Executive Brain: Frontal Lobes and the Civilized Mind* (Oxford: Oxford University Press,

2001), xii and 44. According to Goldberg, "At an early stage of every learning process the organism is faced with 'novelty,' and the end stage of the learning process can be thought of as 'routinization'," the result of the emergence of an effective solution(s)." (See page 44.) This shift of the locus of cognitive control from the right to the left hemisphere occurs on many time scales: from minutes to hours to years and decades (see page 52).

Also, Herbert Simon, Nobel Prize-winning psychologist, believes that learning involves the accumulation of easy-to-recognize patterns of all kinds. See Herbert Simon, *The Sciences of the Artificial* (Cambridge, MA: MIT Press, 1996).

Regarding Hart's stipulation that programs, once learned, can be run off almost automatically, Goldberg adds: "The majority of our mental processes are effortless and automatic, conducted, as it were, on autopilot. By contrast, the effortful and consciously controlled cognitive tasks represent only a minor portion of our mental life." (*The Executive Brain*, 54).

Pattern recognition is described in Goldberg's new book, *The Wisdom Paradox: How Your Mind Can Grow Stronger As Your Brain Grows Older* (NY: Gotham Books/Division of Penquin Books, 2005), 85. By "pattern recognition" we mean the organism's ability to recognize a new object or a new problem as a member of an already familiar class of objects or problems. The capacity for pattern recognition is fundamental to our mental world. Without this ability, every object and every problem would be a totally de novo encounter and we would be unable to bring any of our prior experience to bear on how we deal with these objects or problems.

Part one : **Input stage: Pattern detection** consists of first identifying or recognizing the pattern and, second, making meaning of the pattern including its relationship to other patterns.

and

Part two: **Output stage: Program building** consists of learning to apply what is learned, at first experimentally and consciously, and then, after practice and wiring it up into long-term memory, applying what is learned with the almost automatic ease and skill of the expert.

---

2 Hart, 133.

3 Hart, 151.

4 Hart, 151. Also see Diane Ackerman, *An Alchemy of the Mind*, (New York: Scribner, 2004), 54–55. "The brain is a pattern-mad supposing machine. It maps the known world. Given just a little stimuli it predicts the probable. When information abounds, it recognizes familiar patterns and acts with conviction. If there's not much for the senses to report, the brain imagines the rest.

Pattern pleases us, rewards a mind seduced and yet exhausted by complexity. We crave pattern and, not surprisingly, find it all around us, in petals, sand dunes, pine cones, and contrails. We imagine it when we look at clouds and driftwood; we create and leave it everywhere like tracks."

5 Hart, 142.

6 Quoted by David B. Brown in "Towards a Communication Theory," *Teachers College Record,* May 1977, 453.

7 See *The Human Situation* (Lectures at Santa Barbara, 1959), Pierro Ferrucci, ed. (New York: Harper & Row), 173. Also compare George A. Kelley, *A Theory of Personality* (New York: W. W. Norton, 1963): "Man looks at his world through transparent patterns or templates which he creates and then attempts to fit over the realities of which the world is composed," 17.

8 That the brain learns by detecting patterns among incoming sensory data has been amply confirmed by numerous brain researchers since Hart first published *Human Brain and Human Learning* in 1983. See Stanley I. Greenspan with Beryl Lieff Benderly, *The Growth of the Mind and the Endangered Origins of Intelligence* (New York: Addison-Wesley Publishing Company, 1997), 114 and Candace B. Pert, *Molecules of Emotion: Why You Feel the Way You Feel* (New York: Scribner, 1997; reissued in 1999 by Simon & Schuster with a different subtitle), 147; John J. Ratey, *A User's Guide to the Brain: Perception, Attention, and the Four Theaters of the Brain* (New York: Pantheon Books, 2001); and Elkhonon Goldberg, *Wisdom Paradox: How Your Mind Can Grow Stronger As Your Brain Grows Older* (New York: Gotham Press, 2006).

From Goldberg's new book, *The Wisdom Paradox: How Your Mind Can Grow Stronger As Your Brain Grows Older*, 88, we already know the capacity for pattern formation and pattern recognition is not unique to humans. It is shared by every other species capable of learning. What sets us apart as humans is the powerful capacity for transmitting the repertoire of these patterns from individual to individual and from generation to generation through culture.

9   Alphonse Bertillon (1853-1914) devised an elaborate system for positively identifying individuals in spite of their variety. It was intended primarily for criminal justice purposes. Later, fingerprinting proved far simpler but the system is still used by physical anthropologists.

10 John B. Carroll, speaking of the mature reader, suggests that it may be true, "astounding as it may seem, that reading is based upon a capability of instantly recognizing thousands or even tens of thousands of individual word patterns, almost as if words were Chinese characters not structured by an alphabetic principle." See *Theories of Learning and Instruction, 63d Yearbook of the National Society for the Study of Education* (Chicago: University of Chicago Press, 1964), 341. For actual use of Chinese, see Paul Rozin and others, "American Children with Reading Problems Can Easily Learn to Read English Represented by Chinese Characters," in *Psycholinguistics and Reading*, Frank Smith, ed. (New York: Holt, Rinehart and Winston, 1973), Chapter 9.

We learn attributes of the neocortex memory from Jeff Hawkins, *On Intelligence*, (New York: Times Books, Henry Holt and Co., 2004), 69. The neocortex is not like a computer, parallel or otherwise. Instead of computing answers to problems the neocortex uses stored memories to solve problems and produce behavior. There are four attributes of neocortical memory:

• The neocortex stores sequences of patterns. You cannot tell me everything that happened all at once, no matter how quickly you or I listen. It is because the story is stored in your head in a sequential fashion and can only be recalled in the same sequence.

• The neocortex recalls patterns auto-associatively. An auto- associative memory system is one that can recall complete patterns when given only partial or distorted inputs. Inputs to the brain auto-associatively link to themselves, filling in the present, and auto-associatively link to what normally follows next. We call this chain of memories *thought*, and although its path is not deterministic, we are not fully in control of it either.

• The neocortex stores patterns in an invariant form. Your brain holds an internal pattern. Memories are stored in a form that captures the essence of relationships, not the details of the moment. When you see, feel, or hear something, the cortex takes the detailed, highly specific input and converts it to an invariant form that is stored in

memory. It is the invariant form of each new input pattern that it gets compared to. (The face of a long time friend, how to start a car, how you recognize a song, etc.)

• The neocortex stores patterns in a hierarchy. Rarely are the functions clearly delineated. Functionally they are arranged in a branching hierarchy. The lowest of the functional regions, the primary sensory areas, are where sensory information first arrives in the cortex. (44–45, 47)

You hear sound, see light, and feel pressure, but inside your brain there isn't any fundamental difference between these types of information. An action potential is an action potential. These momentary spikes are identical regardless of what originally caused them. All your brain knows is patterns. Your perceptions and knowledge about the world are built from these patterns. There's no light inside your head. It's dark in there. There's no sound entering your brain either. It's quiet inside. In fact, the brain is the only part of your body that has no senses itself. (56)

11 Much can be learned about the process of learning by observing how young children build their vocabulary and the knowledge of the world that that vocabulary represents. In going about this prodigious feat, children make great use of categorizing down. If something is at first not understandable, children, if unguided, rarely resort to repeated attempts at memorization of the original input or memorization of a definition. Instead, they move on, gulping in massive amounts of new input until they hit upon a kind of input that finally provides a recognizable pattern, triggering the "aha" response.

12 Just because the brain has stored a pattern for "door" does not mean that it has stored all of the attributes of the pattern called door in a single location. A truly startling quality of the brain is that it can access bits of information stored in different locations and array it to make sense, and do so with astonishing speed.

13 See Frank Smith, *Comprehension and Learning* (New York: Holt, Rinehart and Winston, 1975), 1. The "make sense" concept has been widely discussed by many brain researchers. Harry J. Jerison, for example, suggests that reality is "a creation of the brain, a model of a possible world that makes sense of the mass of information that reaches us through our various sensory (including motor feedback) systems." See *The Human Brain* (Englewood Cliffs, NJ: Prentice Hall, 1977), 54. Such early work by Smith and Jeris is accepted fact today.

14 This stage of language acquisition is familiar to many parents, teachers, and others who have contact with children. It has been discussed

by many psycholinguists. See, for example, James Britton, *The Teaching of English, 76th Yearbook of the National Society for the Study of Education* (Chicago: University of Chicago Press, 1977), 11.

15 Rote memory should be kept to a minimum; instead, focus on reaching an understanding via pattern seeking/meaning making. However, when rote memorization is necessary, use CUE—an acronym from the *HET* model representing three methods which help ensure that students will remember. *C* stands for creative, such as use of skits or role playing or writing lyrics to a familiar tune. *U* stands for useful, such as having students make a connection to how a concept or skill is used in their lives. *E* stands for emotional, making an unforgettable emotional impact on students through the fun and adventure of a study trip, the sadness when animals die in oil spills, or the joy and deep satisfaction of making a contribution to others.

16 For a description of what makes concepts or skills age-appropriate, see Lawrence F. Lowery, *Thinking and Learning: Matching Developmental Stages with Curriculum and Instruction* (Black Diamond, WA: Books for Educators, 1995). Dr. Lowery has a rich background in curriculum development, including University of California, Berkeley, professor, Graduate School of Education and member of the board of directors for the Lawrence Hall of Science) and principal investigator for the FOSS project (Full Option Science Systems), developed under the auspices of the National Science Foundation and for the Equals Project (math for girls).

17 Hart, 223.

18 Hart, 141-142.

19 The *HET* model expresses this concept by contrasting the typical input of the traditional classroom life (*second hand* and *symbolic*) and the input needed for fully brain-compatible learning (primarily *being there* and *immersion* when used as follow up to *being there*). The difference in the amount of sensory input, and thus learning, is enormous. Sensory input from *being there* and *immersion* experiences are especially important when learning something new. See Chapter 1.

20 Scientists investigating speech and listening to language have produced an impressive body of knowledge, much of it long established. Yet, apparently, it is all but unknown to most educators, who commonly refer to "auditory" and "listening" skills and similar ideas far off the mark. For an excellent discussion, see George A. Miller,

Language and Speech (San Francisco: W. H. Freeman and Co., 1981), especially Chapter 6.

21 Hart, 134.

22 *A Private Universe* is a fascinating video illustrating the power of concepts generated by full sensory input as a child to override adult learning limited to lecture and reading. Harvard graduates are interviewed in their caps and gowns. The question "What makes for the seasons?" is answered the same by liberal arts students and those with science backgrounds, even including a course in advanced planetary motion—the earth gets closer to the sun in the summer (thus hotter) and farther away in the winter (and thus colder).

23 See *Cooperative Learning* by Spencer Kagan (San Clemente, CA: Kagan, 1994) and Kagan's *Smart Cards*.

24 See Mihaly Csikszentmilhalyi, *Flow: The Psychology of Optimal Experience* (New York: Harper, 2008).

25 The authors believe that our reading and math reforms have failed over the years because we have continue to insist that there is only one way to teach all students instead of finding a best way for individual students. For example, children that learn to read at age four and who can read and spell years ahead of their grade level, have discovered their own patterns for decoding and spelling. It is a disservice to inflict the standard phonics lessons on them. Doing so usually slows down their reading speed and often also diminishes their enjoyment of reading without providing any benefits. The more unconscious their system of pattern seeking, the more space they have in their conscious mental processing to deal with comprehension. On the other hand, students who haven't detected patterns for decoding that work do need the standard phonics lessons. Pattern identification and understanding is as unique as each child's brain. And, it is far more powerful than our brief lessons can ever be. So, observe your students' pattern-seeking processes and outcome carefully. Complement them rather than force them.

Chapter 5: Program Building– Step Two of Learning

Our behavior, and that of our fellow human beings, has long been one of life's greater mysteries. Behavior—its building blocks and why specific building blocks are chosen at any one moment in time—must be understood if we are to create schools that foster real learning.

◉ Learning Is a Two-Step Process

Step One—Input stage: Pattern seeking & meaning making
First, the brain must detect/identify a pattern.
Second, the brain must make meaning of the pattern, including its relationship to other patterns.

AND

Step Two—Output stage: Building programs to use what we understand
Begins with conscious effort (often with guidance)
and then
With practice, becomes almost automatic and wired into long-term memory.

According to Hart, the key to understanding behavior is "the realization that we act very largely by programs . . . a fixed sequence for accomplishing some intended objective." In other words, to carry on activities, one must constantly select a program from among those stored in the brain and put it to use.[1]

Hart defines a *program* as:

"A sequence of steps or actions, intended to achieve some GOAL, which once built is stored in the brain and 'run off' repeatedly whenever need to achieve the same goal is perceived by the person. A program may be short, for example giving a nod to indicate 'yes,' or long, as in playing a piece on the piano which requires thousands of steps. A long program usually involves a series of shorter subprograms, and many parallel variations that permit choice to meet conditions of use. Many such programs are needed, for instance to open different kinds of doors by pushing, pulling, turning, thumbing a

HET Learning Principles

- Intelligence as a function of experience
- Bodybrain partnership —emotion as gatekeeper to learning and performance—movement and cognition
- Multiple intelligences
- Learning as a two-step process
  — pattern seeking/meaning making
  — program building

button or lever, and so on. Language requires many thousands of programs, to utter each word, type it, write it in longhand, print it, and so forth. Frequently used programs acquire an 'automatic' quality: they can be used, once selected, without thinking, as when one puts on a shirt. Typically, a program is CONSCIOUSLY selected, then run off at a subconscious level. In general, humans operate by selecting and implementing programs one after another throughout waking hours."[2]

To understand the power of Hart's statements, consider some everyday examples. Simple ones are such things as a procedure for putting on one's shoes. There are the "right-foot-first" people and the "good heavens, no—the left first" folks. Same with putting on a coat. For high good humor, watch someone in a restaurant offering to help another with their coat. Of course the assistant offers the coat in the manner that he or she would put it on—from the left, high up near the shoulder while the recipient turns to receive the coat low from the right and the awkwardness ensues.

Or, how about the shower? Your favored hand grabs the soap and that soap knows just what to do. Zip! You're done with the shower. But, if for some temporary reason that hand can't get wet, the soap no longer remembers what to do. The result is much fumbling about, a shower that takes much longer, and the feeling of not being quite as clean and refreshed as usual. You can almost hear your mother's voice asking, "Did you wash behind your ears?"

For another example, think how many of us have driven miles with absolutely no recall of the journey. A little scary! Or, after being reassigned to a new school, we find ourselves one morning in the parking lot of our former school. How did that happen!

As John Ratey points out in his book, *A User's Guide to the Brain: Perception, Attention, and the Four Theaters of the Brain*, skill acquisition recruits more cortical neurons to master the skill; then, as the skill becomes more automatic, less of the recruited cortex is used and the function is delegated to lower parts of the brain. "Thus, the brain has a tremendous ability to compensate and rewire with practice."[3]

This shift from full attention to identifying patterns to automatic use of what is learned was outlined in Chapter 4. Please re-read pages 4.2 and 4.3 because they help explain the journey from the first "Aha" to unconscious use of knowledge and skills.

The most fascinating aspect of Goldberg's gradiental model (described on pages 4.2-4.3) with its shifts from right to left frontal, from front to back, and neocortex to older structures is that it provides a physiological explanation for Leslie Hart's definition of learning as a two-step process as shown below. The correspondence is striking.

New definition of learning	Brain activity when learning something new
• Step One: Pattern-Seeking (see Chapter 4)	
Identifying patterns................................	Primarily right frontal lobes shifting to
Making meaning/understanding...............	Primarily left frontal lobes
• Step Two: Program-Building	
Ability to use learning with support.............	Shift from front toward back of brain
Ability to use the learning becomes automatic and part of long-term memory.......	Shift to back and lower/older brain structures

Admittedly, these are broad brush strokes but knowing that different parts of the brain must be engaged to move learning from an initial "Aha" to long-term memory of how to *use* the knowledge or skill gives us a larger view of learning. It allows us to key in to what sensory and motor input students need, what practice *using* the knowledge or skill will move the learning from new to practiced, and the time it takes to make those physiological shifts in the brain. Suddenly, "covering" content and relying on paper-pencil tests to indicate mastery can be seen as the useless strategies that they are.

THE PROGRAM CYCLE

This chapter addresses the second step of learning—developing programs for using what is understood.

The basic cycle in using programs is:

Step 1. Evaluate the situation or need (detect and identify the pattern or patterns). For example, is it a birthday, graduation, holiday, costume, or office party? (Each demands certain consideration, appropriate dress, gift, contribution to the potluck, etc.) Ah, it's a birthday party.

Step 2. In response to the incoming patterns, select the most appropriate program from those stored. For example, because it's a birthday party you prepare to RSVP, buy a present, wear party clothes, and eat a skimpy breakfast and lunch because you know there will be cake and ice cream.

Step 3. Implement the program. For example, you execute your plans by going to the party and having a great time.

The fourth step, wiring into long-term memory, occurs when several birthday parties have been attended, including one's own!

As illustrated in the previous example, the first step in the learning process is detecting pattern. Once a situation has been analyzed, and if action is required, the brain scans its repertoire of stored programs, selecting the one that is most appropriate or calling forth two or more and using them in fresh combinations. Towards a positive end, such capacity to "use old programs in fresh combinations" underlies what we call creativity.[4]

Used negatively, this evaluate—select—implement process is seen in the case of the student who repeatedly misbehaves. Wanting to attract the teacher's attention, this student reaches into his/her mental bag of programs and, as unconsciously as the driver arriving at the wrong parking lot, automatically pulls out a behavior that will attract attention. Unfortunately, the behavior also makes the teacher furious. In such students' mental bag of programs, there are too many of the "wrong" behaviors/programs and too few of the "right" ones, i.e., ones that get the attention of the teacher but without the anger.

Equally somber is the child-grown-adult who has no program for using multiplication for real-world applications such as computing mortgage payments or figuring the real cost of an item he/she let ride on the VISA charge card. Unpleasant consequences flow from lack of appropriate mental programs.

Successful implementation of a mental program is its own

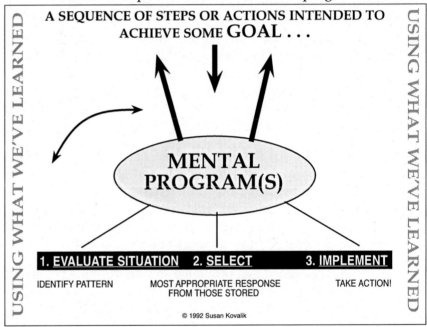

reward, accompanied by feelings of accomplishment and increased satisfaction. Aborting a mental program that doesn't work is emotionally unsettling because it leaves us unsure of what to do next and decreases our sense of self confidence.[5] When orchestrating your curriculum, provide the time and experiences that allow youngsters to master new information and add it to prior knowledge in a meaningful way, thereby creating new mental programs.

Hart, in fact, defines learning as "the acquisition of useful programs."[6] "Learning," such as getting an A on a paper/pencil test, which does not result in acquisition of a mental program is not learning from Hart's perspective because it doesn't stick. Hart points out that information that does not become part of a program is usually unretrievable. For example, recall your sophomore college days and the traditional western civilization class. The characteristics of this stunning experience: yearlong, 99.9 percent lecture, and an enormously fat textbook. For the mid-term and final exams, you used the ubiquitous blue book. Weeks later when the blue book was graded and returned, you glanced inside. To your total shock, there were paragraphs of stuff you didn't even recognize—never heard of before! A classic example of information that never became part of a program and, thus, is unretrievable and often unrecognizable, even a bare three weeks later. In other words, most information that we use is embedded in programs; the corollary is: information that is not used is also not retrievable and, if truth be told, was probably never "learned" in the first place. Thus, "covering information" is a colossal waste of time for both students and teachers.

The implications for the classroom of the 21st century are obvious—students must master concepts and skills with depth of understanding and use what they understand. We in turn need to present less content and give students time to "use" the information again and again in varying settings until the information is recallable in a usable form, i.e., a behavior, a program.

It should be noted that programs and subskills are not identical and have little in common. A program, while it can be enormously complex, such as driving a car, is a sequence for accomplishing some end—a goal, objective, or outcome—an end with meaning to the learner. Subskills, such as the blend *ch* or the short *i* are not a sequence for accomplishing some end; they are experienced as isolated, fragmented pieces. In contrast, the program to be attained is the act of reading—an insight young students can easily miss.

To reinforce the difference between pattern-seeking (making meaning of input) and program building (using what is learned), consider diapering a baby. Everyone recognizes the patterns diaper and baby. But, as Diane Keaton makes clear in the movie, *Baby Boom*, not everyone can diaper a moving baby. The same is true with returning a rental car. Everyone knows what the words *car, return, rental,* and *airport* mean. But not everyone has a mental program of the steps for *returning a rental car to an airport.*

Because this discussion of building programs and wiring knowledge and skills into long-term memory is so critical to what we as teachers do in the classroom, we are providing here part of Hart's description of program building from his book *Human Brain and Human Learning.*

SECOND FUNDAMENTAL OF LEARNING: WE LIVE BY PROGRAMS*

Extraction of patterns—identifying and making meaning of them—constitutes the first of two steps in learning. But plainly enough, we do not live by sitting in an armchair and detecting patterns. We live by doing, by action. Thus, the second step in learning is the development of mental programs to use what we know, i.e., the patterns we have come to understand. Step two in learning is defined as "the acquisition of useful programs.

THE MYSTERY OF BEHAVIOR

For thousands of years, back to the dim origins of humans, behavior has seemed largely a mystery. What people did seemed utterly haphazard, unpredictable, and unexplainable.

Teachers have long struggled with the behavior of their charges, often to the degree that class management threatens to push instruction into a secondary function. Even corporate personnel specialists confess to being frequently surprised and baffled by the behavior of workers, for all the "motivation" that pay and prospects of advancement would seem to offer. More than half of marriages in the United States go astray; the inability of spouses to understand each other, even after years of intimacy, stands out. At any gathering of parents, the difficulties of comprehending the strange worlds children inhabit take a prominent place in the discussions.

---

* Text in this font, from here to page 5.9, indicates excerpt from *Human Brain and Human Learning* by Leslie A. Hart. Used with permission of the publisher.

However, in the last four decades and more, researchers studying the brain and several other disciplines have made progress on many fronts. When their findings are brought together and unified, our understanding of human behavior can take a great leap. This opens the door to revolutionary advances in education and gives us the chance to catch up, at least somewhat, with the discoveries resulting from the dazzling and often upsetting advances in technology.

THE BASIS OF BEHAVIOR: PROGRAMS

The key to understanding human behavior is the realization that we act very largely by programs. The word *programs* need not alarm us with visions of robots. It means simply a fixed sequence for accomplishing some *intended objective.* In other words, we act to carry out some purpose, some personal, individual, and usually self-selected purpose—the exact opposite of robot behavior.

Suppose, for example, that I wish to telephone my dentist. I pick up the phone, push the buttons in a certain order, and put the receiver to my ear to wait for the call to go through. I have executed a program for making a phone call. Should I call him again tomorrow, I will go through just about the same procedure.

Should I wish to phone a local store, I may have to use an additional program to find the number. I get the phone book, look up the listing, then dial—a variation of the program I used to call my dentist.

If now I want to visit the store, I must implement a longer program. I go to my car, take out my keys, find the right one, unlock the door, open it, get in, put the key in the ignition switch, fasten the seat belt, turn the switch and start the engine, release the parking brake, put the car in gear, press the accelerator pedal—just to start on my trip. To get there in my accustomed way I go through a series of dozens of steps, including the right choices of turns at street intersections. Yet I can "reel off" this program with the greatest of ease, hardly giving any attention to what comes next, much as I can put a cassette in a player and have the tape reel off a musical or other program.

Clearly, one of the reasons for our huge brain is that as humans we need and use a great number of programs to carry on our complex activities—thousands of times as many as the most intelligent of other animals. Exactly how that is achieved remains unknown, although the progress of researchers in the neurosciences suggests that we may have a good start toward understanding the neuronal, chemical, and molecular mechanisms involved within another few years.[7]

The Source of Programs

Present knowledge makes clear that programs can be acquired in two distinct ways: transmitted with the genes or learned after birth. As a general rule, the more brainpower an animal has, the more it learns after birth. The more neocortex or new brain it possesses, the greater the relative reliance on after-birth learning. We see once more why the laboratory rat and other small experimental animals can shed so little light on human learning: Their programs are largely species wisdom, transmitted genetically, while humans use the splendid new brain to do most learning after birth, over many years.

No aspect of being human appears more dominant than this incessant accumulation of programs. The process, of course, is most rapid in the earlier years then gradually tapers off. But since we live in a world that changes constantly, we are under far greater pressure than our forebears to continue to learn, to continue acquiring new programs. The man of 75 who is given a video tape recorder to honor that birthday must master some new programs to operate his new machine. A few centuries ago the programs acquired by age 25 would pretty well see one through a full life; today much of what is learned by age 25 will become obsolete. Failure to keep on learning can prove restrictive, costly, or embarrassing.

How Programs Work

To carry on activities, one must constantly *select* a program from those that are stored in the brain and *implement* it—put it into use.[8] Even to walk across the room, one must use an extremely complex program involving many of the body's 600-plus muscles and the shifting of weight from one side to the other as the feet alternate in moving forward. The program has to be repeated every two paces, with continual fine adjustments to change direction or to pick up and carry articles. To walk, one program is used; to go up stairs, another; to go down stairs, a third. To take a stroll outside one may have to use programs for going uphill, downhill, crossing rough ground, jumping over a puddle, or running a few steps to avoid traffic. *Each time, the program in use has to be switched off and another selected and switched on.* The brain does this so smoothly that we ordinarily are not aware of the switches being thrown, but this is the main key to our present insight into behavior.

If I am getting dressed in the morning and open a drawer full of shirts, I must make a conscious selection of which I will wear. After I have made that choice, opening up the shirt, putting it on, and buttoning it up "runs off" as a kind of automatic program to which I don't have to give any conscious attention unless something goes wrong—I find a button missing—and interferes.

Which shirt will I select? It depends on a perception of the *pattern* I will be dealing with. If I am going to a business meeting, I select a dress shirt; if I plan to make some repairs, I choose a work shirt; if I plan to exercise, I choose another type of shirt. Even more subtle patterns may influence me: I may want a conservative dress shirt for the meeting or a brighter one if the meeting will become a celebration with old friends. Though the decision may be trivial, I cannot act until some decision is made. (Following fixed habits or rituals, where possible, avoids decisions and so may seem more "comfortable.")

In much the same way, we select the most appropriate program from those stored in the brain to deal with what is happening at the time. For example, seeing stairs ahead, I select a going-up-stairs program. Having accidentally jostled somebody, I choose an offering-apology program. Facing an arithmetical problem, I tap my division program. Meeting a neighbor, I select a greeting program, complete with smile, nod, and suitable words.

THE PROGRAM IMPLEMENTATION CYCLE

In each of the above examples, a basic cycle is plainly in use:

1. *Evaluate* the situation or need (detect and identify the pattern or patterns being dealt with).

2. *Select* the most appropriate program from those stored.

3. *Implement* the program selected.

Human behavior looked at in these terms may hardly seem simple but such a perspective provides more penetrating insight.

Key Observations

For educators, viewing behavior as a function of the program implementation cycle significantly expands our ability to observe and analyze student behavior during the learning process. Key observations include:

1. Unless the learner can reasonably and accurately evaluate the need or problem at hand (that is, detect and identify the patterns involved), the cycle goes astray at the outset. The student simply does not know what to do.

   A familiar example is the student trying to cope with an arithmetic problem couched in words. Unable to detect the pertinent pattern,

the student flounders, wondering whether to add, or divide, or give up entirely. Another example is spelling of longer words. Lacking any sense of the structure or pattern of the word, the student tries to simply remember the order of the letters—perhaps producing some weird versions.[9]

2. People can access and use only those programs they already possess. However much one may be coerced or urged, or motivated or rewarded, there is no way to perform the program *unless it has already been stored.* He or she does not know how to do it. No program, no ability to perform the needed action.

   There is no way to force a person to ride a bicycle, or play Chopin on the piano, or write a scientific paper, if those programs have not previously been acquired. That many other people can do these things has no bearing. Yet in almost any classroom, at any level, this principle is ignored. On the playground, one may hear a child being called "clumsy" or "poorly coordinated" when the real difficulty is that the child has not yet learned certain programs. In homes, parents scold children; in businesses, bosses scold employees—all in the same futile way for the same futile reason. *If the program has not been acquired, the solution is to acquire it,* not in criticizing, labeling, or giving a poor mark, practices that prove devastating to learners.

3. A student cannot implement a program unless given the chance to do so.

   A test question might ask, "How can you verify the correct spelling of a word?" The answer intended is, "Look it up in a dictionary." A student who gives that answer, we must note, is not using that program. Rather, he or she is *using a program for answering a question on a test.* So commonly are tests used in instruction that this all-important difference may be overlooked; students may pass tests yet often be unable to carry out the programs themselves—a complaint loudly uttered today. Similarly, if students are always *directed* to use certain programs, there is no way to know whether they can detect the pattern, have a program to select, and can implement it. Rather, they are implementing programs *for following directions.* Such "learning" may prove fictitious.

As I indicated earlier, a program always has a goal, an objective—it is an activity to achieve some intended outcome. What happens if the program selected and implemented does not work?

WHEN PROGRAMS DON'T WORK

During the program implementation cycle, the brain asks, "What *pattern* am I dealing with; what *program* should I choose to deal with it?" The most appropriate program is then implemented. Usually it will work. If it aborts, the brain must recycle—pattern detection, program selection, implementation. Let's say that I have taken out my keys to open the car door. I insert the key but it won't turn—the program *aborts.* I must now go through the three-step cycle again: reevaluate the situation, select another program that seems appropriate, and implement that. Perhaps I have the wrong key, in which case I recycle to find the right one and try again. Perhaps the lock has jammed, so I recycle to the unusual program of going around to the opposite door.

Aborting Programs Is Disturbing

Aborting a program *always causes some degree of emotional shift* because the failure of a program to work is in general disturbing and *threatening,* especially when no workable alternative program can be found. The degree to which programs usually work when implemented to achieve the intended goal serves as a direct, continuous measure of how well one has "made sense of the world," how competent we generally are. Programs *should* work. When they do, confidence in oneself increases; when too often they don't, confidence diminishes.[10]

Impact on Self-Confidence. Teachers have long sensed that self-image and the belief that one can successfully learn is important to self-concept and, in turn, to learning. Brain research now concurs. An individual's confidence rises or falls when programs do or do not work. We can see, too, that children whose parents or teachers have over-directed their activities and over-stressed second-person estimates of achievement, may mistrust their own ability to evaluate situations and select appropriate programs.[11]

This program view of behavior, I submit, is consistent both with present scientific understandings of the brain, and with what we can clearly see—once we know where to look—in the normal functioning of children, other adults, and ourselves. True, we cannot see into another person's brain to observe what pattern-detecting abilities and programs have been established there. However, we can see with new insights what happens when that person is allowed to use what he or she considers the most appropriate program—or when the individual has none to apply, or can't identify the pertinent pattern to begin with.

THE ACQUISITION OF USEFUL PROGRAMS

The word *useful* in "acquisition of useful programs" deserves attention. Primarily, it means useful to the individual who will possess the program—in that person's view, rather than in someone else's view or to satisfy some supposed social or other standard. While it is true that one can be coerced into acquiring a program and may use it under duress, such programs are likely to become unused as soon as the duress ceases, if good mental health prevails. If use of the forced program does continue, it usually will signify either superstitious ritual, with anxiety that something dreadful will occur if it is not used, or the inappropriate behavior that goes under the common name of neurosis. *Inherently, the use of a freely learned program satisfies; that of a coerced program brings back the old fears under which it was built.* We see this in mild form when people do arithmetic with obvious pain and reluctance and, in more serious degree, when individuals who have been forced to learn a musical instrument well cannot bear to play before an audience in later life.

Transfer of Learning

In a far wider sense, *useful* conveys the possibilities of *transfer* of learning, which can greatly increase the speed of new learning. For example, a program for roller skating can readily transfer to ice skating; one for using a typewriter keyboard can easily be extended to using a computer keyboard which then can serve as a mental anchor for learning new information about the computer. *The ability to transfer some of these behavioral building blocks, adapting and adjusting them to new needs, explains why some individuals can master a new task far more rapidly than others* who lack the programs to transfer, or who in some cases may not yet have recognized the similarity of pattern involved which leads to and permits transfer.

Source of Creativity

The capacity to use old programs in fresh combinations seems to underlie what we call creativity. Greater sensitivity to pattern similarities facilitates the transfer. While I would doubt that sensitivity can be directly taught, it seems probable that it can be facilitated.

THE POWER OF PROGRAMS

The implications for education of the program concept of behavior—*evaluate, select, implement* program cycle—are stupendous, bringing not only fresh insights into human behavior but also generating some major guidelines for improving learning achievement.

To summarize:

1. We live by programs, switching on one after another, selecting from those that have been acquired and stored in the brain.

2. As humans, we are far more dependent on programs acquired by the tens of thousands after birth, in contrast to animals that rely more on programs genetically transmitted.

3. A program is a fixed sequence for accomplishing some end—a goal, objective, or outcome. Our human nature makes the working of a program pleasurable; the concept of some after-the-event "reward" is neither necessary or valid. However, feedback is essential to establish that the program did work more or less as intended.

4. We can use only those programs that have already been built and stored. What programs another person has, or many people have, has no bearing. If a person does not possess a program, efforts to force its use are absurd.

5. We routinely use a three-step cycle: evaluate the situation (involving pattern detection and recognition), select the program that seems most appropriate from our store, and implement it.

6. The abortion of a program—upon its failure to work—calls for recycling. When a high proportion of self-selected programs work well, confidence rises; when too many programs are aborted, confidence is reduced and the learner may become far less able to self-select programs.

7. Although laboriously built, fully acquired programs have an automatic quality that can easily lead one to forget that other individuals may not have acquired these programs.

8. Learning can be defined as the acquisition of useful programs.

9. Learning progress can be properly evaluated only by observing *undirected* behavior.[12] Questioning and testing dealing primarily with *information* can reveal little. It shows only poorly what individuals can *do*.

10. Effective transfer of learning depends on using established programs in new applications and combinations. (Skill in putting together new combinations may equal "creativity.") The learner who can adapt established programs to new tasks, by seeing similarities of patterns involved, learns much more rapidly than one who cannot.

11. In general, if we regard human learning and behavior in terms of continually asking "What program is being used?", sharp new insights can be gained, and many confusions avoided.

When extracting patterns and building programs, specific information may be helpful to the task or even required. But, this does not imply that there is necessarily any great virtue in "stuffing the head with facts."

It can be handy to carry in memory certain information that will be frequently used. For example, we may store the phone numbers of a dozen people we often contact so we don't have to look them up each time. If patterns are involved, such information is much more easily remembered as when one knows that Tim, Linda, and Vance all work in the same office, and can be reached through its main number, at hours when that office will be open.

In our real world today, there exists vastly more information than can be memorized and it tends to change or obsolete rapidly, so that trusting memory can be treacherous.

A better strategy than trying to collect facts is to possess programs for finding various information—knowing what reference books are available and how to use them, or where to obtain help. But until specific information is linked to need for pattern or program, it serves little purpose. When such needs exist, learners typically "gobble up" information at an astonishing rate because they see it has immediate and meaningful application.

TRANSLATING BRAIN RESEARCH INTO ACTION USING THE NINE BODYBRAIN-COMPATIBLE ELEMENTS

Of the four principles of learning gleaned from recent brain research, the redefinition of learning is the most revolutionary. As mentioned earlier, our billion dollar a year testing industry stops far short of measuring learning by this new definition. So, too, do all the traditional tools teachers have inherited, with the possible exception of rote memorization. That schools teach until students can use what they learn in practical, real-world ways—and remember what they've learned years later—is a wholly new expectation. It is long overdue but nevertheless a bit unnerving.

Bodybrain-Compatible Elements

- Movement
- Meaningful Content
- Immediate Feedback
- Mastery
- Adequate Time
- Enriched Environment
- Choices
- Collaboration
- Absence of Threat/ Nurturing Reflective Thinking

Where to start? Right here, with lots of commonsense.

First, what do we want students to understand? Look at this from a parent's point of view. Ask them. Survey your own life's lessons. What do you wish you had understood much earlier in life before the lessons got so expensive? Better interpersonal skills, a better understanding of interest and financing, auto mechanics for drivers, savings from conserving (electricity, water, recycling garbage, and so forth), gourmet cooking on a budget, how to create and stick to a budget, investment strategies, tips on child rearing. Probably these and much, much more.

Also, look at what's worth knowing from your students' point of view. Every generation faces its unique challenges as well as those that plague us all. What are those special challenges facing your students? What knowledge and skills would help them most? The answers to these questions will help you focus your curriculum on what's important to know and be able to do.

The question that will help you revamp your instructional strategies is "What do we want them to do with what they understand?" Whatever that is, students must begin to do it. That doing will transform your classroom.

MOVEMENT

Because it is the movement centers of the brain that sequence thinking, it is essential that movement—doing—be part of learning from beginning to end, from the conception of curriculum content to instruction to assessing outcomes. Said more strongly, restriction of movement and all forms of passivity restrict learning. So, whether such active learning is a personal preference or not, we owe it to our students to make learning in our classroom the active, joyful process that it naturally is.

Using Movement to Enhance Program Building

The bodybrain-compatible element of movement enhances program building in many ways.

Curriculum Development

- Develop inquiries that ask that students *use* what they understand in real-world ways and situations. Make sure your inquiries clearly state what students are to **do** with what they understand.
- Provide the real-world tools and materials needed to produce the product called for in the inquiry.
- Design inquiries that ask students to act out the sequence of steps or processes inherent in the key point.

- Always include inquiries that require use of bodily-kinesthetic intelligence for solving problems and producing products.

Instructional Strategies

- During direct instruction, checking for understanding, and groupwork, include as many forms of the dramatic arts as you can; for example, role playing, miming, simulations, planned and impromptu skits, impersonations (of people and machines), and so forth.

- Reduce, if not eliminate, worksheets until the end of the learning process so that students learn how to describe what they have done linguistically. This is important not only to test-taking but also being able to acquire additional information through reading.

- Assign moment activities not just for the sake of movement but to activate the bodily-kinesthetic intelligence.

MEANINGFUL CONTENT

Just as beauty is in the eyes of the beholder, so too is meaningfulness in the eyes of the learner. The brain is ruthless in its judgments about what is worth sending to long-term memory versus what will simply fade away from short-term memory. Its most important criterion is whether something is meaningful to the learner, something that is useful, that will be called upon again.

Using Meaningful Content to Enhance Program Building

The bodybrain-compatible element of meaningful content enhances program building in many ways.

Curriculum Development

- Ensure that your *being there* locations allow for doing, not just looking, and that those responsible for hosting the

visit are prepared for students to actively research the key points—ask questions, compare answers, delve into behind-the-scenes information, and so forth.

- Make sure your inquiries ask students to apply the key point to situations that are part of students' current world as well as future situations.

- Ask students to write inquiries for your key points that apply the concept or skill to their lives. Select those that best relate to students' current experiences and assign them to students for homework which they can share with parents and siblings, for groupwork which will give them more perspective, and for individual work which will provide reflection time.

Instructional Strategies

- Provide adequate time for students to reflect on what they're learning—how it applies to their lives now and in the future, to their community and the world.

- Require journal writing every day; include at least one assignment that asks students to reflect on what they've learned today and two ways they can apply it during the coming week.

- Involve students in self-assessment processes.

IMMEDIATE FEEDBACK

Creating programs, especially accurate ones, is impossible without feedback. Assembling sensory input into understandable pieces then wholes, training the muscles to use what is understood—at every step along the way our learning is a set of approximations under refinement.

The best feedback is that built into the learning situation and materials—inherent, immediate, consistent. For example, learning to ride a bike, play a saxophone, use a hand lens or microscope, match yesterday's colors for painting in oils or water color, and so on. In each case, learners knows immediately if they have successfully performed the action. No one needs to tell them.

The most hazardous kind of feedback for learners to rely on is teacher feedback. Why? Because it is external not internal, and therefore can't be replicated by the learner, and because it is rarely immediate due to the demands on the teacher by other learners. Grading papers overnight, even by the end of the day, does little to help a learner develop accurate programs. To be useful, feedback must come at the time the learner is engaged in using the knowledge or skill. This axiom is urgent when learner and new material meet.

This discussion brings up some interesting observations about homework. From a brain research point of view, it is clearly a mistake to assign a page of division problems if students have not yet mastered division because it is likely that they will get as much practice doing division wrong as they will doing it right. This only serves to deepen the confusion and makes reteaching more difficult the next day. On the other hand, if students have already mastered division, why should we burden them with a page of busywork? In our opinion, homework should consist primarily of students applying concepts and skills to real-life situations around the home and neighborhood through meaningful projects.

Because some learners need more feedback and thus more time to learn a particular concept or skill, homework assignments are a way to vary the time and number of practices.

Using Immediate Feedback to Enhance Program Building

The bodybrain-compatible element of immediate feedback enhances program building in many ways.

Curriculum Development

- For every inquiry you develop for students, think through what means and level of feedback students will receive in the process. Will the situation and materials provide the needed feedback? If not, can Learning Clubs do an adequate job or are all the members at ground zero relative to the concept or skill to be learned? How available are you as teacher? Can you shift your role to guide on the side so that you can freely roam and provide sufficient feedback to all?

- If adequate feedback can't come from the learning situation and materials of the inquiry, make sure the forms of feedback vary, as they do in real life. Among the choices, include inquiries that:
    - Require students to develop rubrics for self assessment and to practice the 3Cs of assessment.
    - Require Learning Club members to provide feedback to each other. Have students assess both the quality of the feedback received and what they learned in the process of analyzing and providing the feedback.

- Develop long-term projects such as the Yearlong Research Project, social/political action projects, service projects, Kids Vote America, and so forth.

Instructional Strategies

- Ask students frequently—on a scale of 1-10—how well they think they will remember what they are learning 10 years from now. If less than 9.5, ask them what it would take for them to wire the knowledge/skill into their long-term memory. Have them write their own inquiries, building in those suggestions. Assign those you approve of to be done as homework or in-class assignments. Your goal here is for students to learn to become responsible for their learning outcomes. If you've chosen your content well, they will willingly take up this responsibility.

- Commit yourself to effective first teaching goals and strategies. Intend to make your first lesson so effective that additional teaching or, heaven forbid, re-teaching/remedial teaching is unnecessary. Guided practice allows you to ensure that early learning is correct and sufficient to override previously-held misconceptions.

- Develop a deep repertoire of feedback strategies, such as ask three-before-me (three students before the teacher), peer response, self-assessment with rubrics and the 3Cs, target talk, coaching by knowledgeable peers and experts, teaching a younger buddy (through the act of teaching, they discover what is not well understood), and so forth.

MASTERY/APPLICATION

Mastery and an accurate program wired into long-term memory are one and the same thing. They are the outer and inner manifestations of each other.

To help students reach mastery, see the recommendations for curriculum development and instructional strategies for the other eight bodybrain-compatible elements discussed in this chapter.

ADEQUATE TIME

Those who liken the brain to a computer fail to appreciate the true biological nature of the brain. While it may take nanoseconds to switch from 0 to 1 and back again, the gist of learning in computers, learning in the brain requires physiological growth of neurons, dendrites, axons, and time for mylination to occur. Such growth takes time.[13] Wish as we may, wish as we might, there are no short cuts except going at it as if we understood how the brain works. That would call for teaching it well once, guiding practice of application in varying circumstances (not just rote memorization), and having students use it—without birdwalking—until the physiological process is completed and learning has been hard-wired into long-term memory. Teaching the concept and skill of division in a single, uninterrupted day is a perfect example of adequate time in action. Please see the video, *Divide and Conquer: A Concept in a Day,** by Martha Kaufeldt. Division Day has been replicated in schools and

districts across the country over the past 15 years; the results are always the same. Mastery for all students that day and a program wired into long-term memory that doesn't slip away over time.

Using Adequate Time to Enhance Program Building

The bodybrain-compatible element of adequate time enhances program building in many ways.

Curriculum Development

- Use your *being there* locations to naturally integrate content and skills. Thus, a one-hour writing assignment about their favorite ecosystem equals two hours of learning because language arts and science are both used simultaneously. This helps free time for practicing basic skills, such as writing, math, speaking, and so forth, without ever losing focus on the study of ecosystems. Similarly, if the focus were on math, you could explore the math possibilities at your current *being there* plus revisit earlier sites while maintaining focus on math.

- Develop, and have your students (from grade three and up) help you develop, lots of inquiries—more than you think you'll need. For substantive concepts, that means a dozen or more. For significant knowledge key points, perhaps five to eight inquiries. There is no magical number of inquiries that are needed. The richness of the sensory input, extent of prior related experience, degree of personal interest, all affect the speed and depth of learning.

Instructional Strategies

- Eliminate pull-out programs. Invest your resources in more effective instructional strategies and improved curriculum in each classroom.

- Eliminate rigid schedules; use time flexibly. Make the schedule from day to day fit the learning. On some days, science is the focus all day with skills hitchhiking along as a means to practice a concept or significant knowledge.

- Take advantage of teachable moments.

- Teach students to assess their progress toward building a program. Have them assess where they are almost hourly:

Step One: Recognizes the pattern

Understands the pattern

Step Two: Can apply/use what they understand with assistance

Can apply/use what they understand without assistance and almost automatically

ENRICHED ENVIRONMENT

With the goal of developing programs in mind, any discussion of enriched environment will have to bury the "rich for the sake of richness" idea. Planning for an enriched environment is a calculated process, not an artistic fling. Every item you allow through the doors must relate directly to the concepts and skills being studied for the month. Further, most of the items should allow learners to handle and do something with them as they practice applying what they understand.

Using Enriched Environment to Enhance Program Building

The bodybrain-compatible element of enriched environment enhances program building in many ways.

Curriculum Development

- Give each item that you bring in the acid test: Is it needed for an inquiry or for direct instruction? If not, don't bring it. There is a huge difference between interesting things and related things. Stick with those things that are concep-

tually related and significant to acquiring an understanding of the concept.

Instructional Strategies

- Plan your immersion environment to not just look good but to be user friendly.

- When experts visit the classroom, ask them to bring items that students can handle and do something with. Look-and-admire items are nifty but from the bodybrain learning partnership's point of view, nowhere near as powerful.

- Invite students to contribute to the immersion environment. Their items can be kept in a guest corner, available for only a couple of days.

CHOICES

Because every brain is different— in wiring, in prior experiences, in interests—every student goes about using what they understand differently. For example, remedial readers use reading skills much more fully if they get to choose the content—car magazines or fashion magazines, spy novels or *Ranger Rick*, sports magazines or romance novels. This is true for all learners. If we can see ourselves in the action, we are more able to learn and remember something.

Using Choices to Enhance Program Building

The bodybrain-compatible element of choices enhances program building in many ways.

Curriculum Development

- When developing inquiries, make sure that there are some for each intelligence so that students can choose their level of difficulty. If the content is unfamiliar, allow them to begin with their intelligence of strength. As they become more adept at using the knowledge or skill of the key point, encourage them to use inquiries calling for intelligences that are less developed.

- Encourage students to develop inquiries that would allow them to apply the key point in an arena of personal interest.

Instructional Strategies

- Encourage students to expand their interests, to develop hobbies, and to explore careers. Use those interests as examples for concepts and skills you are teaching.

COLLABORATION

The number one cause of passivity in the classroom is being stuck in the role of listener. As listener, there is no chance to check one's thoughts for understanding, to explore possibilities, or to try out how to use something. Collaboration pulls the learner out of passivity and thrusts him/her into using what is learned through conversation, joint problem solving, and the work of carrying out a project. In effect, collaboration multiplies the number of teachers in the room, increases the amount of practice applying key points, and increases the level of challenge.

Using Collaboration to Enhance Program Building

The bodybrain-compatible element of collaboration enhances program building in many ways.

Curriculum Development

- Design inquiries that can't be done by any one member of the Learning Club working alone. Increasing the challenge and making real the need for each member to participate forces students to dig deeper and seek connections and relationships that would otherwise remain hidden.

Instructional Strategies

- Don't fly by the seat of your pants when framing collaborative tasks. The potential of collaboration to cement

learning into long-term memory is too great to be handled casually. Be purposeful and on target. See *Designing Groupwork: Strategies for the Heterogeneous Classroom* by Elizabeth Cohen.

ABSENCE OF THREAT/ NURTURING REFLECTIVE THINKING

Although absence of threat is listed last, it should be understood from reading previous chapters of this book that it must be teachers' first and continuing consideration and that, for this discussion of program building, it is accepted here as a given. Academic learning is all but impossible without an atmosphere of no threat. But absence of threat is only the beginning of the emotional continuum. In-depth learning begins to occur when the learning environment nurtures reflective thinking.

Using Absence of Threat/Nurturing Reflective Thinking to Enhance Program Building

The bodybrain-compatible element of absence of threat/nurturing reflective thinking enhances program building in many ways.

Curriculum Development

- Create inquiries requiring students to practice what they understand on their own—through homework, individual projects, and the Yearlong Research Project. Require them to personalize/adapt an inquiry to an area of special interest to them.

Instructional Strategies

- Create a daily journal entry assignment: How does/ could this concept or skill apply to your personal life?

ENDNOTES

1 To grasp the significance of Hart's conceptualization and definition of learning as a two-part process, consider for a moment what is required of a student taking a typical standardized test with its multiple choice and true-false items. With both kinds of test items, the right answer is present. The student has only to detect the answer (pattern) that is most familiar (a process usually accompanied by a small niggling in the back of the brain that says, "Hey, we've heard of that one before!" "Familiar" doesn't represent understanding of the concept inherent in the test question; ability to apply in a real-life setting is clearly light years away. Thus, in essence, the multi-billion dollar testing juggernaut assesses only the first half of the first stage of learning. To push this realization further, consider the Friday quiz, also typically weighted heavily toward multiple choice and true-false items. Sometimes 80% is accepted as indication of mastery; sometimes it is considered sufficient to just record the letter grades, A-F, and then the whole class moves on to the next topic.

If America is disappointed in the student outcomes of its public schools, it must examine what definition of "learning" is serving as the basis for the design and implementation of its curriculum and instructional practices. If Hart's two-part definition of learning were adopted, outcomes would—and do—soar because it forces profound and radical change at the very core of the business of teaching-learning. See Leslie A. Hart, *Human Brain and Human Learning,* 3rd ed (Black Diamond, WA: Books for Educators, 2002), 166.

2 Hart, 156-157.

3 John J. Ratey, *A User's Guide to the Brain: Perception, Attention, and the Four Theaters of the Brain* (New York: Pantheon Books, 2001), 21.

4 Hart, 166-167.

5 Hart, 167.

6 Hart, 161.

7 Recent research suggests that memory storage is not restricted to the brain only but is a bodybrain function (see Chapter 5). However, until researchers can provide a clear, detailed picture of how this functions, we will continue to refer to the brain as the location for storing programs.

8 Dr. Jose M. R. Delgad has stated this as: "To act is to choose one motor pattern from among the many available possibilities and inhibitions are continually acting to suppress inappropriate or socially unacceptable activities." See "Intracerebral Mechan-isms and Future Education" in *New York State Education* (February, 1968), 17. Today we know that the motor part of the brain is also involved in sequencing thought. See Elkhonon Goldberg, *The Executive Brain: Frontal Lobes and the Civilized Mind* (Oxford: University Press, 2001); John Ratey, *Spark: The Revolutionary New Science of Exercise and the Brain* (New York: Little, Brown and Company, 2008); and John Medina, *Brain Rules: 12 Principles for Surviving and Thriving at Work, Home, and School* (Seattle, WA: Pear Press, 2008).

Delgad's comment is still true 40 years later and applies to academics as well as behavior.

9 James Doran, director of Algonquin Reading Camp, Rhinelander, Wisconsin, has demonstrated to me a simple, quick technique for giving students a sense of pattern that produces startling gains in their competency in spelling. His brain-compatible methods also produce large, rapid gains in reading.

For truly surprising gains in reading, see *The Auditory Discrimination in Depth (ADD)* and the *Visualizing and Verbalizing for Improved Comprehension and Thinking* and related programs by Lindamood-Bell. For information, contact the Lindamood-Bell Reading Processes Center, San Luis Obispo, California 800-233-8756.

10 Self-esteem or self-concept programs have long had a questionable base, primarily a "touchy-feely" approach aimed at "feeling good about yourself" as a result of others' telling you that you are a "good person" (sometimes in the face of evidence to the contrary). Current brain research tells a different story about the brain's producing and receiving its own opiate-like molecules as a response to mental programs that work, to a sense of competence in handling the world. See Candace Pert, Ph.D., *Molecules of Emotion: Why You Feel the Way You Feel* (New York: Scribner, 1997); Stanley I. Greenspan, M.D. with Beryl Lieff Benderly, *The Growth of the Mind and the Endangered Origins of Intelligence* (New York: Addison-Wesley Publishing Company, 1997), 104; and Robert Sylwester, "The Neurobiology of Self-Esteem and Aggression" in *Educational Leadership* (February, 1997, Volume 54, No. 5), 75-78.

11 Parents might well ask if this over-emphasis on valuing of performance by a second person might not also contribute to the extraordinary

power of peer groups and peer pressure during the teen years (and beyond). See Alfie Kohn, *Punished by Rewards: The Trouble with Gold Stars, Incentive Plans, A's, Praise, and Other Bribes* (Boston: Houghton Mifflin, 1993) and *Beyond Discipline: From Compliance to Community* (Alexandria, VA: ASCD, 1996).

12 Teachers "driving" a conventional class and initiating most activity have little chance to observe what students do on their own. In a true Montessori setting, for example, teachers can readily become observers because they have time and can be more detached. Students feel relaxed and absorbed in their work rather than on guard against criticism or a bad mark.

13 We speak here of academic learning. Some kinds of life-and-death experiences cause the brain to grow dendrites instantly, ready to assess the situation and respond during the incident. Academic learning, however, must travel a slower learning route.

Part B

Getting Started: Implementing Stage 1

Because the *HET* model is so all-encompassing—providing a single framework for viewing the entire range of curriculum development and instructional strategies needed to translate current brain research into the classroom—it is essential that teachers avoid trying to do it all the first year. Full implementation of the model is a three- to five-year effort. The experience of thousands of *HET* teachers can be distilled into several pieces of hard-won advice:

1) Start at the beginning.

2) Do first what brain research says needs to be done first. Don't jump ahead to the things you most like to do, such as integrating curriculum, when you're just starting Stage 1.

3) Do thoroughly and well those parts that you begin with before moving onward. Drips and drabs aren't sufficient to make for real change in outcomes. Make an agreement with yourself to move through any discomfort you might experience rather than to avoid it.

4) Consciously maintain practices from prior stages as you begin a new stage of implementation.

5) Be kind to yourself and enjoy the journey as you go!

As you proceed, know that the *HET* model has many resources to support you. One of the most valuable is *HET Your Personal Guide to Implementing HET in the Classroom* by Karen D. Olsen. The rest of this book is organized around the stages of classroom implementation. Each goal or benchmark for curriculum and instructional strategies is accompanied by practical how-to suggestions for achieving that goal.

Stage 1 of the *ITI/HET Classroom Stages of Implementation* describes where and how to begin. Chapter 6 outlines what to do before students arrive; Chapter 7 addresses what to do the first day of school, and Chapter 8 discusses what needs to be accomplished before moving on to Stage 2. The criteria for assessing Step 1—making the environment bodybrain compatible—is applied 100% of the day.

Stage 2 of the *HET* Classroom Stages of Implementation *is* is explored in Volume Two—making curriculum and instruction bodybrain compatible and what needs to be accomplished before moving on to further improving curriculum. The criteria for implementing Stage 2 is applied only for that portion of the day, week, or year for which the teacher has developed bodybrain-compatible curriculum using the *HET* model.

Volume Three also provides practical steps for making curriculum more powerful as described in Stages 3-5.

The *HET* Classroom Stages of Implementation were distilled from the experiences of more than 500 teachers who implemented the *HET* model over a 10-year period while improving science education in the Mid-California Science Improvement Program. The stages were designed to provide a road map for teachers and their coaches; they have continued to evolve over the intervening years. Much hard-earned wisdom is packed into these descriptions of curriculum and instructional strategies.

The stages of implementation are an invaluable guide. They help clarify pictures of end goals as well as next steps. They are also a useful tool to assess progress toward implementing a bodybrain-compatible learning environment individually and as a group.

As a rule of thumb, Stage 2 should be completed within one year, two at most.

Guidelines

The stages described in HET Classroom Stages of Implementation are:

- *Stage 1: Making the learning environment bodybrain compatible*
- *Stage 2: Making curriculum bodybrain compatible*
- *Stages 3-5: Advanced levels of curriculum work to refine and expand conceptual curriculum*

BEFORE SCHOOL

Stage 1.1

Making the learning environment bodybrain compatible —
Before School

CURRICULUM

- Gets a class list of students with phone numbers and addresses.

- Becomes familiar with state and district health/environment standards.

- Learns about and prepares to teach students to recognize and fix conditions in their environment that are unhealthful, not aesthetically pleasing, and/or cluttered.

- Becomes familiar with state and district curriculum standards and assessment practices.

- Selects *being there* locations that best match the curriculum to be taught.

- Selects a professional and/or peer coach(es) who can/will support the implementation of a bodybrain-compatible teaching/learning environment. Establishes and maintains a schedule for meeting frequently. Prepares thoroughly for each meeting; schedules follow-up time to learn from each session.

INSTRUCTIONAL STRATEGIES

- Before school starts, sends each student a postcard or letter of welcome to class; introduces self to students and tells them a little about what they will be learning.

- Posts relevant health/environment standards in a class binder to share with parents and students (as age appropriate).

- With other adults at the school (custodial, cafeteria, transportation, and office staff, classroom aides, and parents) have taken the necessary steps to identify and fix environmental problems in the classroom.

- Visits potential *being there* locations that could provide real-world experiences with the concepts/skills of the standards.

- Establishes/updates list of promising guest speakers and topics.

- Creates and maintains a healthful, aesthetically pleasing, and uncluttered classroom:
  - Healthful—free of toxins, clean, well lighted, well ventilated with fresh air, ambient temperature, pleasant smelling (the smell of freshness, not of artificial odors), and safe
  - Aesthetically pleasing (calming colors and music, living plants, and well laid out for multiple uses)
  - Uncluttered yet reflects what is being learned.

- Arranges seating in clusters with easy access to work tools.

FIRST DAY OF SCHOOL AND THEREAFTER-CONTINUED

CURRICULUM

- The bodybrain-compatible element of absence of threat and nurturing reflective thinking is taught as an important and on-going part of the curriculum. Such curriculum contains the following five areas:

  1) The Lifelong Guidelines, including the LIFESKILLS

  2) The power of emotions to enhance or impede learning and performance

INSTRUCTIONAL STRATEGIES

- Models the Lifelong Guidelines and LIFESKILLS as the basis for classroom leader-ship and management. Leads rather than controls; inspires rather than manipulates. Creates/maintains an atmosphere that is participatory rather than dictatorial.

- Uses Life Lingo and teachable moments daily to reinforce and extend student understanding and practice of the Lifelong Guidelines and LIFESKILLS.

- Systematically introduces the meaning and importance of each of the Lifelong Guidelines and selected LIFESKILLS through formal lessons (key points and inquiries) and the context of classroom life. The Lifelong Guidelines and selected LIFESKILLS are posted and readable from a distance.

- Bases "discipline" on helping students develop the personal and social skills and behaviors needed to successfully practice the Lifelong Guidelines/LIFESKILLS rather than on a system of externally imposed rewards and punishments.

- Formally introduces age-appropriate lessons about the power of emotion to drive attention and learning. The role of emotion is discussed daily in multiple ways, such as during reflective thinking questions, Town Hall meetings, and teacher feedback to individual students as well as during planned lessons.

- Provides consistency and emotional security for students:
  - Meets students at the door at the beginning and ending of every day (greeting and farewell).
  - Uses agendas every day to provide focus for learning, to enable students to direct their own learning, and to encourage learning time-management strategies.
  - Uses written procedures for all frequently occurring events/activities to provide consistency, continuity, and emotional security for students. Visuals include graphics as well as words.

- Provides a place and time in the classroom—an "Australia" to help students bring their emotions and behavior back under control.

- Frequently uses collaborative learning, as appropriate, to extend and deepen learning and to create a sense of community.

FIRST DAY OF SCHOOL AND THEREAFTER-CONTINUED

CURRICULUM	INSTRUCTIONAL STRATEGIES
3) The important role of movement and daily aerobic exercise in academic learning	• Models and teaches students about using movement and daily aerobic exercise to enhance learning.
	• Uses movement to enhance learning. Provides daily movement sessions to energize, calm, and assist in understanding and remembering concepts, significant knowledge, and skills. Uses such resources as *Brain Gym* and teacher-designed movement activities that grow naturally from curriculum content.
	• Includes movement and other bodily-kinesthetic action in direct instruction of key points as well as in follow-up activities and inquiries.
	• Ensures that students get 35 minutes of aerobic exercise every day to kick start brain chemistry for optimum learning.
4) Personal and social skills for collaboration	• Models and formally teaches the personal and social skills needed to work collaboratively.
	• Organizes students into Learning Clubs. Teaches how and when to use various group processes, such as leading, supporting, listening, encouraging, sharing, "3-before-me," and so forth.
	• Leads students in activities, including Town Hall Meeting and Acknowledgment Box, that are appropriate for each stage of group development—developing a sense of belonging, creating common ground, and taking action. The resulting sense of community serves as the basis for achieving high academic performance as well as enhancing personal and social growth.
	• Uses collaborative learning to achieve specific goals daily.

FIRST DAY OF SCHOOL AND THEREAFTER-*CONTINUED*

CURRICULUM

5) How to nurture and utilize reflective thinking.

INSTRUCTIONAL STRATEGIES

• Uses a calm voice, synchronizes his/her heart-brain coherence, and stays emotionally centered.

• Provides a variety of processes and structures throughout the day that enhance students' reflective thinking, such as wait time, journal writing, reflecting on the daily agenda (beginning and end of the day), making choices that allow students to direct their learning, forecasting how to take on a learning task, reflecting on what one has learned academically, the process of collaborative work (before, during, and after and when asking about content, social, and personal outcomes), providing adequate time for students to complete assignments, and strategies to help students refocus.

• Selects a professional and/or peer coach(es) who can/will support the implementation of the bodybrain-compatible element of absence of threat and nurturing reflective thinking. Establishes and maintains a schedule for meeting frequently. Prepares thoroughly for each meeting; schedules follow-up time to learn from each session.

WHAT TO ACCOMPLISH BEFORE MOVING ON

CURRICULUM

- Formally teaches the concept of multiple intelligences — defined as problem-solving and product-producing capabilities — to students early in the year.

- Uses the multiple intelligences when developing inquiries and as a frequent, on-going topic for reflective thinking about the processes and products of collaborative work.

INSTRUCTIONAL STRATEGIES

- Includes real-life experiences — *being there*, immersion, hands-on materials, and visiting resource people — to supplement classroom instruction and provide rich input for each of the multiple intelligences.

- Is learning how to provide students with multiple ways to understand, solve problems, produce products, and demonstrate what they understand and can apply through:
  - Use of the multiple intelligences as a guide when lesson planning, selecting instructional strategies, and developing/selecting inquiries and other assignments for students, including homework
  - Use of the multiple intelligences during direct instruction of key points and other instructional strategies
  - Flexibility in allocating time for students to complete their work
  - Student choice of tasks, materials, and processes used for completing projects whenever appropriate

- Has mastered the instructional skills identified in Stage 1.2 and continues to use them daily:
  - Modeling of the Lifelong Guidelines and LIFESKILLS
  - Life Lingo
  - "Discipline" based on using the Lifelong Guidelines & LIFESKILLS
  - Daily agenda
  - Written procedures
  - Models movement to enhance learning and uses it with students to energize and calm
  - Collaboration to enhance personal and social growth and increase achievement (includes the three phases of building community — developing a sense of belonging, creating common ground, and taking action)
  - Calm voice, heart-brain coherence, and emotionally centered
  - Nurturing reflective thinking through numerous strategies

WHAT TO ACCOMPLISH BEFORE MOVING ON

CURRICULUM

- Is developing a lesson planning process and format for providing a bodybrain-compatible learning environment.

- Selects a professional and/or peer coach(es) who can/will support the implementation of the bodybrain-compatible element of multiple intelligences and use of a variety of instructional strategies. Establishes and maintains a schedule for meeting frequently. Prepares thoroughly for each meeting; schedules follow-up time to learn from each session.

INSTRUCTIONAL STRATEGIES

- Is developing a variety of instructional strategies to ensure students can identify/understand *patterns* and develop *programs* for using what they understand understand and wire them into long-term memory. Such instructional strategies include:
  - Modeling how to be a lifelong learner and participating citizen
  - Expanded and deepened use of movement and daily aerobic exercise to enhance learning
  - Direct instruction, usually limited to 16 minutes per hour
  - Nurturing reflective thinking
  - Graphic organizers
  - Discussion and questioning
  - Role-playing
  - Literature
  - Songs
  - Video clips, great artwork, and photographs
  - Journal writing to enhance social and personal growth and academic learning
  - Celebrations of Learning

- Designs time frames for HET conceptual curriculum to fit the content rather than a rigid daily schedule; is learning to adjust time frames to best accommodate needed instructional strategies and to give students adequate time to complete their work.

Note: Stage 1 of implementing *HET* begins not with themes or integration but with the brain research relevant to creating a bodybrain-compatible environment in which learning can occur.

Although a bodybrain-compatible learning environment cannot be fully realized until curriculum becomes bodybrain compatible, curricular changes have little impact if the learning environment is not consistent with how the brain learns. Therefore, implementors are advised to proceed slowly with curriculum development until significant strides toward maintaining a bodybrain-compatible learning environment are achieved.

Stage 1, entry level into a bodybrain-compatible environment, is to be applied to the classroom 100% of the time unless specified otherwise. Note that this stage is broken into three parts in order to give teachers greater focus on where and how to begin.

Chapter 6: What to Do Before Students Arrive

Stage 1.1

BEFORE SCHOOL

Making the physical environment bodybrain compatible —
Before School

CURRICULUM	INSTRUCTIONAL STRATEGIES
• Gets a class list of students with phone numbers and addresses.	• Before school starts, sends each student a postcard or letter of welcome to class; introduces self to students and tells them a little about what they will be learning.
• Becomes familiar with state and district health/environment standards.	• Posts relevant health/environment standards in a class binder to share with parents and students (as age appropriate).
• Learns about and prepares to teach students to recognize and fix conditions in their environment that are unhealthful, not aesthetically pleasing, and/or cluttered.	• With other adults at the school (custodial, cafeteria, transportation, and office staff, classroom aides, and parents) have taken the necessary steps to identify and fix environmental problems in the classroom.
• Becomes familiar with state and district curriculum standards and assessment practices.	• Visits potential *being there* locations that could provide real-world experiences with the concepts/skills of the standards.
• Selects *being there* locations that best match the curriculum to be taught.	• Establishes/updates list of promising guest speakers and topics.

HET Classroom Stages of Implementation **Stage**

Making the physical environment bodybrain compatible —
Before School **1.1**

BEFORE SCHOOL

CURRICULUM

INSTRUCTIONAL STRATEGIES

• Creates and maintains a healthful, aesthetically pleasing, and uncluttered classroom:

— Healthful

- Free of toxins

- Clean

- Well-lighted

- Well-ventilated with fresh air

- Ambient temperature

- Pleasant smelling (the smell of freshness, not of artificial odors)

- Safe

— Aesthetically pleasing (calming colors and music, living plants, and well laid out for multiple uses)

— Uncluttered yet reflects what is being learned.

• Arranges seating in clusters with easy access to work tools.

• Selects a professional and/or peer coach(es) who can/will support the implementation of a bodybrain-compatible teaching/learning environment. Establishes and maintains a schedule for meeting frequently. Prepares thoroughly for each meeting; schedules follow-up time to learn from each session.

GETTING STARTED . . . FIRST IMPRESSIONS

Where and how do you begin your program improvement efforts? Start with brain research firmly in mind. Your number one goal is to make your classroom a bodybrain-compatible environment. Once that is in place—for you as well as for your students—powerful learning will occur.

Much of the foundation work for Stage 1 occurs before the school year even begins. Take seriously what architects have known for centuries: form dictates function, and the behaviors that drive it. Students come to typical classrooms with "school behaviors," a reaction to bureaucratic institutionalism. These school behaviors are often far from the polite behaviors expected when they visit a friend's house and want to earn the right to come again. A change in the environment (form) will makes changes in students' perception of school and thus their behavior in school (function).

First Impressions

As any substitute teacher or Dale Carnegie workshop presenter can testify, first impressions mean a great deal, making the kind of long-term relationships in a classroom easier to build or poisoning them from the beginning. To get your year off to a good start, take the time to invest in a positive, strong first impression. Send each student a postcard or letter before they arrive; this will predispose them to look forward to and enjoy their first day of school and every day thereafter.

For a mailing list, ask the school secretary if she could print out a set of labels for you. Share with students how excited you are to meet them and what they can expect—what you will study the first month (and more if appropriate) and the *being there* experiences they can look forward to. Following this personal invitation, the first day of school is more like a reunion than a first meeting. You've set the tone and are off to a good start.

FIRST THINGS FIRST . . . MAKING THE ENVIRONMENT SAFE

Reading up on environmental hazards may not at first seem like requisite reading for teachers. But times have changed. The staggering increases in special ed students and classifications of disabilities has led many researchers to believe the causes go beyond genetics; many environmental toxins, especially neurotoxins, are known culprits. Become familiar with your district and state health/environmental standards and the resources referred to in this chapter. The actions you take to free your classroom of toxins may well be your most important gift to students this year.

Find out if your school has a functional committee responsible for investigating and resolving environmental issues. Ask to join the committee and encourage others to attend its meetings. Share what you have learned and ask for copies of the research the committee has operated on in the past. Collect this information in a format you can share with students and parents. Keep it handy for ready reference.

Prepare to Teach Students

The key to identifying and resolving environmental hazards is to educate, educate, educate. And that includes students. Prepare age-appropriate curriculum to present to your students. Extend your lessons into homework assignments so students can apply what they learn to other indoor environments.

In this dawning of the 21st century, knowledge of chemical hazards is no longer solely the domain of chemists. For our own health and welfare, we must become knowledgeable about our exposures and risks. We must learn to look out for ourselves and learn how to take action to correct unacceptable risks to our health and well-being.

THE CLASSROOM IS HEALTHFUL

Negative "messages" from the environment often set off behaviors that impede student learning and frustrate teachers. For example, a dirty, ill-kempt classroom tells occupants that they aren't valued; if no one cares, why should students?

And, as life in the 21st century becomes more technology-based, our environment—indoor and outdoor—is becoming increasingly more chemical-laden. Forty years ago, healthful was defined as clean, an absence of dirt.

Today, the definition of healthful must include the invisible as well as the visible—the presence of toxic off-gassing. We must look at the dark side of noise-snuffing carpets, energy conservation measures dictating that heating/cooling systems restrict inflow of fresh air and windows be sealed shut, high-tech machines that spew gases (copiers, laser printers, and more), art and science chemicals, the ubiquitous and potent cleaning compounds, and the effects of poor maintenance (allergens, toxic molds, and chemicals). We must take a new look at our classrooms and school campuses using a 21st century awareness of healthful. We must inform ourselves and take responsibility for acting upon our knowledge.

> ## GUIDELINE
>
> The classroom is healthful—
>
> - Free of toxins
> - Clean
> - Well-lighted
> - Well-ventilated, air fresh
> - Pleasant smelling
> - Ambient temperature

Free of Toxins

A growing body of evidence makes it clear that unhealthy environments can and do cause serious learning and health problems for students and staff alike. Learning and behavior problems include: breathing difficulties, asthma, headaches, fatigue, weakness, exhaustion, listlessness; depression, easy crying; moodiness, anger, confusion; excessive talking, explosive speech, stuttering, slurred speech; inattentiveness, disruptive behavior, impulsiveness; nervousness, irritability, agitation; a short attention span, inability to concentrate; memory loss, learning problems; numbness and/or tingling of face, hands, arms; dizziness, clumsiness; restless legs, finger tapping, tremors, tics; excessive fatigue, nightmares; hyperactivity, wild unrestrained behavior, and increased sensitivity to odors, light, sound, temperature, touch and pain.[1]

Medical problems resulting from major, long-term toxic exposure include measurable abnormalities in the blood, nervous and immune systems, and in the brain. These health effects can be permanent, including later reproductive problems, or can even cascade into "spreading syndrome," a condition in which previously tolerated chemicals become intolerable. In serious "sick building" situations, Norma Miller, editor of *The Healthy School Handbook: Conquering the Sick Building Syndrome and Other Environmental Hazards In and Around Your School,* suggests that 80 percent of those who become sick get better in six to 12 months; 15 percent do not improve; and five percent may become worse in spite of therapy, moving into spreading syndrome, their health forever compromised and their future in jeopardy.[2]

> ## Self Check
>
> **When toxins are eliminated:**
>
> - There is a decrease in hyperactivity, absenteeism, complaints of feeling ill, and trips to the nurse's office.
>
> - Behavior at home and school is congruent.
>
> - There is an overall sense of well-being for students and staff.

These are shocking statistics. Unfortunately, there are many scientific and medical studies that suggest that a significant portion of misbehavior, learning problems, and even the dramatic increases in special education enrollments and classifications, such as A.D.D., may be a result of chemical poisoning. Creating and maintaining a healthful environment must become the number one priority of teachers, administrators, school boards, and parents.

A sage comment about education is, "If you think education is expensive, try ignorance." Likewise, if we think environmental issues are too expensive to face, we are not looking at the exponential increase in costs of rising special education enrollments and lifelong damage to student and adult health.

At a research conference at Texas Woman's University to establish ecological guidelines for a healthful school building, 60 environmental specialists from 26 states and two other countries gathered to share concerns about construction and maintenance of healthful school buildings. The top ten major areas, listed in order of importance, are:[3]

1. Heating, cooling, and ventilation
2. Pest controls
3. Cleaning products
4. Chemicals
5. Fragrances
6. Site selection
7. Lighting
8. Remodeling the school building
9. Floors
10. Art supplies

The pervasiveness of toxins suggested by this list is hair-raising. The symptoms caused by the chemicals involved reads like a Who's Who of reasons why students are sent to the principal's office. For a list of particularly toxic chemicals, their location, and symptoms, see page 6.6.

Pesticides. Pesticides are not harmless. They are intended to kill target organisms. Even in small quantities in larger animals, they can poison. Many believe that the mushrooming numbers of children with learning problems is attributable to the increase in toxins in the environment. According to Norma Miller, "Classroom environments can be extremely volatile sites, constantly off-gassing pesticides that have been applied repeatedly for years in the same routine fashion. The general application of pesticides fails to address those micro-environments where insects actually live. Instead, poisons are placed within the confines of the classroom, making it possibly the most toxic place a child will spend time during his or her entire life."[4]

As Norma Miller points out, most school systems don't have a policy that specifically addresses issues surrounding pesticide use. She recommends that such a policy include:

- "Establishment of specific contractual amendments that will attract vendors capable of delivering services to contract specification. Policies that have allowed for low-bid acceptance as the norm should be modified. A stringent policy of bid acceptance that emphasizes value for dollars spent based on a 60% technical and 40% value standard will better serve both the contractor and the school system.

- Discontinuance of the practice of routine spraying.

- Reduction of pesticide use, targeting specific amounts (percentages) over a given period of time. Not many school systems are equipped to move from one approach to another overnight. It is important, therefore, that time constraints be imposed, and that appropriate scheduling be followed when the practice of routine spraying is discontinued.

- Determining that staff members understand the pesticide regulations and the reasons for them. Staff members who apply pesticides either should be state-certified or should practice under the guidance of certified applicators. Anyone who violates pesticide regulations during the application of a pesticide, especially by applying a pesticide prohibited by the policies of the system or state, should face disciplinary action. Contractors who send in workers without proper documentation should be dismissed.

- Notification of all concerned when pesticide application is scheduled.

Chemical	Where It Is Found	Effect
Benzene	Adhesives, anthraquinone colors, art class, auto exhaust, cigarette smoke, degreaser/solvent, eggs, fossil fuel, fungicide, gasoline, glue, paint, paint stripper, plastics, room deodorizers, solvents, spot removing products, synthetic fibers, tobacco, smoke, VOCs*, water, wood finish	**Cause of cancer. Immunotoxic.** Anorexia, aplastic anemia, blurred vision, bone marrow and central nervous system depression, chromosomal abnormalities, dermatitis, disorientation, drowsiness, drunken behavior, euphoria, irritation of eyes and gastrointestinal and respiratory tracts, fatigue, headache, leukemia, leukopenia, lightheadedness, loss of appetite, multiple myeloma, pancytopenia, paralysis, polyneuritis, reproductive hazard
Toluene	Adhesives, carpets, classrooms, cleaners, composite wood products, room deodorizers, floor tile, fossil fuel, fuel additive, gasoline, furniture, glue, insulation, lacquer, liquid paper/white out, paint, paint thinner and stripper, petroleum products, polyethylene, polyurethane wood finish, printing materials, solvents, tobacco smoke, varnish, wallcoverings, water	**Cause of cancer. Narcotic.** Brain malfunction, central nervous system damage, depression, disorientation, irritation of eyes, lung, nose, and skin, fatigue, hoarseness, irritability, kidney, liver and spleen damage, loss of coordination, bone marrow suppression, reproductive hazard, and, with prolonged exposure, permanent neurological damage
Methylene chloride	Adhesives, classrooms, coffee, epoxy, furniture, glue, paint, paint remover, pharmaceuticals, phenolic thermosetting resins, wallcoverings	**Suspected carcinogen. Mutagen.** Bronchitis, central nervous system and heart damage, irritation of eyes, lung, and skin, metabolizes to carbon monoxide in blood, pulmonary edema or lung fluid
Trichloroethane	Art class, duplicating fluid, vinyl floor tile, VOCs, degreaser/solvent, dry cleaning fluid, fumigants, insecticides, insulators, paint, solvent, water	**Cause of cancer.** Dizziness, headaches, possible liver damage

---

* VOC = volatile organic compounds

Taken from *The Healthy School Handbook: Conquering the Sick Building Syndrome and Other Environmental Hazards In and Around Your School*, Norma L. Miller, Ed.D., Editor, page 9.

- Documentation of all chemically sensitive students, teachers, and other persons who are involved in the daily function of the building.

- Providing when requested full disclosure of the materials used by both the school system and its contractors.

- Establishment of standards for pesticide use. It should be determined which pesticide will have the least negative impact on human beings and which areas will be acceptable for the application of the pesticide."[5]

Cumulative Effects. The dangers of one-time exposure are considerable enough but the real problem that educators must face is the accumulated effects of multiple toxins. The figure on the previous page illustrates the total-body-load theory of human disease and ill health. No single factor is the complete culprit but each factor adds a burden to the body's adaptive capacity; disease develops when the body's ability to adapt has been exceeded.

From *The Healthy School Handbook: Conquering the Sick Building Syndrome and Other Environmental Hazards In and Around Your School* by Norma L. Miller, Editor. Washington, DC: National Education Association, 1995, p. 228.

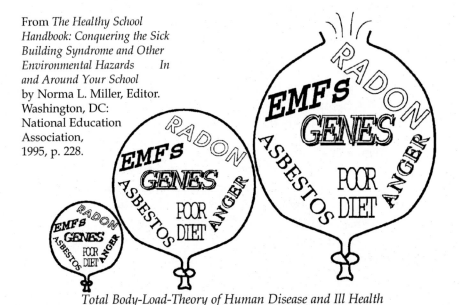

Total Body-Load-Theory of Human Disease and Ill Health

How to Locate and Eliminate Toxins

- Get educated. Two resources to begin with are: *The Healthy School Handbook: Conquering the Sick Building Syndrome and Other Environmental Hazards In and Around Your School* by Norma Miller and *Talking Dirty with the Queen of Clean* by Linda Cobb (New York: Simon & Schuster, 1998).

- Know your students' allergies before the first day of school and make sure that the materials, live animals, and *being there* locations will not trigger an allergic or asthmatic attack.

- Give colleagues and students the benefit of the doubt when they tell you they don't feel well at school but okay at home. Listen to their complaints and take action.

- Create a school committee composed of staff and parents to investigate complaints. Set policies and procedures to determine priorities for eliminating toxins. Budget resources each year to handle situations as they arise.

- Set and closely monitor school policies for chemical use for pests, weed treatments, and cleaning—which, how, when.

- Where possible, enlist the assistance of students to help identify and solve problems.

- Recognize that this is a community problem and the community deserves to know the extent of the problems their children face. Enlist the support of parents and community—time and talents as well as money donations.

The Classroom Is Clean

Clean is clean. It is the clean you make your house when special guests are coming. It means absence of dirt. It means shiny windows, beautiful ceilings and walls with good paint and no water stains, gleaming floors/carpets unstained and free of dust, molds, and other allergens. It means desks without last year's fingerprints, art project mishaps, and gum. It means clean.

Somehow we've come to accept a second-rate standard for cleanliness in our schools. Whether we like it or not, the degree of cleanliness signals clearly how much we value our guests and ourselves. If we want students to choose to be in our classrooms, we need to let them know by our deeds that they're welcome and valued. Nothing you do can mask a dirty environment or mute its messages to students, parents, and colleagues. A dirty environment clearly signals that there are no standards here, people have to be here, and are powerless to change their situation. These are all the wrong messages for a school to telegraph to its students.

If you think we're over-reacting here, guess again. Children love cleanliness and classy surroundings (think Disneyland standards). Standards of cleanliness, tidiness, "classiness," and professionalism do matter.

Making the Most of Resources. Although insufficient resources for proper maintenance and repairs is the rule rather than the exception, before you campaign for an increase in your maintenance budget, analyze what is or is not happening now. It is always possible to make better use of what we have. The most frequent culprit is lack of agreed-upon policies and procedures—an overall plan of the priorities. Or, the plan is written but unknown to most and followed by few.

Here are some questions to ask:

- Exactly what cleaning is done daily? What are the standards?
- How do day-to-day procedures build in time for non-daily, rotational needs such as washing windows, sanitizing desks, washing walls, cleaning carpets, and so forth?
- Who should be notified when things are not done according to the plan? When first reports aren't responded to, what is the follow-up process?

Often maintenance staffs are not under the direct supervision of the principal or, even worse, their needs and priorities are theirs alone. They are said to run the school. If so, make some changes. Create a maintenance/repairs advisory committee composed of teachers, parents, community members (especially those who have earned good reputations for supervising high quality maintenance and repair services), the principal, and the maintenance staff. Put the cards on the table. Hammer out agreements and priorities. Politics must be made to bow to the health needs of children.

Recruit and Delegate. For the most part, teaching is a solitary act. But the issue of a healthful environment is too important to allow a single custodian to dictate what happens. If your school administration doesn't insist on clean and won't assign anyone to help you, recruit help from parents and students. Don't be bashful. They have as much a vested interest in the classroom as you do.

Need tissues in the classroom but it's not in your school's budget? No soap in the bathroom? Ask for donations. Bathrooms superficially cleaned and a health hazard? Let parents press for higher standards. This is their school for their children.

Also, recruit students for tasks similar to those chores they would perform at home. If you want the maintenance staff to perform more of the major cleaning projects such as window washing, cleaning walls, sanitizing desks, etc., then make the students responsible for cleaning up their own daily messes . . . just as they are responsible for them at home so that their parents can spend their time on real cleaning and repair tasks.

Getting Started. As we know from cleaning our own home—and keeping it clean—cleaning is difficult if our space is cluttered. To get your space really clean, you may first have to conquer clutter (see discussion on page 6.20). Before attempting to clean, remove clutter—all of it. If possible, move everything but the furniture out into the hall. Then, scrub, sanitize, paint. Scrutinize the carpet. If it's not cleanable to acceptable health (not just visual) standards, have it removed immediately; if cleanable, get it cleaned immediately using as chemical-free a process as possible.

Before you move anything back in, make sure that it is absolutely essential to what you are studying this year. If not, don't let it through the door. Keep visible only those things that will be used this month; store things needed for the rest of the year in cupboards that have doors (or solid colored curtains) and thus can be kept out of sight.

Items that will not be used this year should be removed from your classroom. Recycle (give them to teachers who can use them), give them away, throw them away, or store them off-site. Then, clean the room and everything in it. Make floors and walls and everything within sanitary as well as tidy.

Don't stop until the room meets your standards for your own home . . . you know . . . if your future mother-in-law were coming to visit for the first time. Now that's clean!

Don't Overlook the Restrooms. The bathrooms your students regularly use are a big part of maintaining a healthful environment.

If your bathrooms are frequently trashed by students, perhaps students are expressing their discontent about the lack of cleanliness and the inadequate supplies (no toilet paper or soap or towels). If you want to turn things around, hold a bathroom celebration on the weekend. Invite parents and students to the party. Deep clean, paint, and decorate the bathroom. Make it look as much like yours at home (or what you'd like yours to look like!). Add a touch of wallpaper or special paint for color and class. Post relevant LIFESKILLS and procedures where necessary but don't make it look like a military camp. And add a sign telling users how to report a problem, e.g., "If you find something wrong in this bathroom, come to room X to report it. Thank you for helping us keep our bathroom clean."

Also take note of in-classroom sinks and drinking fountains. Not only should they be visually clean but also they must be kept sanitary.

Mastering the Art of Clean

- Make the most of your resources by ensuring there are daily procedures both for day-to-day cleaning and for larger jobs, parts of which need to be done each day to ensure they are completed as expected.

- Make sure that the daily procedures are performed as expected.

- Involve parents and the community in maintenance issues. It is their school and their children. Ask their advice, recruit their assistance, and delegate tasks.

- Involve students; help them become responsible for cleaning up their own daily messes so that maintenance staff can address larger cleaning issues.

- In your own classroom, raise the bar. Insist on standards of cleanliness at least as high as those you maintain at home.

- Before school starts, find out what allergies your students have. Plan materials and resources accordingly.

- Pay attention to the bathrooms.

- Schoolwide, create a maintenance/repairs advisory committee of teachers, parents, community members, the principal, and the school maintenance staff. Hammer out agreements about standards and priorities within current resources and determine if additional resources are needed, where, and why.

Hanging in There. To maintain this new standard of clean, talk with your custodian. Share your intentions and standards for your classroom. Ask what you can do to help achieve and maintain your goals. Pride is a powerful motivator. Help both of you to be proud of your classroom.

Tell your maintenance person what allergies you and your students have. Together select cleaning products for use in your classroom. Choose those that don't leave toxic fumes; naphtha, creosol, lye, formaldehyde in disinfectants and ammonia, ethanol, or chlorine bleach in scouring powders are particularly bad. For nontoxic alternatives, see *Talking Dirty with the Queen of Clean* by Linda Cobb. See also the discussion of pollutants and ventilation, pages 6.12-6.-6.15.

Self Check

The Classroom Is Clean

Clean to meet the evaluative yardstick of our senses:

- Visual—no dust bunnies, streaks and smears, discoloration, dullness/lack of shine; nothing broken or mis-functioning; no clutter (no furniture, resources, materials not in current use)

- Smell—no odor, no allergens/antigens such as molds, bacteria, dust. Air filters are cleaned every two months or more often as needed; carpeting is deep-cleaned twice a year and removed when it can no longer be cleaned to standards. Air purifiers are installed in each classroom that needs one.

- Touch—no stickiness or roughness (from dried materials on surfaces or from scraps and cracks)

- Sanitation—absenteeism due to illness by school contagion less than one percent

The Classroom Is Well-lighted

Lighting in schools has been examined from various points of view over the past 50 years. Sufficient light to easily read a book, see work on one's desk, and see the board have long been the accepted standards for classroom lighting. More recently, energy conservation issues have prevailed. Aesthetics is also a consideration. However, recent research goes beyond these typical issues and makes it clear that light—amount, intensity, and color spectrum—has a profound effect on people of all ages, not just children. For those new to the body of research about the effects of light on physical, emotional, and brain function, the findings are quite startling. The implications for teaching and learning are huge.

Effects of Lighting on Physical and Emotional Health. John Ott, pioneer and giant in the study of the effects of light on humans, believes that "humans are photosynthetic," that full-spectrum light acts as the ignition switch for all human biological functions: "The light-mediated process known as photosynthesis in plants is, in my opinion, the same thing as metabolism in humans."[6] According to Fritz Hollwich, M.D., "Light is a primal element of life. Artificial light may be an optic substitute but is by no means equivalent to nature's light in physiological terms."[7] Light from the sun synchronizes most body functions; its absence or imbalance can cause a reduction in our physiological, emotional, and intellectual functioning.[8]

Light not only permits us to see but, through its stimulation of the pineal and hypothalamus glands, also affects virtually every function of the body. The spectral properties of sunlight are fundamental to the:

- Endocrine system, biological clock, immune system, circulatory system, respiratory system, and sexual development
- Ability to control stress and fatigue
- Healthy functioning of the nervous system[9]

Most of us spend the majority of our waking hours drenched in light whose spectral characteristics differ markedly from those of sunlight. Artificial sources of light fail to duplicate the full spectrum of natural sunlight which casts a broad, continuous rainbow of colors.[10]

Most indoor artificial light tends to be weak in strength and density and distorted in terms of color.[11] One component of natural light, which we rarely receive indoors, is ultraviolet light. It is virtually absent from incandescent lighting, shielded in standard fluorescent tubes, and blocked by normal window pane glass and eyeglass lenses. According to Faber Birren in *Light, Color, and Environment,* UV stimulates blood circulation, lowers blood pressure, prevents rickets, increases protein metabolism, decreases fatigue, stimulates glandular activity, stimulates white blood cell activity, increases the release of endorphins, and enhances the production of vitamin D, thereby increasing the absorption of calcium and phosphorus.[12]

According to Richard J. Wurtman, M.D., 16 hours of artificial lighting provides less physical and emotional benefit than one hour of natural lighting.[13] Prolonged exposure to artificial lighting has been associated with:

- Irritability, eyestrain, headaches, fatigue
- Hyperactivity, allergies, frequent minor illnesses
- Inability to concentrate, vision problems
- Susceptibility to osteoporosis and rickets
- Increased incidence of dental cavities
- Changes in heart rate, blood pressure, electrical brain wave patterns, hormonal secretions, and body rhythms
- Depression/Seasonal Affective Disorder, alcoholism, suicide (the third leading cause of death for young adults), weight gain, anxiety, and insomnia.[14]

In short, natural sunlight is a key ingredient in maintaining our health and mental acuity for learning—*a vital nutrient.* Lack of sufficient light affects many children and adults so much that their behavior, learning, and performance are significantly impaired.[15]

◈ Using Light to Improve Learning & Performance

- Conduct a thorough analysis of the light in your classroom and other areas where students spend a lot of time. Check for:
  - Amount of lighting for near and far work (the old-fashioned measurement of whether a student can see his/her work at desk and board)
  - Intensity (high enough to prevent eye strain but without glare)
  - Color spectrum (the color spectrum matches natural sunlight).

- Remove the omnipresent, blue-spectrum fluorescent tubes; substitute full-spectrum tubes that mimic natural sunshine. Replace or repair lights that hum.

- Add incandescent lighting to special reading areas and the teacher's desk.

- Install/Repair window treatments that block the glare of direct sun but allow sunlight in (shades that mount at the bottom of the window and pull up are often more useable than those that hang from the top).

- During design and renovation of schools, insist on windows in every classroom and all offices, full spectrum fluorescent lights, and separate switches for each bank of lighting.

- Consider visual needs and sensitivities of students when drawing up student seating assignments.

- Keep exposure to computer screens, videos, and TV to a minimum.[21]

Effects of Lighting on Brain Function and Achievement. Modern in-door life, with its radical changes in the amount, intensity, and color spectrum of our lighting, challenges our brain in many ways that make learning more difficult for all of us. The difficulties arise indirectly from physical symptoms described previously, and directly, due to actual changes in brain waves and disturbances in producing various neurotransmitters.

Studies show surprisingly strong effects of lighting on brain function. For example, lack of natural light from the sun results in:

- Increased incidence of anxiety and irritability, an inability to tolerate stress, difficulty in getting started in the morning, crying spells, and an overall decrease in activity levels, specifically in the fall semester[16]

- Overeating, oversleeping, and sluggishness[17]

- Increased absenteeism (more than double)[18]

- Lower achievement scores[19]

Given the billions of dollars spent on public education each year, it makes no sense to "stack the cards against educational success by ignoring issues of polluted light."[20]

Self Check

Well-Lighted Classroom

- Lighting includes natural sunlight supplemented by full spectrum and incandescent light; lighting is cheerful but without harshness or glare.

- Burned out elements are repaired in a timely manner or, in overly bright areas, rearranged to pair them with working elements.

- Winter depression (SAD) is minimal. Students are cheerful and healthy.

Well-Ventilated

The two most essential fuels for the brain are glucose and oxygen. Proper diet supplies the first. Fresh air provides the second. Without fresh air—oxygen—learning is impossible. Fresh air means an absence of neurotoxins and biological allergens/antigens such as molds, bacteria, viruses, dust mites, dust, pollens, and so forth.

The importance of fresh air to a healthful environment can't be overemphasized. Most of the pollutants discussed earlier off-gas into the air and thus become a ventilation/fresh air problem. For example, all of the issues in the top 10 most serious indoor sources of pollution identified in the Texas Woman's University study (see page 6.5), except lighting, impinge on air quality—adequate oxygen and absence of toxins. Thus, the adequacy of a school's ventilation system should be the first system analyzed and have first call on resources.

The authors have yet to see a large building whose HVAC (heating, ventilation, and air conditioning) system really works, i.e., provides a pleasant environment (good air quality and appropriate temperature) for everyone year round.

Before the advent of so many chemicals, the biggest challenges to air quality were the products of human bodies—carbon dioxide, moisture, odors. Now, like cleanliness, we need to recognize a 21st century definition of well-ventilated: complete absence of toxins and full presence of fresh oxygen, pleasant smelling (the absence of odor), and a constant, appropriate temperature.

For an excellent discussion of current challenges for ventilation and toxin removal, see *The Healthy School Handbook: Conquering the Sick Building Syndrome and Other Environmental Hazards In and Around Your School* by Norma Miller, often cited in this chapter, and her videotape, *Environmentally Sick Schools—What You WANT and NEED to Know: A Guide for Parents and Teachers.*

Providing oxygen—fresh air with no neurotoxins and allergens—to the brain is the most important contribution to learning that educators and taxpayers can make. The formula is a simple one: "No oxygen, no learning."

⠿ Improving Ventilation and Providing Fresh Air

- Listen to those who complain about poor air and not feeling well. They are your "canaries"—your indicators of air quality.

- Check the intake and outflow points of your system(s) to make sure that outflow from the ventilation system and any other outflow points do not feed dirty air into the "fresh air" intake.

- If you have windows that open, open them (monitor when the outside might be unsafe). Your goal is to have fresh air at head height. Make a point of asking yourself, "How's the air in here right now?" Ask this question at least once every hour. Does it smell of body odor, is the air stale, do students look alert yet calm?

- Insist on the maximum percentage of fresh air exchange allowed by law in your state. Reducing fresh air intake to conserve energy is absurd—far less expensive than lost learning due to inattention caused by low oxygen levels to the brain and or the presence of neurotoxins and allergens. If the allowed exchange rate is inadequate, lobby your legislature for exemptions for those schools that can prove a need for more fresh air intake. If your school is located in an area of high outdoor pollution, widen your political action focus.

- Thoroughly clean the system, including duct work, each year before school starts. Replace the air filters at least every two months. Add purifying systems to areas of high concentrations of chemicals or classrooms whose students or teacher is particularly sensitive to poor ventilation.

⠿ Improving Ventilation and Providing Fresh Air
continued

- Given the rate of introduction of new chemicals into the environment, analyze the chemical composition of every item that comes onto the campus, from construction materials to cleaning agents, computers to book print, white board markers to science and art supplies, particularly items brought on to the campus in large quantities.

- Eliminate artificial fertilizers, pesticides, or herbicides from playgrounds and athletic fields because these chemicals are tracked in and can build up in high concentrations.

- When designing or remodeling a single story building, compare the long-range costs (purchase, maintenance, and repair) of a heat pump HVAC unit for each classroom versus the large, centralized unit. Individual units over time are often more cost-effective, not to mention pleasant, because each classroom can have the temperature the occupants want, contaminants from elsewhere in the building spread less readily, and each room has access to fresh, high-oxygen outside air.

Pleasant Smelling

The most pleasant-smelling environment is one that has no particular smell, just a sense of air that is fresh and well-oxygenated. That means absence of smell from cleaning chemicals, body odor, mold from air conditioners and other sources, stale air, dust, old books with mites, and so forth.

Use of potpourri and air fresheners on a regular basis is not desirable because some of your students may be allergic to them. On an occasional basis, to heighten an immersion or hands-on experience, adding an odor can be very useful, provided of course that no student has an allergic reaction to the fragrance used.

When adding a smell to the classroom, use natural rather than artificial sources, such as natural oils from real plants.

Ambient Temperature

A steady, reliable temperature of 68 degrees in the winter and 76 degrees in the summer helps students stay focused on learning. Yet few centralized systems can deliver. Our recommendation is careful monitoring of windows that open and, whenever possible, a separate HVAC unit for each classroom.

Safe

That our public schools provide a safe environment is assumed, at least a minimal level of care. But the truth is that delayed maintenance and repairs often present real safety hazards. Examples include: an electrical supply inadequate to the demands of the classroom, broken or missing plates for electric plugs and switches, furniture that is ill-fitting, unsteady, chipped, cracked, or splintery. Other hazards include tears in the carpet, loose throw rugs, coats and boots on the floor due to lack of hangers, and so forth. The list goes on.

Unfortunately, timely maintenance is a common budget-cutting target. School board members and administrators need your support and input as they address competing priorities.

AESTHETICALLY PLEASING

Aesthetics is defined as the study or theory of beauty and of the psychological responses to it. It is the branch of philosophy dealing with art, its creative sources, its forms, and its effects. While this is more inclusive than necessary for our purposes here, the sense of rigor is important to the classroom. That is to say, the scientific research behind the physiological, mental, and emotional impact of color and other elements of design, versus interior design based on personal preference or tradition, is critical. By basing classroom design on research findings, we can create classrooms that nurture reflective thinking for the highest possible percentage of our students.

For a workaday definition of aesthetics, we will focus on two areas: art and design. Art is usually thought of in terms of line, shape or form, value, texture, and color. Design is often thought of in terms of space, color, composition, different materials and techniques, and purpose or use.

Our ultimate criteria of acceptability and excellence in these areas is not how chic or groovy or cool a classroom may look but rather how well it nurtures reflective thinking. Questions to ask under each category of art and design include the following:

Purpose in Design. To what extent do the elements allow you to implement the bodybrain-compatible elements to best advantage? For example, does the form of the room allow such functions as Learning Clubs, Town Hall meeting, and other group projects? For intrapersonal space and time, a time-alone space (often called an "Australia")? For movement, immersion and hands-on-of-the-real-thing, and ready access to needed resources, materials, and tools? Does it provide an attractive entry that provides transition into the room?

Space. Is there a sense of spaciousness yet a location for every purpose and a place for everything and everything in its place without clutter and crowding? Does the layout allow for flow and freedom to move about? Has all unnecessary furniture been removed? Is the teacher's desk in an inconspicuous place?

Color. There is plenty of hard data about the physiological, emotional, and mental effects of color. To ignore it when designing and remodeling schools and even a single classroom is to squander public resources. There is great power in color. We need to learn to harness it as a way to enhance learning. For example, intense reds, yellows, and oranges over-stimulate students, making it difficult for them to focus on learning; the incidence of discipline problems is high. Other colors, especially the cool colors, greens and blues, are soothing and calming, inviting reflection and introspection.

As color emits its effects on students every minute of every day, it should be considered one of our strongest instructional allies. Accordingly, color should be selected with great care.[22]

Historically, elementary schools have used either institutional colors such as drab greens and grays or the ubiquitous white, or they have used bright, vivid colors such as red, orange, and yellow. Recent color research would have us avoid both extremes. Recommended colors for classrooms that enhance intellectual work include the following:[23]

- For preschool and elementary grades, light salmon, soft warm yellow, pale yellow-orange, coral, and peach. For example, such combinations as light salmon walls and forest green floors

- For upper grade and secondary classrooms, beige, pale or light green, and blue-green; where students face one direction, side and back walls in beige, sandstone, or light tan with front wall in medium tones of gold, terra-cotta, green, or blue

- For libraries, pale or light green (creates a passive effect that enhances concentration)

If we want to nurture reflective thinking, we should choose the colors that most enhance it.

Like any well-decorated five-star hotel, color schemes should consist of a basic color and not more than two or three accent colors on the walls. Multiple patterns, such as bears around one bulletin board and crayons or geometric patterns around another, are a violation of every good design principle. If you wouldn't do something in your own living room, rethink it for the classroom. Somehow we've developed some strange traditions for color and interior decoration for school classrooms.

The design principles of understated and simple elegance are as important for the classroom as they are for the board room of a multinational corporation.

Color and light go together. Color should not allow glare and should maximize the visual appeal of the classroom.

Texture. Because classrooms must be so utilitarian, they often consist of one smooth artificial surface after another. Very boring to the eye. Plants, a fabric-covered couch or wooden rocker, desk lamps with fabric window shades, and a handwoven rug or ceramic floor tile all help add texture and eye appeal to the classroom. Conversely, limit the number of doorless/curtainless shelves; their "stuff," be it book spines or piles of papers, provides the kind of texture that amounts to clutter.

Line. What lines catch the eye? Rows of desks/tables that make the room appear long and skinny? Chaotic lines from haphazard arrangement of chairs, bookcases, and such? Consider a three-to-four- inch-wide, solid-accent color strip around the room about three to four feet from the ceiling. This draws the ceiling down, making the room more kid-sized and gives the eye a line to follow to view the room from one end to the other.

Value. Could a visitor entering your room identify what you and your students value in the learning process? What you are currently studying? What is your focus?

UNCLUTTERED, YET REFLECTS WHAT IS BEING LEARNED

Somewhere along the line, we have confused an enriched environment with a cluttered environment. If we don't have things hanging from the ceiling, floor to ceiling word walls, student work from the last month(s), bulletin boards in multicolors (even 3-D), and more, then we feel we don't have an enriched environment. Unfortunately, the very students who have the most difficulty focusing on learning are the ones most distracted and most likely to experience sensory overload in the midst of clutter.

However, architectural and interior designers of 5-Star hotels are under no such illusions. Their goal is to make people feel welcome and relaxed, not distracted and over-stimulated.

The goal of *HET* is an uncluttered but rich environment. The theme wall sets the itinerary for the month and where that fits within the yearlong theme. Print and non-print material support the content being learned. An uncluttered, well-designed room significantly improves student and teacher performance and enjoyment. It's well worth the effort. (See classroom designs on pages 6.18 -6.19 and the video *One Day Makeover for Your ITI/HET Classroom* with Dottie Brown.)

SEATING IS ARRANGED IN CLUSTERS WITH EASY ACCESS TO WORK TOOLS

Of all the images of school that bespeak a mindless bureaucracy at work, rows of desks bolted to the floor in rigid rows win the academy award. No talking, do your own work, keep your eyes to yourself. A recipe for restricting sensory input and brain activity.

In the bodybrain-compatible classroom, students need flexible seating to fit the nature of their work, particularly collaboration time or, in the *HET* model, Learning Club time. If possible, trade your desks for tables and chairs.

The size of the clusters—two to five students—will depend upon the collaborative skill of your students. If you think your students will have difficulty handling participation in a group of five, begin with two (or, if need be, a committee of one) and work upward.

Each Learning Club should have their own work tool basket and student binder—each color-coded for that group.

The work tool basket should, at a minimum, include the following, each color-coded to match the tool basket: a pair of scissors for each student (with the handles matching the basket colors), a glue stick for each student, a box of 24-48 crayons, one set of about 12 fine point markers, one set of about 8-12 broad tipped markers, a ruler for each student, one eraser, some extra pencils/pens, a small dictionary,

Cluttered Classroom Illustration
by Sue Pearson, *associate*, Susan Kovalik and Associates

LIFELONG GUIDELINES

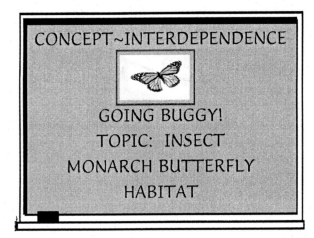

CONCEPT~INTERDEPENDENCE

GOING BUGGY!

TOPIC: INSECT

MONARCH BUTTERFLY

HABITAT

LIFESKILL
OF THE WEEK
CARING

Focused Classroom Illustration
by Sue Pearson, *associate*, Susan Kovalik and Associates

and, once in awhile, something special needed for the day such as magnifying glasses, tweezers, and so forth.

The Learning Club student binder, also color-coded to match the work tool basket, should, at a minimum, contain the following: Lifelong Guidelines and their definitions; LIFESKILLS and their definitions; the written procedures for the classroom; job descriptions of common collaborative rolls such as reporter, recorder, encourager, and so forth; information about Town Hall meetings; a map of the state; and a few strategies (such as, when your stuck on an assignment, try these strategies). If you've chosen binders that have clear plastic covers on the outside, slip in a piece of paper with the name of the class inside the front plastic; in the back plastic pocket, put a copy of the yearlong curriculum mindmap. The Learning Club student binder should also have a stripe of color that matches the work tool basket.

Color coding these items makes identification and return to their proper place an easy and quick task so that each morning begins afresh and well organized.

BECOME FAMILIAR WITH STATE AND DISTRICT CURRICULUM STANDARDS AND ASSESSMENT PRACTICES

No matter what your tools—textbooks or teacher written curriculum—allow state/district standards to frame what is expected of your students. Within this frame, dedicate yourself to making the content as conceptual and engaging as possible.

SELECT "BEING THERE" LOCATIONS

That *being there* experiences greatly enhance learning is hardly a new notion. It is confirmed by our own experiences as learners, by educational research from John Dewey to the present

day, and by current brain research. And yet, we ignore our wisdom day after day. We complain that "it's not in the budget" or "I don't have time" or "my kids couldn't handle such a trip." However, the school grounds and neighborhood only need shoes that can go a-walkin'' or a public transportation bus pass; study trips need not be expensive or distant. *Being there* study trips are a powerful use of time, promoting far more learning than the same amount of seat time; and kids can and will rise to the occasion and the opportunity to learn something exciting.

Matching the curriculum with real-world experiences that demonstrate how and why that learning is important is key to creating a bodybrain-compatible learning environment.

Before you take students, visit the locations yourself. See them through the eyes of your students. Ask yourself how well the people at these locations (workers and visitors) demonstrate the concepts and skills of your state standards. For more discussion about selecting and using *being there* locations, see Chapter 12.

IDENTIFY GUEST SPEAKERS

Guest speakers are a great way to introduce and extend the excitement generated by *being there* study trips. They provide that critical context for students—who uses these concepts and skills, how, and why.

If your guest speakers represent famous persons or periods in history, have them come in dress and role play the issues of the time.

MEETING FREQUENTLY WITH A PROFESSIONAL OR PEER COACH

As you plan for students, remember to plan for your own needs. Set aside the necessary resources, especially time, to ensure that you have opportunities to meet frequently with a professional or peer coach who has mastered the *HET* model in his/her own classroom and can support your implementation of a bodybrain-compatible learning environment.

Support is critical to your success. Make sure you get needed assistance through both formal and informal venues.

Finding a Coach

Insist on frequent, at least monthly, support from a coach who has implemented the *HET* model at Stage 3 or higher. While peer coaching (two peers at nearly the same level of implementation) can work, the process is agonizingly slow. The blind leading the blind, both strangers to the landscape, is too costly in terms of time, effort, and lost opportunities.

In addition to your coach, find a colleague who is committed to implementing the *HET* model and who is willing to share deeply about professional issues and growth. The combination of a coach and a partner is very powerful. Ask the coach to work with the two of you as a team. Triads are also a good size for coaching.

ENDNOTES

1. Norma Miller, ed., *The Healthy School Handbook: Conquering the Sick Building Syndrome and Other Environmental Hazards In and Around Your School* (Washington, DC: NEA Professional Library, 1995), 5.

2. Miller, 23.

3. Miller, 64

4. Miller, 244.

5. Miller, 247-248.

6. John Ott, photobiologist and trailblazing researcher as quoted in Miller, *Healthy School Handbook*, 203.

7. Miller, 195. See also Fritz Hollwich, M.D., *The Influence of Ocular Light Perception on Metabolism in Man and Animals*.

8. Miller, 196.

9. Miller.

10. There are numerous books and articles that catalog the detrimental effects on health and brain wiring in children who spend too much time in front of computer and TV/video screens. See also Miller, Chapter 10, especially pages 195-206.

11. Miller, 197.

12. Faber Birren as quoted in Miller, *Healthy School Handbook*, 208.

13. Richard J. Wurtman quote in Miller, *Healthy School Handbook*, 197.

14. Miller, 196. Seasonal Affective Disorder (SAD) is a common companion, if not a major source, of childhood and adult depression. It is believed that winter's feeble light rays, some 70% weaker in intensity and duration than summer sunlight, are responsible for the deep depression experienced by 5% of the population and for the less serious *winter blahs* familiar to some 30-40% of the population. This is significant because the pineal gland, "the light meter and conductor that orchestrates our body clocks, plays a vital role in every aspect of human function, regulating reproduction, growth, body temperature, blood pressure, motor activity, sleep, tumor growth, mood immune function, and even longevity. And, interestingly, the *activity of the pineal gland is governed by environmental light.*"

Dr. Thomas A. Wehr of National Institute for Mental Health believes that SAD has "a tremendous impact on children's ability to function in school. They start out the school year fairly strong, thinking they will enjoy it. In November, it starts to fall apart. They sleep 12 hours a day. They're not creative. They've lost the spark. Those with winter depression are slowed down." Miller, *Healthy School Handbook*, 212-213.

15 "Energy- and money-saving concerns have created classroom lighting conditions that foster the 'sunlight starvation syndrome.' The light distribution in our schools tends to be so deficient in most parts of the natural spectrum that we may just be fighting an uphill battle, attempting to teach students in 'the twilight zone.' It's time to acknowledge that light is a *cooperating teacher* in every classroom." Miller, *Healthy School Handbook*, 196-197.

16 Miller, 213.

17 Ubell as quoted by Miller, *Healthy School Handbook*, 213.

18 Wohlfart as quoted by Miller, *Healthy School Handbook*, 209.

19 Dozens of studies detail increased achievement when typical fluorescent tubes are replaced by full spectrum tubes or natural sunlight. See Miller, *Healthy School Handbook*, Chapter 10.

20 Miller, 213.

21 Jane M. Healy, Ph.D., *Failure to Connect: How Computers Affect Our Children's Minds* (New York: Touchstone, 1998).

22 We highly recommend Frank H. and Rudolf H. Mahnke, *Color and Light in Man-Made Environments* (New York: John Wiley & Sons, 1993).

23 Frank and Rudolf Mahnke are deeply committed to color and design based on hard science rather than on personal preferences and style, as color has specific physiological effects on humans that are universal rather than culture dependent.

NOTES TO MYSELF

Chapter 7: What to Do the First Day of School & Beyond

FIRST DAY OF SCHOOL AND THEREAFTER

CURRICULUM

- The bodybrain-compatible element of absence of threat and nurturing reflective thinking is taught as an important and on-going part of the curriculum. Such curriculum contains the following five areas:

  1) The Lifelong Guidelines, including the LIFESKILLS

INSTRUCTIONAL STRATEGIES

- Models the Lifelong Guidelines and LIFESKILLS as the basis for classroom leadership and management. Leads rather than controls; inspires rather than manipulates. Creates/maintains an atmosphere that is participatory rather than dictatorial.

- Uses Life Lingo and teachable moments daily to reinforce and extend student understanding and practice of the Lifelong Guidelines and LIFESKILLS.

- Systematically introduces the meaning and importance of each of the Lifelong Guidelines and selected LIFESKILLS through formal lessons (key points and inquiries) and the context of classroom life. The Lifelong Guidelines and selected LIFESKILLS are posted and readable from a distance.

- Bases "discipline" on helping students develop the personal and social skills and behaviors needed to successfully practice the Lifelong Guidelines/LIFESKILLS rather than on a system of externally imposed rewards and punishments.

HET Classroom Stages of Implementation **Stage**

FIRST DAY OF SCHOOL AND THEREAFTER

Making the learning environment bodybrain compatible —
First Day and Thereafter **1.2**

CURRICULUM

2) The power of emotions to enhance or impede learning and performance

- Formally introduces age-appropriate lessons about the power of emotion to drive attention and learning. The role of emotion is discussed daily in multiple ways, such as during reflective thinking questions, Town Hall meetings, and teacher feedback to individual students as well as during planned lessons.

- Provides consistency and emotional security for students:
  - Meets students at the door at the beginning and ending of every day (greeting and farewell).
  - Uses agendas every day to provide focus for learning, to enable students to direct their own learning, and to encourage learning time-management strategies.
  - Uses written procedures for all frequently occurring events/activities to provide consistency, continuity, and emotional security for students. Visuals include graphics as well as words.

- Provides a place and time in the classroom—an "Australia" to help students bring their emotions and behavior back under control.

- Frequently uses collaborative learning, as appropriate, to extend and deepen learning and to create a sense of community.

3) The important role of movement and daily aerobic exercise to enhance academic learning

- Models and teaches students about using movement and daily aerobic exercise to enhance learning.

- Uses movement to enhance learning. Provides daily movement sessions to energize, calm, and assist in understanding and remembering concepts, significant knowledge, and skills. Uses such resources as *Brain Gym* and teacher-designed movement activities that grow naturally from curriculum content.

- Includes movement and other bodily-kinesthetic action in direct instruction of key points as well as in follow-up activities and inquiries.

- Ensures that students get 35 minutes of aerobic exercise every day to kick start brain chemistry for optimum learning.

FIRST DAY OF SCHOOL AND THEREAFTER

CURRICULUM	INSTRUCTIONAL STRATEGIES
4) Personal and social skills for collaboration	• Models and formally teaches the personal and social skills needed to work collaboratively. • Organizes students into Learning Clubs. Teaches how and when to use various group processes, such as leading, supporting, listening, encouraging, sharing, and "3-before-me," and so forth. • Leads students in activities, including Town Hall Meeting and Acknowledgment Box, that are appropriate for each stage of group development— developing a sense of belonging, creating common ground, and taking action. The resulting sense of community serves as the basis for achieving high academic performance as well as enhancing personal and social growth. • Uses collaborative learning to achieve specific goals daily.
5) How to nurture and utilize reflective thinking	• Uses a calm voice, synchronizes his/her heart-brain coherence, and stays emotionally centered. • Provides a variety of processes and structures throughout the day that enhance students' reflective thinking, such as wait time, journal writing, reflecting on the daily agenda (beginning and end of the day), making choices that allow students to direct their learning, forecasting how to take on a learning task, reflecting on what one has learned academically, the process of collaborative work (before, during, and after and when asking about content, social, and personal outcomes), providing adequate time for students to complete assignments, and strategies to help students refocus. • Selects a professional and/or peer coach(es) who can/will support the implementation of the bodybrain-compatible element of absence of threat and nurturing reflective thinking. Establishes and maintains a schedule for meeting frequently. Prepares thoroughly for each meeting; schedules follow-up time to learn from each session.

MAKING THE MOST OF ANTICIPATION

The big day has arrived. You are ready and the students are full of anticipation. For sheer exuberance and excitement, nothing beats the first day of school. Kindergartners have been talking about school for months. Their mothers are full of anticipation and dread simultaneously. First graders "can't wait." Who is my teacher? What kind of person is she/he? Will my teacher like me? Will I like her? Will my classmates like me? Will I like them? Even upper grade students have geared up their curiosity about what it will be like this year. "Will any of my friends be in my class with me?" "What will my teacher be like?" "Will school be fun?" The excitement is contagious.

Capitalize on this openness of students. They are their most hopeful the first day of school and the most willing to join the teacher in creating an extraordinary year for themselves.

Leading Versus Managing the Classroom

For teachers, this is your most powerful moment. As any self-improvement, Dale-Carnegie kind of course will tell you, first impressions are powerful and lasting. And, as any substitute knows, we have 60 seconds in which to establish who we are and what we're about, that our classroom isn't about typical school with worksheets and boredom, anxiety and dread.

The first day of school is a social event of importance; treat it that way. Model what your parents taught you about being a host/hostess. Follow the same procedures you would if you were inviting yet-to-be-met guests to your home.

Few of us like to be managed; we'd rather be led by a leader who possesses both vision and common sense and who, above all, keeps our best interests at heart—collectively and individually. The *HET* approach to the issue of classroom management and discipline is to be proactive—to lead rather than control, to inspire rather than manipulate. Thus, the leadership you display on the first day must be your finest in the classroom for the entire year. Even before the first day of school, there are several leadership steps that will make your first moments together go smoothly.

The Invitation. First, send a written invitation to your students—a real note through the U.S. mail.[1] Welcome them, tell them how pleased you are that they will be coming to your classroom, that you look forward to spending the year with them. Tell them something about yourself and what you have planned for them. Give the date for your classroom's Back to School Night; ask that they invite their family.

The Greeting. Greet your students as you would greet guests coming to your house. Greet them at the door. Shake each one's hand. Exchange a word of welcome with them. Tell each one you're glad he/she came and that you're looking forward to the year. Let your work in preparing the room for them tell them that they are important to you. Point out the posted procedures[2] for arriving to class and help each student understand and follow them. As students pass by, give each a piece of puzzle that they will use to find their fellow Learning Club members.[3] Plan to greet students at the door each and every day.

Settling In. As you would at a sit-down dinner, invite them to find their name tag, where to put their personal belongings, what they can do to settle in and feel comfortable.[4] Preparation says that you care, you value their coming.

Introductions—Developing a Sense of Inclusion/Belonging. Once students have settled into their assigned seat, give them an inclusion activity with fellow members of their Learning Club to help them get to know each other.[5] At the dinner table, this is the equivalent of the host or hostess introducing each guest by providing a key piece of information about them and directing the conversation along those lines until comfort levels have been established and conversation takes on a life of its own.

ABSENCE OF THREAT AND NURTURING REFLECTIVE THINKING

The bodybrain-compatible element of absence of threat and nurturing reflective thinking should be taught as an important and on-going part of the curriculum. The first of the five areas is the Lifelong Guidelines, including the LIFESKILLS.

Even young students are capable of understanding basic concepts from brain research. For content, review Chapter 1 and the curriculum examples at the back of this chapter.

There are numerous ways to implement absence of threat and nurture reflective thinking. Key among these are: modeling the Lifelong Guidelines and LIFESKILLS; using Life Lingo; teaching the meaning and importance of each Lifelong Guideline and selected LIFESKILLS to represent Personal Best; using written procedures, daily agendas, and calm voice; and collaborative learning.

THE LIFELONG GUIDELINES AND LIFESKILLS

Implementation of the Lifelong Guidelines and LIFE-SKILLS must be the first thing on your agenda the first day of school and the highest priority thereafter. Use both planned curriculum and teachable moments that occur. These guidelines are the basis of your leadership of the classroom and the foundation for students' academic success.

Modeling

The single most powerful instructional strategy—regardless of what you are teaching—is modeling. And the statement that, "Do what I do" is always more powerful than "Do what I say." is not just folklore. One of the greatest discoveries in recent brain research, one Bob Sylwester compares to the discovery of DNA in biology, is the existence of mirror neurons—a handful of exceptionally large neurons adept at turning observation into copycat behavior. This observe-and-mimic capability vastly speeds up the learning process. Infants continually amaze us with such prowess. For example, the forbidden swear word delivered with just the same intonation and body language as the father in similar circumstances, the pushing the right buttons to turn on the TV, petting the cat nicely, locking the car doors, and on and on. Adult examples also abound: When you move your arm, you suddenly feel that that's exactly how your mother gestures, cutting a friend's hair in college after watching how it was done a couple of times, diapering a baby, etc.

Every complex behavior—reading, writing, teaching, figure skating, becoming a manager, driving a car, becoming a person—all are tasks whose learning is significantly speeded up or even made possible thanks to our mirror neurons.

Thus, consistent modeling of the values and beliefs of a lifelong learner and a contributing citizen—core goals of the *HET* model—are a must. But doing so is more easily said than done. Be prepared for some self-evaluation.

For example, when preparing to teach the Lifelong Guidelines and LIFESKILLS, reflect on your own conduct and be open to fine tuning anything less than perfect manners, attitudes, and conduct. Muster the courage to make appropriate changes. Model for your students how to make changes in long-standing patterns of behavior. Remember, modeling isn't about being perfect, it's about showing others how to be the best human being possible—imperfect perhaps, but always improving and always willing to make amends for mistakes.

To model is to commit to making one's outer and inner life—words and actions—congruent and consistent. Learn how to discuss with your students those times when you fall short. Modeling is not about being perfect but about continually improving.

Do As I Do. As teachers, we are some of the most powerful role models in the lives of our students. They study us carefully, whether they appear to or not. They watch to see if we offer up only "token" lessons about being a learner or productive citizen, or if we truly believe that such skills are important social and behavioral guidelines for *all* to follow—at home and elsewhere. Take time to visualize exactly the kind of person you want to be and what you want mirrored in your students' behaviors. Then, define and write down strategies that will achieve these personal goals. Remember, you're on stage and actions always speak louder than words.

Modeling of the Lifelong Guidelines/ LIFESKILLS is a daily priority.* What students see in their teacher is that the guidelines are not rules to be blindly followed in the classroom but rather they are guidelines for succeeding in life. Your high expectations of yourself and for your students create an environment in which students can internalize responsibility for their behavior. By the end of Stage 1.3, "discipline" programs that depend on external control and rewards should be eliminated. Teacher and students should be operating with the Lifelong Guidelines and LIFESKILLS as guidelines to behaviors that enable us to succeed in life, not as "rules" to be resisted. We strongly urge you to jump ahead to Chapters 8 and 9.

It should be noted, however, that full use of the Lifelong Guidelines/LIFESKILLS hinges on engaging content based in *being there* experiences. With that in mind, teachers should look forward to Stage 2 with relish. Stage 2 enhances all that you have strived for in Stage 1; conversely, continuance of Stage 1 instructional strategies makes Stage 2 possible.

Life Lingo

The second most powerful strategy for teaching skills and behaviors such as the Lifelong Guidelines and LIFESKILLS is to acknowledge their use as they occur, taking advantage of the teachable moment—when appropriate behaviors or skills are demonstrated and deserve comment or should be used and the consequences need to be discussed. These spontaneous moments occur naturally and can be more powerful than preplanned lessons. Life Lingo* provides your students an opportunity to understand what the behavior or skill looks like, sounds like, and feels like, and does

---

* Because Life Lingo and modeling are the two most powerful ways to teach the Lifelong Guidelines and LIFESKILLS, both strategies must be fully mastered, becoming second nature, automatic, a program wired into long-term memory.

not look, sound, or feel like, in varying situations. Such on-the-spot feedback helps build shared understanding of the Lifelong Guidelines and LIFESKILLS as a common language to discuss the behaviors that go with them. You'll be surprised how quickly your students, regardless of age, will make Life Lingo comments about the behavior of others . . . and you. Be prepared!

The Goal of Life Lingo. Misbehavior is a teaching opportunity. It's a symptom that students don't know enough of the appropriate behaviors and/or know too many of the wrong behaviors. By helping provide clear pictures of expected behaviors, Life Lingo is extremely effective for teaching students desirable behaviors and skills such as the Lifelong Guidelines and LIFESKILLS.

Additional pictures of what a behavior or skill does and doesn't look, sound, and feel like are essential, especially when that behavior or skill is conceptually rich and its application to real life is complex. Mastering the Lifelong Guidelines and LIFESKILLS is a lifelong pursuit. For example, the attributes of truthfulness are not only complex but often subtle; frequently, the difference between truthful and tactless depends on circumstance. Be patient.

Students need lots of opportunities for guided practice and heaps of patience by the teacher—the ability to apply many of the nuances come with experience and maturity. Learning to apply behaviors, attitudes, and/or skills, such as the Lifelong Guidelines and LIFESKILLS, is a lifetime endeavor, a work in progress. Have patience, knowing that social and self-awareness don't spring full blown but unfold over time. Continue the dialogue of Life Lingo on a daily basis so that it becomes part of the fabric of classroom life.

How to Use Life Lingo. Life Lingo is simple to use if you leave behind any habits of lavishing praise for behavior or overusing/misusing "I statements." For example, saying "I like the way [John] is using his time while he waits for . . . ." is a bondage statement that may control behavior for the moment but keeps the focus on pleasing the teacher rather than on students developing their own sense of what's right or wrong, appropriate or inappropriate. Life Lingo helps students develop responsibility for their behavior.

Life Lingo in Three Steps. The three steps of Life Lingo are short and to the point. For example:

- First, use the student's name. "Mike, . . ."

- Second, label the Lifelong Guideline/LIFESKILL that the student is using. "Mike, you were using the Lifelong Guideline of Active Listening. . ."

- Third, identify the action. "Mike, you were using the Lifelong Guideline of Active Listening when you faced the speaker, looked interested, and were able to tell in your own words what the speaker meant."

With these three steps, verbal feedback is quick and easy. The same steps should be used for short written acknowledgements—from the teacher and from other students. Written acknowledgements are important because they provide a long-lasting communication, a treasured note that can be referred to again and again. An easy device for capturing such written comments is the Acknowledgement Box (see below).

Avoid Value Judgments. Life Lingo is best without value judgment. As the Sergeant in the TV series *Dragnet* would say, "Just the facts, ma'am." The facts are *who*, *what* Lifelong Guideline or LIFESKILL was demonstrated, and *how* it was used. Such clear statements provide immediate feedback about use of the desired behaviors. Students see the Lifelong Guidelines and LIFESKILLS in action and make their own judgments about how useful they are. This independent analysis is critical to building character traits, values, and attitudes—and their related behaviors—that will last a lifetime.

Acknowledgements Box. Comments for the Acknowledgments Box can be written by both teacher* and students, signed or anonymous. They should be brief, nonjudgmental, and follow the three-step format described above: "I want to acknowledge Jack for using the Lifelong Guideline of No Put-Downs when he gave me useful feedback about grammar and spelling on my thank-you letter to the Governor." Whenever you have a spare moment during the day,

such as when getting ready to move on to a new activity, simply pull three or four acknowledgements from the box and read them aloud to the class. Students are always eager to hear positive things others have to say about them.

Remember, the purpose of giving and receiving acknowledgments** is to encourage your students to reflect on their behavior and build their own internal dialogue about it. They will soon begin to feel the acknowledgement inside because they themselves said so, not the teacher, not another student; the student's own perspective then becomes the motivator and guide of behavior. This decreases the power of peer pressure now and later.

Using Life Lingo to Correct Misbehavior. Life Lingo is a potent teaching tool to deal with misbehavior and it is easy to use. First ask "What happened here?" Then, "What Lifelong Guidelines and/or LIFESKILLS didn't you use?" Lastly, "What Lifelong Guidelines and/or LIFESKILLS could you have used to have prevented this situation?" Remember to remain neutral in tone. This is the teaching phase of correcting misbehavior. And always make sure students understand how their misbehavior affected that person and how it made that person feel. Strengthening students' awareness of how their behavior affects others is a critical step in helping them internalize the Lifelong Guidelines and LIFESKILLS.

There is no punishment or "getting even" phase when working with the Lifelong Guidelines and LIFESKILLS. But there are consequences—natural or logical results to an action. The consequences phase—which is vastly different than punishment—should always be in proportion to the gravity of the act and should be directed at "cleaning it up" and/or experiencing a consequence that helps the offender understand the damage he/she has caused.

Consequences should also be related to the situation in which the misbehavior took place and in proportion to the degree of physical or emotional harm that occurred. the consequences should be grave.

---

* Teachers should take care to ensure that no student is left out. Anonymous acknowledgements written by the teacher can ensure that all students receive an acknowledgement each week.

** Acknowledgements differ from compliments in subtle but powerful ways. Compliments arise from the speaker having applied his/her criteria for what's good or commendable. Acknowledgements are a way of applying generally accepted criteria for behavior, such as the Lifelong Guidelines and LIFESKILLS. The goal is to redirect students from relying on external standards to relying on internal ones.

For example, if serious misbehavior took place on the playground, the student should not be allowed to be on the playground with others for a specified period and/or to do so only under specified conditions. If the misbehavior was bad language or teasing another student in class, perhaps suspension of a classroom privilege would suffice. If the misbehavior was hitting and hurting someone, a Town Hall meeting is in order and serious consequences should be applied.

Don't overreact if the misbehavior was irritating but didn't cause injury or damage. Also, if the misbehavior occurs due to unclear expectations, such as lack of procedures that spell out the expected personal and social behaviors (see the instructional strategies for Stage 1.2, Volume One), point the finger back to yourself. Such misbehavior is hardly the student's fault and it's a teaching opportunity.

Before jumping to consequences, always discuss with the student the impact of his/her behavior on the other person(s). Make sure the student understands and has some emotional feel for what that person suffered. And, always ask the misbehaving student how he/she could "clean it up" or make amends with the wounded party and what consequences would help him/her to remember not to do such things again. Often students are harder on themselves than adults would be.

If such conversations between you and a student fail to curb the behavior, add an audience—the injured student plus whoever else was present; if necessary, add all of the members of his/her Learning Club or even the entire class. However, do so only after you have created a sense of community in the classroom—a community in which that student is fully a member. In our experience, the only students who continue to misbehave are those who feel no connection to others and therefore feel they have nothing to lose by misbehaving. Students want to belong, they want to matter, they want to be loved and respected. When they are included, when they belong, they value what their peers think.

Systematically Introduce Meaning and Importance of Each Lifelong Guideline

Teachers should never make assumptions about what understandings students bring to school. This is particularly true in the realm of the Lifelong Guidelines and LIFESKILLS. From America's diversity come multiple points of view and beliefs about what is appropriate behavior, about what makes for a sense of community. It is the job of the teacher to create a common set of understandings, the basis for a common culture in the classroom, a shared sense of community, which in turn becomes the foundation for high academic achievement.

Chapters 8 and 9 discuss the Lifelong Guidelines and LIFESKILLS and ways to begin systematically introducing the meaning and importance of each.

Teaching the Lifelong Guidelines. Although we adults might think of curriculum as the stuff of state standards and textbooks, for students, curriculum is what we ask them to do and how we ask them to do it. Where we might think curriculum hasn't begun until the textbooks have been passed out, students see curriculum in the way the bus driver treats them, how (or if) and principal greets them at the door of the school, and what the teacher says from the moment students see him/her.

Put your best foot forward. Make sure that the first things communicated to students are the most important things. They want to know that their teacher is someone they can like and respect, that their classmates will be their friends—the kind you keep for life—and that what they'll study is important and useful in the real world.

Our advice is to keep the textbooks and other traditional materials on the shelf during the first week of school. Focus full time on the curriculum content described for Stage 1 of the *HET Classroom Stages of Implementation.* Also see the schedule for the first day of school beginning on page 18 of this chapter

Basis for "Discipline"

Perhaps one of the most disconcerting implications of brain research is that conventional "discipline" programs—those that depend upon externally imposed rewards and punishments—are brain antagonistic. They are inconsistent with both brain research, as discussed in Part A of this book, and sociological research, as illustrated in Alfie Kohn's book, *Punished by Rewards: The Trouble with Gold Stars, Incentive Plans, A's, Praise, and Other Bribes.*

Such discipline programs are also inconsistent with the central goal of a democratic society—the development of a citizenry willing to commit to nurturing a society that works for all.

[Note: If your school requires schoolwide adherence to a particular disciplinary program and process that is brain antagonistic, make sure that you talk with your principal about how you intend to use the Lifelong Guidelines and LIFESKILLS in a brain-compatible way. Get his/her agreement about how you will proceed.]

THE POWER OF EMOTIONS TO ENHANCE OR IMPEDE LEARNING AND PERFORMANCE

Although the Prussian roots of our educational system have taught us that discipline and cerebral function define both the goals and the processes of public education, brain research tells us a different story (review Chapter 2). As we now know, emotion drives attention which drives learning, memory, and almost everything else. If we want students to learn and remember, we must learn how to create a learning environment which uses the power of emotion in positive and effective ways.

Teaching Students About Absence of Threat and Nurturing Reflective Thinking

Because the purpose of your being together is learning, tell your students that you want them to understand how their brain works. Make models,[6] introduce the role of emotion in learning and performing. Start the first day of school and teach an aspect of how our brains work each day for the first month; after that, use every teachable moment to reinforce what they've learned and to help them learn to apply it in practical ways.

How much you choose to teach students about how their brain learns depends on their age. It is our experience that students K-6 can grasp the concepts; it is the vocabulary that may need adjusting. And yet, don't underestimate them! Just as kindergartners love the sound of big words, such as the names of dinosaurs, they can pick up on many of the brain terms, cerebral cortex, molecules of emotion, limbic system, frontal lobes, and so forth.

The Role of Emotions in Learning and Performing. The content about the pivotal role of emotions in learning and performing is presented in Chapter 2; for examples of key points and inquiries for first and fourth grades, see Chapters 16 and 17.

In truth, we *cannot control* our emotions, nor the feelings they produce. Feelings are our bodybrain's way of letting us know what's going on inside.[7] But we **can control our responses to our feelings.** This is a critical distinction for students to understand and a critical choice to make every time an emotion comes up. Because we feel something doesn't mean we have to act on it. For example, everyone gets angry, even furious, from time to time but we can choose to **not act** on that anger. Likewise, everyone feels jealous from time to time but we don't have to attack or undermine the person we envy. Model having control over your responses and include it as a topic during class meetings and other appropriate forums.

Also discuss with students how their emotions filter their perceptions of what's going on around them. For example, the person with a negative outlook on life tends to see all the things that are wrong or not good enough while the person with a positive view sees what's good.

The Lifelong Guidelines and LIFESKILLS. Teaching **and using on a daily basis** the Lifelong Guidelines and LIFESKILLS is the heart of Stage 1 of implementation and is the ongoing foundation for all later stages of implementation. They provide a set of standards for behavior by students, staff, and parents. They set the expectations and tone for all interactions that occur every school day—adult-adult, student-adult, and student-student. Chapters 8 and 9 explain the Lifelong Guidelines and LIFESKILLS and how to teach them. We also highly recommend *Tools for Citizenship and Life: Using the HET Lifelong Guidelines and LIFESKILLS in Your Classroom* by Sue Pearson. With a separate chapter for each of the Guidelines and LIFESKILLS, it describes why and how to practice the guideline/skill, what it looks like in the real world, what it looks like in school, 500 inquiries (whole group and small group/individual), signs of success, suggested literature (by grade spans: primary, intermediate, and middle/high school), and sample family letters.

The Lifelong Guidelines and LIFESKILLS form the fabric of your classroom. They are always front and center, always a topic of the teachable moment when student behavior is particularly conducive to learning and citizenship as well as when it goes awry.

For the first day of school, introduce students to Life Lingo and the Acknowledgements Box.[8]

Daily Agendas

Once students have settled in and met the members of their Learning Club, introduce the daily agenda. Like written procedures, the daily agenda is a key element in your classroom leadership. Posted for all to see through the day, it continues to put forth your intentions for the day—what students will do and the key pieces that you will do. It is also an important means of teaching time management skills to students. As each task is completed, check it off your classroom agenda and have each student learn to check it off the agenda they copy down each morning upon entering the classroom.

Keep in mind that the agenda is not a time schedule. The only times written on it are for special events for which students can't be late, such as the bus for a study trip, class photo appointment, and so forth. The agenda is a mindmap of the important tasks of the day

from the students' point of view. It is not the same outline as for lesson planning.

Completion of a daily agenda is occasion for a mini-celebration and the LIFE-SKILL of Pride. The top agenda is appropriate for primary grades; the second, for intermediate.

Be sure to include on your first agenda the date for your classroom's Back to School Night. [Note: We strongly recommend that you hold your Back to School Night for your classroom during the first or second week of school—even if the rest of the school holds one later.]

Written Procedures

Procedures are not "rules" nor are they the directions for completing an assignment. Written procedures are a multi-purpose instructional strategy—a systematic and unambiguous way to describe for students the personal and social skills needed to be successful as a learner and team player during a specific activity. They are also a primary tool for extending your classroom leadership during times when students are working independently or in groups.

Use written procedures for all frequently occurring events/ activities to provide consistency, continuity, and emotional security for students. Include graphics as well as words; visuals help students, especially younger students and English learners, learn and remember the steps.

Before the first day of school, have the following written procedures ready to go. Others can be developed later with the participation of students.

- Morning entering the classroom
- Leaving at the end of the day
- Leaving and re-entering during the day for regular events, such as recess and special subjects, and for special events, such as schoolwide assemblies
- Lunch room procedures
- Learning Club
- Town Hall Meeting
- Quiet time

Procedures should be written and posted, either on a flip chart or in student binders where they can be readily accessed.

Think your procedures through carefully; involve students in developing them. Most importantly, be 100 percent consistent in having students adhere to them. These are guides for success—now and in the future—the stuff useful habits of mind are made of.

See examples on the next page.

THE ROLE OF MOVEMENT IN ENHANCING ACADEMIC LEARNING

Few among us consider ourselves movement specialists. We haven't mastered movement and exercise for ourselves much less our students. There are clear reasons in our minds why we chose not to become a P.E. specialist. Are we striking a familiar chord here? If so, rest assured that what we are talking about with movement here is a far cry from such discussions.

The motivation behind movement as a critical bodybrain-compatible element in the *HET* model is not movement for the sake of movement or exercise because it's good for you but rather because movement is critical to the functioning of the brain and therefore to learning for all age groups. And it's not just any movement, it is the kind of movement associated with using what is learned and also movement to reset students' emotional states to a level appropriate to the next activity. This can include the typical letting off steam as well as focusing the brain for learning, reenergizing for a shift to a new topic of learning, or simply relaxing and taking a break.

Movement and Emotion. Because emotion drives attention and all other aspects of learning, the emotional states of students are critical to your success as a teacher (and to your students' successes as learners). Thus, you must learn to teach students how to handle their emotional life so they can maximize their learning.

We all know there are times that we feel so keyed up we can't concentrate or so listless that we can't get going. It's the same for our students. There are times when we need to help them slow themselves down and times when we need to help them speed themselves up. Movement can do both.

When and how? Well, some of those times are predictable; others are serendipitous.

Planning for Movement. Because movement is so key to optimum functioning of the bodybrain learning partnership, it should

Good Morning!

1. Greet Mrs. Kay with a handshake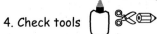

2. Hang up your coat, hat & pack

3. Put homework & notes in basket

4. Check tools

5. Greet learning club members

6. Work on Journal

Office Procedures

1. "Good morning."

2. "My name is _____. I am in _____'s class."

3. "I am here for _____."

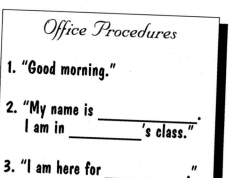

🌲 Quiet Place

1. One person

2. Sh-h-h-h

3. Turn timer

Group Work PROCEDURE

1. Cooperate

2. Soft voice

3. Take turns talking

4. See ③ before me

5. Share ideas

6. Do your personal best

7. Clean up

Examples appropriate for elementary school

Morning Procedure

1. Greet your Learning Club members with a smile.
2. Copy the agenda.
3. Work on any unfinished inquiries.
4. Select a LIFESKILL goal to work on today. List 2 actions 7o reach that goal.

End of the Day Procedure

1. Organize your materials, Learning Club's basket, books, & folder.

2. Clean up your area.

3. Copy Homework Assignment. Check for understanding with a partner.

4. Say, "Good-bye," or, "See you tomorrow," to the teacher and your Learning Club members.

Intrapersonal Procedure

1. Work alone.

2. Work silently.

3. Quietly ask the teacher or a partner for help if you don't understand something.

4. Check your finished work for evidence that it is an example of "PERSONAL BEST."

Examples appropriate for middle school to adult

be planned for as carefully as for the 3 Rs. Plan carefully for the predictable moments and be prepared for the unpredictable moments.

Predictable Moments. The predictable moments when movement is helpful include coming back to the classroom after recesses, lunch, and schoolwide events; changing activities, especially from a high-energy task to a low-energy one or vice versa; or in the middle of a long task such as test-taking or working on a challenging inquiry. Movement facilitates smooth transitions and a flow from one activity to the next.

For such predictable moments, develop movement activities that grow out of subject content.

Unpredictable Moments. When unpredictable moments may occur can be a surprise but that they will occur is virtually guaranteed. So, develop a handful of movement routines that you can do at a moment's notice. For example, if you see glazed eyes that signal little learning is taking place, shift gears and energize with simple stretches, deep breathing, or Brain Gym movements. Such activities may have nothing to do with the content of the theme but they will get the job done.

Resources. Good resources for these activities include:

- *Hands on: How to Use Brain Gym in the Classroom* by Isabel Cohen and Marcell Goldsmith

- *Freeze Frame: One Minute Stress Management* by Doc Childre.

- *Let's Get Moving: Movement in the Classroom* by Diane Berry (95-minute video and booklet)

- *Minds in Motion: A Kinesthetic Approach to Teaching Elementary Curriculum* by Susan Griss

- *Learning on Their Feet: A Sourcebook for Kinesthetic Learning Across the Curriculum, K-8* by Carol Glynn

Things to Avoid. Resist the urge to stifle movement, even irritating and distracting movement. Instead, redirect it. Highly bodily-

kinesthetic students simply can't keep still and even if they could it would shut down their most powerful intelligence for learning. Redirect, redirect, redirect. For example, for those who can't keep their hands still or to themselves, give them a spongy, squishy ball to manipulate; the procedure is that they can handle it any time they want or feel they need to, as long as they don't bother others.

For students who constantly pop up and walk around, seat them in the back of the room and allow them to move around whenever they feel they need to, as long as they don't bother others.

What you're dealing with in these instances is not short-term behavior problems but students who need to develop lifelong strategies for handling themselves in appropriate ways—ways that enhance their ability to learn and to be considerate of other's needs.

PERSONAL AND SOCIAL SKILLS FOR COLLABORATION

The personal and social skills for collaboration are the skills that make our lives work. They are the basis for making and keeping friends, getting along with co-workers, and, most importantly, maintaining a loving and healthy family. They are also the interpersonal skills that widen and deepen our resources for learning throughout our lives. Knowing this, don't lose patience and give up on what might at first seem like a waste of time.

Furthermore, the power of collaborative learning—academically as well as socially and personally—is perhaps the most well documented and compelling area of educational practice. The difference in the quality and depth of learning that occurs once a sense of community or class family has been achieved is phenomenal—believable only when you've experienced it. Be patient. Keep at it.

Model the Personal and Social Skills Needed to Work Collaboratively

Because our popular media so enshrines competition and the necessity of being #1, many students not only have few personal and social skills to collaborate, they don't value collaboration. It's for dweebs, not successful folk.

Nor is the field of education noteworthy for a collaborative tradition. "Go to your room, shut the door, and do whatever you want to do" is the time-worn approach to teaching.

Against such a backdrop, consistent modeling is essential. Students must be able to see, hear, and feel collaboration and its power to enhance not only academic learning and performance but joy and satisfaction in one's personal life.

Modeling in the Classroom. To model collaboration, teachers must shift their role from sage on the stage to guide on the side, from autocratic disciplinarian to a leader who invites students into helping design the learning environment. Teachers must also model their citizenship skills in the way they work with colleagues to improve the school's program and environment.

Resources. The most important personal and social skills for collaboration are included in the Lifelong Guidelines and LIFESKILLS. Useful resources for modeling collaborative skills are:

- Chapters 8 and 9

- Curriculum and instructional strategies for collaboration discussed in detail in Chapters 1-5 as one of the nine bodybrain-compatible elements of the *HET* model

- *Tools for Citizenship and Life: Using the Lifelong Guidelines & LIFESKILLS in the Classroom* by Sue Pearson

Teach the Personal and Social Skills Needed to Work Collaboratively

Given the diversity in student backgrounds, no teacher can assume that students come with the personal and social skills needed to work collaboratively. Plan to start from scratch and teach every element through each of the stages of group development. Furthermore, don't assume that the adults at your school—teachers, classified staff, and parents—possess a common view of what these skills are and how to practice them. We strongly recommend that you:

- Begin with teaching the Lifelong Guidelines/LIFE-SKILLS and build a comprehensive and uniform understanding, among adults and students, of what each of those behaviors looks, sounds, and feels like (and does not look, sound, or feel like).

- Understand that written procedures are part of a larger picture, not just a short cut to better behavior in the short run.

Resources. Resources for teaching students the personal and social skills needed for powerful collaboration include:

- *Designing Groupwork: Strategies for the Heterogeneous Classroom* by Elizabeth Cohen

- *Cooperative Learning, All Grades* by Spencer Kagan and Kagan's *Smart Cards: Cooperative Learning* which summarizes 56 cooperative structures.

Organize Students into Learning Clubs

Every group of students brings to collaborating their own unique blend of personal and social skills, or lack of, and their own preferences for collaborative structures. Thus, while Learning Clubs of four students may be ideal, you may need to begin with pairs and work your way methodically and carefully to your desired number. As you proceed, remember that the goal of collaboration is singular: To create a sense of community that enhances each student's academic achievement. In the process, you will also enhance social and personal growth.

Resources. Resources include those cited above for collaboration plus how to structure a Town Hall Meeting (see pages 9. 7-9).

Living Citizenship

Citizenship is not learned by true-false or multiple choice questions. It must be learned by doing. Ongoing Town Hall Meetings are a critical part of that experience in the *HET* classroom. See Chapter 9, Getting Started with the Lifelong Guidelines and LIFESKILLS.

Lead Students in Activities Appropriate for Each Stage of Group Development

Group development and a sense of community don't happen by accident, nor are they simply a product of time. They must be worked on daily. Luckily, there is a blueprint. Most experts in group development recognize at least three stages, each with its predictable behaviors and process needs. See pages 9.2-6 for an *HET* model version of these three stages.

As you proceed, keep in mind the three levels of community-building. Make sure the strategies you select don't require a greater sense of community than the stage your students are actually in at the moment.

The most common error is selecting an activity that requires coming to a decision or vote—handling the pressures of persuasion, the influence of higher social status, and the desire to control—before students have developed the trust and leadership-followership skills to handle such processes. The second biggest error is not letting students truly engage in meaningful group projects once they have developed the skills to do so.

Analyze your favorite collaborative strategies according to the stage of community building you are working on.

Creating a Sense of Belonging—Activities that help build a sense of inclusion ask participants to do a task together, such as mill to music, share a favorite hobby, what they like most in a friend, or create a visual using a T-shirt outline that shares something about where they were born, their family members, etc.—all for the purpose of getting to know others and letting others get to know you.

Daily use of the Lifelong Guidelines and LIFESKILLS is essential for creating an environment that welcomes everyone to become a part of the group and ensures that each person feels they belong.

Acceptance of who we are and of differences is an essential condition during these activities. Inclusion activities must be safe interactions with no potential criticism of performance or test of status in the group.

Inclusion activities should **not** ask individuals to share something they might consider personal or private, such as the origin of their name, where their ancestors came from, what jobs their parents hold, whether they live in a house or an apartment, and so forth.

These activities also do **not** ask that a product be created that can be judged or evaluated, such as a group project made by a study group. Nor do these activities ask members to vote on or agree to something, a process that requires some boundary bumping and use of persuasion and personal influence that comes from social status in the group—all part of the next stage in developing community, creating common ground.

Brainstorming activities protected by the DOVE rule which prohibits judging the ideas offered are good ways to meld curriculum content with this stage of group building. [DOVE stands for **D**efer judgment, **O**pt for the original and offbeat, **V**ast numbers of ideas are better than only a few, and **E**xpand and piggyback on ideas.]

List your favorite activities for creating a sense of belonging for ready reference.

Creating Common Ground—Creating a sense of common ground is essential for effective work as a citizen. Activities that create common ground must elicit an appreciation for members' strengths and capabilities and engender mutual respect so that the exercise of creating common ground is not a competition but a give-and-take interaction, through which students learn to handle and temper the pressures of persuasion (facile verbal skills), the influence that comes from higher social status, and desire to control. In this stage, students learn how to transition from leader to follower, follower to leader smoothly as appropriate to the task at hand and in response to the ever-changing roles among the group (assigned or self-assigned) rather than to ego or power. At its core, this stage of group development means that you listen respectfully when I speak and I listen respectfully when you talk, with the intent of understanding each other. We see value in each other and are willing to work cooperatively with each other.

Activities to develop this stage require high levels of trust among team members; clearly, a strong sense of inclusion must be built before embarking on the task of creating common ground.

This is the stage when students learn to trust in the power of the group and let go of the need to control while at the same time learning how to be a leader in a democratic setting—using persuasion, influence, and power in a positive way for the benefit of the group rather than to be self-serving. And, conversely, become willing to allow others to lead.

Activities for this stage include building a group project, making decisions about what group project to undertake and how to proceed, solving problems facing the class or a Learning Club, and so forth. In the early stages, tasks should be teacher-generated and involve emotionally-neutral tasks, gradually evolving into .

This stage can take quite a while, depending upon the personal and social skills of students.

List your favorite activities for creating common ground for ready reference.

Taking Action—Taking action to improve the well-being of the community as a whole and the individuals within it requires **and further develops** group cohesion and a deep sense of respect, trust, and affection in the group. With the goal of growing responsible citizens, the activities chosen for this stage should be genuine tasks worthy of citizen activity. Celebrations of Learning and Social/Political Action Projects are ideal. Start with small but meaningful projects, which will likely be largely teacher directed, and then let students' commitment to building a better world for themselves and others take over the planning and execution of activities.

List your favorite activities for preparing students to take action for ready reference.

HOW TO NURTURE AND UTILIZE REFLECTIVE THINKING

Reflective thinking is the basis for many skills, personal and academic. Personally, it enables us to check our anger, think before we burst out with a comment we'll later regret, put ourselves in other people's shoes, etc. Academically it allows us to guide ourselves through alternative approaches to solving a problem, explore how we might need a skill or concept in the future, imagine how things might fit together, plan alternative courses of action, etc.

Calm Voice

A voice of calm is the voice of someone who picks his/her words carefully. Repetition of directions and expectations soon begins to reflect impatience. Daily agendas and written procedures do much to allow teachers to speak calmly because there is no need to repeat directions or scold when students don't comply with the teacher's expectations. Save your voice and your students' willingness to listen for the important things.

Processes and Structures

There are many ways to help students develop reflective thinking as a habit of mind. For example, wait time, journal writing, reflecting on the daily agenda (beginning and end of the day), making choices that allow students to direct their learning, forecasting how to take on a learning task, reflecting on what one learned academically, the process of collaborative work (before, during, and after and asking about content, social, and personal outcomes), providing adequate time for students to complete assignments, and strategies to help students refocus.

Nurturing reflective thinking should be a daily, even hourly, endeavor.

SCHEDULE AND LESSON PLAN FOR THE FIRST DAY OF SCHOOL

As any parent, or author, knows, it's risky to offer advice; it unerringly finds its way to that person's stubborn streak, however small and well hidden that streak might be. So, with apologies in advance, we offer some great ideas from a gifted teacher and associate of Susan Kovalik & Associates, Sue Pearson. Pick and choose as you like but our best advice is to make a trusting leap and try Sue's recommendations. Do everything. By Christmas, you'll find yourself weeks ahead of where you usually are.

The first daily schedule and lesson plan is for primary grades, the second for intermediate grades.

IDEAS FOR MY LESSON PLANNING

IDEAS FOR MY LESSON PLANNING

PRIMARY GRADES—SCHEDULE* FOR THE FIRST DAY OF SCHOOL

8:30	ARRIVAL
8:45	STANDARD TASKS
9:00	INTRODUCTIONS/INCLUSION
9:15	DAILY AGENDA
9:30	MOVEMENT/SNACK/BATHROOM
9:45	KEY POINTS & INQUIRIES ABOUT COMMUNITY
11:00	MOVEMENT/MUSIC
11:15	DIRECT INSTRUCTION/INQUIRIES
11:50	LUNCH ROOM PROCEDURES
12:00	LUNCH
12:30	STORY/REST TIME
1:15	DIRECT INSTRUCTION/INQUIRIES
1:45	MOVEMENT
2:00	NURTURING REFLECTIVE THINKING
2:15	REVIEW COMMUNITY, BRAIN MODEL, BRAIN SONG
2:30	LEARNING CLUB CLOSURE
2:45	LEAVING PROCEDURES/DISMISSAL

* Please note that these time frames are VERY tentative; their purpose is for lesson planning. Be flexible. Alter time as needed to complete the project at hand.

PRIMARY GRADES—LESSON PLAN FOR THE FIRST DAY OF SCHOOL

➤ Note to Teacher: Your goal is quality of experience, not quantity of information; be sure to provide adequate time for each inclusion activity and key point. These key points need extensive development using literature, discussion, reflection, journaling, and real-life experiences.

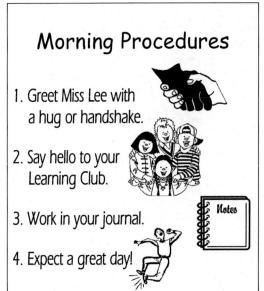

Morning Procedures

1. Greet Miss Lee with a hug or handshake.

2. Say hello to your Learning Club.

3. Work in your journal.

4. Expect a great day!

8:30   ARRIVAL: Await students at the classroom door; welcome them with a handshake, "high five," or a hug. Give each student a "puzzle piece" (see Puzzle Inclusion Activity on page 7.28-7.29). Make sure each student reads and follows the "Morning Procedures."

8:45   STANDARD SCHOOL TASKS: Allow time for opening ceremonies (pledge of allegiance, songs, and so forth) and for standard school procedures such as taking attendance and lunch count, collecting notes, and performing any other tasks required by your school district.

9:00   INTRODUCTIONS: Introduce yourself. Share some hobbies, interests, and family information. Introduce "Mike's On" procedures. Then, within each Learning Club, have each student introduce him/herself to members of the Learning Club using the Mike's On procedures : "My name is _____ and I like to _____."

➤ This symbol indicates a note to the teacher.

➤ Note to Teacher: Walk around the room offering support for the shyer students and to ensure that no one student in a group monopolizes the time. Allow students a few minutes to exchange information.

9:15   DAILY AGENDA: Tell the students that an agenda—the plan for the day—will be posted every morning on the board (overhead, flannel board, white board) and that it is their responsibility to copy it in their spiral notebook.

"Mike's" On Procedure

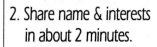

1. One person holds the "mike" & shares.

2. Share name & interests in about 2 minutes.

3. Others use Active Listening.

4. Pass the microphone to another.

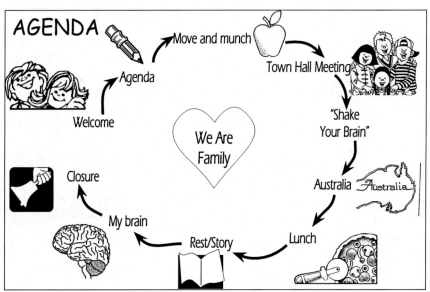

AGENDA

Welcome → Agenda → Move and munch → Town Hall Meeting → "Shake Your Brain" → Australia → Lunch → Rest/Story → My brain → Closure

We Are Family

Snack Time Procedure

1. Clear off desk or table.
2. Get your snack.
3. Join your group.
4. Eat quietly.
5. Clean up when done.

Explain that the agenda is a time management and organizational tool that will be used every day. and that both students and teacher will benefit from its use. Explain every part of the agenda, why it will be used every day, and that any items not completed will be assigned as homework or done the next day. Invite students to predict the written words by observing the accompanying graphics. Allow them sufficient time to copy the agenda, words, and graphics. As the day unfolds, check off each item on the agenda as it is completed. Have the students do the same on their own agendas.

9:30 MOVEMENT/SNACK/QUIET TIME/RESTROOM

You may wish to introduce the following movement activities from *Brain Gym* by Paul E. and Gail E. Dennison: Lazy 8s, Thinking Cap, and Hook-ups. Also see *Hands on: How to Use Brain Gym in the Classroom* by Isabel Cohen and Marcell Goldstein.

Quiet Time Procedure

1. Find your personal space. Stay there during quiet time.

2. Listen to music. No talking.

3. Read a book, write, or draw.

Restroom Procedure

1. Quietly signal the teacher.

2. One at a time.

3. Wash hands.

4. Come right back.

To evaluate snacks, use the "three-before-sugar rule." Permit students to bring only those items whose top three ingredients are not sugar or another form of sweetener.

Play soft instrumental music, approximately 50-60 beats per minute. Ask students to use only their 12–inch voice (loud enough to be heard no more than 12" away) while talking with each other.

9:45 KEY POINTS & INQUIRIES ABOUT COMMUNITY

Conceptual Key Point—

A spirit of community doesn't just happen in a neighborhood or classroom because people live or work in the same area. Each member—young and old—must take responsibility for creating and enhancing a sense of community throughout each day, month, and year. Creating a sense of community is a three-step process:

- Developing a sense of inclusion or belonging
- Creating common ground, and
- Taking action

Our beginning point for step 1, developing a sense of inclusion, is using the Lifelong Guidelines and LIFESKILLS:

- TRUSTWORTHINESS
- TRUTHFULNESS
- ACTIVE LISTENING
- NO PUT-DOWNS
- PERSONAL BEST/LIFESKILLS

Inquiry for Direct Instruction—

Think about your best friend; recall three things that you like best about him/her. Share those qualities with the class. Discuss with your Learning Club what your best friend has taught you about the Lifelong Guidelines. Share with your Learning Club which Lifelong Guideline you most appreciate your best friend using when you're together.

Record student responses on the board and group their responses as best you can. Then have students compare the list they generated to the Lifelong Guidelines.

Inquiry for Whole Class Discussion—

Identify the three most common qualities your Learning Club values in best friends. Have the recorder for your Learning Club read these to the rest of the class.

Skill Key Point—

Present the procedures for the community circle. They should replicate some of these examples:

TOWN HALL MEETING Procedures

1. Come to the meeting area when your Learning Club is called.

2. Find a place on the rug (oval, line, etc.) to sit. Sit where you can see everyone and everyone can see you.

3. Sit comfortably in your own personal space.

4. Remember to use the Lifelong Guidelines throughout Town Hall Meeting time.

5. When you hear the chimes, it's time to use Active Listening.

➤A simplified version of these procedures for primary grades can be sung to the tune of "Supercalifragilisticexpialidocious." Those words are: "Push in chair, walk quietly, and sit in listening shape. Come and make a circle at our favorite gathering place." Then repeat.

Introduce the chimes as a reminder to "actively listen." Ask the students to name the tool and parts (chimes, mallet) and to observe how the hammer is used to gently strike the metal rods. Ask them to identify the number of tones the chimes can make (one per metal rod/cylinder). Instruct them to show active listening (you/me, ears, eyes, heart, and undivided attention) when they hear the chimes. From here on, use the chimes as one of the strategies to call for active listening from the students.

Conceptual Key Point—

In a community, people come together to create a safe place to live and work. In order for our class community to be safe for everyone, there are certain guidelines that community members must be willing to follow. When problems occur, people talk together to solve them in peaceful and fair ways.

➤Topics for Whole Class Discussion—

• What guidelines would make our community a safe place to learn? Hint: Think about what we learned about our best friends.

• Discuss student answers to the above question and the Lifelong Guidelines as acceptable behaviors for our classroom community. Get agreement which Lifelong Guidelines and LIFESKILLS the students want to begin with.

• Recite Lifelong Guideline Pledge:*

"I am Trustworthy, Truthful, and an Active Listener, too.
I will do my Personal Best and give No Put-Downs to you!"

Significant Knowledge Key Point—

Our brains will help us learn many new things this year. When our brains feel safe and are protected from danger, they learn and remember more information. We, as a community, can all help each other's brains by practicing certain safety rules and learning ways to solve our problems. In our classroom, we will all work hard to build a community based on using the Lifelong Guidelines and the LIFESKILLS. The Lifelong Guidelines are the behaviors we will use with each other so that we can be successful in school and life.

➤Tips for Direct Instruction About the Lifelong Guidelines-

• Lead a general discussion on each Lifelong Guideline. Record what students think each guideline means on a classroom wall where everyone can see and refer to them.

---

* This pledge is just an example. We recommend you involve your students in developing your own once students have a full understanding of the Lifelong Guidelines.

- Teach a sign for "Active Listening" that can be used immediately, such as American Sign Language or hand in the air with fingers spread apart to represent the five elements of active listening—you, eyes, ears, heart, and undivided attention.

- Provide examples of working together, such as "Community Jobs." Introduce these community jobs; use real-world terms when possible, e.g., horticulturist (plant care-taker), messenger (delivers materials to the office), personal trainer (in charge of recess equipment). Brainstorm the performance standards for each of these jobs. Choose volunteers to demonstrate/pantomime the task being done incorrectly and then correctly. Invite the students to describe one more job that they feel is needed in the classroom.

Inquiries for Choice — For Learning Clubs or Individuals

1. Illustrate at least five people other than your family (or for young students, within the family) upon whom you depend for food, safety, and services each week. Describe to your Learning Club what at least two of these people do for you and why that's important. Identify one person the group has in common and be ready to share your information with the class.

2. Identify at least five community services that you and your family depend on to stay healthy and safe. Record your finding on the T-chart under the following headings: HEALTH, SAFETY, CONVENIENCE, FUN.

3. Write a story or draw a picture that shares a time when you cooperated with another person and it helped both of you. Share your product and explain what happened as a result of your cooperation.

4. Brainstorm with your Learning Club two or more ways you will work to build a community using the Lifelong Guidelines of Trustworthiness, Truthfulness, Active Listening, No Put-Downs, and Personal Best. Prepare your ideas for class sharing time.

5. In your journal, write about a time or draw a picture of a time you used one of the Lifelong Guidelines. Explain your choice to a partner.

11:00 MOVEMENT/MUSIC

Teach one of the brain songs (e.g., "Shake Your Brain" by Red Grammer on the CD *Teaching Peace* or one of those listed at the end of this lesson plan). Allow the students to create movements that demonstrate the meaning of the lyrics. Practice the song twice. Afterwards, provide reflection time asking questions such as: How did this song make you feel? Which motions will be the easiest for you to remember? What changes do you notice in your feelings? Does anyone know another brain song that the class could sing later in the week?

11:15 DIRECT INSTRUCTION

Significant Knowledge Key Point—

Our brains will help us learn many new things this year. When we feel safe, our brain learns and remembers more. As a community, we can all help each other feel safe by following certain agreements. Agreements to use the Lifelong Guidelines and the LIFESKILLS will help us get to know and respect one another so that we can be better learners.

Direct Instruction with these materials: A copy of *Franklin Goes to School* by Paulette Bourgeois or *Chrysanthemum* by Kevin Henkes plus chart paper and colored markers (blue, green, red, black).

Anticipatory Set: Ask questions such as: Did anyone feel a little nervous about coming to school today? What made you feel nervous? How did your body let you know it was nervous? What did you do to try to feel less worried? Were any of you excited? What feelings did you have? Share a personal story of your own first day at school. Explain that you have a story where the main character shares some of their same feelings.

Direct Instruction: Read aloud the book you chose. Ask the students to do a "thumbs up" when they have the same feelings that Franklin (or the character in your book) does. Use a "thumbs down" when they have different feelings. Obviously, there will be some story parts when there will be "thumbs up" and "thumbs down" simultaneously depending on each student's individual experiences and personal feelings. Ask questions that focus on feelings. For example, how did you feel on your first day of kindergarten? How did your family help you prepare for school? Do you still feel nervous or excited when school is starting? Why do you suppose you feel that way?

▶ Acknowledge that each of us can and does have different reactions to things and that our reactions change over time. By asking questions such as these, you also provide an opening for you to share your own childhood recollections of school as well as an opportunity to share your excitement as the teacher of this class! Participate in the discussion as well as supervise it. Let your students know who you are.

Inquiry —

Compare your feelings about the first day of school with Franklin from the story *Franklin Goes to School*. Tell your partner how your feelings and Franklin's are alike. Share how your feelings are different than Franklin's. Listen to your partner's feelings. Explain your feelings about school to your classmates when the teacher invites you to share.

Skill Key Point: Using a T-chart —

There are many kinds of T-charts. The common element is that they have two or more columns which allow us to compare or contrast information about a topic. Two T-charts we will use often are the KWL and LSF (see pages 10.14 and 9.15-9.16).

T-Chart of My Feelings Before School

LOOKS LIKE	SOUNDS LIKE	FEELS LIKE
smiling	"I can't wait to go!"	happy
crying	"I'm scared!"	nervous
laughing	"It will be fun."	good
unhappy face	"I don't want to go!"	scared

Review some of the answers offered by the students. Emphasize the variety of feelings that were shared. Suggest that the class revisit the chart in one week for another check on feelings and any changes that may occur.

11:50 LUNCH PROCEDURE

12:00 LUNCH/RECESS

12:30 REST TIME/ STORY TIME

Go To Lunch Procedure

1. Clean work area.

2. Get your coat & lunch.

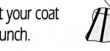

3. Line up at the door and stand quietly.

4. Proceed to cafeteria.

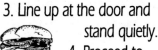

Rest Time Procedure

1. Find your quiet space and stay there during rest time.

2. May listen to music. No talking.

3. If you don't feel sleepy, take a book or toy with you and play quietly.

Younger students may require a short rest time after lunch for the first few days until they are back into the routine of school. This is an excellent time to play some quiet, classical music with 40-60 beats per minute which helps to regulate the heartbeat after strenuous activity.

12:45 DIRECT INSTRUCTION

Significant Knowledge Key Point (continued) —

Our brains will help us learn many new things this year. When we feel safe, our brains learn and remember more. As a kind of community, we can all help each other feel safe by following certain agreements. By agreeing to use the Lifelong Guidelines and the LIFESKILLS, we will get to know and respect one another so that we can be better learners.

Story: *Alexander and the Terrible, Horrible, No-Good, Very Bad Day* by Judith Viorst

Predictable story: Invite students to repeat chorus whenever it appears: "It was a terrible, horrible, no-good, very bad day."

Judith Viorst's story centers on a young boy, Alexander, for whom everything is going wrong. His response? "I'm going to Australia!" Use Alexander's experiences as an introduction for your class's own personal "Australia," a small corner of the room where the students can visit to relax, refocus and reflect. Lead the students to this special area.

The following items are suggested for Australia

- Some type of chair (rocking, Adirondack, stuffed, bean bag, large pillows)

- Procedures for visiting Australia

- Small table covered with cloth

- Lamp

- Quiet timer such as an executive-style oil drip timer (up to about 10 minutes)

- Headset with classical music tapes in basket ~ optional

- Stress relief "squeeze ball"

- Small class photo or inspirational quotation in a frame. Invite students to visit "Australia," a "safe" place for the brain to reflect and the heart to heal. A comfortable place in the classroom with a rocking chair, Adirondack lawn chair, bean bag, pillows, or cushions. Teaching strategy: Tell each student to write his/her name on a small piece of paper. Pull names out, one at a time, for visits to Australia on this first day, thereby preventing a rush to Australia.

Demonstrate the use of any special items (e.g., timer, headset). Write procedures for using Australia with the students. Choose two or more students to demonstrate the procedures.

Inquiry —

Draw a picture of a "safe place" you go to when you are feeling sad, mad, angry, or stressed. Share this special place with your teacher. Add it to your "My Special Place" Book. ("My Special Place Book" can be as simple as a binder with plastic sleeves. Slip each drawing into one of the sleeves and add a title page.)

"Australia" Procedure

1. Wait your turn. One person at a time.

2. Start the timer (only 10 minutes).

3. Sit; relax; listen to quiet music; slow your breathing.

3. Put items back in their place.

4. Return to your seat when time is up.

1:15   MOVEMENT

The activities from *Brain Gym* can be repeated with simple aerobics added.

1:45   DISCOVERY INQUIRIES

Conceptual Key Point –

Learning is the result of a partnership between our brain and our body. Our brain talks to our body and our body talks to our brain. The number one topic of conversation is our emotions. How we feel affects how we learn.

Significant Knowledge Key Point —

The heart and brain tend to match each other. If your heart is racing, you brain is also in a high state of emotional override. If your heart slows, your brain calms down and more fully engages the thinking part of the brain.

Inquiry —

Have students discuss with a partner:

— What emotions are you feeling now?

— Can you feel your heart beating? How many times per minute is it beating? (Have students count for 15 seconds and then multiply by four.)

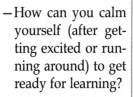

— How fast is your brain working?

— How can you calm yourself (after getting excited or running around) to get ready for learning?

— Share your findings with your Learning Club.

➤ Today is but an introduction to these ideas. Continue studying about the impact of emotions for 15 minutes a day over the next two weeks and into the school year.

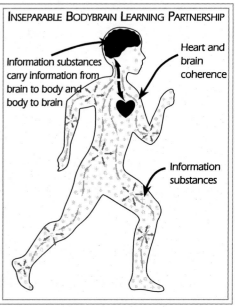

INSEPARABLE BODYBRAIN LEARNING PARTNERSHIP

Information substances carry information from brain to body and body to brain

Heart and brain coherence

Information substances

2:00   REFLECTIVE THINKING: Quiet Time with Music

➤ Many students need time alone to think while their brains begin to integrate new information. Build this into each day. Suggest that your students reflect on their experiences today.

Inquiry —

Take time to calm your heart and brain. When your heart and brain are both calm, think about your day. Discuss the following questions with your Learning Club, then have your recorder share two of the most memorable things with the class.

• What have you learned today that you want to share with your family?

• What would you like to remember forever?

2:15 REVIEW KEY POINTS OF THE DAY

Guide a review of "What makes a community?" and "How brains work best when people feel safe and why." Sing the song "Shake Your Brain." Invite two or more students to model the movement/motions for the rest of the class.

2:30 CLOSURE: Learning Club

Review the sign(s) for "Active Listening." Teach the students to use the "Mike's On" procedure (a defunct microphone or look-alike item should be a standard item in each Learning Club basket of materials). Start with one student in each group (wearing the most red, blue, green, etc.) who will share. Question: What one word describes how you feel right now? Proceed around the group until each student has shared (right to pass is always an option).

2:45 LEAVING PROCEDURES

➤Introduce "end-of-the-day procedures" for the students to complete before leaving the classroom.

2:55 DISMISSAL

➤Be present at the door to share a "good-bye" handshake, hug, or "high five" with each student as he/she leaves.

End of Day Procedure

1. Clean your area.

2. Help others straighten up.

3. Put items in your pack.

4. Say goodbye to others.

5. Share 1 thing you learned.

INTERMEDIATE GRADES—SCHEDULE* FOR THE FIRST DAY OF SCHOOL

8:30	ARRIVAL
8:45	STANDARD SCHOOL TASKS
9:00	INTRODUCTIONS
9:15	DAILY AGENDA
9:30	INCLUSION ACTIVITY
10:00	DISCOVERY INQUIRIES
10:20	REFLECTIVE THINKING
10:30	MOVEMENT/SNACK/RESTROOM
10:45	CONCEPTUAL KEY POINT
11:00	WHOLE CLASS INQUIRY
11:15	MOVEMENT/MUSIC
11:30	TOWN HALL MEETING
12:00	LUNCH PROCEDURES/LUNCH
12:45	REVIEW MORNING
1:00	INQUIRY
1:45	RECESS
2:00	KEY POINT/INQUIRY
2:45	SIGNIFICANT KNOWLEDGE KEY POINT
3:15	PLEDGE/LEARNING CLUB CLOSURE
3:30	DISMISSAL

* Please note that these time frames are VERY tentative; their purpose is for lesson planning. Be flexible. Alter time as needed to complete the project at hand.

INTERMEDIATE GRADES—LESSON PLAN FOR THE FIRST DAY OF SCHOOL

▶ Note to Teacher: Your goal is quality of experience, not quantity of information; be sure to provide adequate time for each inclusion activity and key point. These key points need extensive development using literature, discussion, reflection, journaling, and real-life experiences.

8:30 ARRIVAL: Await students at the classroom door; welcome them with a handshake, "high five," or a hug. Give each student a "puzzle piece" (see My Piece of the Puzzle directions that follow). Make sure each student reads and follows the "Morning Procedures." Tell them to look for procedures every morning.

8:45 STANDARD SCHOOL TASKS: Allow time for opening ceremonies (Pledge of Allegiance, songs, and so forth) and for standard school procedures such as taking attendance and lunch count, collecting notes, and performing any other tasks required by your school district.

9:00 INTRODUCTIONS: Introduce yourself. Share some hobbies, interests, and family information. Introduce "Mike's On" procedures. Then, within each Learning Club, have each student <u>introduce</u> him/herself to members of the Learning Club using the

▶ This symbol indicates a note to the teacher.

Morning Procedures

1. *Be Friendly*. Greet Mr. Smith with a handshake or hug.

2. *Be responsible*. Hang coat/sweater on the hook by your name.

3. *Be organized*. Remove school materials from your pack.

4. Place pack by your coat and take school materials with you.

5. Sit where you see your name.

6. *Be caring*. Greet 3 or more students with a big "Hello!"

7. *Be ready*. Copy the agenda.

Notes

Mike's On procedures : "My name is _____ and I like to _____."

▶ Note to Teacher: Walk around the room offering support for the shyer students and to ensure that no one student in a group monopolizes the time. Allow students a few minutes to exchange information.

9:15 DAILY AGENDA: Tell the students that an agenda—the plan for the day—will be posted every morning on the board (overhead, flannel board, white board) and that it is their responsibility to copy it in their spiral notebook.

Explain that the agenda is a time management and organizational tool that will be used every day. and that both students and

---

"Mike's On" Procedure

1. Take the mike from the basket.

2. Follow directions for who goes first. Only one at a time.

3. Pass the mike by handing to the next person.

4. Actively listen to the person holding the mike.

5. Last person to share returns the mike to the basket.

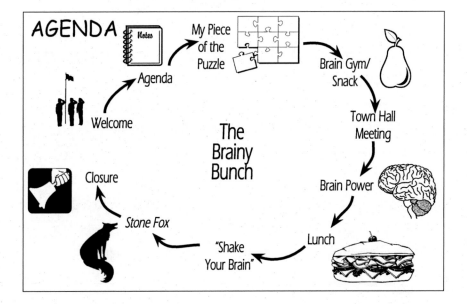

teacher will benefit from its use. Explain every part of the agenda, why it will be used every day, and that any items not completed will be assigned as homework or done the next day. Invite students to predict the written words by observing the accompanying graphics. Allow them sufficient time to copy the agenda, words, and graphics. As the day unfolds, check off each item on the agenda as it is completed. Have the students do the same on their own agendas.

9:30 **INCLUSION ACTIVITY:** "My Piece of the Puzzle"

➤Check to ensure that every student received a puzzle piece as he/she entered the room. Then, post the "My Piece of the Puzzle" Inquiry so all can easily see it.

➤*Directions for preparing "My Piece of the Puzzle"*—

"My Piece of the Puzzle" Inquiry

1. When the music starts, stand up, push in your chair, take your puzzle piece, and walk around the room.

2. Without talking, find puzzle pieces that fit with yours. When you find a match, stay with that person. Continue to find students with other pieces that fit with yours.

3. When you have all the pieces that fit together to make a rectangle, send a messenger to the teacher for a piece of oaktag paper.

4. Working together, paste all the pieces on the oaktag paper to make a completed jigsaw puzzle.

5. Choose a name for your Learning Club and print it with a dark marker at the top of your poster.

6. Hang the poster on our "Getting to Know You" bulletin board.

For each group, gather up one piece of 9"x 12" construction paper and one piece of 12"x 18" oaktag (make sure the paper and oaktag are of different colors), and one black marker.

1. Right before school begins, use your class list and divide the students into groups or what *HET* calls "Learning Clubs."

2. Determine how many students will sit together and where the location of the groups will be. (For example, five students in a group: Group 1 near the door, Group 2 by the teacher's desk, Group 3 next to the classroom library, Group 4 by the windows, and Group 5 near the overhead.)

3. Using one piece of construction paper start with the first group. Divide the paper into puzzle pieces, one for each student in the group. Using the marker, write one student's name on each piece. Make the patterns of the cut unique for each group.

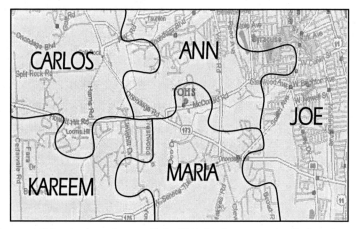

4. Repeat this pattern for each individual group until done.

5. Cut out the pieces.

6. Be ready to hand each student his/her own piece upon entering the classroom.

➤Give the students parameters for selecting a name for their Learning Club, such as a name that represents powerful learners or the power of the brain.

LEARNING CLUB:
THE BRAINY BUNCH

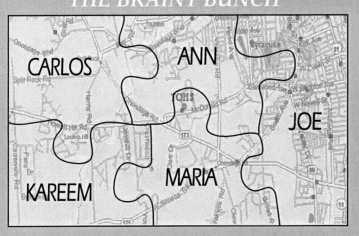

CARLOS
ANN
JOE
KAREEM
MARIA

Inquiry —

 After completing the puzzle, each Learning Club conducts a "Spotlight" interview of each of its members. Each student is asked two questions by each member of the group to learn more about his/her hobbies, interests, and family.

Reflective Thinking Inquiry —

As a Learning Club, reflect on this set of activities to build a sense of belonging. Ask questions such as: What did you like best about this activity and why? What was the most difficult part for you? The easiest part? What would you do differently next time to learn more about each other?

▶Tell the students that membership in the Learning Clubs will change often (about once a month) and will also start with inclusion activities that are fun. For example: a variety of codes, word searches, several clues on index cards to lead the students to find the other members of a new Learning Club. The purpose is to give them opportunities to get to know each other well and to practice using the LIFESKILL of Friendship — making and keeping friends.

10:00 DISCOVERY INQUIRIES

Conceptual Key Point —

 Learning is the result of a partnership between our brain and our body. Our brain talks to our body and our body talks to our brain. The number one topic of conversation is our emotions. How we feel affects how we learn.

Significant Knowledge Key Point —

 The heart and brain tend to match each other. If your heart is racing, your brain is also in high gear. If your heart slows, your brain calms down.

Inquiry —

 Have students discuss with a partner:

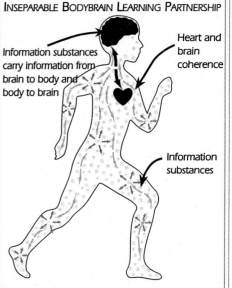

INSEPARABLE BODYBRAIN LEARNING PARTNERSHIP

Information substances carry information from brain to body and body to brain

Heart and brain coherence

Information substances

—What emotions are you feeling now?

—Can you feel your heart beating? How many times per minute is it beating? (Have students count for 15 seconds and then multiply by four.)

—How fast is your brain working?

—How can you calm yourself (after getting excited or running around) to get ready for learning?

—Share your findings with your Learning Club.

▶Today is but an introduction to these ideas. Continue studying about the impact on emotions for fifteen minutes a day over the next two weeks and revisit it throughout the school year.

10:20 REFLECTIVE THINKING: Quiet Time with Music

▶ Many students need time alone to think while their brains begin to integrate new information. Build this into each day. Suggest that your students reflect on their experiences today.

Inquiry —

Take time to calm your heart and brain. When your heart and brain are both calm, think about your day. Discuss the following questions with your Learning Club, then have your recorder share two of the most memorable things with the class.

- What have you learned today that you want to share with your family?

- What would you like to remember forever?

10:30 MOVEMENT/ SNACK/RESTROOM BREAK

Allow the students to create movements that demonstrate the meaning of the lyrics to at least two Lifelong Guideline/ LIFESKILLS songs (see back of book for songs by Jeff Pedersen and Judy Eacker.

Restroom Procedure

1. Quietly signal the teacher.
2. Wash hands.
3. Come right back.

▶ You may want to introduce the following movement activities from *Brain Gym* by Paul E. and Gail E. Dennison: Lazy 8s, Thinking Cap, and Hook-ups. Also see the book and video, *How to Make Learning a Moving Experience* by Jean Bladyes. Preview the video so you will have an appropriate activity to show to the students.

Snack time can include quiet music playing, students talking with Learning Club members, etc. Just add what you want to the snack time procedures.

Snack Time Procedure

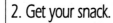
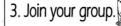

1. Clear off desk or table.
2. Get your snack.
3. Join your group.
4. Eat quietly.
5. Clean up when done.

10:45 CONCEPTUAL KEY POINT

Conceptual Key Point: Community

A spirit of community doesn't just happen in a neighborhood or classroom because people live or work in the same area. Each member—young and old—must take responsibility for creating and enhancing a sense of community throughout each day, month, and year. Creating a sense of community is a three-step process:

- Developing a sense of inclusion or belonging
- Creating common ground, and
- Taking action

Our beginning point for step 1, developing a sense of inclusion, is using the Lifelong Guidelines and LIFESKILLS:

- TRUSTWORTHINESS
- TRUTHFULNESS
- ACTIVE LISTENING
- NO PUT-DOWNS
- PERSONAL BEST/LIFESKILLS

Whole Class Inquiry —

Think back over your school experiences. Choose the year you feel you were an enthusiastic, successful learner. Using pencil or fine point markers, create a mindmap sharing five or more reasons you feel that the class supported your needs as a learner. Share the results with your fellow Learning Club members during Round Robin (sharing information in a clockwise way in the group).

▶ See *Cooperative Learning* by Spencer Kagan. Bring your mindmap to the Town Hall Meeting later in the morning.

11:15 MOVEMENT/MUSIC

This is an opportunity to move around the room, either in a structured way (exercises) or non-structured (explore the classroom and find out where materials are located as you listen to the music). This is a good time to introduce the Lifelong Guidelines songs with the video *Spread Your Wings* by Jeff Pedersen.

11:30 KEY POINT / TOWN HALL / T-CHART

➤Introduce the chimes as an "active listening" tool. Teach the other signals that you plan to use when students need to be active listeners, such as American Sign Language for "to listen" or hand in the air with fingers spread apart to represent the five elements of the Chinese Tang symbol— you/me, eyes, ears, heart, and undivided attention.)* Also see *Spread Your Wings: the Life-long Guidelines* by Jeff Pedersen, CD and video which has a song for each of the Lifelong Guidelines. Creating new lyrics for common melodies is also a fun activity.

Significant Knowledge Key Point—

Step 2 in building a sense of community is creating common ground. Through this process, we discover and come to respect each others' strengths and gifts and become willing to lead and to accept the leadership of others to maximize the capabilities of the community.

➤Discuss the concept of community: Guide the students through a discussion of community. Utilizing their real-life stories, literature, and other topics, draw out a definition of community.

---

* The Chinese symbol is an excellent visual because it contains all the important elements for active listening. See *Reaching All by Creating TRIBES Learning Communities* by Jeanne Gibbs.

- Invite the students to share information from their mind-maps about characteristics of classrooms in which they were successful learners.

- Write the attributes on a chart tablet either in list or mind-map form. Use this information as a lead-in to adopting the Lifelong Guidelines (and LIFESKILLS) as acceptable behaviors for everyone (adults included), to use in the classroom. Using the Lifelong Guidelines will build community and promote successful learning.

- Introduce each of the Lifelong Guidelines and assess the students' understandings of these concepts by having them record their ideas on a chart.

- Decide as a group which Lifelong Guideline to first focus on. (Hint: No Put-Downs is especially critical in intermediate grades and secondary schools.)

➤This is a good time to show video clips of TV shows that use put-downs continuously, e.g., Snoopy movies.

Town Hall Meeting Inguiry

➤MATERIALS: The individual handouts of Lifelong Guidelines and LIFESKILLS, plus chart paper, and markers.

Lifelong Guidelines—

Create a T-Chart using the Lifelong Guideline the students have selected as their starting point. Use a large chart tablet so you can collect information for all of

TOWN HALL MEETING
Procedures

1. Come to the meeting area when your Learning Club is called.

2. Find a place on the rug (circle, line, etc.) to sit. Sit where you can see everyone and everyone can see you.

3. Identify and sit comfortably in your own personal space.

4. Remember to use the Lifelong Guidelines throughout the Town Hall meeting.

5. When you hear the chimes, it is time to use active listening.

the Lifelong Guidelines/ LIFESKILLS in one place. Ideas can be added throughout the school year. Following is an example of how such a chart might look:

T-Chart with Put-Downs

LOOKS LIKE	SOUNDS LIKE	FEELS LIKE
arms crossed	You can't play with us!	left out
laughing at clothing	Where'd you get that old thing?	humiliation
laughing at answer	"You sure are stupid!"	hurt
no one noticing	"Who's she/he?"	isolation

➤For the second day of school, plan on doing a second version of this chart so that it looks like the following chart.

T-Chart with NO Put-Downs

LOOKS LIKE	SOUNDS LIKE	FEELS LIKE
Students greeting each other	Hi! How are you today? Want to play at recess?	welcome
High fives!	Great job! You mastered the 7 times tables.	capable
Someone waving	"Maria, come join us."	belonging

Additional ideas can be put on the chart as students notice them in literature, common experiences, newspaper articles, biographies, and real-life adventures.

12:00   LUNCH PROCEDURES/ LUNCH

12:45   REVIEW MORNING

Circle up by birthday and share with two other persons what you learned from this morning. Check the agenda and cross off the items that have been accomplished. Discuss why the procedures will help the students.

Go to Lunch Procedure

1. Clean up your work area.

2. Get your coat & lunch.

3. Line up at the door and stand quietly.

4. Proceed to cafeteria.

1:00   INQUIRY

Design a poster on 12" x 18" paper that encourages our school community to eliminate put-downs and use put-ups in their place. Using pencil, write a catchy heading and add drawings that illustrate your suggestions. Print your name in the lower right hand corner and ask a partner to check your work for any areas that may need improvement. Color your poster when you know that you have done your personal best. Share the poster and ideas with your Learning Club. Hang your work in the hallway with any other posters from the class. Complete your work before class starts tomorrow.

1:45   RECESS

2:00   KEY POINT/INQUIRY

Significant Knowledge Key Point

Step 3 in creating a sense of community is taking action. Communities are dynamic; they are either vibrant and growing or diminishing and dying. Maintaining community requires taking actions that nurture and expand the well-being of the group.

➤MATERIALS: One copy (or class set) of *Stone Fox* by John Reynolds Gardiner. This story:

• Is written at a third/fourth grade reading level but revered by students in grades 2-8 (regardless of students' reading level)

• Includes each Lifelong Guideline and LIFESKILL (great for beginning of the year introductions)

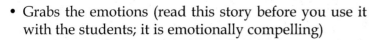

- Grabs the emotions (read this story before you use it with the students; it is emotionally compelling)

- Develops the concepts of community/survival

- Focuses on problem-solving skills

- Centers on a non-traditional family (grandpa and grandson)

- Is only ten chapters long (short enough to complete in one or two weeks).

While this book is a favorite, there are many others (*My Side of the Mountain, Where the Red Fern Grows, Charlotte's Web,* or a personal choice) that provide a basis for developing the concept of community, Lifelong Guidelines, and LIFESKILLS through literature.

> ### Pre-reading strategies:

- Locate your state in relation to Wyoming on a U.S. map. Determine if any students have visited Wyoming.

- Determine what kind of pets, if any, the students have at home. Lead a discussion of the kinds of "jobs" dogs do.

- Discuss the Husky as a canine breed—where and why the breed was developed.

- Have students write in their journals their predictions for why the book is titled *Stone Fox* and what they think the story plot will be.

- Review strategies for decoding new words.

> ### Reading: Chapters 1 and 2 can be read aloud by the teacher, individually by each student, with a partner, or in the Learning Club.

Inquiry —

 Develop a mindmap that focuses on Lifelong Guideline/ LIFESKILLS used by the three main characters (you may include an animal as well as humans) in the first two chapters of *Stone Fox*. Choose two of your favorite characters; for each, identify two

 Lifelong Guidelines and/or LIFESKILLS used by each character uses. Write that word on a line; include the page number where this example can be found. Defend your choices with your Learning Club during inquiry share time. For example:

Little Willy and Grandpa used the LIFESKILL of Sense of Humor when they. . . .

2:45 CONCEPTUAL KEY POINT REVIEW - TOWN HALL MEETING

> Guide your discussion with the following ideas:

- Ask students to review the information from their mindmaps and the T-chart created in the morning.

- Present the LIFESKILL of Cooperation as a goal for Learning Club projects/inquiries. Brainstorm attributes of the LIFESKILL of Cooperation. Ask the students to locate the word in class dictionaries to be sure of the definition.

- Invite the students to reflect on an activity/ situation/ inquiry when they have been part of a collaborative group. Provide time for a "popcorn" share (strategy where group members may "pop" out their answers in any order providing they still follow the Lifelong Guideline of Active Listening.

- Practice writing "Pop-corn Procedures" together (students and teacher).

3:15 PLEDGE/LEARNING CLUB CLOSURE

Inquiry

 With your Learning Club members, create a Lifelong Guidelines Pledge. Use rhyme or free verse, including the names of the Lifelong Guidelines and the word "community." Motions/signing may also be included. Share this pledge tomorrow during Town Hall Meeting.

Note: During the next Town Hall Meeting, students can continue to discuss or, if they desire, develop additional versions of a class pledge.Or, the best parts of each pledge can be combined to make a unique verse.Once they have agreed upon a pledge they feel best expresses the principles they want for their classroom community, they should recite it after the Pledge of Allegiance.

3:30   DISMISSAL

Follow the end-of-the day procedures.

End-of-Day Procedure

1. Organize the items in your area.

2. Help others straighten up the Learning Club materials.

3. Put important items in your pack.

4. Say goodbye to others.

5. Share one thing you learned with the teacher on the way out the door.

MEETING WITH A PROFESSIONAL AND/OR PEER COACH

As discussed in Chapter 7, pages 7.18-7.19, coaching on a regular basis is critically important. If you don't already have a coach assigned to you by the end of the first day of school, don't hesitate. Ask for one. Schedule yourself to meet for an hour or two every two weeks if at all possible. Again, frequent small amounts of time are more productive than all day twice a year. Also find a peer coach to work with you and join you when you meet with your professional coach.

ENDNOTES

1 The invitation should be a personal note. It needn't be lengthy or detailed. The important message is that you're inviting them to share a wonderful year with you.

2 For examples of procedures, see Chapter 7, 7.10-7.11..

3 For a description of this community building process, see Chapter 9, 9.2-9.8.

4 If you live in a northern climate requiring lots of heavy clothing or if your classroom has nowhere to hang coats and carry bags, your procedures should be detailed. Also, when elements of the classroom are new, consider an invitation to explore the classroom for 2-5 minutes before they sit down.

5 Developing a sense of inclusion/belonging is a critical first step in any classroom. See pages 9.2-8.

6 Although the triune brain theory has largely been eclipsed by for a larger view of how emotion affects learning, there is still value in teaching students (adjusted for the age of your students, of course) about their brain and its functions; for example, brain stem and cerebellum, limbic system, and cerebral cortex.

7 Antonio Damasio, *Looking for Spinoza: Joy, Sorrow, and the Feeling Brain.* (New York: Harcourt, 2003), 85.

8 For more information about the Acknowledgements Box, see pages 7.7-7.8.

Chapter 8: The Lifelong Guidelines and LIFESKILLS

THE LIFELONG GUIDELINES

The Lifelong Guidelines are a result of asking the question: "What qualities do you want in a lifelong partner?" Conversely, these Lifelong Guidelines also ask you to consider what qualities you should possess to make someone want to spend a lifetime with you. Also, what qualities would you hope a stranger on the street would have? A neighbor? However you ask the question, under whatever the circumstances or length of time of interaction, these five qualities come out high on the list. They form the foundation for positive, valued relationships and make learning joyous and powerful. They are also the keystone to good classroom leadership and, more than instructional strategy, help eliminate threat and enhance reflective thinking. The Lifelong Guidelines must become internalized. They shape the culture of the classroom.

An invaluable tool for teaching the Lifelong Guidelines and LIFESKILLS is *Tools for Citizenship and Life: Using the ITI/HET Lifelong Guidelines and LIFESKILLS in Your Classroom* by Sue Pearson. With a separate chapter for each of the Guidelines and LIFESKILLS, it describes why and how to practice the guideline/skill, what it looks like in the real world, what it looks like in school, more than 500 inquiries (whole group and small group/individual), signs of suc-

cess, suggested literature (by grade spans: primary, intermediate, and middle/high school), and sample family letters.

For a discussion of the Lifelong Guidelines, see the following excerpt from *Tools for Citizenship & Life: Using the ITI/HET Lifelong Guidelines and LIFESKILLS in Your Classroom*, pages 8.2-8.13.

Lifelong Guidelines

TRUSTWORTHINESS: To act in a manner that makes one worthy of trust and confidence

TRUTHFULNESS: To act with personal responsibility and mental accountability

ACTIVE LISTENING: To listen attentively and with the intention of understanding

NO PUT-DOWNS: To never use words, actions, and/or body language that degrade, humiliate, or dishonor others

PERSONAL BEST: To do one's best given the circumstances and available resources

---

TRUSTWORTHINESS

To act in a manner that makes one worthy of trust and confidence

What Is Trustworthiness?

If we were artists commissioned to paint a masterpiece representing the Lifelong Guideline of Trustworthiness, we would choose for our model a mother rocking her infant child, the baby's eyes intently studying her mother's face, a tiny hand reaching up to touch her mother's cheek. The purest form of trust in life is child to mother. The parent provides food when the child is hungry, warmth when cold and comfort when hurt. This relationship between mother and baby is a child's first experience with trustworthiness.

Yet we know there are other pictures in which food is late or lacking, comfort is in short supply, and warmth is missing. What do such babies begin to learn about trustworthiness? They learn that "people in my world are not reliable." Such early experiences with family and caretakers impair a child's ability to have confidence in other people.

Trustworthiness: An Umbrella in Stormy Weather. Trustworthiness, identified by specific attributes such as reliability and dependability, is vital because it is an umbrella under which we protect ourselves from stormy weather. Each one of us needs at least one such umbrella for protection—if not a trustworthy friend, at least a parent or close family member with whom we can talk and know that our words will go no further. We need to trust that those close to us will adhere to the Lifelong Guidelines and LIFESKILLS. Likewise, we need to be the umbrella of protection for other people by providing confidentiality, steadiness, and support during those occasional drizzles, steady rains, and torrential downpours that life presents.

Trustworthiness Is a Double-Sided Coin. But trustworthiness is more than an umbrella in stormy weather for us as we seek out those who are trustworthy, safe, and comfortable to be with. Trustworthiness is a double-sided coin, a two-way street. It isn't just what we receive; we in turn must be trustworthy for others.

Students must be taught that they can't expect the gift of trustworthiness from others if they are not trustworthy in return.

The Lifelong Guideline of Trustworthiness requires that parents and teachers teach both sides of Trustworthiness—how to give it and how to receive it. To do so, we must teach children the signposts for recognizing this characteristic in others. Who really deserves their trust so others don't take advantage of them? How do they extend their trust so that relationships of all levels can deepen and enrich their lives?

Why Practice Trustworthiness?

The Lifelong Guideline of Trustworthiness forms the basis of relationships—effective working partnerships, close friendships, healthy family bonds, and the long-lasting intimate relationship of husband and wife. If people can't trust us, they don't want to be around us—it's too risky. The lower the level of trustworthiness, the more distant people remain. And, because few pursuits in life are solitary, most goals require the participation of others. If we are to succeed in our goals, we must become trustworthy people.

For Staff. The higher the stakes become, the more crucial trustworthiness becomes. Designing seal rings for the space shuttle booster rocket, problem-solving safety design issues on the Boeing aircraft assembly line, doing customer service in a small business whose owner has just invested his entire life savings into his business are examples of everyday work environments in which our trustworthiness and ability to work as a team can have life-and-death or life-changing impact.

Can your colleagues feel secure that you are dependable (the job gets done), consistent (high quality of work), and reliable (follows directions and meets deadlines)? Does your word have credibility? Does your supervisor have confidence that you'll complete a task he/she assigns or keep confidential information secure?

As our trust-building skills improve, we are more likely to be included in upper-level planning and decision making. Such involvement is a key element in satisfaction in the workplace.

For Students. Close relationships of any kind, including teacher-student and student-student, cannot exist without trustworthiness. It is the cornerstone of respect and liking. One can love someone without liking and respecting him/her—a common burden of children abused by their parents. Trustworthiness is also the source of one's sense of security, safety, and confidence.

A key ingredient in the Lifelong Guideline of Trustworthiness is emotional consistency—that the student knows the teacher cares about him/her and that the teacher's emotional and physical behaviors are consistent with that love, that no matter what happens, the student knows he/she will be fairly treated.

When students feel safe and secure in the classroom, learning becomes paramount because the bodybrain can focus on learning. The atmosphere in the classroom, instead of tense and suspicious, is calm and steady. The teacher can be relied on to keep her word when students share problems. Consistency is the standard for student and teacher actions, both in application and outcome.

For Families. When a teacher is known to be trustworthy, relationships with students' families will flourish. A teacher who consistently and fairly applies rules and consequences wins respect from both students and adults. Family members recognize that we are working with them, not against them, in the education of their child. Generally, the more we know and understand about a child's circumstances, the greater the possibility that the teacher can provide emotional support, which in turn will promote academic learning. The parent-teacher relationship exudes confidentiality, whether relating to family or school concerns; this raises the level of trustworthiness for all involved, leading to additional exchanges of pertinent information.

Note: The only time a teacher must divulge confidential information from a student is when some form of abuse is apparent. Many states have laws requiring that this information be disclosed, and indeed, the penalties are severe if they're not reported. A student sharing this type of information is crying out for help and trusting that we will provide guidance, backing, and support.

How Do You Practice Trustworthiness?

We practice being trustworthy by not abusing others' trust; we don't share confidences, ignore deadlines, spread rumors, talk behind backs, lie, cheat, steal, or exhibit any of the other behaviors that would abuse trust.

The beginnings of trustworthiness lie deep within our childhood experiences. As infants, was food consistently there when we felt the pangs of hunger? Were we changed when wet and uncomfortable, rocked when ill, comforted when frightened? If the answers to these questions are yes, then we trusted our caretaker. On the other hand, were we left to wonder if food would come or if someone would take care of us when we were ill or frightened? Did our caretakers keep their word? Did they model good judgment and integrity? Clearly, the development of trust and trustworthiness in the classroom comes more quickly for some students than for others. Whatever it takes, however, it is our job as educators to develop future citizens who are trustworthy and who are capable of trusting those who have earned their trust.

Making Wise Choices. Trustworthiness is the result of making wise choices over time—some wise, others not so wise. The ability to do so, however, isn't automatic. It takes practice, in the midst of which we make mistakes—lots of them! For instance, when sent to deliver a message, does the student attend to the task at hand or slowly meander through the hallways disrupting other learners by waving in classroom windows? Do you remember some of these situations from your own childhood experiences? One friend shares a secret with another, who promises not to tell. The two are part of a trust-building pact. Did the secret get told as soon as another warm body was in sight or remain private? Remember going to a friend's house and promising to return home by dinner time? Were you at your place at the dinner table or nowhere to be seen? Remember finding money around the house or at school? Did you search for the owner or pocket the cash? These are all examples of early trust-building opportunities.

At school, does a trip to the bathroom take a few minutes or is it necessary to dispatch an escort to accompany the unreliable student back to class? Can the child be trusted to complete her own work and not to copy someone else's work? Will the child tell the truth even though negative consequences may result? Does the student return forms and homework on time, turn in "found" objects and money, work hard to eliminate put-downs from his vocabulary, and do his personal best consistently?

As adults, every action we take, every deed we accomplish, every word we utter, creates the person others see us to be. People either believe us or they don't. Building trust is a definitive example of actions speaking louder than words because all of the good intentions and promises in the world cannot compensate for jobs undone, deadlines ignored, secrets revealed, and promises broken. Therefore, tell the truth, work to your personal best, keep your word, exceed expectations—be a person viewed as reliable, dependable, and believable.

Building a Reputation Takes Time. A reputation of trustworthiness is earned slowly since it is based on a collection of positive experiences among people over time. Consistency, reliability, and honest actions all typify a person who is worthy of our trust. The same is true for each of us. Our actions and reactions will be watched for awhile, before we are known to be trustworthy.

Adults must recognize that trustworthiness develops in stages. Expectations of trustworthiness for five-year olds should be more basic than expectations for fifteen-year olds. Students must understand that each time trust is broken, it takes longer to be restored; sometimes trust can be irrevocably broken.

TRUTHFULNESS

To be honest about things and feelings with oneself and others

What Is Truthfulness?

Truthfulness has many aspects; its complexity unfolds as students mature. It is a difficult Lifelong Guideline to practice. Its attributes are complex and often depend on circumstances. The definition of truthfulness that follows is the result of brainstorming by a class of teachers and administrators at U.C. Davis, California.

"To be truthful means being honest about things and feelings . . . being honest with ourselves and with others. Being truthful is not always easy because truth is not absolute (black and white) and two seemingly contradictory statements could both be true depending upon the perspectives of the observers (for example, the blind men discovering the elephant). It takes courage to be truthful because others may disagree.

"Being truthful requires good judgment about:
- What to say (possible risk to our source of information)
- When to say it (in private or before others)
- To whom to say it (to the person responsible for the problem/situation or as a complaint to anyone who will listen)
- How to say it (with sensitivity and tact or intended to hurt) [1]

"Truthfulness is a critical building block for human relationships and therefore has significant consequences, both short-term and long-term, for each of us."[2]

Preserving the Truth. Preserving the truth depends on each one of us refusing to exaggerate, change, or vary the facts we share. This requires careful observation and clear thinking as we perceive and analyze a situation; it also requires precise communication when sharing.

Whether it's the policeman asking, "What happened here? Which driver caused the accident and how?" or the parent asking, "How did this happen? Who started this?" the situation calls for the truth. How well did we observe the incident? Do we stick to the facts or make inferences that may or may not be true? Are we committed to telling the truth despite consequences?

Why Practice Truthfulness?

Most people believe what they hear (especially from someone they know or from someone who is supposed to be trustworthy) unless the information is proven to be inaccurate. After that, the informant's word is not as good as it used to be; people listen with a sense of disbelief or the feeling that they should check another source. Recall the story from Aesop's Fables about the boy who cried wolf. The boy lied so many times about the wolf being after the sheep that when the wolf really did attack, none of the villagers responded to his cries for help. If we aren't truthful at all times, people—especially family and friends—will be suspicious when we share stories; they'll want proof or verification from other sources. The greater the number of lies and careless statements that pass through our lips, the more corroboration our listeners will need.

It is important, sometimes even a matter of life or death, that people believe us. Nothing is as precious as our reputation that we say what we mean and mean what we say. Truthfulness is the bedrock of trustworthiness.

Effective Relationships Rely on Truthfulness. Based on a survey of more than 15,000 people, 88 percent chose honesty as the key trait of effective leadership.[3] Honest people have credibility; credible leaders gain the trust and confidence of their followers. They keep their promises and follow through on their commitments. In contrast, people who consistently lie are shunned, have few friends, and have fewer options for well-paying employment.

In personal relationships, if we can't be trusted to tell the truth even with insignificant information, how can anyone believe that our important ideas are true? By always telling the truth, friends, family, and co-workers will believe what we say. We become respected and valued members of our families and communities.

When the Lifelong Guidelines of Truthfulness and Trustworthiness are present, a sense of community develops. Then, all members are less likely to be dishonest because each is genuinely cherished for who he/she is. When we belong, we have something to lose if we break the norms of our group. When we belong, there is no need to create some persona bigger and better than in real life.

Benefits to Telling the Truth. According to Dr. Abraham Kryger, D.M.D., M.D., there are real benefits to telling the truth. Among them are: greater success/personal expertise, an increased sense of grounding/confidence, less anxiety/worry/guilt, increased ability to deal with crises/breakdowns, improved problem-solving abilities, improved interpersonal relationships, greater emotional health/control of one's emotions, increased ability to influence others, better sleep, better health, increased ability to think well/reason soundly, less need to control, good humor, and greater self-expression and self-satisfaction.[4] Do those sound like qualities you'd like in your life? Truth—and its dark twin, lies—drive world events, nudge the fall of civilizations, and sculpt our lives like no other character trait.

Consequences of Not Telling the Truth. There are also consequences that result from not telling the truth. Some of these consequences according to Dr. Kryger are: more frequent failures/frustrations in life, being distrusted by others, lack of self-esteem/self-confidence, dysfunctional interpersonal relationships, inability to self-correct, and stress of many kinds. Almost all types of human stress can be traced to not telling the truth at one level or another.[5]

How Do You Practice Truthfulness?

Always tell the truth! It was Mark Twain who said, "If you tell the truth, you don't have to remember anything."[6] It is easier to remember what really happened, what words were really spoken than to try to recall a made-up story or a distorted version. You also practice the Lifelong Guideline of Truthfulness by telling the entire truth immediately rather than telling the story a little bit at a time until finally the whole truth emerges. Credibility is easy to destroy with some simple untruths told in a moment to either create a better impression, deny involvement, or refuse to acknowledge that an incident has occurred. As a teacher, you're on stage; be honest with your class. Remember, what you do is more important than what you say you do!

Recognize That There Are Barriers to Telling the Truth. When teaching students about the Lifelong Guideline of Truthfulness, we must admit to ourselves and to them that there are formidable barriers to telling the truth in our society. Perhaps the biggest is refusing to accept that it is possible to tell the truth. A widespread but false belief held by many is that it isn't humanly possible to tell the truth. That is just a handy excuse that absolves us of the need to question our lack of truthfulness.

A second powerful barrier is fear of consequences if we tell the truth. For example, the boss firing us, someone close to us losing respect for us, people may retaliate if we challenge their belief system, or we may not know how to disagree with a friend whose "truth" is far different from our own.[7]

Practice, Practice. Have students share stories and repeat information as accurately as possible. Teach them to write terms and facts on paper so they can refer to them if needed. Show them the importance of being willing to recheck any data that seem to lack credibility by going back to the source of the information. Teach students many problem-solving strategies; when logical, natural choices are available, a student is less likely to lie. Avoid setting a trap for a student, as when you already know the answer but ask the question anyway. All you accomplish is catching him/her in a falsehood. Why not catch someone when telling the truth and thus reinforce the desired, rather than the negative, behavior?

Seek Workplaces and Friendships That Value Truthfulness. Telling the truth isn't always easy. Often, telling parents, friends, the boss, and co-workers the truth brings unpleasant consequences.

However, telling a lie under these circumstances almost always has far-reaching consequences, often of greater severity than if we simply spoke the truth up front and accepted the consequences, as unpleasant as they might be. Once we're caught lying, people lose faith and confidence in us. In work relationships and with friends, this is devastating.[8]

One final caution. Sometimes people in power will ask for our honest opinion about plans, choices, and situations. If the level of trust in that business or organization is high, we feel comfortable in sharing our thoughts. If it's low, our risk is much greater, particularly if our true beliefs are not what the person in power wants to hear. Rather than be part of a lie that will have unwanted consequences for us and others, we should look for work settings where truthfulness is truly valued. During interviews, ask questions that will reveal the level of truthfulness in that culture. By gathering as much information as possible before accepting a position, we can make more informed decisions.

ACTIVE LISTENING

To listen with the intention of understanding what the speaker intends to communicate[9]

What Is Active Listening?

Hearing is an inactive, involuntary process that occurs when the ears pick up sound waves being transmitted by some kind of vibration and forward them to the brain. Listening, however, is an active, voluntary process which includes recognizing, and intending to understand the messages received. Listening requires participation, patience, energy, and the **intention** to "get it"—not just what the speaker says but what he/she intends to communicate.

To actively listen, the brain must be physiologically active. Not only must it perceive the sounds correctly but it must also compare words to emotional nuances for consistency, then convert words into images that can be analyzed, compared, and stored for future reference. This is an extremely active process requiring neural wiring that, unfortunately, one out of four students hasn't developed by the time he/she starts school.[10] However, such wiring can easily be developed in the classroom. For more information about how to create the needed wiring, contact Lindamood-Bell Learning Processes Center, San Luis Obispo, California, (800) 233-1819.

Most people listen passively. That means the sound acts on them—enters their ears—but they don't actively and consciously participate in the process; they don't exert effort in order to listen and attend to what they are hearing. An example is listening to a book on tape while driving or a music CD while cleaning the house. In contrast, active listening is far more complex.

A wonderful metaphor for active listening, and an excellent way to teach it to students, is illustrated in the TANG, a Chinese character for "to listen"—to listen with our eyes, ears, heart, and give undivided attention.[11] If we do so, we are truly acting upon our intention to understand what the speaker intends to communicate.

The active listener is more than a receiver. In many ways, he assists the speaker to deliver his/her message by providing encouragement, such as attentive body posture, full eye contact, positive body signals, and multi-tiered acknowledgements, such as "Mmm; uhuh; yes; I understand; I agree; yes, interesting; I heard something about that yesterday . . . tell me more." The listener is saying to the speaker, "Your ideas and message are important to me and to others in the room. I will listen while you communicate with me and then I will ask questions if I disagree or don't understand. Above all, I respect your opinions and your right to speak." And, eventually, "I understand what you are trying to tell me."

Why Practice Active Listening?

Active listening is critical because it is the doorway to understanding. Whether in social settings, at work, or with family and friends, not getting it can cause serious problems. At best, it is embarrassing and makes us feel like outsiders. All too often it is

also costly in our relationships with others and expensive for our employers when we misinterpret instructions. Furthermore, it is difficult to be successful in life if we are not taking in accurate information about the world and how it works.

On a daily basis, our sense of hearing collects a wide range of information that we need to protect ourselves and to enhance our problem solving. What might happen, for instance, if a jogger, wearing headphones and listening to music, is crossing the street against the walk sign and can't hear a persistent honking horn? Or, if a worried parent is unable to focus on the doctor's directions for the baby's medicine and care? Wouldn't you feel sad if you missed your plane to Disney World because you didn't hear the final boarding call? Since one of the ways we stay safe and make informed decisions includes listening to sounds collected from the real world, isn't it common sense to concentrate on what we hear?

Unlike reading, we can't regulate the pace of someone else's speech, replaying it again to check an unfamiliar word. Thus, we may miss important information reported to us and respond in a peculiar way. To immediately understand what we hear, it's crucial that we perfect the skill of listening well. We can only talk intelligently about a topic when we can grasp what is said to us. To be able to listen well gives us confidence when communicating with others. Listening in the real world is an everyday skill.

Spotlight on Brain Research. Most educators don't realize that active listening—turning words into mental images that can be processed and stored in short- and long-term memory—requires neural wiring that over 25 percent of the population does not have or has not developed sufficiently to succeed in school. Nanci Bell, author of *Visualizing and Verbalizing for Improved Language Comprehension*, describes typical symptoms of oral language processing difficulty, any one of which would increase difficulty and frustration in learning as well as in social settings. Unfortunately, most people who have difficulty with language processing display more than one of these symptoms. It is a sobering list:[12]

"1. *Individuals may frequently not understand jokes.* Language humor depends on imagery, whereas sight humor (pie in face) does not and is more easily understood. Almost everyone gets sight gags but not everyone gets language-based humor.

2. *Individuals may not understand concepts of cause and effect.* To process cause and effect relationships you must be able to process a gestalt from which to judge an effect.

3. *Individuals may not respond to explanations given in language.* If a student's performance needs correcting, a "talking to" may be only partially understood or not understood at all because the student is connecting to only a part of the oral explanation.

4. *Individuals may ask and re-ask questions that have already been answered.* The individual hears the answer but is unable to process and connect to the given information and will therefore ask the same question again, only phrased differently. Such individuals are often not aware that they are asking the same question over and over, only with modified language.

5. *Individuals may not grasp the main idea or inferences from television shows or movies, although they may get a few details.* Individuals may seem to miss concepts or nuances from movies they've seen. In discussions with them, they don't interpret the movie or story sequence well.

6. *Individuals may lose attention quickly in conversation or lectures.* Students who are unable to connect to the gestalt of language will find that in a few minutes, often less, they are "lost" and may drift away mentally and/or physically.

7. *Individuals may have weakness in auditory memory and in following directions.* These symptoms may be severe and labeled as aphasia[13] . . . [or] be subtle weaknesses that cause others to suspect lack of intelligence or lack of motivation. In fact, individuals with these symptoms will frequently doubt their intelligence."

Ms. Bell also points to a link between listening difficulties and oral language expression:

"The oral language comprehension weakness is often accompanied by an oral language expression weakness. Individuals experience difficulty organizing their verbalizing and expressing themselves easily and fluently or they are verbal but scattered, relating information out of sequence. For example, a student on academic probation, with severely impaired auditory and reading comprehension, frequently interjected irrelevant comments in conversation. His comments were disjointed both unto themselves and to the topic. Consequently, he was often viewed as mentally disabled."[14]

Every teacher can list students who have exhibited these frustrating symptoms. There is more to being an active listener than most people realize.

How Do You Practice Active Listening?

If these listening difficulties sound familiar, you owe it to yourself and your students to read Nanci Bell's book. Use it as a teacher's manual with your entire class every day for 30 minutes for at least six weeks. You'll be astounded at the transformation in academic capability of individual students and the class as a whole.

Once the necessary neural wiring is in place, more traditional classroom strategies for teaching students to pay closer attention, try harder, focus more, and so forth, can be used with greater success.

Proficient listening requires the neural wiring to process language plus the social skills our society has come to expect of listeners. There are many ways for students to practice these social-based listening techniques.

Using the Chinese Symbol for Listening. The Chinese symbol which depicts "to listen" as an act involving ears, eyes, heart, and undivided attention[15] is a good place to start. It offers a handy visual and helps turn intention into tangible action. Listening with intention helps the listener "hear" with an open mind and rid him/ herself of any preconcieved notions that would corrupt the speaker's message. Many poor listeners get so involved in the speaker's style of delivery or their judgments about the speaker that they miss the message. Listening with ears, eyes, heart, undivided attention, and with the intention to receive the intended message are keys to active listening.

Social Expectations

In Western culture, certain behaviors are expected of a good listener, including "attending skills" and "follow-up skills." Attending skills include not interrupting the speaker, listening for what he/she intends to say rather than what we want or think he/she will say, holding eye contact, using open body language, and offering some encouraging responses ("Wow!" "Then what happened?" "Really?") and actions (nodding, smiling).

Personal Behaviors. To form a more accurate impression of a speaker's intended message, we must pay constant, careful attention. When we lose our concentration, we also lose much of the information. There are a number of ways to help ourselves focus on listening and collecting information.

- Limit distractions. Change places to promote concentration.

- Look at the speaker. Observe body language (open versus closed), listen to the tone of voice (pitch, quality, and timbre), and note facial expressions as clues to emotions. In many instances, the medium is the message—most of the message is communicated non-verbally.[16]

- Focus your attention on the meaning of the words; use signals (head nodding, smiles) to indicate you understand.

- Create pictures in your mind of what you're hearing.

- Visualize how this information fits with what you already know and what it means to you. Expect to act upon what you hear.

NO PUT–DOWNS

To not use words, actions, and/or body language to degrade, humiliate, or dishonor others

What Are Put-Downs?

Put-downs are words and body language that imply, "I am better than you. I have more money than you, I am smarter than you, I have more options than you." The objective is to elevate the speaker's social standing and power. By creating a laugh at someone else's expense, the speaker gains power in the situation by controlling the behavior of others and undermining relationships of those in the audience have with the targeted person. Put-downs are also a way of avoiding the real issues of the moment. They often reveal unconscious feelings of jealousy, anger, fear, or inadequacy. Whether from one person or a group, the goal of put-downs is always the same—humiliation, power, control, and increased social status.

The body language of put-downs—actions and body movements, such as rolling the eyes, tapping the forehead, caricaturing, and so forth—are honed to an art in sitcoms and other popular media in our society. They are every bit as powerful as words.

Sometimes put-downs affect us more deeply than usual. For example, when they're spoken by people we like and trust or by people we want to like us, the results are devastating. We feel betrayed. If the people whose opinion we so value express something negative about us, then it must really be so. Also, if the comments are aimed at a sensitive area (e.g., physical changes during puberty, being overweight or underweight, being an immigrant with beginning English skills), students often feel shame about something over which they have little or no control. Similarly, when we receive put-downs in front of our peers, the humiliation and shame deepen as we lose face.

Why Practice No Put-Downs?

Put-downs among adults produce a lack of trust which is extremely detrimental to an educational agency, especially when it trickles down to influence students' attitudes and behaviors. If a staff is to pursue efforts to improve the school program, put-downs must be eliminated. To be open to learning is to be vulnerable. We're open to snickers when we make mistakes or admit we can't answer a question. Every student should be able to approach new opportunities and learning experiences without dreading verbal abuse.

When we refuse to allow put-downs in the classroom, we're teaching respect for all people, ideas, and situations. We're building a positive emotional climate in our classroom so that our students feel comfortable enough to risk an answer, offer a thought, and try some new skill without worrying about mocking remarks or gestures. This is particularly important for children in the middle position of sibling birth order whose skills and knowledge can't match their older sibling but who don't have the safety of being the baby.

Prohibiting the use of disparaging remarks is akin to constructing an invisible shield that protects and nurtures.

How Do You Practice It?

To change a negative habit to a more positive one, we first must recognize the negative behavior. Thus, we must teach students to recognize put-downs and become sensitive to their effects despite their pervasiveness in our mass media and society. Many students look on the word plays of put-downs as a form of humor, overlooking that it's at the expense of others.

Next, we must create an action plan to eliminate put-downs and encourage respect for others.

Recognizing the Need to Change. Select a video clip ripe with put-downs. Have your students identify and count the put-downs they hear and see. Discuss with your students how they would feel if they were on the receiving end of these put-downs. Next, focus on comments heard in the classroom and school common areas. Ask your students to observe the participants. Who is handing out the put-downs? Who is the brunt of the put-downs? Who has power and social position and who doesn't? Refer to Glasser's needs list: belonging, power, fun, and freedom.[17] Which of these fundamental human needs is the speaker missing? If put-downs occur in your classroom, what's missing from your classroom environment? Look for patterns that demand change and then, with your students' help, create an action plan.

The Importance of Modeling. Creating an environment free of put-downs requires constant modeling by all adults. The entire school staff (administrators, teachers, aides, custodial workers, cafeteria staff, and parent volunteers) need to understand their role as role models for students. A "Do as I say but not as I do" atmosphere doesn't work. Post the Lifelong Guidelines/LIFESKILLS around the school for all to see and follow. Initiate discussions about the harmful effects of put-downs. If a put-down is heard, deal with it immediately using a calm, rational manner before the situation escalates.

Taking Responsibility for Eliminating Put-Downs. Everyone plays a part in eliminating put-downs. To begin cleansing your class-room of put-downs, eliminate the put-down banter that is passed off as humor. Recall a comment that had dual interpretations and then the speaker quickly said, "Just kidding!"—but you never knew the intent for sure. As the saying goes, "Many a true word is said in jest." Second, agree on a "cancel" signal. Whenever someone says a put-down, other family members simply say, "Cancel." The hurt is canceled, the power play is canceled.

PERSONAL BEST

One's best possible performance given the time and resources available

What Is Personal Best?

For those using the *HET* model, the Lifelong Guideline of Personal Best is defined by the 19 LIFESKILLS defined here. To pursue one's personal best means working to develop and strength-en each LIFESKILL.

Quality work is never an accident; it is always the result of combining clear goals, high standards, knowledge and skills, and genuine effort. It represents the wisest choice among many options matched with commitment, perseverance, and wise use of time, talents, and resources. There is no one way to achieve a sense of fulfillment, but doing one's personal best on a consistent basis is the best road we know to reach that end.

The Lifelong Guideline of Personal Best is not about treats, rewards, or bonuses; it's about a deep sense of personal satisfaction for a job well done, mastering a skill, or making a contribution.

Personal Best Is Not a Fixed Standard. Personal Best is not about perfectionism. Personal Best is the result of our consistent pursuit of a moving target within an ever-changing terrain. Our performance in the same activity looks different over time. As our

competence grows, our performance improves. As the tools, time, and resources available to us improve, our performance improves.

For example, while supporting your family (emotionally, financially, and physically), you might take up jogging. You try hard to improve your running technique but you struggle to complete the course. You're doing your personal best in both areas—family life and jogging—but your jogging skill and capabilities in no way compare to those of a professional athlete who devotes full focus and time to his/her athletic pursuits. Personal Best is using the utmost effort possible and striving for a heightened stage of excellence. This may or may not translate into being Number 1, the winner, the hero; in the real world, such status is rare. But all of us can achieve our personal best.

The Lifelong Guideline of Personal Best is one's best possi-ble performance at the time, under the circumstances of the moment, and using the tools, time, knowledge/skill, and resources available at the moment. This, of course, takes into account the LIFESKILL of Resourcefulness!

Personal Best Is a Mindset. What drives you to do your per-sonal best? The most important element is a clear vision of your goals and personal performance standards and love of what you are doing. When such vision and love are united, you want to do your best! The secret about goals is to make them personal—to focus on your performance, not on the status or glamour of the project, job, or assignment. Athletes strive to surpass their previous personal accomplishments. This provides a vision that pushes them to constantly improve. Then, love the process of working toward your goals, celebrating each step toward your vision.

Doing one's personal best is a way of life, not an isolated incident.

LIFESKILLS

CARING: To feel and show concern for others

COMMON SENSE: To use good judgment

COOPERATION: To work together toward a common goal or purpose

COURAGE: To act according to one's beliefs despite fear of

CREATIVITY: To imagine ways to solve a problem or produce a product; to invent something original or redesign something adverse consequences

CURIOSITY: A desire to investigate and seek understanding of one's world

EFFORT: To do your best

FLEXIBILITY: To be willing to alter plans when necessary

FRIENDSHIP: To make and keep a friend through mutual trust and caring

INITIATIVE: To do something, of one's own free will, because it needs to be done

INTEGRITY: To act according to a sense of what's right and wrong

ORGANIZATION: To plan, arrange, and implement in an orderly way; to keep things orderly and ready to use

PATIENCE: To wait calmly for someone or something

PERSEVERANCE: To keep at it

PRIDE: Satisfaction from doing one's personal best

PROBLEM SOLVING: To create solutions to difficult situations and everyday problems

RESOURCEFULNESS: To respond to challenges and opportunities in innovative and creative ways

RESPONSIBILITY: To respond when appropriate; to be accountable for one's actions

SENSE OF HUMOR: To laugh and be playful without harming others

Why Practice Personal Best?

Aristotle wrote, "We are what we repeatedly do. Excellence, then, is not an act, but a habit."[18] The Lifelong Guideline of Personal Best is transferable from one sector of life to another—in family and social life, in one's job, in religious experiences, and in recreational activities. You can't work on excellence in one area and not have it show up in other areas. But the converse is also true: Refusing to do your personal best in one area will show up as laziness or avoidance in other areas.

Some people start out by thinking, "Doing my personal best is too difficult! I'll have to work really hard." But think of the opposite— do you really want to work toward personal worst or mediocrity? You may have to expend the same amount of effort to achieve less. Does that make sense? Self-respect—and the respect of others—depends heavily upon performing consistently at our personal best.

How Do You Practice It?

As we're sure the Army has discovered, the slogan "Be all that you can be!" is far more easily said than done. Not that it is a mystery. But to achieve our personal best requires a broad range of personal and social skills that need to be learned early and practiced daily until they become dependable habits of mind rather than now-and-then skills we pull up when we get in a pinch.

The Lifelong Guideline of Personal Best is defined by 19 LIFESKILLS as shown on the previous page. To the surprise of many, children seem to have an intuitive grasp of the LIFESKILLS. The word and concept of "perseverance," for example, is no hurdle at all for kindergartners. And they seem delighted to be let in on the secret of how to succeed at things—when they want something, they know how to go about getting it. What a wonderful gift so early in life. One might say that the road to success in life is paved with 23 yellow bricks: the 19 LIFESKILLS and five Lifelong Guidelines.

In addition to keeping our feet on the yellow brick road, we must also:

- Identify a vision, set personal goals.

- Continuously self-evaluate in order to improve as needed (attitude, performance, or goal-setting) and to revise or completely redesign our plans as needed.

- Welcome suggestions from others who have different perspectives and who may have unique experiences to share.

- Understand that we will make mistakes but that we can turn them into life lessons; realize that we have discovered a way *not* to do something and must fine tune our thinking. Thomas Edison discovered over 2,000 ways not to make the light bulb before he found a way that worked.[19] We should expect to refine our methods, thinking, and techniques—any variation that might improve us or our product. We can feel pride in our heart when all of these LIFESKILL efforts combine as one and provide us with the experience of doing our personal best.

Does this sound like a recipe for adults only? Not true. Even five year olds can set a vision of what they would like to be when they grow up although it often changes weekly. At five, many of the skills children learn have feedback built into the learning event; they don't have to ask, "Teacher, is this right?" They are able to judge for themselves. As for welcoming suggestions from others, they are used to getting plenty of advice from grown ups! And when it comes to learning from mistakes, young children do it with much more grace than adults do.

Can children younger than five learn these aspects of doing the Lifelong Guideline of Personal Best? In their own age-appropriate ways, absolutely! It may in fact be more difficult for high school students and adults to learn the Lifelong Guideline of Personal Best because they must first shed old attitudes and habits of mind.

A REMINDER

For in-depth guidance on how to implement the Lifelong Guidelines and LIFESKILLS in your classroom, see *Tools for Citizenship & Life: Using the HET Lifelong Guidelines & LIFESKILLS in Your Classroom* by Sue Pearson (see books4educ.com). The book provides a separate chapter for each Lifelong Guideline and LIFESKILL and discusses what it is, why it is important, and how to practice it. Most importantly, the book contains 500 inquiries, activities ready-to-go for teaching and student practice of each Lifelong Guideline and LIFESKILL. It also recommends high quality literature books whose characters illustrate the Lifelong Guidelines and LIFESKILLS—successes and possible life consequences if they are not used. We strongly recommend this book to you. It will make your first day of school and succeeding weeks much, much easier.

A companion book, *Character Begins at Home*, provides 500 additional inquiries that be assigned for homework that parents can be involved in.

BEFORE YOU BEGIN

Before you begin implementing the Lifelong Guidelines and LIFESKILLS, determine whether you will be implementing solo or as part of a team. The answer is critical to your planning. Where are your peers? What knowledge and commitment to body-brain-compatible education do they share?

As any parent knows, consistency is critical when it comes to behavior guidelines. So it is with the Lifelong Guidelines and LIFESKILLS of Stage One. Schoolwide implementation as a team effort is clearly the best way to go, the more so with older students. But students will respond to consistent use of the Lifelong Guidelines and LIFESKILLS in their classroom. The solo approach does work for students but, as with most tasks, working alone is harder.

HET schools that use the Lifelong Guidelines and LIFESKILLS begin implementing them in a variety of ways. Some just dive right in! The staff agrees that these behaviors will help expedite the learning process by providing absence of threat for the students and by helping nurture reflective thinking. The school wants such social and behavioral guidelines, they want them now, and they also want them schoolwide.

Other sites reach schoolwide consensus more slowly. They often begin with initiating schoolwide discussions, hold book talks around key *HET* books and then bring in *HET* trainings (e.g., the Lifelong Guidelines and LIFESKILLS PowerPack provided by Susan Kovalik & Associates) and other opportunities for the staff to practice and learn brain research-based strategies.

In other schools, teams of teachers begin using Lifelong Guidelines and LIFESKILLS in their classrooms, using the resources of the team for support and maintaining an ongoing dialogue with other colleagues about the progress of their students.

Implementation moves more quickly and is more rewarding if others at your school have adopted the Lifelong Guidelines and LIFESKILLS as their model for interacting with students. But never overlook the power of one—a single teacher leading the way.

Whatever your situation, you can start now. Start in your own classroom and let the Lifelong Guidelines and LIFESKILLS grow from there. They have a way of taking on a life of their own as students, parents, and other staff embrace their use.

The Advantages of Implementing Schoolwide

Agreeing to implement the Lifelong Guidelines and LIFESKILLS schoolwide has many advantages. First, there is a common vocabulary that, over time, builds a commonly shared belief system about how children learn and how adults should treat students and each other, a necessary building block for developing a sense of community. Second, consistency from class to class results in more rapid change in student and adult behavior. Last, the "spill-over" factor is high: The students will take the desired behaviors into other areas of their lives outside school—at home and in group situations such as neighborhood play, sports, scouts, and so forth. With everyone involved at the same time, there is an opportunity to build common understandings and buy-in very quickly.

Implementation by a small group (grade level or team) is harder because students receive mixed messages about the importance of using the Lifelong Guidelines and LIFESKILLS as community-building strategies by those outside the team which interfere with the learning process. In addition, lack of consistency—between the classroom and other locations within the school—makes the process slower, especially for students having behavior problems.

Solo Implementation

If you are doing this alone, you will have to work hard to create an alternative culture on campus, one which your students will see as viable and valuable. The process of implementation at the classroom level is, however, the same whether implementing solo, as a team, or schoolwide. In general: Start the first day of school, work intensively during the first four to five weeks, and reinforce daily thereafter.

ENDNOTES

1   Karen D. Olsen, instructor, extension course in brain-compatible learning at the University of California, Davis, 1993.

2   James M. Kouzes and Barry Z. Posner, *The Leadership Challenge,* Fourth Edition (San Francisco, CA: Jossey-Bass, Inc., 2008), 21-22.

3   Dr. Abraham Kryger, D.M.D., M.D., *Benefits of Telling the Truth.* (http:www. wellnessmd.com/tellingtruth.html). See also Bill Moyer, *The Truth About Lies,* videotape, 1987.

4   The lie detector test is based on physiological evidence of the body's reaction to lying—more rapid pulse and rise in blood pressure. Also see *The Orman Health Letter* published monthly by TRO Productions, Inc., Baltimore, M.D., and http://www.wellnessmd.com/tellingtruth.html

5   Kryger.

6   Mark Twain, *Notebook,* 1984.

7   Kryger.

8   Kryger.

9   This definition of listening comes from an *est* communication workshop developed by Werner Earhart in the 1970s. Earhart believed that communication is an act of intention: The listener must intend to "get" what the speaker intends to say; the speaker must intend to speak the truth about what he/she thinks and feels.

10 Not surprisingly, the more hours spent in front of a television, the less time spent developing language. See Nanci Bell, *Visualizing and Verbalizing for Improved Language Comprehension and Thinking* (Palo Alto, CA: Gander Publishing, 2007),. 21.

11 For a discussion of the meaning of the Chinese symbol for "to listen," see Jeanne Gibbs, *TRIBES: A New Way of Learning and Being Together* (Windsor, CA: CenterSource Systems, LLC, 2001), 93-94.

12 Bell, xxi.

13 Aphasia is the loss of one's ability to speak or understand spoken or written language due to disease or injury of the brain.

14 Bell, xxi.

15 Gibbs, 93-94. The book also provides many ready-to-go activities for students to practice active listening.

16 "The Importance of Effective Communication," (Northeastern University, College of Business Administration, October, 1999. http://www.cba. neu.edu/~ewertheim/interper/commun.htm)

17 William, Glasser, M.D. *Choice Theory: A New Psychology of Personal Freedom,* (New York: HarperPerennial, 1998), 31-41.

18 Aristotle, *Nicomachean Ethics,* 350 BC., (W.D. Ross, translator, *The Internet Classics Archives/Works by Aristotle,* http://classics.mit. edu/ Browse/browse-Aristotle.html).

19 Jack Canfield and Mark Victor, *A 2nd Helping of Chicken Soup for the Soul: 101 More Stories to Open the Heart and Rekindle the Spirit* (Deerfield Beach, Florida: Health Communications, Inc., 1995), 253. See also *Thomas Alva Edison Home Page,* (http://www. thomasedison.com)

NOTES TO MYSELF

Chapter 9: Getting Started with the Lifelong Guidelines and LIFESKILLS

THREE PURPOSES OF ONGOING USE OF THE LIFELONG GUIDELINES/LIFESKILLS

The Lifelong Guidelines and LIFESKILLS provide the basis for three important functions of a bodybrain-compatible learning environment:

- They are the agreed-upon behaviors for all and thus replace the *rules* of traditional "discipline" programs.

- They provide a safe environment for creating and maintaining a sense of community

- They describe the behaviors of civil discourse which are the foundation of citizenship

THE LIFELONG GUIDELINES/LIFESKILLS AS AGREED-UPON BEHAVIORS

The difference between agreed-upon behaviors and rules is not subtle; it is the difference between behavior that is internally motivated and monitored versus behavior that is externally imposed and controlled—and therefore typically resisted. Your goal is to have students who commit themselves to living the Lifelong Guidelines and LIFESKILLS because they make their lives work, not because they're what the teacher makes them do.

Most of this chapter is about how to teach the Lifelong Guidelines/LIFESKILLS in a way that enables students to understand their power to make their lives work—in the classroom today and, more important, now and later in life. See pages 9.9 through the end of the chapter.

BUILDING A COMMUNITY OF LEARNERS THROUGH THE LIFELONG GUIDELINES/ LIFESKILLS

Because creating and maintaining a community of learners is such a powerful engine for improving academic performance, it should be your number one goal beginning the first day of school and every day thereafter.

In the *HET* model, creating community occurs in three stages:

Developing a Sense of Belonging

The need to belong is just that—a psychological imperative, not a luxury.[1] Once it is taken care of, students can direct their attention to other matters of importance in the classroom. All five Lifelong Guidelines plus the LIFESKILLS, particularly Caring, Cooperation, and Friendship, provide a useful foundation for creating a safe environment in which a sense of belonging can develop.*

If we want to belong to a group, we must in turn be willing to extend an invitation to others to be included. This sense of reciprocity helps override the in-group, out-group, us-vs.- them mentality of cliques and gangs. It builds the foundation for tolerating diversity and accepting differences. It's the basis for respect and self-respect.

Willingness to include others is modeled by the teacher in the welcome letter to students before school starts, by standing at the door every morning to give a personal good morning (more than a polite hello, this includes an emotional check-in), and saying farewell at the end of the day (with a thank you for a good day and looking forward to seeing you tomorrow). This willingness to be inclusive, rather than exclusive, is modeled throughout the day in equitable and appropriate treatment of students—no favorites, none ignored or addressed with short temper, all accepted as full members of the group. This equity and respect of others is also put forth as a clear expectation of each student and his/her treatment of others.

The LIFESKILL of Friendship is multifaceted; learning it begins the first day of class. We must teach students the importance of being inclusive in our relationships with others, to understand that a close friendship with one person does not mean we can't also have a close friendship with another or several others. Opening ourselves up to multiple close friendships is not a sign of disloyalty or an indication that one of the friendships is less valuable to us. Instead, it may be an indication of many personal interests, hobbies, personality comfort zone, or proximity (neighborhood or groups we belong to that meet weekly).

At this first stage of community development, students need lots of interaction to get to know each other and practice the Lifelong

---

* Although time spent developing a sense of community may initially seem to be an unaffordable luxury in the face of today's curriculum demands, the many school shootings and tragedies tell us otherwise. Common descriptors of such students include: he never belonged, he was a loner who kept to himself, he was never accepted, he was different, he was an outcast, he was teased/bullied, no one had any idea that he was struggling with so many problems . . . he was just a quiet kid that kept to himself.

Guidelines—Trustworthiness, Truthfulness, Active Listening, No Put-Downs, and Personal Best. They need opportunities to explore life's perennial questions: Who are we? What will we do together? How will we treat each other? Will I be safe? Will I be allowed to be myself? All of such discovery requires that students move beyond stereotypes to see each classmate as an individual yet as a member of their classroom and Learning Club and to understand and appreciate each other's gifts and talents. This stage of building a community of learners parallels the formin' stage, the first of four stages described by Bruce Wayne Tuckman, a pioneer in group development, in 1965.[2] Tuckman's descriptions of group development are widely used in business and governmental settings as well as in education.

Developing a sense of belonging is built over time through many shared activities that add meaning to students' lives. Be aware that you will need many such activities because this stage must be nurtured throughout the school year. It is not something initially achieved and then left behind; it must be reinforced and nurtured all year long, becoming stronger over time in order to support work that challenges the group because it surfaces disagreements, demands resolution of problems, and necessitates compromise.

Plan activities daily for the first month of school no matter the grade level. Continue at least weekly the remainder of the school year (more frequently if you have new students joining your class). When your students start to wrangle with each other, you'll know it's time to bring out more activities and do some reteaching.

Don't try to reinvent the wheel; there are excellent, ready-made resources. We recommend you own a copy of the following: *Cooperative Learning* and a set of *SmartCards* both by Spencer Kagan. There are also many on-line resources. Using Google, search keywords such as professional development activities, team building activities, inclusion activities, and ice breakers. You will find many activities in the public domain that can be used in any way you choose without copyright infringement.

See examples of how to weave these activities into the first day of school in Chapter 7, beginning on page 7.18 for primary grades and page 7.26 for intermediate grades.

Keep in mind that this stage may take days or months depending upon factors such as the following:

- The level of personal and social skills your students bring to the classroom

- Student turnover in your class

- The amount of group disruption due to extensive pullout programming

- The consistency of your modeling and expectations

- The focus you give to community development (frequency and intensity of initial teaching/practice, reteaching, use of the teachable moment, and so forth)

Whatever the challenges, **do not** succumb to the urge to move on before this stage is solidly in place.

Students Are Showing Signs of Developing a Sense of Belonging When They

- Know each other's names

- Are participating members of their Learning Club

- Are actively listened to when they speak and actively listen when others speak

- Feel free to speak up during class and Town Hall Meetings

- Enjoy coming to school and indicate they like their classmates and teacher

- Use the Lifelong Guidelines and LIFESKILLS with others and expect others to use them in school interactions

- Refrain from Put-Downs and readily and sincerely give appreciations of others

- Are willing to work with a new study partner or group

- Welcome and immediately include new students and visitors into their Learning Club and the class

- Know and appreciate the strengths of each individual in the class

- Are sensitive to what is happening to others in the class and consistently use the LIFESKILLS of Caring and Friendship so that there are no loners or isolated students

Students Need More Practice Developing a Sense of Belonging When They

- Do not feel free to speak up or share ideas during Learning Club, class, and/or Town Hall Meetings

- Do not actively participate in Learning Club and class activities

- Do not use the Lifelong Guidelines and LIFESKILLS in classroom interactions

- Do not actively listen to others

- Do not welcome new students and visitors into their Learning Club and class

- Put others down

- Treat people preferentially; have special buddies and exclude others from membership in their circle of friends

- Notice someone alone and do nothing to invite him/her to join in (classroom, playground, cafeteria)

- Don't create a sense of inclusion for new students and other visitors

- Don't offer help and directions to a visitor on campus

Creating Common Ground

To create common ground, you must help students to:

- Create and maintain the conditions that make it safe to disagree

- Understand that it is okay to hold differing opinions

- Realize that it is equally okay to change one's mind without it being considered a sign of weakness or of losing face

Just as we expect citizens in our melting pot of nationalities, races, creeds, religions, socioeconomic status, and languages to work together to make our democratic government work, so we expect it in the classroom. Just realize in advance that this takes lots of practice, patience, and perseverance—all guided by a high level of intention that common ground can and will be achieved.

This is the stormin' stage described by Tuckman,[3] characterized by challenging the leadership (yours and the group's), experimenting with power and how to wield it, sticking to a position out of pride and refusal to back down before one's peers, learning when and how to lead and when and how to follow, etc. Conflict at this stage, and in life, is inevitable. Your goal must be to help students learn effective skills and strategies to navigate through conflict rather than to minimize or shrink from it.

In this stage of creating community, students must make a commitment to community—Spock's mantra (of Star Trek), "the good of the many outweighs the needs of a few." They must also transition from following the Lifelong Guidelines/LIFESKILLS as agreed-upon behaviors to using the Lifelong Guidelines/ LIFESKILLS as foundation stones with which to build their lives.

Even with daily work on this stage, expect that it will take time for students to internalize the processes. There are no magic formulas. Use your common sense, your knowledge of developmental levels of students (primary, intermediate, middle school, high school), and your knowledge of this particular group of students. What you're creating is an experience of what is possible when people commit themselves to work together to accomplish tasks that make a difference in the world. Citizenship succeeds or fails at this step in community building—in a classroom, a homeowners' association, or a city council.

The depth of coming to know and respect others while creating common ground helps open up a grasp of the richness of the wider world and a curiosity to explore it. The sooner students discover that there is more than one valid point of view to consider, the sooner they can begin to appreciate and participate in the role of informed citizen.

For resources supporting the developing of this stage, see those mentioned on page 9.3 plus the discussion of conducting a Town Hall Meeting that follows.

Students Are Showing Signs of Creating Common Ground When They

- Are willing to remind each other to use the Lifelong Guidelines and LIFESKILLS

- Feel free to express their opinions in their Learning Club and the classroom

- Feel free to disagree and yet are willing to change their position when the facts warrant it or when the majority votes for another position

- Focus on the facts and merits of an issue, not on the person who advocates it

- Look forward to solving problems and making decisions because they are confident in the group's (Learning Club and class) ability to do so and feel safe during the process

- Are willing to iron out differences for the good of the group rather than press for a win-lose solution

- Have developed skills to resolve conflicts one-on-one or through more formal means such as mediation and Town

Hall Meetings

- Are comfortable with being the leader for a project yet willing to allow and support someone else to lead when that person has been assigned that responsibility by the group

Students Need More Practice Creating Common Ground When They

- Refuse to listen to classmates who are trying to remind them to use the Lifelong Guidelines and LIFESKILLS

- Continue arguing for their position because they don't want to give in even when it is not the solution or course of action voted on by the group

- Refuse to support the action agreed to by the group because it wasn't their idea

- Argue positions based on who advocates it rather than on its facts and merits

- Cause disruptions so the group can't reach agreement or bring an issue to a vote

- Have to win at all costs and neglect to think of the good of the group

- Undermine implementation of an agreed-upon course of action

Taking Action

Taking Action is the use of community to achieve academically—individually and as a group—and to perform any number of tasks, especially social/political action projects that emerge from studying the curriculum.[4] As Herbert Spencer, English philosopher noted: "The great aim of education is not knowledge, but action."[5]

The goals of this stage of group development are to:

- Strengthen the sense of belonging through working together to accomplish an agreed-upon task

- Give students practice in applying the personal and social skills needed to create and maintain common ground

- Provide practice using the concepts and skills of our curriculum in real-world situations

- Give students practice in using the levers of our democratic society to change for the common good

Teaching students how and when and why they should Take Action is the ultimate purpose of public education, the reason we have tax payer-supported free education in this country.[6] That we should have taught them the basic skills at high levels is a given. That they should understand the concepts and issues before them is a given. That there has been rigor and high expectations is a given. Thomas Jefferson understood that a democratic society was and continues to be dependent upon public education for all, public education that understands and remains true to its mission to create an informed, participating citizenry.

Students Are Showing Signs of Taking Action When They

- Help develop inquiries for curriculum content and select those that most challenge their ability to apply the concepts and skills to real-world situations

- Invite classmates to join them in self-generated projects

- Take responsibility for helping set the agenda and conduct Town Hall Meetings

- Understand the need to give and serve others in the community and larger world (citizens acting individually and in groups)

- Generate ideas for Social/Political Action Projects

- Carry the majority of the responsibility for planning and carrying out Social/Political Action Projects

- Self-organize within their Learning Club to take on projects to improve the school and community and to help those less fortunate

Students Need More Practice Taking Action When They

- Need frequent reminders to use the Lifelong Guidelines/ LIFESKILLS

- Remain unfocused; do not take charge of their own learning; are content to let time slip by; don't set personal or group learning goals

- Need to be motivated or prodded by their teacher to work on their projects

- Wait for their teacher to select and plan Social/Political Action Projects

- Don't understand the need to help improve their school or community or to help those less fortunate than they

PUTTING IT ALL TOGETHER: IMPLEMENTING THE LIFELONG GUIDELINES & LIFESKILLS THROUGH TOWN HALL MEETINGS

As stated before, the Lifelong Guidelines and LIFESKILLS are not meant to be the basis for a rule-based discipline program; they are the ingredients necessary to build a community of learners. They are for everyone—a common language for agreed-upon behaviors of all staff (certified and

classified), students, and parents. They solve the mystery of how to be successful in the classroom, the school, and in life. Their use is a tangible commitment to creating a sense of group—a community of learners—a prerequisite to improving academic outcomes. They are both context and vehicle for practicing citizenship in the classroom through Town Hall Meetings.

Why Town Hall Meetings

Community does not happen accidentally or overnight. Both teacher and students must share this goal and be intentional about developing it. Getting together in formal and informal ways in order to get to know one another better and solve problems facing the group is as old as time and critical to the democratic processes of our society.

The commonsense core of group-building is this: You can't build a sense of community if you don't get together and act like a community. Town Hall Meetings provide opportunities to teach students how to become involved, informed citizens. The Lifelong Guidelines and LIFESKILLS provide the context for being together (the behaviors and skills that allow community to develop) and, often, the agenda items for the meeting (the behaviors not being followed that cause problems among members of the group).

The purposes for calling a Town Hall Meeting are to:

- Nurture ongoing community building at each stage of group development through a variety of agendas such as:

  — Selected activities at each stage of group development

  — Sharing acknowledgements

  — Celebrating accomplishments

  — Introducing a new student to the classroom

  — Planning and carrying out Social/Political Action Projects

- Solve problems affecting the entire class

- Develop or revise written procedures and other guidelines or rubrics to create greater student self-direction in learning and self-governance of the classroom

- Make decisions about class projects

- Learn the necessary skills to lead and participate in formal meetings

- Experience firsthand the civics lessons described in the state/district curriculum standards[7]

Town Hall Meetings as a Vehicle for Group Development

Not all activities to create a community of learners occur in Town Hall Meetings. However, an important goal of every Town Hall Meeting is to further develop a sense of community. Therefore, always make sure that the task you ask of students in a Town Hall Meeting is clearly articulated, appropriate for the age of your students, and suitable for the stage of community development at the moment. For example, don't expect students to handle the pressure of persuasion or influence based in social standing and still come to agreement on something before you've built a sense of belonging and they've learned to work through conflict to create common ground. (Refer to pages 9.2-6.)

How to Start

For the first two weeks of school, Town Hall Meetings should be conducted every day, led by the teacher. However, as student skill develops, students may request a meeting and may co-chair selected meetings as appropriate.

After two weeks, evaluate your students' progress. Do they need more experience with Town Hall Meetings to master the personal and social skills needed? Or is the need for group problem solving a daily occurrence? If so, continue meeting frequently, daily if needed. As students become more adept at creating common ground, try scheduling Town Hall Meetings just twice a week, adding additional meetings as needed.

Let agendas for meetings emerge from the needs of the classroom. For example:

- Build a sense of community

- Implement the Lifelong Guidelines/LIFESKILLS

- Develop/revise written procedures for guiding personal and group behaviors (such as morning entry or end of day procedures)

- Share acknowledgments

- Solve behavior problems that affect the class

TEACHING STUDENTS STRATEGIES FOR COPING AND CLEANING THINGS UP

Living the Lifelong Guidelines and LIFESKILLS requires two key strategies: Coping when others don't follow the Lifelong Guidelines and LIFESKILLS and cleaning things up when we (students and teacher) don't follow them.

Coping Strategies

Strategies for coping:[8] include

- Ignore it.

- Walk away or do hook-ups (see *Brain Gym).*

- Go to another activity.

- Talk it out.

- Use an "I" message. I feel ____ when ____. I need ____.

- Go back and try again.

- Apologize if needed.

- Tell him/her/them to stop.

- Stop to cool off.

- Count from 1 to 25 to cool off.

- Take 10 deep breaths and release them slowly.

- Problem-solve with a friend or with your Learning Club.

- Add the issue to a Town Hall Meeting agenda.

- Draw a picture to show what happened; share it with someone.

- Write about the incident in your journal.

- Do a "freeze frame" (see *HeartMath Solutions).*

Strategies for Cleaning Things Up

Strategies for cleaning things up include:

- Make sure you understand how you made the person feel when you didn't follow the Lifelong Guidelines and LIFESKILLS.

- Apologize with more than a simple "I'm sorry." Be specific. Restate the harm that you did, such as hurt their feelings, humiliated them in front of others, bruised their arm, or broke something.

- Ask what you can do to repair the harm and what you can do to make it up to them. If it's within reason and appropriate to the damage inflicted, do it without delay and do it sincerely.

- Learn from your mistakes. Ask yourself why you did what you did. Was it to feel important? To avoid looking weak or less than perfect? To avoid consequences for earlier misbehavior? Remember, whittling away at others never makes us feel better about ourselves. Figure out how to meet your own needs. That is your responsibility, something no one else can do for you.

Reflective thinking so that we understand why we did what we did and how it affected the other person is critical to learning to change and master our behavior—to have emotions but not be run by them. Never underestimate the importance of questions that cause students to reflect on their internal thoughts and reactions to external events. It is the examined life that Socrates so prized.

See discussions of reflective thinking on pages 1.27-1.28, 2.9-2.12, 3.16-17, 4.23-24, 5.16, and 10.12-10.13.

HOW TO TEACH THE LIFELONG GUIDELINES AND LIFESKILLS

There are innumerable ways to begin using the Lifelong Guidelines and LIFESKILLS. This chapter contains advice from those who have gone before you as described in *Tools for Citizenship and Life*[9] by Sue Pearson. We highly recommend you own your own copy of this book and use it daily.

To get off to a good start, plan thoroughly before you begin. Some steps are mechanical, such as setting and sticking to an organized schedule and using a variety of instructional strategies to teach, reteach, and reinforce (see Chapters 7, 10, and 15.). Other steps will require personal transitions. Be open to the power that the Lifelong Guidelines and LIFESKILLS can have in your life and in that of your students. Your most rewarding and satisfying years of teaching are just around the corner!

Consider the following planning steps:

- Take time to reflect; do a self-evaluation of your own understanding and practice of the Lifelong Guidelines and LIFESKILLS; set personal goals for improving.

- Start with the Lifelong Guidelines; begin the first day of school.

- Create a schedule for teaching and implementing the Lifelong Guidelines and LIFESKILLS for the first four to five weeks; know what you want to teach and the activities the students will do each day.

- Teach the Lifelong Guidelines/LIFESKILLS through weekly (daily in the early weeks of the year) literature selections that you read aloud to the class and for other reading assignments.

- Use graphic organizers to make the behaviors associated with the Lifelong Guidelines and LIFESKILLS.

- Use real-world events and to capture the teachable moment.

Take Time to Reflect

Before you begin, take time to assess your own personal understanding of the Lifelong Guidelines and LIFESKILLS.

The Importance of Self-Evaluation. Evaluate yourself in relation to each of the Lifelong Guidelines and the LIFESKILLS. Which ones are strengths for you? Are some "just okay?" Are some not as strong as they need to be? Remember, these behavior guidelines are something you must live and model, not just teach about.

If you're like co-author Karen Olsen, some will make you squirm. Organization? Karen had to jump up from the computer and start organizing and cleaning her house. You can't just talk about the Lifelong Guidelines and LIFESKILLS, you have to live them! (See the discussion about modeling in Chapter 10.)

Bring It Home. The classroom is your living room and students need to feel welcome. As you reflect on your own use of the Lifelong Guidelines and LIFESKILLS as a teacher, it often helps to picture how you would want your own children, nieces and nephews, or grand-children treated; then, commit yourself to treating other people's children that same way. The quality and nature of the connections between the teacher and his/her students, and among students, are the basis for all else in the classroom, especially academic learning. Model the behaviors you would show to honored guests visiting your home and business—behaviors that exemplify the Lifelong Guidelines of Trustworthiness, Truthfulness, Active Listening, No Put-Downs, and Personal Best defined by the LIFESKILLS.

Start with the Lifelong Guidelines the First Day of School

What usually works best is to introduce all five Lifelong Guidelines at once as a collection of behaviors to enhance learning and being together for everyone. Then, go back and teach each Lifelong Guideline in-depth using the instructional strategies described in Chapters 7, 10, and 15.

Enhancing the Physical Environment. The physical environment sends a continuous message to students. So, design it with care. Choose a focal point in the classroom/school to display the Lifelong Guidelines and LIFESKILLS for immediate reference. The back of the room, for instance, is not a handy place. Until everyone is totally familiar and comfortable with the Lifelong Guidelines, daily visual reminders will help in recognizing and identifying expectations. With the terms and definitions posted, it's easier to remember to use Life Lingo (see Chapter 21) as a reinforcement strategy. Some teachers also prepare copies of the Lifelong Guidelines (and later, the LIFESKILLS) for every student to place in his/her binder or notebook. Providing copies for parents helps to provide a basis for common vocabulary between the home and school and allows for reinforcement and connections outside of the school day.

Parent/Family Involvement. Parents want to know what is happening in the classroom. The Lifelong Guidelines and LIFESKILLS are easy to share with parents and readily understandable. Whether you're part of a schoolwide effort or working alone in your classroom, it's important to keep family members informed of the behaviors that are expected in class.

A newsletter is one vehicle for building understanding of the Guidelines. First, send a general introduction to all the Lifelong Guidelines and LIFESKILLS (see the sample letters at the end of this chapter). In future issues, offer more information about the specific activities students will be doing.

For parents who want to reinforce the Lifelong Guidelines and LIFESKILLS at home, we recommend the parent version of *Tools for Citizenship and Life: Using the Lifelong Guidelines and LIFESKILLS in Your Classroom* called *Character Begins at Home: Using the ITI/HET Lifelong Guidelines and LIFESKILLS in Your Home* by Sue Pearson and Karen D. Olsen. These two books work as companions to nurture the home-school partnership.

Create a Schedule

Good teaching is not an accident. You must have a month-long plan that tells you what to do from day to day. The following plans are recommended by numerous *HET* practitioners and associates of Susan Kovalik & Associates. Adopt or adapt to fit the needs of your students.

Plan #1: One a Week. The "one a week" plan is a popular one with *HET* teachers. Its strength is that it allows you to focus in depth on one Lifelong Guideline (and later on, one LIFESKILL) at a time. This is particularly important with younger students.

- Week One—Trustworthiness
- Week Two—Truthfulness
- Week Three—Active Listening
- Week Four—No Put-Downs
- Week Five—Personal Best

The following outline offers suggestions for teaching and providing practice for the Lifelong Guideline each day during each of the five weeks. For example, for the first week focusing on the Lifelong Guideline of Trustworthiness:

- Monday—definition of the Lifelong Guideline of Trustworthiness illustrated through literature and song

- Tuesday—video segment showing both use and lack of use of Trustworthiness plus discussion and role playing

- Wednesday—song, T-chart, and literature illustrating Trustworthiness

- Thursday—role playing and literature illustrating Trustworthiness

- Friday—song, role playing, and journal writing illustrating Trustworthiness

For the second week focusing on the Lifelong Guideline of Truthfulness, you could use the same combination of teaching strategies as shown above or change them as you see fit. Likewise, for the third, fourth, and fifth weeks focus on the remaining Lifelong Guidelines of Active Listening, No Put-Downs, and Personal Best. Follow the suggestions or feel free to change them according to your intuition.

For descriptions of the teaching strategies referred to above, see Chapter 7 and 10.

Plan #2: One a Day and Repeat. The "one a day and repeat" plan is also easy to use. Designed by Joy Raboli, it allows students to see where they are going by the end of the first week. This is useful for older students from upper elementary through high school. You decide based on your own students' needs, learning patterns, and temperament.

Under this plan, set aside a small portion of each day to develop a deeper understanding of the Lifelong Guidelines. The time of day isn't important, although most teachers prefer to have a set schedule so they are sure to teach them each day. This plan focuses on a particular Lifelong Guideline each day of the week and repeats the week throughout the month.

- Monday—Trustworthiness

- Tuesday—Truthfulness

- Wednesday—Active Listening

- Thursday—No Put-Downs

- Friday—Personal Best

For example, a schedule for Plan #2 might look like the graphic on the next page.

Plan #3: Your Choice. A few teachers have asked why they even have to have a plan for introducing and teaching the Lifelong Guidelines and LIFESKILLS. They have felt that it should just be taught naturally, whenever the circumstances are appropriate. We, too, believe in teaching them in the most natural way possible during the teachable moment. But, we also know that current curricular demands have a way of pushing the best of intentions aside. The result, all too often, is that focus is lost and so are the lessons to be learned.

Communicating with Parents / Families

Whichever schedule for incorporating the Lifelong Guidelines and LIFESKILLS you adopt/adapt, be sure you communicate to families what you are doing, how, when, and why. The letters to parents on pages 9.18-9.19 can help open a teacher-parent dialogue about first the Lifelong Guidelines and then later the LIFESKILLS.

Using Literature

There are innumerable ways to use literature to introduce, reteach, or reinforce the Lifelong Guidelines and LIFESKILLS. Here are but a few. Remember to think of changes you would make for your own students and your literary choices. The examples here are

LIFELONG GUIDELINES
TRUSTWORTHINESS   TRUTHFULNESS
ACTIVE LISTENING   NO PUT-DOWNS
PERSONAL BEST

		Mon	Tue	Wed	Thu	Fri
		DAY ONE **TRUSTWORTHINESS**	**DAY TWO** **TRUTHFULNESS**	**DAY THREE** **ACTIVE LISTENING**	**DAY FOUR** **NO PUT-DOWNS**	**DAY FIVE** **PERSONAL BEST**
WEEK	ONE	**TRUSTWORTHINESS** Define~Story~Discuss	**TRUTHFULNESS** Define~Story~Discuss	**ACTIVE LISTENING** Define~Story~Discuss	**NO PUT-DOWNS** Define~Story~Discuss	**PERSONAL BEST** Define~Story~Discuss
	TWO	**TRUSTWORTHINESS** Video~Tally~Graph	**TRUTHFULNESS** Video~Tally~Graph	**ACTIVE LISTENING** Video~Tally~Graph	**NO PUT-DOWNS** Video~Tally~Graph	**PERSONAL BEST** Video~Tally~Graph
	THREE	**TRUSTWORTHINESS** T-chart~Role Play~Real Life	**TRUTHFULNESS** T-chart~Role Play~Real Life	**ACTIVE LISTENING** T-chart~Role Play~Real Life	**NO PUT-DOWNS** T-chart~Role Play~Real Life	**PERSONAL BEST** T-chart~Role Play~Real Life
	FOUR	**TRUSTWORTHINESS** Creative Writing~Journal	**TRUTHFULNESS** Creative Writing~Journal	**ACTIVE LISTENING** Creative Writing~Journal	**NO PUT-DOWNS** Creative Writing~Journal	**PERSONAL BEST** Creative Writing~Journal
		The Bears on Hemlock Mountain, The Velveteen Rabbit, The Secret Garden	*Berenstein Bears Tell the Truth, Sam, Bangs and Moonshine, Pinocchio*	*3 Little Pigs-Wolf's Point of View, Charlotte's Web, Horton Hears a Who*	*Ugly Duckling, Ira Sleeps Over, Crow Boy, Whipping Boy, Charlie Brown books*	*Amazing Grace, Stone Fox, The Giving Tree, The Three Little Pigs, Brave Irene*

the target word on the ray and the action below the ray. For example, based on *Charlotte's Web*, put the name Wilbur in the center circle. Add a ray; above it write Perseverance; under the ray write the descriptors of action from the text, e.g., "He thought and thought until he created a plan to help save his friend Charlotte, the spider." (See an example of such a character web on the next page.)

- Identify three Lifelong Guidelines or LIFESKILLS that were used to solve a problem in the story. Identify two Lifelong Guidelines or LIFESKILLS that were not used and thus contributed to problems.

- Read a traditional story such as *The Three Little Pigs*. Rewrite the ending as if the pigs had used the Lifelong Guideline of Personal Best to solve their problem with the wolf.

for teaching a Lifelong Guideline or LIFESKILL. (See *Tools for Citizenship and Life: Using the HET Lifelong Guidelines and LIFESKILLS in Your Classroom.*)

- Character Web: Read a book that exemplifies one of the Lifelong Guidelines or LIFESKILLS. Write the name of one main character in the center of a piece of chart tablet paper. Draw a circle around the name. Add rays coming out from the circle, similar to a child's drawing of the sun. (For very young students, consider using a felt story board with images rather than words.) Have your students identify a Lifelong Guideline or LIFESKILL that this storybook character used to solve problems and reach his/her goals. Write

- After reading a biography or autobiography, label three or more Lifelong Guidelines or LIFESKILLS that the person used well. Link them to actions from the book. Next, invite members of your Learning Club to share their experiences in developing these same Lifelong Guidelines or LIFESKILLS. Using a Venn diagram, identify the behaviors associated with the selected LIFESKILLS that the book character and your learning-club members have in common and which behaviors are different. Again using a Venn diagram, compare two LIFESKILLS you use to do your personal best with those used by a character in the story.

- After completing several stories, play "Who Am I?" Choose a character from a previously read book. Share the Lifelong Guidelines/LIFESKILLS used along with one or two related actions to carry out the Lifelong Guidelines/LIFESKILLS. Invite other students who have read the book to guess who the character is.

- Compare three LIFESKILLS used by two well-known people. Select people from different time periods and settings such as Madame Curie and Rosa Parks. List three LIFESKILL strengths they have in common. List three weaknesses that each one has. Discuss whether or not the LIFESKILLS are unique to the time period/setting of the story.

- Find local newspaper articles describing problems that are occurring because people didn't use the Lifelong Guidelines/LIFESKILLS. Read the articles with your students and have them determine which Lifelong Guideline or LIFESKILL was or wasn't used. Ask students to share their thinking with other members of their Learning Club.

Hopefully these few ideas will have you thinking in many different directions. Perhaps you remember a favorite biography and think, "Of course, why didn't I ever mention perseverance when we read about Thomas Edison or Rosa Parks?" Or, perhaps you recall a link to humor using *Charlotte's Web*? How about the courage shown in *The True Story of Ruby Bridges*? Eventually, you'll wonder why you ever thought it would be hard to make connections. They'll be popping up everywhere!

A character web for the book entitled *Charlotte's Web* could look like the following.

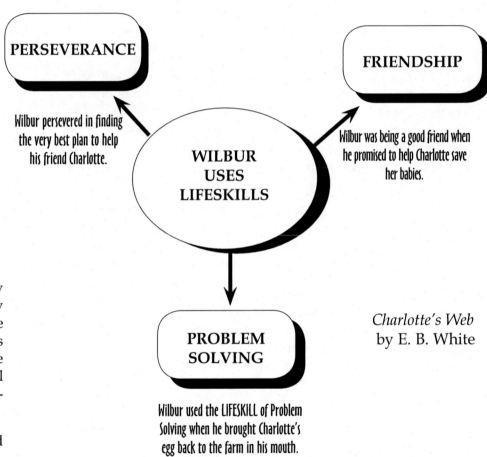

PERSEVERANCE

Wilbur persevered in finding the very best plan to help his friend Charlotte.

WILBUR USES LIFESKILLS

FRIENDSHIP

Wilbur was being a good friend when he promised to help Charlotte save her babies.

PROBLEM SOLVING

Wilbur used the LIFESKILL of Problem Solving when he brought Charlotte's egg back to the farm in his mouth.

Charlotte's Web by E. B. White

Graphic Organizers

There are many kinds of graphic organizers; each has its purpose. Students should learn how to use all of them, a task they can do very easily if their use is modeled by the teacher during direct instruction and required by those inquiries for which they are particularly useful. (See also pages 10.13-10.15)

T-Charts are an excellent graphic organizer to help introduce, reteach, or reinforce a Lifelong Guideline or LIFESKILL.

Kinds of T-Charts. There are many kinds of T-charts. The common element is that they have two or more columns which allow students to compare or contrast information about a topic. The two most common T-charts are the LSF chart (looks, sounds, feels like) show on the next page and the KWL (know, want to know, have learned) chart (see also pages 10.14-10.16).

The LSF T-chart asks students to analyze a concept or skill for relevant attributes—what something *l*ooks like, *s*ounds like, and *f*eels like and then what it does not look, sound, and feel like. The simple and more comprehensive versions of such T-charts are illustrated on 9.15-9.17 using the Lifelong Guideline of Trustworthiness.

How to Use T-Charts. Using a large chart tablet, write the name of the concept or skill across the top of the page; select two or more attributes that will help students focus on key aspects of the concept or skill. Create and name these columns. By adding a comparison of what something is to what it isn't, students can more easily develop a broader and deeper understanding of what they are learning.

Then, ask students to think of personal experiences at school or situations from stories they have read that will fit into each category. Allow them sufficient time to think to fill in the spaces with minimal prompting. Let them use their own words (for younger students, draw simple pictures to illustrate the meaning). Once students can connect new learning to previous personal experiences, learning speeds up significantly. As for the Lifelong Guidelines and LIFESKILLS, students' intuitive understanding of them is often surprising.

Save the T-chart(s) and add to the columns daily throughout the first week of study and weekly thereafter as students identify more attributes. The more pictures students have for a concept or skill, the more adept they will become in applying them in real-world settings and the more likely the concept/skill will become wired into long-term memory.

Use Real-World Happenings to Capture the Teachable Moment

The real power in teaching the Lifelong Guidelines and LIFESKILLS comes from making them part of daily living. This means using real-world happenings to capture the teachable moment rather than depending on an occasional, carefully prepared or canned lesson.

For a discussion of daily teaching strategies that will allow you to capture the teachable moment, see Life Lingo, pages 7.6-7.8.

The curriculum content of the teachable moment lies right at your finger tips—your own experiences with school as a child and your students' current and past experiences with school. For older students, include current events from community, nation, and world.

Teacher's Childhood Experiences at School. Since students love hearing stories of their teacher's experiences, begin by telling about your own learning experiences in school. When did you feel safe enough in school to take a risk? What things happened that kept you from being the best student you could be? What mistakes do you still regret? What were your most embarrassing moments? Use your LIFESKILL of Sense of Humor. Avoid becoming preachy. Let children know that, for all of us, our lives are a work in progress and that the Lifelong Guidelines and LIFESKILLS are lifelong pursuits.

Invite students to share examples of situations when they have felt safe and comfortable enough for learning to take place. Ask for examples of behaviors that prohibit or limit learning for them. Provide time for small groups to create a mindmap or other visual organizer detailing conditions that promote learning for everyone. Then present the Lifelong Guidelines (or later, the LIFESKILLS) and suggest that the Learning Clubs organize their responses to match up with a Lifelong Guideline/ LIFESKILL. For example, if one Learning Club's mindmap has, "It helps us when people listen to our ideas," this would support the Lifelong Guideline of Active Listening. Another group may have, "When people speak respectfully to us, we can concentrate on learning," and might decide that this links to the Lifelong Guideline of No Put-Downs. After all of the positive learning behaviors have been categorized, agree that these guidelines will be part of classroom life.

Students' Experiences at School. From a student perspective, a school day is full of experiences—good and bad. Use these events and interactions at school as the context for discussing the Lifelong Guidelines and LIFESKILLS. During Town Hall Meetings, invite the students to share some of the problems they have experienced during school, past and present, that kept them from concentrating on learning, e.g., fights on the playground, name calling, use of put-downs, a bully who frightened them, and friends telling lies.

Current Events. For older students, a discussion of current issues in the news can lead into the Lifelong Guidelines and LIFESKILLS. Pose pertinent questions to promote analysis of what Lifelong Guidelines or LIFESKILLS helped the people to solve the problem or accomplish what they did. And what Lifelong Guidelines and LIFESKILLS didn't the people use that landed them in the predicament described in the news articles. What characteristics in people do the students admire?

TRUSTWORTHINESS

Looks Like	Sounds Like	Feels Like
students sharing ideas	"I've got something to share!"	safety
people working together	"Will you teach me how to do that?"	comfortable
student running an errand	"Please take this to Mrs. X down the street."	I'm trusted
students helping one another	"Would you help me?" "Yes."	friendliness
student turning in found object	"I found this. It belongs to someone else."	honesty

TRUSTWORTHINESS

Looks Like	Sounds Like	Feels Like	Doesn't Look Like	Doesn't Sound Like	Doesn't Feel Like
going on an errand alone	"You can do it!	special	someone supervising you	"I know you can't get there without getting into trouble."	sarcastic
borrowing a library book	"I know you will take good care of it."	honored	losing a library book	"I think somebody stole it!"	distrust
finding money	"Thank you for bringing the money to the lost and found."	trusted	pocketing found money	"Finders keepers! Losers weepers!"	suspicion
going to a friend's house	"Be home on time."	someone depends on me	sneaking out of the house	"I wouldn't do that. Trust me!"	lying

Are these the only lessons that teach about the Lifelong Guidelines? No. There are many more. Our purpose is to offer some beginning points. Go back to your own roots and experiences for hooks that will help you make the Lifelong Guidelines and LIFESKILLS memorable and part of the fabric of classroom life.

IT STARTS WITH STAFF

Implementing the Lifelong Guidelines and LIFESKILLS must begin with the adults on campus—all staff, not just teachers and classroom aides. This means bus drivers, coaches, cafeteria personnel, maintenance staff, parent volunteers, and visitors. Everyone. To get each one on the same page, generate a T-chart just as you would with students. The T-charts on the next page were generated by teachers and administrators at a Summer Institute[10] training. The differences between what should be and what should not be make a drastic difference in community. The Lifelong Guidelines and LIFESKILLS are something everyone does. "Do what I say, not what I do" has never worked and never will.

LIFELONG GUIDELINE—*when used by staff with staff*

Trustworthiness

Looks Like:	Sounds Like:	Feels Like:
communal resources	addressing issues directly	equality
whole staff collaboration, professional mutual respect	sharing useful information	team effort productive
laughter	sharing ideas/curriculum	safety, family
living up to responsibilities; keeping one's word	adequate time to discuss differences	support is dependable

Behaviors Should No Longer Look, Sound, or Feel Like:
▪rumors ▪favoritism ▪missing materials ▪frequent absences ▪terrified new teachers ▪competition ▪power struggles ▪put downs of children ▪fear of failure ▪betrayal ▪empty promises ▪gossip

LIFELONG GUIDELINE—*when used by staff with staff*

Truthfulness

Looks Like:	Sounds Like:	Feels Like:
eye contact	ownership by using "I" statements	safe, non-threatening
active listening	open communication	respectful
cohesiveness, okay to disagree	verbal reinforcement, compliments	opinion is valued
calmness	constructive feedback	validating, supportive

Behaviors Should No Longer Look, Sound, or Feel Like:
▪withholding ▪dishonesty ▪deceit ▪gossip ▪cliques ▪labeling others

LIFELONG GUIDELINE——*when used by staff with staff*

Active Listening

Looks Like:	Sounds Like:	Feels Like:
eye contact	respectful silence awareness on speaker	non-judgmental
open body language	collegial, refreshing, connected	energized
nodding, smile	respond with respect, calm voices	respectful, trusting
focused attention	one voice at a time	positive atmosphere

Behaviors Should No Longer Look, Sound, or Feel Like:
▪misunderstood ▪rude interruptions ▪feelings of inequality ▪excluded ▪isolation ▪anger ▪frustration

LIFELONG GUIDELINE— —when used by staff with staff

No Put-Downs

Looks Like:	*Sounds Like:*	*Feels Like:*
energized gatherings	authentic conversations	supportive/understanding of peers
cooperation	no blaming someone else	loyalty to those not present
collaboration	appreciating input	willing to risk
a well functioning community	willing to hear other perspectives	safe teaching and learning environment

Behaviors Should No Longer Look, Sound, or Feel Like:
▪sarcasm ▪personal attacks ▪insults ▪demeaning ▪power trips ▪prejudice

LIFELONG GUIDELINE— —when used by staff with staff

Personal Best

Looks Like:	*Sounds Like:*	*Feels Like:*
professional appearance	open communication willingness to share	relaxed
self-confidence	comments of appreciation	positive, warmth
organized	open to others' perspectives	team pride
walk the LIFESKILL talk	talk the LIFESKILLS talk	contagious atmosphere of excellence

Behaviors Should No Longer Look, Sound, or Feel Like:
▪negative, unwillingness to improve ▪blaming others for problems ▪sloppy ▪refusal ▪apathy

WHEN TO TEACH THE LIFESKILLS

Remember that the LIFESKILLS are not separate from the Lifelong Guidelines; they define the Lifelong Guideline of Personal Best. Begin teaching the LIFESKILLS only when you are ready to teach the Lifelong Guideline of Personal Best.

To teach the LIFESKILLS, use the same approaches that worked well for you when teaching the Lifelong Guidelines. Remember that developing habits of mind and heart take time. Master the instructional strategies described in Chapters 7, 10, and 15 so they are readily available for daily use. Above all, have fun with your students. Learning values and appropriate behaviors may be serious business but it need not be joyless! Enjoy watching your students (and yourself!) grow.

Date _____

Letters to Parents

Dear Family,

Who doesn't want to have a sense of community whether it be in the neighborhood, an organization, a church, or workplace? Community is that sense of belonging one feels when many hearts and minds come together to work toward a common goal and live by a common set of behavioral standards.

In our classroom, we will follow the Lifelong Guidelines of:

- TRUSTWORTHINESS   • ACTIVE LISTENING • PERSONAL
- TRUTHFULNESS   • NO PUT-DOWNS   BEST

These five Lifelong Guidelines are the agreed upon behaviors for our classroom—what behaviors to expect from ourselves and others. They are the social outcomes we set for the community. They also ensure that all students are in an environment that encourages exploring, discovering, and learning.

These behaviors contribute to a sense of workability in life, not only in our classroom now, but also as adults.

Sometime during the sixth century B.C., Lao-Tzu (a name meaning "old sage") wrote:

"The journey of a thousand miles begins with a single step."

As we venture into learning and living each guideline, I invite you to join us on our journey and provide an important supportive role in the development of our classroom community. We will keep you up-to-date with our progress through letters, newsletters and projects.

Sincerely,

Your child's teacher

Date _____

Dear Family,

Our class has been working hard to learn to live by the Lifelong Guidelines in our classroom community. Our efforts will continue throughout the year as we attach new meanings and deeper understandings of their application. At this time, we are ready to progress from group standards and expectations, the Lifelong Guidelines, to those that are more individual, the LIFESKILLS.

The fifth Lifelong Guideline, "PERSONAL BEST," is defined by 19 LIFESKILLS:

		CARING
COMMON SENSE	FLEXIBILITY	PERSEVERANCE
COOPERATION	FRIENDSHIP	PRIDE
COURAGE	INITIATIVE	PROBLEM SOLVING
CREATIVITY	INTEGRITY	RESOURCEFULNESS
CURIOSITY	ORGANIZATION	RESPONSIBILITY
EFFORT	PATIENCE	SENSE OF HUMOR

The Lifelong Guidelines and LIFESKILLS will be introduced in our community one at a time. This will assure that all students arrive at common understandings of the meanings of each and how to practice them.

Margaret Mead, a famous anthropologist, provides an inspiring quote to spark our journey:

"Never doubt that a small group of thoughtful, committed people can change the world. Indeed, it is the only thing that ever has."

Once again, we invite you to learn with us as we venture forth in creating our classroom community.

Sincerely,

Your child's teacher

ENDNOTES

1 William Glasser, *Control Theory in the Classroom* (New York: Harper & Row, Perennial Library, 1986). According to Glasser, there are four needs that must be met in the classroom (beyond survival): To belong and love, to gain power, to be free, and to have fun.

2 In 1965, Bruce Wayne Tuckman published his now famous article on group development entitled "Developmental Sequence in Small Groups." (*Psychological Bulletin*, 63, 384-399). The article was reprinted in *Group Facilitation: A Research and Applications Journal* - Number 3 (Spring 2001). It is also available at http://www.dennislearningcenter.osu.edu. He describes four stages and their characteristics: formin', stormin', normin', and performin'. Most current discussions of group development parallel these stages. In the *HET* version of building community, Tuckman's last two stages are grouped together. Hence, the three stages of developing community described in this book are: Developing a sense of belonging, creating common ground, and taking action.
Tuckman later added a fifth stage, adjourning.
Other resources for providing "getting to know you" exercises include: *Reaching All by Creating TRIBES Learning Communities* by Jeanne Gibbs and

3 Tuckman hoped that if people understood the stages that groups naturally progress through, they could work more effectively together and reach optimum functioning more quickly. Many groups, however, fail to break through the stormin' stage.

4 In a democratic society, taking action to preserve our democratic system is not an option. If we pay attention to the process of group development, we can learn to take action in ways that strengthen, not weaken, the glue that holds us together.

5 Hert Spencer, 1820-1903. Quote taken from "Education Quotes-The Quotation Page": http://www.quotationspage.com/subjects/education/

6 See Carl Glickman, *Renewing America's Schools* (San Francisco, CA: Jossey-Bass, 1993) for a powerful discussion of the purpose of public education in America and a call to action to fulfill that purpose.

7 Because creating an informed citizenry is the reason we provide free public education, you will find many state curriculum standards that apply to Town Hall Meetings. For example:

National Standards for Language Arts—K-12

NL-ENG. K-12.4 Communication Skills—Students adjust their use of spoken, written, and visual language (e.g., conventions, style, vocabulary) to communicate effectively with a variety of audiences and for different purposes.

NL-ENG. K-12.7—Students conduct research on issues and interests by generating ideas and questions, and by posing problems. They gather, evaluate, and synthesize data from a variety of sources (e.g., print and non-print texts, artifacts, people) to communicate their discoveries in ways that suit their purpose and audience.

NL-ENG. K-12 Developing Research Skills—Students use a variety of technological and information resources (e.g., libraries, databases, computer networks, video) to gather and synthesize information and to create and communicate knowledge.

NL-ENG. K-12 Applying Language Skills—Students use spoken, written, and visual language to accomplish their own purposes (e.g., for learning, enjoyment, persuasion, and the exchange of information).

National Standards for Civics and Government—K-4

NSS-C.K-4.1 What is government?

NSS-C.K-4.2 Values and principles of democracy

NSS-C K-4.3 Principles of democracy

NSS-C.K-4.5 Roles of the citizen

National Standards for Civics and Government—Grades 5-12

NSS-C.5-8.1; 9-12.1—Civic life, politics, and government

NSS-C.5-8.2; 9-12.2—Foundations of the political system

NSS-C.5-8.3; 9-12.3—Principles of democracy

NSS-C.5-8.5; 9-12.5—Roles of the citizen

8 List developed by Sue Pearson, associate, The Center for Effective Teaching.

9   This book plus posters of the Lifelong Guidelines/LIFESKILLS and their definitions are available through Books for Educators at books4educ.com

10 Summer Institutes are sponsored by Susan Kovalik & Associates, now known as The Center for Effective Teaching. They are designed to provide an overview of the *HET* model for teachers, administrators, board members, parents, and community members. For more information, or for a free brochure, call The Center for Effective Teaching or visit their Web site at www.thecenter4learning.com.

Chapter 10: What to Accomplish Before Moving to Stage 2

WHAT TO ACCOMPLISH BEFORE MOVING ON

CURRICULUM

- Formally teaches the concept of multiple intelligences—defined as problem-solving and product-producing capabilities—to students early in the year.
  Uses the multiple intelligences when developing inquiries and as a frequent, on-going topic for reflective thinking about the processes and products of collaborative work.

INSTRUCTIONAL STRATEGIES

- Includes real-life experiences—*being there*, immersion, hands-on materials, and visiting resource people—to supplement classroom instruction and provide rich input for each of the multiple intelligences.

- Is learning how to provide students with multiple ways to understand, solve problems, produce products, and demonstrate what they understand and can apply through:
  - Use of the multiple intelligences as a guide when lesson planning, selecting instructional strategies, and developing/selecting inquiries and other assignments for students, including homework
  - Use of the multiple intelligences during direct instruction of key points and other instructional strategies
  - Flexibility in allocating time for students to complete their work
  - Student choice of tasks, materials, and processes used for completing projects whenever appropriate

ACCOMPLISH BEFORE MOVING ON

HET Classroom Stages of Implementation
Making the learning environment bodybrain compatible —
Before Moving On

Stage 1.3

CURRICULUM

INSTRUCTIONAL STRATEGIES

- Has mastered the instructional skills identified in Stage 1.2 and continues to use them daily:

    - Modeling of the Lifelong Guidelines and LIFESKILLS
    - Life Lingo
    - "Discipline" based on using the Lifelong Guidelines & LIFESKILLS
    - Daily agenda
    - Written procedures
    - Models movement to enhance learning and uses it with students to energize and calm
    - Collaboration to enhance personal and social growth and increase achievement (includes the three phases of building community — developing a sense of belonging, creating common ground, and taking action)
    - Calm voice, heart-brain coherence, and emotionally centered
    - Nurturing reflective thinking through numerous strategies

ACCOMPLISH BEFORE MOVING ON

CURRICULUM

INSTRUCTIONAL STRATEGIES

- Is developing a variety of instructional strategies to ensure students can identify/understand *patterns* and develop *programs* for using what they understand understand and wire them into long-term memory. Such instructional strategies include:
  - Modeling how to be a lifelong learner and participating citizen
  - Expanded and deepened use of movement and daily aerobic exercise to enhance learning
  - Direct instruction, usually limited to 16 minutes per hour
  - Nurturing reflective thinking
  - Graphic organizers
  - Discussion and questioning
  - Role-playing
  - Literature
  - Songs
  - Video clips, great artwork, and photographs
  - Journal writing to enhance social and personal growth and academic learning
  - Celebrations of Learning

- Selects a professional and/or peer coach(es) who can/will support the implementation of the bodybrain-compatible element of multiple intelligences and use of a variety of instructional strategies. Establishes and maintains a schedule for meeting frequently. Prepares thoroughly for each meeting; schedules follow-up time to learn from each session.

- Designs time frames for HET integrated curriculum to fit the content rather than a rigid daily schedule; is learning to adjust time frames to best accommodate needed instructional strategies and to give students adequate time to complete their work.

- Is developing a lesson planning process and format for providing a body-

WORKING WITH THE MULTIPLE INTELLIGENCES

Of the areas of brain research discussed in Volume One of this book, none are more immediately experienceable than the multiple intelligences. Just look around you at the range of occupations of extended family and close friends. For example, the contractor who can estimate time, materials, and costs within minutes; the businesswoman who at a glance can identify an emerging pattern in monthly financial reports; the newspaper reporter who can cut to the chase and write a pithy, accurate story under a deadline of minutes, not hours; the mother who awakens from a dead sleep because she can "hear" that something is wrong with her infant five rooms away; the interior designer who can see different hues within a color that the rest of us see simply as off-white; the musician who sees mathematical perfections and chord progressions in music that others of us describe merely as something we either like or don't like but can't tell you why; the junior high student who finds her dissection kit, an out-of-character Christmas present, an irresistible introduction to the world of the animal kingdom in her yard and the discovery of a life-long occupation as science teacher. Well, you get the picture. Each of these occupations activates a different part of the brain.

The goal of the *HET* teacher is to create Renaissance minds—students who are proficient in using all the intelligences to solve problems and produce products. Such multi-faceted people are invaluable employees, friends, and family members. Perhaps most importantly, these are people with a wide range of interests, abilities, and satisfactions. They are people who have joined the ranks of lifelong learners and capable, committed citizens.

Unfortunately, traditional education primarily builds on only one of these areas, linguistic intelligence. Math is typically taught as a talk-about-it set of arithmetic skills done on worksheets. Few of us receive any real music or art training through the public school system; mostly we dabble and experience art as a form of self-expression rather than as a set of specific skills. Science is typically a drawn-out exercise in vocabulary with little practical application, mostly through textbooks and their inevitable end-of-the-chapter questions limited to Bloom's knowledge and comprehension levels. History/social studies is taught as a linguistic survey of knowledge rather than as a way of thinking or as a lens to analyze events.

Perhaps most egregious of all, students that are not high in linguistic intelligence, approximately 80 percent of the population, leave school feeling inadequate. As dropouts, pushouts, or squeak-bys, they doubt their ability to learn; yet, when using the intelligences they're strong in, they are powerful learners and valuable community members.

Multiple Intelligences As Curriculum Content

Introducing students to the multiple intelligences is a way to open doors to the reality that, in fact, all students can learn, all students can succeed but they will go about it differently. Luckily, students have an intuitive grasp of the multiple intelligences. For many students, having language to talk about the multiple intelligences often provides immediate relief for the years they may have felt inadequate in the classroom.

There are three ways to proceed: First, teach the multiple intelligences as curriculum content. Expect all students to recognize, understand, and maximize their gifts and learning strengths and to understand how to build other areas of intelligence. Invite them into the challenge of becoming Renaissance minds.

Second, alter your instructional strategies and curriculum development processes to create a learning environment conducive to learning in multiple ways. Mastery of each of the instructional strategies identified in Stages 1.2 and 1.3 is a good beginning.

Third, after a short introduction of the multiple intelligences, rely on teachable moments and questions that guide reflective thinking about collaborative work. For example, have students reflect on what intelligence(s) they'll need to accomplish a learning task, individually and as a Learning Club. After the task is completed, ask students to reflect on what they learned about the multiple intelligences—their own and others'—that they used to tackle and complete the task. Always ask what they learned from each other; acknowledge multiple intelligences using Life Lingo and as a regular concluding activity in Learning Club. The best way to strengthen an area yet to be developed is to see it modeled, talk about it, and then practice it in a supportive environment.

Multiple Intelligences Through Real-Life Experiences.

Including the multiple intelligences in your instructional strategies is easier than you might think. The two most effective ways are to provide *being there* experiences for students—study trips to locations that best illustrate the concepts and skills you want your students to learn—and to bring resource people to the classroom.

Being There. Any slice of life illustrates the multiple intelligences because the world is multidimensional. Except for assembly lines, real work requires a range of capabilities to move a job from beginning to end. Let students see for themselves how important it is to become as well-rounded as they can.

Analyze the intelligences required for each task and assignment. Make it an ongoing topic for reflecting about collaborative work. Keep the topic of multiple intelligences alive through teachable moments.

Resource People. If possible, have resource people come dressed in the clothes typical of their occupation or role in history and surrounded by as many immersion and hands-on-of-the-real-thing tools as possible. Briefly explain the multiple intelligences to each resource person. Ask that they refer to the intelligences required to do their work. Have them explain the activities in their youth that allowed them to develop such intelligences. This personalization of key figures encourages students and provides an example of a life map they might draw from for their own growth and development.

Encourage resource people to take the students through at least one activity using some of the hands-on, real items used during their presentation.

Providing Multiple Ways to Think and Perform

For too long, school has predominantly been an experience of lecture, reading, recitation—processes and products of linguistic intelligence. If we're committed to ensuring that all kids can learn, we must significantly reduce our reliance on linguistic intelligence, using it to supplement, not lead, instructional approaches. We must provide students ample opportunities to learn and perform using all the intelligences. Our goal should be a classroom that uses non-linguistic intelligences at least 50 percent of the time.

Use of the Multiple Intelligences As a Guide to Classroom Life. Stage 1.3 introduces teaching the multiples intelligences to students, explores how students can use their strengths to understand the content and skills of their curriculum, and then how students can use what they understand in real-world ways. Full implementation of the multiple intelligences occurs in curriculum development in Stage 2.

Stage 1.3 also invites you as teacher to begin to explore your own strengths in intelligences other than linguistic. Because we teach the way we learn, we must first become aware of our own intelligences and consciously work to strengthen and use each of them. Only then can we help our students to grow in all intelligences.

Don't be afraid to invite students into this exploration process. The sage on the stage is a lonely role and will only slow your progress. Invite them to join you in thinking through how the knowledge and skills of your curriculum are used in real life at the *being there* location you have chosen. Create assignments that ask them to perform a task that is typical of the *being there* location. These real-world uses **always** involve multiple intelligences, usually two or more simultaneously. Use these contexts or scenarios to help you expand your instructional strategies and assignments to utilize all the intelligences.

One last reminder: Collaborative tasks are excellent structures for eliciting many intelligences at once. However, don't forget to provide students ample intrapersonal time—time to explore and think things through on their own and time to reflect on what each has learned through journal writing and planning projects.

Flexibility in Allocating Time. Because no two brains are alike in how they process or in what prior experiences they bring, each student will need different amounts of time to seek patterns and develop ment programs. "Less is more" is the best piece of advice we can give ourselves. Avoid "covering" material; focus on less content but take learning to application and mastery and long-term memory. [See the two part definition of learning below.]

We suspect that one of the enduring attractions of a solely linguistic approach to teaching is that a teacher can describe con-

---

Part one : **Input stage: Pattern detection** consists of:

- Identifying or recognizing the pattern and

- Making meaning of the pattern including its relationship to other patterns.

and

Part two: **Output stage: Program building** consists of:

- Learning to apply what is learned, at first experimentally and consciously, and then,

- After practice, wiring it up into long-term memory and applying what is learned with the almost automatic ease and skill of the expert.

---

tent faster than he/she can lead students through discovery processes or collaborative assignments. Thus, the false impression arises that more learning takes place through lecture and other applications of linguistic intelligence. However, as we well know from our own college days, high test scores, even on essay exams, don't necessarily translate into long-term memory. Most of us can recall shockingly little of our college content and probably even less from high school.

We recommend that you mount the new definition of learning that emerges from brain research on your desk to serve as a daily reminder of your purpose as teacher.

There are many ways to provide time; none are new but must be implemented with the intention of improving the likelihood that students will **learn** as defined above.

- During direct instruction, use such techniques as wait time, think-pair-share, check with your Learning Club, 3 Before Me, and so forth.

- During collaborative work, use the techniques described in Elizabeth Cohen's *Designing Groupwork* and Spencer Kagan's *Cooperative Learning* and *SmartCards*. Especially important is rotating leadership and other specific roles so as to give each student ample opportunity to talk about and process what they are learning.

- For complex or large tasks, create frequent progress checks and adjust time as needed.

For additional advice on how to implement the multiple intelligences in Stage 1.3, revisit Chapter 3. For advice on how to use the multiple intelligences when developing curriculum, see Chapters 16 and 17.

Choices. Providing choice is more than a nice-thing-to-do option, it is a bodybrain learning partnership imperative. To make school a success for everyone, we **must** provide choices that invite all of the multiple intelligences to come out to play. This can be done in many, many ways, such as during direct instruction, the materials and supplies we provide for students to use, the nature of the assignments, projects, and homework we assign, the use of collaboration, flexibility in time allocations, and, yes, how we assess/test students.

Student choices of tasks, materials, and processes to complete projects is bodybrain-compatible on a number of levels. Psychologically, choice is an important part of William Glasser's theory about what makes people tick. He identifies four essential human needs—to belong and to love, to have freedom, to gain power, and have fun.[1] When appropriate, choice of task, materials, and processes for completing projects helps meet the last three of Glasser's needs:

- Choosing something that coincides with a special personal interest, such as writing an essay about a personal passion such as cars or horses, makes learning more **fun**.

- Choosing among alternatives, such as which intelligence to use to show that we understand something rather than always having to take a paper and pencil test, gives us **freedom** in how we go about learning.

- Choosing materials and projects that allow us to be successful gives us a sense of **power**.

Also, for many students, being able to select the tools they will use for a task is highly motivating and elicits a burst of interest and keen attention to the task. However, that same set of supplies and materials may be new to others and thus a complete distraction. Just as birds must learn the fine points of flying, each of us must learn to make the most of our bodybrain partnership. Allowing students to choose their supplies and materials is an important step toward becoming a self-directed learner capable of maximizing the likelihood that they will master new learning.

MASTERY AND CONTINUED USE OF INSTRUCTIONAL STRATEGIES IN STAGE 1.2

All of the instructional strategies identified in Stage 1.2 are continued on a daily basis and the teacher has developed a mental program for using them on a moment's notice. These strategies include:

- Modeling of the Lifelong Guidelines/LIFESKILLS
- Life Lingo

- "Discipline" based on using the Lifelong Guidelines & LIFESKILLS
- Daily agenda and written procedures
- Movement to enhance learning
- Collaboration
- Calm voice, heart-brain coherence, and emotional centeredness
- Nurturing reflective thinking

DEVELOPING A VARIETY OF OTHER INSTRUCTIONAL STRATEGIES

Stage 1.3 is also the time to launch additional instructional strategies in preparation for Stage 2 and entry into making curriculum bodybrain compatible. The strategies for Stage 1.3 include:

- Modeling how to be a lifelong learner and participating citizen
- Expanded and deepened use of movement to enhance learning
- Direct instruction, usually limited to 16 minutes per hour.
- Nurturing reflective thinking
- Graphic organizers
- Discussion
- Literature
- Songs
- Video clips, great artwork, and photographs
- Journal writing to enhance social and personal growth and academic learning
- Celebrations of Learning

Modeling Being a Lifelong Learner and Participating Citizen

The single most powerful instructional strategy—regardless of what you are teaching—is modeling. As you already know, "Do what I do" is always more powerful than "Do what I say."

If you're not sure what you're modeling as a lifelong learner and participating citizen, do a self assessment and also ask a colleague whose opinion you value. Here are some questions to ask.

Do you read daily? For how many minutes? Do you read multiple genre, e.g., magazines, newspapers, professional literature, fiction, nonfiction, poetry? Do you read more than one book at a time? Do you talk about what you're reading with others—family, friends, colleagues, your students? Are you passionate about learning something new? Do you express wonder and awe? Are you enthusiastic about students' work to plan and carry out a Celebration of Learning or is it just one more item in your lesson plan book?

Are you registered to vote? Do you vote in every election at your precinct? Do you eagerly apply what students are learning to current events in the school, community, nation, and world (as age appropriate)? Do you donate regularly to a charity or two? Do you volunteer to help those less fortunate? Do you share with students how you live your life so that you make a difference? Do you engage in supporting students' Social/Political Action projects with enthusiasm and spirit or as just another job to be done?

If you have answered no to any of the above questions, you might want to consider the fact that you are working at cross purposes with yourself. On the one hand, you are working hard to educate the nation's young; on the other hand you are demonstrating to them that someone other than they will take up the responsibility to somehow make the world a better place, help those less fortunate, and preserve our democratic way of life.

Movement

Brain research makes it very clear that movement plays a key role in the learning process. There is a strong connection between movement and emotion and the part of the brain that controls physical movement also helps sequence thinking. Movement in the classroom is not a luxury, it's a necessity.

Movement to enhance emotional receptivity to learning is a daily consideration. As you approach Stage 2, the role of movement to help students let off steam and to reenergize and refocus must expand and to enhance learning and memory of concepts and skills.

Movement and Content. Movement should be implicit in learning, that is, most learning involves, or should involve, application to real-world situation. So the more completely we base our curriculum in being there locations, the more doing we can build into our students' day. Similarly, the more we teach to the brain-based definition of learning—continuing to develop mental programs to use what is learned and wiring it into long-term memory—the more movement we need from students. Allow and encourage them to use their bodies to increase sensory input, practice ways to use what they understand, and to hard-wire learning into long-term memory. For example, make study trips truly exploratory not just look and see. Develop role-playing plots and actions that illustrate the concepts and skills to be learned.

Movement as a mnemonic is also very powerful. Hand jives, dance steps, whole-body movements/postures, finger tapping rhythms—all involve additional areas of the brain in the recall process. The important thing is having the movements grow out of the content rather than trying to fit predesigned movements to content. Students are wonderfully creative when it comes to making up movements. Invite them in creating movements, then pick the best one(s) for the class to use.

Resources. Good resources for these activities include:

- *Stage 2 of the ITI/HET Stages of Implementation: Intelligence Is a Function of Experience* (DVD, 14 minutes)

- *Let's Get Moving: Movement in the Classroom* by Diane Berry (DVD, 95 minutes, with manual)
- *ITI/HET in the Urban Middle School* by Nicole McNeil-Miller (DVD, 15 minutes)
- *Multiple Intelligences and the Second Language Learner* by Jo Gusman (DVD, 40 minutes)
- *Smart Moves: Why Learning Is Not All in Your Head* by Carla Hannaford

The above resources are available through books4educ.com

See also Chapter 2 and pages 1.20-1.21, 2.7-2.8, 3.22, 4.15-4.16, and 5.10-5.11.

Direct Instruction

Many people define direct instruction as lecture. Lecture has its place but it is a limited one. It is the driest version of direct instruction which typically provides little sensory input beyond hearing and seeing the speaker. Lecture is but a small part of good direct instruction.

There are many models for direct instruction. Perhaps the most widely known is the ITIP model (Instructional Theory into Practice) created by Dr. Madeline Hunter of UCLA (University of California, Los Angeles). We briefly describe an *HET* adaptation[2] of it here as an example of deliberate, intentional steps to foster learning. Any solid model well implemented will serve the purpose for *HET*.

The steps proposed by Madeline Hunter were a result of her research into what effective teachers do. However, she always cautioned people not to make it a static formula and not to believe that every step must be used every time the teacher chooses to use direct instruction as the most appropriate strategy. She acknowledged that teaching is heavily contextual and that only the teacher, with full knowledge of the subject matter and his/her students, can know what is best done at any one moment.

What Is Direct Instruction? Direct doesn't mean boring. It does mean focused, clear, interactive, well paced, and readily under-

standable by students. According to Linda Jordan, *HET* Associate and Professor at Hope College, School of Education, in Holland, Michigan, direct instruction is:

- A teaching method through which the teacher maintains a highly structured environment for teaching specific concepts and skills
- A process that enables the teacher to maximize student engagement and time spent on task.
- Is characterized by teacher direction on an academic focus followed up with student practice and application.

When Is Direct Instruction Effective? Direct instruction is effective when other means to discover and explore are insufficient or frustratingly inefficient.

Direct Instruction in the *HET* Model. The Hunter ITIP model was widely promoted by states and districts during the 1970s and it resurfaces whenever educators look for a training model for direct instruction. We believe it is a very valuable tool. What follows is an *HET* version of ITIP.

By direct instruction in the *HET* model, we mean an orchestrated presentation by the teacher that is limited to 11-16 minutes per hour and that is accompanied by full sensory input to as many of the 19 senses as possible when working within an immersion environment.

Direct instruction should be looked at not as an end in itself—the way to teach—but rather as the catalyst to student work on inquiries. Direct instruction can lead the way or follow a discovery process. It can be most powerful during the teachable moment when students are already fully engaged in their work and hungry for more answers.

Steps in Planning and Conducting Direct Instruction. The steps in planning and conducting direct instruction are simple and straight forward. Each has a basis in brain research.

Anticipatory Set. The anticipatory set works at two levels:

- It creates an emotional hook or bridge to the new learning. In the words of Dr. Robert Sylwester, "Emotion drives attention which drives learning, memory, problem solving, and just about everything else."[3]

- It accesses prior experiences by illustrating how, where, and why this concept or skill is used in real life and how students might use it. This starts the pattern-seeking, meaning-making operation of the brain—looking for related patterns in its memory banks, a beginning place for processing incoming data.

Anticipatory sets common in the *HET* model are:

- Being there experiences
- The *HET* Discovery Process
- Visit by an expert
- A hands-on-of-the-real-thing activity
- An inclusion activity which asks students to recall an experience common to all classmates

The goal of an anticipatory set is to get students motivated, curious, excited about the concept or skill, and aware of how the concept or skill is used in real life.

Learning Objective The learning objective in an *HET* classroom is the key point to be learned. For grades 2 and up, the key point should be written and posted—on the wall or in their notebooks. For K-1, the key point is usually represented by a pictorial mindmap that students who cannot yet read can understand.

This key point, a sentence or two, tells students specifically what is expected of them, what they are to learn.

Purpose or Rationale. Purpose or rationale is always answered by how, where, and why this concept or skill is important to know and be able to do in real life. No students should be told by a teacher, as one of the authors was in her high school algebra and trig classes, "I don't know when and where you would use this. Just learn it."

In the *HET* classroom, purpose or rationale should be part of the anticipatory set. Apply it to your students' lives and the *being there* experiences you've selected.

Input. This is the teacher's opportunity to give his/her best shot at making the patterns in the concept or skill meaningful, useful, and memorable. This is the "teaching" part. Will you provide a *being there* experience, immersion experience, demonstration using hand-on-of-the-real thing, a structured discovery process? Will you engage students in a set of questions for discussion by Learning Clubs or partners?

Remember, just as curriculum development is a pattern-enhancing activity, so too is the input part of your lesson. Your input should be planned to make pattern seeking by students inescapable. Think about what you are teaching from the students' point of view:

- What information do they need (don't bury them);
- What are the patterns/programs or chunks of the task (analyze the tasks but don't splinter it into a zillion meaningless pieces)
- In what order should I teach those them? Which will be picked up effortlessly through the *being there* experience?
- What teaching strategies should I use?

Modeling. Choose a whole-class inquiry that asks students to use the knowledge or skill of the key point. Carry out the inquiry, or first part of it, as a model, showing students what they need to do and how. Again, make sure that the inquiry requires application to real life; include as many of the multiple intelligences as possible.

Check for Understanding. During modeling, ask questions to test student understanding. Use collaborative structures, such as check with a partner, or think-pair-share and, for individual response, allow plenty of think time. Check to see who agrees or disagrees. Most importantly, urge students to talk about what they think they understand and how they would use it.

Checking for understanding is to ensure that the end of Step 1 in learning—understanding the pattern(s)—is completed (see Chapter 4, especially pages 4.1-4.2).

Guided Practice. After modeling and checking for understanding, select another inquiry for students to complete collaboratively, either whole Learning Club or pairs. As they work, circulate among the groups, checking for accuracy and completeness of understanding. The key to providing guided practice is immediate feedback.

If misconceptions appear or if students aren't getting it, use the teachable moment to reteach an individual or the class; of course, use a different way using different examples.

Guided practice is the beginning of Step 2 of the new definition of learning—applying what is understood to the real world (see Chapter 5, especially pages 5.1-5.2) Don't move on until understanding is accurate and sufficient to complete other related inquiries, first in collaborative settings and, eventually, alone.

Independent Practice. Select an inquiry for individual work. Again, make sure that the inquiry reflects real-life use of the concept or skill.

Independent practice ensures that each student can apply the concept or skill to real life and that they are wiring this learning into long-term memory.

Students should be given several inquiries at this stage. Hard wiring comes from applying knowledge and skills over time. The teacher must use his/her best judgment about whether students have developed a program for using the knowledge and skills and if it will be retained years into the future.

Working independently gives students time to reflect on the depth and breadth of their understanding (or lack of) and their ability to apply their knowledge. With this information, they can begin to direct their own learning.

Closure. Closure to a lesson does not equal completion of wiring into long-term memory. However, the strength of the closure will likely determine whether students will persevere through sufficient practice to commit a concept or skill to long-term memory.

One of the most powerful elements of closure is time for reflective thinking. Ways to nurture reflective thinking include journal writing, personal think time (in writing) before sharing with a partner, writing a thank you note to the visiting expert listing the things learned/appreciated, writing a paragraph to parents describing what the student has learned and how it can be applied immediately in their life, creating a graphic organizer that represents what they learned, writing additional inquiries that the student thinks would help create long-term memory of the key point, and so forth.

Teachers also need closure and time for reflective thinking. For the teacher's sake, there must be reflection time to recap the key point and to clarify and check again that students learned the key point as intended. Do you move on to another key point or do you plan additional inquiries for the students to practice until the information/skill gets wired into long-term memory?

An Analogy. A useful analogy for direct instruction is teaching someone to bake bread. Linda Jordan describes this as follows:

Steps in Direction Instruction	Baking Bread Analogy
Anticipatory set	The aroma brings you in
Stating the key point (objective)	The recipe
Stating the rationale/purpose whom?	What are we cooking? For
Input	Choosing the ingredients
Modeling	Showing how bread is baked
Checking for understanding	Tasting the bread
Guided practice as	Give them the recipe and help needed
Independent practice	New baker takes over kitchen
Closure	Reflect on how to improve the product next time

Although Hunter's instructional model predates brain research on this subject, her instincts were right on target.

Elements of ITIP Model Learning	The *HET* Definition of Learning
Anticipatory set	Identifying or recognizing the pattern
Stating the key point	
Stating the rationale/purpose	
Input	Making meaning of the pattern
Modeling	
Checking for understanding	
Guided practice	Learning to apply/use what is understood (a program)
Independent practice	
Closure	
	Stored in long-term memory

Nurturing Reflective Thinking

Life in the 21st century is anything but conducive to reflective thinking and becoming more difficult by the year. Students come to us with a revved up sense of time while more demands are heaped upon us from year to year. The pressures seem endless. But brain research and our common sense tell us that reflective thinking is a essential—personally as well as academically.

Thinking about information and skills—deciding how they relate to our lives or those we admire, thinking about how something new relates to what we already understand, wondering about how we could ever use something—gives the brain an opportunity to process them in numerous locations of the brain, enriching our understanding and increasing the likelihood that it will become retrievable.

Nurturing reflective thinking is more a habit of mind than a specific instructional strategy, more an intention to do so than a silver bullet from our bag of instructional strategies. There are a variety of processes and structures to nurture reflective thinking, old and new. For example, wait time, journal writing, reflecting on the daily agenda (beginning and end of the day), making choices that allow students to direct their learning, forecasting how to take on a learning task, reflecting on what one learned academically, the process of collaborative work (before, during, and after and asking about content, social, and personal outcomes), providing adequate time for students to complete assignments, strategies to help students refocus, making detailed drawings of an object, homework assignments that require action to apply something to real-world settings, the Three-Before-Me rule, action-oriented individual projects, and much more.

As you approach Stage 2, intensify your focus on academic reflections while continuing to include inner musings.

To keep journal writing vital and vigorous, add an element of audience. For selected journal writings, assign or let students choose a real person to write to. Encourage them to actually mail some of these "letters." Of course, one of those people could be the student him/herself. From time to time, announce in advance a journal entry that you will respond to. A good rule of thumb is that you will write back as much as they write to you.

Vary the assignments, the point of view, and the content. Encourage students to use their journal writing to explore their own thoughts and feelings and to reflect on how their new knowledge and skills can/will apply to their life in the future.

To invigorate learning from the product and process of group and individual work, give students time and, in the beginning, the questions to reflect on prior to work, during work, and after. Creating a reliable "voice in the back of the head" that helps us learn from the past and operate more intelligently in the future is the heart of becoming a successful lifelong learner as well as a successful student in the classroom.

When it comes to reflecting on personal work, make sure you include homework. For more information, see pages 1.27, 2.9-12, 3.16-17, 4.23-24, and 5.16.

Graphic Organizers

Graphic organizers are important learning tools because they can show the rich relationships that exist among concepts, ideas, and elements. Although this is very important for all students, it is especially critical for students high in spatial intelligence and those who have difficulty seeing the whole picture (see Appendix A). No other instructional process can illustrate such relationships as clearly or efficiently.

Kinds of Graphic Organizers. There are various kinds of graphic organizers:

- Pictorial representations of content, such as mindmaps, flow charts, time lines, story boards, and so forth

- Illustrations of important interrelationships, such as more complex mindmaps, webs, bridges, and so on

- Data formats that invite comparisons of quantities or qualities, such as those from the fields of science and mathematics (axis graphs, bar charts, Venn diagrams, pie charts, etc.)

Why Use Graphic Organizers. The strength of graphic organizers is that they record information in ways that make information more understandable by focusing our attention and enabling us to see relationships which in turn pushes us to see a bigger picture. They also bring up questions that would never have occurred to us. The pursuit of answers to such questions happily leads us further into the concepts, into ways to apply them in similar and differing situations.

Examples of Graphic Organizers. Some graphic organizers deal with precise comparisons and relationships such as the axis graph and bar charts; these work well when dealing with quantities. Others illustrate interrelationships of many facets of many items

such as mindmapping and Venn diagrams; these work well when dealing with qualitative aspects such as the attributes of concepts. Others simply transform information from words to pictures.

The KWL T-chart is developed over time. It is used to record what students already **know** about a concept or skill before you begin instruction and what they **want to know** about it. This is important information. Not only does it pique students' interest but it also helps the teacher know if their are any misconceptions that need to be corrected and what examples of a concept hold the most interest for students. Over time, once a week, students add on what they have **learned.**

Choose the form of graphic organizer that would best assist the reader to perceive and interpret the data that you most want him/her to analyze and understand. Useful, and easy to use, graphic organizers include:

- Bar graphs and pie charts assist the observer to compare quantities of numerous items.

- Axis graphs assist in observing for directions or trends in the quantitative interaction of two things. They also indicates how much of which of two ingredients must be increased or decreased in order to reach a desired goal.

- Venn diagrams assist the observer in comparing two entities for differences and similarities.

- Column charts simply separate out the data by designated characteristics (e.g., bookkeeping formats and decision-making formats such as P.M.I. or plus, minus, and interesting/neutral effect).

- Mindmaps are capable of presenting a large amount of data and, most importantly, showing the interrelationships among that data. Because it is a visual format, it gives the brain more clues for analyzing relationships and remembering the big idea and its relevant details.

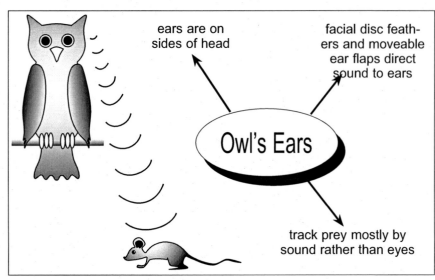

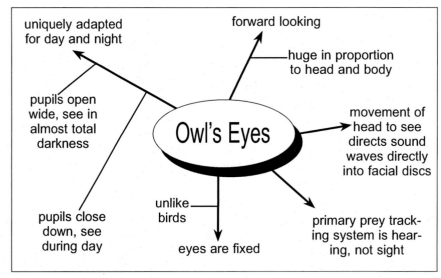

For more information about visual organizers, see *Visual Tools for Constructing Knowledge* by David Hyerle and *Mapping Inner Space: Learning and Teaching Visual Mapping* by Nancy Margulies. Also see *Graphic Organizer Smart Card* by Jerome Kagan and computer software *Kidspiration* (primary grades) and *Inspiration* (upper grade through adult).

- The mindap shown previously on the topic Body Brain Compatible Elements is an example of a graphic organizer illustrating a study for a year or month. It helps a learner remember the information at a glance. Color adds another dimension, especially for those high in spatial intelligence.

- The mindmaps showing the topic "owl's Ears" are examples of mindmaps for key points—for primary grades and for intermediate.

- The T-Charts shown on the topics of "Absence of Threat" and "Trustworthiness" are graphic organizers that help organize and record information.

Discussion

Discussion is powerful because it gives students multiple opportunities to turn an idea over in their minds, to try it out for size, to sharpen meaning by exploring the boundaries of what something is and isn't, and to see how it applies to the world they live in and the world of the *being there* location. Often, we're not sure what we really think about something until we hear ourselves talk about it. Discussion helps uncover misconceptions about things, misconceptions we can't correct until we realize they're there.[4]

As any professional facilitator will tell you, there is an art and science to framing questions that generate rich discussion. This in contrast to questions that lead to a single, correct answer.

ABSENCE OF THREAT — T-Chart

What Will See	What Will Hear	Result
students sharing ideas	"I'd like to share something."	safety
people working together	"Will you teach me how to do that?"	comfortable
student running an errand	"Please take this to Mrs. X down the hall."	I'm trusted
students helping one another	"Would you help me?" "Yes."	friendliness
student turning in found object	"I found this. It belongs to someone else."	honesty

TRUSTWORTHINESS — T-Chart

Looks Like	Sounds Like	Feels Like	Doesn't Look Like	Doesn't Sound Like	Doesn't Feel Like
going on an errand alone there you	"You can do it! without getting into trouble."	special	someone	"I know you supervising	sarcastic can't get
borrowing a library book	"I know you will take good care of it."	honored	losing a library book	"I think somebody stole it!"	distrust
finding money	"Thank you for bringing the money to the lost and found."	trusted	pocketing found money	"Finders keepers! Losers weepers!"	suspicion
going to a friend's house	"Be home on time."	someone depends on me	sneaking out of the house	"I wouldn't do that. Trust me!"	lying

Go on line and pick up a synopsis of how to lead discussions that fits your situation. An excellent resource is Jamie McKenzie's "The Question Mark" at http://questioning.org

A few commonsense rules to keep in mind:

- Discussion is most powerful when it occurs immediately after the trigger event.
- Give students a window on what discussion looks like. Take them to see "discussion" in action, at school board meetings, city council meetings, PTA meetings, and so forth.
- Involve students in developing written procedures for different kinds of discussion, from informal classroom discussions to formal Town Hall Meetings.

An excellent resource for structuring discussions and other forms of groupwork is *Cooperative Learning* by Spencer Kagan. Also see the discussion of Town Hall Meetings on page 9.7-8.

The KWL T-chart is developed over time. It is used to record what students already **know** about a concept or skill before you begin instruction and what they **want to know** about it. This is important information. Not only does it pique students' interest but it also helps the teacher know if their are any misconceptions that need to be corrected and what examples of a concept hold the most interest for students. Over time, once a week, students add on what they have **learned.**

Literature

There is nothing better than a great story to pique students' interest and curiosity and, in the process, to teach a meaningful lesson. For your daily focus or story time with students, select a story rich with examples of what you want to teach, such as the Lifelong Guideline or LIFESKILL you are currently focusing on, on what addresses an important incident/situation from the day, or on the concept or skill you are teaching. Which stories offer strong exam-

ples of Trustworthiness? Truthfulness? Active Listening? Integrity? Which teach the destructiveness of Put-Downs? Which support development of Personal Best or Resourcefulness? Select emotion grabbers such as *Chrysanthemum* by Kevin Henkes, *Leo, the Late Bloomer* by Robert Kraus, *Charlotte's Web* by E. B. White, *Stone Fox* by John Reynolds Gardiner, *Shiloh* by Phyllis Reynolds Naylor, *My Side of the Mountain* by Jean Craighead George, and *Where the Red Fern Grows* by Wilson Rawls. The strong characterizations created by the various authors make youth and adults identify with the characters, giving a vicarious but intense experience with the dilemmas faced in the stories.

Selecting Books. Always have a good story going for students. Invite them into other worlds, other possibilities for their yet-to-be-seen futures. Find a good children's librarian at your school or local library or even at a child-oriented bookstore. Ask what kids select to read and select from those kid-tested book list, then use your personal experiences and judgment to determine which stories are good choices for your own students, both in content and age appropriateness.

Pre-Reading Student Books Is Important. It is important that you read each story before you read it aloud to your students. First, you will want to determine if the story content and language are consistent with what you want your students to experience. Such previews allow you to sidestep objectionable language, skip parts that students might find upsetting, determine if the content and language are appropriate for your students, and to consider its fit with your students' life experiences.

By pre-reading you also familiarize yourself with the story and find comfortable discussion spots and those places in the plot that will most effectively highlight the importance of a concept, skill, or behavior you want to teach and connect to your students' experiences. It also allows you to add a bit of drama to your reading.

This same care needs to be given to books that you assign to the class. Just because a book is on the school's literature list doesn't mean it would be a good match for your students.

Songs

Songs are a wonderful teaching device and, along with story-telling, the best mnemonic available. They combine the power of memorable melody and the rhythm and rhyme of poetry and significantly increase the likelihood that what is learned will become stored in long-term memory. They also provide powerful hooks for retrieving memories. To test this power, think of your favorite song and the vividness of memories that reappear every time you hear it. Every chunk, topic, of *HET* integrated curriculum you develop should have its own "theme" song.

Some songs come ready made, perfect words to a catchy melody. But don't be afraid to write your own lyrics to familiar melodies in order to capture the content you are teaching, be it science, math, art, or P.E. Students delight in this creative task.

Singing is fun and something that all can do; musical talent and training are not required (but desirable!). Make curriculum-based songs a hallmark of your classroom.

Some examples of content lyrics to famous tunes appear on the previous page.

Video Clips, Great Artwork, and Photographs

Art has often been called the window to our inner life. Certainly it carries and preserves the images of our civilization. Images grip us and speak to us on many levels; truly, a picture is worth a thousand words.

When using video clips, be sure you select just the clip that introduces or reteaches or tests the concept or skill of your curriculum. Don't play the entire segment from the point of view of the video; just the segment that hits your goal. Don't allow the tail to wag the dog.

When choosing great art or photographs, enlist the watchful eyes of your nearest librarian. Show her/him your curriculum and ask for recommendations. To display your art piece or photograph, clear a space on the wall, at least 10' x 10'. Leave the wall bare so

Pride, Great Pride
(to the tune of
Ain't She Sweet?)

Pride, great pride
Feel it way down deep inside.
When you just can't rest
Until you do your best,
Feel that PRIDE.

Mastery,
Just remember "CCC"
When it's correct, complete,
And comprehensive
How proud you'll be.

When you've got pride
You'll aim much higher.
That little spark
Becomes a fire.

Pride, great pride
Feel it way down deep inside.
When you just can't rest
Until you do your best,
Feel that pride!

© Jean Spanko

Resourcefulness
(to the tune of *This Old Man*)

When you face problems tough,
Resourcefulness will be enough
Look around for answers,
Change your point of view.
Great ideas will come to you.

Keep your mind focused well;
Stay away from folks that tell you
That "This won't work,
we tried it once before."
Show those people out the door.

If you fail, don't give in
Try your first ideas again.
The solution may be
Just a step away.
Be resourceful every day.

When you're stumped, you can ask
Trusted friends to share your task.
They can listen well
And dream along with you...
Give a different point of view.

Think in ways new and strange.
There's a world that you can change.
Be resourceful and you'll
See the answer clear.
All the world will stand and cheer.

that it doesn't compete with the art. This is especially important with students who are easily distracted.

Journal Writing

Journal writing is an excellent device to help students reflect on what they are learning or thinking about a topic. With no one looking over their shoulder or judging their words, they can reflect on what they truly think and feel. Since writing is thinking on paper, the very act of writing requires students to sort through their thoughts, reflect on their feelings, and organize their ideas.

Journal writing provides opportunities for students to reflect, respond, react, and reply to a wide variety of ideas, comments, and stories. It is a powerful instructional tool. Use it daily to offer students chances to revisit, review, and renew previous beliefs and thoughts and to compare them to new ones. It is particularly useful to provide adequate time to reflect about their experiences relating to the Lifelong Guidelines and LIFESKILLS.

A simple strategy for journal writing is to have students write in their journal every day. Once a week, have them indicate the one or two things they want you to respond to (which you should do in writing in their journal for them to keep). This addition of a real audience makes the journal more than an academic exercise and establishes the standard for writing—what real people use in the real world.

Note: A journal differs from a diary which primarily records day to day occurrences. Journals reflect one's personal journey. Periodically you should invite students to write something to you, something that you will respond to. Rule of thumb: Write as much back as the student writes to you. This encourages length and depth in their writing.

Although reading student writing can sometimes be overwhelming due to the sheer volume of it, keep in mind that "writing is the inking of our thinking"—it's as close as we can get to seeing what goes on in the students' heads.

Celebrations of Learning

As the saying goes, "All work and no play makes Jack a dull boy." The same goes for Jill and for teachers and parents as well. Celebrating successes, big and small, is very, very important. Such celebrations provide markers for our progress, announce to us and others that we have hit a new milestone and, very importantly, that we have left some old behaviors and beliefs behind.

Change, for students and adults, is not about adding new crusts to our outer layers but about truly leaving behind some old behaviors and beliefs that no longer serve us and are no longer appropriate to who we are becoming.

Celebrating to Internalize Change. Leaving old behaviors and beliefs behind is obviously a critical part of learning to live the Lifelong Guidelines and LIFESKILLS. And the way to do so—with grace and the support of those we live with—is to celebrate those milestones. In the *HET* model, we call these Celebrations of Learning. Be they markers of small accomplishments or large, they are public and full of hard-won pride. They are not, however, "I/we are #1" or "Student of the week" episodes. They are a way to share with others what one has learned; they state one's intent to continue moving forward. In the case of students and staff, this means moving forward together.

In Stage 1, Celebrations of Learning focus heavily on the Lifelong Guidelines/LIFESKILLS. By the end of Stage 1.3, Celebrations of Learning should also include curriculum content. However, regardless of the content focus, Celebrations of Learning help wire learning into long-term memory. Remember, all learning is a two-step process—pattern seeking through developing programs to use what is understood, a progression summarized on the next page in Chapters 4 and 5.

Celebrating, Not Rewarding. Do not confuse celebrating with giving rewards. There is a world of difference between a deep sense of personal satisfaction and an ice cream cone. As discussed on page 17.3, external rewards extinguish the very behavior for which the reward was given. In contrast, celebrations in the *HET* model stoke an internal sense of pride and satisfaction; they are public acknowledgments of a student's (or teacher's) growth that he/she has already internally acknowledged and values. Celebrating as a group allows each individual to acknowledge and value the same accomplishment by others.

Celebrating Growth in Using the Lifelong Guidelines. Because internalizing and consistently using the Lifelong Guidelines and LIFESKILLS are key to academic growth, on-going celebrations of growth in these behaviors are an important investment in future academic achievement and in creating future citizens.

There are many ways to celebrate growth toward learning to apply the Lifelong Guidelines and LIFESKILLS. These are starters for you:

- A LIFESKILLS Fair for Parents, a special evening during which your students plan LIFESKILL "booths" — demonstrations of what his/her favorite LIFESKILL means and how to use it. Students can work as a learning club, in partners, or individually.

- A LIFESKILL Day planned for the entire class during which students, as members of a small group of 2-5 students, carry out their plans to practice that Lifelong Guideline or LIFESKILL for the entire day (or whatever time period is chosen). Projects can be carried out on campus (Caring and Friendship with younger buddies, reading to them, helping them learn to use the library), at a nearby public park (Effort and Cooperation, clean up projects, trail restoration), or at a museum or aquarium (Curiosity, a behind the scenes tour). The possibilities are endless. On return to class, have each group give a 3-5 minute presentation of how the LIFESKILL of the day helped make that day special for them — more interesting, more fun, more friendships.

Taking time to acknowledge students' success in implementing the Lifelong Guidelines and LIFESKILLS helps students experience that deep sense of personal satisfaction that comes from doing one's best, contributing to the group, doing something because it's the right thing to do. These celebrations provide the initial external feedback that promotes an internal sense of pride — earned and deserved.

Celebrating Academic Growth. Academic growth is often considered an invisible activity made manifest only by tests and grades. Nonsense! There are many ways to make academic growth visible, tangible, experienceable — something always appreciated by parents and essential to students in their journey to becoming self-directed, lifelong learners. Celebrations of Learning are one of the best ways to do so.

FLEXIBLE TIME FRAMES

Inadequate time is the 21st century's foremost stressor. Those of us caught up in it don't need brain research to remind us that rigid time schedules loyal to the needs of bureaucracy rather than the needs of individual learners are killers. They frustrate learning and performance of students and staff alike.

Although freighted with tradition, there is not a shred of brain research to support the typical time schedule allocating set amounts of time per subject each day. Indeed, a growing and convincing body of evidence suggests that such schedules are counterproductive. Students need time to engage, explore, try out, master, and commit concepts and skills to long-term memory. Time frames should flex with the needs at the moment. Fortunately, integrating subject content through *being there* experiences enables us to make time frames longer, such as all afternoon or two-thirds of the morning. Sheltering a significant block of time during each day or each week ensures adequate time to focus, explore in depth, and practice the use of new mental programs.

When planning time frames, keep in mind the new, body-brain-compatible definition of learning as a two-step process summarized below. (Also see Chapters 4 and 5).

As a rule of thumb, time frames should be planned to ensure that each of the four steps of learning described above can be accomplished by students. If so, future study and practice can add depth and increase expertise.

The effects of inadequate time can be very detrimental. For example, a student studying a new math skill only gets a peremptory swipe at it and, as a result, does not "get" it. The coinciding emotional message is often, "I'm not good at math," or, "I don't like math", or both. The next time the concept/skill is presented, it comes freighted with negative emotional baggage. So, not only does the student start from ground zero academically but the task is made all the more difficult by negative emotions.

MEETING FREQUENTLY WITH A COACH

Goals to work on for you and your coach include ensuring that you master all of the elements initiated during Stage 1.2 and continue using them on a daily basis and that you work systematically to accomplish each of the curricular and instructional strategies of Stage 1.3. Go for mastery of one thing at a time rather than jumping into everything at once. Be kind to yourself!

Also, find tools that support you. A "must have" tool is *Your Personal Guide to Implementing HET* by Karen D. Olsen. It describes five stages of implementation starting with what to do before school starts, the first day and beyond, what to accomplish before moving to Stage 2, beginning stages of integrating curriculum, etc. Each stage describes what to do for curriculum development and for instructional strategies. In addition it describes what the classroom will look like and feel like as students join in, called "The Dance," and when students begin to internalize what is happening, called "Taking Flight." These pictures provide a needed road map to direct you and also provide a means of assessing progress. The document is intended to be used with your coach. No secrets, both of you on the same page.

ENDNOTES

1   William Glasser, M.D. *Quality School: Managing Students Without Coercion, The.* New York: HarperCollins, 1998. Also see William Glasser, M.D. *Control Theory in the Classroom, revised* New York: Perennial Library, 2001.

2   This description of ITIP applied to the *HET* model was developed by Linda Jordan, a trainer for Susan Kovalik & Associates and Assistant Professor at Hope College, School of Education, Holland, Michigan.

3.   Dr. Robert Sylwester, "The Role of the Arts in Brain Development and Maintenance." (An unpublished paper). See also *A Celebration of Neurons: An Educator's Guide to the Human Brain.* (Alexandria, VA: ASCD, 1995), especially Chapter 4.

4   "A Private Universe" is a fascinating window on interviews with Harvard University students on their graduation day. The question put to them is "Explain the reason for the seasons." Even those who had taken astronomy classes gave the "Hot, baby, hot" explanation: When the sun gets closer, our season gets warmer. It is a powerful illustration of the power of misconceptions to override subsequent learning. Instructional strategies such as discussion and collaboration work are excellent tools for rooting out and correct stubborn misconceptions.

Chapter 11: Dealing with Challenging Behaviors

IT'S NOT JUST YOUR IMAGINATION

With 30 students in a classroom—each one with unique brain wiring and prior experience—behavior which disrupts learning is as inevitable as death and taxes. Toxins in the environment, prescribed and recreational drugs, shattered families, stressful living that leaves little time to connect with family members, violence in society and inside our schools—all these and more contribute to changes in brain wiring. And, make no mistake, behavior is neurologically driven.[1]

How to respond? Many teacher behaviors make the situation worse. Some "fix" the problem in the moment but do nothing to keep it from reoccurring. Some dramatically improve the situation in ways that have long-term ability to reduce or eliminate problem behavior.

SEARCHING FOR SOLUTIONS: BALANCING OLD BELIEFS AND NEW SCIENCE

There are many schools of thought about how to handle challenging behaviors. Some are home grown, such as "Spare the rod, spoil the child." Others seem to seep from the woodwork of our schools, such as "Don't smile until Thanksgiving." Behavioral psychologists, the Skinnerian model of punishments and rewards, have had a strong influence on education. Consequently, candy and detention, carrot and stick are the premise of many "classroom management" programs. However, whatever our roots and our current beliefs about behavior and how to handle it, we owe it to our students, and ourselves, to take a fresh look at the issue and come to a balanced perspective—a 21st century combination of the best of old beliefs and the best from brain research.

This new perspective must be a blend of behavioral science, psychology/sociology, and brain research. First let us dig up our deeply held beliefs, examine them in the light of the 21st century, and integrate their best elements for today's challenges.

The most useful application of new brain research to the classroom that we have found is the work of Dr. Sigurd Zielke.

Through his intensive work over the years with adjudicated teens, crisis residency centers, and research study, he has put together a program that can help teachers see with new eyes those students whose behaviors place them at risk.[2]

Taking a Fresh Look at Challenging Behaviors in the Classroom

The first step in dealing with the challenge of extreme behavior in the classroom is to examine what our deeply held beliefs are and where they came from. For the most part, new teachers arrive steeped in theories and assumptions from the schools of behaviorism and psychology (cognitive-rational) but with precious little information about what brain research has to say about behavior.

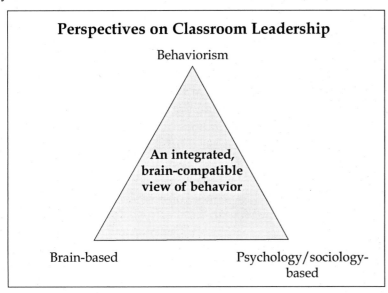

Perspectives on Classroom Leadership

Behaviorism

An integrated, brain-compatible view of behavior

Brain-based

Psychology/sociology-based

© Zielke & Zielke, 2004

Behaviorism. The school of behaviorism, whose best known proponent was Dr. B. F. Skinner, was built on the stimulus-response view of human behavior. Provide the proper stimulus—either a reward or a punishment—and you can evoke the desired response.

The reward and punishment approaches to classroom management combine M&Ms and other "carrots" plus punishments, creating highly controlling environments in which all authority and judgment is held by the adults.

Psychology-Based Approaches. Psychology-based approaches focus on creating a need-fulfilling environment and interactions. Examples include those centered on Maslow's hierarchy of needs, Glasser's choice theory (the need to belong/love, gain power, have freedom, and have fun)[3], and Gossen's restitution (make amends/clean up what you did).[4]

Brain-Based View of Behavior. Looking at behavior from a brain research perspective requires that we shift our thinking from behavior as a set of choices to be manipulated or redirected to behavior as being neurologically driven, a mix of genes and childhood experiences, what Dr. Bob Sylwester calls the "genes and jeans" from our parents/primary caregivers.

This is not a fatalistic view of behavior, that you are your wiring, but it suggests that much misbehavior is beyond a child's ability to correct simply by choosing to do so.

Taking an Integrated, Brain-Compatible View of Behavior

Brain research suggests that, while the behaviorist approach is effective and even necessary in the short run, it is counter-productive in the long run.[5] Unfortunately, most teacher preservice training does not take us beyond this short-term approach to help us develop strategies for the long haul.

Brain research also suggests that the psychological/sociological approaches can be valuable immediately and in the long run, but they don't provide the tools to delve deeply enough into the extremely challenging behavior of individual students to help them change the mental wiring that produces their at-risk behavior.

For most of us, this message is unsettling to say the least. Didn't we grow up in a system that embraced such notions and strategies? Didn't these assumptions go unchallenged through our teacher prep classes? For most of us, the answer is a yes. And no doubt we hear them woven into political debate and even family get-togethers, a reflection of generationally held beliefs.

What we need is to balance these outlooks, working from within the triangle, using an integrated approach that allows us to make commonsense choices as we move through our day, interacting in ways most effective for each student.

What is needed is consistent teacher-student and student-student interaction in a bodybrain-compatible environment that builds new neurological pathways that produce the kinds of behaviors that allow the student to be successful academically and socially.

Analyzing the Problem: One Size Does NOT Fit All

There are many barriers to analyzing behavior problems. The most significant is that most serious misbehavior needs one-on-one intervention which is often impossible to achieve given that we operate in a group setting—usually 25-35 students. The most common mistake is designing a behavior management program for the entire class when only a few students need the intervention.

As you analyze student behavior, focus on each individual.

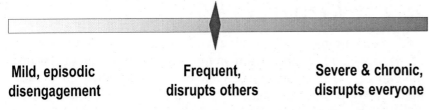

Mild, episodic disengagement   **Frequent, disrupts others**   **Severe & chronic, disrupts everyone**

On one end of the spectrum, misbehavior can be described as mild and episodic, the result of being disengaged from the curriculum or unclear about procedures or expectations. Or, the student may just be reacting to/following the lead of a more disruptive classmate.

Resolution of these problems is entirely under the control of the classroom teacher and requires orchestrating the environment primarily by using group structures and processes.

On the other end of the spectrum, misbehavior can be described as severe and chronic, disruptive to everyone, fed by brain dysfunction and/or severe, repeated trauma. Resolving these problems requires orchestrating the environment using group structures and processes AND one-on-one interventions.

Once you've analyzed the degree of severity of misbehavior for each student, determine how well the group solution—your Lifelong Guideline/LIFESKILLS-based, classroom-wide leadership program—will handle these misbehaviors. Will it suffice or do you need to add one-on-one interventions?

Group solutions usually adequate   **Need group solutions & one-on-one interventions**

For group solutions, the first step is developing a sense of belonging. (See the description of how to build a sense of community in Chapters 9 and 7.) This is a critical drive for humans; when thwarted, it creates a major disturbance in a child's growth and development, even in learning as the child's attention to his/her world is overridden by the search for connection with a primary caregiver and others. Antisocial behavior is but a natural manifestation of this wiring in search of completion. (For a fascinating discussion of this neurological drive to connect to others, see *Hardwired to Connect: The New Scientific Case for Authoritative Communities . . . A Report to the Nation from the Commission on Children at Risk.*[6]

Getting Real: My Part in the Problem

Before you begin to analyze individual students to "see what's wrong," first analyze how you orchestrate your environment—curriculum, instruction, and group structures and processes.

You may well find that there are things you are doing and not doing that make student behaviors worse, not better. In other words, are you adding fuel to the fire? Before you begin to plan one-on-one interventions or class-wide fixes, first throw away the combustibles.

Teacher's Belief System. How you view challenging behavior is critically important. Teachers who have trouble with "classroom management" tend to take misbehavior personally—a deliberate attempt by students to bedevil their teacher; it's an aggravation, something to be controlled and eliminated. Teachers with the greatest success with misbehavior view it as a teaching opportunity. Simply put, a student has too many of the wrong behaviors or too few correct behaviors or perhaps can't tell when to use the appropriate behaviors.[7] In any case, it's a learning opportunity for the student, not a major disruption in the teacher's day.

If you feel the heat of frustration or anger, students will stoke it for you. To succeed, you must remain calm and centered.

Lack of Personal Relationship Between Teacher and Student. If students don't feel they have a relationship with their teacher, they have nothing to lose by causing the teacher grief, so why not misbehave? And, besides, pushing the teacher's buttons and watching his/her veins pop out on the neck is a fun thing to do!

If students have nothing to lose by misbehaving, the incentive is to misbehave, show off, get a laugh. Eliminate this incentive by establishing a relationship with them that makes them identify with your situation.

Lack of a Sense of Community in the Classroom. Learning new correct behaviors and when to apply them is most efficiently acquired through imitating the behaviors of the group. When fully a member of the group, the incentive is to behave within the norms of the group.

Failure to Provide for Student Needs. According to Glasser, there are four essential needs a classroom must provide: to belong and to love, to gain power, to be free, and to have fun. Teachers ignore these at their peril.[8]

Instructional strategies and curriculum must be adjusted to ensure that they respond to these needs.

Lack of Emotional and Procedural Consistency. For students trying hard to keep a rein on their behavior, the anxiety caused by unpredictable events or a teacher's mood swings can be the straw that breaks their control. Teachers must model the Lifelong Guidelines/LIFESKILLS at all times and use agendas and written procedures every day to provide a sense of predictability, and thus of safety and security.

Lack of Engaging Curriculum. Re-evaluate your curriculum. Avoid curriculum that is boring because it's too easy or irrelevant to students' lives, too difficult because it requires skills that students don't have, or age-inappropriate (students can't understand it and must therefore resort to memorization). Such content is unengaging and no trickery of instructional strategies can overcome its deficits.

Overuse of Lecture and Worksheets. Limited instructional strategies is also a significant source of boredom and increased distractibility as the brain is always on the prowl for sensory input. Also, instructional strategies can help meet or thwart students' needs to gain power and be free (be self-directed) as well as have fun.

TEACHING AS A CONTACT SPORT

Old approaches to dealing with students attempt to minimize or insulate emotion during human interaction, thus reducing friction. In contrast, the new, integrated view of working with students promotes the opposite. Dr. Zielke refers to teaching as a "contact sport" requiring that the teacher keep bumping the child's boundaries so as to nudge him/her toward experiences and responses that help with this rewiring. The idea here is not to eliminate conflict but to help students learn how to learn from it and deal with it in productive ways.

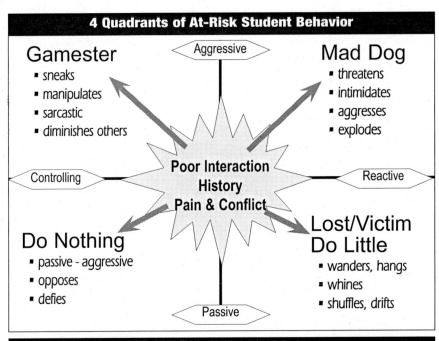

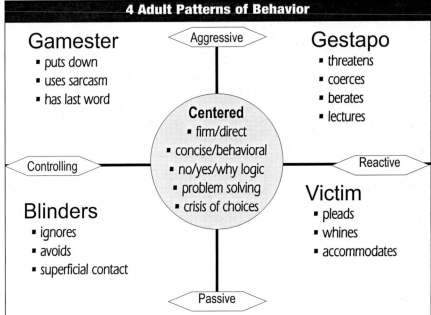

During this "contact sport," teachers need tools from the fields of behaviorism and psychology/sociology but they must keep their eye on brain research, using it to set the vision of where they are going, what tools to use along the way, and when to use those tools or abandon them.

Solutions

The best antidote for misbehavior is building a sense of community. The Lifelong Guidelines/LIFESKILLS—modeling them, formally teaching them, reteaching them, reinforcing them moment-by-moment through target talk—provide an excellent vehicle for boundary bumping in a supportive and nurturing environment.

Second, create an environment with absence of threat. Review Chapters 2 and 7.

Third, stay centered. Students delight in pushing adults' buttons. It's a big energy rush for them—power and fun. Zielke points out why by showing four quadrants of student misbehavior juxtaposed against related quadrants of adult response. When teacher behavior enters the same aggressive quadrant as the student's behavior, the situation becomes explosive. If the teacher enters one of the passive quadrants, the students take over. The more a teacher interacts from the center, the greater the ability to pull students from the outer edges of their quadrants into the middle.

If teachers allow themselves to stray from an emotional set pointing away from centeredness, the fireworks begin.

Silver Lining

However difficult behavior problems can become, your silver lining is this: Humans are hardwired to connect with others—to be loved and cared for and to love and care for others.[9] This is a biological imperative. However unreachable a student may seem, inside him/her is a powerful, neurological drive to connect. With this knowledge, we must commit ourselves to establishing a personal relationship with each student through which to model healthy interactions with others and help each become capable of creating healthy connections with others.[10]

ENDNOTES

1   Sigurd Zielke, Ph.D. "An Introduction to Neurobehavioral-Developmental & Social Classroom Management," a presentation to Susan Kovalik & Associates on January 20-22, 2005.

2   Dr. Zielke is currently producing books and a videotape about his work. We strongly recommend his publications. They are the best tools for dealing with challenging behavior that we have seen in over 30 years.

3   William Glasser, M.D. *Quality School: Managing Students Without Coercion, The.* (New York: HarperCollins, 1998). Also see William Glasser, M.D. *Control Theory in the Classroom, revised,* (New York: Perennial Library, 2001).

4   Diane Gossen, *Restitution: Restructuring School Discipline*, (New York: Perennial Library, 1986). This book offers a process to redirect the individual, leading away from traditional methods of discipline towards a more research-based approach.

5   Every field of endeavor—from business to education—has studies that indicate that long-term, external manipulation of behavior doesn't work; it squashes the development of internal motivation and intrinsic drive to perform at high levels. For example, employers complain that employees develop a "what's in it for me" attitude about every work assignment, even the basic work load, never mind the over-and-above performance levels that they wish to encourage with rewards. In the classroom, students want to "negotiate" the minimum.
The external imposition of rewards is deadly. See Alfie Kohn, *Punished by Rewards: The Trouble with Gold Stars, Incentive Plans, A's, Praise, and Other Bribes,* (Boston: Houghton Mifflin, 1993).

6   *Hardwired to Connect.* A collaborative work by the Commission of Children at Risk. Sponsored by YMCA of the USA, Dartmouth Medical School, Institute for American Values, 2003.

7   Pat Belvel, TCI Consulting of San Jose, CA, specializes in trainings on classroom management and peer coaching. See also Belvel's *Rethinking*

Classroom Management, 2nd ed. (Thousand Oaks, CA: Corwin Press, 2010).

8   Glasser, *Control Theory in the Classroom*. New York: Perennial Library, 1986.

9   *Hardwired to Connect.*

10 Connection to another is real. The Lifelong Guidelines and LIFESKILLS must become part of who we are, not things we ask of students in order to control their behavior. Likewise, the classroom can't become a community of learners until every student internalizes the Lifelong Guidelines and LIFESKILLS.

Part **C**

Making Curriculum & Instruction Bodybrain Compatible:

Implementing Stage 2

IMPLEMENTING STAGE 2

Chapters 12 through 15 describe how to implement Stage 2 of the *HET Classroom Stages of Implementation*—making curriculum an instruction bodybrain compatible. It assumes that you have already made significant progress in implementing Stage 1 to make the learning environment bodybrain compatible.

How to Use Stage 2

Whereas Stage 1 applies to the classroom 100% of the time, Stage 2 should be applied only to that portion of the day, week, or year for which curriculum using the *HET* model has been developed. **The goal for Stage 2 is to implement** *quality* **bodybrain-compatible learning. Quality is more important than quantity.** *Keep working at Stage 2* **until at least 10-15 percent of the curriculum** for the total year meets the criteria for bodybrain compatibility.

The time frames and content that teachers select to begin implementation of their bodybrain-compatible curriculum vary widely. Typically teachers begin where they feel they will be the most successful and expand from there. Whatever the starting point, however modest or bold, these descriptors at this stage apply only during the time when a teacher is implementing his/her bodybrain-compatible curriculum.

The actions that teachers must take, for curriculum and instructional strategies for Stage 2, are outlined on the following pages.

As a rule of thumb, Stage 2 should be completed within one year, two at most.

CURRICULUM GOALS FOR STAGE 2

Your primary curriculum development goals for Stage 2 of the *HET Classroom Stages of Implementation* are to develop curriculum that:

- Fits how the brain learns

- Is based in *being there* locations

- Starts with an important concept that can integrate subject areas and basic skills together in ways students experience in their own lives

- Is taught in a bodybrain-compatible manner

- Provides a conceptual framework for state standards

As you proceed, look for a concept(s) that helps pull together what the people at the *being there* site need to understand and be able to do AND the content from your state/district standards.

Also, note that integration should begin at home. Be sure you integrate areas *within* a subject area, such as physical, earth, and life sciences and technology and history, geography, civics, and economics, plus sociology/psychology and other windows on understanding man.

When integrating basic skills, let the circumstances of the *being there* location invite the skills into the curriculum in a natural way; ask yourself what the people there must be able to do.

Chapter 12 discusses developing curriculum based on *being there* experiences. Chapter 13 describes how to write integrated curriculum. Chapter 14 examines how to start organizing your curriculum through concepts.

NOTE: The following descriptors apply only when the bodybrain-curriculum described in this and subsequent chapters is being implemented.

HET Classroom
Stages of Implementation

Stage
2

MAKING CURRICULUM & INSTRUCTION BODYBRAIN COMPATIBLE

CURRICULUM	INSTRUCTIONAL STRATEGIES
• Bases curriculum on a physical location that students can and do frequently experience through *being there* study trips.	• Takes students to each *being there* location at the beginning of study as well as at the end and in between as needed for students to see concepts in action.
• Chooses at least four such *being there* locations. Selects concepts and skills and develops curriculum for each as described below.	

• Selects the most powerful, intrinsically engaging concepts and skills captured by the overlapping answers to two questions:	• Teaches concepts and skills through the lives of those at the *being there* location rather than through the perspective of textbooks. Utilizes on-site interviews, visiting resource people, situational role-playing, and other instructional strategies that make the concepts and skills come alive for students. Includes role-playing to help students learn to apply concepts and skills and to build C.U.E. (creative, useful, emotional) into the teacher's instructional strategies and inquiries.
— What do people need to know and be able to do at this site? (This question includes includes workers, visitors, and users/consumers.)	
— What content and skills from my curriculum standards describe what one needs to know and be able to do at this site?	

• Organizes and integrates content and skills from multiple curriculum areas as naturally occurs at the *being there* location and as people need to know and use them. Such integration is neither forced nor artificial.	• Integrates skills from other content areas whenever necessary in order to provide the tools students need to accomplish their learning tasks.

• States clearly and succinctly each concept students are to understand. Determines what significant knowledge about the concept students must understand in order to achieve a deep understanding of the concept.	• Posts the key point(s) currently being studied on the curriculum wall or in student binders. For younger students, includes visual symbols to help convey the meaning of the content.

• Provides students with choices through multiple opportunities for real-world application through daily inquiries; such inquiries allow multiple ways of solving problems and producing products.	• Regularly provides choices honoring both personal interests and the multiple intelligences through activities/inquiries and other means.

HET Classroom
Stages of Implementation

Stage
2

MAKING CURRICULUM & INSTRUCTION BODYBRAIN COMPATIBLE

CURRICULUM

- For every key point—concept, significant knowledge, and skill—to be taught, provides sufficient inquiries typical of those activities at the *being there* location to ensure sufficient practice to wire those concepts, knowledge, and skills into long-term memory.

- Uses an organizing concept to pull together content and skills from multiple subject areas. This organizing concept unifies study for the year.

- For at least two chunks of conceptual curriculum during the year, includes a Social/Political Action Project and concludes with a Celebration of Learning.

- Completes writing curriculum (key points and inquiries) before beginning to plan lessons.

Note: The goal of Stage 2 is to develop and implement conceptual curriculum for 10-15% of the year.

INSTRUCTIONAL STRATEGIES

- Provides each student ample time to complete sufficient inquiries to master the key points. Ensures that students are allowed to work through their strengths through the first three stages of learning (see the New Definition of Learning, page 5.3) and, during the last stage of learning, provides opportunities to strengthen other intelligences.

- Displays a mindmap of the current curriculum—component and its topics—on the curriculum wall along with immersion items for the current *being there* location in order to heighten student interest, elicit prior related memories, and help students see connections and relationships among patterns.

- Uses Social/Political Action Projects and Celebrations of Learning to provide real-world contexts for learning and using knowledge and skills, to provide real audiences for developing/practicing language arts and math skills, and to provide students opportunities to practice responsible citizenship.

- Has developed and regularly uses a lesson planning process and format for organizing key points and inquiries and selecting instructional strategies best suited to teach student the concept, significant knowledge, or skill at hand.

- Selects a professional and/or peer coach(es) who can/will support the implementation of the bodybrain-compatible element of multiple intelligences and use of a variety of instructional strategies. Establishes and maintains a schedule for meeting frequently. Prepares thoroughly for each meeting; schedules follow-up time to learn from each session.

HET Classroom **Stage**
Stages of Implementation

MAKING CURRICULUM & INSTRUCTION BODYBRAIN COMPATIBLE

2

CURRICULUM

INSTRUCTIONAL STRATEGIES

• Expertly uses all the instructional strategies identified in Stages 1.2 and 1.3 everyday, throughout the entire school day for both *HET* conceptual curriculum time and for other curriculum as well.

• Expertly uses instructional strategies for *introducing and reteaching* the concepts, significant knowledge, and skills of the *HET* integrated curriculum:

— *Being there* experiences which are enhanced and deepened through lead-up activities, assignments during bus rides, focused follow-up activities including return trips to the *being there* location, visits by resource people, immersion and simulations, personalized homework assignments, and so forth.

— The *HET* Discovery Process as a frequent alternative to direct instruction and an important means of helping students learn how to learn.

— Teaching concepts and skills through the lives of those at the *being there* location rather than through the perspective of textbooks. Utilizes on-site interviews, visiting resource people, situational role playing, and other instructional strategies that make the concepts and skills come alive for students. Includes role playing to help students learn to apply concepts and skills and to build C.U.E. (creative, useful, emotional) into the teacher's instructional strategies and inquiries.

• Expertly selects and uses strategies for *HET* conceptual curriculum time that ensure that *students reach mastery*, i.e., that students identify/understand patterns and develop programs for using what they understand in real-world ways. Such additional instructional strategies include the following:

— Modeling being a lifelong learner and participating citizen

— Movement routines to help students identify and understand patterns and sequences of events/processes and to build mental programs for using concepts and skills and retaining them in long-term memory

MAKING CURRICULUM & INSTRUCTION BODYBRAIN COMPATIBLE

CURRICULUM

INSTRUCTIONAL STRATEGIES

Strategies to ensure that *students reach mastery* continued —

— Collaboration on an ongoing basis including formally teaching students the personal and social skills necessary for effective collaboration. The content of the inquiries assigned for collaborative work is specially designed so that no one student can complete an inquiry alone. Collaborative work sessions include identifying in advance the Lifelong Guidelines and LIFESKILLS necessary to successfully complete an assignment plus reflective thinking at the end of the work. When possible, the structure and roles within the collaborative group are an extension of the content to be learned, such as roles of people in a court room (judge, jury, legal stenographer, and so forth).

— Knowledge of temperament, considered during instruction and when designing inquiries in ways that speed up and deepen learning.

• Expertly uses instructional strategies to *enhance wiring into long-term memory* and for *assessing student progress* through the new definition of learning:

— Clear performance criteria for students through inquiries and rubrics that describe the performance levels expected of them, including the expectations for materials, process, time, and quality as appropriate. These statements of expectation are written and do not require explanation from the teacher.

• For at least two chunks of integrated curriculum during the year, includes a social/political action project and concludes with a celebration of learning.

— Social/political action projects that grow naturally out of students' study at a *being there* location (or from a related current event/situation in school, community, nation, or world) and that provide students practice in using the democratic processes of our government and society and in contributing to others.

— Celebrations of learning that heighten emotional involvement in applying the key points and help wire learning into long-term memory.

• Selects a professional and/or peer coach(es) who can/will support the implementation of the bodybrain-compatible curriculum delivered through the use of a variety of instructional strategies selected to best suit the key points and inquiries at hand. Establishes and maintains a schedule for meeting frequently. Prepares thoroughly for each meeting; schedules follow-up time to learn from each session.

Note: The goal of Stage 2 is to develop and implement conceptual curriculum for 10-15% of the year.

Chapter 12: Developing Curriculum Based on a *Being There* Experience

CURRICULUM

- Bases curriculum on a physical location that students can and do frequently experience through *being there* study trips.

- Chooses at least four such *being there* locations. Selects concepts and skills and develops curriculum for each as described below.

- Selects the most powerful, intrinsically engaging concepts and skills captured by the overlapping answers to two questions:

  — What do people need to know and be able to do at this site? (This question includes workers, visitors, and users/consumers.)

  — What content and skills from my curriculum standards describe what one needs to know and be able to do at this site?

- Organizes and integrates content and skills from multiple curriculum areas as naturally occurs at the *being there* location and as people need to know and use them. Such integration is neither forced nor artificial.

INSTRUCTIONAL STRATEGIES

- Takes students to each *being there* location at the beginning of study as well as at the end and in between as needed for students to see concepts in action.

- Teaches concepts and skills through the lives of those at the *being there* location rather than through the perspective of textbooks. Utilizes on-site interviews, visiting resource people, situational role-playing, and other instructional strategies that make the concepts and skills come alive for students. Includes role-playing to help students learn to apply concepts and skills and to build C.U.E. (creative, useful, emotional) into the instructional strategies and inquiries.

- Integrates skills from other content areas whenever necessary in order to provide the tools students need to accomplish their learning tasks.

12.1

ANCHORING CURRICULUM IN REAL-LIFE LOCATIONS

In our opinion, the two most convincing areas of brain research are: 1) the importance of emotion and movement in the bodybrain learning partnership[1] and 2) the need—the absolute requirement—for full sensory input to the brain through all 19 senses.[2]

For teachers, this means that content must be meaningful and mentally and physically engaging and that the amount of sensory input must be vastly increased over that of the traditional tools of textbooks, worksheets, lectures, and an occasional video or Internet scan. Anchoring curriculum and instruction in *being there* locations meets both requirements handily.[3] Don't teach from a book, teach from the real world—a backyard, a mall, a park in the neighborhood, a grocery store. Teach from real places where real people go to meet their needs—as shoppers, business people, people looking for a place to play, relax, or be entertained.

Some readers may complain that their district doesn't allow money for field trips. We're not talking about *field trips* or end-of-the year *travel rewards*. We are talking about **study** trips designed in accordance with brain research findings about how the human brain learns. Is there a difference? You bet! Is it doable? Affordable? Absolutely, *if* we choose locations near the school that we and our students can revisit frequently by walking or by taking a short ride on public transportation.

Are we talking about throwing away textbooks? No. But we are suggesting that textbooks be used as one of many resources, not as *the* curriculum and paramount instructional tool.

Are we talking about ignoring state standards? Absolutely not. Standards adopted by the district tell us what we as teachers are expected to teach our students. We owe our students a curriculum with no gaps and no repetitions as they progress from grade to grade. Curriculum standards—be they state driven, district adopted,

or school generated—are an essential foundation for good curriculum planning at the classroom level.

Anchoring curriculum in real-life locations gives students clear pictures of **what we want them to understand** and **what we want them to do with what they understand** because they can see how and when people use such knowledge and skills. The richness of these pictures also allows students to make connections both to other locations and among other content areas.

Examples of Engaging Being There Locations

Look for sites that are immediately accessible—the school yard, a walking trip of 15 minutes or less. First look for sites on campus, such as the cafeteria, bus barn, or maintenance center. Next, branch out into the neighborhood within walking distance. Then, look for sites that can be reached by inexpensive public transportation.

Be creative. The most intriguing study trips are often the ones right under our noses—locations where we have gone innumerable times but never thought to take a behind-the-scenes look, such as grocery stores, malls, our own school cafeteria or bus system. Examples: [4]

Kindergarten: Animals living in or visiting the classroom; man-made pond on the school grounds; school yard; backyard of a nearby home (for the natural world and for hobbies); nearby pond or creek, park, or empty lot; or pet store.

First grade: Any of the above locations plus underground aspects of those locations, local habitats that are rich in animal and plant life, farm, garden (on the school grounds or nearby home), larger bodies of water such as lakes, rivers, ocean, and a zoo, aquarium, or pet store.

Second grade: Any of the above locations plus natural history museums, taxidermy shop, construction and repair shops where a variety of tools are used, and local businesses.

Third grade: Any of the above locations plus nearby road cuts that expose changes, fast or slow, in landscape, before and after flood scenes, a variety of construction projects that illustrate new building and remodeling, recycling operations from pick-up to remanufacturing to resale, and lots of in-classroom and neighborhood illustrations of life cycles, physical science cycles, machines, and so forth. Also, community landmarks, businesses (grocery store, mall, mom-and-pop stores of any kind), and city agencies and resources such as police, fire, and medical hospitals, clinics, etc. And, don't forget observation of daily weather and the nighttime sky.

Fourth grade: Any of the above locations plus those a little farther afield, including state agencies and state historical sites or their replications.

Fifth grade: Any of the above from the perspective of systems or change and sites of national significance.

Sixth grade: Any of the above observed with a specific perspective based in a concept from state standards that would pull together concepts from both science and history/social studies.

How to Bring Together Real-Life Locations and Curriculum Standards

Just as a magnet attracts metal shards, a *being there* experience helps attract important concepts and skills from your state standards/district-adopted curriculum. At this stage of your implementation, allow this magnetic quality of *being there* locations to do your curriculum integration and development work for you. Rather than trying to chase down various curriculum pieces, allow the intrinsically interesting aspects of the *being there* location and the most important points from your curriculum standards to simply pull together, a natural fit of related patterns. Curriculum for this stage of implementation should be intriguing and enjoyable to both you and your students. Remember, this is your entry into conceptual, location-based curriculum. Make it fun. Give yourself the best chance at succeeding.

Ask these two pivotal questions when developing curriculum based on a *being there* location:

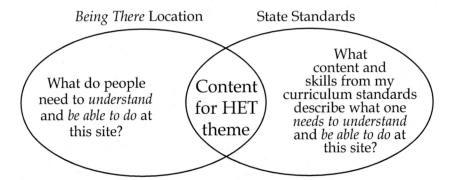

The answers to these two questions help you analyze your real-life location and your curriculum standards so that you can:

- Extract what is most meaningful and important for students to learn and then select and organize the most engaging, relevant concepts and skills from your state standards.

- Create a basis for authentic assessment (see Chapter 19) by building in real-life standards and expectations for what a capable person should understand and be able to do at this location.

The answers to these two questions give you the content for your curriculum. Curriculum development in the *HET* model requires an eye for the practical and lots of common sense; it is not a theoretical exercise.

Older students enjoy exploring the question, "How would this location and its operation be different if people really understood the content and skills we are learning?" This question allows/forces the teacher and students to "think outside the box" and look afresh at the question, "What's worth teaching/learning?"

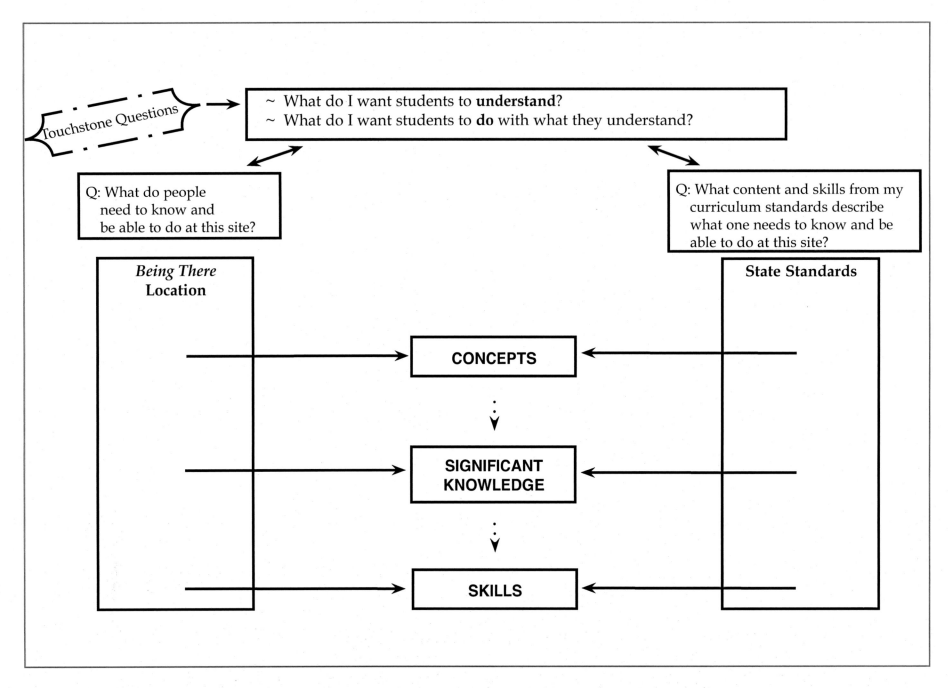

Touchstone Questions

~ What do I want students to **understand**?
~ What do I want students to **do** with what they understand?

Q: What do people
need to know and
be able to do at this site?

Q: What content and skills from my
curriculum standards describe
what one needs to know and be
able to do at this site?

Being There
Location

State Standards

CONCEPTS

**SIGNIFICANT
KNOWLEDGE**

SKILLS

Choosing a physical location as the anchor for curriculum is critical to the *HET* model for several reasons:

- The best way to ensure that students quickly grasp an accurate and comprehensive understanding of the concepts and skills of the curriculum is to allow them to experience those concepts in their real-world contexts.

- Once students understand concepts in one location, they can generalize them to other locations and use them to explain past events and make predictions about events in the future. *This speeds up and deepens the pace of future learning.*

- Each of us must understand how our community works to become an informed citizen.

For more ideas for all school environments—urban, suburban, or rural, see *Ten Minute Field Trips.* Renowned educator Helen Russell Ross describes more than 200 short, close-to-home field trips that explore new dimensions of familiar spaces and objects. Brick walls, rock outcrops, lawns, broken pavement, weeds, and trees are all targets of exploration. The book is divided into topic sections (plants, animals, Earth science, etc.); each includes pre-field trip classroom activities, teacher preparation, and a list of trip possibilities. For urban areas, a special cross-referenced list of field trips for hard-topped school grounds is included.

GUIDELINES FOR SELECTING BEING THERE *LOCATIONS*

Selecting physical locations upon which to build your curriculum is the most critical curricular decision you will make for the year. Like any builder, choose your site with care. The more solid the foundation, the more empowering your curriculum can be.

Before selecting a physical location, do your homework. Think through the following steps.

Step 1: Analyze the Potential of a Site to Teach What Your Students Need to Learn

Remember, you are not developing curriculum for separate subjects which must have a designated amount of seat time per day. Let the locations extract and integrate the aspects of subject areas and skills naturally. For example, don't just focus on the biological aspects of a location; examine your *being there* location in its full science context, including technology and physical and earth science. When looking at the historical aspects, include today's problems created by similar social, economic, and governmental forces. Then, if halfway through the year or semester one area needs more study, concentrate on it during your last *being there* experience or address it during the gaps between your chunks of *HET* curriculum. Remember, let the world integrate your curriculum naturally.

Also, focus on the fact that real life is all around you. A location need not be far afield to be powerful. Consider first your school campus, the immediate neighborhood accessible on foot, and then those locations that you can access via public transportation. Avoid the traditional "field trip" location that is too expensive to visit more than once.

For example, consider the common grocery store. Been there a million times? Of course. But have you ever been behind the scenes and looked at it from a business perspective? Would you be amazed to discover that the typical profit margin for grocery stores is two to three cents on the dollar? Ever wonder how many items change price? When? How often? The possibilities for study are unlimited: profit/loss, employer/employee relationships, the demographics of the clientele/producer, legal restrictions, health inspections, competition, energy costs, OSHA requirements, and so forth.

Step 2: Visit the Site

First, go to each location with new eyes. Pretend you've never been there before. Get curious! Look everything over from a fresh perspective. Look behind the scenes. Imagine what others see—those who work there, those who come there to shop, visit, enjoy. What do these folks need to know to perform their roles well? What do visitors need to know to get the best value for their dollar, to make the wisest decisions, to avoid being taken advantage of, or to enjoy it most fully? Here's an interesting challenge: How would the location and its operations be different if people fully understood the content and skills you plan to teach your students? Second, interview people—those who create the environment (employees and owners) and those who come here (clients/customers and sightseers). Skip past the knowledge and comprehension questions of Bloom's Taxonomy and dive right into the levels of application, analysis, evaluation, and synthesis. That's where the fun and engagement are! Ask the interviewees why they choose to work or shop here. What about this place makes them proud to work/visit here?

Third, put yourself in your students' shoes. What is gripping about this location? What would bring you back again and again?

Step 3: Expand Your Knowledge Base

Solid curriculum can't be developed from information off the top of one's head and our typical curriculum tools are limited; state standards/district curriculum offer an outline, textbooks provide only summary, superficial information. Expect to become a learner. Open yourself up to the joy of discovery. Don't expect to have all the answers. Long gone is the era when what you knew by age 25 would carry you through a lifetime. Learning how to learn and learning to embrace the necessity for learning with enjoyment are the demands of our time. Model this and let your excitement and passion transfer to your students.

Pursue concepts that you believe will allow students to unlock meaning in other settings. Ask yourself several questions: What can be generalized and what can be used to predict events or happenings in other locations? From the students' points of view, what's useful? What are the most empowering concepts and skills you can help them understand?

Keep in mind that the availability of resources is an important consideration when you select a location. You should expect to have at least 50 resources in your room, such as books (e.g., *Eye Witness, Usbourne* series), magazines, print of all kinds written at a range of reading levels (including children's books that provide clear explanations and lots of visuals), plus multi-media options which capitalize on today's technologies (Internet, video, encyclopedias on CD, and so forth). And, very importantly, real things for hands-on exploration.

STEP 4: Revisit Your Curriculum

However small or large this chunk of curriculum for the *being there* experience, is it as conceptual as you can make it? (See discussion in Chapter 11 and Part C.) Have you prioritized the content so students will have time to *understand* and learn to *apply* the most important concepts, significant knowledge, and skills? Are your curriculum choices solid and acceptable to your supervisors? Can you explain them thoroughly to the parents? If so, you are ready to begin developing key points and inquiries.

INTEGRATION MADE EASY

The usual way to prepare to integrate curriculum is to take the prescribed content of traditional subject areas, schedule them one at a time, and then search for ways to make them come alive for your students. In contrast, the *HET* approach makes integration easy and natural by allowing *being there* locations to effortlessly bring together curriculum so that it matches the world we see when we look out the window, walk down the street, or window shop in the mall. Science is everywhere we look, the results of history and social interaction are unavoidable, the arts are everywhere we turn, and all are going on together.

Integrating Subject Content and Basic Skills

If you're still on the fence, not yet ready to base your curriculum in *being there* locations, consider this: *Being there* locations are the great mixer—not only blending together subject areas but also content with skills, in natural and engaging ways.

Be assured that the basic skills—basic and universally essential—can be taught using any location where they are used in real life. Any location drips with numbers; all you have to do is decide what mathematic functions and concepts you want to apply to those numbers.

Use the numbers built into your physical location to make algebra and geometry, as well as basic math, come alive—how far, how long, how tall, how wide, how much, what volume, what angle, which direction, how many years since, how much per square foot/mile, and so forth. Keep a running list of numerical data inherent in each *being there* location. When test-practice time comes, have students use data from these lists instead of that from dull worksheets so students can create their own problems demanding skills they are studying. Make geometry and algebra come alive.

Reading? Writing? Oh my, yes. *Being there* locations offer students something real to read about and a real audience to write to. Have students communicate their discoveries and thank resource people who helped them learn.

For a comprehensive discussion of how to incorporate the basic skills, see Chapter 18.

Being there locations also bring together all the other subject areas in a natural, effortless way—science, social studies, the arts, and so on. Almost any mixture of natural and man-made settings will demonstrate the concepts, significant knowledge, and skills you have chosen from your state standards to include in your *HET* curriculum. As for history/social studies, just add people to your location and you will have a window through which to view human nature past, present, or future. All other content areas can be similarly accessed.

HET Curriculum and Assessment

Anchoring curriculum content in the real world also allows us to develop assessment that mirrors performance standards that students and teachers encounter in their everyday lives. For example, we write a letter with perfect grammar and spelling because we want a real person to take our opinion seriously; we want to calculate math problems accurately when the answers impact our personal lives.

For more information about assessment, see Chapter 19.

Self Check

Ideal *being there* locations:

- Capture student, and teacher, interest and enthusiasm in order to sustain willingness to learn over time, leading students to eagerly ask and pursue questions.

- Provide a powerful illustration of how the concepts and skills are used — why, how, when, by whom.

- Provide maximum sensory input (using as many of the 19 senses as possible).

- Invite authentic use of the concepts and skills you have selected from your state/district curriculum standards.

- Are readily accessible (time and expense) so that the class can visit regularly, allowing for in-depth exploration.

- Have significant carry-over potential, i.e., if students come to understand this setting well (the scientific and technological aspects as well as the historical and social science concepts that drove the setting's creation and continuance), they will be able to immediately understand a great deal about other similar settings.

- Become a prototype for learning *how* to learn about the real world.

ENDNOTES

1   See Chapter 2 for an in-depth discussion of the power and role of emotion and movement to effect learning and performance.

2   See Chapter 1 for a discussion of sensory input and its importance to learning.

3   Gerald A. Lieberman, Ph.D. and Linda I. Hoody provide a range of studies illustrating the power of context and *being there* experiences. See *Closing the Achievement Gap: Using the Environment As an Integrating Context for Learning* (Poway, CA: Science Wizards, 1998).

4   Karen D. Olsen, *Science Continuum of Concepts for Grades K-6* (Black Diamond, WA: Books for Educators, 2009).

Chapter 13: Tools for Developing Bodybrain-Compatible Curriculum

CURRICULUM

- States clearly and succinctly each concept students are to understand. Determines what significant knowledge about the concept students must understand in order to achieve a deep understanding of the concept.

- Provides students with choices through multiple opportunities for real-world application through daily inquiries; such inquiries allow multiple ways of solving problems and producing products.

- For every key point—concept, significant knowledge, and skill—to be taught, provides sufficient inquiries typical of those activities at the *being there* location to ensure sufficient practice to wire those concepts, knowledge, and skills into long-term memory.

INSTRUCTIONAL STRATEGIES

- Posts the key point(s) being studied on the curriculum wall or in student binders. For younger students, includes visual symbols to help convey the meaning of the content.

- Regularly provides choices honoring both personal interests and the multiple intelligences through activities/inquiries and other means.

- Provides each student ample time to complete sufficient inquiries to master the key points. Ensures that students are allowed to work through their strengths through the first three stages of learning (see the New Definition of Learning, page 5.3, *Exceeding Expectations*) and, during the last stage of learning, provides opportunities to strengthen other intelligences.

TIPS FOR DEVELOPING CURRICULUM FOR STAGE 2

Since the goal of Stage 2 is to develop curriculum for only 10-15% of the school year, select *being there* experiences and content that you consider most engaging to students and that most interest you as well. Don't start with the "dry" stuff in your state standards; pull out the enlivening concepts that are best illustrated at the *being there* location. All else builds on these decisions.

Don't worry about how to integrate. That's the easy part. As discussed in the previous chapter, simply allow the context of the *being there* experience to integrate your subject areas and skills naturally—as you see it in real life at the *being there* location.

The hardest part about developing conceptual curriculum is being clear about what you want students to understand and what you want them to do with it. This is different from a generalized question about what you want students to *know.* Such vagueness often leads us into a sea of factoids—details, dates, and definitions—and we quickly end up drowning in a soup of overwhelming possibilities.

Again, begin by asking yourself what jumps out at you as the big idea, the most important concept, the most needed skills at this location. Then, look through your state standards and identify the concepts and skills that are a good match. State what you want students to understand clearly and crisply—preferably as a single sentence. Never use more than three or four sentences for each idea. Keep it short, simple, and clear. These are key points.

Next, think through what you want students to be able to do with what they understand and how they can practice applying those concepts and skills in the context of the *being there* experience or a simulation of it. These are inquiries.

One concept and a handful of significant knowledge and skill key points with inquiries attached will get you through a mini-curriculum structure or topic lasting half days for a week or more.

Have we made this sound too easy? Well, the mechanics aren't that difficult. Again, the hard part is getting clear on what *exactly* you want students to understand and *exactly* what you want them to do with it.

Always start with a concept, something that students can carry with them to unlock meaning in new situations, something generalizable and transferable. Then add on from there. Once you're clear about the concepts and skills and how students will use them in real-world ways, the actual process of writing them down on paper is an easy writing task, much like writing one short paragraph at a time.

Just as business admonishes us to think outside the box, it is helpful to think beyond the usual questions about what may be on the test. Instead, ask what students need to know to understand their world and what skills they need to act on it.

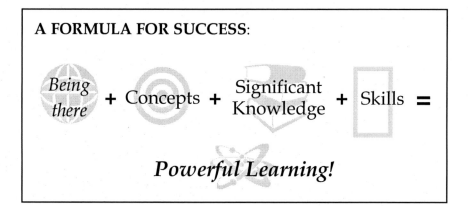

A FORMULA FOR SUCCESS:

Being there + Concepts + Significant Knowledge + Skills =

Powerful Learning!

MAKING CURRICULUM FIT THE BRAIN

The purpose in writing your own curriculum is to make it more powerful for students. Otherwise, why bother? To make it more powerful, curriculum should be developed to fit how the brain learns (review brain research presented in Chapters 4 and 5—the brain as pattern seeker and meaning maker and learning as the acquisition of mental programs). Powerful, bodybrain-compatible curriculum:

- Builds on local *being there* experiences that provide maximum sensory input, engage the body in learning, and level the playing field for students who lack prior experience with the concepts and skills to be learned.

- Is conceptual

- Carries the learner through the four steps of the *HET* brain-based definition of learning (see below)

- Is tailored to your specific students' interests, needs, and ways of learning in ways that unleash positive emotions and deepen commitment to learning.

Definition of Learning

Part One—**Input stage: Pattern detection** consists of first identifying or recognizing the pattern and then making meaning of the pattern, including its relationship to other patterns.

and

Part Two—**Output stage: Program building** consists of learning to apply what is learned, at first experimentally and consciously, and then, after practice and wiring it into long-term memory, applying what is learned with the almost automatic ease and skill of the expert.

TOOLS FOR WRITING CURRICULUM FOR STAGE 2

Once you have selected the most engaging concepts and skills based on the overlap between your *being there* location and your curriculum standards as described in Chapter 12, you are ready to begin writing your curriculum. Curriculum writing is made much easier if you ask yourself two questions:

- ***What do I want my students to understand?***

  This question helps you focus on what you want to teach—the concepts and skills identified during your work in Chapter 12. It also requires that you write clear and specific statements of what you want students to understand.

  These statements are your ***key points***. (See pages 13.4-8).

- ***What do I want students to be able to do with what they understand?***

  This question helps you figure out ways students can apply what you are teaching in real-world—and thus memorable—ways, beginning with uses at the *being there* location and then generalizing to other situations. This is the step that ensures mastery and long-term memory, gives you a solid foundation for authentic assessment, and ensures success – yours as a teacher and your students' as learners.

  These statements are your ***inquiries***. (See pages 13.9-16)

KEY POINTS: WHAT I WANT MY STUDENTS TO UNDERSTAND

The most important thing to say about key points is this: Make them as conceptual as you can. Avoid writing down a string of factoids. Factoids are good for playing Jeopardy but aren't useful in real life.

Conceptual Key Points

Go for big ideas/concepts that will engage your students. Use the GUTS criteria to guide you:

G = generalizable—a principle or conclusion that can be used to explain specifics; pulls idea into general use

U = understandable by students this age

T = transferable to new locations/situations

S = succinct and clear

Generalizable. "Teacher, why is this important? What's this good for?" All students deserve curriculum that answers these questions. In our mind, it's curriculum that can be generalized to a big idea or concept that explains an important aspect of our world and that can be transferred to similar but different situations. Such curriculum empowers students and makes teachers more effective and efficient.

Always ask yourself what you want your students to understand and why.

To write powerful curriculum, you must be willing to do some independent research and to learn to play the Bump Up game.

Research Is a Must. One can't extract concepts out of district/state curriculum standards or a textbook without a solid knowledge base. Writing factoids? That's easy; they are every-

where. But conceptual statements that can be generalized and applied in similar but different situations require a knowledge base beyond that which is needed to teach from published curriculum tools and curriculum frameworks.

A good beginning place for research is the information available at the *being there* location, such as brochures, pamphlets, booklets, magazines, and books. Next, follow up on any references found in these sources. Then, branch out. Visit the Internet as well as your library and media center.

Your goal is to obtain enough knowledge to write key points that can be generalized and transferred.

Bumping Up. The Bump Up game is a search for big ideas/concepts to organize, ideas that give meaning to what we expect our students to learn. Here are some examples of the Bump Up game applied to information found in a brochure on dog worms—research for a *being there* visit to a vet's office. Let's assume that the relevant state standards you have chosen are about parasites.

As you read through this brochure about parasites, you find lots of information about worms, especially heartworms. However, you want to make the information as transferable as possible so that students who have a pet other than a dog can also relate to the problem. Ultimately, your students should be able to transfer some of the knowledge about parasites in dogs to parasites in other animals, including humans.

Your task is to "bump up" the contents of the brochure to make it more conceptual. Begin by checking your state standards. Are there relevant concepts about parasites? If so, you're ready to write key points. If not, you will need to extract concepts from the brochure using your knowledge of parasites.

The brochure about heartworms on the next page is typical of information sources we run across in our day-to-day lives—specific information about a specific topic. Unfortunately, such information often does not help us generalize to other situations. For example, suppose we have a cat in the house. What does this brochure tell us about taking care of our cat to ensure against parasites? Not much. But, with more research, we can state the important concepts rather than just restating these specifics; our students can then learn a great deal that they can transfer to other situations now and in the future. They can know something about cats, rabbits, hamsters, and any other pet they may choose. Concepts provide post office boxes in the brain to which new information can be sent for comparison, add-on, updating, etc. This makes learning more efficient.

For example, look at the heartworm brochure on the next two pages. Facts and factoids abound. The challenge is to recognize what is really important for students to understand and be able to use. First pull out the concepts; then look for significant knowledge necessary to build a conceptual understanding of internal parasites that is sufficient to help one become a competent pet owner and apply the concept of parasitism more broadly to other species, including humans. Select those facts that help students more fully understand our concept about parasites.

As you can see, the details stated in the "facts and factoids" column, although interesting, can't be generalized or transferred. Their use ends with dogs and, if one doesn't own a dog, the information is largely forgettable. However, when bumped up to a conceptual statement about parasites, the learner can acquire an understanding that has wide application.

Where heartworm disease comes from...

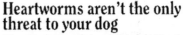

Mosquitoes transmit heartworm disease by biting an infected dog, then passing the infection on to other dogs they bite. Developing heartworms migrate to the dog's heart, where they can grow up to 14 inches in length as they mature. If not removed, they can cause permanent heart and lung damage and even death. But you may not see any signs before it's too late. And once diagnosed, the treatment for heartworm disease can be dangerous and costly.

Mosquitoes transmit heartworm disease.

How it spreads....

Heartworm infections are common along the Atlantic and Gulf coasts and the Mississippi River Valley and its tributaries, and now have been reported in every state in America, including Alaska, and in Canada as well. Some mosquitoes have a flight range of over 15 miles enabling them to spread the infection over great distances. In addition, dogs tend to travel more with their owners each year, and this also can increase the spread of heartworm disease.

When the weather begins to turn cold, mosquitoes often try to find protected areas such as inside your home or doghouse. So even dogs kept mainly indoors can become infected. They are also at risk when taken for walks or released in the yard.

Heartworms can grow up to 14 inches in length.

The American Heartworm Society has documented an increase in cases of heartworm disease.

Heartworms aren't the only threat to your dog

Roundworms (Ascarids) and Hookworms: There are two important species of ascarids and hookworms that commonly infect all dogs. These intestinal parasites can cause poor growth—and even death. Dogs of all ages are at risk, but puppies are particularly vulnerable. Your veterinarian can diagnose these infections in your dog by examining a fecal sample to determine if eggs are present.

Puppies are often born with roundworms (Ascarids)...

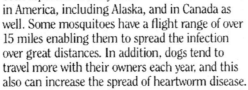

Many puppies are born with roundworms, which they contract from their mothers before birth. These worms can also be passed in egg form through a dog's feces. Roundworms live and grow in a dog's intestines, and can

Roundworms (ascarids) Toxocara canis

reach lengths of up to 7 inches. Dogs suffering from a heavy roundworm infection appear potbellied, have a dull coat, and may experience vomiting and diarrhea. Lung damage, pneumonia, and liver damage may also occur.

Roundworm (ascarids) Toxascaris leonina

Hookworm can be fatal...

Hookworm
Ancylostoma caninum

Hookworms are also common in puppies. If left untreated, heavy infections can cause a puppy's death within weeks.

Hookworms can be passed through the mother's milk, or in egg form via the feces. Infection can also occur as the result of larvae penetrating the skin (causing a local rash), after which they migrate via the bloodstream to the intestines. Hookworms can cause diarrhea, severe anemia, and weakness. Dogs may also lose weight due to the bloodsucking of hookworms.

Hookworm
Uncinaria stenocephala

Taken from "To protect your dog . . . Ask for heartworm preventive that has a heart." Heartgard

Note: **Some concepts are global** enough that they provide an **umbrella for study across subject areas.** For example: "Prevention is the best cure." This concept can be applied to history (the importance of resolving conflicts which escalate into war); to economics (controlling theft in a business before the business runs out of money or controlling inflation in the stock market to prevent deep, long-lasting depressions or failure to make and enforce laws controlling large corporations, e.g., Enron, WorldCom, Savings & Loans, and so forth); to geography (the value of taking steps to avoid catastrophic floods); to sociology (the end cost of restricting access to quality education by the poor, such as larger prison populations and higher recidivism rates), and so forth.

Playing the Bump Up Game

From These Facts & Factoids and a Knowledge Base . . .	*Come These Conceptual Key Points:*
• Heartworms in dogs are transmitted by mosquitoes. • Roundworms in puppies and dogs can be contracted before birth and through feces. • Hookworms in puppies and adult dogs can be passed through the mother's milk or via feces in egg form; the larvae can also penetrate the skin. • Treatments to kill heartworms can sometimes lead to death because the remains of the heartworms drift into the lungs and cause potentially fatal blood clots. • Mosquitoes, some of which have a flight range of 15 miles, have carried heartworms to all 50 states and Canada.	• Because internal parasites have evolved such a wide array of methods of reproduction and acquiring access to a host, all animals can have them, including pets and humans. Parasites harm and even cause the death of their host if untreated. • Prevention is the best cure.

Parasitic behavior is also a concept that can be applied across subject areas. In addition to biological applications such as pet ownership, commercial animal husbandry, dangers within our food supply system, and personal health, parasitism is a useful concept through which to study areas of economics (from extorting lunch money from younger students to anti-trust behavior of large corporations such as Microsoft and Enron) and sociology (co-dependency, organized crime, and imperialism).

Some concepts, however, provide a **quality study base only within one subject area** such as study of the *methods* by which parasites reproduce. Although not generalizable across subject areas, it nonetheless is a concept that opens the door to a lifetime of study in biology and is very generalizable and transferable across species, including humans.

Understandable. Curriculum content for students must be understandable by students at their age. (For more information on age-appropriate curriculum, see Appendix B). The test for age-appropriateness is this: **If students**—even after a *being there* experience and lots of hands-on-of-the-real-thing input—**still must resort to memorization,** *then the content is not age-appropriate.* Examples include atoms and molecules for third graders, photosynthesis for sixth graders, and so forth. Such content sounds good to politicians and the public but confuses students (and convinces them they can't learn science) and frustrates their teacher.

Transferable. The power of conceptual curriculum is that it can be transferred to new locations/situations. If students understand the idea of habitat in the rain forest, for example, they will also understand the principles of habitat in a desert. They don't have to start from scratch learning about deserts, they already know quite a bit.

Succinct and Clear. As George Bernard Shaw once wrote, apologizing to a friend: "I'm sorry this letter is so long; I didn't have time to write a short one." Writing clear, concise, succinct key points demands the best writing skills you possess and requires mental discipline. This is a time for the Lifelong Guideline of Personal Best!

Significant Knowledge Key Points

If a concept is new to students, it should be accompanied by knowledge key points that help students understand the concept. For example, the significant knowledge key points below help students understand the conceptual key points stated on the previous page:

- Worm infestations can occur in dogs at any age—from before birth through adulthood—and can occur in a variety of ways: via mother's milk, infected mosquitoes, eggs in feces, the mother before birth, and larvae penetrating the skin.

- The three most common parasites in dogs—heartworms, roundworms, and hookworms—are dangerous not only

because they rob nutrients from their host but because their presence can cause permanent damage to heart, lungs, and liver and, if untreated, death. For example, heartworms can grow up to 14 inches long and roundworms up to 7 inches.

- The presence of some internal parasites is often hard to detect until serious damage to the host, even death, has occurred. Therefore, prevention is the best and safest treatment for parasites. Learn about the parasites that are typical to the areas where your dog lives and visits, test your pet as recommended by a veterinarian, and treat accordingly.

These knowledge key points about parasites in dogs help students understand the concept of parasites in a real-world way. This combination of concepts and significant knowledge allows students to achieve competence both for taking tests and operating in the real world; and, it makes learning about parasites affecting cats or even people more efficient, taking but a fraction of the time to learn compared to a first exposure to learning about parasites in dogs. Teaching conceptually—starting with a concept followed by the significant knowledge needed to understand the concept—not only deepens learning but it also makes your teaching time efficient as well as effective.

Skill Key Points

To understand a concept in real-world ways, students may need specific skills. Often these skills are not directly related to the concept; they are basic skills—math, writing, speaking, and so forth. Make sure you identify them and teach them so your students can succeed in using what they understand from the conceptual and significant knowledge key points. Other skills are unique to the context of the application of what we know.

The following skill key points include the need for math skills as well as for pet ownership:

- Precise measurement of dosages of medication (for dogs and humans) is important because an overdose can be lethal and an inadequate dose can be ineffective in treating the problem. Most dosages for humans and animals are now measured using the metric system, in milliliters (ml) or cubic centimeters (cc) rather than ounces because measuring in milliliters or cubic centimeters provides a more accurate and reliable measurement of small quantities. For example, one fluid ounce equals 30 milliliters; five centimeters is about one teaspoon. Because the measurements on the syringe or bottle of medication may differ from the prescription, one must be able to convert measurements from US to metric and vice versa.

- Recommended dosages indicate how many cc's or ml's to administer per x pounds of an animal's weight. To calculate the correct dose for an animal: First, carefully weigh the animal. Second, divide the animal's weight by the number of pounds indicated in the recommended dosage (for example, 10 pounds per one cc of medicine). Third, multiply this number times the number of cc's or ml's to be administered.

> Recommended dosage:
>   5 cc per 10 pounds of animal
> 1) Fido weighs 70 pounds
> 2) Divide 70 by 10 = 7 doses
> 3) Multiple 7 times 5cc's = 35cc's

- Shots for a dog are usually delivered in the loose skin at the top of the neck and shoulders by first pulling up the loose skin and then inserting the needle sideways so as to avoid hitting the spine or muscle.

- Some medications are given to dogs orally. Put the medication in a food morsel. Hold the dog's mouth open, insert the food far back in the mouth, and hold the dog's mouth closed until it swallows.

To summarize, always lead with a concept, then add information necessary to understand the concept. When skills are needed, state them simply and succinctly, just the way you want students to remember them.

Self Check

All my key points:

- Are based in *being there* locations

- Are a marriage between what the people that work at and use that location need to understand and be able to do **AND** content from my state/district standards

My conceptual key points meet the GUTS criteria:

G = generalizable—a principle or conclusion that can be used to explain specifics; pulls idea into general use

U = understandable by students this age

T = transferable to new locations/situations

S = succinct and clear

INQUIRIES: WHAT I WANT MY STUDENTS TO BE ABLE TO DO WITH WHAT THEY UNDERSTAND

Once you have stated what you want your students to understand as conceptually as possible and included significant knowledge and skills, think through ways students can apply these understandings in real-world ways. Go back to your *being there* location and watch how these concepts and skills are applied by the people who work and visit there. Then, keeping in mind the age of your students and what is appropriate for their stage of mental development, start writing these applications down on paper. Jot down as many as you see and others that come to mind. You are now ready to write inquiries.

The ABC+D² Rules for Writing Inquiries

As you write inquiries, keep the following rules in mind:

- **A**lways start with the action in mind.* What are students to do? How can they practice applying what they understand to real-world situations?

- **B**e specific with your directions so that students can see the outcome or finished product in their mind's eye. What is the inquiry asking them to do?

- **C**onnect to the key point. Will doing this inquiry help students both understand and be able to apply the concept, significant knowledge, or skill described in the key point? Never select an activity just because it is fun or clever or cute. If it doesn't help students understand and practice the key point, throw it out. Learning is serious business; stay focused on what you want students to understand and what you want them to do with what they understand.

- Requires **d**eep thinking.

- **D**on't stop writing until you have enough inquiries for each key point to address all the multiple intelligences and to take students through mastery to long-term memory.

Providing Choice

One of the biggest benefits of developing your own curriculum at the classroom level is the opportunity to build in choices for students. Choices allow them to learn through the intelligences in which they are strong and then, while completing the last phase of the Two-Step Learning process, strengthen those less-developed

---

* For action verbs, see the Inquiry Builder chart on page 13.10. Decide which of the multiple intelligences you want students to use (listed along the left of the chart from top to bottom) and the kind of performance you want them to engage in (Bloom's taxonomy along the top of the chart from left to right). Start your directions to students using this verb. [Note: We have revised the order of Bloom's Taxonomy to better fit how the brain learns.]

intelligences. Choices also allow students to expand interests and deepen motivation to learn. Inquiries are your major means of providing meaningful choice; fortunately, it's easy to do. Simply refer to the Inquiry Builder Chart on the next page. Select action words from each segment of the chart and you will be able to write inquiries that meet the multiple intelligences.

The inquiries about parasites on page 13.10 are examples of how a teacher can use inquiries to build in choices for students. The initials after each inquiry indicate which intelligence is needed to carry out the task. Also, some inquiries require collaboration, while others require individual work.

Another important way to build in choices is to invite students, third grade and up, to develop inquiries for your key points. A good starter question is, "What examples of this concept (skill) have you seen today?" Gather up these inquiries and then decide which you would like to offer to the class, Learning Club, or individuals to choose to do.

Examples of Inquiries with Key Points

Examples of inquiries for the key points about parasites could include the following.

Conceptual Key Point #1: Because internal parasites have evolved such a wide array of methods for acquiring access to a host and for reproducing, all animals are host to internal parasites—including pets and humans. Parasites harm and even cause the death of their host if untreated.

Inquiries for Conceptual Key Point #1:

1) Working in pairs for five minutes, write down as much information as you can about parasites you have learned from your own pets and those of friends and neighbors. Share this information with the class during the next inquiry. (L)*

---

* These symbols at the end of each inquiry refer to the multiple intelligences; see the Inquiry Builder Chart on the previous page.

INQUIRY BUILDER

Starting Point with being *there* experience

Ending Point for test preparation

Bloom's Taxonomy (adapted)

MULTIPLE INTELLIGENCES		Application	Analysis	Evaluation	Synthesis	Comprehension	Knowledge
	Logical/ Mathematical	▪apply ▪solve ▪convert ▪expand ▪schedule ▪sequence ▪organize	▪question ▪solve ▪inventory ▪compare ▪distinguish ▪differentiate	▪estimate ▪measure ▪choose ▪predict ▪judge ▪select ▪assess ▪value ▪rate ▪review	▪design ▪infer ▪classify ▪hypothesize ▪prepare ▪formulate ▪propose	▪describe ▪calculate ▪identify ▪explain ▪retell ▪recognize ▪sequence ▪organize	▪label ▪name
	Linguistic	▪apply ▪teach ▪translate ▪interview ▪communicate	▪analyze ▪debate ▪criticize ▪discuss ▪question ▪investigate ▪interpret	▪critique ▪interpret ▪discuss ▪rate ▪relate ▪probe ▪judge ▪justify	▪compose ▪rewrite ▪propose ▪infer ▪adapt ▪debate ▪impersonate ▪produce	▪review ▪describe ▪discuss ▪express ▪report ▪explain ▪restate	▪name ▪tell ▪label ▪recall ▪define ▪record ▪narrate ▪list ▪memorize
	Spatial	▪diagram ▪exhibit ▪translate ▪teach ▪illustrate ▪make ▪apply ▪chart ▪summarize ▪graph	▪disassemble ▪differentiate ▪diagram ▪distinguish	▪predict ▪estimate ▪measure ▪judge	▪formulate ▪plan ▪propose ▪arrange ▪design ▪organize ▪restructure	▪locate ▪sort ▪identify ▪compare ▪describe ▪illustrate ▪recognize ▪relate parts	▪interpret ▪adapt ▪draw ▪match ▪sketch
	Bodily/ Kinesthetic	▪apply ▪rhythm ▪dramatize ▪mime ▪operate ▪(teach) ▪(demonstrate) ▪(practice)	▪interpret ▪disassemble ▪experiment ▪diagram ▪(inventory)	▪rehearse ▪(measure) ▪(debate)	▪convey emotion ▪tell a story ▪(invent) ▪(assemble) ▪(design) ▪(construct) ▪(arrange) ▪(prepare) ▪(classify)	▪perform ▪(locate)	▪imitate ▪play
	Musical	▪perform (solo or group) ▪harmonize ▪(express) ▪rhythm ▪synchronize ▪(characterize)	▪interpret ▪analyze ▪(compare)	▪interpret ▪critique ▪(characterize)	▪create a variation ▪improvise ▪(express) ▪(convey emotion) ▪(symbolize) ▪compose ▪(tell a story) ▪transpose	▪imitate ▪rehearse	▪recite

( ) = could have this quality if so designed.

2) As a class, add as much information as you can to the KW columns of a KWL chart about parasites. (L, LM)

3) As a Learning Club, select a parasite to research that often infects humans. Using the Internet or media center, discover at least one method by which this parasite accesses its host, when the parasite was first discovered and named, and the treatments commonly used over time. Illustrate the life cycle of the parasite on a poster board; make a timeline representing the years when the parasite was discovered and the treatments used for it over time. Present your findings to the class. After your presentation, post your information for a class Gallery Walk. (L, LM, S, BK)

4) Take a Gallery Walk with your Learning Club. Compare your research findings with that of other Learning Clubs. Use a Venn diagram to analyze similarities and differences in content in content between other Learning Clubs and yours. Use another Venn diagram to record similarities and differences in approaches to researching for Inquiry #3. (BK, LM, L)

5) As a class, add more information to the KW** columns of the KWU chart about parasites. (L, LM)

6) As a Learning Club, plan a visit to a veterinarian's office. List five things that you would like the vet to show or explain to you about parasites that infect dogs. (L, LM)

Significant Knowledge Key Point #1: Worm infestations can occur in dogs at any age—from before birth through adult—and can occur in a variety of ways: via mother's milk, infected mosquitoes, eggs in feces, the mother before birth, and larvae penetrating the skin.

Inquiries for Significant Knowledge Key Point #1:

Before going to the vet's office:

** KWU charts are used for brainstorming what students already _know_ and what they _w_ant to know. After study, they capture what has been learned learned.

1) As a Learning Club, choose one of the three most common worms that infect dogs—heartworms, roundworms, or hookworms. Using the Internet or media center, create an illustration on poster board of that worm's life cycle; indicate each stage during which this parasite accesses its host and how the parasite does so. Make a life-sized clay model of your worm and the organ it attacks. Describe the treatments commonly used to treat such infestations. Present your Learning Club's findings, illustration, and models to another class. (L, S, BK)

2) Select a dog owned by a member of your Learning Club or a neighbor. Estimate the dog's weight. Based on this weight, compute how much of the following medicines should be administered to this dog or puppy (or kitten). (L, LM) [See Math Skill Key Point #1.]
   For roundworms, one cc of Pyramtel Paomate per 10 pounds of body weight.
   For hookworms, one cc of Pyramtel Paomate per 10 pounds of body weight.

3) Working in pairs, select four breeds of dogs that interest you. Visit a website to discover the average adult weight of these dog breeds. Compute how much of the medication for heartworms, round worms, and hookworms should be administered to each of these breeds. (L, LM)

Math Skill Key Point #1: Recommended dosages indicate how many cc's or ml's to administer per x pounds of an animal's weight. Use the following three steps to calculate the correct dose for an animal: First, carefully weigh the animal. Second, divide the animal's weight by the number of pounds indicated in the recommended dosage (for example, 10 pounds per one cc of medicine). Third, multiply this number times the number of cc's or ml's to be administered.

> Recommended dosage:
>   5 cc per 10 pounds of animal
> 1) Fido weighs 70 pounds
> 2) Divide 70 by 10 = 7 doses
> 3) Multiple 7 times 5cc's = 35cc's

At the vet's office:

1) As a Learning Club, interview the owner of a dog brought to the vet's office. List the reasons why the owner thought his/her pet might have worms. Next, interview the vet to determine his/her diagnosis. Prepare to present your findings to the class when you return from the vet's office. (L)

2) Observe the vet examining a dog for possible worm infestation. If the vet prescribes treatment for worms, compute the amount of the dose to be administered. Check your computations against the vet's. Observe the vet giving the prescribed treatment. (L, LM)

Back at the classroom:

1) As a Learning Club, decide which member will bring one dog and which will bring one cat. Assign those members to bring that pet to the Classroom Vet Clinic Day. (L)

2) On Classroom Vet Clinic Day, weigh your Learning Club's two pets on an accurate scale before the vet arrives. Ask the vet to explain his/her reasons for diagnosing the presence or absence of parasites in each animal. Check with your Learning Club; do you agree or do you have more questions? Also ask the vet why he/she chose that particular method of treatment. Then, calculate the correct dose for each pet. Ask the vet to check your calculations. Watch the vet closely as he/she administers that treatment. (L, LM)

3) Write a personal thank you letter to the vet for allowing your class to visit his/her vet clinic and for coming to the classroom for Classroom Vet Clinic Day. Share with him/her three things you learned about parasites that most fascinated you. (L)

Language Arts Skill Key Point #1: A letter is a form of written communication that expresses personal thoughts, experiences, or feelings, requests information, services, or products. There are three types of letters, each with a slightly different structure:

1) The **personal letter**, often called a friendly letter, is an informal communication, usually written to a close friend or relative. Personal letters can be handwritten or typed. The structure of a friendly letter includes the following:

- Date
- Greeting
- Body
- Closing
- Signature

Personal letters include thank you notes, letters of condolence, regret, or apology, notes of congratulations, letters to catch the recipient up to date or inquire about his/her life, and so forth. Email communications are also a version of a friendly letter. However, the date is usually left out because the software records the date.

February 29, 2004

Dear Mom,

[Body of letter]

Love,

Karen

A personal letter

The widespread use of the computer and Internet is altering the way we communicate. Today, virtually all business and most personal letters are produced on the computer, rarely handwritten. As a result, a handwritten personal letter is a special occurrence and is appreciated by most people as a special effort to communicate, a special touch.

2) A **business letter** is written from one business or organization to another business or organization. Its purpose is to request information, to discuss a problem or situation, or propose ways the two entities can cooperate together. Because it is written on behalf of one's business or organization, it is the most formal letter. Both its language and its structure are more formal than in a friendly letter.

A business letter includes the following:

- Date
- Heading (name and address of the recipient)
- Formal salutation (usually followed by a colon instead of a comma)
- Body
- Closing
- Signature
- Name, title, and address of sender

A business letter

February 29, 2004

Ms. Joy Hands,
Customer Service Manager
Books for Educators, Inc.
17051 SE 272nd Street, Ste. 18
Covington, WA 98042

Dear Ms. Hands:

[Body of Letter]

Sincerely,

Jack Paperback
Mr. Jack Paperback, President
Paperback Press
131 West Lane
Corporate City, CA 98000

Business letters are usually typed. When sent via email, it is often scanned and sent as an attachment so that the letterhead and signature can be conveyed to the receiver. Like a fax, this electronically conveyed letter constitutes a legally binding document.

If both sender and recipient know each other, are of similar rank in the organization, and are on good terms, the salutation often uses the person's first name followed by a comma. For example: "Dear Judy," If so, the sender then also signs only his/her first name.

3) A **personal business letter** is a combination of a friendly and business letter. It is written to a business from a person representing him/herself, not the business he/she works for; it is therefore slightly less formal than the business letter but not as chummy or familiar as the personal letter. Common uses of a personal business letter are to thank the company or to register a complaint, to send an appreciation to a member of the com-

A personal business letter

February 29, 2004

Ms. Joy Hands,
Customer Service Manager
Books for Educators, Inc.
17051 SE 272nd Street, Suite 18
Covington, WA 98042

Dear Judy,

[Body of Letter]

Sincerely,

Jack
Mr. Jack Paperback, President
Paperback Press
131 West Lane
Corporate City, CA 98000

pany for superior service, or to acknowledge something the company or someone working for the company has done.

A personal business letter has the same seven parts as a business letter: date, heading; recipient's name, title, and address; salutation; body; closing; signature; and sender's name and address (see format for a business letter on the next page). A personal business letter is also usually typed.

In a personal business letter, the salutation usually uses the person's first name followed by a comma (not a colon). The sender also signs only his/her first name.

Inquiries for Skill Key Point #2:

1) As a Learning Club, create movements to represent each part of the three kinds of letters. Use the same movement for the same part if found in all three types of letters. Create additional movements for any new part not found in the other types of letters. Create a chant to accompany the movements that explains each part of each type of letter. Teach the movements and chant to the class. (BK, L, M)

2) As an Learning Club brainstorm at least six situations that would require that a letter be written. Choose one situation. On a slip of paper, write the name of the person (classmate, guest teacher, or business) to whom the letter should be written. Put your scenario in the bag your teacher passes around the room. Then, draw a scenario out of the bag.

Before you begin to write your letter, determine the type of letter you need to write and the structures you will need in the letter. Mindmap the things you would want to say. Write the letter. Have a member of your Learning Club review your letter for correctness of format. (BK, L, LM)

3) As a Learning Club, select a community problem or issue that you think needs action. Determine the type of letter you should write to the editor of your local newspaper expressing your concern. Offer your recommendations for resolving this issue. (L)

4) Create a PowerPoint presentation showing the different parts of all three types of letters. Each slide should include a title, a description of each type of letter, criteria for determining when and why one would select one of the types of letters, and a short sample letter for each with the parts labeled. Show your presentation to the class. (L, S)

5) Compare the similarities and differences among the three types of letters. Illustrate your analysis using a graphic organizer and explain your findings to at least two other classmates. (LM, L)

6) As a Learning Club, analyze the model of each of three letters shown on the overhead projector. Identify the elements of each letter and determine which of the three types of letters each is. Share your responses with the class; be prepared to defend your answers. (LM, L)

7) As a Learning Club, write a business letter to thank the vet for allowing your class to visit the clinic. Include how he/she helped you learn about parasites and prevention. Swap letters with another Learning Club; edit theirs for format, formal language, and clarity. When you get your letter back, make any necessary corrections. Hang your letter on the wall for a Gallery Walk. Prepare a perfect copy to be sent to the vet. Address the envelope and ask your teacher to mail it. (S, L)

8) Write a personal letter to the vet thanking him/her for providing a pet clinic in your classroom. Share about the knowledge

and skills you most valued and describe three things you learned about parasites and their treatment and prevention. Have a member of your Learning Club review your letter. Make any necessary corrections and place it in the mailbag to be mailed to the vet. (L)

Significant Knowledge Key Point #2: The three most common parasites in dogs—heartworms, roundworms, and hookworms—are dangerous not only because they rob nutrients from their host but because their presence can cause permanent damage to heart, lungs, liver, and intestines and can, if untreated, death. For example, heartworms can grow up to 14 inches long and roundworms 7 inches.

Inquiries for Significant Knowledge Key Point #2:

1) As a Learning Club, select a common pet parasite; research it. Write words to a familiar song that would inform dog owners about this common parasite, how it acquires access to its host, the damage it causes, how to to treat it, and how to prevent it. Perform the song for another class. (L, BK)

2) As a Learning Club, research common parasites that infect humans. Complete a KWL chart based on your research. After the doctor speaks to the class and you have had a chance to ask questions, review your KWL chart. Update it, adding information and correcting any misconceptions you had. Rewrite your chart and present it to the class. (L, S, LM)

3) With your Learning Club, select a familiar tune and write lyrics that will teach pet owners important information about worm infestations and how to take good care of their pet. Videotape the performance; send it to the vet so that he/she can create a check-out library for his/her clients. (L, M, S)

4) Create a 3-minute video that presents information about worm infestations and how it applies to pets. Show the video to another class. Give a copy to the vet whose clinic you visited as a thank you. (L, S)

Conceptual Key Point #2: The best and safest treatment for parasites is prevention.

Inquiries for Conceptual Key Point #2:

1) Write a short paragraph or chant describing the damage that a 14 inches long heartworm can do to a dog's heart. Include why such damage is permanent and why treatment can cause death. Read/perform your paragraph/chant to your Learning Club. (L)

2) As a Learning Club, select your favorite paragraph or rap song performed to you. Perform it for the class (choral reading of the paragraph or group performance of the rap song). (L, BK)

3) Select the dog-infesting parasite that most concerns you. Develop a "Parasite Prevention for Your Pet" pamphlet for owners that describes the parasite, how it gains access to its host, the damage it causes, and the best means to prevent and treat it. Use illustrations, graphics, maps, and other graphic organizers whenever possible. Make it informative and colorful. Have your Learning Club check your pamphlet for accuracy. Make 10 copies and have your teacher deliver them to the vet's office to be shared with pet owners. (L, S, LM)

Significant Knowledge Key Point #3: The presence of some internal parasites is often hard to detect until serious damage to the host, even death, has occurred. Therefore, prevention is the best and safest treatment for parasites. Prevention includes learning what parasites are typical to the areas your pet lives in and visits, how to treat your pet for those parasites, and getting regular tests as recommended by a veterinarian to help determine if parasites are present.

1) Homework Assignment: Interview two neighbors who are dog owners. Use a Venn diagram to record similarities and differences in the places their dog has lived and visited during the last year. Based on this information, prescribe a preventative treatment for the dog. If the treatment includes medication, compute the amount of medication the dog needs. Show your math work to determine this dosage. (S, L, LM)

2) Social/Political Action: Plan and carry out a Pet Parasite Prevention Clinic for all the students at your school (grades 4 and up) who have a dog. (LM, L, BK, S)

WORDS OF ADVICE

From the thousands of teachers who precede you on your journey into *HET* curriculum, please heed two pieces of advice:

Start Small. Start small . . . a conceptual, *being there*-based half day or two here and there, then a week of half days. Small chunks of conceptual curriculum that are well planned, well implemented, and occur frequently are more productive than a few large, overwhelming chunks because they are better teachers. A small-amount-frequently approach allows a teacher the best opportunity to practice how to write and teach from conceptual, integrated, location-based curriculum versus textbooks and worksheets and, very importantly, to learn from successes and failures. Quality is far more important than quantity during Stage 2.

Complete Writing Curriculum Before Starting to Lesson Plan. To maintain your focus on what you want students to understand and be able to do with what they understand, complete your curriculum work **before** you begin to think about how you will teach the curriculum. We can guarantee you that if you try to do both simultaneously, your curriculum will suffer.

Self Check

My curriculum:

- Is based in *being there* locations

- Is a marriage between what the people that work and use that location need to understand and be able to do **AND** the expectations of my state/district standards

- Starts with an important concept

- Integrates at least two subject areas, such as science and math

- Integrates at least one basic skill area

- Is completed before lesson planning begins

- Constitutes approximately 10-15% of my year

Self Check

My inquiries:

- Directly relate to a key point

- Meet the ABCs + D rules for writing inquiries

  A = <u>A</u>lways starts with the action in mind

  B = <u>B</u>e specific, clear, and unambiguous

  C = <u>C</u>onnects to the key point

  D = Requires <u>*d*</u>**eep thinking**

  D = <u>D</u>on't stop writing until you have enough inquiries for each key point to take students through mastery to long-term memory.

- Include actions needed at the *being there* locations and similar real-world locations

- Give students sufficient practice in applying a concept or skill to allow them to use it with proficiency and to wire it into long-term memory

Chapter 14: Organizing Curriculum Using Concepts

HET Classroom Stages of Implementation

Making curriculum and instruction bodybrain compatible

Stage 2

CURRICULUM

- Uses an organizing concept to pull together content and skills from multiple subject areas. This organizing concept unifies study for the year.

- For at least two chunks of conceptual curriculum during the year, includes a Social/Political Action Project and concludes with a Celebration of Learning.

- Completes writing curriculum (key points and inquiries) before beginning to plan lessons.

INSTRUCTIONAL STRATEGIES

- Displays a mindmap of the current curriculum—component and its topics—on the curriculum wall along with immersion items for the current *being there* location in order to heighten student interest, elicit prior related memories, and help students see connections and relationships among patters.

- Uses Social/Political Action Projects and Celebrations of Learning to provide real-world contexts for learning and using knowledge and skills, to provide real audiences for developing/practicing language arts and math skills, and to provide students opportunities to practice responsible citizenship.

- Has developed and regularly uses a lesson planning process and format for organizing key points and inquiries and selecting instructional strategies best suited to teach student the concept, significant knowledge, or skill at hand.

- Selects a professional and/or peer coach(es) who can/will support the implementation of the bodybrain-compatible element of multiple intelligences and use of a variety of instructional strategies. Establishes and maintains a schedule for meeting frequently. Prepares thoroughly for each meeting; schedules follow-up time to learn from each session.

CREATING CURRICULUM

The hallmark and heart of curriculum for the *HET* model is that it is based in *being there* locations and that it uses a concept to organize and integrate content and skills from multiple subject areas. Chapter 12 describes how to base curriculum in *being there* locations. This chapter outlines how to use concepts to organize your curriculum.

Concept = Power

Concept = 1. A general notion or idea

2. An idea of something formed by mentally combining all its characteristics or particulars; a construct[1]

In the world of our biological brain, patterns are neural food. They are what our brain seeks and from which it makes meaning. Concepts are rich, powerful patterns for the brain, useful in unlocking meaning around us and much easier to store in long-term memory than curriculum fragments and factoids. To learn fragments and factoids, students mostly resort to memorization; in contrast, concepts allow students to leapfrog from today's lesson to yesterday's personal experience to tomorrow's situations in life. Concepts are powerful curriculum builders.

Concepts: Curriculum Structures Without Borders

Concepts travel. They don't stay where we last put them, such as in science or art. They know no curriculum borders. They are not stopped by time or space. That's why they are so good at integrating curriculum.

Example #1: Consider this statement: "A system is a collection of things and processes (and often people) that interact to perform some function." Clearly this invites an exploration of science—ecosystems, mechanical engineering, and so forth. But it is also a powerful lens through which to view civics: "Our democratic government is a collection of things (laws, government bodies, and citizens) and processes (those described in or allowed by laws). Our federal constitution, including its Bill of Rights, sets the boundaries of our government. Democratic governments are rule-based systems of government rather than power- or people-based forms, such as dictatorships, oligarchies, monarchies, and theocracies."

Economics? Yes. Supply and demand are two interacting components of the capitalist system. Art? Of course. The Munsell Color Wheel is a system of analyzing color combinations and intensity of hue. The potential for integration goes on and on.

Example #2: Consider the rich exploration that could come from study through a related concept: "To study a system one must define its boundaries." For example, in science, a watershed can't be studied if its boundaries aren't established.

History/social studies: Our federal constitution, including its Bill of Rights, sets the boundaries of our government. Laws considered outside this boundary are considered unconstitutional and are set aside or repealed. (Without such boundaries, there would be chaos.)

Boundary lines could also be drawn to include philosophical precursors to our constitution such as the Declaration of Independence, the writings of Thomas Paine, and the constitution of the Iroquois Confederation.

Example #3: Consider the further depth and power from studying another related concept: "Thinking about things as systems means looking for how every part relates to others. Most systems, living and non-living, are made up of smaller parts that, when put together, can do things the parts couldn't do by themselves."

This is a powerful lens through which to study the danger of extinction of animals and plants—together they create a self-sustaining ecosystem but if missing a partner perhaps they will die.

In history/social studies: "Our constitution establishes a system with three parts or subsystems: executive, legislative, and judicial. They are designed to provide checks and balances to preserve a balance of power."

Concepts are like computer worms. Once they infect your hard drive, they never stop moving; once they lodge in your brain, your brain keeps extending the patterns, using them to make sense of more and more of the external world.

GETTING STARTED

Once you have selected your *being there* locations and the concept(s) you want to teach, decide how you want to start organizing your curriculum. Do you want to start small and proceed one step at a time or do you want to start with a yearlong concept in mind? In either case, remember that your goal during Stage 2 of Implementation is only 10-15% of curriculum for the entire year. This modest start allows you to learn from your experiences and master the science and art of developing bodybrain-compatible curriculum before you begin Stage 3.

Starting Small . . . One Step at a Time

A topic is the the smallest piece of conceptual *HET* curriculum. So starting small means starting with one *being there* location and selecting a conceptual key point that is well illustrated by the location, engaging to your students, and in important aspect of your state standards.

Around this nucleus, determine what you want students to understand (key points) and be able to do (inquiries). How to write key points and inquiries is discussed in Chapter 12.

A single, stand-alone topic is like a mini-component. It is often designed for one to three half-days. It's big enough to take you through the tools for building *HET* curriculum but small enough that you can get started with relatively short lead-up time. How long a topic lasts depends on your purpose and planning. The curriculum starting on page 14.6 is designed for 10-12 half days.

You choose the time frames; the *HET* curriculum-building structure will work with time spans long or short, full days or partial, for a month or for a year. However, be aware that curriculum often takes on a life of its own; be prepared to follow the teachable moments. Feel free to extend or shorten any topic as best serves students and your responsibilities for curriculum content.

> **Topic**
> Built upon a concept and based in a *being there* location

Starting Small: An Example for First Grade

> **Topic**
> *Conceptual Key Point:* A habitat is a place where an animal or plant lives while meetings its basic needs.
> *Being there* location: Backyard supplemented with classroom terrariums

Focusing on a single component/topic at a time is a good beginning point for teachers working alone or those who find it easier to work from details to big picture rather than from big picture to details. It allows you to master three critical *HET* curriculum development strategies – basing curriculum in *being there* locations, starting with concepts, and integrating content and skills. As you master these strategies, you will be ready to delve into the power of concepts to create memorable patterns for the brain.

Stepping Out

To reach the goal of Stage 2, having 15% of your year's curriculum be bodybrain-compatible, you will need to take the next step in curriculum development: Writing curriculum for a component with two or more topics—all built upon a concept and based in a *being there* location. This next step allows you to explore the richness of the *being there* location by focusing on related concepts illustrated by the *being there* location, yet ones still related to the concept of the component.

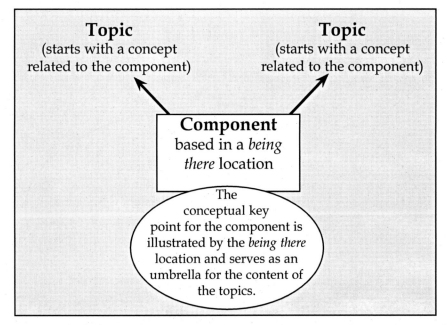

For example, if the *being there* location is a local watershed, the topics might be "Watersheds: An Irreversible System" and "We All Live Downstream." In this example, the concept of the component is systems. You could, however, choose for your concept habitats, such as all things are connected, change, or many others. Because each topic is tats, all related to the concept of the component, the topics are thus related to each other. This conceptual pattern established by the concept for the component serves as the force that organizes and integrates all the subject content and skills for all topics.

Stepping Out: An Example of a Component with Two Topics for Fifth Grade

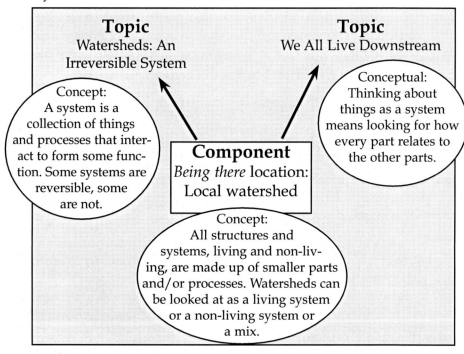

Starting with a skeletal yearlong structure allows you to start small but use the tools for building yearlong curriculum, especially an organizing concept to web together all the content and skills for the year and finding a kid-grabbing title that stirs up student enthusiasm, conveys the essence of the concept, and is memorable.

Starting with the End in Mind

As illustrated on the two previous pages, starting small and stepping out, your first yearlong curriculum can start out small—a topic related to the organizing concept—and then graduate to the level of yearlong content by the end of the year. We strongly recommend this "progressive dinner" approach. It allows you to do small amounts of curriculum frequently while experimenting with conceptual connections that organize chunks of curriculum.

Progressive Dinner Approach to Developing Yearlong Curriculum

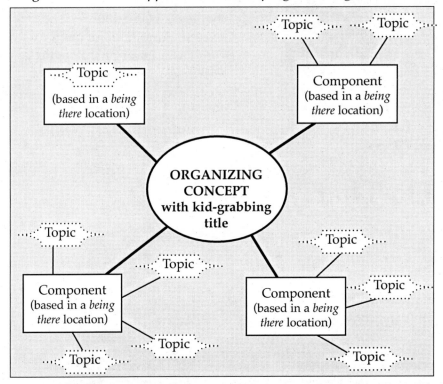

For example, if habitats is the organizing concept for your curriculum, then the *being there* location for the components can be various kinds of habitats such as underground, airborne, pond/lake, tidepools, creek/river, or watershed. Choose those that can be easily visited by your students and readily turned into an immersion experience in the classroom or on the school grounds. Topics for each component then focus on various aspects of the component's concept. For an underground habitat, for example, study animals in the food web or ways they locate and get food.

What's important is ensuring that the pattern or conceptual relationship between the organizing concept and each component and between each component and its topics is obvious to students. The greater the conceptual webbing of the curriculum, the more connections students can make. This quickens and deepens learning and makes efficient use of instructional time. This makes the content easier for the students to understand. It also organizes your content and skills in a natural way that students can recognize as they look out the window, walk down the street, visit a mall, or relax with Mother Nature.

Mastering the tools for developing yearlong conceptual curriculum now will save you time when you begin Stage 3. For more information about the yearlong curriculum structure, see Chapter 18.

SAMPLE CURRICULUM

Beginning on the next page is curriculum developed for 1-3 weeks depending on how much time is devoted to it each day. Notice how each chunk of curriculum begins with a concept which is explored through the significant knowledge needed to understand that concept. Basic skills are practiced, or taught and practiced, in relationship to inquiries, the "doing" part of the curriculum.

Organizing Concept: Form dictates function; function demands form.

Theme Rationale: Understanding the relationship between physical characteristics and use helps students understand how the world around them operates and instructs their ability to invent or design objects in order to solve problems and make our world a better place.

Find the Way

- Tools for Life - Lifelong Guidelines (citizenship)/LIFESKILLS
- Leading the Way (mapping)
- Hand Tools (designing, using, changing, inventing)

Concept: Form and Function

***Being There* Locations:** School, Neighborhood

Fly Like a Bird

- Bionic Me – similarities of Human Body and Simple Machines

*** Birds: Wings, Beaks, & Eyes (animal body parts/functions)

- Similarities of Animal Bodies & Hand Tools

Concept: Form and Function

***Being There* Locations:** Zoo, Pet Store

- Inventions Convention (non-living things, magnetism)
- Innovative Mechanical Devices
- Our Community Environment (community service, research)

Concept: Form and Function

***Being There* Locations:** Museum, City Hall

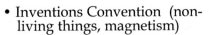

How Did You Do That?

Build a Machine!

Travel Like a Plant

- Plant and Soil Characteristics
- Dig It! (hand tools and modern technology)
- Stems that Bend (weather and adaptations for protection)

Concept: Form and Function

***Being There* Locations:** School Garden, Neighborhood

Sample Curriculum

Model Teaching Week Curriculum by Brenda Russell
Adapted by Curriculum Team, Susan Kovalik & Associates ©2005
Appropriate for 2nd–4th Grade

Organizing Concept for the Yearlong Curriculum:
Form dictates function; function demands form.

Kid-Grabbing Title: How Did You Do That?

Component Kid-Grabbing Title: Fly Like a Bird

Concept for Component: Form and function

Being There Locations for the Component: playground, bird viewing preserve, state park

Guest Speakers for the Component: state park rangers, naturalist, and Audubon member

Conceptual Key Point for the Component:

Form dictates function is a rule based on observations of nature and how the world works. This means that the shape of something and what it is made of determines how it can be used and what it can do. Conversely, a task or function to be done requires a particular form to be possible or efficiently or effectively done. Our observations of form and function have influenced man-made designs and inventions.

Guided Practice Inquiries:

1. With your Learning Club, describe the physical characteristics (form) you have that allow you to meet your basic needs (function). Create a list of the physical characteristics and what each does and what basic need it helps you to meet. Compare your list to the list of at least one other Learning Club. (LM, L)*

___

Note: The letters in parenthesis represent the multiple intelligences; the letters following the parenthesis indicate a state standard on page 14.14.

2. As a Learning Club, observe the animals in the two classroom habitats. Create a T-chart for each animal showing the physical characteristics (form) that allow the animal to meet each of its basic needs (function). In the left column list the basic need to be met and in the right column, the physical characteristic used to meet the basic need. On the back of your T-Chart, create an illustration that shows at least one physical characteristic (form) of one of the animals and write a brief summary describing how this characteristic helps this animal meet its basic needs (function). (BK, LM, LS)

Inquiries:

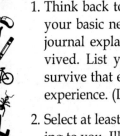

1. Think back to a situation in which you may have felt that your basic needs were in jeopardy. Write an entry in your journal explaining what you did to be sure that you survived. List your physical characteristics that helped you survive that event. Write how you felt during and after the experience. (L, LM) (Science state standard 21.3.2)

2. Select at least five items in our classroom that look interesting to you. Illustrate each item and write a brief description of the attributes (form) of each item. On a Post-It Note, describe the use (function) of each item. With your Learning Club, pantomime the form and function of at least one of your items. Record in your science journal at least one other item that is similar in form or function to one you chose. Example: pencil, long and narrow; similar to a pen, both are used to write. (L, LM, BK)

3. Make a poster showing how you do something that helps you survive. Include both words and illustrations on your poster showing your understanding of form and function. Explain your poster to your Learning Club. (L, LM, S)

4. Observe any birds and other animals you see while on a nature walk. Select at least three to explain to a partner. Describe to him/her the different body parts and how each part was used. Record and illustrate your findings in your journal. (S, L) S4.21

5. With your Learning Club, brainstorm at least five characteristics of birds or other animals that help them meet their basic needs. List three questions you have relating to how birds and animals survive. Have your recorder write the results on lined paper, compare your results with other Learning Clubs, and create a final list for a class research project. (L)

6. With at least two other students, select four or more pictures of animals from the cards on the resource table. Create a four-column chart. Write the name of one of the pictured animals at the top of each column. List the characteristics the animal uses to meet its basic needs in the column below the name of the animal. Share your chart with another trio of students. (S, L, LM)

7. With a partner, choose two of your favorite animal cartoon characters and write a short paragraph for each one naming their body parts and describing how each part helps the animal meet its basic needs. Read your paragraphs to another pair of students for feedback. (LM, L)

Topic: Birds - Wings, Beaks, and Eyes

Significant Knowledge Key Point #1:

One of the most important physical characteristics (form) of birds is their wings. The function of a bird's wing is to lift it in flight. Wings allow birds to get around effectively in the environment to find food, water, shelter, a mate, and protection. Birds' wings are covered with feathers that function to smooth the wing surface to create the air flow that is necessary for flight. Not all birds fly in the same way. Some birds soar for hours without flapping a wing while other birds might flap their wings over 70 times a second as they hover, fly forward, or even backwards. Many birds can be identified by these flight patterns. These flight patterns have been developed to help them meet their basic needs. SCI 6.3.3, 8.3.2, 9.3.2, 15.3.2, 15.4.2

Guided Practice Inquiries:

1. Mimic various birds' wing movements after the teacher demonstrates each one. With a partner, use the Wing Beat Chart as a guide to practice flapping as a hawk, crow, chickadee, robin, starling, pigeon, and hummingbird. One person should keep the time while the other person flaps. Take turns. Try to flap in time with each of the birds on the chart. Discuss how your arms feel when you finish flapping like a particular bird. Try to identify the bird your partner is mimicking and predict how the wing-beat patterns impact at least two birds' flight. Record your observations in your science journal. (L, S, BK) Math 1.3.1, 1.4.2, 1.3.3, 1.4.3, 3.3.6, 5.3.1, 5.4.1

2. Study the illustration your teacher has placed on the overhead projector/computer screen. Working with a partner, discuss, compare,. and contrast the illustration of the bird's wing to your own arm. Using your arms, show your partner how a bird's wing works. Write a paragraph describing a bird's wing in your science journal. (L, BK)

Inquiries:

1. Make a model of a bird's wing with pipe cleaners and feathers. Be ready to explain how the wing (form) helps the bird fly (function). (L, S)

2. Write either a story or a movie scene* that describes a situation where a bird must use its flying abilities (form) to escape from danger (function). Include details about how the bird's wing works, its flight patterns and the environment that it lives in. (L) R5.3.3, 5.4.3
(*See Language Arts Skill Key Point #1)

3. Write a haiku poem* about a specific bird. Use your previous experiences with the Wing Beat inquiry to describe the bird and the way it flies. Illustrate your poem and add it to our class book to be donated to a local children's hospital. (L, S) (*See Language Arts Skill Key Point #2)

4. Using the pictures of birds and airplanes in your packet, complete a Venn Diagram* that shows how the form of a plane and a bird are alike and different. Describe in your Science Journal how each part of a bird and each part of a plane affects their flight. (S, LM, L) (*See Math Skill Key Point #1)

5. With your Learning Club research at least five birds of your choice. Design a bar graph that shows the speed each bird flies. Describe the special attributes of at least two birds' wings noting what impact each bird's wings (form) has on the bird's flight capabilities (function). (Differentiation: Research the flight speed of at least three birds, calculate the time it would take each bird to fly 50 miles, 100 miles and 135 miles.) (S, LM, L)

Significant Knowledge Key Point #2:

Birds are the only animals in the world with feathers. The form of the feather determines its use. Contour feathers, which are found on the bird's body, wings, and tail, are stiff and have barbs that lock them together so they can push air for flight. Contour feathers also provide camouflage (coloring that blends in with a bird's typical environment). Down feathers, which are fluffier, softer, and lie close to a bird's body under the contour feathers, help provide warmth and protection from the weather.

Guided Practice Inquiries:

1. Observe the large contour feather on the screen. Notice how the barbs stick out from the shaft with tiny barbules that grow from each. Illustrate a contour feather (form); label what makes it contour and describe the function of each feature (function). (L, S, BK)

2. Predict how far a Styrofoam ball will move when the teacher flaps down feathers and contour feathers near it. Share your prediction with your Learning Club. Observe the demonstration and use your understanding of form

and function to explain why your prediction was right or wrong. (LM, L)

3. With your Learning Club, select from among the different environments shown on the overhead/computer the one that best matches the bird you have been given. Be prepared to share why you made your choice, based on the physical features of the bird. Describe how the physical features (form) of at least three of these birds influence the survival (function) of the bird in this environment. (S, L)

4. List and illustrate at least one human-made product that mimics the form of the contour feather. Describe its function. Discuss your observations with your Learning Club. (L, S, BK)

Inquiries:

1. Select and observe a contour feather and a down feather. Draw a picture of each, label what kind of feather it is and describe the special features and function of each of the feathers. (L, S, BK)

2. With your Learning Club, sort your bag of feathers into two groups: contour and down. Record a list of attributes of each kind of feather. Compare your list to others' and edit yours to your personal best. Record at least five important feather words in your personal dictionary. (S, BK)

3. Use the Internet to research the form and function of your favorite bird's feathers. Describe such attributes as color, size, and special features of your bird's feathers. Illustrate one contour and one down feather from your bird. Draw a picture of the kind of environment that would help camouflage your bird. Save this work for a future project. (L, S, BK) R 11.3.2, 11.3.5, 11.4.5, 5.3.1, 5.4.1

4. Explain the function of each kind of feather (contour and down) to one other person so that he/she understands how the feathers help the bird move and survive. (L, S)

5. Write a poem or song of at least two verses about the two different kinds of feathers (contour and down). Explain how birds use these feathers. (L, BK, M)

6. Explain, in writing, why down feathers won't help a bird fly and contour feathers do. (LM, L)

7. With your Learning Club draw and color a bird that will be camouflaged in the environment given to you. Explain to a partner how camouflage helps protect a bird. (S, LM, L)

Significant Knowledge Key Point #3:

Each species of bird has a special beak adapted for gathering its food and preparing it for eating. Knowing what a bird's beak looks like helps predict what it will eat and how it will eat it. Knowing what birds eat helps us predict what their beaks look like.

Guided Practice Inquiries:

1. Visit each of the eight different feeding stations. Try to "eat" the food with each of the three different "beaks." Record which beak works best for each type of food. (L, S, BK) SCI 22.3.1, 22.3.3, R 4.3.6, 4.4.6, 4.3.4, 4.4.4

2. View the Eyewitness video "Birds" to observe different bird beak forms and their functions. Discuss with your Learning Club the physical characteristics (form) of four or more different bird beaks and what they allowed the bird to do (function). Share with the class. (BK, LM, L)

3. Use your prior experience to help you describe at least one kind of bird with each of the beak examples you see in the feeding stations. Describe the kinds of food for which this sort of beak is best suited. Explain why the other beaks would not function in specific environments such as grass, mud, water, and trees. (L, S, BK) SCI 22.3.1, 22.3.3, R 4.3.6, 4.4.6, 4.3.4, 4.4.4

Inquiries:

1. Observe pictures of five or more birds and their beaks. Make a list of different beak types and the kind of food you think the bird eats based on the beak type. Describe the kind of environment this bird must live in to find the food for which its beak is best suited. Create a beak/food game that will challenge your peers. Include at least five birds and their beaks. Write the directions for playing your game. Ask two members of your Learning Club to play the game and give you feedback on the directions and the game. (L)

2. Illustrate a poster of at least three different types (form) of bird beaks and the jobs for which they are best suited. Print the job (function) the beak does under the picture of each one. (L, S)

3. From clay create a bird beak and a model of the food that it might eat. Display your beak with a written description telling how the beak (form) impacts what the bird can eat (function). (S, BK) SCI 20.3.1

4. Write a poem or a song about at least three different kinds of bird beaks describing how they are different and how they are used. (L, BK, M)

5. With your Learning Club, create and perform a skit about bird beaks and the different ways they are used. Include at least four of the different beaks in your skit. (L, BK, M, S)

Significant Knowledge Key Point #4:

What a bird must do to find food and escape predators determines where the eyes are placed on the head. Most birds have eyes on the sides of their heads allowing each eye to focus on a different image (monocular vision). This allows the bird to see a different view with each eye and gives a broader range of vision. Birds of prey, like people, have forward facing eyes, fixed in their heads, which allow them to focus on a single image with both eyes at the same time (binocular vision).

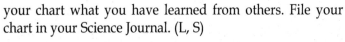
Guided Practice Inquiries:

1. Make an eye patch with a small piece of black paper and a piece of yarn. Adjust it so that it will fit on your head like a pirate's eye patch. When all your classmates are ready, play "Fowl Ball" with them. With a partner, talk about how you felt while playing the game. Be ready to share how this experience helped you understand monocular vision. (S, BK, L)

2. With your Learning Club, discuss the bird pictures that the teacher shows from the overhead or computer. Create a T-Chart to record whether they have monocular vision or binocular vision. List the name of the bird under the category in which it belongs. Compare your T-Chart with those of another Learning Club, and edit yours for accuracy. (L, LM,) SCI 2.3.2

Inquiries:

1. Create a monocular viewer and a binocular viewer using your hands. For the monocular, use your right hand to make a circle with your index finger and thumb. Shut your right eye, place your right hand circle on your left eye, and look straight ahead with your left eye. Stand next to a partner and take turns describing all that you see through the monocular without moving your head. To create the binoculars, use your index finger and thumb on both hands to make the viewer. Put your right hand up to your right eye and your left hand up to your left eye (just like binoculars). Take turns describing your experience with a partner and discuss the differences between the two forms of viewers and what you were able to see/not see (function). Discuss your findings with your Learning Club. (BK, S, L)

2. Working with a partner, create two T-Charts labeled Monocular Vision and Binocular Vision. Record the advantages and disadvantages of each kind of vision. Compare your charts with those of another Learning Club; add to

your chart what you have learned from others. File your chart in your Science Journal. (L, S)

3. Choose a bird with either monocular or binocular vision. Imagine what you could see if you were that bird. Write a paragraph that describes the form and function of that bird's vision. (L)

4. Working alone, divide a group of bird picture cards into two piles. Label one pile monocular vision and the other binocular vision. Record your findings in your science journal. Share your work with another group. Correct before returning. (L, LM)

5. With your Learning Club, create a skit demonstrating monocular and binocular vision and how birds use each kind of vision to get their food and escape predators. (BK, L)

Language Arts Skill Key Point #1:

A scene in a movie is a unit of related actions that take place at a single location. Full-length television shows, animated cartoons, and movies are made by editing together a series of selected small units or scenes.

Guided Practice Inquiries:

1. With your Learning Club, watch a short video clip. Identify three or more different scenes that were in the clip. Discuss the criteria you used to select the scenes. Share your group's conclusions with the class and how watching the clip or the process helped you understand a movie scene. (BK, L, S, LM)

2. With your Learning Club, recreate a short scene from a movie or television show that you have seen. Present to the class and have the class determine if your small product was or was not a "scene." (BK, L)

Inquiries:

1. With a partner, watch a television show or situational comedy. Select a single scene of your choice. Create a poster with a drawing or diagram that shows the essential actions or events that made up the scene. Show the class the clip, read your explanation, and have the class share how it helped them better understand a scene. (BK, LM, L, S)

2. With at least five classmates, create a single scene showing one of the LIFESKILLS or Lifelong Guidelines being used by a group of students. Ask the class to list the things that made up the scene. Process as a class how this scene helped everyone gain a better understanding of a movie scene. (BK, LM, L)

3. Clip three or more cartoon strips from a local newspaper or go on the Internet to www.comics.com, and print out a cartoon. With your Learning Club discuss and be able to explain how each frame of the strip can be the same thing as a single scene in a move or play. Cut out one frame and paste the remaining frames back together. Share with the class how the cartoon changed when one scene or frame was removed. (BK, LM, L, S)

4. Bring in a DVD of an appropriate film or cartoon. Select and show one of the scenes deleted in the editing process before the film was released. With your Learning Club, discuss and share at least one reason why the scene was deleted. Process why filming one scene at a time is important to the final product. (BK, LM, L, S)

5. With your Learning Club, compile a written list of plays, ice shows, television shows, cartoons, and movies. Each member selects a scene he/she remembers from one of the items and shares the highlights. The Learning Club selects one to share with the class. Include why it was chosen and how it is an example of a scene. (L, LM)

Language Arts Skill Key Point #2:

Haiku poetry allows us to express our feelings through a three-line poem. The first line has five syllables, the second line has seven syllables, and the third line has five syllables. R 9.3.4, 9.4.4

Guided Practice Inquiries:

1. With your group read and share together the sample haiku poems the teacher provides. Using the Internet or research books, find one other example of haiku poetry. Share it with the class. (L, LM)

2. With the class write a haiku poem that describes the class. Plan a movement for each line. (L, BK)

Inquiries:

1. Choose one haiku poem from those shared. Write a paragraph telling what the poem means to you. (L)

2. Write a haiku poem about a bird that we have observed. Share it with your group. (L, LM)

3. Write a modified haiku poem by adding a fourth line with five syllables. Illustrate your poem. (L, LM)

4. Write a haiku poem that explains or compares binocular and monocular vision. (L, LM)

5. Write a haiku poem that explains form and function. (LM, L)

Math Skill Key Point #1:

A Venn diagram is a graphic organizer made of at least two overlapping circles. It can be used to compare two or more attributes to see how they are similar and how they are different. Shared attributes are written in the area where the two circles overlap. R 6.3.2, 6.4.2

Guided Practice Inquiries:

1. Make a class Venn diagram comparing the heights of students. (L, S)

2. With a partner make a Venn diagram using similar and different attributes of something you choose. (L, S)

Inquiries:

1. Using all of the LIFESKILLS and Lifelong Guidelines, make a Venn diagram comparing our class community to a bird's community. After you decide which Lifelong Guidelines and LIFESKILLS describe the behaviors of both yourself and birds, compare your Venn Diagram with a member of your Learning Club. (L, S, LM)

2. Create a Venn diagram question that will compare humans and birds. Write the attributes to be compared above each circle and ask your partner to complete the Venn Diagram. (L, S, LM)

3. Make a Venn diagram to compare monocular vision and binocular vision. Compare directions eyes are facing and the number of images one sees. (L, S, LM)

4. Make a Venn diagram to compare your arms to a bird's wings. (L, S, LM)

5. Make a Venn diagram to compare how a bird meets its basic need for survival to how you meet your basic need for survival. (S, L, LM)

Social/Political Action Inquiries or Celebrations of Learning:

1. With a partner, research the National Audubon web site to find information regarding the national annual bird count done in the United States. Find out the procedures for a volunteer counters in your area. Create a chart showing the procedures an individual must follow to be one of the

volunteers. Present the information to the class. Create a list of volunteers and follow the procedures so all can become annual counters. (BK, LM, S, L)

2. Do an Internet search for the web site of your state's Department of Natural Resources. Search throughout the site to determine if there are any endangered or threatened bird species in your area. Choose one as a focus for a class project to inform the community of the bird and why it is endangered or threatened. Include at least three suggestions for what people can do to help the species get removed from the endangered or threatened list. (BK, LM, L)

3. With a group of classmates, go on a walking tour of an area near your school or home. Determine the species of birds that live or feed in that area. Create a plan to help improve or maintain the area so the birds that live there will be able to find food and shelter. Share your plan with at least two other groups. Have them critique the plan and give you feedback. After preparing a final copy of your plan, present it to the local Audubon Society. (BK, LM, L)

STANDARDS/BENCHMARKS FOR THE CONTENT ADDRESSED IN THIS TOPIC

Reading

2.3.3 & 2.4.3 Summarizing, paraphrasing, drawing conclusions
2.4.4 Note taking, outlining, summarizing
4.3.4 & 4.4.4 Drawing conclusions
4.3.6 & 4.4.6. Read & follow directions
5.3.1 & 5.4.1 Locate sources for research
5.3.2 & 5.4.2 Writing letters
5.3.3 & 5.4.3 Writing narrative stories
6.3.2 & 6.4.2 Organize ideas with graphic organizers
6.3.3 & 6.4.3 Write compositions with paragraphs
6.3.4 & 6.4.4 Revise drafts
6.3.5 & 6.4.5 Edit for Standard English
6.3.7 & 6.4.7 Share writing with others

8.3.2 & 8.4.2   Listen to connect prior experiences
9.3.2 & 9.4.2   Public speaking
9.3.4 & 9.4.4   Poetry
10.3.1   Speak and listen in group discussions
11.3.2   Use variety of media for research
11.3.5, 11.4.5 Present research findings

Math

1.3.1 & 1.4.1   Addition and subtraction facts
1.3.2 & 1.4.2   Operations with regrouping
3.3.6   Identify elapsed time
5.3.1 & 5.4.1   Collect & organize data

Science

2.3.2   Sort & classify objects
6.3.2 & 6.4.2   Investigate, compare, & contrast identifiable characteristics of plants and animals
6.3.3   Investigate & describe how plants and animals require certain conditions to survive
8.3.2   Investigate & describe how some living things are alike in appearance and behavior; others are not
9.3.2   Explain how particular features of plants & animals help them live in different kinds of places
15.3.2, 15.4.2 Identify & describe variables that affect the survival of organisms within an ecosystem
18.3.1   Use science as a process that involves observing & asking questions
18.3.2, 18.4.2 Scientific observation
18.4.4   Exchange scientific observation & ideas
20.3.1   Compare a model with what it represents
21.3.1   Ask questions & investigate to get answers
21.3.2   Record observations in a journal
22.3.1   Follow verbal & written directions
22.3.2   Create illustrations, graphs, charts
22.3.3   Cooperate & contribute ideas within a group
24.3.3   Identify & gather tools & materials needed in an investigation

RESOURCES

Teacher

Print–

Braus, Judy. Ranger Rick's Nature Scope: Birds, Birds, Birds, Washington, D.C.: National Wildlife Federation, 1992.

Hume, Rob. Birdwatching. New York: Random House, 1992.

National Audubon Society First Field Guide: Birds. New York: Chanticleer Press, 1998.

Stokes, Donald & Lillia. Stokes Field Guide to Birds. Boston: Little, Brown and Company, 1996.

Web Sites–

www.audubon.org/states/nv
www.nbii.gov/education.birds.html

Video–

Eyewitness Videos: Birds, Sight, Flight (available from Amazon.com)

Student

Print–

Hume, Rob. Birdwatching. New York: Random House, 1992.

National Audubon Society First Field Guide: Birds. New York: Chanticleer Press, 1998.

Stokes, Donald & Lillia. Stokes Field Guide to Birds. Boston: Little, Brown and Company, 1996.

Literature–

Avi. Poppy. New York: HarperCollins Publishers, Inc., 1994.

Cannon, Janell. Stellaluna, San Diego: Harcourt Brace & Co., 1992.

Yolen, Jane. Owl Moon, New York: Scholastic, Inc., 1987.

Video–

Eyewitness Videos: Birds, Sight, Flight (available from Amazon.com)

National Audubon Society, Owl Up Close, Nature Science Network, Inc., Carrboro, NC, 1991.

Bluebirds Up Close, Nature Science Network, Inc., Carrboro, NC, 1991.

Hawks Up Close, Nature Science Network, Inc., Carrboro, NC, 1991.

Hummingbirds Up Close, Nature Science Network, Inc., Carrboro, NC, 1991.

Cardinals Up Close, Nature Science Network, Inc., Carrboro, NC, 1991.

Websites–

www.audubon.org/states/nv
www.surfbirds.com
www.cityofhenderson.com
www.springmountainranch.com
www.birds.cornell.edu
www.dnr.state
www.library.thinkquest.org
www.nbii.gov/education.birds.html
www.erin.utoronto.ca/~w3bio325/325lab1.html

Music–
"Land of the Loon" by Dan Gibson and John Herberman from Solitudes
"Piano Songbirds" by Dan Gibson and John Herberman from Solitudes (http://www.somersetent.com/WebMusic/cdmshow.wws)

Artifacts/Models–
1. A collection of bird figures. Some with "chirping" are available from National Geographic.
2. Bird feathers collected on a bird walk

Guest Speaker–
Naturalist from local zoo who specializes in birds

Lesson Design– SK&A Team © 2005

Anticipatory Set–
Read orally the first chapter of Poppy by Avi. Discuss the owl's feeding habits.

Inclusion Activity–
Each Learning Club will try to open and eat a walnut without using a nutcracker and share strategies they used with the class.

Lesson Objective–
Significant Knowledge Key Point #3 Each species of bird has a special beak adapted for gathering its food and preparing it for eating. Knowing what a bird's beak looks like helps predict what it will eat and how it will eat it. Knowing what birds eat helps us predict what their beaks look like.

Rationale/Purpose: To help students see the application of form and function in nature

Guided Practice Inquiries:

1. Visit each of the eight different feeding stations. Try to "eat" the food with each of the three different "beaks." Record which beak works best for each type of food. (L, S, BK) SCI 22.3.1, 22.3.3, R 4.3.6, 4.4.6, 4.3.4, 4.4.4

2. View the Eyewitness video "Birds" to observe different bird beak forms and their functions. Discuss with your Learning Club the physical characteristics (form) of four or more different bird beaks and what they allowed the bird to do (function). Share with the class. (BK, LM, L)

3. Use your prior experience to help you describe at least one kind of bird with each of the beak examples you see in the feeding stations. Describe the kinds of food for which this sort of beak is best suited. Explain why the other beaks would not function in specific environments such as grass, mud, water, and trees. (L, S, BK) SCI 22.3.1, 22.3.3, R 4.3.6, 4.4.6, 4.3.4, 4.4.4

Independent Practice Inquiries:

1. Observe pictures of five or more birds and their beaks. Make a list of different beak types and the kind of food you think the bird eats based on the beak type. Describe the kind of environment this bird must live in to find the food for which its beak is best suited. Create a beak/food game that will challenge your peers. Include at least five birds and their beaks. Write the directions for playing your game. Ask two members of your Learning Club to play the game and give you feedback on the directions and the game. (L)

2. Illustrate a poster of at least three different types of bird beaks and the jobs for which they are best suited. Print the job the beak does under the picture of each one. (L, S)

Closure: Learning Clubs process the feeding activity by completing their "Fill the Bill" record sheet. Learning Clubs share their sheets with the class. The class plans the next learning activity based on the consensus of the group.

Instructional Strategies:

- Learning Clubs
- Group Roles
- Direct Instruction
- Brainstorming
- Demonstrations
- Bird Walk

- Pairs

- Internet

- Models

IMPLEMENTATION TIPS

Teaching from key points and inquiries based on a *being there* location is considerably different from teaching from textbooks and worksheets. Our advice to you is this:

- Start early in the year, October at the latest, to give yourself maximum time between components—time to learn from experience before starting another curriculum chunk and time to do your personal best when planning and implementing the next component. Remember, doing small amounts of curriculum frequently is a much better learning experience than attempting a few large chunks.

- Keep your focus on the two main goals of Stage 2 curriculum:

  - Developing curriculum based on a *being there* location

  - Starting with a concept which can organize and integrate content within and among subjects and skills and making all curriculum as conceptual as possible

- However you start, be sure you always post your curriculum mindmap on the wall for students to see. Add immersion items to it. For second grade students and up, also post your key points as you go. For the benefit of students who are high in spatial intelligence but not in linguistic intelligence, use graphics to represent the content. Remember, you want your theme to focus students' attention on what is to be studied and to connect it with what they have previously studied and will study in the future.

ENDNOTES

1 *Webster's New Universal Unabridged Dictionary.* (New York: Barnes & Noble, 1996).

Chapter 15: Instructional Strategies for Stage 2

STAGE 2 INSTRUCTIONAL STRATEGIES

CURRICULUM

INSTRUCTIONAL STRATEGIES

• Expertly uses all the instructional strategies identified in Stages 1.2 and 1.3 everyday, ***throughout the entire school day*** for both *HET* curriculum time and for other curriculum as well.

• Expertly uses instructional strategies for ***introducing and reteaching*** the concepts, significant knowledge, and skills of the *HET* integrated curriculum:

— *Being there* experiences which are enhanced and deepened through lead-up activities, assignments during bus rides, focused follow-up activities including return trips to the *being there* location, visits by resource people, immersion and simulations, personalized homework assignments, and so forth.

— The *HET* Discovery Process as a frequent alternative to direct instruction and an important means of helping students learn how to learn.

HET Classroom Stages of Implementation **Stage**

Entry level for making the learning environment
bodybrain compatible

2

CURRICULUM

INSTRUCTIONAL STRATEGIES

Strategies for *introducing and reteaching* continued —

— Teaching concepts and skills through the lives of those at the *being there* location rather than through the perspective of textbooks. Utilizes on-site interviews, visiting resource people, situational role playing, and other instructional strategies that make the concepts and skills come alive for students. Includes role playing to help students learn to apply concepts and skills and to build C.U.E. (creative, useful, emotional) into the teacher's instructional strategies and inquiries.

• Expertly selects and uses strategies for *HET* conceptual curriculum time that ensure that students **reach mastery**, i.e., that students identify/understand patterns and develop programs for using what they understand in real-world ways. Such additional instructional strategies include the following:

— Modeling being a lifelong learner and participating citizen

— Movement routines to help students identify and understand patterns and sequences of events/processes and to build mental programs for using concepts and skills and retaining them in long-term memory

— Collaboration on an ongoing basis including formally teaching students the personal and social skills necessary for effective collaboration. The content of the inquiries assigned for collaborative work is specially designed so that no one student can complete an inquiry alone. Collaborative work sessions include identifying in advance the Lifelong Guidelines and LIFESKILLS necessary to successfully complete an assignment plus reflective thinking at the end of the work. When possible, the structure and roles within the collaborative group are an extension of the content to be learned, such as roles of people in a court room (judge, jury, legal stenographer, and so forth).

— Knowledge of temperament, considered during instruction and when designing inquiries in ways that speed up and deepen learning.

HET Classroom Stages of Implementation **Stage**

2

STAGE 2 INSTRUCTIONAL STRATEGIES

*Making curriculum and instruction
bodybrain compatible*

CURRICULUM

INSTRUCTIONAL STRATEGIES

• Expertly uses instructional strategies to *enhance wiring into long-term memory* and for *assessing student progress* through the new definition of learning::

— Clear performance criteria for students through inquiries and rubrics that describe the performance levels expected of them, including the expectations for materials, process, time, and quality as appropriate. These statements of expectation are written and do not require explanation from the teacher.

• For at least two chunks of integrated curriculum during the year, includes a Social/Political Action Project and concludes with a Celebration of Learning.

— Social/political action projects that grow naturally out of students' study at a *being there* location (or from a related current event/situation in school, community, nation, or world) and that provide students practice in using the democratic processes of our government and society and in contributing to others.

— Celebrations of learning that heighten emotional involvement in applying the key points and help wire learning into long-term memory.

• Selects a professional and/or peer coach(es) who can/will support the implementation of the body-brain-compatible curriculum delivered through the use of a variety of instructional strategies selected to best suit the key points and inquiries at hand. Establishes and maintains a schedule for meeting frequently. Prepares thoroughly for each meeting; schedules follow-up time to learn from each session.

IMPROVING INSTRUCTIONAL STRATEGIES: THE CHALLENGE

Before you can profit from powerful curriculum, there are two prerequisites: You must provide a bodybrain-compatible environment (discussed in Stage 1 of implementation) and you must possess expertise in a variety of instructional strategies.

Why? Because the day is long for elementary school students. From their point of view, variety in instructional strategies from hour to hour is a must, not a luxury. Limited instructional strategies leads to monotony, putting both students and teacher at risk. Lecture, textbook reading assignments, and worksheets can't be sustained all day long. Students won't sit still for it; they couldn't even if they wanted to. Movement and full engagement of the sensory system is the biological nature of young students. When students tire of their teacher's limited instructional strategies and leadership, they take over the class themselves and the tug-of-war begins.

We believe that improving instructional strategies should be the first priority during Stage 2 and should garner 80 percent of the staff development and support resources. Our schools won't improve until every teacher can and does effectively use a wide variety of instructional strategies.

Stage 2 is a clarion call to you to deepen and master a wide variety of instructional strategies, a foundation for your continuing work to improve curriculum.

USING A VARIETY OF INSTRUCTIONAL STRATEGIES

Instructional strategies must vary and they must increasingly become a natural extension of the content to be learned, not pre-designed, publisher-provided activities. At Stage 2, instructional strategies used during Stages 1.2 and 1.3 must deepen and be crafted to best deliver the content at hand. This represents an important shift from Stage 1 in which movement to enhance learning, for example, focused mostly on movement which help students reset their emotions. Then, the content of these movements was unimportant as long as they achieved the goal of energizing or relaxing students. However, in Stage 2, movements must also be crafted to help deliver the content to be learned. Whether teacher-made or student-made, these movements must help students understand, use, and store the content of the current key points in long-term memory.

In similar fashion, the songs and literature used during Stage 2 must help students understand, use, and remember the content of the key points. If your favorite songs and literature don't help teach your key points, they must be left behind. Collaborative learning activities must also pass this acid test; the structure of roles within the Learning Clubs should help teach the content of the day's/week's key points.

In short, your use of instructional strategies in Stages 2 and beyond must be designed to deliver the content you are teaching. To do so, your use of each strategy must deepen and become a natural outgrowth of your content—the best possible way to teach the content of the moment.

CONNECTING INSTRUCTIONAL STRATEGIES TO CONTENT

For Stage 2 and beyond, it is essential that you extend and deepen your use of strategies so that they become more content driven than formula. Implement them not only during the *HET* curriculum but all day every day.

Movement to Enhance Learning

In Stage 1, movement mostly centered on ways to energize and calm students. In Stage 2 and beyond, your use of movement must connect to and grow out of the curriculum you are teaching—the key points and inquiries of your *HET* curriculum. Examples:

body mapping[1] to learn the continents of the world, steps of the scientific thinking process, body movements to form the letters of the alphabet, and so forth.

Movement should be daily, sometimes even hourly, so that students not strong in linguistic intelligence (approximately 80% of our students) have another avenue through which to learn and remember.

Content for Movement. Your first goal in using movement is to integrate it with the content being studied. Encourage students to use their bodies to increase sensory input, practice ways to use what they understand, and hard-wire learning into long-term memory. For example, make study trips truly exploratory not just look and see. Develop hand jives and whole-body movement routines as mnemonic devices. Develop role-playing plots and actions that illustrate the concepts and skills to be learned. Create dance routines based on the concepts or skills. Add movement to songs. Be creative. Above all, have fun!

Once you get started, the ideas will flow. Don't be afraid to involve students. Invite them to write inquiries to develop explorations, hand jives, role-playing scenarios, dance routines, songs, and so on.

To get you started, the following resources provide pictures that will stir your imagination:
- *Stage 2 of the ITI/HET Stages of Implementation: Intelligence Is a Function of Experience* (video, 14 minutes)
- *ITI/HET in the Urban Middle School* by Nicole McNeil-Miller (video, 15 minutes)
- *Multiple Intelligences and the Second Language Learner* by Jo Gusman (video, 40 minutes)

For more information about movement to enhance learning, see pages 1.18-19, 2.14-15, 3.18-3.19, 4.12-14, and 5.10-11.

The motivation behind movement, a critical bodybrain-compatible element in the *HET* model, is not movement for the sake of movement or exercise because it's good for you but because movement is critical to the functioning of the brain and therefore to learning. It's not just any movement, it is the kind of movement associated with using what is learned as well as to reset students' emotional states to a level appropriate to the next activity. This can include the letting off steam as well as focusing the brain for learning, reenergizing for a shift to a new topic of learning, or simply relaxing and taking a break.

Collaboration

Collaboration is far too rich a topic to adequately address here. For specific strategies, see *Designing Groupwork* by Elizabeth Cohen and *Cooperative Learning* by Spencer Kagan. In addition, make sure that:

- Students receive formal instruction in the personal and social skills necessary to make collaboration work

- The content of collaborative inquiries is specifically designed so that no one student can complete an inquiry by him/herself, thus forcing full participation by each student.[2]

- Collaborative work begins with an analysis of the Lifelong Guidelines/LIFESKILLS needed and ends with reflective thinking questions about the process and content of the collaborative work.

Also, from Stage 2 on, the structures of collaboration—especially the roles assigned within Learning Clubs—should be an extension of the content currently being studied in the component or topic. For example, instead of the usual roles of chair, recorder, timer, supporter, etc., the roles should be those inherent in the key points for the week(s), such as judge, prosecutor, defender, jury; or, labor and management negotiators, consumers, and public opinion experts.

The roles in collaboration groups should be as natural and fluid as those in real life. Collaboration is a means of extending and deepening student experience with content and skills. Collaboration is not an end goal; creating a sense of community is a means to greater academic achievement and practice in citizenship.

For more information about collaboration, see pages 7.14-7.17 plus 1.18-1.19, 2.14-2.15, 3.18-3.19, 4.25, and 5.16.

Providing for Temperament

"He's been like this since the day he was born . . . all smiles and easy going," "I knew she'd be interested in this job because as a child she was always intrigued by such things." Such comments recognize that many of our personality preferences are innate, part of who we are. Accommodating such personality traits, rather than resisting them, makes life in the classroom much more productive for both teacher and students.

What Makes Us Tick? Temperament, factors of one's personality, strongly impact the learning process, affecting:

- How we take in information

- How we organize during learning and applying learning

- What we value when making decisions

- Our orientation to others

We are born with these preferences or temperaments. The place we call home—where we feel most comfortable on the sliding scale for each of these four areas of behavior—remains relatively unchanged throughout life.

The Power of Temperament. The power of temperament upon school participation and achievement is enormous. First, we should stop expecting everyone to be like us; we need to begin to understand and appreciate our differences and learn how to make them an asset, rather than an irritant, in the daunting task of succeeding in life.[3]

Second, we must keep foremost in our minds that powerful learning (greatest depth, speed, ability to apply) occurs when students operate consistently with their mental wirings. Thus, we must recommit ourselves to the idea that schools must remold themselves to fit children rather than expecting children to fit schools. For a discussion of temperament and how to make them work for you through the nine bodybrain-compatible elements, see Appendix A.

INSTRUCTIONAL STRATEGIES FOR INTRODUCING AND RETEACHING

To get the most power out of your *HET* curriculum, you must master three more instructional strategies:

- Using *being there* experiences as the basis for both curriculum and instruction

- Teaching concepts and skills through the lives of those at the *being there* location

- The *HET* Discovery Process

Using Being There Experiences

As you spend more time studying each *being there* location, allow the *being there* experience to push you into more real-life application of concepts and skills. Abandon workbooks and worksheets; rely more on practice of skills and concepts using the situations at the *being there* location. For example, teach/practice math using interesting situations at the site, such as profit/loss, costs of running a business, computing taxes, number of people who come and go, etc. Examine law making and enforcement, historical comparisons of then and now, and so forth. Invite students, third grade and up, to write inquiries from which you select those that offer challenge for both individual and group work.

Be creative. Be real. Give students a window into the real world; help them understand what goes on behind the scenes so they better understand what they see and hear.

Teaching Through the Lives of Those at the Being There Location

Children are extremely adept at learning by imitation. Develop inquiries that require them to become someone at the *being there* location—a business owner, clerk, customer, customer service rep, biologist, water treatment engineer, college student.

Use role playing frequently. Each time a student plays a person at the *being there* location, it broadens his/her horizons. If you can imagine it, you can do it. If they can imagine themselves doing many different roles, they can also imagine more career possibilities.

Role playing is also highly appealing to those in the audience; there is action to watch, dialogue to hear, and a story line to follow. The emotional impact makes it easier for students to see connections to real life.

Role playing is especially powerful for teaching concepts that students have difficulty learning because they are abstract or because students hold misconceptions.[3]

Role playing can be formal—with time allowed to prepare and rehearse an assigned scenario—or spontaneous. Both are powerful. Role playing is especially effective for teaching students alternative responses.

Be playful. And be rigorous. Know that for many students, hearing about something is seldom as powerful as seeing it. And, because education is about giving students options in life, what better way than to have them experience those options now through role playing in the safe environment of your classroom.

The HET Discovery Process

The *HET* Discovery Process is designed to encourage curiosity and initiative—key LIFESKILLS for becoming a lifelong learner and a contributing citizen. It's an opportunity to present students with an object, specimen, or problem and let them discover both the questions and the answers. This process is exciting and allows Learning Clubs to orchestrate their own learning. It's used most effectively when the Lifelong Guidelines and the LIFESKILLS are in place.

The steps in the Discovery Process are:

1. Stimulating curiosity

2. Setting standards and expectations

3. Providing lead-up time

4. Orchestrating the exploration

5. Providing small group follow-up time

6. Capturing the teachable moment

7. Assessing student learning

8. Creating long-term memories through outreach

Curiosity, the Great Motivator. When to use the Discovery Process? Whenever you introduce a firsthand item—a specimen (owl pellets, worm farms, kiwi fruit), something unusual (starfish, oak galls, nests, etc.), something about which you want to pique student interest.

The Discovery Process takes full advantage of a child's natural curiosity. It is an opportunity to explore both the questions and answers, to explore connections between prior experiences and new, fact and fiction, to lead one's own learning.

In the *HET* model, the Discovery Process is usually a Learning Club activity. In the spirit of two heads are better than one, working together usually uncovers the most patterns and the richest, most complex connections.

Step 1—Stimulating Curiosity. This is your chance to open the doors to wonder and awe for your students and a chance for them to experience being active, self-directed learners. This isn't direct instruction time, it's a time to pose "what if's," and drop amazing facts. Have fun! Get excited yourself! Tell your students that they are going to have a most amazing time.

Step 2—Setting Standards and Expectations. Setting standards and expectations for behavior and performance is critical. In addition to the everyday expectations to use the Lifelong Guidelines and LIFESKILLS, clearly establish standards and expectations specific to the nature of the event.

In ten minutes or less:

- Identify the necessary procedures for working with a specimen (live or otherwise).
- Discuss use of exploratory tools, procedures, or other special equipment they will use.
- Review what teamwork looks and sounds like and does **not** look and sound like.

It's critical that the teacher is an enthusiastic leader. Yes, handle the snake, touch the shark, open the owl pellet, reach for the worms, and watch the live owl with fascination.

A KWU (know, want to know, and now understand) T-chart (see Chapter 10) is an effective tool to help students focus their thoughts. For the *K* column, have them list what they already *k*now (and think they know); in *W* column, list what they *w*ant to know. This discussion helps them set their expectations and begin to develop strategies for exploring. Afterwards, in the third column, have them list what they learned.

Step 3—Providing Lead-Up Time. Before beginning the Discovery Process, students need time to assimilate what they have heard, seen, and experienced during Steps 1 and 2. This should be done both individually and as a group. Provide time for students to discuss their mindmaps, share something from their personal experience, ask themselves, "Where does this fit into my knowledge/

experience base?" and so forth. This is the time to communicate, a time during which students must actively and purposefully manipulate information to extract as much meaning from it as possible so that information is accurately stored in the brain.

The internal dialogue that occurs in answer to the question "How does this affect me?" is critical to activating the brain's attention mechanisms and decision to store something in long-term memory.

During this settling in, getting comfortable period, students might be sketching a specimen, comparing pictures with the real thing, hypothesizing about what they're going to discover, or sharing their personal experiences related to the lesson. This is their motivational lead-up for what they are about to do. For many students, this is the time to overcome fears and apprehensions about the unknown, e.g. a scary-looking owl. Not everyone is ready to jump in when the teacher says, "Go." Lead-up time is invaluable even if only ten minutes.

During lead-up time, decisions must be made about who's responsible for each group task. For example, "I'll be the recorder." "John draws well; he can sketch the parts." "Who wants to label?"

Sometimes it's appropriate for the teacher to select who will do specific jobs. This guarantees that students have an opportunity to practice various roles exercising leadership and responsibility. An efficient way to identify who does what is to assign every student in the group a number. All the teacher has to do is say, "For today, number 1 is the recorder, number 3 is the organizer, and number 5 is the facilitator," and so on. Another way is to post job assignments identifying specific jobs (one for each member of the group) that can be rotated. Possible roles are:

- Facilitator—sees that each group member has the opportunity to share ideas; reviews ground rules (if any) and initiates the discussion; helps restart discussion when things bog down

- Inquisitor—asks at least two questions about the subject or topic to reveal the concept (big idea)

- Connector—looks for and shares connections between the topic and personal experiences

- Illustrator—draws a picture of the most important elements of the topic

- Summarizer/recorder—summarizes discussions to clarify content or how to proceed; records events, procedures, conclusions for the group

- Reporter—reads the instructions or information aloud and reports the outcomes

- Organizer—makes sure the work area is organized and clean

- Quieter—notices when the teacher signals for active listening

Assignment of job responsibilities does not mean that such tasks interfere with the primary responsibility of full participation, in "doing" the activity, working with firsthand materials, and so on. Everyone is a learner, all must participate in the activity. The jobs assigned to the group are in addition to the job of learning as individuals. Equal opportunity to experience responsibility and leadership is a cornerstone commitment in an *HET* classroom.

Step 4—The Exploration. The students are mentally ready to proceed. Let them explore, guide when it is necessary, help them interpret what they find. Shift your role from sage on the stage to guide on the side.

Step 5—Providing Small Group Follow-Up. Can you remember how important it seemed to you when a teacher gave you positive, instructive feedback? Remember how good it felt and how pleased you were that he/she noticed you personally? Such feedback is critical, yet finding time to interact with students more frequently is difficult. Usually students who receive most of our time are those with behavior problems or special needs. To solve this dilemma, limit the time allotted for direct instruction, suggest students ask each other for help ("Ask Three Before Me"), and then take this purloined time to purposefully circulate during the groupwork activity.

"Purposefully circulate" means that you will especially target groups and individuals to reteach, redirect, and/or reenergize. This is the teacher's time to observe, listen, and analyze student responses and to give immediate feedback. This is also a perfect opportunity to acknowledge the use of the Lifelong Guidelines, especially Personal Best as defined by the LIFESKILLS.

Step 6—Capturing the Teachable Moment. The teachable moment is when the student's curiosity is sparked and the teacher can enhance learning by drawing on his/her own knowledge base. It is an opportunity for the teacher to model being an active and competent learner. Taking advantage of teachable moments requires a broad knowledge base, willingness to extend learning on the spur of the moment, or even digress when appropriate.

In this information age, we're both frustrated and excited by the bombardment of knowledge all around us. To find time to increase your knowledge base, take 20 minutes a day (10 in the morning and 10 in the afternoon or evening) to read about the concepts, significant knowledge, and skills of your theme. Read books, magazines, newsletters, and professional journals; listen to CDs; watch DVDs; and examine any other materials that relate. When you are an *HET* teacher, your conceptual curriculum will help you assimilate information and hold it organizationally in your mind. Teachers must be active learners committed to mastering how to use information and skills, not just talk about them.

Remembering how good it feels to learn—reliving the feeling each day—enables us to recognize when learning is actually taking place in the classroom and to capture the teachable moment.

Step 7—Assessing Learning. Because the Discovery Process is so multidimensional, assessment should be so also. In addition to checking for context, we should assess the strength of our students' emotional involvement in learning. How students feel about learning determines whether that learning will get wired into long-term memory.

Assessing Emotional Impact. Assessing the emotional impact of a lesson is just as important as assessing content. Feelings while learning something new become the attitudes we hold for the rest of our lives. How often have we heard, "I wasn't good in that when I went to school, so I'm not surprised my child isn't doing well either," or "I've never liked math or science or reading."

A daily journal is one way students can express their emotional responses to what they're learning. After a vigorous lesson such as dissecting owl pellets, it's imperative to allow students to ponder how they feel about what they learned and how this experience will affect learning in the future. Never discount your students' feelings; acknowledge that feelings are a part of being alive and, more importantly, they are the gate keeper to the cognitive domain. Everyone has emotions; unguided or ignored emotions usually hinder learning rather than assist.

If an activity has generated feelings of indignation, outrage, or heightened personal interest and concern, it is time for political action, a time to write letters to the editor, school board, planning commission, Save-the-Whales committee, a chemical company, the President of the United States, local businesses, Sierra Club, and the like. Learning and internalizing information are not enough in today's society. Individuals must realize they have a right and a responsibility to become involved and that their opinions and concerns need to be heard.

Taking action on social issues imparts a sense of importance to lessons learned at school. It provides a real-world context in which to fully explore concepts and skills and gives an audience (and a reason) for exercising a wide range of communication skills.

Assessing Academic Learning. The current "authentic assessment"[5] movement is a pleasant breath of spring across the educational landscape. Brushing aside contrived, trivial standardized assessments, Grant Wiggins, Fred Newmann, and other authentic assessment leaders admonish us to measure ability to use knowledge—producing knowledge rather than reproducing it. Thus the phrase "authentic expressions of knowledge."

In the *HET* model we speak of mastery/competence in terms of performance. There's a large gap between knowing about, and selecting choice *A*, *B*, *C*, or *D* and being able to apply information to a real-life situation. Measuring the ability to use what we know is what authentic assessment is all about.

The exploration phase of the Discovery Process is just the beginning and should lead onward to specific demonstrations of what is learned during the Discovery Process. See Chapter 19 for a discussion of assessment in the *HET* model.

Step 8—Creating Long-term Memories Through Outreach. Outreach is the purposeful connection of classroom activity to someone or something outside the classroom—a way of applying lessons to reality.[5] Outreach can be planned by contacting a resource person or it can be spontaneous such as when students suggest a course of action. Outreach asks the question, "Knowing this information leads me where or to whom?" To have knowledge and skills is to be responsible. Does it demand we take action? In a democracy, if we don't take action to correct problems or social ills, who will? Perhaps the students want to share with other classes or schools, produce a videotape, invite someone in to answer questions, start an information center, or set up a display at the local library or school district office. Educating others is a major responsibility of us all. Outreach demands application of what is studied. It may have long-range effects or short-term impact, but it is an important classroom activity, one which gently prods both the students and the teacher into looking at content in an active, meaningful way.

When looking at outreach, called "political or social action" in the *HET* model, we should use the language arts skills of reading, writing, listening and speaking. Outreach activities provide real audiences and a clear sense of purpose. What better environment in which to master these skills? In students' minds it becomes clear that these skills are a means to an important end—the ability to cope in the real world.

The best tools we know to assist you in planning outreach is *Kid's Guide to Social Action: How to Solve the Social Problems You*

Choose — And Turn Creative Thinking into Positive Action and *The Kid's Guide to Service Projects: Over 500 Service Ideas for Young People Who Want to Make a Difference,* both by Barbara A. Lewis. These books are filled with practical suggestions for getting involved and vignettes of student political action from around the country. They will assist your students with form, content, addresses, procedures, and presentations. They are comprehensive and written as user's guides. *Enriching Curriculum Through Service Learning,* edited by C.W. Kinsley and K. McPherson, is another fine resource.

Enjoy the moment. Your students certainly will!

INSTRUCTIONAL STRATEGIES FOR LONG-TERM MEMORY AND ASSESSMENT

If students don't wire curriculum content into their long-term memory, the brain does a short-term memory dump and nothing remains except an emotional memory of whether they enjoyed the subject/skill or disliked it and a grade, even an *A,* on a test paper. We have wasted their time and ours. This is an important idea from brain research. It explains why spiral curricula, in which students are exposed to different parts of something each year with the expectation that they will add up at the end, don't work. And, it underscores the wisdom of "less is more," why covering content results in little long-term memory.

To revisit Chapter 1, learning is the result of real — observable and measurable — physiological growth/change in the brain. If we are to take students to long-term memory, we need to provide curriculum which is highly engaging, a task that *being there* experiences do well, and we must carry out instructional strategies that heighten and prolong the engagement.

Clear Performance Criteria

The beauty of inquiries that call for applying concepts and skills to situations at the *being there* location is that the tasks are real

to students and they can readily see that real-world standards should apply. Rather than resistance to classroom "stuff," they can readily accept that performance standards are just how it is and if you want to succeed in life, get to it. For example, students grumble about grammar rules but they will work diligently on a letter to the mayor to make a good impression and thus increase the likelihood that their request will be taken seriously.

Whenever possible, let students discover what the real-world standards are for themselves. Younger students can interview people at the *being there* location; older students can also visit websites, especially those connected to professions such as unions, construction codes, work performance evaluation criteria, and rubrics of all kinds, scoring tools that list criteria for a piece of work. A useful website for school related rubrics is http://rubistar.4teachers.org

For information about how to make your inquiries better assessment tools, see Chapter 19.

Celebrations of Learning

Celebrations of Learning are a unique kind of party. They are events that make public what students have learned, give them a showcase for proving it, and let them bask in the delight of an important accomplishment. The audiences are real — parents and other students. The LIFESKILL of Pride is real. The resulting competence-induced confidence and pride are real.

Celebrations of Learning can come before or after a Social/Political Action Project and can be an integral part or completely independent. It all depends upon what you want to achieve and whether the content has taken on a life of its own (which frequently happens!). So, you may change your mind as you work through the component or topic of study.

For more information about conducting Celebrations of Learning, see Chapter 10, 10.18-10.19.

Social/Political Action Projects

Social/Political Action Projects are at the heart of the *HET* model for three reasons:

- They are the most powerful combination of curriculum and instruction you can devise

- They create an informed, involved citizenry—the ultimate purpose of public education

- They teach students how to become a lifelong learner

For more information about Social/Political Action Projects, see Chapter 21, 221.1-21.2.

ENDNOTES

1   Some useful resources for body mapping include:

Sandra and Matthew Blakeslee, *The Body Has a Mind of Its Own: How Body Maps in Your Brain Help You Do (Almost) Everything Better.* New York: Random House Trade Paperbacks, reprint edition, 2008.

Susan Griss, *Minds in Motion: A Kinesthetic Approach to Teaching Elementary Curriculum* (Portsmouth NH: Heinemann Press, 1998.).

Helen Landalf, *Moving the Earth: Teaching Earth Science Through Movement.* (Lyme, NH: Smith and Kraus).

Carol Glynn, *Learning on Their Feet: A Sourcebook for Kinesthetic Learning* Shoreham. VT: Discover Writing Press, 2001.

Sheila Kogan, *Step by Step: A Complete Movement Education Curriculum.* Champagne, IL: Human Kinetics Publishers, 2003.

Billye Ann Cheatum and Allison Hammon, *Physical Activities for Improving Children's Learning and Behavior.* Champage,IL: Human Kinetics Publishers, 2000.

2   Elizabeth G. Cohen, *Designing Groupwork: Strategies for the Heterogeneous Classroom, Second Edition* (New York: Teachers College Press, 1994), 64-65. When no one person could easily do a task alone, members find it necessary to exchange ideas. Elizabeth Cohen calls this kind of collaboration an "equal exchange model." Cohen points out that "if only one person can do the task alone, then there is no motivation for a free exchange of ideas; the only issue is whether the person who know how to do the job will help those that don't." Cohen refers to this kind of interaction as a "limited exchange model of working together." Studies show a significant difference in performance levels of high thinking skills between these two kinds of collaborative work.

3   David Keirsey, *Please Understand Me II: Temperament, Character, Intelligence* (Del Mary, CA: Prometheus Nemesis Book Company, 1998).

4   "A Private Universe" is a fascinating window on interviews with Harvard University students on their graduation day. The question put to them is "Explain the reason for the seasons." Even those who had taken astronomy classes gave the "Hot, baby, hot" explanation: When the sun gets closer, our season gets warmer. It is a powerful illustration of the power of misconceptions to override subsequent learning. Instructional strategies such as discussion and collaboration work are excellent tools for rooting out and correct stubborn misconceptions.

5   Fred Newman, one of the primary leaders of the authentic assessment movement, states, "The idea of authentic achievement requires students to engage in disciplined inquiry to produce knowledge that has value in their lives beyond simply proving their competence in school."

6   The power of outreach experiences to cement learning is well documented through a plethora of studies. Sarah S. Pearson, *Finding Common Ground: Service Learning and Education Reform, A Survey of 28 Leading School Reform Models* (Washington, DC: American Youth Policy Forum, 2002), 72-75.

Making Curriculum More Powerful: Implementing Stage 3

CURRICULUM DEVELOPMENT: OPPORTUNITY AND CHALLENGE

As discussed in Chapter 12, the purpose of writing your own curriculum is to make it more powerful for students by:

- Capturing the power of local *being there* experiences to engage the bodybrain learning partnership and naturally integrate all content and skills

- Providing pattern-rich content for the brain's inherent pattern-seeking nature

- Providing a vehicle for tailoring curriculum to **your** students' specific interests, needs, and ways of learning in ways that help students build mental programs and wire them into long-term memory.

These are the opportunities. The challenges lie in the fact that *teacher-made curriculum is better than publisher-developed curriculum* **only if it is**.

To ensure that your curriculum is more powerful than canned curriculum available off the shelf, it must be developed to fit how the brain learns. Recall the brain research presented in Chapters 4 and 5—the brain as pattern seeker and meaning maker and learning as the acquisition of mental programs.

The Goals of Curriculum Development

The crucial curriculum development goals for Stages 2 were to master the art of basing content and skills in a *being there* location and making curriculum more conceptual. Maintain these building blocks.

The curriculum development goals for Stage 3 and beyond are to master writing curriculum that:

- Enhances students' ability—through *being there* experiences, key points, conceptual curriculum—to detect and understand patterns

- Promotes—through *being there* experiences and inquiries—development of mental programs to use in real-world ways what students understand

Stage 3 requires that you deepen your understanding of how to make the glove fit the hand—how to make curriculum fit the brain. This chapter will explore how to make key points and inquiries that better fit your students.

MAKING CURRICULUM MORE POWERFUL

CURRICULUM

- Maintains, expands, and deepens all the aspects of integrated curriculum described in Stages 1 and 2.

- Develops curriculum that is conceptually based in order to enhance students' ability to identify patterns and make meaning:

  - Uses an organizing concept to unify study for the year and to integrate subject areas.

  - Conceptual key points are the focus of all *HET* curriculum.

  - Significant knowledge key points are selected with care in order to provide students with the knowledge needed to understand and apply the concepts in real life.

  - The curriculum enhances pattern seeking; factoids have been eliminated.

- Provides inquiries sufficient in variety and number to:

  - Utilize and strengthen each of the multiple intelligences

  - Develop mental programs to store in long-term memory.

INSTRUCTIONAL STRATEGIES

- Continues and deepens use of the instructional strategies described in Stages 1 and 2. Reviews twice a year (October and February) these descriptors and compares them to student responses. Makes the necessary adjustments in instructional strategies before continuing on with curriculum development for Stage 3.

- Regularly provides sufficient choices through inquiries and other means; includes ample opportunities to practice solving problems and producing products.

- Ensures that the primary sensory input provided to supplement and extend *being there* experiences is immersion and hands-on-of-the-real-thing. Uses technology primarily after *being there* sensory input to supplement full sensory input, not replace it.

- Allows adequate time for students to complete their work.

- Varies instructional strategies and chooses the most effective methods for the particular content at hand, e.g., direct instruction and *HET* Discovery Processes, collaboration and personal study time, mindmapping, organizing materials, and cross-age/multi-age interaction.

MAKING CURRICULUM MORE POWERFUL

CURRICULUM

INSTRUCTIONAL STRATEGIES

- Provides practice using interpersonal intelligence and effectively uses collaboration to enhance learning for academic, personal, and social growth..

- For grades K-6, uses science as either the core or a prominent part of curriculum integration because science is everywhere and in everything and explains how the universe works, thus providing universal concepts for integrating content in a natural and powerful way. Provides an understanding of science and technology as vital to the role of citizenship in the 21st century.

  For grades 7-12, focuses on conceptual key points that are fundamental to all subject areas and serve to integrate the subject areas in a natural and powerful way. Significant knowledge key points provide the knowledge needed to understand how that concept is applied to each content area in real-world ways.

- Includes in the curriculum many of the elements that appear as a natural part or extension of the *being there* focus, e.g., science, technology, history/social studies, fine arts, as well as mathematics, reading, writing, and oral expression. Integration of content is natural, not contrived.

- Supports the theme with multiple, varied, and rich resources, including 50+ books, magazines, newspapers, and DVDs brought in by teacher and students plus Internet access.

- Resource people and experts are regular visitors to the classroom.

- Visits to off-campus learning sites are frequent and serve as the focal point and context for the curriculum being studied.

MAKING CURRICULUM MORE POWERFUL

CURRICULUM

- Prominently displays the organizing concept and components and topics on the wall so they can serve as the framework for teaching and learning. Bases at least 25-35 percent of instruction during the school year upon the bodybrain-compatible curriculum developed for this stage of implementation.

- Provides practice in citizenship through inquiries and other Social/Political Action Projects that are natural outgrowths of *being there* experiences and other related study.

INSTRUCTIONAL STRATEGIES

- Refers to the curriculum wall frequently to point out connections and relationships to prior and future study.

- Creates a 3-D immersion wall for the current *being there* location. Includes key point(s), artifacts, models, charts, photos, and whatever resources that will make the content come alive for students.

- Includes a social/political action project based on the needs at the *being there* location and related topics under study.

- Concludes each significant chunk of *HET* curriculum (at least each component) with a Celebration of Learning.

- Encourages students to experience in-depth learning (becoming an "expert" about a topic of their choice) through completion of a Yearlong Research Project.

MAKING CURRICULUM MORE POWERFUL

CURRICULUM

- Ensures that content is age-appropriate.

INSTRUCTIONAL STRATEGIES

- Completes writing curriculum (key points and inquiries) before beginning to plan lessons. Has developed and regularly uses a bodybrain-compatible lesson planning process and format.

- Selects a professional and/or peer coach(es) who can/will support the implementation of the bodybrain-compatible curriculum delivered through the use of a variety of instructional strategies selected to best suit the key points and inquiries at hand. Establishes and maintains a schedule for meeting frequently. Prepares thoroughly for each meeting; schedules follow-up time to learn from each session.

Note: The goal of Stage 3 is to develop and implement integrated curriculum for 25-35% of the year.

Chapter 16: Making Curriculum More Conceptual: Key Points

Improving a school is neither simple nor easy. Your journey to Stage 3 has likely taken 2-3 years. But don't become discouraged. As the saying goes, "If the task was easy, someone else would already have done it for you." Congratulate yourself for a long, hard job done well and know that the full payoff for your efforts lies in Stage 3 and beyond. Here, students bloom and dreams become reality. You will see achievement levels soar, the projects that students eagerly engage in will amaze you, and you will enjoy teaching more than you ever thought possible. Stage 3 is where you want to be. Enjoy this segment of your journey!

The challenge at Stage 3 is to make your key points more conceptual. To do so, you will need to:

- Revisit key points and what they are supposed to do

- Continue to base your key points in *being there* locations. Let the experience of the location unfold naturally, integrating the science, mathematics, technology, history/social studies, fine arts, reading, writing, and oral expression as you see it happening.

- Make science either the core or a prominent part of your curriculum. Use its universal concepts to organize all subjects and skills. (See the concepts on pages 16.5-16.6.)

- Look with new eyes at everyday locations and select concepts that will enhance responsible citizenship. Stretch yourself to find a few powerful concepts that will explain a lot of things instead of collecting a lot of content under many organizers.

- Improve the quality of your key points

Good key points enhance students' capacity to extract meaningful patterns and develop useful mental programs. Good key points help students build larger, more abstract conceptualizations and generalizations about the world. Knowledge is power.

KEY POINTS DEFINED

A key point is a clear, concise statement of what you want students to understand and be able to apply. A key point presents a pattern—usually a collection of related patterns—that when taken together add up to something worth knowing, something that can be used in real life. For example, sharp pointed ears, a long tail, and a meow sound are attributes or parts of the pattern called cat. Two metal objects pulling toward each other in absence of an outside force such as a push or gravity suggests one of the metal pieces is a magnet. Or, here comes Calvin home from school and Hobbes is stalking through the house. You guessed it. Whooosh! An overly exuberant tiger knocks Calvin flat. We live our lives by identifying and interpreting such patterns.

From the humor that makes our day (Calvin and Hobbes) to the minute-by-minute conversations that make up the fabric of our lives, from job training to learning parenting and relationship skills, detecting and understanding patterns is the brain's way of making meaning of our world. It follows then that *we should view curriculum development—and the lesson planning that follows—as a pattern-enhancing activity. Your job is to write curriculum that makes recognizing and understanding patterns engaging, even gripping, and totally unavoidable.* In other words, all students can and will master each key point.

Curriculum As a Pattern-Enhancing Activity

Patterns are everywhere.[1] Our job is to enhance students' ability to identify and understand them.

For example, suppose we want students to understand the following science concept: "Interactions among animals and plants to meet the need for food within a habitat are called a 'food chain' or 'food web.'" There are at least four large and fairly complex patterns essential to understanding this idea—interactions, need for food (different ways plants and animals take in food), habitat, and food chain/food web. Once these four patterns are understood, students can begin to grasp the significance of the concept or pattern represented by the concept.

The Pattern Called "Need for Food." Students should understand that plants have various ways to take in food, such as through the roots, the air, ingesting meat (Venus fly traps), making their own food through photosynthesis, and so forth. They also should understand that animals have an even greater variety of ways to take in food and what "food" is needed varies tremendously among species. Pulling in prior knowledge or previously understood patterns, speeds up and enriches the learning process.

The Pattern Called "Interactions." Plants and animals don't take in food in isolation. Interaction implies give and take. Exploring the ways plants and animals interact (who eats whom/what, who assists whom by doing what) to have food available, to find it and to take it in lays the foundation for understanding a habitat and the interdependence of its inhabitants. Animals and plants can interact in hundreds of ways. Things are becoming interesting!

The Pattern Called "Habitat." The concept or pattern of habitat—all who live in this location—tells us what to include in our food web. The garden, the neighborhood, the city, an old oak tree—all create unique and diverse habitats. Theory can become experience at a *being there* location.

The Pattern Called "Food Chain/Food Web." Pulling forward what students already understand about chains—bicycle chains, key chains, and figures of speech—deepens and speeds their learning. For example, chains are only as strong as their weakest link or the chain of events drove everyone onward. Lose a link and the chain becomes too short to do its job (the loss of one animal may cause one or more animals or plants in the habitat to die off).

Once students understand the idea of a food chain, they'll also understand the complexity of a food web—multiple overlapping chains. In a very short time, their understanding of this concept can become very rich, broad, and forever memorable, all through connecting previous smaller patterns with new ones and finally creating one large pattern to capture the concept.

Once these four large and complex patterns are understood, they provide post office boxes in the brain where new information can be sent to and added to quickly and effortlessly.

Collectively, key points constitute the common core of knowledge and skills that all students are to understand and be able to apply.

Three Kinds of Key Points

The *HET* model uses three kinds of key points:

- **Conceptual** key points are those that capture big ideas that apply worldwide; they are universal truths about how the world works. They can be generalized and transferred to multiple settings.

- **Significant knowledge** key points provide information necessary to understand the concept locally where it can be directly experienced at *being there* locations.
- **Skill** key points describe those basic skills needed to explore and utilize the big ideas.

Why three kinds of key points? Early in the development of the *HET* model, there was just one kind of key point. We learned two lessons. First, when content is truly integrated, even students didn't recognize they were learning math or how to write a paragraph. Designating skill points as such helps teachers communicate to students, parents, peers, and supervisors that skills are being taught and learned, which ones, and when. Second, we learned that teacher's key points tended to mirror the district's/school's curriculum which, until the recent state standards movement, consisted primarily of factoids. Factoids deaden interest; concepts

When we think back over the enormous volume of information we ourselves covered during high school and college and the almost equally enormous volume of information we no longer remember, we should be more humble and honest about curricu-

lum planning for today's students. If covering volumes of details—dates, definitions, names of famous people, and other fill-in-the-blank items—didn't stick with us, why do we pass it on? Especially when brain research clearly tells us why it doesn't work.

If you search for one strategy that would most satisfy the demands of the brain, it is this—basing curriculum in *being there* locations, letting the real world organize or integrate content and skills as it naturally occurs, and visiting that site often (before, during, and at the end of study). The importance and power of this strategy cannot be over emphasized.

Although science may not be your favorite subject, its universal, what-makes-the-world-tick concepts are far and away the versatile set of concepts to engage students and to readily organize content at a *being there* location. Our advice to you, based on coaching thousands of teachers through curriculum development, is to make science the core of your planning.

Why are we so keen on focusing on science? Because science is the great equalizer. The differences in student backgrounds in science are the least whereas the differences in student background in language arts are the greatest. Also, students love to explore their world—its objects, what they can do, how they are made, and why. This is science.

Science is also far and away the subject that elicits the most sensory input. As we have learned from brain research, the greater the sensory input, the greater the physiological change in brain; the greater the physiological change, the greater the learning.

How Conceptual Key Points Drive the Curriculum:

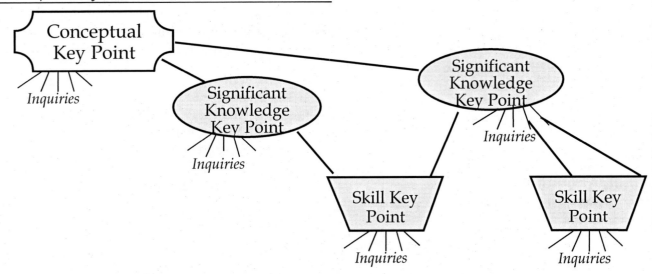

For a user-friendly list of science concepts by grade level, see *Science Continuum of Concepts for Grades K-6*. The main science idea for each grade level K-6 appears on the next page. Many of these concepts could be carried through high school and be highly challenging to students.

Look with new eyes at everyday locations and select concepts that will enhance responsible citizenship. Stretch yourself to find a few powerful concepts that will explain a lot of things instead of collecting a lot of content under many organizers.

Carefully pick through your standards to identify concepts and to "chunk up" ideas to make them more conceptual. This chunking up process is vital, the only way to eliminate factoids which are largely devoid of patterns and thus appear meaningless to the students.

WHAT MAKES A CONCEPT POWERFUL?

What makes a concept powerful? It's universal—it explains a great deal about many things—and it can be directly experienced (seen and touched). The main science idea for each grade level of the *Science Continuum* is a powerful concept for organizing all subjects. For example:

Kindergarten: OBSERVATION — People can learn about things around them by observing them carefully—what they are made of, how they are put together, what they do, and how they are similar and different. Observing and comparing similarities and differences is a key way to help interpret and understand our world. Often we can learn even more about these things if we do something to them and note what happens.

First grade: BASIC NEEDS* or *HABITATS—All living things, including humans, have basic needs (food, water, air, protection from weather, disease, and predators, and to reproduce). A habitat is the place where the animal or plant lives while meeting these needs.

Second grade: FORM AND FUNCTION—The physical characteristics of animals and plants vary greatly and determine what they can do and how they do it to meet their needs. Similarly, the physical characteristics of non-living things vary greatly and determine what changes can occur in them and how they can be used.

Third grade: CHANGE— Things are changing around us all the time. Change can occur in a variety of ways (reversible, irreversible; controllable, not controllable; steady or repetitive and thus fairly predictable or not steady or repetitive and thus unpredictable) and for different reasons. The rate and size of change may not be observable with human senses; we need tools to measure such change. Change can be helpful, harmful, or neutral.

Fourth grade: INTERDEPENDENCE—Plants and animals interact with each other and their environment in ways that allow them to meet their basic needs. Keep in mind that humans are animals.

Fifth grade: SYSTEMS—All structures and systems, living and non-living, are made up of smaller parts and/or processes.

Sixth grade: CHANGE IN SYSTEMS—Both living and non-living systems have situations in which they change in some way and other situations in which they remain essentially unchanged or constant. Why situations in such systems change and why they remain constant can be explained in terms of particular variables. Much change in our world is human-made; some is intended and some inadvertent.

Just as students have to learn and practice how to write in different genres, such as essay, short story, journaling, technical writing, poetry, etc., so must teachers. Writing key points is definitely a different genre—part essay, part technical writing, advertisement, and part revelation of one's soul (or at least your prior life's experiences and knowledge base).

To guide you in improving the quality of your key points, keep the following guidelines in mind:

GUIDELINES FOR IMPROVING KEY POINTS

Here are some guidelines—the S.T.U.D.E.N.T.S. rule—to help you improve your key points:

GUIDELINES FOR WRITING KEY POINTS— S.T.U.D.E.N.T.S.

S = *Succinct* and clear, *simple* but not simplistic

T = *Tied* to real-world situations

U = *Universal* concepts that naturally integrate all subjects and skills at a *being there* location

D = *Designed* for students

E = Understandable by *every* student (age-appropriate)

N = *NOT* lesson planning

T = Worthy of the *time* of teacher and students

S = Tight connection between *significant* knowledge key points and the conceptual key points they are to support

---

S = Be <u>succinct</u> *and clear,* <u>simple</u> *but not simplistic.*

Learn to cut to the chase to say exactly what you wanted to say, no more and no less. Keep a copy of Strunk and White's pithy little book, *The Elements of Style,* on how to be pithy.

T = <u>Tie</u> *your key point to real-world situations.*

Select concepts and skills from your state/district standards that students see illustrated at their *being there* locations. Context is very important to the brain when seeking patterns. Context enables students to see what something is and what it is not in addition to how and when it is used and why. The understandings reached are **always** deeper and broader than when the concept or skill is taught in the classroom isolated from its real-world context.

U = *Look for* <u>universal</u> *concepts that will naturally integrate all subjects and skills at a being there location.*

Today's future citizens face challenges ever so much bigger than we did. Yesterday's curriculum with its overload of factoids must be replaced with curriculum that allows students to make more connections, see bigger pictures.

Factoids are statements of fact that offer little potential for detecting patterns because they represent such a small dot of life and thus offer few attributes for students to grab on to. Factoids rarely make it past short-term memory processing. A week after the test, all is forgotten. Unfortunately, most textbooks consist primarily of factoids and thus are difficult to learn from. Their content is watered down, written in short, simple sentences for low readability, and summarized so briefly as to be cryptic and seemingly unrelated to real life or student experiences. Most curriculum—state standards as well as district level—has traditionally been overweighted with factoids. Examples: weekly vocabulary-building lists in English classes that do not relate to concurrent areas of study, definitions in science that students have no prior or current experience with, and strings of historical dates for which students have little context.

D = <u>Design</u> *the key point for students.*

State exactly what you want them to understand so they can use that concept or skill. State it just as you want it remembered, just as they will retrieve it to use it in the real world. Avoid starting with " The student will. . . ." For example, don't say "The student will understand why civilizations fail." State that "Civilizations fail for five main reasons which are . . . ."

E = *Be sure the content is age appropriate so that* <u>every</u> *student can understand it.*

Be aware that much content in today's curriculum standards, while it may impress the public, is not age appropriate. For example, compare the table of contents of your science textbook with the concepts in the *Science Continuum of Concepts.* You'll find many concepts should be moved upward to later grades when students' brains are organized to process the content, not just memorize it. See discussion of age appropriateness in Appendix D.

N = Writing key points is __not__ lesson planning.

Always complete writing key points and inquiries before you begin to lesson plan.

For example, a skill key point about journal writing might look like this: "Journal writing helps us clarify our thoughts, make connections, summarize things to help us remember them, and/or sort through our emotions."

However, mixed in with lesson planning or advice to yourself, it could well end up like: "Journal writing is a learning tool based on the ideas that students write to learn. Students are actively engaged in using the journals to write about topics of personal interest, to note their observations, to imagine, to wonder and to connect new information with things they already know."

The above key point fails on several key criteria: First, it does not state clearly what students are to understand and remember nor is it concise. It also treats students as third persons not present for or part of the conversation. Writing key points and lesson planning at the same time ALWAYS distorts the key points.

T = Make sure what you write is worth the __time__ spent on it- yours and your students.

For all the criticism of textbooks and related worksheets, homespun curriculum is no better if it is more of the same and doesn't fit how the brain learns. As you gather information about your components and topics, you become more knowledgeable about the world around you and thus better able to craft your key points. Spend your time well.

S = Tighten up the connection between __significant knowledge key points__ and conceptual key point.

Make sure the significant knowledge key points are what students need to know to understand how the conceptual key point applies locally at their *being there* location and elsewhere in their area. Resist the temptation to toss in tidbits that, although interesting in themselves, don't actively contribute to understanding the conceptual key point.

EXAMPLES OF KEY POINTS

For examples of good key points, see Chapter 14 and those below.*

KINDERGARTEN: Observing and comparing

Conceptual Key Point #1: People, and animals, use their many senses to explore and find out about their environment, each other, and themselves. Exploring and finding out about is a process called observing, a process that involves much more than "watching" or "looking at." Good observation requires the use of all our senses because different senses provide different information during observation.

Significant Knowledge Key Point #1.1: Tools, such as magnifiers, thermometers, X-ray machines, often give more information about things than can be obtained by observing things with our senses without their help.

Significant Knowledge Key Point #1.2: Different information can be taken in by moving closer to or further away from the thing being observed and by comparing and contrasting them to something else.

The following examples of concepts and significant knowledge to be learned are excerpted from *A Continuum of Concepts: Science Curriculum for Grades K-6* by Karen D. Olsen.[2]

FIRST GRADE: Basic needs
Conceptual Key Point #4: Everybody can "do" science, invent things, and have ideas. "Doing" science is a way of observing and thinking and learning about the world.

Significant Knowledge Key Point #4.1: Describing things as accurately as possible is important in science because it enables people to compare their observations and understandings with those of others. Tools such as rulers, magnifiers, thermometers, balances, and scales allow us to observe and describe things more completely and accurately.

Significant Knowledge Key Point #4.2: Tools are used to do things better or more easily and to do some things that could not otherwise be done at all.

Significant Knowledge Key Point #4.3: When people give different descriptions of the same thing, it is usually a good idea to make some fresh observations instead of just arguing about who is right.

SECOND GRADE: Form and function:
Conceptual Key Point #3: Circles, squares, triangles, spirals, and other shapes are patterns that occur in nature and in human-made things. They are the building blocks of nature and human creations.

Significant Knowledge Key Point #3.1: Each shape has its advantages.

- The circle holds the most mass relative to surface area; thus, most animals with self-regulated body temperatures are roundish in shape in order to reduce surface area compared to body mass. In contrast, most reptiles have flat bodies which increase surface area to body mass, therefore allowing them to use the environment to heat and cool their body.

- The triangle is the strongest shape. It is a common shape in bridges, buildings, and structures which must bear weight.

- Squares and rectangles are a good shape for efficient stacking, such as some support structures in plants or storing items in a closet or warehouse, and for measuring, such as in surveying and computing distance and volume (acreage, perimeter, and so forth).

- Hexagons, such as in bee hives, maximize the enclosed region and minimize the perimeter construction materials. Also efficient for stacking and, when stacked, it makes a strong structure (the concept behind the method of timber shoring developed in the Comstock Mines of Virginia City, Nevada).

THIRD GRADE: Change
Conceptual Key Point #2.1: Change can be steady or repetitive and therefore fairly predictable. An example of repetitive change is a cycle.

Significant Knowledge Key Point #2.1.1: Cycles are changes that occur in a pattern which repeats itself. Examples of cyclical change include night-day, seasons, life cycles (such as the butterfly), water cycle, phases of the moon, etc.

Significant Knowledge Key Point #2.1.2: A garden is a complex microcosm of change that illustrates many cycles, such as reproduction, growth, dying, decaying, recycling, etc.

Significant Knowledge Key Point #2.1.3: Cycles and change happen over time. Some take place over short periods of time, such as the life cycle of a butterfly, and others over long periods of time (such as the seasons of the year, generations of a family, or even millions of years, such as the change in the horse from the size of a rabbit to today's horse).

Significant Knowledge Key Point #2.1.4: Some physical objects, plants, and animals change in some way when they are part of a cycle, such as the metamorphosis of a butterfly from caterpillar to butterfly. Other physical objects may also change but not be part of any cycle, such as changes in a hillside as a result of mining for gold or coal.

FOURTH GRADE: Interdependence
Conceptual Key Point #1: Within a habitat, the resident plants and animals interact with other plants and animals and the environment in ways that allow each to meet its basic needs (food, water, oxygen, sunlight, protection from predators, weather, and disease, and reproduce). This interaction is called interdependence.

Conceptual Key Point #1.1: Interactions to meet the need for food within a habitat are called a "food chain" or, more accurately, a "food web." The disappearance of even one animal or plant can have a cascading effect on the food web.

Significant Knowledge Key Point #1.1.1: Food webs are significantly and often disastrously disrupted by human activities, such as land development and pollution.

Significant Knowledge Key Point #1.1.2: Food preferences can usually be predicted based upon the physical characteristics of the plant or animal (Note: Refer to the organizing concept for second grade, form and function) and can be categorized as carnivorous, herbivorous, and omnivorous.

FIFTH GRADE: *Systems*
Conceptual Key Point #1: Thinking about things as systems means looking for how every part relates to others.

Significant Knowledge Key Point #1.1: Living systems—Every plant and animal is a living system; each is made up of smaller parts whose processes are essential to the survival of that plant or animal.

[Note: A simultaneous study of plants and animals, the similarities and differences of their structures will provide a useful compare and contrast, discovery-oriented context and thus minimize rote memorization. For example, microscope examination of the difference in thickness of cell walls of plants and animals, source and distribution of nutrients, etc.]

Significant Knowledge Key Point #1.2: Non-living systems—Non-living systems are also made up of smaller parts, each contributing to what the system can do.

Significant Knowledge Key Point #1.3: Some systems are a combination of living and non-living parts or processes. For example, in a watershed, the non-living parts of the watershed system are sunlight, soil, water, air, and gravity. The living parts are fungi, bacteria, algae, animals, and plants.

Significant Knowledge Key Point #1.4: In manmade systems, such as the Boeing 747, there are often redundant or backup systems that are/can be activated if the first system fails.

Conceptual Key Point #1.1: Something may not work as well (or at all) if a part of it is missing, broken, worn out, mismatched, or mis-connected.

Significant Knowledge Key Point #1.1.1 [related state standard that is illustrated at the being there location . . . as many made into key points as needed for students to master this conceptual key point]

Conceptual Key Point #1.2: In something that consists of parts, the parts usually influence each other. When parts are put together, they can do things that they couldn't do by themselves.

Significant Knowledge Key Point #1.2.1 [related state standard that is illustrated at the being there location . . . as many made into key points as needed for students to master this conceptual key point]

Conceptual Key Point #1.3: No matter how parts of an object are assembled, the weight of the whole object made is always the same as the sum of its parts. Likewise, when a thing is broken into parts, the parts have the same total weight as the original thing. For example, all the individual parts for a bicycle or car weigh the same as the assembled bicycle or car.

Significant Knowledge Key Point 1.3.1: [related state standard that is illustrated at the being there location . . . as many made into key points as needed for students to master this conceptual key point]

ENDNOTES

1 See the discussion of pattern seeking and making meaning as the first stage of the new, brain-based definition of learning in Chapter 4.

2 See A *Continuum of Concepts: Science Curriculum for Grades K-6* by Karen D. Olsen (Black Diamond, WA: Books for Educators, 2009).

Chapter 17: Making Curriculum More Memorable— Inquiries

This we know. The antidote to poor learning is action. And that is what inquiries do. They frame the action students will take to explore and use concepts and skills until the learning becomes wired into long-term memory.

Well-written inquiries make every day memorable. Parents know when their children are learning because there is an answer to the question, "What'd you do in school today?" The children chatter endlessly. They were excited about learning and they remember it well enough to regale their parents hours later.

THE NOT-SO-SECRET INGREDIENTS FOR MAKING THINGS MEMORABLE

The list of not-so-secret ingredients for making things memorable is not a long one:

- Revisit what inquiries are and what they're supposed to do

- Maintain a sense of community that supports learning and nurtures reflective thinking

- Connect to prior experience, knowledge, and skills

- Allow students to see and practice applying concepts and skills in a real-world context so critical details are available for ready reference, especially the *being there* location on which the curriculum is based

- Offer opportunities to apply concepts and skills to areas of learners' interest

- Provide choices so students may use their most developed intelligence(s) to explore concepts and skills in order to arrive at an accurate understanding; then, encourage them to use their less developed intelligences as they wire learning into long-term memory.

• Improve the quality of your inquiries

The purpose of inquiries is to add action to learning so that students can achieve an accurate understanding, develop mental programs for using concepts and skills, and wire learning into long-term memory. Inquiries complete step two of the new definition of learning. (See Chapter 5 for a discussion of learning as the acquisition of new programs.)

Inquiries Defined

🔷 Learning Is a Two-Step Process

Step One — Input stage: Pattern seeking & meaning
            making

First, the brain must detect/identify a pattern.

Second, the brain must make meaning of the pattern, including its relationship to other patterns.

AND

Step Two — Output stage: Building programs to use what
            we understand
    Begins with conscious effort (often with guidance)
    and then
    With practice, becomes almost automatic and wired into long-term memory.

Inquiries, a key curriculum development structure in the *HET* model, are activities that enable students to understand and apply the concept, skill, or significant knowledge of a key point. The primary purpose of inquiries is to enable students to develop mental programs to apply the key point in real–world situations. They make learning active and memorable. They answer the question: *What do you want students to do with what they understand?*

What Makes a Good Inquiry?

We owe it to our students to prepare them for their most important role—informed, active citizenship.

If we can't come up with a real-world use of a key point, then one of two things is true: The information or skill is in fact not key and teaching it would be a waste of student and teacher time *or* our own knowledge base is insufficient. In either case, expect the writing of inquiries to dredge up some surprises and some questions that may not be comfortable to answer. What you will discover, and what thousands of *HET* teachers before you have discovered, is that much of our traditional curriculum is brain antagonistic. If our intent is to implement the best of what we know about recent brain research, we must make our curriculum bodybrain-compatible. For most states, the state standards developed during the late 1990s are a step in the right direction.

A test of curriculum: How can students apply the following concepts? How can the knowledge empower students? How can they use them in real-world situations? If you cannot answer these questions, you cannot write powerful inquiries. For example, the following are typical concepts from state standards. While they may seem abstract and distant from students' lives as they are stated, inquiries, such as those on the next page, can bring them home and make them real.

- When warmer things are put with cooler ones, the warm ones lose heat and the cool ones gain heat until they are all the same temperature. A warmer object can warm a cooler one by contact or at a distance.

- There are three ways in which heat can go into or out of something:
  Conduction is the transfer of heat from one thing to another by direct touching, such as a frying pan sitting on top of an electric stove or the heating element in an electric water heater.
  Convection is the transfer of heat through moving air currents such as in the circulating air in forced air furnaces or cold air entering the house through cracks around poorly insulated windows and doors.
  Radiation is the transfer of energy through light such as the heat generated by an electric light bulb, a computer, or warmth from the sun.

- We can affect these heat transfer processes by using insulation, materials that are poor conductors of heat. [i]

Very real applications for the concepts on the above key points include the following:

- Analyze your home (house or apartment) identifying all the ways the family attempts to stabilize temperature by adding heat via conduction, convection, radiation, and insulating against heat loss. Analyze incidental/accidental ways by which heat is added and lost. Determine how effective/adequate the attempts to insulate are. List three ways insulation could be made more effective; estimate savings over a 10-year period and 30-year period.

- Record your information on a chart or poster. Share your findings with an adult family member and record his/her response. Share what you have learned about the heat loss and gain to your Learning Club.

- Compare your home to a friend's home. Determine which home is easier to keep stabilized and which is more economical. Record in your journal at least three reasons to explain your conclusion.

Would you be interested in this issue if we told you that you could save from $40,000 to $70,000 over a lifetime plus keep the coastal intertie system from brown-out or going down altogether? And be more comfortable in your home? Such applications satisfy us that we have some concepts worth learning, that we're on the right track. So, now we can develop inquiries that will help students understand and apply these concepts in real-life, in memorable ways.

MAINTAIN A SENSE OF COMMUNITY

As previously discussed, there is a wealth of research confirming the power of a sense of community to promote not only personal and social growth but academic achievement as well. Nurture this sense of community daily; take its temperature every week. The emotional climate in your classroom is either deepening or it is fading; it is either focused on learning or it is sliding into becoming a social club. Make sure your curriculum has a receptive audience when it arrives in the classroom.

See building a learning community in Chapter 9.

CONNECT TO PRIOR EXPERIENCE

Learning is far more efficient and powerful when the brain already has a "post office address" established in the brain where new learning can be processed and added on to. This allows the brain to compare patterns, a rapid way to reach new understandings of a new *being there* location or a new idea.

Make sure you develop inquiries that ask students to compare prior experience to new experiences.

Allow Students to See and Apply In Real-World Contexts

A picture really is worth a thousand words. Don't reply on lecture and reading assignments to explain what you want students to learn—show them and let them apply content in real and meaningful ways. Write inquiries that let them experience firsthand the real-world standards of performance, the joys and the frustrations. Give them windows on life that they can study and master . . . one window at a time.

Offer Opportunities to Apply in the Learners' Area of Interests

Since conceptual key points, and basic skills, apply worldwide, there are many settings in which to study how to use them. Whenever possible, give students choices about the context in which they are studied. If a student is fascinated with cars, let him/her apply geometry to map reading and trip planning. Or let a student captivated by trains use them as a vehicle for studying geography. For a student fascinated by statistics and baseball, let her put the two together. And so forth.

The more conceptual your curriculum, the most opportunity there is to build in student interests.

PROVIDE CHOICES THROUGH THE MULTIPLE INTELLIGENCES

Traditionally, our schools cater to those high in linguistic intelligence. For the majority who are not, who have other strengths when taking in information, solving problems, and producing products, our failure to provide a balanced instructional program is a serious barrier to their success. Allow students to see concepts and skills in action in *being there* settings and apply what they understand in those settings—not on a paper and pencil test. This significantly levels the playing field.

Write enough inquiries to allow all students to operate from their strengths while they strengthen their less developed intelligences. Visit the *being there* location as often as you can, at least in the beginning of study, the middle, and the end.

Invite your students into the process of writing inquiries. From third grade and up, they do a wonderful job. Just teach them the ABCs + D^2 Guidelines (see page 13.9) and give them the a copy of the Inquiry Builder chart (see page 13.10). Then, you choose those you want students to consider.

For examples of inquiries addressing the multiple intelligences, see the DVD *I Can Divide and Conquer*, which depicts 50 third through fifth graders mastering division in a single day, and *Mission Addition*, which shows first graders mastering their addition facts in one week.

IMPROVE THE QUALITY OF YOUR INQUIRIES

To improve the quality of your inquiries, build in more action and greater use of the *being there* location. Use the ABCs + D Guidelines and the Inquiry Builder chart. Consider labeling each inquiry, noting what intelligence(s) is required, so that you know in advance the kinds of choices you are offering.

Most importantly, remember that less is more. Stick with a concept or basic skill until students have developed a mental program for applying it at the *being there* location and through social/political action. Don't move on until students have wired it into long-term memory. If you have chosen powerful concepts that apply around the globe as well as in the backyard, the time will be well spent.

A well-written inquiry can also be used as an assessment tool. See Chapter 19.

ENDNOTES

1   See *Science Continuum of Concepts, K-6* by Karen D. Olsen (Black Diamond: WA: Books for Educators, 2009).

Chapter 18: Integrating & Teaching Basic Skills

MISCONCEPTIONS

There are two misconceptions about including or integrating basic skills into *HET* curriculum. One is that the *HET* model is fine for the content areas, such as science and social studies, but not for teaching the basic skills—reading, writing, and arithmetic. This is not true. The *HET* model does, however, recommend that these basic skills are best taught as a means to an end, not as an end in themselves, and that they therefore be taught with and through engaging subject content.

The second common misconception is that the basic skills are the sole domain of first and second grade teachers and language arts and math specialist. Other teachers are thus exempt from any responsibility to teach or reinforce basic skills. Wrong. It is everyone's responsibility in public education to ensure that our citizens are literate and fully capable of engaging in the significant debates of the day. It is everyone's responsibility to ensure that our citizens can make informed judgments about both policy and funding issues, the environment, and who their leaders should be.

TEACHING THE BASIC SKILLS IS SERIOUS BUSINESS

Although test scores across the nation strongly suggest that we must change how we teach the 3Rs, experience suggests that we shouldn't burn our bridges until we are on solid footing on the other side.[1] Before you abandon the old reading program and leap to a new approach, make sure you are well trained in the new before you stop teaching the old. In other words, make sure that you have rigorous training in the new approaches so students can achieve at least as much as before. This is not a time for leap of faith. The futures of your students hang in the balance. Become fully prepared before you leap.

Thus, our advice about beginning to include or integrate the basic skills with content is to first use the high-interest *being there* and immersion experiences of the *HET* curriculum to *practice* applying basic skills in real-world situation. Then, when you're trained and prepared, begin to teach basic skills through the *HET* curriculum.

This chapter describes five ways to integrate the basic skills in the context of other subjects and real life:

- Full inclusion of all subjects and skills in the "Classroom of the 21st Century" (see pages 18.2-10)

- An integrated day to teach a basic skill—division—in a single day (see pages "A Concept-in-a-Day," 18.11-14.

- How to anchor math in real life (see *'Anchor' Math*, pages 18.14-16.

- A list of 50+ real writing experiences that can be used to practice or teach writing skills (see pages 18.17)

- How to organize a yearlong research project (see page 18.18)

Classroom of the 21st Century*

Skills are taught in the *HET* classroom but they do not drive the curriculum. Content drives the curriculum and skills are taught as they relate to the content, as their usefulness becomes apparent. Before public education took hold in this country, many young boys were apprenticed to skilled workers in a variety of fields. This is a perfect example of the power of relevant context for learning skills. As they learned a trade, boys learned all the skills associated with that trade, and there was never a doubt as to why?

Skills only have meaning within the larger context of their usefulness. When they are useful, they are learned. Children do not learn to speak because adults want them to; children learn to speak because it is useful. This is true of adults as well; we know it from our own experience. I took five years of Spanish while attending public schools, but it wasn't until I moved to an ethnically diverse area that I needed to know Spanish. Suddenly it became useful; there was a reason to learn a second language. Reason and purpose accelerate learning.

Thus, skills are taught in the brain-compatible classroom, but only within the context of the content of the integrated theme. The difference is that skills do not drive the curriculum. Instead, they are placed within a meaningful framework. For example, learning the sound "a" in isolation has no meaning without the larger context of a word. The word "heel" only has meaning within the larger context of a sentence because the "heel" of a shoe is different from the "heel" who broke last night's date. Likewise, learning how to compute the area of rectangles has no meaning without the context of a useful application such as "How many cans of this color paint do we need for this part of the room?" Without the context of the theme, the mastery of the skill becomes meaningless. The

---

* Pages 18.2-10 are taken directly from the ITI/HET book, *Classroom of the 21st Century* by Robert Ellingsen, a companion to the DVD of the same title. The book documents Robert's classroom application of the *HET* model as a framework for integrating all basic skills and content areas. Used with the written permission of the publisher.

question invariably will be asked, "Why?" and "Because I told you so" is not a satisfactory answer.

So how does one make something like computing the area of rectangles useful within a theme? I teach the skill within a meaningful framework. Each year my class performs a Shakespearean play. As part of our preparation, the class designs and paints stage flats of scenery for our performance. Each of the five flats are 4' by 8' and the students need to construct scale drawings of their set design. Students find the area formula a useful tool as they construct their own three-dimensional, miniature sets. Frank Smith states that "learning is incidental."[2] Learning takes place within the course of everyday, real activities. It is within the context of this real activity—building a stage set—that students learn the geometric concept of area.

READING

You learn by doing. A child does not learn to speak by learning about speaking; a child learns to speak by speaking. So, first and foremost, when teaching reading, let students read. And since usefulness is a prime motivator, what the students read must relate to the topic being explored in some meaningful way. Sara Zimet notes that conventional "reading texts emphasize skill, and reading is taught for the sake of the skill itself [whereas] we need to shift our emphasis from 'reading to learn to read' to 'reading about something meaningful while learning to read.' By emphasizing the process to the exclusion of meaningful ideas, we sacrifice the raison d'etre for learning to read."[3]

Children's fantasies and realities are so much more exciting than the boring words and scenes of most basal reading texts. For this reason my method has been to use children's novels to teach reading. As I plan my year theme, I brainstorm possibilities for the reading component. During the PATHFINDERS component of my theme, the novel I selected was *My Side of the Mountain*[4] by Jean George. It is the story of a boy who ventures into the wilderness and learns to survive without the trappings of modern life—a perfect fit with our study of Lewis and Clark and the other pathfinders of history.

All students should have equal access to rich, significant literature. Oftentimes educators separate their poor readers from their good readers. And where are these poor readers placed? Into a basal text that is even more simplistic and contrived than the one from which they were pulled, thereby compounding their difficulty in searching for meaning. **ALL students should have an enriched curriculum.**

All students of all abilities in my classroom read *My Side of the Mountain*, some with ease, some with difficulty, but all with fascination and enjoyment. Each day a selection is assigned. Students make the free choice of whether to read silently, with a partner, or orally in a group. The only requirement is that they meet with the teacher at least once a week for an oral reading check. When students are entrusted with the power to make their own choices, they tend to self-select the appropriate placement given their ability. My poorer readers chose to meet with me daily. But when they came to reading group, they were joined by other students making the choice to read orally, a heterogeneous group full of good reading models. Why do we put poor readers only with poor readers? Who will model correct reading behaviors for them?

Heterogeneous reading groups, in addition to being academically sound, have the extra benefit of building self-esteem. There is no "dumb group." It builds the sense that "we're all in this together" and encourages understanding and acceptance of individual differences.

Granted, there are students who can legitimately benefit from extra help. I do think moving to a more enriched curriculum will eliminate the need for some diagnostic/prescriptive services, but not all. What about those students? They do need extra help but that help should be **offered within the bounds of the curriculum and tied closely to the theme** of their classroom experience. And the single most meaningful place for a child is with the classroom teacher. Pull-out programs should be avoided at all cost. I propose, instead, a **pull-in program** where specialists work with students within a self-contained, safe, supportive classroom. Logistics can be a problem to overcome but we need to do what is best for kids, not what is most convenient for the bureaucracy.

Comprehension. The best way to learn to read is to read. But there is more to reading than correctly decoding words. The Spanish alphabet is phonetically regular and I have learned my sounds well. I can go into many classrooms, pick up a Spanish reader and pronounce word after word with only the slightest Anglo accent. But am I reading? Correctly calling words with no understanding is not reading, and phonics, while a helpful tool, is only that—a tool for correct decoding. Phonics does not concern itself with understanding. How is comprehension addressed in the *HET* classroom? Not with worksheets.

I propose to involve students more actively in the comprehension process. Once more I find Bloom's Taxonomy to be an amazing aid in this respect—simple to use, but powerful. Daily, after reading period, the class comes together for a discussion of the day's selection. A copy of Bloom's Taxonomy is placed on the overhead and the class uses this to discuss the story. This copy is the only comprehension worksheet the students receive during the year. At first, the teacher may use it to ask questions, but, with practice, students become quite adept at generating the questions and at knowing the level at which they are being asked to think. This is metacognition at its best—knowing how to learn and knowing when you are doing it.

Once a week I obtain a written record of their work by having learning teams brainstorm questions, present them to the class, and choose a specified number to answer. Students then write the questions and answers neatly, in complete sentences, and with correct spelling and capitalization—a much more active approach than that elicited by most commercially produced worksheets. How, you might ask, do students complete a neat and grammatically correct paper? First, they are held accountable for it. Expectations are everything. Second, in the absence of worksheets, students have

many more opportunities for real writing; the worksheet doesn't do the writing for them. And finally, no one is left without support. Students have their cooperative learning team to assist them and the teacher, as part of the learning team, is constantly circling the room, encouraging and giving **immediate feedback.**

Reading Skills. Although teaching the skills of reading can sometimes be frustrating and tedious, we must accept that these skills are there to support reading. However, if a skill does not directly aid a student in decoding and comprehending of a passage, then its viability needs to be seriously questioned. Skills for the sake of skills—because it's in the workbook—is a grave mistake. For example, I have clear and painful memories of trying to teach students how to identify accent marks in words with a program that even went so far as to differentiate between primary and secondary accents. The irony, of course, is that the students could already read the words. Nevertheless, they failed in that all-important skill: the fine distinctions in stress. The question remains: "Was the skill useful?" And a further question continues to haunt us: "How many of these workbook skills, which consume such a large part of a student's learning time, are necessary to produce successful and lifelong readers?" Teaching skills is not teaching reading; reading teaches reading—the practice of extracting meaning from print. Skills can be a useful aid, but only within a larger context, and only when they are useful. They are not an end in themselves.

When skills are taught when they make the most sense— when they are needed to understand something—they are learned more easily and are more readily wired into long-term memory. For example, teaching students how to use an index when they begin their research projects and find using an index a helpful way to locate information; time lines are taught as students study historical events; and outlining is taught as students write research papers. Workbooks, which present skills in an arbitrary fashion, are both unnecessary and unproductive.

Parts of Speech. We all teach them. Apparently students never learn them--why else do we ALL teach them? My class is introduced to parts of speech during our GEOGRAPHY component. As students study our state, they find one location for each letter of the alphabet, plot it on a grid, compute miles and kilometers from our location, and use that location in an ABC book. This provides ample opportunity for work in a wide variety of skills: alphabetical order, map skills, and mathematical computations. Students then write their own ABC books, using a pattern established in the *Oregon ABC Book*: "Adrian Albright, the adorable actress, anticipates acclaim in Ashland's amphitheater."[5] Children identify proper nouns for people and places, adjectives to describe the nouns, verbs to state the action, and adverbs to describe the verbs. And all this is done within the context of their own writing, about locations they have studied in their home state. This is the teachable moment, that point in time when students are most in tune with the learning. Why? Because it is useful, it is creative, and it is emotional—there is a healthy dose of fun as students stretch their imaginations.

As I developed the skill component of the reading program, I found that the skills are repeated in a cycle. Of the thirty skills taught in the intermediate level of the Houghton-Mifflin reading series, twenty-one are taught at two grade levels, and an amazing seventeen are taught at all three grade levels. Why, then, must students be placed in ability groups, forever labeled, with no chance for reprieve, when all levels are working on the same skills?

In the *HET* classroom, skills are introduced in the large group, students work on the skill only until they have mastered it, and students continue working on that skill until it is mastered. There is no low group, middle group, or high group. Instead there is a guide word group, a syllabification group, etc. Within these temporary, flexible groups are students with a wide range of achievement levels, all of whom need practice with the same skill. Once again, the "we're all in this together" attitude is developed. Artificial demarcations convenient to the authorities are torn down and students work in heterogeneous settings.

Vocabulary. Vocabulary development is an ongoing process. In a meaningful classroom environment it happens continuously at an informal level, just as children originally learn the spoken language. "All children except the most severely deprived or handicapped

acquire a vocabulary of over 10,000 words during the first four or five years of their lives. At the age of four they are adding to their vocabulary at the rate of twenty new words a day. By seven this rate may have increased to nearly thirty words. . . . By late adolescence the average vocabulary is at least 50,000 words."[6] How is this done? Not by worksheets, not by looking words up in the dictionary, not by formal instruction. It is done because the brain is the organ for learning; it will learn what is useful. The 50,000 words children pick up by adolescence are words they find to be useful.

The key to formal vocabulary instruction is to make it useful and meaningful to the student. The obvious method in an *HET* classroom is to closely tie vocabulary instruction to the theme.

Current events are an integral part of the brain-compatible classroom because the brain-compatible classroom focuses on the real world. Knowledge of current events is essential for the politically active populace of a democracy. The brain-compatible classroom is the classroom that prepares students to take on this role as active citizens.

OREGON TODAY is the name given to the current events strand of our curriculum. Each morning one student is responsible for sharing an article related to the theme. That article then becomes part of our classroom collection folder where all articles are filed and classified. Once a week an article is chosen to be the class' reading selection for the day. Learning teams read, mindmap, and discuss the article. They are also responsible for choosing the one word that interests them most. Learning teams share their word with the class and the class then has five new vocabulary words, one word per learning team. These words are entered into the students' personal dictionaries and onto our Oregon Today vocabulary chart for continual reinforcement. Whenever a student finds that word in any other reading, a star is added to the chart. A very simple approach but, tied to the theme, it becomes meaningful. And the probability that the word is learned and stored increases.

WRITING

A pattern is forming: children learn to speak by speaking and to read by reading. Little wonder, then, that children learn to write by writing. That is not to say that merely writing, with no skill instruction, will produce literate citizens. But we do know that heavy doses of skill instruction, separated from the meaningful context of real writing, do not work. The literate student must write every day. And that writing must have purpose and an audience.

The journal approach to daily writing is an exceptional example of real writing assignments. Students keep a notebook full of their own musing: dreams, concerns, and questions, a daily record of their lives. This is real writing in its truest sense because it is student-centered and student-directed. There are no contrived topics or arbitrary limits on length. Writing is useful because it becomes a vehicle by which children connect with the outside world, taking what is within and giving it form and substance.

I have had much success with this method, yet I know that not all teachers have. When I've compared notes with my colleagues for whom it hasn't worked, I find one noticeable difference: I write back to the author—not just a few sprinklings of "great" or "good point," but written feedback of significant length and meaning. If a child writes to me about his/her pets, I write about my pets. If a child writes about favorite foods, I write about mine. The journal becomes a dialogue between us; it establishes rapport. Finally, it provides a meaningful context within which to place skill instruction.

I recommend several different approaches to writing. Journals are but one component of the writing program, writing folders are another. Journals are daily jottings. The writing folder is for long-term story development and is worked on every day during WRITERS' WORKSHOP, a time when students learn the writing process: pre-writing, rough draft, revision, editing, and publishing. Children use the skills developed during writers' workshop to develop their own creative writing. Works in progress are filed in the writing folder until that time the student determines the piece

is ready for publication. Occasionally specific assignments are given if they fit the theme, but more often students are engaged in constructing stories from their own imaginations. Many states have ongoing summer institutes where teachers learn the writing process. The key is that the teacher also becomes a writer and models for the class his own ongoing work. My students assisted me in writing my story "Reggie at the Bat." The students, in a sense, become apprenticed to the teacher as author.

Teaching Writing Skills

The daily journal and the writing folder provide the structure for direct instruction of skills. They are the blueprint. Once they are in place, the skills, which are the building materials, can be used to construct literacy. But where would they be placed with no blueprint as a guide? Teaching skills such as capitalization and noun/verb agreement, apart from any meaningful writing, is like giving the carpenter the 2' x 4's and asking him/her to build a house without a plan. The product would be a haphazard, rickety construction, destined to come tumbling down and ill-fitting the needs of its inhabitants.

Once the framework of real writing is in place, skill instruction can proceed. A variety of methods can be used. Basal English series offer pages of practice, and there is nothing wrong with their occasional use as need dictates. But why go through the book cover to cover? Why let the textbook publisher dictate the curriculum when it is the classroom teacher who is the educational expert? It is the teacher who, having student writing in hand, can diagnose and prescribe skill instruction appropriate to the needs of each particular group of writers.

If, in their writing, students are writing conversations, and writing them incorrectly, then that is the teachable moment—the appropriate time to teach the correct use of quotation marks. If certain words are consistently misspelled, then they become a part of that student's spelling list. If letters are continually formed illegibly, then handwriting instruction is called for.

The theme itself may provide opportune times to address particular skills. During our Shakespeare unit, the class play is *A Midsummer Night's Dream.* This is the perfect opportunity to introduce apostrophes. The play's title becomes a meaningful "hook" on which to attach the skill instruction.

To ensure that skill instruction proceeds at a systematic pace I have a daily editing practice modeled after the DAILY ORAL LANGUAGE series (D.O.L.). Admittedly, the name is a bit misleading. A more accurate title might be DAILY WRITTEN LANGUAGE, as the editing task is with paper and pencil. The program's title stems from the fact that once the written editing assignment is complete, it is processed orally.

A short selection, full of errors, is placed on the board most mornings when students enter the classroom. They know from the posted daily agenda that their first task is to edit this selection. Once again, cooperation is encouraged. Later in the morning the class meets together and orally processes the passage, finally recopying a fully corrected final version. This happens over time until the majority of the class has mastered the skill and can independently write a perfect copy the first time. New writing skills are then introduced, taken from common errors occurring in journals and writing folders. Those students who still have not mastered the original skill continue to meet with me during Writers' Workshop.

MATH

For five years I had avoided integrating mathematics. I was tied to the text, my own math anxiety holding me back. Finally, I had no choice if I wanted a fully integrated classroom—math was the only subject still on the outside. What I found, to my amazement, was that math is the simplest of all skill areas to integrate. All that is needed is statistics, real-life numbers to work with. How lucky! Statistics are everywhere!

Cobblestone magazine is a history magazine for young people. In September, 1980, the entire issue was devoted to Lewis and Clark.

It became our "basal text" for the week, the base of study for all subjects, including math. It is a rich source of statistics about the Lewis and Clark expedition. Those below are only a small sampling of the statistics available, providing many opportunities for real world "story problems." But, given the full immersion of the students into reliving the Lewis and Clark expedition, they become more than mere "story problems"; they become real-life applications.

Available Statistics:

- Lewis and Clark started their journey up the Missouri River on May 14, 1804.

- The entire central basin of North America was purchased from the French for four cents an acre, or a total of $15,000,000.

- A Scotsman named Alexander Mackenzie had published an account of the same region in 1793.

- The Great Falls were a series of five large waterfalls that stretched over 15 miles on the Missouri River.

- From beginning to end, the walk over the Rocky Mountains took three-and-a-half months.

- On their return trip, Lewis and Clark separated for six weeks to explore different regions.

- Lewis and Clark returned to St. Louis on September 23, 1806.

Problems to Be Solved Based on the Available Statistics:

- How many years ago did Lewis and Clark begin exploring the Louisiana Purchase?

- How many acres of land did Thomas Jefferson purchase from France?

- Approximately how many miles were between each of the Great Falls of the Missouri River?

- Assuming that all months are thirty days long, how many days did it take Lewis and Clark to cross the Rocky Mountains?

- Using your previous answer, how many weeks did it take Lewis and Clark to cross the Rocky Mountains?

- How many days were Lewis and Clark separated during their trip?

- 30 days have September, April, June, and November. All the rest have 31, excepting February, which has 28. Knowing this, what was the total number of days of the Lewis and Clark expedition?

This last problem is the most difficult of all. Very few of my fourth graders answered it correctly at first. But I've never seen such excitement, motivation, and problem-solving strategies as when students attempt it.

Problems such as these form the core of THEME MATH, a term I use with students to distinguish it from other components of the math program. Theme math uses **real-world** problems closely tied to the content. Students attack these problems with more motivation than the artificial problems of basal series. The interest is built in; the students have some curiosity to find out more about whom and what they have been studying.

The amount of thinking involved is awesome when compared to a basal text. Students need to identify the problem, find the data necessary to solve the problem, identify the operation needed to solve the problem, and then finally compute the answer. What's more, the statistics are not conveniently listed for them as they are for you here. Students search for them within the context of the historical narrative.

Theme math is a prime motivator for students to learn mathematical skills. Suddenly there is a reason for memorizing those basic facts, to KNOW—**to really know** everything about the Lewis and Clark expedition. In addition, theme math is an excellent way to build conceptual understanding of the four operations (addition,

subtraction, multiplication, and division). Students develop a sense of what addition looks like, how it "feels" and sounds compared to the other operations. *And all the while they are working in the realm of the real world, with real numbers—***APPLICATION!**

It is essential that the teacher understand the purpose of theme math. It is to build *conceptual understanding*, not to drill on memorization of facts and computations. Students who have not memorized their multiplication facts are still capable of understanding the concept of multiplication. *Memorization of facts should not be a prerequisite to opportunities for applying concepts.* If anything, building the concepts should come first, giving the student the meaningful framework before the individual skill bits are put into place.

Math Skills. Mathematical computation is an essential life skill. Theme math does not replace that. But it does enhance computation by giving it meaning and purpose. Computation is still addressed. In fact, within this meaningful context of the theme, computation is learned much more readily.

DAILY ORAL MATH (D.O.M.) is one way to reinforce math skills. Similar to daily oral language (the daily drill in written language), it is a short and sweet math review. Alternating with D.O.L., it may consist of four problems reviewing the four operations, or it may be other math skills more closely aligned with the day's thematic activities. Skills such as a review of the formula for computing area during our Shakespearean set design, or using a scale of miles to compute distance during our GEOGRAPHY component can be reinforced during D.O.M. The daily agenda points out that this is one of the first tasks to be completed. Later in the day, student volunteers solve the problems for the class, modeling correct form and computation.

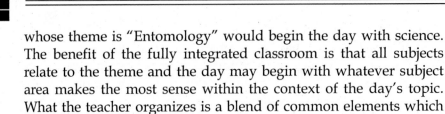

DAY IN THE LIFE OF

So how does it all come together? How does the teacher orchestrate all the various elements of a brain-compatible classroom? The *HET* model is truly unique in that it draws from a wide variety of excellent approaches and sources and synthesizes them into a coherent, seamless whole. Language experience is an excellent approach to teaching reading, but what about math? The university sponsored writing projects teach writing in a brain-compatible way, but what about social studies? Math Their Way is an experiential and hands-on approach to mathematics instruction, but what about science? The *HET* approach seeks to break down these artificial walls between curricular areas, take the best from each, and infuse brain-compatible instruction into all subjects for a truly integrated whole. And it does so with a profound respect for the professional expertise of the classroom teacher.

Flexibility is the key word in planning a fully integrated day, week, month, or year. School schedules are arbitrary demarcations of time and **are highly brain-antagonistic.** Lessons should not be forced into the artificial constraints of a set time period; **the content should determine the schedule.** The self-contained classroom offers the greatest opportunity for fully integrating subject areas.

I hesitate to share specifics of a daily schedule because the model will find a unique implementation in every classroom. **The power of the model lies in its adaptability to individual teaching styles.** The graphic on this page is my plan for the week. Such a plan could take many forms. This picture of a typical day in the life of a brain-compatible classroom starts a schedule for flexible frameworks to be altered as content dictates. My 9:00 A.M. starting time and a 3:30 P.M. closing time made it possible for me to think of the instructional day as being divided into four blocks: two morning periods and two afternoon periods.

I recommend that you begin the day with the theme. It provides students with a focal point for the day's activities. In a classroom not yet fully integrated, this would mean beginning the day with the content area on which the theme is based, e.g., a classroom whose theme is "Entomology" would begin the day with science. The benefit of the fully integrated classroom is that all subjects relate to the theme and the day may begin with whatever subject area makes the most sense within the context of the day's topic. What the teacher organizes is a blend of common elements which maintain a sense of stability and comfort for students, intermixed with a daily flow of ever-changing events and topics—a miniature slice of real life. Here is an example:

Generally, I begin my day[7] with a language arts block. When students enter the classroom, they are greeted by me personally, a daily agenda detailing exactly what will occur that day, and background music playing softly to enhance thinking. The rule is quiet study as students begin their tasks: DAILY ORAL LANGUAGE and/or DAILY ORAL MATH to review skills, then on to silent and/or oral reading of the day's selection, followed by independent

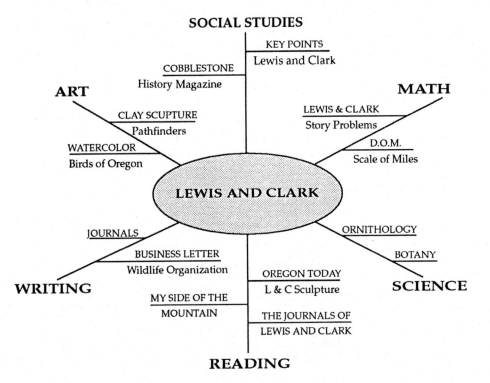

work with ongoing INQUIRY projects. At some point I bring the class together for stretching, aerobics, and relaxation—important techniques which help focus students' bodies and minds on the topic for the day. This is followed by a discussion of the day's reading based on Bloom's Taxonomy and a large group discussion and correction of the skills review. Finally, during OREGON TODAY, the current events article for the day is shared.

The second morning block is reserved for science and social studies. This is when students receive and work with the key points of instruction. Lecture, reading, discussion, films, experiments, and inquiries all receive equal emphasis as conceptual understanding of the major thematic components is built. Each day sees a different focus. Perhaps a lecture and reading on the key points early in the week, moving toward more interactive pursuits by the end of the week, with possible closure of the week, topic, or entire component by Friday.

The first afternoon block is reserved for mathematics. This is equally divided between THEME MATH for concept building and MATH GROUPS for computation practice. Oftentimes the week begins and ends with THEME MATH to provide a frame within which the rest of math instruction is placed.

The final afternoon block returns to language arts. A skill is introduced or reinforced with the large group. This is followed by a large group WRITERS' WORKSHOP where works in progress are shared and elements of good writing are discussed. Students then move on to independent writing time, engaging in real writing activities such as JOURNAL, letters, and creative writing of their own choice. During this independent time the teacher is free to confer with individuals and/or conduct SKILLSHOPS, the small, temporary, and flexible skill groups.

What about other subject areas such as art, music, and computers? They all find a place in the schedule as appropriate. Sketching and watercolor techniques are taught when the day's reading concerns that subject, e.g., Sam's sketching of his falcon. Students work with clay after reading and discussing a newspaper

article about a local sculptor and his Lewis and Clark statues. Pioneer songs and instruments are used to prepare for the class' Oregon Trail adventure. Computers are used during the writing process as students edit and publish their work. Computers are also used when software exists that enhances understanding of the topic, such as the Oregon Trail or Pathfinders simulation games. Everything fits. It's just a new fit. In the traditional classroom, content is made to fit the schedule; in the *HET* classroom, **the schedule is made to fit the content.**

A self-contained, heterogeneous classroom is a superior design for the *HET* classroom. There are fewer interruptions to fragment the day, the sense of belonging is more fully developed, and students aren't segregated according to ability. Because the mathematical problems are selected mostly with an eye to their meaningfulness, assignments and group collaboration guidelines are set up to ensure that all students, of varying degrees of ability, experience success. Problems are solved within the learning team and calculators are allowed.

ORCHESTRATING A CONCEPT-IN-A-DAY: LONG DIVISION*

The teaching of long division drags on for years. The division facts are introduced in the third grade, the algorithm is introduced in the fourth grade, and again in the fifth and sixth grades. Year after year, the same instructional pattern, even into the basic math courses in junior and senior high—the teacher does a problem on the board, the class does a number of "practice" problems at their desks, and then students are responsible for completing ten to twenty problems for homework.

While attending a week-long Susan Kovalik Model Teaching Program, Martha Kaufeldt was challenged to address this problem by orchestrating the learning environment and curriculum in such a way that it would be possible to INTRODUCE and have the students achieve MASTERY of the CONCEPT AND COMPUTATION OF LONG DIVISION **IN A SINGLE DAY!**

Martha's work pioneered the notion of teaching a major concept in a single day—Effective First Teaching at its best. Since her Long Division Day in 1986, thousands of students across the country have been able to master division in a single day using this approach. Likewise, multiplication in a week for third graders, and addition in three days for first graders.

Here is Martha's story.

---

* The description of orchestrating a concept in a day, pages 20.11-20.14, is a summary of Martha Kaufeldt's experience as described in her book *I Can Divide and Conquer: A Concept in a Day!*, a companion to the DVD of the same title. Used with the written permission of the publisher.

For the first three months of school, my thirty-three fourth and fifth grade students worked on sharpening their accuracy in addition, subtraction, and multiplication. Division facts were memorized by rote. Seventeen other fifth and sixth grade students in our school were recommended by their teachers as students who had mastered the skills of multiplication but had failed to master division.

The day before Division Day all fifty students met. I led them verbally through some relaxation techniques and also asked them to see their own success in learning long division. They all took a pretest in division and were given encouraging words about what would happen the next day.

Overview of the Day's Activities

Theme for the day: I CAN DIVIDE AND CONQUER!

In planning the day, I knew I had to address several important areas: how to ensure positive performance, the format for each activity station, and methods of orchestrating learning.

Elements Used to Program Positive Performance

- Students saw their success

- Each student received a "goodie" box with pencil, slate, and name tag

- Students were divided into groups of five. Group building activities included adopting a famous mathematician who would serve as the group mascot for the day

- Incentives were given at every other station

- Mini-stickers were given to anyone who ASKED FOR HELP

- Direct instruction was limited to 11-16 minutes per hour

- Group work was provided at each station (45 minutes)

- Relaxation periods were provided throughout the day

- Lunch was provided by parents. Pizza was divided into different numbers of slices

- Each student earned an "I CAN DIVIDE AND CONQUER" badge and a certificate at the end of the day

- Warm, loving, enthusiastic adult leaders were always available

Format at Each Station

To simplify training of volunteers and to ensure students had the opportunity to think through each activity, the format for each station was the same: tell, show, solve, and check. Each process is written as a direction to the adult responsible for a station.

Tell

- Read problem aloud—(every student)

- Discuss what the problem is asking or describing. Have students restate in own words

- Point out (ask students to identify) DIVIDEND and DIVISOR

- Ask students to close eyes while you help them visualize the problem. Use a soothing voice while using lots of descriptive words. Ask students to see themselves in the picture, doing the sorting or dividing

- Draw students' attention to manipulatives they will be using, e.g., beads, beans, etc. Point out that they are substitutes for the real thing

Show

Have students work out the problem with the manipulatives. If possible, each student should have his/her own set of manipulatives. If not, work it out cooperatively. Have students:

- Repeat the problem two or more times if necessary until they can confidently show the problem

- Identify quotient and remainders, if any (have a special place for the "remainder" to be placed)

Solve

As each student solves a problem, have them:

- Demonstrate how a problem is written as a number sentence

- Identify terms

- Begin a step-by-step approach to the algorithm.—divide, multiply, subtract, bring down—and frequently relate their computation to what has been done with manipulatives

- Have students work out problem on graph paper for accuracy

- Ask each to turn to his/her partner and ask the partner to explain the problem in "MATH SPEAK"

Check

- Demonstrate how to check by multiplying and adding remainder

- If there is time, make variations of the problem and ask students to solve

- Write a comment in each student passport if you feel student has mastered that problem

- If the student needs more help, continue working, or ask the student to come back at free-choice time, or direct student to a roving helper

- Repeat center to next group. Give incentive rewards to students in second center

Methods of Orchestrating Learning

Our Divide and Conquer Day was just that, a single day. I needed to vary the ways to help students learn. Strategies included:

- Using the Library Media Center with assistance from the Media Specialist

- Providing 26 different learning stations, each with concrete examples to illustrate concepts

- Providing choices at those stations students were allowed to choose among

- Adhering to two management standards for the day: No Put-Downs and Active Listening

- Providing a snack station (items such as graham crackers and juice that are set up by parents)

- Having students work through recesses and taking breaks as needed

- Organizing students into groups of five

- Recruiting and training at least 15 adults to help: parents, aides, student teachers, and community volunteers

- Soliciting additional money—mini-grants and parent donations

Maximizing Input to the Brain

Each segment of the day was designed to maximize input to the brain. Every activity and presentation appealed to a variety of intelligences. In addition, students were allowed to make selections that would best assist them.

The problem to be solved was presented on the bulletin board and in the student handbook. Students used manipulatives to SEE the problem.

Every station leader explained each problem. Students in turn explained the problem using Math Speak. A hand-jive was developed for the mathematical algorithm of division—first you divide, then multiple, subtract, and bring it (the remainder) down.

Each of the 26 stations used different sets of manipulatives. Most were common classroom items as well as shells, buttons, small cars, and dominoes.

Kinesthetic activities included Division P.E., Division Drama, Division Art, Division Music, and a hand jive—a set of hand motions representing the algorithm of division: divide (hand clap), multiply (bring your hands together in the form of an X and tap them twice), subtract (with lower arms pointing upward and hands at shoulder height, bend fingers at knuckle keeping fingers flat and parallel to the floor; rotate wrists outward in flipping motion), bring it (the remainder) down (form a fist and pull downward).

Choices

Choices for students included art, music or drama stations, flexible breaks when needed, and more help on a one-to-one basis. Feeling that they were in control of their learning truly empowered students to feel that they "conquered division."

OUTCOMES

At the end of the *seven hour day* (yes, they came early and stayed late!), students received a certificate and a badge.

The post-test was given the following day. Some students improved as much as 150 percent. All mastered single digit division. Post-tests given three months later showed continued improvement and retention. Students have shared with me that they felt this was one of the most important days in their lives!

To see how brain research can be used to teach a single concept and how to apply it to mastery—and to long-term memory—see Martha's video and book of the same name: *I Can Divide and Conquer*. Available through Books for Educators.

"ANCHOR" MATH

Not only did Leslie Hart coin the term "brain-compatible," he has also given us ways to "anchor" math to real-life experiences of children. His book, *Anchor Math: An Informal Book for All Who Teach Elementary Math and Want to Greatly Increase Student Achievement,* is a treasure trove of wonderfully simple but instantly doable ways of making numbers and mathematics real to students.

Hart illustrates how to teach math in ways that create "mental programs." For a starting point, Hart says that it may be helpful, or at least intriguing, to think of math languages in three clusters.

Three Levels of Math Language

Practical Math. "Practical" math help us deal with the mostly concrete world of here and now, including all of our daily transactions, ordering, physical work, current data, etc. Examples: spent $144.75 for clothes, poured 12 cubic yards of concrete, produced 12,000 widgets, have 322 patients in the hospital.

Projective Math. "Projective" math helps us deal with what should, or could, or might happen. You plan out a trip, or work out estimates for a new business, or figure out how fast a rocket will likely be traveling within four minutes after launch, or how many cases of measles could occur within the next two years.

Investigative Math. "Investigative" math helps us dig out significant concepts by using mathematical techniques, e.g., trends and relationships, limits, and interactions. We might analyze election results to see the role played by racial concerns or gain some insight into an intricate chemical reaction. Included would be "game" math, essentially playing with numbers or mathematical elements for no immediate, "real" purpose.

---

* Pages 18.14-18 of this chapter are excerpted from *Anchor Math: An Informal Book for All Who Teach Elementary Math and Want to Greatly Increase Student Achievement* written by Leslie Hart and published by Books for Educators .Used with the written permission of the publisher.

Our purpose, or need, would determine which kind of math we do. Outside of classrooms, nobody does math without some purpose in mind. (That should make us think about some things we do in classrooms.)

THE CONCEPT OF "n-NESS"

Let us assume that a particular student is able to

– Name the digit . . . "five"

– Write the digit

– Count off objects to match the digit

It still may be true that the student does not have the sense of that number, a sense that we can call "five-ness." This sense of number constitutes one of the main foundational elements of grasping math and being able to do or interpret math with ease and confidence. Some people like to say that the student "feels" the number—which is all right if you like that expression.

Another way to put it is to say that the student has acquired a sense of "shape" for that number and a direct approach, not a "counting" approach.

For instance, if the student hears "five" and then counts one-two-three-four-five, that is a slow and cumbersome way, as compared with directly feeling "five-ness."

This sense of "n-ness" can readily be encouraged and developed by the teacher . . . and, as we shall see, it can be applied not only to the digits but to many numbers as they are "anchored." (The term "anchor" will be explained soon.)

Suppose we ask a 10-year-old student: "What is the difference between numbers 23 and 24?" One student may reply, "24 is one more than 23." That is correct but not the reply we are seeking.

Another student says, "Oh, they are very different! 23 is a stiff, awkward number while 24 is wonderful—it can be the hours in a day, or two dozen, or 4 x 6, or 3 x 8. . . . I can do all sorts of things with it." We can exult, "Ah, this student has really learned the "anchor" math way; this student feels the number." Numbers have shapes and characters and personalities, much as do people. Math becomes much more interesting and easier to do when "the numbers come alive!"

INTRODUCING "FLEXING"

We can use the problems of scanty three-ness to illustrate a simple technique for exploring numbers and patterns to which I'll attach the name "flexing." If you don't care for that term for this activity, use another or create your own. The idea is simple: *push the number, or pattern, or quantity around* in all the ways you can think of.

To flex 3, for example, you pose the question to students: how many ways can you arrange 3 markers? (The markers can be plastic chips, coins, beans, bottle caps or pebbles, or marks on paper or chalkboard. It's a good idea to vary the markers so that the patterns become attached to the number, not to the markers.)

On this page are some of the arrangements possible for 3. For higher numbers, the variations increase.

Flexing has several purposes that enhance math learning. To begin with, of course, experience with three-ness can be greatly expanded. Of major general importance is encouraging students to *explore* on their own and as a member of a little team and at times and in ways hinted at or prompted by the teacher. Most of the time there should be no rules—anything goes. (For example, the coun-

ters can be stacked up; who said no?) At other times restraints can be imposed for the moment: the markers must be put in one dimension (or two or three), or must stay within a 2-inch square or other figure given (or must touch), and so on.

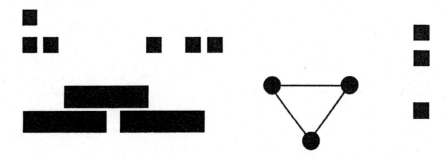

Flex . . . and find patterns.

Such exploration contrasts with sitting meekly in place and doing only what one is told. Youngsters have a strong, genetic drive to *explore*—as we can plainly see by watching any normal toddler. Allowed to explore, learners find math far more interesting, even absorbing. But we can go beyond that benefit, major as it is. In the conventional math schoolroom, numbers push children around. Many become a little gun-shy as they find the numbers given to them to deal with often overpower or intimidate them. In addition, they probably tremble before the "right answer," which must be obtained on penalty of some kind of disapproval or low mark. What a difference when we begin early on to show students that *they* can push numbers! And that, in many instances in math, there is no simple, right, carved-in-stone answer, or at least none that can be found without substantial investigation. When we set students free and "empower" them, they become almost different people. Further, they begin building understanding—from experience—of when a simple calculated answer will do and when it will not. That usually makes them much better at calculating when it is required because they acquire a feeling of confidence that lets their brains work at their best.

One more benefit may be discerned. Flexing gives room for a *creative* approach, as strict calculating does not. So, some students, who might otherwise be considered on the "dumb" side, suddenly show unexpected ability. This can help teachers abstain from judgments about students which are too quick and easy—and perhaps from making unneeded judgments at all.

Get into the act yourself. Can you suggest any flexes of 3 not shown here? Here's a sample of a hint: overlap.

Why do we all need to learn arithmetic? There's a good solid answer to that question: so that we can *measure*. That's what this math is for—measuring. We need to measure how much things cost, how much they weigh, how far away or big something is, how long a trip takes, how many watts a light bulb draws, where on the dial a favorite radio station will come in, our body temperature and much, much more.

REAL WRITING EXPERIENCES

Too many traditional writing assignments lack meaning and purpose—a topic of little interest to students and no real audience (except the teacher's and his/her grade book). Again, using brain research as home plate, no meaning, no engagement. The second most disliked assignment, following closely on the heels of fear of speaking before one's peers, is writing. And yet, the skill of expressing oneself in written form in a variety of circumstances is very important, allowing us to influence people and events.

How do we turn the tide? Often the writing experiences assigned to students are either creative writing or essays. In between these extremes are at least fifty real experiences that we may use in our lifetime.

Real-Life Writing Products

For writing to be meaningful and engaging, rather than contrived and boring, there must be a real purpose and a real audience. The list of writing products below illustrate the possibilities for meaningful writing assignments.

Letters to:
 relative
 friend
 pen pal
 editor of a paper
 association
 service club
 congratulate

 farewell
 complaint
 resignation
Letters of:
 sympathy
 recommendation
 protest
 regret
 apology
 independence
 civil rights
 peace

Speech:
 sales pitch
 sermon
 state of the nation address
 inauguration
 judicial decision
 nomination for office
 political campaign

Newspaper article for:
 front page story
 editorial
 advertisement
 obituary
 movie review
 sports story
 advice column

How-to manuals:
 operate a specific piece of equipment (bicycle, skateboard, Nintendo, DVD)
 survival (wilderness, on the subway, when visiting a foreign country)
 airline safety instructions

Writing for an audience:
 monologue
 dialogue
 poetry
 eulogy
 interview
 (ten questions to ask a famous person)
 recipe
 menu
 dictionary
 encyclopedia entry

*Writing for social/political
action to:*
    president of the U.S.
    federal or state legislative
    representative
    governor
    mayor
    city council
    school board

Special issues such as:
    declaration of war
    declaration of
        independence
    civil rights
    environmental protection

Advertisement for:
    school lunch program
    yearbook
    magazine
    newspaper
    television
    books or movies

Invitation to:
    party (be specific)
    dinner
    weekend outing
    conference (boy scout,
                girl scout,
                4-H, etc.)
    join an organization

The Personal Writing Binder

Encourage each student to have a writing binder with the student's own best examples of how to write, address, and respond to a variety of situations. In addition to the final product, all drafts preceding the final copy are included; these edited pages are good reminders of WHY something is done and the writing/editing skills he/she has developed.

This binder can be added to year by year so that a worthwhile reference will always be at your students' fingertips.

THE YEARLONG RESEARCH PROJECT

Research is the ability to gather, analyze, organize, and eventually synthesize information about a topic. In the *HET* classroom, we invite students of all ages to keep a yearlong collection binder filled with data about a topic of their choosing from within the yearlong theme. Their challenge: to become an expert on that topic.

By the end of the second week of school, all students select a topic for their yearlong research project. Two students may choose the same topic. What's important is that each student has content that fires their interest.

To help facilitate information gathering, ask parents to send their old magazines and newspapers to class. Provide at least 45 minutes a week for students to seek, read, and organize information. In addition, have at least 20 different addresses where students can write for information, such as those in the yellow pages of your phone book, the *Encyclopedia of Associations* at your public library, and so forth).

As they collect information, have the students:

• Highlight important points

• Create a mindmap of three new facts learned from each article

• Begin to organize the information into categories, such as letters sent and received, pictures (of projects, locations, people visited), audio or video interviews, and so forth. Eventually they will organize the information into a document with a table of contents, an index, a summation or executive summary of what was learned, and explanation of the most important content behind the summary.

• Share with a younger buddy every two weeks what they are learning

• By the end of the year, identify and invite to class their favorite resource person

• As a culminating activity, present the highlights of their research through a 10-minute multimedia presentation

The most important lessons from the yearlong research project are:

- Developing an awareness of what it means to truly know something about a topic, to become expert at it ("to know when you know and know when you don't know")

- Spawning a hobby or vocation and paving the way for lifelong interests

- Learning the necessary research skills to find, collect, organize, and synthesize information

ENDNOTES

1 During a mammoth school improvement effort in California during the mid and late 1970s, called Early Childhood Education (ECE), the State Department of Education was pulled up short with a devastating discovery, one borne out by reform programs around the country. Whenever significant change is asked of teachers, the test scores of one-fourth of the teachers—or one-fourth of the schools—experience a drop in test scores for the first year or two before moving back upward and eventually surpassing the original benchmarks. This back sliding occurred primarily when teachers were ill-prepared to succeed with the new tools and methods but had been coaxed into prematurely leaving the old behind.

2 Frank Smith, *Insult to Intelligence: The Bureaucratic Invasion of Our Classrooms* (New York: Arbor House, 1986).

3 Sara Goodman Zimet, *What Children Read in School* (New York: Grune and Stratton, 1976).

4 Jean Craighead George, *My Side of the Mountain* (New York: Penguin USA, 2000).

5 Susan Torrence and Leslie Polansky, *Oregon ABC Book* (T.P. Publications, 1983).

6 Smith.

7 This structure for organizing the day was developed by Robert Ellingsen, over a five-year period. It is offered here as a jumping-off point, not a model. Structure for the day should ensure that the basic skills are included on a daily basis but should also flow with the content and encourage full integration.

Chapter 19: Assessment & Effective First Teaching

It should be no surprise that the Effective First Teaching (EFT) approach to teaching science requires robust assessment—formative assessment as well as summative assessment. Of the two, by far the most important arsenal of tools must reside in formative assessment.

Assessment for EFT has but one goal: Improving teacher effectiveness and student progress in the moment—as a lesson unfolds, not after the fact. The basis of accountability for student progress and teacher effectiveness should be viewed as a by-product of the processes and tools used to meet that goal.[1]

ASSESSMENT AND THE TWO-STEP LEARNING PROCESS

Effective First Teaching (EFT) demands that assessment be done primarily as an extension of instruction along each phase of the two-step learning process—on the fly, as the lesson progresses—so that adjustments can be made immediately, either to extend practice time or to cycle back for reteaching.

At any moment during a lesson, a teacher must be able to ask—and answer—two questions:

- "Where in the Two-Step Learning process is this student?"

- "Are there clues in his/her performance that will help me ensure that the student learns the first time?"

The diagram below illustrates the relationship of assessment to the new, brain-based definition of learning discussed in Chapters 4 and 5.

THE TWO-STEP LEARNING PROCESS			
Detecting/ identifying the pattern	Understanding the pattern	Applying what is understood w/support	Applying what is understood almost automatically/ wired into long-term memory

FORMATIVE ASSESSMENT *SUMMATIVE* ASSESSMENT

BUILT-IN ASSESSMENT TOOLS

Fortunately, curriculum developed for the *HET* model contains the assessment tools needed for both formative and summative assessment:

- What we want students to understand is clearly stated in the key points—concepts, significant knowledge, and skills.

- What we want students to do with what they understand is specifically described in the inquiries.

The Role of Key Points in Assessment

Before investing time and effort to assess what students are learning, make sure that what you're asking students to learn is worth measuring. Authentic assessment of unauthentic curriculum is simply not possible.

To ensure that the time spent on teaching and assessing is well-spent, review Chapter 13 and 16 carefully. Rate each of your key points against the rubrics provided. Use the GUTS criteria for your conceptual key points and the STUDENTS criteria for significant knowledge and skill key points. Revise all key points that don't measure up. The better your key points, the easier the tasks of teaching and formative assessment and the more useful the results in terms of guiding your ongoing lesson planning and selection of instructional strategies.

Key points are a source of accountability for multiple audiences.

- For the classroom teacher, they are the foundation for lesson planning and both formative and summative assessment.

- For students, they clarify expectations, stating exactly what students are to learn and thus allowing them to then put themselves in the driver's seat of their own learning. With a clear sense of what they are to learn—and how it is to be applied (as described in the inquiries)—students can begin to find their own ways to teach themselves and each other.

- For parents, they provide a clear understanding of the content being taught as well as the focus for teacher-parent conferences (and allow the student to be an active participant in such discussions).

- For colleagues, they communicate exactly what you will be teaching and thus how your curriculum fits with your grade level and preceding and subsequent grade levels.

- For administrators, they state the real curriculum of the school (as compared to the over-filled wish statements of textbooks and many state standards); in doing so, they make it possible to determine if the real curriculum aligns with state/district standards. They also provide a clear focus for curriculum leadership and assessment.

Clearly, good key points are multi-purpose and worth the time and effort to make them as effective as possible.

The Role of Inquiries in Assessment

Inquiries call forth the kinds of observable actions by students that allow a teacher, as well as the student, to determine whether progress through the Two-Step Learning Process is occurring and, if not, where the student is stuck. And, because inquiries are based in real-world applications, they contain within them the standards of performance expected of the real world—the workplace of the being there location in which the curriculum is based.

These norms, what we call real-life rubrics, are inherent in being there-based inquiries and provide the benchmarks for norm-referenced, sometimes called criterion-referenced assessments. This is true for both formative and summative assessment. They take the guess work out of making judgments about whether learning is progressing through the Two-Step Learning process.

In addition, because inquiries call for skills needed to apply the concepts of key points, they are also useful curriculum niches for skills outlined in standards and benchmarks.

USING INQUIRIES FOR FORMATIVE AND SUMMATIVE ASSESSMENT

Any inquiry that meets the ABC + D2 rules for writing an inquiry is a good candidate for formative assessment.

THE ABC + D2 RULES FOR WRITING INQUIRIES

- **A**lways start with the action in mind. What are students to do? How can they practice applying what they understand to real-world situations?

- **B**e specific with your directions so that students can see the outcome or finished product in their mind's eye. What is the inquiry asking them to do?

- **C**onnect to the key point. Will doing this inquiry help students both understand and be able to apply the concept, significant knowledge, or skill described in the key point?

- Require **d**eep thinking and real-world applications.

- **D**on't stop writing until you have enough inquiries for each key point to take students through mastery to long-term memory. Ensure that the set of inquiries for each key point utilizes all of the multiple intelligences.

Sharpening the Focus

If you find yourself still in doubt about whether a students has completed a stage in the Two-Step Learning Process, there are two remedies: clarify the expected performance and/or add the 3Cs of assessment.

Clarify the Expected Performance. Uncertainty when judging whether or not a student is progressing through the Two-Step Learning process is usually the result of unclear expectations or standards of performance. Whenever possible, attach the expectation to

a what an employee or visitor to the being there location must know and be able to do. Use the interview process with the on-site resource person to help clarify those standards. Also make them the subject of questions asked of the classroom resource person.

Classroom rubrics[2] are another useful assessment tool because they specifically describe the attributes of a successful product or action. For example, assessing essays or short stories, assessing the planning process for carrying out a Celebration of Learning. Such rubrics provide guidance to students before they begin their task and they make teacher judgments less subjective.

> ## The 3Cs of Assessment
>
> - *Correct—conforming to fact or truth; free from error; accurate*
> - *Complete—having all parts or elements*
> - *Comprehensive—of large scope; inclusive; extensive mental range or grasp, often reflective of multiple points of view*

However, the best rubrics are those unique to the content of the task and built into the task itself so that feedback for students occurs throughout performance of the task when it is most needed—and with only occasional involvement by the teacher. Obvious examples are learning to ride a bike or 19.6-19.7. More challenging are learning to write an effective business letter (the mayor is persuaded to take action as a result of the letter you wrote), speak effectively (you win the election for student body president/mayor) or computing various profit margins for the class business (you strike a good balance between customer perception of value and the profit needed to keep in business).

Rule of thumb: Look for embedded real-life rubrics and help students identify and use them.[3]

The 3Cs of Assessment. Learning in life is largely a self-driven, self-analyzed pursuit. Key to this is developing a sense of when we know and when we don't know, or developing a sense for how much about a topic needs to be understood before one can begin to rely on what one knows as being accurate, then fairly complete, and, finally, comprehensive and therefore trustworthy. Without this sense, life continues to be a trial and error affair, with far more error than success.

The 3Cs of assessment are designed to help the teacher in the short run and students in the long run. They inject some much-needed common sense into the assessment process. They are useful when specific rubrics are unavailable and/or real-life standards are not known.

The 3Cs are a generic rubric, easily used by both teacher and students, and designed to spark that lifelong conversation with the small voice in the back of our head that directs lifelong learning. For example:

When washing a car:

Correct—The outside of the car has been washed and rinsed.

Complete—The outside has been washed and rinsed; windows have been wiped inside and out.

Comprehensive—The outside has been washed and rinsed; windows have been wiped inside and out; mats have been washed and the floor has been vacuumed; "stuff" has been cleared, the trunk has been organized, and receipts have been collected.

When doing the dishes:

Correct—Dishes are in the dishwasher

Complete—Dishes are in the dishwasher; pots and pans are washed and put away

Comprehensive—Dishes are in the dishwasher; pots and pans have been washed and put away; the stove and counter area has been wiped, the table cleaned and place mats shaken; the sink is scrubbed; floor is swept and the

garbage taken out

When assigned to define "egg":

Correct—Female cell of reproduction

Complete—Female cell of reproduction in all species, large and small, delicate and robust; can vary in size and color

Comprehensive—Female cell of reproduction across all species, large and small, delicate and robust; can vary in size and color; can develop inside and outside of the body. Can have different size, shape, and strength of shell, i.e., from very hard, ostrich, to very delicate, frog; can be fertilized in a petri dish; can be harvested and frozen for future use

A WORD ABOUT SUMMATIVE ASSESSMENT

If your goal is to teach effectively the first time, use of summative assessment only is too little too late. However, used in conjunction with effective formative assessment tools and practices, summative assessment can be very useful. It is best reserved for assessing completion of the last phase of the Two-Step Learning Process—whenever it might occur, rather than as an end-of-the-lesson or end-of-the-year snap shot.

Instruments for summative assessment range from standardized tests to criterion referenced instruments, from commercial to the homemade variety. Most fail to provide the kind of feedback that makes accountability a realistic goal.

The Inadequacies of Standardized Tests

Our complaints about standardized tests are three-fold:

• Most standardized science tests consist of items that test reading ability, not ability to apply science concepts and skills.

• Test items fail essential recommendations of the authentic assessment movement:

- To use real-life settings and real-world levels of expectations[4]

- To assess what's worth assessing rather than what's easy to assess

• True-false and multiple choice items, so typical in stan-

TWO-STEP LEARNING VERSUS TYPES OF TEST ITEMS

STEP 1	Pattern Seeking		STEP 2	Program Building	
Making meaning, understanding (input)			Able to use what is understood (output)		
Detecting patterns	Understanding the patterns		Use with conscious effort and guidance	Use automatically and "wired" into long-term memory	
Assessment Questions:	*Q. What do you want students to understand?*		*Q. What do you want them to do with what they understand?*		
Test Item Type	T/F items	Essay questions Multiple Choice	Demonstration with real-world situations	Demonstration over time in different settings	

---

dardized tests because they are less expensive to score, only sample learning in the early stages.[5]

Standardized Tests Versus Two-Step Learning.

Although true-false and multiple choice questions are less expensive to score, they do NOT measure learning as defined by brain research. The following graphic shows what conventional kinds of test items really measure when compared to this new definition of learning.[6]

An Inconvenient Truth. *The inconvenient truth about standardized testing is this:*[7]

• True/False items can be answered based on the barest of recognition, that little bell in one's head that says, "That choice sounds like something I've heard before." Understand it? No, not needed. One can ace a test com-

posed of true-false and multiple choice items without understanding the content. This "sound of familiarity" is quickly dumped from short-term memory.

• Multiple choice questions can also be correctly answered by a combination of bell ringing and cagey test-taking savvy. Understand the content? No, not necessary. Since real-life situations rarely provide us with multiple choice options, test-taking savvy is of little post-school value.

• As for essay questions, memorization can often carry one through the answer— the so-called "parrot back" exercise. In such instances, understanding the content isn't necessary and "application" is usually quite superficial, a memorized application in a limited sphere. Also, even if students do understand the content, and can talk and write about it, doesn't necessarily indicate that they can use what they understand. And certainly it cannot determine if what they understand has been wired into long-term memory. For example, I can still remember my shock when my college Western Civilization blue-book exam was returned (the grading process took about three weeks). In my very own handwriting was information I'd never heard of before! The content I had "learned" lasted long enough in short-term memory to get me an "A" on the exam but completely evaporated shortly thereafter. Sound familiar?

CRITERION-REFERENCED TESTS

The authentic assessment movement has given us solid advice about assessment, perhaps the most important of which is to value norm-referenced assessment—for both formative and summative evaluation. In the HET/EFT model, norm-referenced criteria are drawn from real life, from what one needs to understand and be able to do as an employee, business owner, or visitor at the being there location that anchors the curriculum being studied. Nothing could be more authentic than that, nor more useful to students now and in their future lives. We call these norms real-life rubrics—they are embedded in what students experience in the real-world locations that their curriculum is based in and they represent the pass-fail reality of life itself.

The challenge with criterion-referenced tests, however, is ensuring that the each item can provide a definitive yes/no answer—yes, the student has developed the ability to use a concept or skill and has wired it into long-term memory or no, the student has not.

Fortunately, inquiries are an excellent source of criterion-referenced test items. If they meet the ABC + D2 guidelines for writing an inquiry, you are ready to begin selecting and tweaking. with only a bit of tweaking to make them objective and allow for a clear cut yes/no judgment.

TRANSFORMING INQUIRIES INTO ASSESSMENT TOOLS

Whether for formative or summative assessment, inquiries are an ideal tool. The process is the same.

First, select the inquiry that asks for the most authentic real-world application of the content or skill you wish to assess.

Second, tweak that inquiry so that it can provide a definitive yes-no determination.

Selecting an Inquiry for Assessment

The most important question to ask is which inquiry demands the most authentic real-world application of the content or skill to be assessed? Not the least expensive or easiest to administer but which would be the most convincing proof of ability to apply.

For example, the following inquiries for this fifth grade key point provide a typical foundation for creating an inquiry to carry the load of summative assessment.

Conceptual Key Point: A system is a collection of parts and processes that interact to perform some function. Many things can be looked at as a system or as part of a system. To study a system, one must define its boundaries and parts.

Inquiries:

1) In your Learning Club, analyze a bicycle. Experiment with drawing boundaries which would define systems at least three systems within the bicycle. Draw the boundary for three systems. Record your findings and explain why you chose the boundary you did for each system. Share your findings with at least one other Learning Club. Record in your science journal what you learned from that Learning Club.

2) Select one of the systems identified in Inquiry #1. Analyze the structures and describe the parts and processes that interact to perform some function. Identify the function performed. Record your findings in your science notebook. Share your findings with other members of your Learning Club.

3) Based on what your Learning Club now knows about parts and processes of structures and systems, complete the L column of the class KWL chart (now know, want to learn, learned during study) chart for your Learning Club. Contribute your group's ideas to the creation of a KWL chart for the class.

Question: Which inquiry provides the most authentic assessment of the key point?

Opinion: We would choose the first one. It is the most direct assessment of the concept in the key point.

Question: Could the inquiry be made more reflective of real life, more of a real-world test of understanding and being able to apply the concept?

Opinion: Yes. For example, the student could be asked to analyze the systems in terms of a bicycle repair person looking for the source of brake failure or a propulsion problem.

Remember that from third grade upward, students are write inquiries. And they are very good at it. The actual process of writing an inquiry is another way of applying what they have learned. Like the TV game show Jeopardy, if they know the answer, they can write a doozy of a question.

Also remember that assessment shouldn't be a surprise or a mystery. The learner should know from the beginning what kinds of applications of concept or skill are to be mastered—a known goal to work toward.

Tweaking for a Definitive Yes-No Determination

Successful assess-ment is relatively straightforward. It must answer the basic question: Who will do what, how well, as measured by what, and when?

Elements of a measurable test item:

- Who—all students (not just the advanced students)

- What students should do/know and be able to apply (the concept or skill described in the key point and the application described in the inquiry)

- How well—framed by the inquiries and judged against the rubric(s) of the being there location and the "3 Cs" of mastery

- When—as described in the inquiry (e.g., within the next 10 minutes, by the end of the day, by tomorrow morning, by the end of the week or month)

There are several questions you might ask about an inquiry in order to ensure that both teacher and student can say with conviction, "Yes, the student has completed Two-Step learning for this key point" or "Not yet."

Using Inquiry #1 on the previous page as an example, the thinking process might look like the following:

Q1: Is the action required observable and specific?

Answer: Mostly yes but the action required needs tweaking. For example, the "what" is incomplete. Add "Describe the parts and processes of each of the three systems and the functions these parts and processes create."

Q2: Would this inquiry as written tell you if each member of the Learning Club understood and could apply it?

Answer: Probably not. Tweak it to make it an individual task.

Q3: Does this inquiry provide a time frame for completion?

Answer: No.

Once tweaked as a result of asking the above questions, the inquiry might look like this:

"Working alone, analyze one of the bicycles in the classroom. Then:

a) Sketch the bicycle.

b) Draw the boundaries for three systems: one which would help you analyze a customer's complaints about brake failure, a second that would help you analyze a customer's propulsion problems, and a third system of your choice. Use a different color ink/pencil for each system.

c) Diagram the parts and processes of each system. Describe on the diagram the functions that those parts and processes perform together. Check your work by physically moving the bicycle and comparing its movement to the boundaries you have drawn for each system.

d) Identify what you believe to be the part/process that is the most common cause of failure of that system. Add this information to your sketch. Add your work to your science journal.

e) Complete your work in one hour. Before submitting

your science journal to the teacher to review, look over your work. Analyze it using the 3Cs of Assessment and make sure it is representative of your personal best."

Such tweaking now allows you to answer the question who will do what, how well must they do it, and or within what time allotment:

- Who—a student working alone

- What the learner will do/know and be able to apply—define boundaries of three systems

- How—by analyzing and identifying three systems of a bicycle and describing the parts and processes of each of those systems and the function the parts and processes create

- How well—framed by the inquiries and judged according to the "3Cs" of mastery

- When—within an hour and a half

You now have an assessment tool that will allow you to say quite objectively, "Yes, the student understands and can apply this concept." Or, "No, this student needs more practice applying this concept."

Final question: Has the student truly mastered this concept and wired it into his/her long-term memory? Understanding and applying are the beginning steps. But, in your professional judgment, has the student developed a mental program for long-term memory? If in doubt, ask the student to select his/her favorite toy (must have moving parts). Have him/her do the same inquiry but substitute this toy for the bicycle. Still in doubt, you select a toy or machine and have him/her do the same inquiry again. To quote Leslie Hart: "Learning is the acquisition of useful programs."FN Make sure mastery becomes embedded in long-term memory.

Tweaking and Team Work. Clearly such tweaking to transform an inquiry into a criterion-referenced test item can be done by any teacher working on his/her own and with or without help from students. However, when it comes to summative assessment, it's a task best done as a grade level team and the item then utilized for summative assessment by each member of that team in his/her own classroom.

Such team work and consistent use lightens the work load and greatly improves coherence of curriculum and usefulness of assessment.

ENDNOTES

1 Without question, accountability is essential. However, accountability can be used to coerce or to improve student progress and teacher effectiveness. Under No Child Left Behind, the instruments used and their timing resulted in bludgeoning after the fact and did nothing to improve student learning and teacher effectiveness in the moment—during lessons as they were occurring, which is essential if one's goal is to prevent the need for remediation and provide feedback to enable teachers to teach effectively the first time.

2 For an array of rubrics, see rubistar.com

3 Caine and Caine offer a four relevant indicators for determining master. These real-world test of mastery include:
- The ability to use the language of the discipline or subject in complex situations and in social interaction.
- The ability to perform appropriately in unanticipated situations.
- The ability to solve real problems using the skills and concepts.
- The ability to show, explain, or teach the idea or skill to another person who has a real need to know.

See *Making Connections: Teaching and Learning and the Human Brain* by Renata and Geoffrey Caine (CA: Addison -Wesley, 1994), 156.

Growing Responsible Citizens: Implementing Stages 4-5

IMPLEMENTING STAGES 4-5

Stages 4 and 5 build upon continued implementation of earlier stages. The bodybrain-compatible learning environment created in Stage 1 has been well established and is consistently nurtured and maintained *all day* and the tools for developing bodybrain-compatible curriculum from Stage 2 are consistently and effectively used *during the time targeted for implementing HET curriculum.*

Stage 3 builds on yearlong conceptual curriculum and emphasizes Social/Political Action Projects as training for citizenship. *HET* curriculum also continues. Stage 3 is also the first time that a basic skill area is expected to be taught as well as practiced through the high interest area of the *HET* curriculum. Using the location-based content of the *HET* curriculum to practice and teach the basic skills increases through the stages until all subjects and skills are included.

Stage 4 adds the richness of a micro-community for citizenship training and for increasing student achievement. *HET* curriculum is to be implemented at least 50% of the time.

Stage 5 emphasizes schoolwide implementation, creating multi-age classrooms (preferably a three-year span) and/or using looping patterns by which students stay with the same teacher two to three years, and fully integrated use of technology. Location-based *HET* curriculum is implemented at least 90% of the time. (Note that Stage 5 does not expect that 100% of the day be organized by the organizing concept. It's likely that there will be content areas that a district/school will insist be taught in a specified way that cannot be included in the *HET* curriculum structure. This is political reality; accept it as is. Implementing a truly bodybrain-compatible learning environment for 90% of the day is an enormous gift to students and an extraordinary achievement by a top-flight master teacher.)

CREATING AN INTEGRATED CURRICULUM

CURRICULUM

- All aspects of the *HET* curriculum described in Stages 1-3 are maintained and deepened.

- Curriculum content, as expressed in the key points, enhances pattern-seeking, making it easier for students to perceive and understand the most important ideas and concepts in the curriculum. Inquiries are designed to help students make connections to the real world, to practice using the concepts and skills of the key points, and to develop mental programs and store them for long-term memory. Inquiries that provide experiences in citizenship, such as social/political action activities and collaborative grouping practices, occur weekly.

- The content is conceptual and is consistently used as high interest areas for applying the skills/knowledge in at least one basic skill area (e.g., math, reading, writing).

- An mindmap of the yearlong curriculum, prominently displayed on the wall for both students and teacher, serves as the framework for content development and instruction. On average, more than 50-65 percent of instruction during the school year is based upon this bodybrain-compatible curriculum.

- Curriculum for collaborative assignments is specifically designed for group work.

INSTRUCTIONAL STRATEGIES

- Immersion and hands-on-of-the-real-thing are the primary input used to supplement and extend *being there* experiences.

- All instructional time during the theme is based upon the progression of

> *Sensory input from*
> *being there*
> *EXPERIENCE ☐ CONCEPT ☐ LANGUAGE ☐ APPLICATION TO ☐ LONG-TERM*
> *REAL WORLD   MEMORY*

rather than the traditional progression of

> *LANGUAGE ☐ ☐ ☐ CONCEPT ☐ ☐ ☐ APPLICATION*

- Collaboration is used daily whenever it will enhance pattern seeking and program building.

- Time is allocated in accordance with the nature of the tasks and student and teacher need for adequate time; such time allocations are made in recognition of the need to develop programs for using knowledge and skills in real-world contexts.

- Peers and cross-age tutors substantially increase teaching and practice time for students in areas of individual need.

CITIZENSHIP & INTEGRATION OF BASIC SKILLS THROUGH A MICRO-COMMUNITY

CURRICULUM

- The integrated curriculum serves as the framework for content development and implementation for teaching at least two areas of basic skills (e.g., math, reading, writing, oral expression, second and primary language acquisition) and is used for applying all the basic skills.

- The development and practice of citizenship continues to be a central focus of curriculum. A schoolwide, ongoing micro-community provides realistic and believable experiences in the governing and commerce of our democratic society. These experiences are used to learn, practice, and master the basic skills.

INSTRUCTIONAL STRATEGIES

- Teaches basic skills within the integrated theme and the micro-community as a means to an end, not as an end in themselves.
  [Although the teacher utilizes specific techniques for teaching the basic skills on a daily basis, during integrated theme and micro-community time, the student's primary focus is on the meaningful content which the basic skills help unlock.]

- Takes advantage of the power of incidental learning, especially during micro-community time, to build mental programs applying the basic skills.

- Provides the relevant technology needed to provide a natural extension of students' senses, allowing them to explore and learn beyond what the *being there* sensory input can provide. For example, microscopes, telescopes, radar, and MRIs to extend vision, sonar, oscilloscope, cell phones, decibel meters to extend hearing, etc., as well as computers and Internet access.

- Uses technology in the classroom so that students have full access to databases and communication systems throughout the country and the world. It is used to extend, not replace, the *being there* experience that provides a starting point for understanding and applying concepts and skills in real-world situations.

SCHOOLWIDE IMPLEMENTATION

CURRICULUM

• The integrated curriculum serves as the framework for content development and implementation for almost all basic skills and content 75-90 percent of the day/year. Key points and inquiries effectively enhance pattern seeking and program building resulting in mastery and wiring into long-term memory. Teachers and students guide teaching and learning based on the new definition of learning:

New definition of learning

- **Step One: Pattern-Seeking**

  Identifying patterns

  Making meaning/understanding

- **Step Two: Program-Building**

  Able to use learning with support

  Ability to use the learning with ease

• The curriculum of the district provides each teacher with pattern-enhancing tools for curriculum planning.

• Bodybrain-compatible curriculum is implemented schoolwide, providing consistency for students as they move through the school.

• The curricular elements of Stages 1 and 4 are maintained and deepened, especially the focus on citizenship through social/political action and micro-community.

INSTRUCTIONAL STRATEGIES

• Uses all the instructional strategies identified in Stages 1 through 4 effectively throughout each day.

• Teaches and provides practice in almost all basic skills are taught and practiced through the other subject areas.

• Students have the same teacher for two or more consecutive years (due either to multi-aged classes or the teacher moving on with the students).

• Continues to provide the relevant technology needed to provide a natural extension of students' senses, allowing them to explore and learn beyond what the *being there* sensory input can provide. For example, microscopes, telescopes, radar, and MRIs to extend vision, sonar, oscilloscope, cell phones, decibel meters to extend hearing, etc., as well as computers and Internet access.

• Uses technology in the classroom so that students have full access to databases and communication systems throughout the country and the world. It is used to extend, not replace, the *being there* experience that provides a starting point for understanding and applying concepts and skills in real-world situations. .

Note: The goal of Stage 5 is to develop and implement conceptual curriculum for 75-90 percent of the year.

NOTES TO MYSELF

Chapter 20: More Quality More of the Time

MORE TIME

At last count, there are not enough minutes in the day to meet all the demands of state and federal requirements. Once you add up the minimum minutes for reading, language, math, aerobic exercise, etc., there simply are enough minutes in the typical school day to do each of them. This is a problem multitasking can't solve. Integrating will. An hour of integrated curriculum can easily buy you 40 minutes of science, 10 minutes of math, 25 minutes of reading, 10 minutes of writing (journal reflections and recording findings), five minutes of art, five minutes of history/social studies, and five minutes of music—all depending on the kinds of inquiries that students engage in.

How is it possible to get 100 minutes of study packed into one hour? Easy. Review the sample curriculum on pages 14.7-14.16. Notice how many skills and content areas are woven into each inquiry. For an example, analyze inquiry #2 on page 14.7:

2. Select at least five items in our classroom that look interesting to you. Illustrate each item and write a brief description of the attributes (form) of each item. On a Post-It note, describe the use (function) of each item. With your Learning Club, pantomime the form and function of at least one of your items. Record in your science journal at least one other

item that is similar in form or function to one you chose. Example: pencil, long and narrow; similar to a pen, both are used to write with.

This inquiry calls for art (the illustration would be done as a simple line drawing or using a specific technique recently taught by the art teacher) for 5-7 minutes, writing for 5-10 minutes, oral language (to plan the pantomime) for 7-10 minutes, pantomiming (drama) for 5-8 minutes, and more writing for 3-5 minutes. Students would also be getting 20-30 minutes of science. In this 25-40 time slot, students would be getting 45-70 minutes of curriculum content and skills.

As you read through the sample curriculum, notice the extent of integration—subject areas and skills—that the inquiries require. The time you spend writing inquiries to ensure you address all the multiple intelligences and levels of Bloom's Taxonomy pay you back in time saved—your time teaching and providing practice time in multiple subjects and skills and student time in learning.

Integration of subjects and skills through location-based study is the gift of time that keeps on giving.

MORE QUALITY

The foremost challenge when fully integrating your subjects and skills is quality. Your curriculum must be better than publisher-generated textbooks with their workbooks and worksheets. This is particularly important as you increase the amount of time for integrated curriculum to 50 percent for Stage 4 and 90 percent for Stage 5.

Quality integrated curriculum:

- Enhances pattern seeking

- Provides enough opportunities to apply concepts and skills in real-world ways to ensure development of long-term memory

- Avoids the compulsion to "cover" content

Enhancing Pattern-Seeking

Curriculum development is a pattern-enhancing activity. To enhance pattern:

- Eliminate factoids

- Make your key points as conceptual as possible

- Choose organizing concepts for the yearlong *HET* curriculum that have enough depth to unfold throughout the year

Eliminate Factoids. Because factoids are devoid of pattern and are so small they don't explain much about how the world works, they carry little meaning and are thus extremely difficult for students to learn. As a result, students must resort to memorization with few hooks to assist with retrieval.

If your state standards are lean on concepts and fat on factoids, you must build a bridge for your students. Sweep all the factoids into a pile and begin to sort. What are the concepts that would make these tidbits of knowledge meaningful and understandable? In what settings, besides Jeopardy, would they be useful? State these concepts and identify the settings. Teach from these. Let the factoids tag along. Never lead with them.

Make Your Key Points As Conceptual As Possible. Master the game of bumping up. Also search for the most universal statement in order to increase students' ability to generalize to other ideas and transfer to other settings and applications.

Select Organizing Concepts That Are Rich in Pattern. Select organizing concepts for the yearlong *HET* curriculum that are rich in patterns and have power of organize a year's worth of content and skills.

For example: discovery can help ***organize*** a theme, that is, all the content is about discovery of different kinds by different people in different locales. But, discovery as a concept is one-dimensional. Once you're used the dictionary to define it—the act or process of discovering; something discovered; to make sight or knowledge of something for the first time—there is nothing about the concept as a concept to pursue. What would follow are examples of discoveries made, factoids organized by chronology or country or time period or nationality. Discovery is an example of a concept that has little power to create a pattern for the discoveries that follow to help make them memorable and retrievable.

On the other hand, concepts such as systems, change, form and function, and interdependence in a habitat are each a nest of related concepts that can be explored for a year, even a lifetime. Each related or subconcept enriches and interconnects what came before and what will come after.

For example, see the conceptual map for systems on the next page. The concept is mapped as if it were the basis for a year of *HET* curriculum with components and topics. Unlike discovery, systems is rich and very multi-dimensional, perfect for enhancing and interconnecting pattern seeking in ways that expand meaning and make content more memorable and more retrievable. It's a powerful concept for grades 5 and up.

Concept mapping is one way to obtain strong patterns for students. Another is selecting a well-known entity whose pattern is instantly recognized by students, whose pieces spin off the organizing concept is predictable, natural ways. An example is the curriculum, "We, the People," whose monthly components are the goals of our government expressed in the preamble of our constitution. Recite that sentence and an entire year pops to mind. Again, easy to add on to and easy to recall. A compelling pattern. The glue here is obvious and embedded in the organizing concept of the theme. This concept is also appropriate for grades 5 and up.

Organizing concepts for lower grades are less abstract and more experiential but still conceptual for the developing brain of a student at that grade. For example, an organizing concept for first grade could be built on a powerful, and age appropriate, science concept: "All living things, including humans, have basic needs—for food, water, air, protection (from weather, disease, and predators), and reproduction. A habitat is the place where the animal or plant lives while meeting these needs." Because the ways that animals and plants go about meeting their needs varies dramatically, and therefore how they are interdependent can be surprising, this concept works well for an entire year. The components could be different habitats, different homes, in which those needs get met in different ways. See the curriculum on page 20.5

Rule of thumb: The more content you have to organize, the more powerful the organizing concept must be and the more conceptually interconnected with the each component must be to the organizing concept. Your goal should be greater pattern enhancement as you the amount of *HET* curriculum grows.

Thus, while an idea such as discovery may be adequate to organize a week or two of integrated curriculum, it is weak glue for 50 percent of a year. Likewise, themes which have a different concept for each component with only tangential connection back to the organizing concept are acceptable for early Stages 2 of *HET* implementation and work when integrated curriculum amounts to only 10-25 percent of the year. At Stage 2, the components are typically isolated islands of curriculum, separated by time and lots of

typical curriculum. This is typical of a normal learning curve, experimentation with how to enhance pattern seeking.

However, for Stages 3-5, the organizing concept must be inherently pattern rich. In the three examples that follow, there is powerful glue to hold 80 percent of a year's curriculum together.

Our constitution's preamble, "We, the people," is so well-known that it casts a predictable and tightly connected web. The glue here is a single, culturally-powerful sentence.

Organizing concept: The goals of democracy are to promote the common good, not the benefit of the few.

Rationale: Democracy cannot be sustained if its people do not understand, support, and exercise the responsibilities as well as the rights of democracy on a daily basis.

The organizing concept, systems, on the next page is held tightly together because the concepts nest together, all inherently intertwined by the physical science concepts themselves.

CONCEPTUAL MAP

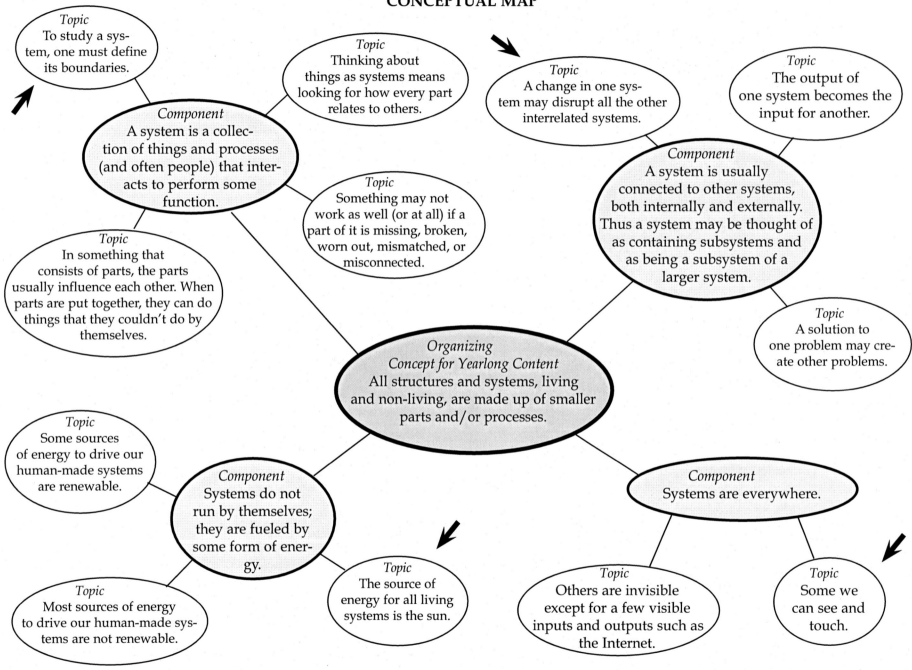

Topic
To study a system, one must define its boundaries.

Topic
Thinking about things as systems means looking for how every part relates to others.

Topic
A change in one system may disrupt all the other interrelated systems.

Topic
The output of one system becomes the input for another.

Component
A system is a collection of things and processes (and often people) that interacts to perform some function.

Topic
Something may not work as well (or at all) if a part of it is missing, broken, worn out, mismatched, or misconnected.

Component
A system is usually connected to other systems, both internally and externally. Thus a system may be thought of as containing subsystems and as being a subsystem of a larger system.

Topic
In something that consists of parts, the parts usually influence each other. When parts are put together, they can do things that they couldn't do by themselves.

Topic
A solution to one problem may create other problems.

Organizing Concept for Yearlong Content
All structures and systems, living and non-living, are made up of smaller parts and/or processes.

Topic
Some sources of energy to drive our human-made systems are renewable.

Component
Systems do not run by themselves; they are fueled by some form of energy.

Component
Systems are everywhere.

Topic
Most sources of energy to drive our human-made systems are not renewable.

Topic
The source of energy for all living systems is the sun.

Topic
Others are invisible except for a few visible inputs and outputs such as the Internet.

Topic
Some we can see and touch.

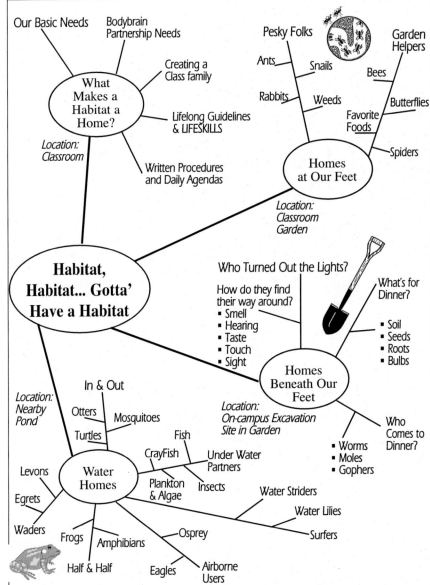

Concept: All animals and plants have the same basic needs; a habitat is where animals and plants interact with each other and their environment to meet those basic needs.
Rationale: Understanding how animals & plants meet their needs in different ,nearby habitats will enable them to predict needs in distant (and thus not experienceable) habitats and become stewards of our world. Also, understanding the diversity of ways animals meet common needs enables students to understand the complexities of stewardship.

The theme on the left is an example of an organizing concept with solid science standing but also intuitively, and thus easily, grasped by a first grader. The mix of solid science and intuitive grasp very powerful glue.

Practice Concepts and Skills in Real-World Contexts

The hallmark of the the *HET* model is basing curriculum in *being there* experiences. This is common sense and brain research combined. We learn what we need to in order to accomplish something important to us; it is easier to learn something we can see in action than something that is only talked about. Review Chapter 12 for a discussion of basing curriculum in *being there* locations.

Suggestions:

- Base your curriculum on science concepts. They are observable and directly experienceable. Transferring them into other content areas makes those areas less abstract.

- After guided practice of a basic skill, provide practice through inquiries, celebrations of learning, and social/political action projects. Eliminate worksheets as practice tools.

- Teach basic skills as tools to better understand and communicate about important ideas rather than as ends in themselves. Spend more time teaching these skills within the context of inquiries calling for action rather than during set time periods of the day (because X number of minutes of such instruction is required).

- Ensure that homework requires application of concepts to real-world situations around the home and neighborhood; embed skill practice into these assignments.

AVOID THE COMPULSION TO "COVER" CONTENT

A pound of common sense is worth a ton of "shoulds." When you examine your curriculum, keep asking yourself why? Why is this important? Is this worth teaching/learning? Would this help students understand the world of today and tomorrow? How, where, under what circumstances could this be useful in the real world?

If you can't come up with compelling answers to these questions, allocate such content to the end of the year, knowing full well that there is already too much content to teach and that this content will fall by the wayside. We call this selective abandonment. Since there is too much to teach, make sure what you leave behind is most deserving of being left behind. In other words, first things first. Put the most important things first and teach them to mastery and long-term memory. Don't feel bedeviled by what you can't control, in this case, limited time coupled with unrealistic expectations.

Tips to help put the most important things first include:

• Consider organizing and teaching history around concepts rather than chronologically. In a chronological study of U.S. history, for example, few students ever get to the Vietnam War and its related civil unrest or the Gulf War or the conundrums surrounding the invasion of Iraq.

• Teach basic skills to mastery in a concentrated way. For example, long division in a day, multiplication in a week, punctuation in half day spurts (apostrophes one time, colons and semi-colons another).

Chapter 21: Citizenship Through Social/Political Action and Micro-community

Preparing students to become participating citizens in our democratic society is a core value of the HET model. It can and should be done in small and big ways on a daily basis. Two of the most effective ways are involving students in social/political action projects and creating a micro-community which gives students a being there experience of community life. While Social/Political Action Projects begin in Stage 3 and progressively deepen through Stages 4 and 5, micro-community begins at Stage 4.

SOCIAL/POLITICAL ACTION PROJECTS

Social/Political Action Projects are central to the HET model and its core goal of growing responsible citizens and for providing students opportunities to apply concepts, knowledge, and skills in real-world ways.

From Knowledge to Action

Social/Political action is a call to action, moving from knowing about to doing something that matters. A project can occur midway into study of a topic or be a culminating activity. It can grow organically out of students' experiences studying the location of the being there locations. It's what students find important and compelling. It might take the form of lobbying the city council for a stoplight at the school, pressing the EPA or local governmental entity to complete a toxic clean up, urging other students not to eat tuna that doesn't carry the dolphin-friendly symbol, picketing the superintendent's office to get the kindergarten toilets fixed and the restroom reopened, replanting mangrove forests, working in a soup kitchen, visiting the elderly, ensuring that homeless children get school supplies, launching an anti-drug campaign at school, and so forth. In the process of such projects, young citizens discover the levers of our democratic system, learn the personal skills to make their opinions heard and considered, and develop the courage and perseverance to press on until problems get resolved. They also develop a commitment to give back to society through service projects, governmental internships, voter responsibility, etc.

Social/Political Action Projects are usually undertaken as an entire class although Learning Clubs could take on separate parts of a class project. There are no hard and fast rules here, just the intent to have students engage in something meaningful and experience the deep sense of satisfaction that comes from making a contribution to the world and helping make it a better place.

Resources

Resources to assist you and your students to identify, plan, and carry out social/political action projects include: *The Kids' Guide to Service Projects: Over 500 Service Ideas for Young People Who Want to Make a Difference* and *The Kids Guide to Social Action: How to Solve the Social Problems You Choose—And Turn Creative Thinking into Positive Action* both by Barbara A. Lewis and *Enriching Curriculum Through Service Learning* edited by C.W. Kinsley and K. McPherson. For ideas about community service projects, also contact Sarah Pearson, American Youth Policy Forum, 1836 Jefferson Place, WE, Washington, D.C., 20036, aypf@aypf.org, 202/775-9731.

Behaviors of Responsible Citizenship

Responsible citizens:

- Participate in community dialog; are informed voters

- Treat others with respect and courtesy

- Obey the law; work through the system to change those laws they believe are unfair or wrong

- Practice conservation

- Maintain a positive work ethic; develop the personal and social skills to be financially self sufficient

- Take responsibility for personal health

- Are committed to family and do their part to make the family a successful unit

- Are tolerant of religious, racial, ethnic, gender, and age differences

---

Remember the Lifelong Guidelines/LIFESKILLS

The Lifelong Guidelines/LIFESKILLS should be an integral part of any Social/Political Action Project. They describe the personal and social skills your students need to take action about a problem or societal issue. This is particularly true if the nature of the topic and the community's position about it result in contentious debate, such as supporting the Endangered Species Act and the spotted owl in a classroom located in the heart of logging country or reacting to the discovery of water registering in the unhealthy range several times a week during a visit to the local water treatment plant. Students should not be told that they can't work on issues of consequence just because there will be consequences that affect someone or some business in their community. The idea behind democracy is, as Star Trek's Spock comments, "The needs of the many outweigh the needs of the few."

Social/Political Action Projects As Assessment Tools

What we know from brain research is that wiring knowledge and skill into long-term memory takes practice—multiple uses in varying situations. While test taking is usually performed from short-term memory, Social/Political Action Projects immerse students in complex projects that extend over time, thus giving rich, engaging practice that ensures mastery and creates long-term memory of a wide range of skills and knowledge.

A MICRO-COMMUNITY

Despite the innumerable achievements of our technological era, we must rank as a major shortcoming our failure to involve children in our adult world. Most children have not a clue what their parents do for a living and thus are learning precious few of the skills necessary to build a successful life.

The reasons are many: It's unsafe for children to roam about the neighborhood as they could 50 years ago; more people are employees, not entrepreneurs or owners of mom-and-pop operations that involved the children from an early age onward; and many jobs have become fantastically specialized so that even if children did accompany their parents to work, they could not understand what their parent was doing. And yet, the challenges facing future citizens continue to mushroom.

A powerful antidote to these conditions is a micro-community on campus—a microcosm of American life, replete with city council, sheriff, court system, bank, currency system, post office, newspaper, radio and TV stations, recycling center, class and individual businesses, and more. All student run. A micro-community not as an add-on, something done after school or on special days, but a fully integrated, daily ingredient in the vibrant life of the school.

Francie Summers, a truly gifted administrator in Las Vegas, Nevada, and her hard-working, capable staff have demonstrated the power of such a micro-community at two schools, providing impressive illustrations of the power of a micro-community to not only induct the young into the roles of citizenship but also to dramatically increase academic performance.

Another fully-developed micro-community was created at Sul Ross Elementary, Waco, Texas, by an equally talented staff with principal Terri Patterson. It, too, experienced sharp increases in academic performance and, quite impressively, with a high minority, very low-income student population.

The Power of a Micro-community

"Our Title I school serves children and families from poverty. HET works for our students because it makes them feel worthy as individuals. It unleashes their natural curiosity in such a way that learning makes sense and the world around them is understandable. They know they can make positive changes in their world and be productive, responsible citizens. HET is powerful and changes the lives of children and the adults who work with them."
—Terri Patterson, Principal , Sul Ross Elementary, Waco, Texas

"HET has had a dramatic impact on students, staff, and the community during the eleven years I have served as principal at two micro-community schools. The students have acquired the knowledge to be successful in school and in life; staff have felt empowered as professionals and are excited about teaching. The communities have been exceedingly supportive because they have reaped the benefits as we 'grew responsible citizens'."
—Francie Summers, Principal, Edith Gareheim Elementary, Las Vegas, Nevada

---

Key features of these two micro-community models include:

• Using the Lifelong Guidelines and LIFESKILLS to shape the culture and define the way we treat others

• Replication of essential elements of community life such as daily mail delivery, a banking system (training provided by a bank), an in-house monetary system capable of exchanging real dollars for "Gareheim Gold," a newspaper and TV station, stores open daily for such necessities as extra pencils and pens, special paper, snacks, a recycling service, and more. Each classroom carried out these functions as its class business.

• Governmental services such as a court system that convenes weekly or more often if needed, a city council that legislates the rules of behavior for its citizens, local EPA, business license bureau, and so forth. Again, classroom businesses.

• Class and individual businesses which operate every week, some daily. "Going to Town Day," which occurs three to four times a year, provides a sales outlet for all businesses—class and individual or partnership—and a breathless exchange of Gareheim Gold in a fast-paced, two-hour period. Prospective business owners must mull through an approvable business plan, buy a business license, arrange for advertising over the schoolwide intercom or student-run TV station and newspaper, and rent retail space.

• Engagement in city projects of importance, such as the fifth grade developing an architectural plan to turn an empty lot across the street from the school into a city park (the plan was accepted by the local authorities and became a reality)

• Community participation through volunteerism, monetary donations, and business partnerships

• Participation of parents and younger siblings

The richer the micro-community, the more real it is to students. The more real it seems, the more fully they embrace participating in it. The micro-community creates a real need to know, making learning deeper and more comprehensive. See *Jacobsonville: An ITI/HET Micro-Society*, a 30-minute DVD of the model developed at Jacobson and Gareheim Schools, Las Vegas, Nevada.

Self Check

A Micro-community

• The micro-community is seamlessly woven into the life of the school. Students participate in some aspect of the micro-community on a daily basis.

• Every student participates in his/her class business (recycling program, convenience store) or schoolwide project (post office, newspaper, TV station, a bank). In addition, many students also run a business in partnership or as sole proprietor.

• Although students are aware that theirs is a micro-community of their own making, they value being a member and realize that they are learning invaluable business and citizenship skills.

• Students understand the importance of learning to use what they learn—from the Lifelong Guidelines to academic concepts and skills to everyday common sense.

• Staff use the high-interest experiences of the micro-community as a proving ground for students to apply basic skills. For example, every business must calculate its expenses and percentage of profit/loss.

• The micro-community is student run; staff serve as guide on the side, not sage on the stage.

Living with Change: Personal & Group Tools, School Structures

LIVING WITH CHANGE

At least in its rhetoric, every school in America is committed to improving its program for students. The schools that go beyond rhetoric are those that have a realistic picture of the challenges of change, have developed the personal and group tools for living with it, and have committed themselves to move forward together on an agreed upon path.

Chapter 22 describes personal tools needed for the journey. Included is advice by William Bridges about transitions necessary for change and a variety of personal tools you will need along your journey. Also included is a discussion of some group tools that will help you and your colleagues become best allies, not enemies, as you pursue profound change in your school.

Chapter 23 describes several structural changes that support change. In other words, how to begin to reshape your school's bureaucratic structures so they support, not thwart, your change efforts.

We dedicate this part of the book to those courageous educators who have committed their lives to making our schools a place where all children thrive and all adults enjoy a professional, challenging, and humane work environment that feeds their souls and enlivens their workday. May every reader of this book join your ranks and contribute to the mission.

Chapter 22: Tools for Living with Change

At least in its rhetoric, every school in America is committed to improving its program for students. The schools that go beyond rhetoric are those that have a realistic picture of the challenges of change, have developed the personal and group tools for living with it, and have committed themselves to move forward together on an agreed upon path.

Personal tools needed for the journey include advice by William Bridges about transitions necessary for change and a variety of personal tools you will need along your journey. Also included is a discussion of some group tools that will help you and your colleagues become best allies, not enemies, as you pursue profound change in your school.

Structural tools include institutional changes that support change. In other words, how to begin to reshape your school's bureaucratic structures so they support, not thwart, your change efforts.

We dedicate this part of the book to those courageous educators who have committed their lives to making our schools a place where all children thrive and all adults enjoy a professional, challenging, and humane work environment that feeds their souls and enlivens their workday. May every reader of this book join your ranks and contribute to the mission.

PERSONAL TOOLS

Given the size of the gap between traditional schools, modeled on the Prussian system of the 1840s, and the way they must become to be bodybrain-compatible, the degree of change needed is truly enormous. A school cannot make the jump in one leap but a clear picture of the landing site can make first steps more purposeful. We hope that the following discussion of change processes will provide some of the needed brush strokes to reveal a landscape for the future.

Transition Versus Change

William Bridges, in his book *Managing Transitions: Making the Most of Change*, points out that, "It isn't the changes that do you in, it's the transitions."[1]

Change Is External. Change, he says, is situational: reassignment to a new grade level or subject area, new team structure or roles, changes in homework policies, different vision by new principal or incoming superintendent or school board, the start of double or triple length instruction periods, converting from dependency on textbooks to developing curriculum based on a physical location, and so forth.

Change occurs in external behavior and events.

Transition Is Internal. In contrast, transition is "the psychological process people go through to come to terms with the new situation."[2] Transitions require that we change our personal programs that attach us to old behaviors and actions and that interfere with being able or willing to carry out new behaviors. For example, in order to design instructional strategies that support the body-brain learning partnership, we might have to toss out decade-old lesson plans, be willing to start from zero and stumble like a novice over an aspect of something that in the past earned us praise and recognition for our expertise.

To choose transition is to choose to reinvent ourself as an educator and as a person, after which change is remarkably easy. Again, "Change is external, transition is internal."[3]

No Transition, No Change

Bridges cautions us that change can't work unless transition occurs. To understand how profound this comment is, think back to your school's last big change effort that went nowhere. The school plan was totally revamped after an extensive needs assessment that included faculty and student involvement. Good ideas were written on the page, complete with detailed calendar and who was to do what. Yet, six months later . . . nothing. No behaviors changed, no new actions were taken. Things remained as before. Why? Because transition—internal shifts—did not occur.

Transition Begins with Endings

Bridges maintains that transition is very different from change. The starting point for change is the outcome to be implemented. The starting point for transition is the ending that you must make in order to leave the old situation, actions, and attitudes behind—the old beliefs, the old reality, and the old identity you had before the change can take place.[4] For example, letting go of textbooks as our curriculum, rigid time schedules, teaching as a solitary act. And, yes, letting go of our established place as "experts."

FOUR LEVELS OF TRANSITION AND CHANGE

Living with change is neither easy nor comfortable. But it can become interesting rather than irritating, a helpful friend rather than a feared foe, if we better understand the personal and group dynamics that accompany it.

There are four levels of transition and change:[5]

- Personal transitions
- Personal learning curve changes
- Group transitions
- Institutional change

Personal Transition

According to Bridges, **"Nothing so undermines organizational change as the failure to think through who will have to let go of what when change occurs."**[6] Ask yourself what endings you need to complete. What beliefs or attitudes or facets of your identity are incompatible with or competes with the new action to be implemented; whatever that is, it must be left behind.

Transition starts with an ending. We begin with letting go of many things, some of which are simply habit, some that we dearly cherish. But letting go need not be a funeral. Some things we are glad to be rid of. Others things served us well and were successful for their time and use, so celebrate them. Thank them for their service and then step forward with a sense of adventure and high hopes, not with regret. Transition and change are swirling dance partners. Enjoy the dance.

Because there is much about our traditional model to let go of and so many vested participants (staff, parents, and even students from intermediate grades and up) who must make the transition, it is unlikely that we will make the transition in one year or even two;

three to five years is more likely. Be patient but be thorough. The challenge in school reform is that we cannot fully succeed in creating a bodybrain-compatible learning environment for students until our fellow travellers join us.

Personal Learning Curve Changes

Typical of the journey to transform one's school is the urge to do everything at once. If it's a good idea to end up with a restructured school, let's restructure it now. If it's a good idea to put everyone in teams to best integrate curriculum, let's require team teaching now. This "Let's start where we want to end up" action plan is a recipe for disaster. In our opinion, it is the foremost reason why school reform efforts fail. Restructuring before staff have the skills to succeed has never worked and never will.

So. . . we beg of you: Start at the beginning; start from where you are. Start with a focus on Stage 1. *Make it your personal goal to complete Stage 1 in one year.*

Stage 2 is also primarily a personal learning curve challenge, especially mastering the instructional strategies described in Stages 1 and 2. By the end of Stage 2, you should be working in close collaboration with colleagues to develop the best curriculum for your students that you can and the best instructional strategies for delivering that curriculum.

Levels of Use. Our journey through transitions and change often feels like an out-of-control roller coaster ride and that "the harder we work, the behinder we get." Understanding Levels of Use can reduce our distress and help us capture a sense of our progress.

Developed by Gene Hall, Susan Loucks, and others at the University of Texas in the mid-1970s, the Levels of Use (see next page) describe the levels of implementation people go through when implementing something new.

When using these levels, remember three things:[7]

- They are not a one-way street; for example, each time you add a new strategy to your collaborative approaches, you go back to Level 0.

- "Skipping" levels does not occur. With luck, one can speed through a stage; with even more luck, one can achieve level 5 and beyond. But there are no guarantees.

- These levels apply to specific subskills, not to a teacher generally, or how a teacher may teach a particular subject area, or to an instructional strategy. It applies to a specific subskill within a curricular or instructional area. For example, the ability to utilize cooperative learning during science experiments or to structure clear roles and responsibilities for each group member. Do not apply this scale on a gestalt level, e.g., saying that as an elementary school teacher, a teacher is at the level of non-use; or, as a teacher of reading, he/she is at preparation. Apply Levels of Use only to a particular subskill.

For more information on using Levels of Use, see Chapter 5, *Coaching for the HET Model: Delivering on the Promise* by Karen D. Olsen.

Levels of Use [8]

LEVEL	INDICES
0 - Non-use	No action being taken. It is not part of the teacher's conversation; if it is, questions indicate a significant lack of understanding or misunderstanding.
1 - Orientation	Teacher is just acquiring information and is exploring, or will soon explore, its potential impact on self and classroom operation. At the last stages of this level, teacher faces the critical decision to implement the skill/task or to turn away. Major consideration: Will there be adequate support?

—————— Major decision point ——————

2 - Preparation	Teacher is preparing to use it and is thus finding out more about it, gathering the necessary resources (materials, management structures, personal skills/knowledge, support, time, etc.). A difficult stage.
3 - Mechanical Use	Teacher's focus is on the day-to-day doing of it and is attempting to master the tasks in a step-by-step process. Typically the "system" at this level is less than its parts and often the whole is not clearly envisioned.
4 - Routine Use	Use is stabilized. The few changes the teacher makes are made in response to the needs of the implementor rather than of the students. This is a fairly comfortable stage; little preparation is needed to sustain the implementation.

LEVEL	INDICES
4 - Routine Use (continued)	Teacher gives little thought of improving use of the skill/task or of its consequences for students. At the last stage of this level, teacher faces a critical decision to make changes in the program to make it work better for students or to stay stuck in a comfort zone. Major consideration: Will the increased benefit to students be worth the effort?

—————— major decision point ——————

5 - Refinement	Teacher changes implementation to increase both long- and short-term results for students (groups and individuals); work to make changes is limited to own students in own classroom only.
6 - Integration/ collaboration	Teacher has made all the refinements possible working alone in his/her classroom at the refinement level and now makes deliberate efforts to collaborate with others to achieve broader changes, a collective impact across several classrooms or even schoolwide.
7 - Renewal	Teacher has made all the refinements and integrations possible and now seeks more effective alternatives—new approaches/systems/goals for self and school. In the latter stages, the teacher faces the decision to abandon the old system (or significant parts of it) and adopt/adapt the new or to fall back to an earlier stage such as routine use. If the decision is to go forward with the new, the next stop is "non-use" and the cycle begins anew.

* The information about Levels of Use is excerpted from *Coaching for the HET Model: Delivering on the Promise* by Karen D. Olsen (Black Diamond, WA: Books for Educators, 2009). Used by written permission of the publisher.

APPLYING LEVELS OF USE: THE BREAD BAKING STORY

Level 0—NON-USE

Barbara notices that when I visit her house, I always go straight to the bread box and help myself to her home-made bread. She concludes, given my obvious interest in bread and her information regarding nutritional superiority of natural vs. wonder bread puff, that I should learn to bake bread. At her first suggestion I begin to ask questions such as, "Well, can I cook it in the microwave? Or how about on top of the stove? I'm always in a hurry."

Clues: Questions about "cooking" the bread in the microwave oven or on top of the stove indicate significant lack of understanding (dare I say misunderstanding?) of how bread is baked and, clearly, non-use of the skill called baking bread.

Level 1—ORIENTATION

Barbara begins to talk with me about the merits of home-baked bread: taste (That one I'm clear on!), nutrition (I'm not impressed), texture (I still like to wad up my bread into a tight round ball from time to time), dinner guests are pleased and impressed with warm-from-the-oven home-baked bread (my friends know better than to come to my house if they're hungry). "Barbara, how long does homemade bread last? Is it still tasty after 3-4 days (I travel a lot during the week)."

"Do you have a simple recipe? Like a 4-H cookbook type recipe . . . you know, one for kids, nice and simple, fail-safe." Barbara says "yes" twice. I say, "I want to do it. If you'll give me a recipe and any other information you think I might need right now,

I'll begin this weekend. First stop, shopping; I have none of the things that this recipe calls for."

Clues: I'm willing to acquire information and I'm considering its impact on my operation (such as it is!). However, notice that in the early stages of this level I haven't yet made a decision to bake my own bread. I'm just shopping for information (and enjoying Barbara's bread in the process!). During my shopping, I reveal what motivates me. Barbara is thus able to determine what information (knowledge, skill, or motivation) will move me forward to the next level of use. In the last stage of this level, I make the critical step— deciding to implement. Barbara loads me up with "stuff" and I go merrily on my way.

Level 2—PREPARATION

Saturday morning, the big day, I take out my 4-H recipe and read the reminder list at the top for ingredients I'll need (So far, so good). Firmly grasping the list, I go to my cupboards. "Oh, oh, no baking soda, no yeast, no pre-sifted flour (Gosh, I don't remember ever seeing them at the store), no Crisco for the pan." (Hmm, this is disheartening.) Off I go to the grocery store. Returning, I put all my ingredients on the counter, get out the plastic recipe book holder; I don't want to smudge up and wear out my recipe the very first time. (Say, this sure looks like a lot of stuff to me. Wonder how many loaves it makes.) Rechecking my recipe, it says it makes only one (One!) loaf 6" x 4" x 4". (Oh, my gosh, I don't have a pan that size!) Back to the store I go. My Saturday is not going smoothly. (Where is that Barbara, anyway? Easy for her to say!! Where is she when I need her?) Shucks, I'm out of time. I'll have to wait until next Saturday.

Clues: I am struggling! And, I'm looking for help. I don't have the materials I need, time is a problem, there is no recognizable management of anything here.

Level 3—MECHANICAL USE

Sparing my reader the gory details, it is now 10 consecutive Saturdays and eight loaves later (it took two Saturdays to get organized). I now have the ingredients (no trip to the store is necessary); I've gotten the task down to 2 1/2 hours; however, I'm still using the plastic recipe holder to protect the recipe because I still read and reread

and reread the recipe each step of the way. I'm also trying to figure out how to speed things up a bit and to ferret out how to eliminate the burning on the bottom (On the top is OK; makes for crunchy crust). Oh, well, finicky is for cats.

Clues: It does happen! The stuff gets mixed up to the correct proportions and it does come out of the oven within the approximate time; however, it's a bit black on the top and bottom. My response: "I can do it, but it's a lot of work and the result doesn't quite match my pictures."

Level 4—ROUTINE USE

At last! I can whip it up in 30 minutes and have mastered the recipe." (I don't have to use the plastic holder anymore; reading it once is enough). And my loaves aren't black on the bottom or the top!! Funny thing though, there is always as much of the loaf left when I get home on Friday as when I left Sunday evening.

Barbara asks how my housemates like the bread. "My housemates?" I ask blankly. "What about them?" (Barbara knows there are three of us at the house.) "Hmm, well, they don't seem to eat much of it, just me, I guess." Barbara

asks why. "I don't know; I'll ask." (Barbara knows!) "Maybe they'd like sesame seeds or something on it."

Clues: From my perspective things are going just fine. Little effort is needed to do the job now. But so far I've not thought much about others' responses. As I begin to think about how what I'm doing works for others, I'm brought toe to toe with an important decision, in fact, a critical turning point. From this point forward, am I willing to direct my attention to how my efforts work for those around me? Finally, I decide to find out why others don't eat my bread and commit myself to do something about it.

Level 5—REFINEMENT

So I begin my quest to discover why it is that people in my household don't eat my bread. The information is specific and concrete, i.e., useful but decidedly discouraging. I consider whether it is worth it to me to make the effort to make the changes necessary to have it work better for them. So I ask them, "Well, what if I add sesame seeds or raisins or some-

thing like that?" I go back to Barbara (my trusted mentor) and ask her for other (still relatively simple but tasty) recipes I might try. She's delighted (Darn her!). I come home with several that include the special things to meet the finicky tastebuds of my household. Dawns the Saturday. This time, in my foresight, I have acquired the right ingredients. I'm ready. I even risk not using the plastic recipe holder (I'm getting good at this stuff!). In less than two hours and a quarter, wonderful smelling, terrific looking, and wow-tasting bread (two loaves this time) pop from the oven, sporting some new ingredients and experimental toppings. Wow! Tasty bread!

CLUES: I am in pursuit of information about how I can make the bread better for others and I am committed to doing so. Notice that my skill in preparing for the new changes is much more advanced than when I first entered the preparation level. (Almost any change, however seemingly slight, will push one back to earlier levels of implementation but, usually, the trip back to the refinement level goes much more quickly than the first journey.)

Level 6—INTEGRATION/COLLABORATION

Am I pleased and confident! I've worked out all the bugs (forgive the computer language reference) in the recipes Barbara has given me, experimented and even made some changes on my own. But my household is demanding and they want more and better! I become the instiga-  tor in setting up a bread baking support group—The International Order of Bread Bakers! We share and share, talk and talk. Our first Recipe Swap Meet is wildly successful (and wild). We are now challenging the time-honored kitchen wisdoms about baking bread. In our collective search for the Better Loaf, we all make significant changes in our individual baking practices.

Clues: Having exhausted my individual resources for adapting my bread baking program, I have gotten together with others to share ideas and solutions. In doing so, I am able to make further changes in my baking to improve the outcome of my labors for the recipients.

Level 7—RENEWAL

After months of collaborating and making changes based on our collective work, we have uncovered a major AH, HA! "There must be a better mousetrap!" My helpful household makes a sug-

gestion: "Forget the bread. How about croissants?" (Oh, no!!!) Visions of my terrible shopping trips, plastic recipe holder, reading, re-reading, and re-re-reading the recipe, and black top and bottom pass before my eyes. I groan out loud. Can I really bear to go back to the level of non-use again and work painstakingly and painfully down through the levels of implementation again? "No, no, no, and NO!" (But I do like croissants!)

CLUES: At this stage I have great skill and expertise in bread baking. I can adapt or make up recipes at will (and are they delicious!). But there is a cloud on the horizon—this just isn't enough anymore. I'm becoming restive. And, yes, bread baking has suddenly become insufficient—there must be something better. I search high and low for the better loaf.

At the later stages of this level, you can easily recognize a dangerous person! Finally, with great relish, I decide to abandon the old bread baking routines and leap into crois-  sant baking. And, if I can convince my fellow international friends of the wonderment of croissants, there will be a whole-lotta' baking going on and the entire bunch of us will go back to the stage of non-use—baking croissants is, after all, a new task. The decision to shift to croissants is a major one, not unlike adoption of a new continuum or new textbook or restructuring the curriculum. However, since there is considerable carryover to some of the related skills and knowledge, this journey will be much easier. Better yet, I have a clear picture (with trained taste buds as well) of what a baker of dough does and needs.

The dog days we complain about are usually times we realize we've gone back to zero in a number of areas. The half-empty glass explanation is that the reform model our school has adopted doesn't work. The half-full glass explanation is that we are making progress but have just added a new element to an instructional strategy that has temporarily taken us back to Level 0.

Also, knowing where you are helps you plan what staff development content you need to move yourself forward. For example, the inservice content should answer these questions:

Level	Content Needs to Be Addressed:
0	What's in this for me? What/how would it improve things for students and for me?
1	How does this work? What exactly do I have to do? Convince me that it's a good idea and doable (Where's the support?) Convince me to say, "Yes, I will do this."
2	Having decided to do this, lay it on me! Give me all the details I need—materials, management structures, knowledge and skills, etc.
3	Come coach me. Watch what I do and tell me what to fix/where I can improve? Why do I seem to be working so hard and getting so little result? Why aren't I getting better results from/with my students?
4	What? Make changes . . . and go back to zero! Convince me that ____ (the "it" you're doing at Level 4) can result in higher outcomes for students and that this would be worth the effort to make these changes.
5	Explain what those changes would be and help me figure out how to do them.
6	Let's get together and share. We need time together.
7	We've exhausted the possibilities of our current approach. We need to search for a better mousetrap. Who/what can help us?

The Levels of Use is an invaluable tool when learning something new or making significant changes in something familiar. It is value free, merely descriptive. It explains our sense of frustration with taking two steps forward and, when things change just a bit, taking one or two steps backward (to orientation or mechanical use).

TOOLS FOR GROUP TRANSITION & CHANGE

However extra-ordinary a teacher may be, he/she is only one person. Providing a world-class education to all students requires a concerted and cohesive effort of each and every staff member. No exceptions. Group change requires the transition stage at a group level—going through whatever psychological processes the group as a group must go through to come to terms with the new demands for improving the school—to reinvent the group as a cohesive staff dedicated to working together to create the best possible education for for all students.

This means that the current social groups must dissolve and new groupings committed to getting real work done must be formed. Any serious attempt to implement curriculum in Stages 2-5 require a healthy and productive group environment. You and your colleagues must be willing to apply to yourselves all that you have learned about nurturing collaborative work capacity in your students. Leadership must be revolving, group success is more important than individual ego and social standing. There must be unanimous commitment to doing one's Personal Best when working on the task to be accomplished, etc.

Group change and development must begin with personal and group transitions. Each individual must answer the question, "What must be left behind?" Are there old grudges or slights that must be set aside? Are there lingering resentments about who has played what roles in the past or who got recognition that was not truly deserved? Are there hurt feelings that have never been resolved? Is there anger about events or words that were unfair? And so forth. If so, transition must occur . . . things need to be left behind, individually and as a group.

Some staff environments are so toxic that an experienced group leader will be needed to help people work through the morass. And not just for one session but on an on-going basis until the environment becomes healthy and productive. Remember, adults can't give to students what they don't themselves have. A healthy and productive group environment is essential.

Know Your Goal—Collegial, Not Congenial

As you move through group change, know that your goal is a collegial environment, not a congenial one. This distinction is vital. This professional-social polarization is addressed by Carl Glickman, in his book *Renewing America's Schools: A Guide for School-Based Action.* He describes the dilemma in terms of collegial versus congenial.[10]

"*Congenial* schools are characterized by an open, social climate for adults. Communications are friendly, and teachers, parents, caretakers, and principals easily socialize with one another. Faculty meetings are pleasant, holiday parties are great, refreshments at meetings are plentiful, and faculty members spend time together away from school (aerobics on Thursday night, stress-management workshops. Members describe their school as a nice place where everyone gets along well.

"*Collegial* schools are characterized by purposeful, adult-level interactions focused on the teaching and learning of students. People do not necessarily socialize with one another, but they respect their differences of opinion about education. Mutual professional respect comes from the belief that everyone has the students' interest in mind. The result of such respect is seen in school meetings, where the school community members debate, disagree, and argue before educational decisions are made. Even in the hottest of debates, people's professional respect for others supersedes personal discomfort. People believe that differences will be resolved and that students will benefit. Social satisfaction is a by-product of professional engagement and resolution, of seeing how students benefit, and of the personal regard in which adults hold one another. They become colleagues in the deep sense of being able to work and play together, and each side of the relationship strengthens the other. Being collegial means being willing to move beyond the social facade of communication, to discuss conflicting ideas and issues with candor, sensitivity, and respect. For many schools, the first job is to move from being conventional to being congenial, but the big job for public education is to become collegial, so that social satisfaction is derived mainly from the benefits derived from efforts on behalf of students."

Conventional	Congenial	Collegial
Isolated	Social	Professional respect; personal caring as a by-product of work
Individual teacher's autonomy	Individual teacher's autonomy	Collective autonomy
School seen as physical site for work	Pleasant and open climate for adults	Purposeful conflicts, resolution on behalf of students

Paint the Picture for All to See—The Four P's

According to William Bridges, to make a new beginning, people need four things:[11]

- The purpose—each person can explain the basic logic behind what is to be implemented

- The picture—each can see a clear picture of how what to be implemented will look and feel

- The plan—a step-by-step plan for implementing the new thing, how to get started, how to proceed

- A part to play—a role for each person that allows him or her to be part of the phasing in and full implementation of the new thing

This is especially true when the change to be made is a group task, such as implementing the *HET* model.

Transitions from old to new can be hastened by helping people shape new, specific behaviors for implementing the new changes. Many HET teams use the following, or an adaptation of it, to frame their work together.

Expectations for Working Together

Failure to become an effective group has many causes. One of the most common reasons is the group's failure to meet the unspoken needs of individual members. Meeting needs is hard enough when we know about them; it's virtually impossible if they remain unknown.

Use this worksheet to elicit the typically unspoken needs of the group's individual members. Each person completes the form and shares it with the group. For example:

Personal Needs

Purpose:
To make more effective use of my time

Picture:
That everyone arrives on time
& everyone shares the load

Plan:
To make work assignments clear

Part to Play:
To do my Personal Best to complete my tasks as promised and on time

Professional Needs

Purpose:
To improve my groupwork skills
To plan curriculum as quickly as
    possible

Picture:
To "walk the talk" of the Lifelong
    Guidelines and LIFESKILLS

Plan:
To divide up the curriculum work
    to save time and to share ideas
    (produce the best curriculum)

Part to Play:
To complete the Group Work
    Tasks form for each task and
    complete tasks as written

Group Agreements for Specific Work Tasks

Date_____

Name of Project_____

Name_____

- Tasks I agree to do to make this project successful/complete

  _____Date_____

  _____Date_____

- Research I agree to do and share with my group

  _____Date_____

  _____Date_____

- Materials I agree to make/bring to help complete this project

  _____Date_____

  _____Date_____

Lifelong Guidelines/LIFESKILLS we agree to use during our work together: _____

_____

_____

Deadline for project completion: _____

Questions for Self- and Group-Monitoring

The most difficult aspect of group work is giving feedback to a group member who isn't keeping his/her agreements for group behavior or who is not doing his/her part on group tasks. John Champion, former superintendent, gives us a clean, nonjudgmental, non-confrontation way to bring a member back on board. It is a simple question, one whose exact wording is agreed to in advance:

- We agreed that (identify agreement)_____.

- I see the following behaviors_____.

- Help me to understand how these behaviors are consistent with our agreements.

These questions, agreed on in advance, make it more comfortable for group members to confront and be confronted about behavior that is inconsistent with necessary group agreements. Agreeing how to disagree provides a safe environment for working together.

Impact of Temperament

During any transition and efforts to change, it is critical that we remember who we are so that we make the most of our strengths and compensate for our weaknesses. No one needs to be Hercules, no one needs to be an Einstein, but all of us need to be effective team players.

We are not robots, we are not alike, we cannot expect others to think like we do or to value what we do in the same way. Thus, when working in teams to plan curriculum, we must keep in mind our personality preferences/temperament. We recommend that you revisit Appendix A frequently, especially pp. ApA.2-ApA4— how we take in information and what we value when we make decisions.

Taking in Information. While working with a partner or partners, do recall that, although the end result is the same, "sensors" and "intuitors" go about taking in information very differently. Be patient with each other. One way is not better than another and remember that dual perspectives will produce the best curriculum.

Expect that you will likely choose different starting points. Sensors will likely choose to begin with state standards; intuitors will likely want to begin with the big idea and concepts of the theme. *To resolve these preferences, our advice is that you both agree to start with a physical location.* Go visit it. Then pull forth the state standards and ideas for an organizing concept.

The bottom line is that, no matter what beginning point you might choose, decisions in one area will make you revisit the others. Planning is not linear, one way from beginning to end.

Making Decisions. Deciding what and what not to include in your curriculum is not as easy as it sounds. First of all, there is too much stuff included in state standards and other district-adopted curriculum. Teaching it all to mastery is not possible. Even covering it all is impossible.

Second, each teacher arrives at the table with his/her own set of favorite activities and topics. The LIFESKILL of Flexibility and willingness to compromise is essential.

Understand that "thinkers" are making decisions primarily based on objective, logical considerations about what content best fits in the overlapping area of the Venn circles:

"Feelers," on the other hand, base their decisions primarily on subjective input, perhaps valuing tradition at the school ("the curriculum we've always done before") and empathizing with team mates who agonize over throwing out a favorite unit.

Introvert, Extrovert. No discussion about personality preferences is complete without considering our orientation to others. Extroverts gain energy during committee meetings and think out loud. They are the first to interject a thought while thinking out loud and may be blunt or even offensive.

In contrast, introverts often leave committee meetings feelings drained and unwilling to return. Due to the time necessary to rethink and edit their comments, they often don't get a chance to talk and become frustrated. They may also complain at the ongoing insensitivity of extroverts and their lack of active listening.

Lifestyle. Since much of the work to change a school depends on schoolwide implementation, and similar results by everyone, it is important to stay vigilant about lifestyle—the way we like life to unfold. Those at the "judging" end of the scale—who like organization, closure—may delay implementation until the plan is specific, detailed, and clear. Those on the "perceiving" end of the scale—who just want to get started and often consider waiting for details to be foot dragging—may accuse their colleague of sabotage.

Remember to make plans specific enough for the judgers and beginning dates near enough to convince the perceivers that action will occur.

Honoring and Respecting Each Other

Clearly, a book similar to *Men Are from Mars, Women Are from Venus* could be written here!

In the heat of disagreements and irritations, it's important to remember that two heads are better than one, not just because the collective I.Q. is boosted, but also because perspectives are multiplied. And although pulling together multiple perspectives may be, and usually is, frustrating and time consuming in the short run, it's better in the long run. It will be more thoroughly thought through and will offer students, whose personality preferences differ markedly from their teacher, a curriculum that allows them to be the learners they are.

In the end, everyone wins. But, in the meanwhile, we must remember to honor and respect each others gifts. We strongly recommend that a staff development session be devoted to taking the Keirsey-Bates temperament test and a discussion of what it means for working together. See Appendix A for the reference to *Please Understand Me: Temperament Character intelligence.*

- No lost time at the beginning of the year teaching classroom norms and procedures (half to two-thirds of the class already know them and help teach and enforce them on your behalf)

As you might guess, the above lists could go on and on. The significant idea here is that the multigrade structure provides instructional opportunities for teachers and students that just aren't possible in an age-graded setting.

ENDNOTES

1 William Bridges, *Managing Transitions: Making the Most of Change* (California: Addison-Wesley Publishing Company, Inc., 1991), 3.

2 Bridges, 3.

3 Bridges.

4 Bridges.

5 Bridges.

6 Bridges.

7 Karen.D. Olsen, *Coaching for the HET Model: Delivering on the Promise* (Black Diamond, WA: Books for Educators, 2009), 82.

8 Adapted from Gene Hall, et al, by Karen D. Olsen, *The California Mentor Teacher: Owners' Manual* (Covington, WA: Books for Educators, 1999), 68.

9 Karen D. Olsen, *The California Mentor Teacher Role*, 71-78.

10 Carl Glickman, *Renewing America's Schools: A Guide to School-Based Action* (San Francisco: Jossey-Bass Publishers, 1993), 22-23.

11 Bridges, 55-60.

Chapter 23:
Structural Tools

Structural tools, like computer equipment, come in two varies, hardware and software. The hardware equivalent is the way we organize the school, classrooms, and staffing. The software equivalent is the decision making criteria we use to shape those elements.

HARDWARE

Our traditional graded system is a bureaucratic device born of administrative convenience. However, if we are to create body-brain-compatible learning environments, we must abandon age-grading, departmentalized, fragmented structures in favor of those that put teachers and students in humane, personal settings. While there are numerous ways to do so, many of which can be combined, the following deserve consideration.

The Year Round School

In the ever-shifting world of synaptic connections, there is one undisputable truth: Use it or lose it. Use those connections that allow us to read, to compute, to name the capitals of each state or to lose them.

During the years when federal programs for low achieving students required fall and spring testing, every Chapter 1 director knew that the subsequent fall test scores of returning students would be lower than those of the previous spring. The students didn't continue using their academic synaptic connections and they were lost. The lesson from this is clear: The students who most need public education are least well served by a long summer break.

Consider changing the school calendar so that every 35-45 days there is a two week break. That's not long enough for students to lose their learning and just long enough for staff to rest up and have some joint planning time and/or inservice training.

The Multi-Graded Classroom

Multi-aged classrooms is certainly not a new idea. In fact, it started as a necessity in sparsely populated areas—the little red school house, grades 1-8 in one room. It's being done now by innovative schools that want to increase the quality and outcomes of learning for their students. It's power to enhance student learning is well documented by John Goodlad in his book *The Multigrade Classroom*. Every educator truly interested in improving student outcomes should read this book.

Co-author Karen Olsen attended a one-room school with grades 1-8, for eight years. From a student perspective there are many advantages. Those she most values as an adult include:

- Learning the skills to be both leader and follower

- Opportunities to teach others increases one's own understanding and provides a chance to note one's own progress. This is in marked contrast to the common perception of low achievers in age-graded structures who always feel inadequate compared to their classmates and rarely get opportunities to see how much they have accomplished. In addition, the ego of the very bright students is held in check as they interact with older students and get a realistic appraisal of what is yet to be learned.

- More one-on-one learning opportunities than are possible when there is only one teacher in the room

- When learning from older, more knowledgeable students, finding out what they used the information for and why they valued it enough to want to pass it on

- Discovering the need for genuine collaboration among all age levels (a simple game of baseball wasn't possible unless the entire student body was on the field)

- Mentors to teach me skills and knowledge in areas of personal interest

- Tolerance of different abilities and interests. As a result of our experiences in school, we expected differences and we respected them. (Could it be that our near phobia of "isms" is an outgrowth of the training in sameness that occurs in our schools? Same age, same books, same instructional processes, etc. Ageism, classism, racism, ethnicism, sexism . . . all are expressions of distrust and fear of differences.)

- Passing through adolescence as if it were no big deal (there were only a handful of us)

- Time and space for small group interactions (because there were older students to serve as leaders and teachers) and for intrapersonal time when we wanted

- Opportunities to do everything—drama, singing, writing for the newspaper, etc., and an expectation that we all could and would try them all

- Lack of stress. What wasn't learned this year would be picked up next year. Intellectual growth spurts didn't have to arrive by a certain month or year.

For the teacher, the advantages were also numerous and powerful:

- A great environment for learning to live, acquiring social skills and personal skills such as the LIFESKILLS

- An effective structure in which to meet individual needs and interests by increasing the number of available teachers, tutors, and mentors

- An effective structure for integrating all subjects and skills (wide range of materials allows all students to study the same unit)

- An easier structure for action-based, project-focused teaching because complex, real-life projects that capture student interest can be readily done with multiple levels of skills and interests

- Makes orchestrating genuine, significant schoolwide and community projects easier because older students can anchor many of the subcommittees

- Lots of opportunities to redirect most potential discipline problems by giving older students leadership responsibilities for significant tasks

- Easy to convey to young learners the use of basic skills and high performance standards (modeled by older students)

• No lost time at the beginning of the year teaching classroom norms and procedures (half to two-thirds of the class already know them and help teach and enforce them on your behalf)

As you might guess, the above lists could go on and on. The significant idea here is that the multigrade structure provides instructional opportunities for teachers and students that just aren't possible in an age-graded setting.

Looping

In the instructional structure called "looping," teachers follow their students from one grade to the next for at least two years (better, three or four) and then loop back to begin again with new students. This structure assists both teachers and students to build a self-sustaining community. It eliminates the need to enter school each fall with the dreaded task of spending the first five to six weeks getting to know each other, assessing academic and social skills, and reviewing the skills and concepts learned the previous year. Instead, teachers and students are free to continue where they left off when school ended the previous year. The practice of looping is used in many schools across the United States and is the accepted practice of HET teachers in Bratislava, Slovakia, where teachers have the same students from grades one to four and from five to eight.

Leaping

Similar to looping, teachers using the leaping structure follow their students from the last year of middle school into their first year in high school or from the last year of elementary into the first year of middle school. This has all of the benefits of looping plus the added benefit of easing the transition from middle school to traditional high school environment or elementary school to middle school.

SOFTWARE

The software of our minds when shaping the structure of our schools provides the criteria for making decisions—from the small, hardly noticed, moment-to-moment to those costing tens of thousands of dollars.

When the software is old and unconsciously used, improvement efforts inevitably fail.

Choice of Curriculum and Instruction

Those most far-reaching choice is the one you've already made. By purchasing and reading this book, you've set yourself on the road to education for the 21st century—applying brain research to the classroom and to the entire school. The *HET* model will take you there.

The journey takes three to five years.

Allocation of Resources Using EFT As Goal and Criteria

However you choose to structure your school, your improvement efforts will be greatly enhanced by adopting the concept of Effective First Teaching. Use it as an over-arching goal for all programmatic decisions and as a criteria for all budgeting decisions—for cutting, reallocating, and for allocating new monies.

When coupled with the *HET* model, the EFT software will ensure you have adequate resources when you need them.

For use of EFT as a criteria for all budgeting decisions, see *What Brain Research Can Teach Us About Cutting School Budgets* by Karen D. Olsen.

Appendices

A: Temperament

B: Age Appropriateness

C: Organizing Study Trips

D: Communicating with Parents

E: Conducting Town Hall Meetings

Notes to Myself

Appendix A: Temperament

Excerpted from *Coaching the HET Model: Delivering on the Promise* by Karen D. Olsen. Used by written permission of the publisher.

WHAT MAKES US TICK?

Although teachers have long understood the effect of personality on getting along with others, personality also strongly impacts learning—how a student takes in, organizes, and uses information. And while brain research is still in its infancy[1] when it comes to explaining temperament or personality types, the need to understand and deal with temperament and personality in the classroom is immediate and ongoing and *very* important to life in the classroom. Therefore, until brain research can provide more definitive guidance, we continue to recommend that teachers consider the work of psychologist Carl Jung and those who have updated his work and made it a practical tool, especially the teams of Myers-Briggs and, more recently, Keirsey-Bates.

A fantastically useful (and fun) book on this subject is *Please Understand Me: Character and Temperament Types*[2] by David Keirsey and Marilyn Bates. Building on the work of Carl Jung and Myers and Briggs, Keirsey and Bates put forth a wonderfully useful framework for understanding what makes people tick. We are born with personality preferences and they remain relatively unchanged throughout our

Intelligence

"Each person is a unique bundle of relatively stable 'personality traits' overlaid by more temporary emotional states and colored by ever-shifting moods and feelings."

William Poole,
The Heart of Healing, 1993

life. Thus, it behooves us to understand them and work with them, not against them—for ourselves and for others. Viewing how they go about learning, moves students yet one more step toward becoming self-directed, lifelong learners.1

Temperament types or personality preferences strongly impact the learning process by affecting four important areas:

- How learners take in information
- How they organize during learning and when applying learning
- What they value when making decisions
- How they orient to others

We are born with these temperament types. The place we call home—where we feel most comfortable on each of these four areas of behavior—remains relatively unchanged throughout life.

However, preferences are just that—preferences. They are preferred ways of behaving but one is not stuck at any one place along a scale. Anyone can slide along the scales if and when he/she chooses. All it takes is the desire to do so, practice to acquire the skills needed to operate from another point along the continuums, and then willingness to be a bit uncomfortable as we leave "home."

It is important to note, however, that the further away our "learned" behavior is from "home" on the scales, the greater the energy drain, the greater the stress but also the greater the range of situations in which one can operate successfully if desired. The scale most stubborn to change (and the scale whose degree of change is limited) is how we take in information.[3] Great change can be made along the other three scales. For example, the woman who is valued by her friends because she is empathetic and always takes people's feelings into account when making decisions but at home must play the role of disciplinarian for the family and model objective and logical decision making; or the worker who works assiduously through the daily to-do list but whose personal life is spontaneous and open to new action every day; or the introvert who becomes an effective keynote speaker.

Although seldom mention in education, temperament theory, sometimes called personality preferences, is used widely in the corporate world. There are numerous magazines and newsletters dedicated to this subject. Our resource for the classroom is *Please Understand Me: Character and Temperament Types* by David Keirsey and Marilyn Bates. It is an extraordinarily readable, practical book. Give yourself the gift of reading about the self inside, hidden beneath the classroom roles of teacher and student. See also www.keirsey.com.

Lifelong Traits

Although born with these personality preferences, we can learn to shift our behavior along the four temperament scales. This is a critical skill when operating in the real world where things are as they are, not as we'd like them to be.

We strongly recommend that you give students, grades three and up, the Keirsey-Bates temperament survey the first week of school. Explain the behaviors typical of the ends of each continuum or scale below plus:

- Where they are on the scales
- Where the members of their Learning Club are on the scales
- That they can learn to slide along the scales when it's important to them to work successfully with another

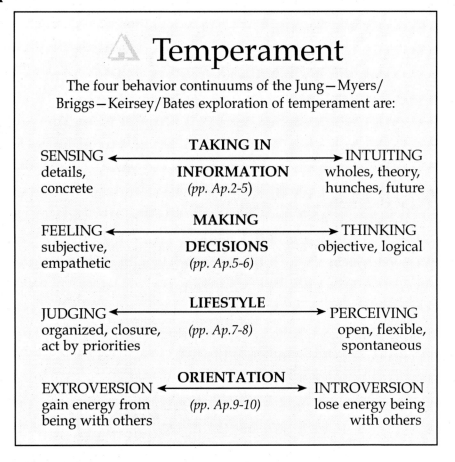

Temperament

The four behavior continuums of the Jung–Myers/Briggs–Keirsey/Bates exploration of temperament are:

	TAKING IN	
SENSING ⟵		⟶ INTUITING
details, concrete	**INFORMATION** *(pp. Ap.2-5)*	wholes, theory, hunches, future
	MAKING	
FEELING ⟵		⟶ THINKING
subjective, empathetic	**DECISIONS** *(pp. Ap.5-6)*	objective, logical
	LIFESTYLE	
JUDGING ⟵		⟶ PERCEIVING
organized, closure, act by priorities	*(pp. Ap.7-8)*	open, flexible, spontaneous
	ORIENTATION	
EXTROVERSION ⟵		⟶ INTROVERSION
gain energy from being with others	*(pp. Ap.9-10)*	lose energy being with others

TAKING IN INFORMATION[4]

Knowing how we and our students take in information is critical both to teaching content and guiding behavior. Differences in this area are at the root of most friction, exasperation and, occasionally, complete inability to get along with family, friends, co-workers, students. Never mind differences in values or interests; if the information we receive isn't what the speaker intended, communication and relationships quickly roll downhill. How we take in information can alter the incoming message, especially if our way of taking in information differs considerably from that of the speaker.

It is important to note that this aspect of temperament describes the internal "wiring" of the mind—*how it works* when it acquires sensory input and munches it about to make meaning of it, to relate it to prior learning, to make it meaningful, to apply it. This is different from the issue of how one acquires information or brings it in from outside. *At issue here is what the brain does with what it gathers and the form it prefers it in as it does so*.

Sensing

Those who prefer to learn via details and concrete input, called sensors, learn by dealing with what can be seen, heard, touched, or otherwise directly experienced. Figuratively, they're from Missouri, the "show me" state. They learn by gathering details, collecting them one after the other, and fitting them together until they snap into place, into a pattern that makes sense. This is much like putting together a puzzle without knowing what the framework or picture is ahead of time. Most of us are this kind of learner—75 percent of the population.[5]

TAKE IN

SENSING	INFORMATION	INTUITIVE
details, concrete		wholes, theory, hunches, future

Sensors on the very end of the continuum need assistance in seeing and applying the big picture—the parts in relationship to the whole and to each other. They often have difficulty dealing with two or more competing ideas or ideas that are not fully compatible.

Ambiguity is unsettling to them. Sensors learn best by being allowed to interact with the real world, not textbooks which are an abstraction of the real world and so fragmented that the pieces never add up. The real world helps them see how the pieces fit together.

Intuiting

In contrast, intuitors are sometimes referred to as the "big W" people—*whole notion*. They prefer to begin with the big picture—a framework or theory to give meaning to the pieces. Intuitors want to know the theory or the why behind a thing before they get into the details about it; they work well going from theory to application. They are "what if" people, preferring to deal with the possible rather than the details of the actual; they deal in hunches, the future, and the abstract. Often they are very impatient with details and consider the typical school curriculum quite boring.

It is important to note, however, that the end result for both sensors and intuitors is the same—a full understanding of the concept and the particulars. What differs is the route and, at times, the speed, in reaching the destination. One kind of learner is not smarter than another. Just different.

Why is this discussion about ways of taking in information important? Because it tells us a great deal about how to write curriculum—both key points and inquiries.

Implications for Sensors. When comparing and organizing, the sensor generally tends to work with smaller pieces. At first glance, our traditional curriculum would seem ideal for these students—small pieces for learners who prefer pieces. Unfortunately, the pieces of the curriculum, e.g., 847 skills for reading, are so small that they don't add up, they don't make sense.

When information is presented via second-hand sources, which it typically is, perceiving meaning is even harder. Worse yet for the sensor is information presented via symbolic sources; learning becomes nearly impossible for most sensors. It's not surprising to find that, of those students who drop out of school before completing the 8th grade, 99.6 percent of them are sensors.[6] A truly shocking statistic! The typical curriculum does not help the sensor develop the capacity to see how the pieces of the curriculum and their world come together. It fails to give sensors a big picture of what's going on and why it's important—crucial triggers that tell the brain to store something in long-term memory.

To improve chances of success for sensors:

- Develop key points that are concepts rather than factoids.

- Always teach concepts and skills in the context of real-life uses familiar to students. Focus on the why and the how. Check for understanding of the big picture as you go.

- Revisit your *being there* location numerous times, going more in-depth and more big-picture each time. Focus on how people use the concepts and skills of your curriculum to be intelligent users/participants at that location.

- Lead with inquiries based on the middle levels of Bloom's Taxonomy—application. Then progress to the upper levels—analysis, evaluation, and synthesis. Finish with comprehension and knowledge—the form of most tests.

Implications for Intuitors. Since most of the curriculum and instructional tools of the traditional classroom are fragmented and piecemeal, intuitors are frustrated and bored much of the time. Extreme intuitors, like the extreme sensor, often act out their frustration. These are the curriculum-induced behavior problems—the under achievers, students we know could and should be doing much better than they are.[7]

To improve chances of success for intuitors:

- Develop key points that are conceptual rather than factoid.

- Always teach concepts and skills in the context of real-life uses familiar to students. Focus on how the theory is applied and the details of how it is done.

- Early in your direct instruction, explain the theory behind

what is being studied so that the details make sense and have a post office box in the brain.

- Lead with inquiries based on the middle levels of Bloom's Taxonomy—application. Then progress to the upper levels—analysis, evaluation, and synthesis. Finish program-building practice with comprehension and knowledge—the form of most standardized tests.

Bloom's Taxonomy and How Students Take In Information

As discussed in Chapter 13, Bloom's taxonomy is a key resource when writing inquiries because it focuses on actions to be taken. Although not truly hierarchical (higher representing "better" thinking), the different levels do require different mixes of "pieces and wholes" thinking—taking in and processing input like a sensor or like an intuitor. Thus, temperament and Bloom's Taxonomy complement each other. When overlaid, they sharpen our understanding of how to help students learn more effectively. The chart below illustrates the nature of pieces-to-wholes mental processing required by curriculum developed at each level of Bloom's Taxonomy: K=knowledge, C=comprehension, AP=application, AN=analysis, E=evaluation, S=synthesis.[8]

For example, intuitive learners prefer working on inquiries that require them to apply, analyze, evaluate, and synthesize information. They typically find inquiries written for knowledge and comprehension quite boring. Sensors, on the other hand, are often frustrated with inquiries written at the evaluation and synthesis levels and are more comfortable with knowledge and comprehension questions.

Given these differences, we recommend that you begin your curriculum writing and lesson planning with a focus on application. This directs your thinking to how the concept or skill to be taught is demonstrated at the *being there* location and provides a common entry point for both sensors and intuitors.

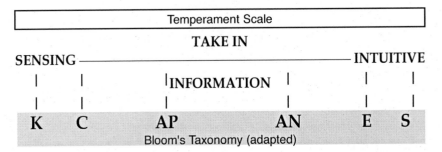

Temperament Scale

TAKE IN

SENSING ———————————————————— INTUITIVE

INFORMATION

| K | C | AP | AN | E | S |

Bloom's Taxonomy (adapted)

Our job as teachers is to help students spread their wings to become proficient learners from all kinds of input in all kinds of settings. Further study should challenge both sensors and intuitors, giving all students ample practice in every level of Blooms' Taxonomy and ensuring a mix to enhance their problem-solving/product-producing capabilities as adults. (For a discussion of how to use Bloom's taxonomy in curriculum development, see pages 13.9-10.)

DECISION MAKING[9]

Effective decision-making is a bedrock skill for lifelong learning. Among many important decisions is the recurring "Do I want to learn this, or not?" "Will mastering this concept/skill move me toward my goals?" "What are my goals as a learner?" "What do I want to specialize in when I grow up?" "What's my answer to peer pressure to use drugs?" And on and on.

The decision-making scale described by Keirsey and Bates examines what people value as they perceive and weigh facts, events, circumstances, their own thoughts and feelings, and those of others, to make a decision. Because decision making is a skill so fundamental to success in life, we must give our students the gift of learning about themselves and others.

Feeling

Those at the feeling end of the scale strongly value *how the decision will affect others,* more so than the logic or principle(s) or the cold, hard facts involved. As a consequence, their decisions tend to be subjective and empathetic. For example, if a "feeling" police officer stopped a car for rolling through a stop sign enroute to the hospital delivery room, he would likely conclude that, under the circumstances, allowing the nervous young father to get the soon-to-be mother in labor to the hospital as quickly as possible was more important than applying the usual consequences for the stop sign infraction. He might even escort them to the hospital.

To improve chances of success for feelers:

- Because the willingness to learn is the learner's choice, remember to provide inspirational pep talks when engaging students in new lines of inquiry. Focus on feelings.

- Guide student reflection on how they felt about working together and how successful they were in sliding along the scale to increase the potential for group success. Ask "How did you feel about _____?" kinds of questions. Use reflective thinking questions following collaborative work to focus their attention on what they value when they make decisions and how they felt during the activity.

- When disciplining the feeling student, always point out how his/her actions made the other person feel.

DECISION

FEELING———————————————————THINKING

MAKING

- When studying literature or history or conducting a class meeting, make sure that you point out the emotional issues and themes, the angst of the situation.

Thinking

The "thinking" decision-makers *value the objective, logical elements*. If the principle is x then the choice of y is obvious and not to be distorted by extraneous circumstances or the reactions of the people involved. Thus, a thinking police officer observing the same stop sign infraction would likely conclude that labor pains do not necessarily signal imminent birth and that the safety of others as well as the mother-to-be and child is of paramount importance. The nervous husband should receive a ticket *and* be monitored for several blocks to ensure that he doesn't speed or run another stop sign.

Life in a Bureaucracy. It is not difficult to imagine the reactions of feelers and thinkers making decisions together in our public school bureaucracy which tends to zigzag between extremes and non-action. For example, zero tolerance drug/weapon policies violate the feelers sense of justice when a bystander is swept up in a dragnet because he/she is a friend of one of the offenders and thus was in the wrong place at the wrong time.

On the other hand, thinkers are driven to distraction when the system turns a blind eye to instances of bad behavior because of political pressure, lethargy of individual staff not wanting to bother applying the consequences, or the issues don't show up on the system's radar screen even though it bugs students. Some inconsistencies in decision making are part of human behavior and teacher judgment about individual differences. However, when students participate in pull-out programs and must deal with multiple teachers, all of whom decide procedures and behavior differently, students become frustrated. The solution lies not in having more rules but in opening up the dialogue about the importance of decisions and how each of us weigh the alternatives.

Life in a Learning Club. Collaborative work can really strain relationships if students aren't aware of temperament. For example,

thinkers often object when procedures aren't being followed properly. A rule is a rule. Feelers often react to the nature and circumstances of an issue and the perceived fairness, regardless of the rules. Needless to say, groupwork goes much more smoothly for students and teacher if students are taught this information about decision-making early in the year as part of group development and LIFESKILLS.

To improve chances of success for thinkers:

- Because the willingness to learn is the learner's choice/ decision, remember to provide convincing arguments and "what if" explorations when engaging students in new lines of inquiry.

- Guide students to reflect on how temperament helped or hindered group work and how successful they were in sliding along the scale to accomplish the task. Ask "What/how well did you think about _____?" kinds of questions. Use reflective thinking questions[10] following collaborative work to focus students' attention on what they value when they make decisions.

- When disciplining the thinking student, always point out the consequences of his/her actions. Ask "what if" questions such as "What if you were Jack and someone did that to you?" "What if Jack had fallen a little harder and broken his arm?" "What would it take for you to control your temper a little bit more?"

- When studying literature or history or conducting a class meeting, make sure that you point out the "what if" questions. For example, what if others had joined in the same behavior, would the society/class/family collapse?

LIFESTYLE[11]

Lifestyle refers to how people like to organize their lives—not lifestyle as in living high on the hog. On one end of the scale are people who live life by judging—not in the sense of good or bad but rather by decree or judgment, e.g., in Camelot, by decree of the king, it only snows between certain hours during certain months of the year. Camelot is a very orderly, predictable world.

On the other end of the scale are the spontaneous folk who attend to what's happening right now, not five minutes ago, not in response to agreed upon priorities (unless that's what's going on now). These people are open, flexible, and tolerate ambiguity.

In any group setting, it is essential to value the qualities on the other end of the lifestyle scale (and anywhere along it). A healthy tension between demand for organization and attention to the events and demands of the moment almost always produces a better result, a better mouse trap, greater learning for students, and better curriculum and instructional programs by teachers.

LIFESTYLE
JUDGING————————————————————PERCEIVING
organized, closure, priorities   open, flexible, spontaneous

Judging

The judging person likes a great deal of organization and closure, avoids surprises and ambiguity, and prefers clear priorities.

These are the makers (and doers!) of to-do lists, people who set and work toward priorities, and who are adamant about closure and nailing down loose ends. The judging person is the one to announce in a loud voice during a meeting, "Well, what's the decision here? We've wasted 25 minutes and no decision has been made! For heaven's sake, let's stop the jawing and make a decision before more time is wasted!" Ambiguity is intolerable, closure (even if the decision is a bad one) is highly valued. Also, judgers do not like surprises in their world. They plan carefully to make things run smoothly and predictably.

To improve chances of success for judgers:

- Realize that being a judger is innate. Ambiguity and unmade decisions are genuinely unsettling and even upsetting. Judgers appreciate and expect directions to be clear and well thought through. Changing directions makes them uncomfortable.

- Be organized. Have an agenda every day and follow it. When you deviate, do so for a good reason and explain why and how you will handle the change, such as when undone tasks will get finished.

- Develop and use written procedures. When many parts of the day are predictable, judgers can then begin to handle small amounts of ambiguity and develop their tolerance for doing so over time.

- Develop inquiries that are clear and unambiguous about what is to be done and what the final product is to look like.

- Judgers often have their own schemes for organizing and may resist the teacher's method. When possible, invite students to come up with ways of organizing, tackling problem solving or producing a product. However, be watchful for the students who insist there is only one good way to do things. Help those students develop more flexibility, to operate based on the circumstances of the moment rather than on a fixed view of the world.

Perceiving

Perceivers, on the other hand, literally perceive their environment *right now*, take in new information, perceive the essence of what's happening now—minute-by-minute and then respond to the "right now" situation. Forget the to-do lists and last week's priorities. The moment is now!

Perceivers are frequently described as open, flexible, spontaneous. And those are the nice words to describe them! Colleagues who are in supervisory or close teaming roles with the perceiver often use other, not-so-kind descriptions! For example, deadline for a perceiver means "It's almost time to start." A loose end, not a problem; it's never too late to rethink an issue or change one's course of action. Ambiguity? No worries. Handle things as they come up; just improvise a little. Got a fire to put out, a crisis to handle? Here is your person! Spontaneity is the hallmark of the perceiver.

Working Together. For the judger and perceiver to work together—as team teachers or as students in a cooperative learning group—is assuredly a strain. For example, imagine traveling together . . . the judging person, in pre-terrorist times, was likely to insist upon arriving at the airport at least an hour in advance, prepaid ticket with pre-assigned seating designation in hand. In contrast, the perceiver was likely to cut arrival time down to the very last minute—no ticket and, not unlikely, no reservation. He/she was the last passenger to enter the plane, giving a slight leap to clear the widening gap as the jetway was pulling back.

In the Classroom. In classroom settings, the perceiving student is an anomaly, a square peg that the highly routinized bureaucracy tries to jam into a round hole. Spontaneity? This is **the** schedule. Flexibility? You may choose the odd-numbered questions for homework or the even-numbered ones. Distracted by the real world outside the window? None of that. Get back to your work.

Although approximately 38 percent of the general population is an SP personality, a combination of sensing and perceiving, only two percent of teachers are SP types. This means that few SP children will ever have an SP teacher who understands and can appreciate their temperament type.

To improve chances of success for perceivers:

- Realize that the rules and essence of bureaucracy create an especially difficult environment for perceivers. Just getting by from minute-to-minute is a strain. Provide moments of relief through humor, guide bird walks gently back to the topic rather than just interrupting and scolding, allow choices, and most of all, appreciate the differences instead of becoming annoyed by them.

- Realize that being a perceiver is not a temporary disability. It is a personality preference from birth onward and it is part of who that person is. The role of education is to expand students' options in life rather than punish them because who they are is frequently and, to a bureaucracy, fundamentally irritating. Therefore, teach perceivers to use their perceiving tendencies to good advantage and to recognize when those tendencies are a disadvantage and how to slide along the scale when circumstances call for it. Teach them the LIFESKILL of Perseverance and encourage them to take responsibility for completing a final product before moving on to the next thing.

- Ensure that choice is available and then help the perceiver to complete the chosen inquiries/tasks.

- Whenever possible, assign perceivers jobs and inquiries that have some unpredictability to them, that call for flexibility and resourcefulness.

ORIENTATION TO SELF AND OTHERS[12]

Extroversion and introversion are two commonly known qualities. Much of the folk wisdom about them is accurate enough to be useful. Not so well known, however, is the energy flow that occurs.

ORIENTATION

EXTROVERSION————————————————INTROVERSION

gains energery from
being with others

loses energy being
with others

Extroversion

Extroverts gain energy from being with others. For example, when completely fatigued, extroverts go where there are people such as to a party—arriving early and going home late, returning refreshed and frisky. They literally absorb energy from others. Thus, many introverts find it exhausting to be around a highly extroverted person.

To improve chances of success for extroverts:

- As teacher, master the ability to gear up and gear down your energy flow to match that of individual students and groups. Model it for students; teach them how to do it.

- Understand that extroverts think out loud and need talking time to learn. Develop a tolerance for "busy noise" when students are talking yet still on task.

- Make sure you build in group interaction time (even groups of two). Include inquiries that call for group work. Vary the nature of the activities to best fit extroverts at times and introverts at others. For example, a steady diet of cooperative learning assignments is as deadly for introverts as an unvarying lecture is for extroverts.

- Provide quiet time for extroverts to learn to appreciate their own company. Teach them to use their inner voice as a learning partner, to talk themselves through things on their own, especially when solving problems and producing products.

Introversion

Introverts, on the other hand, lose energy when around other people. When tired, a party or any grouping of people is the last place introverts want to go. They instead prefer to go off to a quiet place alone and re-energize from the inside out. It is important to note, however, that introverts can behave like an extrovert. Many introverts can socialize and dramatize along with the best of the extroverts. Many have jobs that require a high degree of extrovertive behavior. However, the energy cost to an introvert for such jobs is very high, the basis of burn-out for many.

To improve chances of success for introverts:

- As teacher, master the ability to gear up and gear down your energy flow to match that of individual students and groups. Model it for students; teach them how to do it.

- Active learning requires huge amounts of mental energy that can easily be drained away when introverts interact with others. Classrooms that are out of control or that overuse cooperative learning or have lots of conflict (student-student and student-teacher) can become incapacitating for introverts, stealing the energy they need for learning. Use your classroom leadership to create an environment that doesn't rob energy from introverts. Include choices that call for individual work, work in teams of two rather than five, and so forth. Create quiet corners where introverted students can go during the day to reenergize themselves.

- Teach introverts how to participate in groupwork without becoming uncomfortable and drained of energy.

- Make sure you have a balance of introvert-extrovert activities. For introverts, reflection time and journal writing, SSR reading time, individual projects, and working in pairs rather than as a learning club. For extroverts, collaboration, collaboration, collaboration—with as many people as possible!

THE IMPACT OF PERSONALITY

The impact of personality on school participation and achievement is enormous. We should stop expecting everyone to be like us; we need to begin to understand and appreciate our differences and learn how to make them an asset, rather than an irritant, in the daunting task of succeeding in life.[13]

In addition, we must keep foremost in our minds that powerful learning (greatest depth, speed, ability to apply) occurs when learners are able to operate consistent with their mental wirings. Schools must remold themselves to fit children rather than expect children to change how they learn to fit how schools teach. For example, although 38 percent of the general population are a combination of sensor and perceiver (SP), only two percent of teachers are that temperament type. On the other hand, 56 percent of teachers (compared to only 38 percent in the population at large) are sensor-judgers (SJ).[14] Thus, it is rare for SP students ever to have an SP teacher, someone who understands them. On the

> *We must recommit ourselves to the idea that schools must remold themselves to fit children rather than expect children to change how they learn to fit how schools teach.*

other hand, SJ students have many teachers whose temperament matches theirs; school is a relatively comfortable experience for them.

Most shocking of all, 75-90 percent of at-risk students are SP personalities. They are not "drop outs," they are "push outs." The system is simply too structured, too rigid, too boring, too oppressive.[15] While SJ students have less than a four percent chance of drop outs, SP students have a 34 percent chance of dropping out. This means that SP students are nine times as likely to become casualties of the system and for no other reason than their temperament, the temperament they were born with.

ENDNOTES

1 According to Robert Sylwester, Emeritus Professor of Education, University of Oregon, study of temperament has in the past been "essentially oriented around *mind* and not *brain* research." In the world of brain research, "brain" and "mind" are definitely not interchangeable. Brain research is the stuff of physiology, the biology that can be seen and measured. Mind is explored through observable behaviors. Letter to the authors, August 4, 2003.

2 David Keirsey and Marilyn Bates. *Please Understand Me: Character and Temperament Type.* California: Prometheus Nemesis Book Co., 1984. Although an undated version is available, we prefer this book because of its brevity and clarity.

3 This limit in the degree of possible change is a critical piece of information for curriculum developers. It should not, however, be considered reason to limit to what students are initially prepared to take in. Quite the opposite is true as indicated on page ApA.10. Students need practice taking in information that ranges along the scale but when struggling in the early stages to understand a concept, they need to be given curriculum in the form from which they can best extract meaning.

4 Keirsey and Bates, 16-19.

5 Keirsey and Bates, 160.

6 Keirsey and Bates, 160.

7 It's not just the students who "act out" when the curriculum is boring and/or the instructional strategies don't fit how they learn. Think of your colleagues during inservice trainings. Sensors are driven to distraction by theories (which they tend to call "ivory tower notions"). A successful inservice for them is one with a minimum of theory and a maximum of practicality—specifics and step-by-step how-tos.

Intuitors, on the other hand, are often insulted by step-by-step how-tos, especially those lessons or assignments that are highly detailed and, to them, obvious once they understand the theory or general principles behind the details. They chafe at presentations that do not give them the theory or framework first and then allow them to figure out the details. It just "doesn't make sense" if they have no frame of reference from which to judge the purpose or usefulness of the specifics.

The lesson here is that we teach the way we learn but if we want all children to learn from us, we must teach as intuitor **and** sensor.

8 Olsen, Karen D. *Making Bodybrain-Compatible Education a Reality: Coaching for the ITI Model.* (Covington, Washington: Books for Educators, 1999), Chapter 7.

9 Keirsey and Bates, 20-22. Please note that the use of "feeling" in this discussion does not at all parallel the use of feeling and emotion used in brain research, such as in the work of Antonio Damasio and others examining the emotional system of the brain.

10 Students cannot become self-directed learners until they master the art of reflective thinking, reflecting not only on things after the fact (learning from what they have just done) but also anticipating what is to come (applying previous experiences to the task at hand).

Feelers must learn to keep in mind the facts and the outcomes, not just feelings during the process. Thinkers must learn to keep in mind how people around them feel about the process of an activity and how they feel about the outcome.

Good leaders keep track of both, which enables them to lead a wide spectrum of people, not just those like themselves. While most areas of leadership capability seem to be unconscious, this area can become conscious and thus utilized by students (and adults) on a minute-by-minute basis until it becomes a habit of mind.

11 Keirsey and Bates, 22-24.

12 Keirsey and Bates, 14-16.

13 Keirsey and Bates, 97.

14 Keirsey and Bates, 160.

15 Karen Olsen, An unpublished, study-based survey of more than 100 district administrators in California responsible for reporting and combatting their district's dropout rate, 1985.

NOTES TO MYSELF

Temperament Type of Students I Have Difficulty Connecting With

My Temperament Type

Temperament Type of My Principal

Temperament Type of My Grade Level Colleagues

Appendix B:
Age Appropriateness

A young child's brain is not simply a junior version of an adult brain with less information in it. It processes differently. The human brain unfolds in predictable developmental stages. Each stage is like an ever more complex template laid over the top of the previous one. At each of these stages, the brain is capable of more complex thinking, comparing, and analyzing.

Following is a brief overview of developmental stages based on Dr. Larry Lowery's application of Piaget's work[1] to science education. It is taken from Dr. Lowery's presentations to administrators and teachers of the Mid-California Science Improvement Program (MCSIP, 1987-97)) and in his book, *Thinking and Learning: Matching Developmental Stages with Curriculum and Instruction.*[2]

AGE THREE TO FIRST GRADE—COMPARING THE KNOWN TO THE UNKNOWN

During this stage of life, children learn to understand more words (and the concepts behind them) than they will for the rest of their lives. The child does this by putting real, concrete objects through what is called one-to-one correspondences—putting two objects together on the basis of a single property and learning from these comparisons more than was known before. According to Lowery, the child constructs fundamental concepts about the physical world and its properties (similarity and difference comparisons by size, shape, color, texture, etc.), about ordinal and cardinal numbers (one-to-one correspondence of varying degrees), about all measures (comparison of known to unknown), and about the use of symbols to stand for meaning (word recognitions).[3]

Trial and Error

The major mode of operation at this stage is trial and error. Often, adults mistakenly try to help the child in an attempt to reduce or eliminate error or they reprimand the child for making an error. This is unfortunate because children, liked scientists, learn as much (sometimes more) from errors as from expected, correct results. Whether putting puzzle shapes into the wrong space, putting shoes on the wrong feet while learning to dress, or falling off a tricycle, for the child, an error spurs the learning process along.

One Property at a Time

An important characteristic of this stage is that the child does not yet have the ability to group objects using more than one property simultaneously,[4] such as pairings based on size, color, shape, texture, or speed—all made using one property or characteristic to pair them. The three- to six-year-old may also arrange objects by chaining, i.e., the third object in the chain shares an important characteristic with the second object (which was initially chosen to pair with the first object) based on a different characteristic:

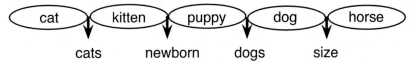

This stage is variously described as the ability to put two objects together on the basis of a single property[5] or learning by one-to-one correspondence. Piaget calls it the pre-operational stage.

According to Larry Lowery, educators "have seldom provided experiences that allow the potential of this stage to develop" because they have not considered the relationships between knowledge of the learner, instruction, and subject matter.[6] As a result, "curriculum materials water down advanced concepts. The cognitive demands of these tasks are often beyond the youngster's level."[7] In contrast, "when teachers challenge children to use this stage of thinking ability, the challenge usually takes the form of a rote-memory/recall routine, something the youngsters can do—but they can do so much more! Unfortunately, teachers predominantly teach the rote-memory/recall routine throughout all the school years."[8]

Age-Appropriate Scientific Thinking Processes[9]

The scientific thinking processes appropriate for this developmental level are observing, communicating, and comparing two items using just one property at a time.[10] At this developmental level, the emphasize should be on exploration, wide-ranging experiences with the real world, sometimes referred to as "messing around" with real things in the real world. Context is important.

Age-Appropriate Curriculum

Organizing concepts recommended by grade level are:[11]

For kindergarten—People can learn about things around them by observing them carefully—what they are made of, how they are put together, what they do, and how they are similar and different. Observing and comparing similarities and differences is a key way to help interpret and understand our world. Often we can learn even more about those things if we do something to them and note what happens.

For first grade—All living things, including humans, have basic needs (food, water, air, protection from weather, disease, and predators, reproduction). A habitat is the place where the animal or plant lives while meeting these needs.

SECOND GRADE TO THIRD GRADE— PUTTING THINGS TOGETHER, TAKING THINGS APART

At this stage a child develops the capability to group all objects in a set on the basis of one common attribute (as compared to putting only two objects together on the basis of a single property). This capacity begins at about age six (late) and is established for most youngsters by age eight.

According to Lowery, "or the first time the student's mental construct is comprehensive and has a rationale or logic to it. . . . Simple rules can be understood and generated by the student if given the opportunity."[12]

Less Trial and Error . . . More Mental Structuring

At this stage students do less trial and error exploration and are more thoughtful about the actions they impose upon their environment; they create an internal mental structure of those manipulations.[13] An important aspect of students' actions is the rearrangement of the materials with which they work. Students also have the capacity to do things in reverse direction without distorting the concept, e.g., 3 + 2 = 5; 5 - 2 = 3. This is one of the powerful aspects of thinking at this stage.[14]

From an adult's perspective, there is a correct and an incorrect way to put things together or take them apart; the child at variance is thus seen as having done the job incorrectly. Rather than just judging the task, however, adults should also examine the reason why the student chose that particular response and then focus on what the answers reveal about the accuracy and depth of the student understands.

To understand that numbers or ideas may be combined in any order, yet it is possible to return without distorting the starting place, is a really big deal for students in second and third grade.

Reversing Direction without Distortion

According to Larry Lowery, "The ability of the mind to do this—reverse direction without distorting the concept—is one of the powerful aspects of thinking at this stage. And the ability to think is this manner separates humans from computers (which cannot solve problems beyond a binary, comparing solution) and other primates (chimps, baboons, and orangutans can solve problems at the comparing stage but not at this stage)."[15]

This stage is variously described as the ability to put all objects together on the basis of a consistent, single property rationale or putting things together and returning things to the way they were.[16] Piaget's term: early concrete operations.

Age-Appropriate Scientific Thinking Processes[17]

The scientific thinking processes appropriate for this developmental level are observing, communicating, and comparing but, at this developmental stage, using two or more properties at a time.[18] At this developmental level, content should become more conceptual, i.e., study of big ideas that form a web that captures many related ideas. While exploration and wide-ranging experiences with the real world remain essential for high levels of sensory input, less concrete ideas can be explored.

Age-Appropriate Curriculum

Organizing concepts recommended by grade level are:[19]

For second grade—The physical characteristics of animals and plants vary greatly and determine what they can do and how they do it in order to meet their needs. Similarly, the physical characteristics of non-living things vary greatly and determine what changes can occur in them and how they can be used.

For third grade—Things are changing around us all the time. Change can occur in a variety of ways (reversible, irreversible; controllable, not controllable; steady or repetitive and thus fairly predictable or not and thus unpredictable) and for different reasons. The rate and size of change may not be observable with human senses; tools to measure such change are needed. Change can be helpful, harmful, or neutral.

FOURTH GRADE TO SIXTH GRADE— SIMULTANEOUS IDEAS

At about age eight to ten, children develop the capacity to mentally coordinate two or more properties or concepts at a time. According to Lowery, when this capacity is in place—which may occur as early as age eight or as late as age ten—students can comprehend place value in math, the need for controlling variables in a science experiment, the use of similes and multiple themes in literature, and can begin to understand, such as the relationships that exist in free trade in social studies.[20] According to Lowery, "As with earlier capabilities, this new one integrates with those preceding it much like a new map of greater abstraction that can be overlaid upon other layers of maps."[21]

Multiple Properties

At this stage, students enjoy puns and can easily learn about homonyms. In their writing they shift to using multiple descriptors: "an old, bent, tired man." They shift from trial and error thinking to contemplating the effects of comparing two or more situations under different situations.[22] Arrangement of objects now indicates the intersection of multiple properties.

However, students at this developmental level are not yet ready to handle the traditional science "experiment" of stating a hypothesis, controlling the variables, and conducting the systematic testing of each variable individually while all others are held constant in order to determine which are relevant and which have no effect. Unfortunately, our traditional school curriculum treats elementary students as young adults. Yet for our young adults—high school students—the curriculum for the non-college bound is a re-run of what students were given in elementary school and, thus, is unchallenging and often boring.

Piaget refers to this stage as late concrete operations; Lowery's term is simultaneity of ideas.[23]

Age-Appropriate Scientific Thinking Processes[24]

The scientific thinking processes appropriate for this developmental level are observing, communicating, comparing, and organizing.[25] At this developmental level, content should be based in concepts which in turn are based in *being there* experiences.

Age-Appropriate Curriculum

Organizing concepts recommended by grade level are:[26]

For fourth grade — Plants and animals interact with each other and their environment in ways that allow them to meet their basic needs. Keep in mind that humans are animals.

For fifth grade — All structures and systems, living and non-living, are made up of smaller parts and/or processes.

For sixth grade — Both living and non-living systems have situations in which they change in some way and other situations in which they remain essentially unchanged or constant. Why situations in such systems change and why they remain constant can be explained in terms of particular variables. Much change in our world is human-made; some is intended and some inadvertent.

IMPLICATIONS

The idea of age-appropriateness is certainly not new. Montessori, Piaget, and countless others have addressed the issue quite clearly. Yet, it just gets pushed aside by tradition when textbooks and state frameworks are being created. A glance through textbooks from the past several decades shows tradition at its most mindless and blind adherence to "the way we've always done it."

So, what does all this mean for integrated curriculum? The closer the curriculum is to the real world, the more likely it will be age-appropriate rather than abstract and calling for mental processing students don't yet possess.

The purpose of looking at what is appropriate at each age level is to make thoughtful decisions about curriculum content. Making "less is more" decisions requires us to emphasize the concepts that are age appropriate, to integrate through concepts so we can group related concepts together across subject areas and thus save time, and to prioritize by deciding what to place "at the end of the list," knowing full well that it is impossible to cover everything on the list into one school year. We call this selective abandonment, an important tool in managing curriculum development.

It is important to note that although the age at which each capacity comes into place is accurate for most students, bear in mind that there will be some students who reach the developmental earlier and some that reach it later. For the late arrivals, if the mental scaffolding doesn't exist for learning a particular concept, they will need much more full sensory, being there experiences. A slower developmental timetable is usually due to fewer relevant, full-sensory experiences.

Another important lesson here is that just because some students can understand something doesn't mean that all students at that age can. Science content is too often selected on the basis of what a few precocious students are capable of understanding, not what all students are developmentally capable of.

END NOTES

1   The pioneering work into the growth of intelligence was done by Swiss psychologist, Jean Piaget, 1896-1980. One of the most significant psychologists of the twentieth century. Since Piaget, others have studied these developmental stages, including Erickson, 1950, Bruner, 1966, Gagne, 1970, and Vygotsky, 1974-97. Larry Lowery, formerly with the Lawrence Hall of Science and instructor at University of California, Berkeley, provides one of the most practical explanations of developmental levels for those engaged in curriculum development.

2   Because Lowery applies the unfolding of developmental stages specifically to science curriculum and instruction, we have chosen to use his point of view. See Lawrence Lowery, *Thinking and Learning: Matching Developmental Stages with Curriculum and Instruction*. (Black Diamond, WA: Books for Educators, 1989 and 1996), 2.

3   Lowery, 17-19.

4   Lowery, 21.

5   Lowery, 19.

6   Lowery, 22.

7   Lowery, 22.

8   Lowery, 22.

9   See *Kid's Eye View of Science: A Teacher's Handbook for Implementing a Conceptual, Integrated Approach to Teaching Science, K-6* by Karen D. Olsen and Susan J. Kovalik (Thousand Oaks, CA: Corwin Press, 2010). Used with written permission of the authors.

10 Lowery, 23.

11 Karen D. Olsen, *Science Continuum of Concepts for Grades K-6* (Black Diamond, WA: Books for Educators, 1995, 2007, 2010), 6.

12 Lowery, 33.

13 Lowery, 35.

14 Lowery, 36.

15 Lowery, 36.

16 Lowery, 34.

17 Olsen and Kovalik, *Kid's Eye View of Science*. Used with written permission of the authors.

18 Lowery, 34.

19 Olsen, *Science Continuum of Concepts for Grades, K-6.*

20 Lowery, 43.

21 Lowery, 39.

22 Lowery, 40.

23 Lowery, 42.

24 Olsen, *Kid's Eye View of Science.*

25 Lowery, 42.

26 Olsen, *Science Continuum of Concepts, Grades, K-6.*

Appendix C:
Organizing Study Trips

GETTING THE MOST OUT OF YOUR BEING THERE STUDY TRIPS

Being there study trips are a powerful way to introduce curriculum because they provide full sensory input to the brain, create an emotional experience, and provide real-world application of concepts and skills. Through a combination of exploration (individual and group) and mediation2 (guided tour with interpretation), they level the playing field, giving students with no prior experience an opportunity to catch up with more advantaged peers. Study trips are a key strategy in applying brain research to the classroom; therefore, they are not to be used as rewards, nor should students be left behind as a punishment.

To ensure that your being there visitation is more than a motivational tool or fun fling, you need detailed planning and a range of instructional strategies not called for when relying on text-books and worksheets.

Begin Before You Start

A successful study trip to a being there location starts before you leave the classroom. Make sure you have completed the curriculum planning work outlined in Chapters 12-17 before you begin planning the study trip. As you plan your study trip, keep in mind these two questions as you proceed:

- What do people (workers and visitors) need to know and be able to do at this location in order to work at/use this site effectively?

- What are the most important concepts and skills from my curriculum standards that describe what people need to know and be able to do at this site?

Preplanning

Although logistics and paperwork may not make the heart sing, they do help ensure that your study trip goes off without a hitch. Complete the following several weeks before the study trip.

On-Site Planning

- Once the site has been chosen, get permission from your principal and district office. Inform the students and parents well in advance.

- Visit the study trip location to finalize what you want your on-site resource person (tour guide, docent, store manager, etc.) to show/explain to your students. Give him/her a copy of the Lifelong Guidelines and LIFESKILLS and your concept and key points (conceptual, significant knowledge, and skill).

- As you tour the site together, be clear what you want him/her to focus on with your students. Often tour guides have their own agenda and want guests to see or tour parts of the site that are not applicable to your concept/key points. Don't go there! Insist that he/she stick to your concept/key points. You are not asking for the usual tour. Leave other content for later trips.

- Share your on-site inquiries with the on-site resource person and ask for ways to improve them. Get feedback on their accuracy, appropriateness, and centrality to what employees and visitors should know and be able to do. Send the final version of the inquiries to the guide before you arrive with students. If possible, also share your follow-up inquiries, especially the social/political action inquiries.

- Ask the guide if it is possible to break the students into smaller groups. One with the guide, the other with you (or another guide) for exploration. (It is almost impossible to hear and stay on task when standing in the back of a pack of 25+ students.)

Preplanning at the School

- Fill out the necessary paperwork to request a bus.

- Find out about procedures for bus dropoff, parking, and pick up.

- Meet with the person in charge of students' medication (school nurse or school secretary). Know clearly who gets what, when, and how to dispense them on the trip. Do not delegate this job; keep this responsibility yourself.

- Organize materials and emergency plans.

- Assemble your clipboard and have it ready to pick up as you board the bus. Information, in addition to what you give students and chaperones for their clipboards, should include:

  - Class list and emergency numbers for school and parents

  - Student allergies

  - Schedule for site and contact person's phone number

  - Bus garage phone number

  - Notes about the site from your pre-visit

  - Blank paper for questions and notes

- Prepare content and logistics for a parent chaperone training.

TRAINING CHAPERONES

Hopefully this is not the first training you have done for your parents because it's best to begin training them on how to help out in your classroom and go on study trips beginning the first week of school. Offer the training several times on different days and times, such as after school, evenings, or even a Saturday morning.

If you cannot get enough parents, recruit qualified candidates wherever you can find them, college students, grandparents, neighbors, friends, classroom aides from other classrooms, etc.

Agenda

There are a number of things that your chaperones need to know thoroughly so they be confident enough about their responsibilities that they can perform them without your presence and support if necessary. Include the following topics:

- Confidentiality—After the trip, do not talk about students, parents, or other chaperones or what you may have heard them say.

- Role—They are here to coach students, to ask questions rather than give answers. Tell them they can answer questions only with a question. For example:

  - What do you think?

  - How could you find the answer to that question?

  - What do you see or notice that is different or the same?

– What do you hear, smell?

– What is that like?

– Why do you ask that?

– Does anyone know the answer to that?

– Good question. Let's write that down and we will ask the tour guide or the teacher.

- Expectations—Chaperones should expect students and other adults to behave in accordance with the Lifelong Guidelines and LIFESKILLS. Remind them that this study trip is not a reward but a serious and central piece to the curriculum of the classroom. (This might be a good time to share some brain research information with them.)
Give parents a copy of any additional behavior guidelines and procedures for this particular study trip

- Target talk—Describe how to use target talk to guide and support students

- Curriculum—Explain what students will be studying. Give them copies of the concept/key points. Also give them copies of all assignments—a blank form and sample completed form—so that the parents have the answers in advance and feel confident about the content students are to learn.

- Procedures—Go over the procedures for the study trip. Remember, most parents have only experienced field trips for fun; they need to develop a new mental program for what an ITI being there study trip is. Typical procedures for all chaperones include:

1. Arrive 30 minutes before the trip for last minute instruction, to review procedures for the trip, and to learn about any last-minute changes.

2. Keep ALL of your students with you at all times. If one has to go to the bathroom, everyone goes totgether, including you, the chaperone!

3. Don't purchase anything for the students, including food, trinkets, or souvenirs.

4. Don't bring any children/students not enrolled in the class.

5. Work with your assigned group only; do not join up with another group so the adults can chat. Students have been placed in small groups for a reason—the opportunity to communicate with you.

6. Don't smoke, eat, or drink (even coffee.) You may have a student snack when the students have theirs (if one is provided).

7. Sit with your student group on the bus.

8. Bring the fanny pack/backpack and materials provided by the teacher (see list that follows). Don't hesitate to contact the teacher in person or via the cell phone (in your pack) if you need to. If students are not using the Lifelong Guidelines/LIFESKILLS or you have an emergency, let the teacher know ASAP.

9. Be on time. Know the time you are to meet with tour guides and the time and sites for each rendezvous during the tour and for departure.

10. Have fun! Enjoy the opportunity to spend some time with your son or daughter and his/her Learning Club friends.

Equipment for Chaperones. Equip your chaperones with the tools and supplies they might need. These items help make their responsibilities concrete and give them confidence that they can handle the job. Ask a local store or other business to provide fanny pack/backpacks for the chaperones. This is an opportunity for local businesses to offer support in a tangible way. Get one for each chaperone (about six).

Include the following items in the packs:

- Cell phone (borrow from teachers, parents, friends, etc., so that every chaperone has one). Be sure you tape the number of your cell phone onto each chaperone's cell phone.

- Kleenex tissue

- Bandaids

- Rubber/latex gloves

- Extra pens/pencils

- Camera (optional)

- A clipboard with the same contents as that on the students' clipboards plus the following:

  - Procedures and responsibilities for chaperones

  - Names of students in his/her group

  - Times his/her group is to meet with the tour guide, for departure, etc.

  - Filled-in version of student worksheets

PREPARING YOUR STUDENTS

Prepare your students for the being there location they are about to visit. Tell them where they will be going and explain why you have chosen this site and how it relates to the curriculum. This does not mean that all the content must be taught before they go; that is an old picture of "field trips" conducted at the end of a unit of study.

Content for the study trip

- Explaining what they are going to see and how it fits in with what they will be studying—the theme on the wall

- Brainstorming the questions they want to ask of those who work at and use the location

Procedures for the study trip

- Engaging students in a discussion of the Lifelong Guidelines and LIFESKILLS they will need to use

- Inviting them to help you write procedures for all to follow

- Creating a bus trip assignment that students will do when going to and returning from the site. Relate these to what students will be studying on site; explain it thoroughly so they know what to do without having to ask a lot of questions once on the bus

- Asking them to predict what they think they might see at such a being there location; keep these responses so that students can test these assumptions when they return

Equipment for Students

Each student should have a clipboard that includes the following items:

- Pencil attached with a string

- Lifelong Guidelines and LIFESKILLS laminated and taped to the back of the clipboard

- Procedures for the bus and when at the being there location

- Assignments for the bus (to and from) and on site

- Blank paper for recording questions and illustrations

- Names of the chaperones

THE DAY BEFORE THE STUDY TRIP

The day before the study trip, double-check your arrangements:

- Review your procedures.

- Call the site to confirm the visit time and your expectations for the tour.

- Call the bus garage to confirm when the bus will arrive at school for departure and when it will return to the school after the study trip.

- Call the chaperones to confirm their assignment and the time they are to arrive. Remind them how important it is that they are on time.

- Form student groups (about 4-5 students per parent/adult chaperone). Unless there is an overriding reason for not doing so, keep students in their Learning Clubs.

- Assign a chaperone to each group. Invite student input; some students do and some do not want their parent as a chaperone for their group.
  [Note: Do NOT assign yourself as a chaperone for a group; you need to be the leader of the total group. Your job is to ensure that each group functions well to maximize learning and to be available to handle an illness, accident, or difficulty a student or chaperone might have.]

- If you do not have an active parent group to act as chaperones on a study trip, consider asking local businesses if they would allow their employees to volunteer. You could also ask grandparents, senior citizens, or even the teacher aides from other classrooms. Remember, you need one chaperone per Learning Club.

30 MINUTES BEFORE THE STUDY TRIP

Just before getting on the bus, meet with parents and with students to review expectations and duties.

With Chaperones

Review the important points with parents. This serves both as a reminder and as a confidence booster. Review the following:

- Standard procedures
- Student assignments (on the bus and at the site)

- How to use target talk for the Lifelong Guidelines and LIFESKILLS

- Any questions about the trip or curriculum content

- The contents of the chaperone backpack

Have chaperones come to the classroom (stand at the back of the room) during your final review with students.

With Students

Before leaving for the bus:

- Introduce the chaperones.

- Review the site procedures (use chart) —
  - Use the Lifelong Guidelines and LIFESKILLS
  - Focus on the LIFESKILL of Curiosity
  - Stay with your group and follow the directions of your group's chaperone
  - Represent yourself and your school in a positive way.

- Hand out the study trip clipboard.

- Answer any questions about what's to be studied.

- Make a final count of the total number of students going on the trip. Have each chaperone count — and remember! — the number of students in his/her group. Have each chaperone say out loud to the class how many students are in his/her group; as they do so, add the numbers on the board to make sure they equal the count for the total class.

For Yourself

Don't forget your clipboard as you board the bus! And, make sure you count the students as they board.

THE BUS TRIP

Don't allow bus time to deteriorate into a bus driver's nightmare. Once students lose their focus, it's harder to refocus them when you arrive at the being there site.

Setting up expectations for travel to and from the being there site is critical:

Getting on the Bus

Start off on the right foot.

- Introduce the bus driver by name and tell students about the Lifelong Guidelines and LIFESKILLS the bus driver will be using to drive them safely to the being there location.

- Introduce the chaperones to the bus driver.

- Review the bus procedures (use chart);

  - Sit with someone from your Learning Club (if uneven numbers, sit with your group's chaperone). Sit as near to your chaperone as possible.

  - Stay in your seat.

  - Talk quietly with your seat mate.

  - Use the Lifelong Guideline of Active Listening and the LIFESKILL of Responsibility at all times.

  - Complete the bus assignment with your seat partner.

- Review the bus assignment and answer questions about how to complete it.

- Count students (and chaperones!) twice—once using a total student count and again by asking each chaperone to give a count of the students in his/her group.

Traveling To the Site

Give students an assignment(s) that will last the length of the drive. This forces students to direct their attention to the world outside the bus and bridges your pre-departure orientation and the visitation. Make sure that the assignment relates to the site to be visited.

Here are some examples for bus time activities while traveling to the site:

- Reading through the field guide and developing at least three questions to ask the guide (the field guide must be developed in advance).

- A from-the-bus window scavenger hunt for items that students think can also be found at the site.

- A variation of an acrostic (a series of lines or verses in which the first, last, or other particular letters when taken in order spell out a word, phrase, etc.) For example:

  L — lake, laundromat, ladies' restroom

  A — aquatic center, airport, arena, airplane

  N — nursery, neighborhood

  D — dog, donut shop

  F — factory, fence

  I — ice, inlet, iron, ice cream parlor

  L — light, leaf

  L — lawn, lip

  - List and tally items for an acrostic based on the name of the being there location.

  - List and tally names for an acrostic based on commercial signs or a key concept to be studied at the being there location.

  - List and tally names for an acrostic based on a category of items chosen by students (the acrostic must be based on the name of a concept to be studied at the being there location).

Traveling Back from the Site

Make sure you have everyone—students and adults! Count students (and chaperones!) twice—once using a total student count and again by asking each chaperone to give a count of the students in his/her group. Then, don't lose momentum. Provide an assignment(s) that lasts the duration of the return bus drive. This time, have them look for examples of something they learned at the being there site. Examples include:

- With a member of your seatmate, review your notes in your field guide. Complete writing down your findings. Compare notes with your partner. Add any information that he/she gathered that you did not. If you have any blank spaces, discuss with someone sitting across the aisle from you to add to your notes. Complete all items in the study guide.

- With your partner, list the Lifelong Guidelines and LIFESKILLS your bus driver used on this trip. Write an acknowledgment thanking him/her for supporting your study trip. Be specific. Give your note to the bus driver as you get off the bus. Also tell him/her thank you in person.

- With your partner, write a thank you note to your chaperone. Be sure to mention specifically what you most appreciated about his/her support during the being there visit.

- As you exit the bus, check for belongings.

RESPONSIBILITIES ON SITE

- Organize the groups. Make sure each chaperone has collected his/her students and they are ready to begin. Check that chaperones and students have their clipboards with them. Make sure each chaperone has his/her backpack.

- Touch base with each group at least once during the trip. Check on the chaperone and provide needed assistance and support. Offer expertise.

- Check on target kids.

- Keep the tour guide on target (time and content).

- Point out Lifelong Guidelines/LIFESKILLS as they occur.

- Provide a time for snacks, drinks, and bathroom breaks.

- Report any accidents to the manager at the site and, on your return, to your principal.

- Follow time schedule.

TEACHER RESPONSIBIILTIES AFTER THE STUDY TRIP

To make sure that you squeeze every ounce of value from your study trip, don't pass up an opportunity to have students review in their minds what they experienced.

On Re-Entering the Classroom

This is a chance to demonstrate the LIFESKILLS of Organization and Initiative for your students.

- As students reenter the classroom, have them remove their papers from the study trip clipboards and put them on their desks. Then, have them sharpen the clipboard pencils and put the clipboards back in the box ready for the next study trip.

- Brainstorm things about the tour guide that you most appreciated learning. If possible, include chaperones in this activity. Have students write personal thank you notes to the guide(s), chaperones, and/or bus drivers.

While the experience is still fresh in their minds (students and chaperones), debrief the being there experience.

- What did they learn? What most impressed/surprised them? What did they learn that they can use this week in the classroom? Outside of school? What did they learn about the concept being studied?

- How did the procedures work? Should any changes be made before the next being there study trip?

- What were the highlights, surprises, disappointments? If we were to do the same study trip again, what changes would we make? And so forth. Preface the discussion with the request that people (students and chaperones) use the Lifelong Guideline of Truthfulness and the LIFESKILLS, including Caring.

Follow-Up Strategies

To carry the momentum of student enthusiasm from the being there experience back into the classroom, choose your most engaging instructional strategies:

- Bring in resource people to further explain what they do at the being there site and why it is important. Before their arrival, have students preoare a prioritized list of what they want the resource person to address and the questions they want to pursue.

- Base your direct instruction on examples from the common experience of the study trip.

- Involve students in role-playing activities so they can explore why the concepts and skills of your curriculum are important and how and when they might use them.

- Engage students in both structured and unstructured discussion.

- Structure Discovery Processes that will carry them deeper into the concepts.

- Invite students to select and pursue their own independent study which extends and deepens the concepts and skills of the curriculum.

- Revisit the site.

ENDNOTES

1 These recommendations for planning and conducting a study trip are adapted from the work of Linda Jordan and Sue Pearson, masters of Highly Effective Teaching (Susan Kovalik & Associates). As most teachers already know, students may or may not come away from a study trip having learned what the teacher intended. Mediation—structuring what students focus on, process, and practice using—is essential.

2 This information is provided in the book entitled *Exceeding Expectations: A User's Guide to Implementing Brain Research in the Classroom*, 5th ed., by Susan J. Kovalik and Karen D. Olsen (Books for Educators, Black Diamond, WA, 2010), Appendix C.

Appendix D: Communicating with Parents

COMMUNICATING WITH PARENTS

Communication with parents and guardians is a completely understated, largely overlooked opportunity for teachers, yet it is one of our most powerful sources of support. Introduce yourself to your parents even before school starts. Let them know that your classroom will be a special experience for their child. Don't wait for the traditional Back-to-School Night in October; it is entirely too late in the fall to serve as a tool for creating an anticipatory set.

Welcome Letter to Students

Begin by sending a letter to their child welcoming him/her to your classroom. In this letter include a personal greeting expressing that you're looking forward to meeting him/her, your commitment to making this year the best ever, and an outline of your plans for the year—the *being there* experiences, the theme, and why you're excited about the year. Also include a request that the child invite his/her parents/guardians to attend a Back to School night held the very first week of school—Thursday night.

Back to School Night

If the first week seems too soon, consider this reality: substitute teachers have less than 60 seconds to establish themselves with students. Four days is more than enough to capture your students' attention and hearts. And, the sooner you communicate with parents, the less time for assumptions or misunderstandings. Your *Highly Effective Teaching (HET)* program may be new and different from what they have known in the past, so capture their attention and spread your enthusiasm in the same way you do with your students. Remember, parents are the first and foremost teachers in the children's lives.

At Back to School night, provide a comprehensive information packet such as the one described here. For parents/guardians unable to attend, send the packet home with their child the next day.

Dear Parents/Guardians,

The *HET* model *(Highly Effective Teaching)* is an innovative and proven method of implementing in the classroom what we know from current brain research. It also integrates skills and content in real-life ways.

The following pages will introduce you to many of the concepts, terms, and resources which will be used in your child's classroom this year. I am looking forward to working with you to create an extraordinary year for your child.

CONTENTS OF THE PARENT INFORMATION PACKET

1. Recommended Books
2. A Week in the Life of My Child
3. The Power of Emotion in Learning and Performance
4. Lifelong Guidelines/LIFESKILLS
5. Food and its Effects on Learning
6. Yearlong Theme
7. Public Library
8. Research Project
9. Mindmapping
10. Homework
11. Letter to Parents
12. Possible Family Study Trips (aka Study Adventures)
13. Contacting the Teacher

1. RECOMMENDED BOOKS FOR PARENTS TO READ

Character Begins at Home: Family Tools for Teaching Character at Home by Karen D. Olsen and Sue Pearson.
Simple, enjoyable activities with hundreds of ideas for nurturing character through the Lifelong Guidelines and LIFESKILLS. Understanding a common language at home and at school helps children develop the social skills of respect and responsible citizenship.

Human Brain and Human Learning by Leslie Hart
The most significant book on "brain-compatible" education (a term coined by this author). His examples of how learning goes astray inside schools will remind all readers of their own experiences as children. This is the foundation book for the *HET* model, its grounding in brain-compatible learning.

Seven Kinds of Smarts: Identifying and Developing Your Many Intelligences by Thomas Armstrong
Armstrong, a leader in translating the multiple intelligences into practical applications at school and home, provides a clear, understandable overview of the theory of multiple intelligences, as well as a 40-item assessment inventory, and everyday examples.

Punished By Rewards: The Trouble with Gold Stars, Incentive Plans, A's, Praise, & Other Bribes by Alfie Kohn
The more we use artificial inducements to motivate children, the more they lose interest in what we're bribing them to do. Offer practical strategies for parents to minimize bribing children to do a job.

The Over-Scheduled Child by Alvin Rosenfeld and Nicole Wise
This book provides choices to the nonstop pressures of over scheduling academic, social, and athletics. The authors offer clear steps to attack this rampant phenomenon of micro-managing every detail of a child's life, thereby encouraging healthier and happier children, and revitalizing the parenting experience.

The Ritalin Nation: Transformation of Human Consciousness by Richard DeGrandpre

The author attributes the disturbing prevalence of inattention and hyperactivity in children to the larger psychological consequences of living in a rapid-fire culture. Practical guidelines for charting a hopeful future and moving away from sensory addiction.

Magic Trees of the Mind: How to Nurture Your Child's Intelligence, Creativity, and Healthy Emotions from Birth Through Adolescence by Marion Diamond and Janet Hopson

Interaction with resources, new experiences, and rich sensory input greatly affects learning. This fascinating book explains how parents and teachers are literally building children's brains.

Boys and Girls Learn Differently by Michael Gurian

An explanation of how learning is affected by the fundamental differences between boys and girls–and what can be done about it. Provides information on brain development, strategies, and tips beginning with preschool through high school.

Teaching Children to Love by Doc Lew Childre

This book provides a wide range of 80 games and fun activities for developing emotional intelligence while increasing learning performance. Helps children make positive and wise choices.

Kid's Guide to Working Out Conflicts by Naomi Drew, MA

This tremendous resource tells how to keep cool, stay safe, and get along by taking a closer look at common forms of conflict, reasons behind them, and positive ways to handle tough situations. Offers tips for countering bullying and dealing with difficult people.

Homework and Kids by William Haggart and Christine Juhasz

This wonderful parent's guide helps to identify how each child learns by discovering their learning styles. You can ensure their success by guiding them through new approaches for completing homework assignments and gaining knowledge.

2. A WEEK IN THE LIFE OF MY CHILD

The grid on the next page is for recording the activities of your child for one week. This is useful for you and your child so that you can get a picture of your child's "education" when outside of school. Remember, you are your child's first teacher. Seeing exactly where and on what your child spends his/her time is the beginning step in examining how you might play a more powerful supportive role with your child this year. Also, I would be happy to discuss your child's schedule with you and its possible impact on your child's learning.

The time chart is broken into four sections to help you capture a full 24-hour day overview of seven consecutive days. Record the adult and peer influences your child experiences each day. How much support time are you able to give your child. The more detailed your information, the more valuable it will be.

3. CURRENT BRAIN RESEARCH

The *HET* model is based upon the findings of brain research from the past 25 years. Gleaned from many fields and supported by research made possible by high tech instruments such as CAT scans, PET scans, MRI, and fMRI, we can now literally watch a brain in action. For 25 years, the research has provided very consistent findings which are summarized in the *HET* model as:

- Intelligence is a function of experiences which cause physiological growth in the brain. Genetics plays a lesser role than generally believed and high levels of sensory input is more important than usually recognized.

- Learning is the result of an inseparable partnership of brain and body. Emotion is the gatekeeper to learning and performance and movement is key to optimal brain function.

	Monday	Tuesday	Wednesday	Thursday	Friday	Saturday	Sunday
BEFORE SCHOOL							
AT SCHOOL							
AFTER SCHOOL							
AFTER DINNER							

- We have at least seven intelligences. An intelligence is defined as a problem-solving and/or product-producing capability. Each of the intelligences functions from a different part of the brain.

- The brain extracts and creates meaning through a pattern-seeking process. It is not logical and sequential when making meaning (however, it can be very logical and sequential when it is *using* information that it has learned).

- Most useful information is embedded in mental programs; information that does not become embedded in a program for using it in real–world applications is largely forgotten.

Because of these findings, the *HET* classroom is dedicated to providing a learning environment with the following bodybrain-compatible elements:

- Absence of threat/
Nurturing reflective thinking

- Meaningful content

- Movement to enhance learning

- Enriched environment

- Choices

- Adequate time

- Collaboration

- Immediate feedback

- Mastery and the ability to use concepts and skills in real life; wired into long-term memory

Each of these concepts about how the brain works and the bodybrain-compatible elements will be discussed at parent night and in home-school communications throughout the year. We will be spending a great deal of time at the beginning of the year on the role of emotion in learning and how to create an environment notable for absence of threat and enhancing reflective thinking. These are key elements of my classroom management and approach to discipline. Also, these are important areas of a strong home-school partnership. I look forward to working with you to help your child learn and grow.

4. LIFELONG GUIDELINES & LIFESKILLS

Our classroom is practicing Lifelong Guidelines and LIFESKILLS (the definition of Personal Best). These differ from regular school rules because they apply to all age groups (adults and children) and in all situations. They form the basis for agreement between teacher and students, and among the students, about behavior and expectations (social and academic). I encourage you to learn about them (ask your child!) and I ask that you reinforce them at home.

 Lifelong Guidelines

TRUSTWORTHINESS: To act in a manner that makes one worthy of trust and confidence

TRUTHFULNESS: To act with personal responsibility and mental accountability

ACTIVE LISTENING: To listen attentively and with the intention of understanding

NO PUT-DOWNS: To never use words, actions, and/or body language that degrade, humiliate, or dishonor others

PERSONAL BEST: To do one's best given the circumstances and available resources

LIFESKILLS

CARING: To feel and show concern for others

COMMON SENSE: To use good judgment

COOPERATION: To work together toward a common goal or purpose

CREATIVITY: To imagine ways to solve a problem or produce a product; to invent something original or to redesign something

COURAGE: To act according to one's beliefs despite fear of adverse consequences

CURIOSITY: A desire to investigate and seek understanding of one's world

EFFORT: To do your best

FLEXIBILITY: To be willing to alter plans when necessary

FRIENDSHIP: To make and keep a friend through mutual trust and caring

INITIATIVE: To do something, of one's own free will, because it needs to be done

INTEGRITY: To act according to a sense of what's right and wrong

ORGANIZATION: To plan, arrange, and implement in an orderly way; to keep things orderly and ready to use

PATIENCE: To wait calmly for someone or something

PERSEVERANCE: To keep at it

PRIDE: Satisfaction from doing one's personal best

PROBLEM SOLVING: To create solutions to difficult situations and everyday problems

RESOURCEFULNESS: To respond to challenges and opportunities in innovative and creative ways

RESPONSIBILITY: To respond when appropriate; to be accountable for one's actions

SENSE OF HUMOR: To laugh and be playful without harming others

5. FOOD & ITS EFFECTS ON LEARNING

There are three books, all very readable, which offer some sound advice and suggestions for feeding children in a healthy manner. I recommend them as a beginning point in understanding the powerful influence food (especially junk food) has upon the chemistry of the brain and, therefore, its ability to learn.

Good For Me! by Marilyn Burns

This is a great book to read with your child. There are also many "things to do" that families will find fun and informational. A quick look at the table of contents gives you an idea of the excitement of this book: Biting In, What's the Use of Food, Anyway?; You Can Hurt Your Stomach's Feelings; The Fizz in Your Diet; The National Meal in a Bun; The Ice Cream Story; Learning to Read Labels; and, Will an Apple a Day Keep the Doctor Away?

Food For Healthy Kids by Dr. Lendon Smith

This provides a thorough look at food, behavior, allergies, and addictions from ages pre-birth to adulthood. Chapter headings include: Hyperactivity and Tension at All Ages; Sugar Cravings—Foods and Moods; Sleep Problems—Foods for Restless Children. Recipes for over 100 healthy and tasty meals for children are included.

The Body's Many Cries for Water by F. Batmanghelidj, M.D.

Hydration also has a big effect on how the brain functions. Make sure your child drinks at least eight glasses of water a day. Sodas are not a water source; they contain chemicals that cause the body to use its water reserves to dilute and eliminate those chemicals. Numerous health and behavior problems are being attributed to dehydration. See www. watercure.com

6. ORGANIZING CONCEPT, KEY POINTS, AND INQUIRIES

The *HET* model is based in the brain research of the past 30 years. It is designed to help make curriculum and instruction best fit the brain's natural way of learning.

Organizing Concept and Key Points

Because brain research tells us that the brain learns through seeking out understandable patterns, our curriculum is designed to enhance students' ability to detect and make meaning of patterns. The staff has worked hard at making our key points conceptual because concepts are big patterns and to organize our content around a single, yearlong theme through which all content and basic skills are taught. This is a dramatic departure from the fragmented day during which each subject is taught separately.

Examples of Key Points.

Key points are statements of what is most essential for students to learn—the essential core of knowledge and skills in each of the subject areas included in our yearlong theme. Key points are identified for each day, week, month, and year. They are the content every student needs to learn and be able to apply.

An example of a *conceptual key point* is: In our complex world we use increasingly more and complicated sources of power and machines to help meet our daily needs. Many tools and machines that help us do our work are powered with electricity. Electricity powers machines that help make our homes light at night, keep us warm in the winter or cool in the summer, keep our food cold so that it won't spoil, as well as many other uses. Electrical energy occurs naturally or can be generated and controlled by man.

An example of a *significant knowledge key point* that supports the conceptual key point is: In order for an electrical current to flow, it must have an uninterrupted conducting path. This is called an electric circuit. There are two kinds of electric circuits. A series circuit has only one electrical path, and any break in the path will interrupt the flow of electricity (for example old-fashioned Christmas tree lights). A parallel circuit has multiple paths. A break in one path will not interrupt the flow of electricity in the other paths (for example a string of lights that remain on when one bulb burns out). Knowing the properties, advantages and disadvantages of each kind of circuit can help us to understand why an appliance may or may not work, make decisions about energy conservation and create more complex electrical environments.

A Yearlong Curriculum. The purpose of the yearlong theme is to provide an umbrella pattern under which everything fits in a way that shows relationships among ideas and thus makes smaller ideas more memorable and retrievable.

The organizing concept for the yearlong curriculum for our classroom is shown below. As you can see, the topics that we will be studying are varied and exciting.

NOTE TO TEACHER:

Paste a copy of your yearlong curriculum

mindmap here so that parents can know

what's coming next.

Inquiries

Inquiries are the activities your child will do to "learn" the concepts and skills identified in the key points. Inquiries require the application of reading, writing, computing, and best of all, thinking!

The intent is to better provide your child with the capabilities that come with understanding at the level of application and the ability to solve problems in the real world versus relying on rote memorization. The two questions I kept in mind as I was developing curriculum for this year were:

- What do I want students to understand?

- What do I want them to be able to do with what they understand?

These two questions will lead us into higher expectations for student performance, especially in the area of basic skills —reading, writing, and 'rithmetic—because they are basic to doing something in the world outside of the classroom. I look forward to sharing with you the key points and inquiries your child will be studying.

In developing inquiries for both work in class and homework for this class, I have also utilized the conceptual framework of Howard Gardner as presented in his book, *Frames of Mind: Theory of Multiple Intelligences*. Gardner defines intelligence as a "problem-solving and/or product-producing capability" rather than an I.Q. number. He says that we are all born with at least seven different, each one operating from a different location in the brain. Each of us develops a propensity for using one or more capabilities in our everyday lives. In the classroom, my goal is to help your child develop all of these areas of intelligence because all are necessary to succeed in life beyond our school years.

Here are some inquiries written for the key points mentioned above. They illustrate the range of problem-solving and product-producing capabilities that can be tapped and nurtured.

They are examples of the types of activities your child will be involved in during our course of study.

1. *Design* and *build* a series or parallel circuit that will light each room in your Learning Club's "house." *Discuss* your plan for wiring your house with each other before you begin. *Propose* to each other how the materials will be used and how the electricity will flow through the house.

2. *Diagram* the wiring in your house. *Label* the electrical parts. *Describe* the circuit. *Determine* if it is a series or parallel circuit and *explain* why.

3. *Create* a flow chart that describes what you know about the flow of electricity through a circuit to make something work. *Read* the article "Relay Race" about telegraphs and discuss the sequence of events in the story as well as the sequence of events that enables a message to travel from the sender in one end of the country to the receiver in the other end of the country. *Illustrate* and *describe* the sequence in a step book.

4. By yourself or with a partner, use the measurements for your Learning Club's house to *calculate* the length of wire you will need to complete the circuit of electricity in your house. *Share* your results with the rest of your Learning Club. *Compare* your results with the others in your Learning Club and together *determine* the total length of wire you will need.

INQUIRIES FOR ASSESSMENT:

1. *Design* and *build* a model for an invention that uses electricity to meet a need that could help make life easier in some way or solve an everyday problem. *Diagram* your invention and how it should work. *Write* a brief explanation of how the invention is helpful and how it should work. If your invention does not work

as you planned it after you build it, *analyze* why you think it did not work and record your analysis in your journal. Be sure to use all of our key points for the week in your invention and your explanations.

2. Edit your research paper first by yourself, then with a partner. Use the rubric to be sure you have included or corrected everything. Rewrite it in its final form. Read it to a partner. Be ready to present it to the class.

As you can see, the inquiries ask students to apply what they are learning to real-world situations. This deepens their understanding, makes learning more memorable, and significantly increases the likelihood that they will remember the knowledge and skills years later. Our assessment inquiries are especially good tests of ability to use knowledge and skills.

To help make this year as rich an experience as possible, I would appreciate any and all support from parents, e.g., serving as a resource person in the classroom, providing materials, generating ideas for possible class study trips, assistance with study trips, etc.

7. THE PUBLIC LIBRARY

Our public library should become your child's favorite place to find information and have questions answered. According to an article published by Northwest Airlines, "There are more than 115,000 libraries serving the American public; libraries employ over 300,000 people and spend almost $3 billion per year on materials and services—less than a dollar a month for every man, woman and child in the United States. America's public libraries circulate more than one billion items per year—everything from books to computer software to children's toys, games, audio cassettes, CDs, videotapes, DVDs, art prints, and films."

It is ironic that some libraries are closing for lack of support in this country. It is the last "free" source of information available to all, regardless of income or education, and deserves to be used

and supported. Interestingly, even during a recession, libraries which are heavily used and strongly supported by their communities are never cut from the budget. Libraries which close are eliminated more because public use is limited, not because public funds are limited. Support your library!

The public library is your closest and easiest vehicle to adventure. And, it's free. If your child does not already have his/her own library card, apply for one immediately. We have application cards available at Parent Night. Set a goal of visiting the library twice a week. Teach your child how to browse through the library and how to use the card catalog (or computerized system!).

Check the schedule for special events for children. Most libraries provide a surprisingly wide array of cultural events for children.

Lastly, teach your child how to read public transportation schedules and how to use public transportation. When your child is old enough, teach him/her to go alone. Going to the library will become as typical an adult behavior as turning on TV to watch the news.

8. YEARLONG RESEARCH PROJECT

As part of the *Highly Effective Teaching* model, each child is requested to choose a topic of interest that relates to our theme and to conduct a yearlong research project. Information can be gleaned from the newspaper, magazines, encyclopedias, and museum pamphlets, at all readability levels designed for both children and adults. This is your child's chance to develop practical, everyday information-gathering skills and discover life-long interests.

Resources are as near as the yellow pages of your phone book and Internet and as far away as those listed in the *Encyclopedia of Associations*, a remarkable publication available through your public library. It contains over 30,000 addresses of public and private organizations that have been formed to "get the word out"—information on all subjects. Writing letters to request free information provides a real audience for your child's writing skills. And when the information arrives in the child's mailbox with his/her name on it . . . well, of course, it will be high interest reading material!

The research project articles should be kept in a three-ring binder. Each article is read, highlighted, and at least three facts that your child thinks are interesting or important are mindmapped; the information is then added to the binder which can be easily reorganized as time goes on. Copies of letters sent and answered belong in the binder. At the appropriate time during the year, the teacher will ask for the expertise of your child to be presented to the class. This is the beginning of a lifelong habit of collecting, analyzing, synthesizing, and using information.

The long-term research project is the best "homework" you can do with your child. It provides a point of discussion and analysis. The end products are pride in accomplishing a significant task, deep knowledge, and lifelong learning skills.

9. MINDMAPPING

This year your child will be introduced to a concept called mindmapping—a way of visually representing how concepts and ideas related to each other. Pictures, as well as colors, enhance long-term memory, and retrieval. Mindmapping is a skill and, like other skills, it demands practice in order to do it well. Learn and practice it along with your child. It is a powerful study skill.

Recommended book: *Mapping Inner Space: Learning and Teaching Mind Mapping* by Nancy Margulies.

10. HOMEWORK

Homework is best assigned when it has meaning and purpose (from the learner's perspective). It should support and expand the skills, content, and concepts that were presented in the class. It

will supplement what has gone on in the classroom that day—something which could not be done at school, either for lack of time or materials necessary to do the job well.

Do not expect your child to bring home "dittos" or "worksheets." Such drills too often kill the joy of learning, and, worst of all, seldom enhance learning. The intent of homework in this class is to give your child practice in using knowledge and skills in everyday life and at real-world standards for acceptability and excellence.

The best homework is the time you spend with your child reading, answering and posing questions, and investigating areas and concepts that will generate a sense of purpose for what your child is learning in the classroom.

11. LETTER TO PARENTS

Because your participation in your child's education is so critical to his/her progress this year, I will send you a letter at least twice a month. The letter will keep you up-to-date with happenings in the classroom—what we are currently studying, how you can support your child in mastering the key points for the month, what you might do to assist your child in learning how to apply what he/she is learning to real life (in your home, neighborhood, community), and, how you might assist the class as a whole—in the classroom or on a study trip.

The letter will typically follow the outline below:

Dear Parents,

We are into our ___ component of this year's theme, and our weekly topics for this month will include:

1.

2.

3.

4.

This week we will be working on inquiries for these key points in our content study:

1.

2.

3.

Our key points in the basic skills area (reading, writing, and mathematics) are:

1.

2.

3.

I invite you to assist your child in understanding those inquiries your child has selected to work on (or that I may have assigned), which support the key points. In particular, I invite you to help your child apply this information to real-life situations.

Your continuing to work with your child on his/her year-long research project is appreciated and makes the efforts all the more worthwhile.

Our resource person for this month (week) will be _____. If you have any additional suggestions

regarding resources, especially non-print ones, please let us know.

Our next study trip:_____

Our next learning celebration event: _____

These are special days. Please mark them on your family calendar.

12. POSSIBLE FAMILY STUDY ADVENTURES WITHIN A 50-MILE RADIUS

Parents are not only the first teachers of their children but also the most important. Schools are but a supplement to the educating process of the parents. Your modeling of lifelong learning is the most important gift you can give your child. Make a list of all the possible educational locations within a 50-mile radius of your home (for small towns, increase the radius to 75 or 100 miles; rural areas, 100–300 miles). For example:

- Parks and historical sites
- Museums
- Cultural centers
- Natural environments: lakes, rivers, mountains, oceans, etc.
- Neighboring cities
- Plays and concerts
- Fairs
- Other

Set as your goal at least one study adventure every four weeks. Remember, intelligence is a function of experience. The more experiences children have, the greater is their ability to make connections.

13. CONTACTING YOUR CHILD'S TEACHER

If you need to contact me, please feel free to call the school and leave a message with the school secretary.

I appreciate your willingness to spend quality time with your child, investing in the role of "first teacher," modeling the behaviors and values of lifelong learners and contributing members of society. Do know that I will be doing everything possible in the classroom to support those goals for your child and I am looking forward to forming a close working partnership with you so that together we can ensure that your child fulfills his/her potential.

Sincerely,

Your Child's Teacher

Appendix E: Conducting Town Hall Meetings

Written for this appendix by Sue Pearson,
Associate, Center for Effective Teaching

WHY TOWN HALL MEETINGS

Since the main goal of the Highly Effective Teaching model is that of GROWING RESPONSIBLE CITIZENS, it is imperative that day-to-day life in the classroom provides opportunities to practice democracy. Town Hall meetings were the way business was conducted in the early years of our country. In fact, some smaller communities still use this structure today—a pure form of democracy in action.

However, Town Hall meetings—formal and informal—don't just happen. The skills of civil discourse so essential to an effective citizenry and the processes for making decisions and taking action within a democratic framework must be taught.

Gathering in both formal and informal ways provides opportunities to get to know one another better and to solve problems facing the group. This practice is as old as time and critical to the continuance of democratic process of our society. When teachers incorporate Town Hall Meeting into classroom life, they are reinvigorating American democracy by engaging our young citizens in the public discussions and decisions that most impact their lives.

In the real world, as adults, we pursue this goal by becoming active in our communities-attending committee meetings, partici-

pating in school board sessions, coaching for little league, becoming a girl scout/boy scout leader, speaking for/against a proposal at city council meetings, serving as an appointed member of a study committee, serving as an elected official, to name just a few.

Foundation of Civil Discourse— A Sense of Community

The foundation of civil discourse is the creation of a sense of community. Community, however, does not happen accidentally, automatically, or overnight. Creating and maintaining it must be a common goal for both teacher and students and must be carried out with intentionality.

Purposefulness

Building community requires purposefulness – a reason for us to come together both informally and formally to get to know one another and solve community problems. So, just as many of our neighbors and governments turn to tradition, so do we—that of the Town Hall Meeting as a vehicle to support the democratic processes of our society. In the classroom/school, Town Hall meetings provide opportunities for students to learn the skills and processes necessary for effective citizenship:

STEP ONE: Building a Sense of Belonging

STEP TWO: Creating Common Ground

STEP THREE: Taking Action

How to implement each step, plus the variety of purposes it can serve, are discussed below.

STEP ONE:
BUILDING A SENSE OF BELONGING

As the recent rancor and ideological stalemates of the U.S. Congress has illustrated, failure to connect, failure to create a sense of all together in a lifeboat, destroys a sense of working toward "we the people, for the people, by the people." Thus, a fundamental condition of democracy is building a sense of belonging in each and every venue where citizens gather. The classroom is no exception.

Ways to Create a Sense of Belonging in Town Hall Meetings

Schedule Town Hall meetings on a regular basis and on a spur of the moment basis as needed, such as to welcome a new student to class. Ways to build a sense of belonging in Town Hall meetings include:

- Develop, with student input, written procedures for Town Hall meetings

- Provide a sense of consistency by using an agenda for every meeting

- Continually model/teach the Lifelong Guidelines (starting with Active Listening and No Put downs) and LIFESKILLS—have the students develop what each would look like/sound like/feel like in a Town Hall meeting

- Build community-building activities into each agenda

- Teach listening/speaking skills needed for participating in Town Hall meetings

- Build a variety of reflection activities into the agenda

- Set personal goals for Town Hall Meeting steps

- Support student in setting personal goals and goals for the Learning Club

- Provide time for reflection-spoken/written, personal/group

- Invite students to share individual experiences

- Introduce new students

- Provide "Citizenship in Action Box" and comment forms

- Invite students to share appreciations and acknowledgments

- Identify district/state curriculum standards, especially language arts and social studies, that can be integrated into Town Hall meetings

- Teach the history of Town Hall meetings as a form of pure democratic process for decision making process, citizenship, and making and following an agenda

- Read/Share stories of individuals in history, challenges faced, and their impact on our nation

- Provide community-building activities that develop a sense of belonging

Signs That a Sense of Belonging Is in Place

Students:

- Follow the basic Town Hall procedures

- Can read and explain a town Hall agenda

- Practice using the Lifelong Guidelines/LIFESKILLS
- Willingly participate in inclusion-building activities
- Understand and play their part in establishing the necessary conditions/atmosphere for learning
- Accept personal accountability/responsibility
- Are willing to work with new partners/groups/Learning Cubs without hesitation
- Welcome and include new students in class
- Participate in the agenda and community-building activities with enthusiasm
- Speak up without fear of unkind comments or retribution
- Develop personal goals for participating in Town Hall meetings
- Practice reflection in small and large groups
- Recognize when classmates are practicing citizenship an provide encouragement for doing so
- Willingly share thoughts/ideas/feelings

Remember that a sense of belonging must be solidly in place before moving to step two which requires the courage, and acceptance, to state differing opinions.

STEP TWO:
CREATING COMMON GROUND

Creating common ground is the lifeblood of compromise which can lead to the best outcomes for the most people with the least harm to the fewest. It's ever a balancing act between adhering to personal principles and searching for the public good. The classroom, again, is no exception.

Ways to Create Common Ground in Town Hall Meetings

Ways to create common ground in Town Hall meetings include:

- Initiate Town Hall Meetings on a regular basis, sometimes at the request of the students

- Continue to provide activities that assist students in maintaining the personal and social skills needed to build community building and develop common ground

- Continue to include in the agenda community-building activities that lead to a sense of "we" as well as support students in developing a healthy sense of "me"

- Continue to recognize group citizenship actions/practices through the CAB box process

- Invite students to submit class problems/issues

- Encourage students to add to the agenda other items of concern/interest to the whole class

- Review previously taught procedures

- Write new procedures as a group (student input) (see examples on page 7.10-7.12 and 7.19-7.20)

- Teach group problem-solving skills

- Create, maintain, & model procedures for disagreeing

- Teach conflict resolution strategies

- Teach the language arts skills of discussion, discourse, and debate and the tactful language for disagreeing

- Model changing one's mind to show that this is not a sign of weakness or "losing face"

- Offer team-building exercises and activities

- Select common group conflicts/problems and develop solutions

- Model/Teach strategies team-building and group processing

- Provide support for each other in times of difficulty or crisis

- Identify class problems/issues and try to resolve them

- Resolve individual conflicts

- Provide adequate time for journal writing/reflection/sharing in regard to Learning Club/team membership

- Walk students through group goal development and practices

- Provide opportunities for students to participate in goal setting and planning for such events as being there study trips, building immersion walls, Celebrations of Learning, and social/political action projects

- Identify/label/practice basic parliamentary procedures

- Begin to turn over the leadership of the Town Hall meetings to students

- Lead students to develop a classroom constitution

- Provide direct instruction on the Bill of Rights, the United State Constitution and its Amendments

- Teach students more about government documents and institutions

- Develop a Class Constitution containing a preamble, Bill of Rights, and amendments (as needed); place a copy in each Learning Club's binder

- Read/Share stories of groups/organizations that have historically come together for the common good and taken successful action

- Identify/work on group projects/inquiries

- Identify a school/community issue; develop a Social/Political action project to alleviate or solve the problem

Signs That Common Ground Has Been Developed

Students:

- Select community-building activities that identify commonalities

- Practice the Lifelong Guidelines/LIFESKILLS outside of the classroom when teacher is not present

- Identify and name class issues that interfere with learning

- Disagree in a civil manner

- Create a Classroom Constitution for all to abide by

- Help write new procedures when needed

- Work with a variety of classmates; no grumbling

- Plan being there experiences with help from an adult

- Volunteer to work on immersion walls

- Willingly visit other classes to share information/key points

- Use the LA skills of polite discourse

- Plan classroom celebrations-each group providing one part or section

- Congratulate fellow students when practicing responsible citizenship

- Reflect on personal and group goals; set new ones as needed

- Identify a social/political action problem, and with guidance from the teacher, alleviate it to the best of their ability.

- Role play problems to practice problem-solving skills

When there is sufficient agreement about common ground, the class is ready to commit to taking action.

STEP THREE: TAKING ACTION

As Granny D was fond of saying, "Democracy isn't something you have, it's something you do." And in so doing—be it on the world stage or in the classroom or anywhere in between—care must be taken to do so in ways that continue to build a sense of belonging and create common ground.

Ways to Take Action in Town Hall Meetings

Creating ways to take action in Town Hall meetings include:

- Provide opportunities for students to develop deeper "pictures" and practices of the Lifelong Guidelines and LIFESKILLS—from the classroom and school out into the community; continue to provide reminders (verbal/written) when individuals/groups need to improve in their use of the LG/LS when those involved fail to self correct

- Continue to include in the agenda community building activities and other opportunities to ensure a sense of belonging, development of a sense of "us" and a healthy sense of "me"

- Shift your role from sage-on-the-stage to guide-on-the-side as much as possible in order to
  - Allow students to participate in/set (as age appropriate) the agenda and carry-out Town Hall meetings (provide guidance only when necessary)

- Encourage students to develop procedures to guide their planning and carrying out action
  - Turn over as much as possible of planning and implementing according to plan development of immersion walls, Celebrations of Learning, social/political action projects, and other worthwhile endeavors

- Guide students in developing rubrics for evaluating their goals and actions

- Develop and carry-out plans to solve "real world" problem/issue

- Reflect on any projects to identify what worked well and what didn't

- Share articles identifying individuals/groups that are taking action to make the world a better place

- Identify ways to use the concepts and skills of district/state curriculum through real-world problems and issues

- Take students on being there study trips to experience how people taking action to improve things in the real world

- Guide students in setting reasonable, reachable goals

- Extend problem-solving skills into the larger community and develop projects to help the greater good

- Support students in selecting, planning, and completing projects that extend into the community at large

- Teach students to serve as conflict resolution managers in the classroom and for identified schoolwide issues

- Teach presentation skills and assist students in preparing and delivering presentations to share with the community (e.g., Chamber of Commerce, Town Council, City Council, Mayor, State Legislators, Governor, President)

- Teach students how to write persuasive letters of concern or suggestions for solving a problem to organization, both public and private

- Develop list of acceptable/democratic protest actions

- Share newspaper, news, magazine, Internet stories of groups (children/teens/young adults) working together for a common cause

Signs that Taking Action Has Been Developed

Students:

- Are excited about being part of something "larger" than themselves

- Identify BIG problems and formulate solutions

- Share their accomplishments with others

- Recognize the LG/LS being used/not used by people outside of the classroom and school

- Practice and recommend suggestions for conflict resolution when problems occur

- Can explain their goals/projects to other groups (e.g. other grades, school board, city council)

- Plan and carry out class Celebrations of Learning on their own

- Can explain how their Class Constitution works

- Write letters to those in power or control in order to change a situation

- Can model and teach others how to resolve conflicts

ELEMENTS FOR SUCCESSFUL TOWN HALL MEETINGS

Success working as a group is a hard-won victory. There are many elements to consider for improving your chances of success.

Building Blocks for Setting Agreed Upon Behaviors

Long accepted as the positive character traits for success in life—family, business, church, recreation, and other pastimes—the Lifelong Guidelines and LIFESKILLS provide that framework for behavior at Town Hall Meetings. They are an extension of the classroom and life lessons leading one to responsible citizenship. (See Chapter 8 and *Tools for Citizenship and Life: Using the Lifelong Guidelines and LIFESKILLS in Your Classroom*, 4th ed. by Sue Pearson.)

No Town Hall meeting can succeed unless these behavior guidelines are understood, agreed upon, and actively practiced. How are these behaviors taught and practiced? We use a brain-compatible strategy called writing, modeling, and practicing *Procedures*.

Procedures

Any activity as important as Town Hall meetings needs and deserves written procedures-therefore a MUST is the establishment of procedures that clearly state the expected behaviors coming to, during, and returning from a meeting. Procedures are conspicuously posted on charts, the overhead, Smart/White board, binder, etc. These procedures identify the actions needed to successfully show the behaviors. They will be modeled, taught and re-taught as necessary. Some procedures may include:

- Coming to and returning from town hall meeting

- Sharing

- Listening

- Disagreeing

- Giving compliments

- Teaching a problem-solving model

- Any other behaviors needing guidelines

While initially (and especially when first introduced), the teacher may determine and write the procedures for many of the classroom behaviors, it is expected that a group of responsible citizens (students) be involved in/take over the process at some point in time. Students may start out by rewriting/refining current procedures and then creating their own as new behaviors need defining/addressing. As you read the sample procedures notice that students are given the actions "to do" rather than the actions "not to do". Also take note of the fact that each sentence begins with a verb-a call to action, so to speak.

Examples of Town Hall Procedures for Primary Grades:

GOING TO TOWN HALL PROCEDURE

Stand and push in your chair

Walk quietly to Town Hall

Sit in listening shape

Use Active Listening

SHARING IN TOWN HALL

Wait for the "talking stick" to come to you

Speak so all can hear

Share your idea

Pass the Taking Stick to the next person

Example of Town Hall Procedures for Intermediate Grades:

CALL TO TOWN HALL MEETING

Check the agenda for Town Hall time

Carry your chair to meeting area

Form a circle with chairs

Listen for the starting chimes

Example of Town Hall Procedures for Middle School and High School:

TOWN HALL MEETING PROCEDURE

Add items to the agenda

Join the group at meeting time

Bring needed materials/ and/or work

Show respect by using Active Listening

Wait for leader to begin announcements

GETTING STARTED

Before you launch your first Town Hall meeting, give careful attention to where you will hold the meetings, the schedule, resources to incorporate, and the process you will follow.

Establishing a Meeting Place for Town Hall

After identifying the behaviors that will support the Town Hall structure, look around your room. How will you identify the area, or physical space, where the meetings will be held?

In Larger Classrooms. If you have larger classroom, there may be a special area that can be designated as meeting space-a place where special things happen and special actions take place.

In Smaller Classrooms. On the other hand, your classroom may be smaller, perhaps in a temporary building, where you are lucky to have room enough for all your students let alone finding a permanent space for your Town Hall Meetings. We offer several options for this situation.

Students remain at their desks. Perhaps there is a photo/ clip of a "Town Hall" on either the Smart Board, White Board, overhead or tri-fold poster board (the kind for science displays) to help set the tone/mood of the meeting.

Invite the students to move to another part of the building-cafeteria, auditorium, library, all-purpose room, empty classroom. Perhaps there is a part-time teacher who is willing to offer his/her classroom space (when not in residence) for your get-togethers. It does help to set the tone if you can bring along a physical representation of the meeting—tri-fold poster board, etc.

Think outdoors! If you are in an area that has great weather year-round, these might be options for your class: outdoor amphitheater, grassy knoll, under a tree, by benches in the outdoor areas, near school steps, or whatever other common space your school has to offer. Perhaps you have a small pond – think of the calming effect that water has on the human body because of the negative ions found in the immediate area. If you live in an area where winter weather is not conducive to outdoor meetings, try them in the fall and spring. Again, bring along a physical representation of your meeting.

How will you make the Town Hall Meeting place visible and distinct? Some suggestions that will help to visibly identify the location/site of your meetings include:

Transforming the Physical Space. Simple, inexpensive ways to transform your environment include:

- Town Hall meeting tri-fold board
- Plastic pillars
- Class and/or United States flag
- Dramatic backdrop/mural of government-type building
- Poster designating this space for the meeting
- Curtain with painting on it
- Lettering (Town Hall Meeting) on the wall
- Projected image on a Smart/White Board

- Special carpeted area
- Town Hall Meeting chair for leader

Designated "Talking Stick." Some suggestions include a:

- "Play" microphone
- Stress ball/object
- Simple sign that has the word "citizen" on it that gets passed from speaker to speaker
- Gavel. If your class has a mascot (stuffed symbol) this can be passed from speaker to speaker. In older grades, the "talking stick" might be something more representational of government: gavel, ballot, or even a speaker's podium.

Post Needed Resources. Hang posters/charts that identify the Lifelong Guidelines and LIFESKILLS on the wall for ready reference. (See books4educ.com for a range of resources.)

Town Hall Meeting Schedule

When will you hold your Town Hall meetings? How often? How long should they be? Rule of thumb is to start with daily meetings because of the importance of building community early on in the process and the need to keep building these important skills throughout the year. This type of schedule also provides a sense of predictability; it's good for the brain to know what's going to happen and when.

The length of your meetings will depend on your goals. When well planned and conducted with consistency and continuity, these meetings will help your students practice responsible behaviors, make important decisions, and become competent problem solvers.

Once your class has developed a sense of belonging, the meetings may come more on an "as needed" basis but at least once or twice a week. This is needed to reinforce the concept of democracy and immediacy-we can follow a process to plan and/or resolve issues, then move ahead.

Some teachers start the day with a meeting while others end the day with a meeting-some do both! The meeting time may also depend on availability of the class as a whole and the meeting site (if meeting outside of the classroom). Practice flexibility!

Resources

The more resources at your fingertips, the more organized your efforts. Consider the following:

Procedures of the expected behaviors. Post and discuss the agenda for the Town Hall meeting. This will be created by you, the teacher, when your meetings first start. A mindmap will provide information for visual and spatial learners. As your students develop as citizens, post a partial agenda and ask students to add their issues to the plan for the meeting. Anything that is not discussed will be carried over to the next meeting. Many teachers post the agenda the previous day-by meeting time some issues may have been worked out by the students on their own.

Citizens Action Box (CAB): When you or your students observe a class member practicing citizenship, write it down! Then place it in the box. To provide an opportunity to acknowledge these actions, simply pull these papers out and read them during your Town Hall meeting.

Note for teachers: You may have to "salt" the box to get the process started and/or to provide examples/models of appropriate content. Watch for students who are NOT being recognized; catch them being responsible citizens and add your acknowledgment to the box. Everyone wants to be noticed. Everyone deserves to be acknowledged for their accomplishments. In the upper grades, the citizen recognition may be more formal and contain additional thoughts/words. Two samples for the primary grades follow:

> I saw [Insert name]_____
> being a responsible citizen when he/she
> (write action here) _____.
> My name is_____

> **RESPONSIBLE CITIZEN**
>
> [Insert name]_____
> used the Lifelong Guideline/LIFESKILL of
> _____
> when he/she [insert action] _____.
> I appreciate this because _____
> [Signed by]_____ [date]_____

Scrapbook (optional): Invite a small group to develop, maintain, and share a scrapbook of the class's activities as the year progresses provides a visual reminder of the accomplishments of a small group of citizens. This book can include copies of documents/letters, photographs, newspaper clippings and testimonials.

Technological Support: This can also be managed by a class group. Record, videotape, DVDs, PowerPoint slide shows, photographic examples of "citizens in action," such as Celebrations of Learning, theme in a day, presentation of yearlong research projects, social/political action projects.

Town Hall Meeting Processes

Provide an agenda and some special practices for your Town Hall Meeting – not only the physical aspects, but the emotional and academic ones as well. Plan for the following:

• Common Agenda (often in mindmap form)

- Opening practice (Lifelong Guideline Pledge, Class-generated pledge, Pledge of Allegiance)

- Class song (maybe the beginning and ending meeting of the week); can consist of a popular tune (e.g. "We Are Family" by Sister Sledge, "I Can See Clearly Now" by Johnny Nash, or a familiar tune with newly-generated lyrics. Could also be sung at the end of a meeting.

- Procedure reminders (if needed)

- Presentation of the finalized agenda/goals

- Activity/Practice that supports one of the three steps of Town Hall Meetings

- CAB (Citizens Action Box) to collect acknowledgments to be read, presentation of recognition notes to named students

- Discussion of agenda topics: If you run out of time, carry over any topic not discussed or completed to the next meeting.

- Other Issues: Something of importance that has developed since the creation of the agenda

- Reflection/Closure: Offer students an opportunity to express their thoughts on that particular meeting process-what went well, what needs additional work, Lifelong Guidelines/LIFESKILLS practiced and those needing work, perhaps another group practice (e.g., class song, group recitation of quotation, personal quotation from each child).

TEACHING ABOUT TOWN HALL MEETINGS THROUGH BEING THERE *EXPERIENCES*

One of the most effective ways for students to begin understanding the Town Hall Meeting process is by providing an on-site visit to a genuine meeting in your area. When you do make arrangements for a visit, plan on taking photos (ask permission), gather brochures and pamphlets, collect maps and any other materials that are available, and use them to create an immersion wall upon the class's return. Young students may just visit the "actual" meeting room and meet a few of the government officials who preside over the event. Intermediate students may be able to attend a meeting during the day while older students can attend alone, or with parents or other class members, at night. Include any photographs/newspaper articles about the visits in your scrapbook. Intermediate grades through high school students may be able to visit a state government site and even participate in lobbying for education while there.

TOWN HALL MEETING: ADDRESSING CURRICULUM STANDARDS

Many of you may be thinking, my teaching time and the students' learning time is already so crammed pack, why should I even consider holding Town Hall Meetings.

One of your concerns is ensuring that you teach the skills and content identified in your state standards. Since the readers of this book come from many different states, we decided to use the National Standards, many of which are the same or similar to yours, in order to identify content and skills that can be taught in context by providing town hall meetings for your students. Following are some samples for Grades K-12. Some standards maybe more heavily invested at certain grade levels and/or the level of Community Building.

National Language Arts Standards

NL-ENG.K12.4 Communication Skills – Students adjust their use of spoken, written, and visual language (e.g., conventions, style, vocabulary) to communicate effectively with a variety of audiences and for different purposes.

NL-Eng.K12.5 Communication Strategies – Students employ a wide range of strategies as they write and use different writing process elements appropriately to communicate with different audiences for a variety of purposes.

NL-ENG.K12.6 Applying Knowledge – Students apply knowledge of language structure, language conventions (e.g., spelling and punctuation), media techniques, figurative language, and genre to create, critique, and discuss print and non-print texts.

NL-ENG.K12.7 Evaluating Data – Students conduct research on issues and interests by generating ideas and questions, and by posing problems. They gather, evaluate, and synthesize data from a variety of sources (e.g., print and non-print texts, artifacts, people) to communicate their discoveries in ways that suit their purpose and audience.

NL-ENG.K12.11 Participating in Society – Students participate as knowledgeable, reflective, creative, and critical members of a variety of literacy communities.

NL-ENG.K12.12 Applying Language Skills – Students use spoken, written, and visual language to accomplish their own purposes (e.g., for learning, enjoyment, persuasion, and the exchange of information).

The above information is found at Education World: http://www.educationworld.com/standards/national/lang_arts/english/k_12.shtml

National Social Studies Standards (by grade levels)

NSS-C.K-4.1 What is government?

NSS-C.K-4.2 The basic values and principles of government

NSS-C.K-4.3 Principles of Democracy

NSS-C.K-4.5 Roles of the Citizen

Grades 5-12

NSS-C.5-8.1 Civic Life, Politics, and Government

NSS-C.5-8.3 Principles of Democracy

NSS-C.5-8.5 Roles of the Citizen

All of these standards, either directly or indirectly, can be addressed during Town Hall Meetings. Depending on the social/political action projects your class adopts, there will probably be science, math, and technology standards that will fit. For example, develop an environment project in grades K-4 and you will be meeting the specifications for: NS.K-4.6 Personal and Social Perspectives. Trying to solve the mystery of contaminated water in a nearby pond with 5th through 8th graders? Well, guess what. The standard for that: NS.5-8.1 Science as Inquiry! Having a discussion about drug prevention with 11th graders? There's a standard for that too! NS.9-12.3 Life Science.

Getting Specific

Listed here are only the general overarching standards. Your standards will be specific, allowing you to zero in on each particular skill. For example, in the newly proposed New York State Common Core State Standards for English language Arts and Literacy in History/Social Studies and Science, Speaking and Listening Standards for Grade One, we can find a more specific example that will definitely be used during Town Hall Meetings.

Ask questions to get information, clarify something that is not understood, or gather additional information. Other examples can be viewed at: http://www.emsc.nysed.gov/ciai/common_core_standards/elastandards.pdf

Check your own state's standards and curriculum to find matches between the content and skills you are expected to teach and find skills your students need to be a successful citizen in a Town Hall Meeting process.

RESOURCES

There are a number of resources (human, print and virtual) available that can provide support for this topic.

Organizations

Government Officials and Offices: Contact local officials to make arrangements for guest speakers, on-site visits, class/school presentations with social/political action projects. These human resources can be found in villages, towns, cities, counties, states and, last but not least, at the Federal level.

League of Women Voters (http://www.lwv.org) The League of Women Voters, a nonpartisan political organization, has fought since 1920 to improve our systems of government and impact public policies through citizen education and advocacy. The League's enduring vitality and resonance comes from its unique decentralized structure. The League is a grassroots organization, working at the national, state and local levels.

The American Legion (http://www.legion.org/) The American Legion was chartered and incorporated by Congress in 1919 as a patriotic veterans organization devoted to mutual helpfulness. It is the nation's largest veterans service organization, committed to mentoring and sponsorship of youth programs in our communities, advocating patriotism and honor, promoting a strong national security, and continued devotion to service members and veterans.

Public Citizen (http://www.citizen.org/) Public Citizen serves as the people's voice in the nation's capital. Since their founding in 1971, they have delved into an array of areas, but our work on each issue shares an overarching goal: To ensure that all citizens are represented in the halls of power.

PRINT RESOURCES

Primary (K-4)

Shh! We're Writing the Constitution. Jean Fritz. New York: G.P. Putnam's Sons, 1987. Presents a "behind-the-scenes" look at the trials and tribulations of the Founding Fathers as they wrote the U.S. Constitution during the summer of 1787. Weaves into the narrative descriptions of several of the personalities who drafted and debated the Constitution; explains Federalist and Anti-Federalist forces; describes the ratification process; and discusses the debate over creating a Bill of Rights. Includes the full text of the Constitution.

We the Kids: The Preamble to the U.S. Constitution of the United States. Illustrations and foreword by David Catrow. New York: Dial Books for Young Readers, 2002. Grades K-5. An explanation of the preamble to the U.S. Constitution in language that kids can understand. Contains a foreword and an easy-to-understand glossary ("establish justice" means "to make things fair and honest for everyone"), followed by the story of a dog who leads three children on a camping trip. The story is told through the preamble. The illustrations relate to each phrase in the preamble.

Intermediate (5-8)

Constitution Translated for Kids, 3rd ed. Cathy Travis. Austin, TX: Synergy Books, 2006. Grades 4-7. Provides a line-by-line translation of the U.S. Constitution: the text of the original document is laid out on the left-hand side of the page and accompanying explanatory paragraphs are set out on the right-hand side. Also includes historical context, student exercises, a glossary, and "fast facts." The book was written by a staffer for a U.S. representative.

What Do You Stand For? For Kids: A Guide to Building Character, Barbara A. Lewis, Free Spirit Publishing, 1999. True stories, inspiring quotations, thought-provoking dilemmas, and activities help elementary school children build positive character traits including caring, fairness, respect, and responsibility.

Middle School/High School

Our Constitution. Donald A. Ritchie. New York: Oxford University Press, 2006. Young adults. Begins with a background on how and why the U.S. Constitution was created, the rights it protects, how it has expanded over time, and how it is interpreted. Most of the book comprises detailed descriptions of each clause and article of the Constitution, with "what it says" and "what it means" explanations.

INTERNET RESOURCES

The Internet provides access to an abundance of websites about our U.S. Government-its history, branches, divisions and more. Following are just a few of our favorite websites.

America Speaks. For more than a decade, AmericaSpeaks has used its 21st Century Town Meeting® model to bring together more than 145,000 citizens in deliberations about critical policy issues, and then connect the results to decision-makers: http://www.americaspeaks.org/

Ben's Guide to Government for Kids. This site provides learning tools for K-12 students, parents, and teachers. These resources will teach how our government works, the use of the primary source materials of GPO Access, and how one can use GPO Access to carry out their civic responsibilities: http://bensguide.gpo.gov/

Child & Youth Rights. Join the largest online community of youth interested in global issues and creating positive change: http://issues.tigweb.org/youthrights

Citizen's Handbook: Practical assistance for those who want to make a difference. The Citizens Handbook is meant to encourage the emergence of more active citizens—people motivated by an interest in public issues and a desire to make a difference beyond their own private lives. Active citizens are a great untapped resource, and citizenship is a quality to be nurtured. While this web site is actually for Vancouver residents there is a wealth of information that is applicable in other communities: http://www.vcn.bc.ca/citizens-handbook/

Constitutional Rights Foundation: Constitution Day. A 2005 act of Congress states that all educational institutions receiving federal funding must observe September 17 as Constitution Day, which celebrates the 1787 signing of our founding document: http://www.crf-usa.org/constitution-day/constitution-day.html

Education Place Activity: Holding a Town Hall Meeting. Children experience democracy in action by taking part in a town meeting: http://www.eduplace.com/ss/act/meeting.html

Learning to Give: Philanthropy. Learning to Give, the curriculum division of The League, is the world's leading developer of lessons and resources that teach giving and volunteerism, civic engagement and character through service learning: http://www.learningtogive.org/

MPC-Media & Center Policy Foundation. The MPC is a groundbreaking and award-winning media foundation dedicated to building better communities through empowering productions and localized outreach: http://www.mediapolicycenter.org//

The American Promise. The American Promise is a Web site devoted to helping teachers, professors and educators bring democracy to life in their classrooms: http://www.farmers.com/AmericanPromise/index.html

The Democracy Project: How Does Government Affect Me? http://pbskids.org/democracy/

Town Hall – Curriculum Guide and Online Activities. This activity is designed for high school natural or political science classes. Students will participate in a decision-making exercise that emphasizes team work, problem solving, and critical thinking: http://www.nps.gov/archive/grsa/resources/curriculum/high/town_hall.htm

Town Mouse and Country Mouse go to a Town Hall Meeting. Town Mouse and Country Mouse Go To Town Meeting. This short downloadable booklet was designed to teach students grades 3-5 about Vermont's Town Hall Meeting process: http://www.sec.state.vt.us/kids/pubs/TM_upper_elem_curric.pdf

USCIS (United States Citizenship and Immigration Services. USCIS promotes instruction and training on citizenship rights and responsibilities and provides immigrants with information and tools necessary to successfully integrate into American civic culture: http://tinyurl.com/ter3b

U.S. Government Web Sites for Kids (part of Ben's Guide to Government). Included are contact websites for almost any agency, branch and/or division of the Federal government from agriculture to transportation. Did you know that the CIA, the FBI and the State Department are just a few of the agencies that have web sites for kids? Also included are excellent web sites for educators and parents: http://bensguide.gpo.gov/pt/subject. html

Young Yorkers Leaflets: Every Vote Counts. Students learn the rights and responsibilities attached to being a citizen. (teacher and student edition): http://www.yorkers.org/leaflet.htm

Young Yorkers Leaflets: Of the people – Community Government. By examining their own community's government, students learn how government makes laws and meets people's needs for protection, public health, education, transportation, and other services necessary for a safer and better life. (Teacher and Student edition): http://www.yorkers.org/leaflets/ofthepeople.htm

Young Yorkers' Leaflets: Town Meetings Teach the Bill of Rights. Using the Bill of Rights as the starting point, students determine how the Constitution affects them in their daily lives through discussion in a series of Town Meetings. (Teacher and student edition): http://www.yorkers.org/leaflets/town.htm

NOW MORE THAN EVER

A resurgence of the Town Hall Meeting process occurred during the last Presidential election. These Town Hall meetings, then and since, provided a forum for residents of an area to voice their opinions and make their feelings known. By providing Town Hall Meetings to teach about democracy and our government, students are better prepared for the role of participating citizen — both in school and as adults.

Given the current economic and political turmoil, the Town Hall meeting process is needed now more than ever.

Glossary
Bibliography
Index

Glossary

3Cs of Assessment
A set of criteria for assessing student work used by both students and teachers. The Cs stand for: Correct—conforming to fact or truth, free from error; accurate; Complete—having all parts or elements; the assignment is done to the defined specifications; Comprehensive—of large scope, inclusive, extensive mental range or grasp; reflects multiple points of view, thorough.

Absence of Threat/Nurturing Reflective Thinking
One of the nine Bodybrain-Compatible Elements of the *HET* model. See Chapters 1-5.

Adequate Time
One of the nine Bodybrain-Compatible Elements of the *HET* model. See Chapters 1-5.

Age-Appropriate
Concepts and/or facts which are understandable (versus memorizable) by students, given the current degree of development of the brain. These biological stages of thinking and learning gained attention through the work of Piaget.

Assessment/Evaluation
A process by which student achievement is assessed. In an *HET* classroom the expectation is for mastery of key points by all students on an "A/no credit yet" basis.

"Australia"
A small corner of the room where the students can go to relax, refocus, and reflect. Used to assist students who are highly upset—angry or sad—to reset their emotions so they can return to learning.

Being There

The most powerful input to the brain is being in a real world location that activates all 19 senses, thereby significantly increasing learning (pattern identification and program building).

Bloom's Taxonomy
A model by Benjamin Bloom, et al, originally designed for developing questioning strategies for college exams. In the *HET* model, the process verbs characterizing each level are used to develop inquiries.

Bodybrain-Compatible Elements
These are nine conditions that enhance and support powerful learning, the basis for the *HET* model. They are: Absence of Threat/Nurturing Reflective Thinking, Meaningful Content, Movement to Enhance Learning, Enriched Environment, Choices, Adequate Time, Collaboration, Immediate Feedback, and Mastery/Application.

Bodybrain Learning Partnership
One of the four concepts from brain research upon which the *HET* model is based. Includes emotions as the gatekeeper to learning and performance and movement to enhance learning.

Brain-Compatible Learning
Coined by Leslie A. Hart in his book *Human Brain and Human Learning*, it is a key goal of the Kovalik *HET* model. A brain-compatible environment is one which allows the brain to work as it naturally, and thus most powerfully, works. Recent brain research has updated this term to "bodybrain-compatible" learning.

Celebrations of Learning
An activity to not only acknowledge accomplishments but to also practice using the knowledge and skills mastered through demonstrating and teaching others, particularly parents.

Choices

One of the nine Bodybrain-Compatible Elements of the *HET* model. See Chapters 1-5.

Collaboration

One of the nine Bodybrain-Compatible Elements of the *HET* model. See Chapters 1-5.

Common Core of Knowledge

Defined in the *HET* model to mean those concepts, significant knowledge, and skills all students are expected to master and that are considered essential to success in life (school and adulthood) and to sustain a democracy and participate in our high-tech society.

Component

An integral structure of the *HET* model based on a *being there* location. In a yearlong theme, components are related to the organizing concept of the yearlong theme; components, a framework designed for approximately one month of study is broken into topics, important aspects of the concept for the *being there* location.

Emotion As Gatekeeper to Learning and Performance

One of the two aspects of bodybrain learning partnership, a brain research concepts upon which the *HET* model is based. See Chapter 2.

C.U.E.

An acronym describing the three ways information can be presented in order for the learner to readily retrieve it. The "C" stands for creative, the "U" for useful and the "E" for emotional bridge.

Direct Instruction

The 11 to 16 minutes of teacher presentation of a key point which provides the focus of the classroom activities; direct instruction is only one way of orchestrating key points.

Effective First Teaching

A commitment to doing the job right the first time—teaching through ability to apply what is understood and wiring into it long-term memory. Should be the rallying cry for today's school reform efforts. Now possible to do if current brain research is applied to curriculum development and instructional strategies. The ITI/*HET* model is such a vehicle.

Enriched Environment

One of the nine Bodybrain-Compatible Elements of the *HET* model. See Chapters 1-5.

Hands-On Experience

A term describing two levels of sensory input: hands-on of the real thing and hands-on of something symbolic or representative of a real thing. Hands-on of symbolic or representational things provides significantly less sensory input, and thus less stimulation of the brain, than does interacting with the real thing.

Group Development—3 Stages of

In the *HET* model, group development and creating community occurs in three stages: Developing a sense of belonging, Creating common ground, and Taking action. The end result is a sense of community that increases academic learning as well as enhances personal and social growth. See Chapter 9.

Immediate Feedback

One of the nine Bodybrain-Compatible Elements of the *HET* model. See Chapters 1-5.

Immersion

An environment that simulates as richly as possible the real-life environment being studied, e.g., transforming a classroom into wetlands or a pond or a period of history, allowing students to experience or role-play as if they were actually there.

Input, Types of

1. *Being there*, physically being in the real world environment; 2. Immersion—full simulation of the real world environment, includes many real world things; 3. Hands-on of the real thing, (e.g., frog); 4. Hands-on of representation (e.g., plastic model of a frog); 5. Second-hand—pictorial representation, written word (e.g., pictures, videos, or stories about frogs); and 6. Symbolic—mathematics, phonics, grammar (scientific definition of a frog)

Inquiries

A key curriculum development structure in the *HET* model, inquiries are activities that enable students to understand and apply the concept, skill, or significant knowledge of a key point. The primary purpose of inquiries is to enable students to develop mental programs for applying, in real-world situations, the key point and wiring such knowledge and skills into long-term memory. Inquiries make learning active and memorable.

Inquiry Builder

A chart that organizes the process verbs of Bloom's Taxonomy of Cognitive Objectives according to five of Howard Gardner's seven intelligences

Inseparable Bodybrain Learning Partnership

Current brain research indicates that the limbic system is part of a larger emotional system involving "information substances" produced and received throughout the body. In other words, the brain talks to the body and the body talks back to the brain. Learning is the result of an inseparable bodybrain partnership.

Instructional Strategies

A variety of instructional strategies are critical to implementing the *HET* model at each stage. See Stages 1.2, 1.3, and 2.

Integrated

Combining or coordinating separate elements so as to provide a harmonious interrelated whole (as defined by *Webster's Encyclopedia Unabridged Dictionary of the English Language* 1996).

ITI (Integrated Thematic Instruction)

The name given to a bodybrain-compatible, fully integrated instructional model developed by Susan Kovalik. It is a comprehensive model that translates the best of what we know about learning from current brain research into effective teaching strategies and meaningful curriculum. Now referred to as the *HET* (Highly Effective Teaching) model.

Key Point

Essential concept, skill, or significant knowledge all students are expected to master (know and be able to use). The primary purpose of key points is to enhance students' ability to detect pattern, i.e., to readily identify the collection of attributes that is essential for understanding the concept, skill, or significant idea of the key point. They also provide a clear focus for the teacher for instructional planning and for orchestration of learning.

Learning, a Two–Step Process

Defined by Leslie Hart as a two-part process: 1. Detecting and understanding patterns—a process through which our brain creates meaning. 2. Developing meaningful mental programs to use what is understood and to store it in long-term memory—the capacity to use what is understood first with assistance and then

almost automatically.

Learning Clubs

Learning Clubs are collaborative student groups, the composition of which may change monthly to every six weeks. Getting to know others well accelerates learning, prevenets cliques, and increases opportunities for growth. Learning how to get to know others, and be comfortable doing so, is a critical personal/social skill. For Stage 1 and beyond, see Chapter 7.

Lifelong Guidelines

The parameters for classroom/schoolwide interactions with other students and staff. They are TRUSTWORTHINESS, TRUTHFULNESS, ACTIVE LISTENING, NO PUT-DOWNS, and PERSONAL BEST.

LIFESKILLS

The 19 LIFESKILLS are the day-to-to-day definition of the Lifelong Guideline of Personal Best. The LIFESKILLS are the personal/social parameters for everyone—students and adults. They are: Caring, Common Sense, Cooperation, Courage, Creativity, Curiosity, Effort, Flexibility, Friendship, Initiative, Integrity, Organization, Patience, Perseverance, Pride, Problem Solving, Responsibility, Resourcefulness, and Sense of Humor,.

Mastery

One of the nine Bodybrain-Compatible Elements of the *HET* model; see Chapters 1-6. Mastery in the *HET* model means completion of both steps in the new definition of learning (see Chapters 4 and 5); it means being able to apply what is understood in real-world ways and practicing how to use that skill or knowledge until it becomes wired into long-term memory.

Meaningful Content

One of the nine Bodybrain-Compatible Elements of the *HET* model. See Chapters 1-6.

Mindmapping

A way to visually represent information, usually as a web or cluster around the main idea with symbols and colors, rather than in traditional outline form.

Movement to Enhance Learning

One of the two aspects of bodybrain learning partnership, a brain research concepts upon which the *HET* model is based.

See Chapter 2.

Multiple Intelligences

One of the four concepts from brain research upon which the *HET* model is based. Defined by Howard Gardner as "problem-solving or product-producing capabilities." The first seven intelligences identified by Gardner are: logical-mathematical, linguistic, spatial, bodily-kinesthetic, musical, intrapersonal, and interpersonal. Humans are born with all the intelligences but will develop each according to family and cultural preference, demands of one's environment, and the individual's inclinations and experiences. Gardner has subsequently added an eighth intelligence, naturalist. The multiple intelligences are a key ingredient of inquiries.

Pattern Seeking

A key concept of bodybrain-compatibility; describes the means by which the brain makes meaning from incoming sensory input. Together with program building, is one of the four concepts from brain research upon which the *HET* model is based.

Procedures, Written

Written procedures are an important classroom leadership strategy in the *HET* model. They state the social and personal behaviors are expected for commonly occurring events, such as entering and leaving the room, lunchroom behaviors, and so forth. By describing what social and personal behaviors are expected, these procedures allow students to be successful.

Program Building

A key concept of brain-compatibility describing how the brain stores and uses what it learns. It is defined as "a personal goal achieved by a sequence of steps or actions" which becomes stored in the brain for later retrieval when an action is required. Every goal we accomplish is due to implementation of a program or programs. Together with pattern seeking, is one of the four concepts from brain research upon which the *HET* model is based.

Social/Political Action

An integral part of the *HET* model which provides students a vehicle for applying what they learn to real-world problems. It assists students in becoming contributing citizens. Begins in Stage 2.

Symbolic Input

The most difficult way for the brain to grasp new information such as phonics, grammar, and algebraic equations.

Temperament or Personality Preferences

Based on the work of Carl Jung, Myers and Briggs, and Keirsey and Bates, these four behavior scales strongly affect learning. The behavior areas are: taking in information (sensor or intuitor), decision making (feeling or thinking), lifestyle (judging or perceiving), and orientation to others (extrovert and introvert)

Target Talk

A key instructional tool to teach the Lifelong Guidelines/LIFESKILLS. Labels a behavior in context without value judgment.

Topics

A curriculum development structure of the *HET* model for dividing each component into important topics or areas of the concept for the component's *being there* experience. In the yearlong theme, topics are planned for approximately one week.

Yearlong Research Projects

Topics students choose during the first two weeks of school to become the "expert" on for the class. Students research their project throughout the year and present it to the entire class (and others students as well).

Yearlong Theme

The yearlong theme is the central organizer for integrated curriculum in the *HET* model. It is a concept that organizes all the concepts, significant knowledge, and skills to be learned during the theme. It is represented by a kid-grabbing title.

Bibliography

ABC News Prime Time. *"Your Child's Brain"* with Diane Sawyer. January 25, 1995.

Ackerman, Diane. *An Alchemy of Mind: The Marvel and Mystery of the Brain*. New York: Scribner, 2004.

Armstrong, Thomas. *In Their Own Way*. Los Angeles: Tarcher Press, 1987.

Armstrong, Thomas. *7 Kinds of Smart: Identifying and Developing Your Multiple Intelligences*. New York: Penguin Putnam, 1999.

Beane, James A. *A Middle School Curriculum: From Rhetoric to Reality*, second edition. Westerville, Ohio: National Middle School Association, 1993.

Bell, Nanci. *Visualizing and Verbalizing for Improved Comprehension and Thinking: A Teacher's Manual*. San Luis Obispo, CA: Gander Educational Publishing, 2007.

Brady, Marion. *What's Worth Teaching? Selecting, Organizing, and Integrating Knowledge*. Covington, WA: Books for Educators, 1989.

Bridges, William. *Managing Transitions: Making the Most of Change*. California: Addison-Wesley Publishing Company, Inc., 1991.

Caine, Renata and Geoffrey. *Making Connections: Teaching and the Human Brain*. California: Addison-Wesley, 1994.

Calvin, William H. *How Brains Think: Evolving Intelligence, Then and Now*. New York: BasicBooks, 1996.

Calvin, William H. *"The Mind's Big Bang and Mirroring,"* unpublished manuscript. Seattle, WA: University of Washington, 2000.

Castelli, Darla, C. H. Hillman, S. M. Buck, and H. E. Erwin, "Physical Fitness and Academic Achievement in Third- and Fifth-Grade Students, *Journal of Sport & Exercise Psychology*, 29, 2007.

Childre, Doc. *Freeze Frame: One Minute Stress Management*. Boulder Creek, CA: Planetary Publications, 1998.

Childre, Doc and Martin, Howard with Beech, Donna. *The HeartMath Solution*. San Francisco: Harper, 2000.

Childre, Doc and Deborah Rozman. *Transforming Stress: The Hearmath Solution for Relieving Worry, Fatigue, and Tension*. Oakland, CA: New Harbinger Publications, 2005.

Cohen, Elizabeth. *Designing Groupwork: Strategies for the Heterogeneous Classroom*, Second Edition. New York: Teachers College Press, 1994.

Cohen, Isabel and Marcelle Goldsmith. *Hands On: How to Use Brain Gym in the Classroom.; A Practical Photo Manual for Educators, Parents, and Learners.* Ventura, CA: Edu-Kinesthetics, Inc., 2003.

Csikszentmihalyi, Mihaley. *Flow: The Psychology of Optimal Experience*. New York: Harper, 1990.

Cytowic, Richard E. *The Man Who Tasted Shapes: A Bizarre Medical Mystery Offers Revolutionary Insights into Emotions, Reasoning, and Consciousness*. New York: Tarcher/Putnam, 1993.

Damasio, Antonio. *Descartes' Error: Emotion, Reason, and the Human Brain*. New York: G. P. Putnam Sons, 1994.

Damasio, Antonio. *Looking for Spinoza: Joy, Sorrow, and the Feeling Brain.* New York: Harcourt, 2003.

Damasio, Antonio. *"Thinking about Emotion,"* presentation at Emotional Intelligence, Education, and the Brain: A Symposium. Chicago, IL: December 5, 1997.

Diamond, Marion and Hopson, Janet. *Magic Trees of the Mind: How to Nurture Your Child's Intelligence, Creativity, and Healthy Emotions from Birth Through Adolescence.* New York: Penguin, 1998.

Gallese, Vittorio and Goldman, Alvin. "Mirror Neurons and the Simulation Theory of Mind-Reading" in *Trends in Cognitive Sciences*, Vol. 2, 1998.

Gardner, Howard. *Frames of Mind: Theory of Multiple Intelligences.* New York: Basic Books, 1983.

Gardner, Howard. *Intelligence Reframed: Multiple Intelligences for the 21st Century.* New York: Basic Books, 1999.

Gibbs, Jeanne. *Discovering Gifts in Middle School: Learning in a Caring Culture Called Tribes.* Windsor, California: CenterSource Systems, LLC, 2001.

Gibbs, Jeanne. *TRIBES: A New Way of Learning and Being Together.* Windsor, California: CenterSource Systems, LLC, 2001.

Glasser, William, M.D. *Control Theory in the Classroom.* New York: Perennial Library, 1986.

Glickman, Carl. *Renewing America's Schools: A Guide to School-Based Action.* San Francisco: Jossey-Bass Publishers, 1993.

Goldberg, Elkhonon. *The Executive Brain: Frontal Lobes and the Civilized Mind.* Oxford: University Press, 2001.

Goldberg, Elkhonon. *The Wisdom Paradox: How Your Mind Can Grow Stronger As Your Brain Grows Older.* New York, NY: Gotham Books/Division of Penquin Books, 2005.

Gopnik, A., A. Meltzoff, and Patricia Kuhl. *The Scientist in the Crib: Minds, Brains, and How Children Learn.* New York: William Morrow and Company, 1999.

Gossen, Diane. *Restitution: Restructuring School Discipline.* Chapel Hill, NC: New View Publications, 1996.

Greenspan, Stanley I. with Beryl Lieff Benderly. *The Growth of the Mind and the Endangered Origins of Intelligence.* New York: Addison-Wesley Publishing Company, 1997.

Grissom, Jim. "Physical Fitness and Academic Achievement," *Journal of Exercise PhysiologyOnline* (JEPonline), Vol 8, Number 1, February 2005.

Grissom, Jim. "California Physical Fitness Test: A Study of the Relationship Between Physical Fitness and Academic Achievement in California Using 2004 Test Results." California State Department of Education, 2004.

Hannaford, Carla. *Smart Moves: Why Learning Is Not All in Your Head.* Alexander, North Carolina: Great Ocean, 1995.

Hannaford, Carla. *Playing in the Unified Field: Raising and Becoming Conscious, Creative Human Beings.* Salt Lake City, UT: Great River Books, 2010.

Hardwired to Connect. A collaborative work by the Commission of Children at Risk. New York: sponsored by YMCA of the USA, Dartmouth Medical School, Institute for American Values, 2003.

Hart, Leslie A. *Human Brain and Human Learning*, 3rd ed. Covington, WA: Books for Educators, Inc., 2001.

Hawkins, Jeff with Sandra Blakeslee. *On Intelligence: How a New Understanding of the Brain Will Lead to the Creation of Truly Intelligent Machines.* New York: Times Books/Henry Holt and Company, 2004.

Healy, Jane. *Endangered Minds: Why Children Don't Think – and What We Can Do About It.* New York: Simon & Schuster, 1990.

Healy, Jane. *Failure to Connect: How Computers Affect Our Children's Minds – And What We Can Do About It.* New York: Simon &

Schuster, 1998.

Hillman, C. H., M. B. Pontiflex, L. B. Raine, D. M. Castelli, E. E. Hall, and A. F. Kramer. "The Effect of Acute Treadmill Walking on Cognitive Control and Academic Achievement in Preadolescent Children," *Neuroscience* 159, 2009.

Hyerle, David. *Visual Tools for Constructing Knowledge*. Alexandria, VA: Association for Supervision & Curriculum Development, 1996.

Iacoboni, Marco. *The New Science of How We Connect with Others: Mirroring People*. New York: Farrar, Straus and Giroux, 2008.

Jacobsonville: An ITI/HET Micro-Society, 30-minute DVD. Black Diamond, WA: Books for Educators, 1997.

Kagan, Spencer. *Cooperative Learning*. San Clemente: CA Kagan, 1994.

Kagan, Spencer. *SmartCards*. San Juan Capistrano, CA: Kagan, 2003.

Kaufelt, Martha Miller. *I Can Divide and Conquer: A Concept in a Day*. Black Diamond, WA: Books for Educators, 1987.

Keirsey, David. *Please Understand Me II: Temperament Character Intelligence*. Del Mar, CA: Prometheus Nemesis Book Company, 1998.

Kinsey, C.W. and McPhearson, K, editors. *Enriching Curriculum Through Service Learning*. Alexandria, VA: Association for Supervision and Curriculum Development, 1995.

Kohn, Alfie. *Punished by Rewards: The Trouble with Gold Stars, Incentive Plans, A's, Praise, and Other Bribes*. Boston: Houghton Mifflin, 1993.

Kouzes, James M. and Barry Z. Posner. *The Leadership Challenge*, Fourth Edition. San Francisco, CA: Jossey-Bass, Inc., 2008.

Kovalik, Susan. *Integrated Thematic Instruction: The Model*, 3rd ed. Covington, WA: Susan Kovalik and Associates, 1997.

Kovalik, Susan J. & Olsen, Karen. *Kid's Eye View of Science: A Teacher's Handbook for Implementing and Integrated Thematic Approach to Science, K-6*. Thousand Oaks, CA: Corwin Press, 2010.

LeDoux, Joseph. *"The Emotional Brain,"* presentation at Emotional Intelligence, Education, and the Brain: A Symposium. Chicago, IL: December 5, 1997.

LeDoux, Joseph E. *The Emotional Brain: The Mysterious Underpinnings of Emotional Life*. New York: Simon and Schuster, 1996.

Lewis, Barbara A. *Kid's Guide to Social Action: How to Solve the Social Problems YOU CHOOSE – and Turn Creative Thinking into Positive Action*. Minneapolis, MN: Free Spirit Publishing, 1981.

Lewis, Barbara A. *Kid's Guide to Service Projects: Over 500 Service Ideas for Young People who Want to Make a Difference*. Minneapolis, MN: Free Spirit Publishing, 1995.

Lewis, Thomas. *A General Theory of Love*. New York: Random House, 2000.

Lowery, Lawrence F. *Thinking and Learning: Matching Developmental Stages With Curriculum and Instruction*. Kent, Washington: Books for Educators, Inc., 1995.

Mahnke, Frand H and Rudolf H. Mahnke. *Color and Light in Man-Made Environments*. New York: John Wiley & Sons, Inc., 1993.

Margulies, Nancy. *Mapping Inner Space: Learning and Teaching Visual Mapping*. Tucson, AZ: Zephyr Press, 2002.

McGovern, M. K. "The Effects of Exercise on the Brain." serendip.brynmawr,edu/bb/neuro/neuro05/web2/mmcgovern.html.

Medina, John. *Brain Rules: 12 Principles for Surviving and Thriving at Work, Home, and School*. Seattle, WA: Pear Press, 2008.

Miller, Norma, ed. *The Healthy School Handbook: Conquering the Sick Building Syndrome and Other Environmental Hazards In and Around Your School*. Washington, DC: NEA Professional Library, 1995.

Motluk, Alison. "Read My Mind" in *New Scientist*, Jan. 27, 2001.

Olsen, Karen D. *Coaching for the HET Model: Making Bodybrain-Compatible Education a Reality*. Covington, Washington: Books for Educators, 1999.

Olsen, Karen D. *Science Continuum of Concepts, K-6*. Black Diamond, WA: Center for the Future of Public Education, 2010.

Olsen, Karen D. *What Brain Research Can Teach About Cutting School Budgets*. Thousand Oaks, CA: Corwin Press, 2010.

Pearson, Sarah S. *Finding Common Ground: Service Learning and Education Reform*. Washington, D.C.: American Youth Policy Forum, 2002.

Pearson, Sue. *Tools for Citizenship and Life: Using the Lifelong Guidelines and LIFESKILLS in Your Classroom*, 2nd ed. Black Diamond, WA: Books for Educators, 2005.

Pert, Candace. *Molecules of Emotion: Why You Feel the Way You Feel*. New York: Scribner, 1997.

Posner, Michael and M. K. Rothbart. *Educating the Human Brain*. Washington, DC: American Psychological Association, 2007.

Ramachandran, V. S. *Mirror Neurons and Imitation Learning As the Driving Force Behind "The Great Leap Forward" in Human Evolution*. www.edge.org/documents/archive/edge69.html

Ratey, John. *Spark: The Revolutionary New Science of Exercise and the Brain*.

Ratey, John J. *A User's Guide to the Brain: Perception, Attention, and the Four Theaters of the Brain*. New York: Pantheon Books, 2001.

Rivlin, Robert and Gravelle, Karen. *Deciphering Your Senses*. New York: Simon and Schuster, 1984.

Rizzolatti, Giacomo and Arbib, Michael. "Language Within Our Grasp" in *Trends in Neurosciences*, Vol. 21, 1998.

Rizzolatti, Giacomo and Corrado Sinigaglia, translated by Frances Anderson. *Mirrors in the Brain: How Our Minds Share Actions and Emotions*. New York: Oxford University Press, 2006.

Samples, Bob. *Open Mind, Whole Mind*. California: Jalmar Press, 1987.

Sax, Leonard. *Boys Adrift: The Five Factors Driving the Growing Epidemic of UnMotivated Boys and Underachieving Young Men*. Philadelphia, PA: Basic Books, 2007.

Sax, Leonard. *Why Gender Matters*. New York: Doubleday, 2005.

Shores, E. F. "Howard Gardner on the Eighth Intelligence: Seeing the Natural World," *Dimensions of Early Childhood*, Summer, 1995.

Simon, Herbert, *The Sciences of the Artificial*, Cambridge, MA: MIT Press, 1996.

Smith, Frank. *Insult to Intelligence: The Bureaucratic Invasion of Our Classrooms*. New York: Arbor House Publishing Company, 1999.

Smith, Frank. *to think*. New York: Teachers College Press, 1990.

Sylwester, Robert. *A Celebration of Neurons: An Educator's Guide to the Human Brain*. Alexandria, VA: ASCD, 1995.

Sylwester, Robert. *How to Explain a Brain: An Educator's Handbook of Brain Terms and Cognitive Processes*. Thousand Oaks, CA: Corwin Press, 2005.

Sylwester, Robert. "The Role of the Arts in Brain Development and Maintenance." An unpublished paper.

Zielke, Dr. Sigurd. "An Introduction to Neurobehavioral-Developmental & Social Classroom Management," a presentation to Susan Kovalik & Associates, January 20-22, 2005.

Index

Implementation Ideas

Susan J. Kovalik

Susan J. Kovalik, classroom teacher and curriculum innovator for over 35 years, has spent the past 25 years developing a model for curriculum and instruction based on brain research. In 1980, she developed the ITI Model Teaching Week, an innovative way to show teachers how ITI (now known as the *Highly Effective Teaching, HET*) strategies work with students in their own school. Since that beginning, more than 40,000 teachers have attended the one-week experience watching how their students respond to brain-compatible curriculum and instructional strategies and becoming inspired to begin their own *HET* journey.

Susan Kovalik & Associates, Inc. was created in 1988 and today sends associates, experienced HET instructors, to work around the world teaching and coaching educators. They share the power of working with a model that can be replicated for all students in all situations.

In 1998, Susan was nominated a NASA Woman of the Year.

In 1999, the *HET* model was selected for inclusion in the college text, *Instructional-Design Theories and Models: A New Paradigm of Instructional Theory* edited by Charles Reigeluth, Indiana University. In that same year, Susan was awarded a medal of honor for her work in Slovakia, formerly part of Czechoslovakia, for the eight years that she and her associates worked with school leaders to create an alternative to the communist education system.

In 1999, *HET* qualified as a replicable model for the federally-funded Comprehensive School Reform Demonstration Program (CSRD). It is now included in the national *Catalog of School Reform Models*, opening the doors to schools that are willing to embrace a model whose results can be replicated to benefit all children.

Today thousands of educators and hundreds of schools around the world are actively engaged in creating bodybrain-compatible schools using the *HET* model. *Exceeding Expectations: A User's Guide to Implementing Brain Research in the Classroom* is an implementation guide to creating a bodybrain–compatible education for all children and a satisfying teaching and learning experience for teachers.

Susan Kovalik's brain–compatible books include: *Teachers Make the Difference, Kid's Eye View of Science*, and *ITI: The Model*. She has produced over a dozen videos documenting brain-compatible learning in action.

Karen D. Olsen

Karen D. Olsen brings a wealth of experience to her writing. The product of a one-room school for grades 1-8 and growing up on a ranch, Karen has forever retained her insistence that what we learn should be usable in very practical as well as academically rigorous ways. Following doctoral studies at Columbia University Teachers College, she worked for the California State Department of Education for 12 years. Her assignments included planning and development—writing schoolwide planning and quality program review documents and processes—and management of the school consortium unit serving districts highly committed to school change.

Karen was one of the original founders of California Institute of School Improvement, a non-profit foundation designed to support schools and districts in a wide range of school change issues. As Program Director, she conducted seminars ranging from implications of recent legislation to schoolwide planning and quality review processes, to the role of change agent for mentor teachers. During this time she wrote an insightful mentor book, *California Mentor Teacher Role*, which grew out of her experiences working with more than 7,000 mentor teachers throughout the state.

As Executive Director of the Mid-California Science Improvement Program, a ten–year effort funded by the David and Lucile Packard Foundation to improve the quality of science education based on the *HET* Model, Karen wrote *Continuum of Science Concepts, K-6* and *Classroom Stages of Implementation* to support that effort. Karen also served as Executive Director of the Bay Area Middle School Program, a project to create model middle schools.

Karen co-authored, with Susan Kovalik, *ITI The Model; The Kid's Eye View of Science: A Teacher's Handbook for Implementing an Integrated Thematic Approach to Science, K-6*, and this book. Since that time she has been the author, co-author, or contributing editor of HET books for middle schools, high school, coaching the *HET model*, and providing schoolwide leadership for change. She also updated *Human Brain & Human Learning* by Leslie Hart; Karen has held the intellectual integrity of the ITI/HET Model for more than 20 years.

Karen's most recent book is entitled *What Brain Research Can Teach Us About Cutting School Budgets*, published by Corwin Press.

What Readers Have to Say
About This Book

"This is a "must read" book for every educator who would like practical methods for applying brain research. Throughout the world, international and national schools are using the *HET* conceptual framework to develop responsible citizens. The *HET* model is applicable to any classroom and applies well to all cultures. At our K-12 school in Kobe, Japan we have found that the nomenclature is easy to teach to children of all nationalities. LIFESKILLS are the cornerstone for our program of character/values education and parents are able to understand the concepts and reinforce these values at home. But more important, the *HET* model gives our multinational teaching staff common language to use in their professional day-to-day life."

—David Ottaviano, Ed.D.
Headmaster, Canadian Academy
Kobe, Japan

"If there were just one book that I could buy to be a more effective teacher, it would be *Exceeding Expectations*. This book is an effective coach for the first year teacher as well as for me, a 20-year teacher. The explanations and examples make the *HET* model clear and understandable. I found "meat" in every section of every chapter.

The book is elegantly written—no wasted words—just clear, precise, beautiful language. The personal examples of Karen Olsen helped me to understand the model more completely even though I have been implementing *HET* over eight years now. I also appreciate the research and the sources provided at the end of each chapter, many of which have a short overview that gives you an idea of what that book is all about and its usefulness to you.

Exceeding Expectations goes beyond being a step-by-step guide for *HET*; it's a guide book for effective teaching for all teachers of all experience levels. I still don't know how the authors accomplished this task but they did. This is an award-winning book if I've ever seen one."

—Barbara Norris, 6th Grade Teacher
Florida